Commercial Law Textbook

Sale of Goods, Consumer Credit and Agency

4th edition

Edited by P A Read
LLB, DPA, Barrister

HLT Publications

HLT PUBLICATIONS
200 Greyhound Road, London W14 9RY

First published 1990
4th edition 1993

© The HLT Group Ltd 1993

All HLT publications enjoy copyright protection and the copyright belongs to The HLT Group Ltd.

All rights reserved. No part of this publication may be reproduced or transmitted in any form or by any means, electronic, mechanical, photocopying, recording or otherwise, or stored in any retrieval system of any nature without either the written permission of the copyright holder, application for which should be made to The HLT Group Ltd, or a licence permitting restricted copying in the United Kingdom issued by the Copyright Licensing Agency.

Any person who infringes the above in relation to this publication may be liable to criminal prosecution and civil claims for damages.

ISBN 0 7510 0309 3

British Library Cataloguing-in-Publication.
A CIP Catalogue record for this book is available from the British Library.

Acknowledgement
The publishers and author would like to thank the Incorporated Council of Law Reporting for England and Wales for kind permission to reproduce extracts from the Weekly Law Reports.

Printed and bound in Great Britain

Contents

Preface *vii*

Table of Cases *ix*

Table of Statutes *xxxi*

Introduction *xliii*

Sale of Goods

1 Scope of the Sale of Goods Act *3*

Introduction – Scope of the SGA 1979: property in the goods – Sales and agreements to sell – Price – Categories of goods – Sale distinguished from other transactions

2 Formation of the Contract and Formalities *19*

Formation in general – Mistake – Auction sales – Formal requirements

3 Types of Obligations Created *23*

Introduction – Representations – Conditions and warranties – Innominate terms or intermediate stipulations

4 Duties of the Seller I: Title, Delivery and Quantity *43*

Introduction – Title – Delivery – Quantity

5 Duties of the Seller II: Quality *63*

Introduction – Implied terms about description – Implied terms about quality: common factors – Implied terms about merchantable quality – Implied terms about fitness for purpose – Sales by sample – Other implied terms

6 Duties of the Buyer *100*

Duty to pay – To take delivery

7 Exclusion of Liability *102*

Introduction – Judicial control: incorporation – Judicial control: interpretation – The Unfair Contract Terms Act 1977 – Terms rendered void by the Act – Terms subject to the reasonableness test – The reasonableness test – Anti-avoidance provisions – Miscellaneous provisions – Conclusions

8 The Passing of Property *133*

Introduction – Unascertained goods – Specific goods – Reservation of rights of disposal: s19 – Acceptance: s39

9 Risk, Impossibility and Frustration *157*

Risk – Antecedent impossibility and frustration – The seller's bankruptcy

10 The Transfer of Title by a Non-Owner *165*

Introduction – Estoppel – Sale under common law or statutory powers of sale or under court order – Sale in market overt – Sale under a voidable title – Sale by an agent – Sale by a mercantile agent under the Factors Act 1889 – Sale by a seller in possession – Sale by a buyer in possession – Motor vehicles subject to a hire purchase or conditional sale agreement – Sale by an unpaid seller exercising his statutory rights – Other miscellaneous exceptions to *nemo dat*

11 Real Remedies *208*

Introduction – The meaning of 'unpaid seller' – The unpaid seller's right of lien: ss39, 41, 42 and 43 – The unpaid seller's right of stoppage in transit: ss39, 44, 45 and 46 – The unpaid seller's right of resale: s48

12 Personal Remedies of the Seller *223*

Introduction – The action for the price of the goods sold – The action for damages for non-acceptance of the goods

13 Remedies of the Buyer I: the Right to Reject the Goods *229*

Introduction – Time and method of rejecting the goods – The effects of rejection of the goods by the buyer – Instalment contracts – Situations in which the buyer loses the right to reject – Where the buyer accepts part of the goods: severable and non-severable contracts

14 Remedies of the Buyer II *241*

Rescission for innocent misrepresentation – Damages for non-delivery – Damages for breach of condition or warranty: s53 SGA – Damages in tort – Damages for misrepresentation – Specific performance – Recovery of the price by the buyer

15 Consumer Protection *248*

Introduction – The Consumer Protection Act and product liability – Manufacturer's guarantees – Consumer Protection Act, Part II – Miscellaneous consumer protection statutes – Fair trading legislation

16 The Supply of Goods and Services Act 1982 *261*

Introduction – Contracts for the transfer of goods which are not sale of goods contracts – Contracts of hire – Contracts to supply services

Consumer Credit

1 Introduction *277*

Introduction – Definitions – Multiple agreements – Linked transactions – Total charge for credit – Variation of agreements – Licensing

2 Formation of the Contract *298*

Advertisements – Making the contract – Formalities – Withdrawal – Cancellation – Canvassing

3 **The Creditor's Obligations** *316*
   Implied terms – Debtor's remedies – Transfer of ownership – Information

4 **Default by the Debtor** *330*
   Breach of contract – Default notices – Repossession – Acceleration clauses – Minimum payment clauses – Security

5 **Termination** *357*
   Early settlement – Creditor terminating – Debtor terminating – Termination, breach and settlement

6 **Judicial Control** *365*
   Enforcement orders – The debtor's protection – Extortionate credit bargains

7 **Credit Cards** *382*
   The agreement – The goods – Loss and misuse

Agency

1 **Introduction** *389*
   Agency defined – The creation of agency – The consent model revisited – A general principle?

2 **The Creation of Authority** *397*
   Introduction – Creation by agreement – Creation by estoppel – Creation by ratification – Creation by operation of law – Usual authority

3 **Powers of Attorney** *424*
   Definition – Construction of powers of attorney – The Powers of Attorney Act 1971 – Irrevocable powers of attorney

4 **Contracts Made by Agents** *432*
   Introduction – Disclosed principal – Undisclosed principal – Agent acts outside his authority

5 **Torts Committed by Agents** *446*
   Introduction – Fraud – Other torts

6 **Obligations of Principal to Agent** *452*
   Remuneration – Indemnity – Enforcement

7 **Obligations of Agent to Principal** *460*
   Introduction – Obedience – Due care and skill – Conflict of interests – Secret profits – Delegation

8 **Termination of Agency** *471*
   Method and effect of termination – Irrevocable agencies – Period of notice required

Index *475*

Preface

HLT Textbooks are written specifically for students. Whatever their course, they will find our books clear and concise, providing comprehensive and up-to-date coverage. Written by specialists in their field, our textbooks are reviewed and updated on an annual basis.

While there has been no new legislation since the previous edition of this volume, there have been a number of new cases. Included are *Stewart Gill* v *Horatio Myer & Co Ltd* and *Kordas* v *Stokes Seeds Ltd* (on exclusion clauses and reasonableness); *Davy Offshore Ltd* v *Emerald Field Contracting Ltd* (on the passing of title in sale of goods contracts/supply of goods and services); *Warwickshire County Council* v *Johnson* (as to interpretation of s40(1) of Consumer Protection Act 1987); and *Kelly* v *Cooper* and *Sears Investment Trust Ltd* v *Lewis's Group Ltd* (on agents' obligations toward the principal.)

Cases and materials up to 16 April 1993 have been taken into consideration.

Table of Cases

Adams v Morgan [1924] 1 KB 751   *457*
Ailsa Craig Fishing Co Ltd v Malvern Shipping Co Ltd [1983] 1 WLR 964   *109*
Aitken Campbell & Co Ltd v Boullen & Gatenby (1908) SC 490   *240*
Alan & Co Ltd v El Nasr Export & Import Co [1972] 2 All ER 127   *383*
Aldridge v Johnson (1857) 7 E & B 885   *13, 136, 137, 139, 142*
Allam & Co Ltd v Europa Poster Services Ltd [1968] 1 WLR 638; [1968] 1 All ER 826   *469*
Alpha Trading Ltd v Dunnshaw-Patten Ltd [1981] QB 290; [1981] 1 All ER 482   *456, 457, 472*
Aluminium Industrie Vaasen BV v Romalpa Aluminium Ltd [1976] 1 WLR 676; [1976] 2 All ER 552   *144, 151, 152, 153, 327*
Anangel Atlas Compania Naviera SA v Ishikawajima-Harima Heavy Industries & Co [1990] 1 Lloyd's Rep 167   *465*
Anchor Line, Re [1937] Ch 1; [1936] 2 All ER 941   *143*
Anderson v Pacific Fire & Marine Insurance Co (1872) LR 7 CP 65   *24*
Andre & Cie v Michel Blanc & Fils [1979] 2 Lloyd's Rep 427   *26, 34*
Andrew v Ramsay & Co [1903] 2 KB 635   *455, 466*
Andrews Bros (Bournemouth) Ltd v Singer & Co Ltd [1934] 1 KB 17   *110*
Andrews v Hopkinson [1957] 1 QB 229; [1956] 3 All ER 422   *319, 320*
Anglo-Auto Finance Co Ltd v James [1963] 1 WLR 1042; [1963] 3 All ER 566   *349*
Anglo Overseas Transport Ltd v Titan Industrial Corporation (UK) Ltd [1959] 2 Lloyd's Rep 152   *458*
Archer v Stone (1898) 78 LT 34   *440*
Arcos Ltd v E A Ronaasen & Son [1933] AC 470   *60, 68, 69*
Ardath Tobacco Ltd v Ocker (1930) 47 TLR 177   *178*
Arenson v Casson Beckman Rutley & Co [1977] AC 405; [1975] 3 All ER 901   *462*
Armagas v Mundogas, The Ocean Frost [1986] AC 717; [1986] 2 All ER 385   *404, 406, 407, 410, 449, 451, 467*
Armaghdown Motors Ltd v Gray Motors Ltd [1962] NZLR 5   *236*
Armour v Thyssen Edelstahlwerke AG [1990] 3 WLR 810   *153*
Armstrong v Jackson [1917] 2 KB 822   *38, 464, 465*
Armstrong v Stokes (1872) LR 7 QB 598   *442*
Arpad, The [1934] P 189   *244*
Asfar v Blundell [1896] 1 QB 123   *162*

Table of Cases

Ashbury Railway Carriage & Iron Co v Riche (1875) LR 7 HL 653   *415*
Ashington Piggeries Ltd v Christopher Hill Ltd [1972] AC 441; [1971] 1 All ER 847   *64, 65, 66, 69, 88, 91, 249*
Associated Distributors v Hall [1938] 2 KB 83; [1938] 1 All ER 511   *347, 351, 361*
Associated Japanese Bank (International) Ltd v Credit Du Nord SA [1988] 3 All ER 902   *121*
Astley Industrial Trust Ltd v Miller [1968] 3 All ER 36   *187, 190*
Aswan (M/S) Engineering Establishment Co v Lupdine Ltd [1987] 1 WLR 1; [1987] 1 All ER 135   *76, 81*
Atlas Express v Kafco [1989] 1 All ER 641   *20*
Attwood v Small (1838) 7 Cl & Fin 232   *28*
Attorney-General for Ceylon v Silva [1953] AC 461 (PC)   *408*
Australian Knitting Mills v Grant (1933) 50 CLR 387; reversed sub nom Grant v Australian Knitting Mills, qv   *76, 78, 81*
Avon Finance Co Ltd v Bridger [1985] 2 All ER 281   *381*
Azemer v Casella (1867) LR 2 CP 177   *67*

Badgerhill Properties v Cottrell (1991) The Independent 12 June   *433*
Badische Anilin und Soda Fabrik v Basle Chemical Works [1898] AC 200   *141, 142*
Badische Co Ltd, Re [1921] 2 Ch 331   *164*
Bain v Fothergill (1874) LR 7 HL 158   *9*
Balsamo v Medici [1984] 1 WLR 951; [1984] 2 All ER 304   *470*
Bank of England v Vagliano Bros [1891] AC 107   *3*
Bank of Kuwait v Hammoud [1988] 3 All ER 418   *408, 449*
Baring v Corrie (1818) 2 B & Ald 137   *443*
Barker v Bell [1971] 1 WLR 983; [1971] 2 All ER 867   *205*
Barnett, Hoares & Co v South London Tramways Co (1887) 18 QBD 815   *402*
Barrett v Deere (1828) Moo & M 200   *412*
Barron v FitzGerald (1840) 6 Bing NC 201   *458*
Barrow, Lane & Ballard Ltd v Phillip Phillips & Co Ltd [1929] 1 KB 574   *161*
Bartlett v Sydney Marcus Ltd [1965] 1 WLR 1013; [1965] 2 All ER 753   *78, 83, 90*
Barwick v English Joint Stock Bank (1867) LR 2 Exch 259   *448*
Bass plc v Customs and Excise Commissioners (1991) (unreported)   *272*
Beale v Taylor [1967] 1 WLR 1193; [1967] 3 All ER 253   *65, 70*
Beck v Szymanowski & Co Ltd [1924] AC 43   *110*
Bedford Insurance Co Ltd v Instituto de Resseguros do Brasil [1985] QB 966; [1984] 3 All ER 766   *416*
Beecham & Co Pty Ltd v Francis Howard & Co Pty Ltd [1921] VLR 428   *78*
Behnke v Bede Shipping Co Ltd [1927] 1 KB 649   *247*
Behrend v Produce Brokers' Co Ltd [1920] 3 KB 530   *61*

Bell v Lever Bros [1932] AC 161   *465*
Belmont Finance v Williams Furniture (No 2) [1980] 1 All ER 393   *30*
Belvoir Finance Co Ltd v Stapleton [1971] 1 QB 210; [1970] 3 All ER 664   *363*
Bentinck v Cromwell Engineering Co [1971] 1 QB 324; [1971] 1 All ER 33   *339*
Benton v Campbell Parker & Co [1925] 2 KB 410   *436*
Bentworth Finance v Lambert [1968] 1 QB 680; [1967] 2 All ER 810   *190*
Berndtson v Strang (1868) 3 Ch App 588   *219*
Bernstein v Pamson Motors (Golders Green) Ltd [1987] 2 All ER 220   *77, 79, 83, 238*
Beswick v Beswick [1968] AC 58; [1967] 2 All ER 1197   *412*
Bethell & Co Ltd v Clark & Co Ltd (1888) 20 QBD 615   *217*
Biggar v Rock Life Insurance Co [1902] 1 KB 516   *400*
Biggs, ex parte (1859) 28 LJ Ch 50   *28*
Binstead v Buck (1776) 2 W Bl 1117   *419*
Bishopsgate Motor Finance Corporation Ltd v Transport Brakes Ltd [1949] 1 KB 322; [1949] 1 All ER 37   *165, 179*
Bissett v Wilkinson [1927] AC 177   *24*
Blackburn Bobbin Co v Allen & Sons [1918] 1 KB 540   *163*
Blades v Free (1829) 9 B & C 167   *472*
Blyth Shipbuilding Co Ltd, Re [1926] Ch 494   *141, 142*
Boardman v Phipps [1967] 2 AC 46; [1966] 3 All ER 721   *464, 465*
Bolton v Lancashire & Yorkshire Railway (1866) LR 1 CP 431   *218*
Bolton Partners v Lambert (1889) 41 Ch D 215   *417*
Bond Worth, Re [1980] Ch 228; [1979] 3 All ER 919   *152*
Booth SS Co Ltd v Cargo Fleet Iron Co Ltd [1916] 2 KB 570   *220*
Borden (UK) Ltd v Scottish Timber Products Ltd [1981] Ch 25; [1979] 3 All ER 961   *152*
Borrowman v Drayton (1876) 2 Ex D 15   *60*
Borrowman Phillips & Co v Frere & Hollis (1878) 4 QBD 500   *230*
Boston Deep Sea Fishing and Ice Co Ltd v Ansell (1888) 39 Ch D 339   *466*
Boston Deep Sea Fishing and Ice Co Ltd v Farnham [1957] 1 WLR 1051; [1957] 3 All ER 204   *414, 417*
Boulton v Jones (1857) 2 H & N 564   *440*
Bovington & Morris v Dale & Co Ltd (1902) 7 Com Cas 112   *157*
Bowes v Shand (1877) 2 App Cas 455   *52, 67*
Bowra (John) & Son v Rodoma Canned Foods Ltd [1967] 1 Lloyd's Rep 183   *96*
Brady v St Margaret's Trust Ltd [1963] 2 QB 494; [1963] 2 All ER 175   *331, 335*
Brandon v Leckie (1972) 29 DLR (3d) 663   *203*
Branwhite v Worcester Works Finance Ltd [1969] 1 AC 552; [1968] 3 All ER 104   *300, 319, 320*
Bridge v Campbell Discount Co Ltd [1962] AC 600; [1962] 1 All ER 385   *278, 326, 338, 340, 347, 348, 349, 350, 351*

Briess v Woolley [1954] AC 333; [1954] 1 All ER 909   *499*
Bristol Tramways Co Ltd v Fiat Motors Ltd [1910] 2 KB 831   *75, 87, 89*
British Airways Board v British Airports Authority (1981) The Times 8 May   *124*
British Bank for Foreign Trade Ltd v Novimex Ltd [1949] 1 KB 623; [1949] 1 All ER 155   *453*
British Bank of the Middle East v Sun Life Assurance Co of Canada (UK) Ltd [1983] 2 Lloyd's Rep 9   *402, 407, 408, 410*
British & Commonwealth Holdings Plc v Quadrex Holdings Inc [1989] 3 WLR 723   *100*
Brook v Hook (1871) LR 6 Ex 89   *413*
Brook's Wharf & Bull Wharf Ltd v Goodman Bros [1937] 1 KB 534; [1936] 3 All ER 696   *458*
Brown (B S) & Son v Craikes Ltd [1970] 1 WLR 750; [1970] 1 All ER 823   *78*
Bryant, Powis and Bryant Re, v Banque de Peuple [1893] AC 170   *425*
Buchanan-Jardine v Hamlink 1983 SLT 149   *71*
Budberg v Jerwood (1934) 51 TLR 99   *186*
Bunge Corporation v Tradax SA [1981] 1 WLR 711; [1981] 2 All ER 513   *41, 42*
Burial Board of the Parish of St Margaret, Rochester v Thompson (1871) LR CP 445   *468*
Business Applications Specialists v Nationwide Credit Corporation [1988] RTR 332   *80*
Butterworth v Kingsway Motors Ltd [1954] 1 WLR 1286; [1954] 2 All ER 694   *45, 46, 47, 318*

Cahn v Pockett's Bristol Channel Co Ltd [1899] 1 QB 643   *155, 200, 213, 219*
Calico Printers' Association v Barclays Bank (1931) 145 LT 51   *469*
Cameron & Co v Slutzkin Pty Ltd (1923) 32 CLR 81   *96*
Cammell Laird & Co Ltd v Manganese Bronze & Brass Co Ltd [1934] AC 402   *15, 92*
Campanari v Woodburn (1854) 15 CB 400   *472*
Campbell Mostyn (Provisions) Ltd v Barnett Trading Co [1954] 1 Lloyd's Rep 65   *228*
Capital & Counties Bank v Warriner (1896) 12 TLR 216   *199*
Capital Finance Co Ltd v Bray [1964] 1 WLR 323; [1964] 1 All ER 603   *338, 363*
Capital Finance v Donati (1977) 121 SJ 270   *349*
Car & Universal Finance Co Ltd v Caldwell [1965] 1 QB 525; [1964] 1 All ER 290   *33, 181, 198, 202*
Carlill v Carbolic Smoke Ball Co [1893] 1 QB 256   *256*
Casey's Patents, Re [1892] 1 Ch 104   *452*
Cehave NV v Bremer Handelsgesellschaft, The Hansa Nord [1976] QB 44; [1975] 3 All ER 739   *41, 42, 75, 81, 82*
Central Newbury Car Auctions v Unity Finance [1957] 1 QB 371; [1956] 3 All ER 905   *170, 192*

Chalmers, ex parte (1873) 8 Ch App 289   *210*
Champanhac & Co v Waller & Co [1948] 2 All ER 724   *98*
Chapleton v Barry Urban District Council [1940] 1 KB 532   *105*
Chapman Bros v Verco Bros & Co Ltd (1933) 49 CLR 306   *17*
Charge Card Services Ltd, Re [1988] NLJ LR 201; [1988] 3 WLR 764   *18, 383, 385*
Charrington Fuel Oil v Parvant (1988) The Times 28 December   *407*
Charringtons Ltd v Smith [1906] 1 KB 79   *376, 377, 379*
Charter v Sullivan [1957] 2 QB 117; [1957] 1 All ER 809   *226*
Chartered Trust plc v Pitcher (1987) The Times 13 February   *338, 340*
Charterhouse Credit Co Ltd v Tolly [1963] 2 QB 683; [1963] 2 All ER 432   *326*
Chaudhry v Prabhakar [1988] 3 All ER 718   *463*
China Pacific SA v Food Corporation of India, The Winson [1982] AC 939; [1981] 3 All ER 688   *418, 419, 420*
Choko Star, The [1990] 1 Lloyd's Rep 516   *420*
Christoforides v Terry [1924] AC 566   *461*
Clark v Dickson (1858) EB & E 148   *38*
Clarke v Mackintosh (1862) 4 Giff 134   *29*
Clarkson, Booker Ltd v Andjel [1964] 2 QB 775; [1964] 3 All ER 260   *443*
Clayton v Leroy [1911] 2 KB 1031   *178*
Clerk v Laurie (1857) 2 H & N 199   *474*
Clough Mills Ltd v Martin [1985] 1 WLR 111; [1984] 3 All ER 982   *328*
Coastal International Trading Ltd v Maroil [1988] 1 Lloyd's Rep 92   *243*
Cobec Brazilian Trading and Warehousing Corporation v Toepfer [1983] 2 Lloyd's Rep 386   *53*
Cohen v Kittell (1889) 22 QBD 680   *461*
Coldunell v Gallon [1986] QB 1184; [1986] 1 All ER 429   *380, 381*
Collen v Wright (1857) 8 E & B 647   *444*
Collins v Associated Greyhound Racecourses Ltd [1930] 1 Ch 1   *441*
Comet Group plc v British Sky Broadcasting [1991] TLR 211   *389*
Commonwealth Trust Ltd v Akotey [1926] AC 72   *169, 170*
Compagnie Commerciale Sucres et Denrées v C Czarnikow Ltd [1990] 1 WLR 1337   *49*
Comptoir d'Achat v Louis de Ridder, The Julia [1949] AC 293; [1949] 1 All ER 269   *159*
Cooden Engineering Co Ltd v Stanford [1953] 1 QB 86; [1952] 2 All ER 915   *348, 349*
Cooke v Wilson (1856) 1 CB NS 153   *437*
Corfield v Sevenways Garage Ltd [1985] RTR 109   *70*
Cornwall v Wilson (1750) 1 Ves Sen 509   *416*
Couchman v Hill [1947] KB 554; [1947] 1 All ER 103   *105*
Couturier v Hastie (1856) 5 HL Cas 673; (1856) 8 Exch 40   *160, 419*

Coventry Shepperd & Co v Great Eastern Railway Co (1883) 11 QB D 776   *173*
Crane v London Dock Company (1864) 5 B & S 313   *178*
Crocker Horlock Ltd v B Lang & Co Ltd [1949] 1 All ER 526   *456*
Cronin (Trading as Cronin Driving School) v Customs and Excise Commissioners [1991] STC 333   *271*
Crowther v Shannon Motor Co [1975] 1 WLR 30; [1975] 1 All ER 139   *79, 83, 93*
Cundy v Lindsay (1878) 3 App Cas 459   *21, 171, 180*
Cunliffe v Harrison (1851) 6 Exch 903   *61*
Cunliffe-Owen v Teather & Greenwood [1967] 1 WLR 1421; [1967] 3 All ER 561   *403*
Curtis v Chemical Cleaning and Dyeing Co Ltd [1951] 1 KB 805   *104*
Curtis v Maloney [1951] 1 KB 736; [1950] 2 All ER 982   *176*
Customs (R & B) Brokers Co Ltd v United Dominions Trust Ltd [1988] 1 All ER 847   *71, 115*
Cutter v Powell (1795) 6 Term Rep 320   *164*

Danziger v Thompson [1944] KB 654; [1944] 2 All ER 151   *440*
Darlington (Peter) & Partners v Gosho Co Ltd [1964] 1 Lloyd's Rep 149   *99, 266*
Daun v Simmins (1879) 41 LT 783   *422*
Davies v Directloans Ltd [1986] 1 WLR 823; [1986] 2 All ER 783   *380*
Davies v London & Provincial Marine Insurance Co (1878) 8 Ch D 469   *27*
Davies v Sumner [1984] 3 All ER 831   *70, 113, 115*
Davy Offshore v Emerald Field Contracting Ltd [1992] 2 Lloyd's Rep 142   *143*
Dawson (Clapham) Ltd v H & G Dutfield [1936] 2 All ER 232   *13*
De Bussche v Alt (1878) 8 Ch D 286   *468*
De Vries v Smallridge [1928] 1 KB 482   *375*
Dean v Keate (1811) 3 Camp 4   *334*
Debenham v Mellon (1880) 6 App Cas 24   *421*
Debenham's Ltd v Perkins (1925) 133 LT 252   *436*
Debtor, Re a [1903] 1 KB 705   *376*
Debtor, Re a (No 627 of 1936) [1937] Ch 156; [1937] 1 All ER 1   *355*
Delfini, The [1990] 1 Lloyd's Rep 252   *154*
Demby Hamilton Ltd v Barden [1949] 1 All ER 435   *158*
Denmark Publications Ltd v Boscobel Productions Ltd [1969] 1 QB 699; [1968] 3 All ER 513   *472*
Dennant v Skinner & Collom [1948] 2 KB 164; [1948] 2 All ER 29   *146, 151*
Derry v Peek (1889) 14 App Cas 337   *30, 31*
Dickinson v Dodds (1876) 2 Ch D 463   *306*
Dimmock v Hallett (1866) LR 2 Ch App 21   *24, 27*
Ditcham v Worrall (1880) 5 CPD 410   *414*
Dixon v Stansfield (1850) 10 CB 398   *459*
Donoghue v Stevenson [1932] AC 562   *250*

Dowson and Jenkins, Re [1904] 2 Ch 219   *425*
Doyle v Olby (Ironmongers) [1969] 2 QB 158; [1969] 2 All ER 119   *33*
Drakeford v Piercy (1866) 7 B & S 515   *443*
Drew v Nunn (1879) 4 QBD 661   *472, 473*
Drummond (James) & Sons v Van Ingen & Co (1887) 12 App Cas 284   *96*
Du Jardin v Beadman Bros [1952] 2 QB 712; [1952] 2 All ER 160   *198*
Duke v Jackson (1921) SC 362   *86*
Dunkirk Colliery v Lever (1878) 9 Ch D 20   *226*
Dunlop Pneumatic Tyre Co Ltd v New Garage and Motor Co Ltd [1915] AC 79   *348*
Dunne v English (1874) LR 18 Eq 524   *465*
Dyal Singh v Kenyan Insurance Ltd [1954] AC 287; [1954] 1 All ER 847   *176*
Dyster v Randall & Sons [1926] Ch 932   *440, 441*

Eastern Distributors Ltd v Goldring [1957] 2 QB 600; [1957] 2 All ER 525   *170, 171, 172, 194, 411*
Ebrahim Dawood Ltd v Heath Ltd [1961] 2 Lloyd's Rep 512   *56, 240*
Edgington v Fitzmaurice (1888) 29 Ch D 459   *25, 29*
Edmunds v Bushell and Jones (1865) LR 1 QB 97   *422*
Edwards v Ddin [1976] 1 WLR 943; [1976] 3 All ER 705   *138*
Edwards v Vaughan (1910) 26 TLR 545   *149, 197*
Elafi, The see Karlshamns Oljefabriker v Eastport Navigation Co
Elbinger Act, Fur Fabrication von Eisenbahn Material v Claye (1873) LR 8 QB 313   *437*
Elphick v Barnes (1880) 5 CPD 321   *150*
Elwin v O'Regan & Maxwell [1971] NZLR 1124 NZ Sup Ct   *203*
Enichem Anic SpA v Ampelos Shipping (1989) The Times 11 August   *154*
Epps v Rothnie [1945] KB 562; [1946] 1 All ER 146   *440*
Esso Petroleum Co Ltd v Mardon [1976] QB 801; [1975] 1 All ER 203   *35*
Esso Petroleum Co Ltd v Commissioners of Customs and Excise [1976] 1 WLR 1; [1976] 1 All ER 117   *17, 263*
Esteve Trading Corporation v Agropec International, The Golden Rio [1990] 2 Lloyd's Rep 273   *242*
European Asian Bank AG v Punjab and Sind Bank (NZ) [1983] 1 WLR 642; [1983] 2 All ER 508   *401, 461*
Evans (J) and Son (Portsmouth) Ltd v Andrea Merzario Ltd [1976] 1 WLR 1078   *105*

Faccenda Chicken Ltd v Fowler [1986] 1 All ER 617   *466*
Fairlie v Fenton (1870) LR 5 Exch 169   *434*
Falcke v Gray (1859) 4 Drew 651   *247*
Farnworth Finance Facilities Ltd v Attryde [1970] 1 WLR 1053; [1970] 2 All ER 774   *324, 326*

Farquharson Bros v King & Co Ltd [1902] AC 325   *167*
Federspiel (Carlos) v Charles Twigg & Co Ltd [1957] 1 Lloyd's Rep 240   *137, 139, 140*
Felthouse v Bindley (1863) New Rep 401   *300*
Ferrier, Re [1944] Ch 295   *150*
Finance (F C) Ltd v Francis (1970) 114 SJ 568   *337, 338, 339*
Financings Ltd v Baldock [1963] 2 QB 104; [1963] 1 All ER 443   *41, 330, 331, 332, 335, 348, 349, 365*
Financings Ltd v Stimson [1962] 1 WLR 1184; [1962] 3 All ER 386   *300, 319*
First National Bank v Syed [1991] 2 All ER 250   *373*
Firth v Staines [1897] 2 QB 70   *414*
Fleming v Bank of New Zealand [1900] AC 577   *417*
Fletcher v Knell (1872) 42 LJQB 55   *26*
Florence, Re (1879) 10 Ch D 591   *149*
Flynn v Mackin [1974] IR 101   *13*
Foalquest v Roberts (1990) 21 EG 156   *433*
Foley v Classique Coaches Ltd [1934] 2 KB 1   *7*
Folkes v King [1923] 1 KB 282   *188*
Forman & Co Pty Ltd v The Liddesdale (Owners) [1900] AC 190   *416*
Formby Bros v Formby (1910) 102 LT 116   *439*
Forward Trust v Whymark [1989] 3 WLR 1229   *335, 357*
Four Point Garage Ltd v Carter [1985] 3 All ER 12   *327*
Fred Drughorn Ltd v Rederiaktiebolaget Transatlantic [1919] AC 203   *439, 440*
Freeman & Lockyer v Buckhurst Park Properties (Mangal) Ltd [1964] 2 QB 480; [1964] 1 All ER 630   *400, 404, 405, 407, 408, 410*
French (L) & Co Ltd v Leeston Shipping Co Ltd [1921] 1 AC 451   *457*
Friend v Young [1897] 2 Ch 421   *472*
Frith v Frith [1906] AC 254   *473*
Frost v Aylesbury Dairy Co Ltd [1905] 1 KB 608   *72, 89, 93*
Fullwood v Hurley [1928] 1 KB 498   *465*

Gallagher v Shilcock [1949] 2 KB 765; [1949] 1 All ER 921   *222*
Garnac Grain v Faure & Fairclough [1966] AC 1130n; [1967] 2 All ER 353   *392*
Geddling v Marsh [1920] 1 KB 668   *72, 85, 86*
Geier v Kujawa [1970] 1 Lloyd's Rep 364   *106*
Genn v Winkel (1911) 28 TLR 483   *149, 150*
Gillespie Bros Ltd v Roy Bowles Transport Ltd [1973] QB 400   *111*
Godley v Perry [1960] 1 WLR 9; [1960] 1 All ER 36   *77, 89, 97, 98, 245*
Godts v Rose (1854) 17 CB 22   *138*
Gokal Chand-Jagan Nath v Nand Ram Das-Atma Ram [1939] AC 106; [1938] 4 All ER 407   *464*
Goker v NWS Bank plc (1990) The Times 23 May   *342*

Golding Davies & Co Ltd, ex parte [1889] 13 Ch D 628   *219*
Goldsworthy v Brickell [1987] 1 All ER 853   *381*
Gordon v Street [1899] 2 QB 642   *28*
Gosforth, The (1987) (unreported)   *134*
Goulston Finance Co Ltd v Clark [1967] 2 QB 493; [1967] 1 All ER 61   *353*
Gower v Van Dedalzen (1837) 3 Bing NC 717   *85*
Grafton v Armitage (1845) 135 ER 975   *15*
Grant v Australian Knitting Mills Ltd [1936] AC 85   *90, 251*
Great Northern Railway v Swaffield (1874) LR 9 Ex 132   *419*
Greaves & Co (Contractors) Ltd v Baynham Meikle and Partners [1975] 1 WLR 1095; [1975] 3 All ER 99   *272*
Green v Whitehead [1930] 1 Ch 38   *425*
Green (R W) Ltd v Cade Bros Farm [1978] 1 Lloyd's Rep 602   *123*
Greenman v Yuba Power Products Inc (1962) 377 P (2d) 897   *252*
Greer v Downs Supply Co [1927] 2 KB 28   *441*
Grenfell v E B Meyrowitz [1936] 2 All ER 1313   *67*
Griffiths v Peter Conway [1939] 1 All ER 685   *88*
Grover and Grover v Matthews [1910] 2 KB 401   *415*

Hadley v Baxendale (1854) 9 Ex 341   *243*
Hall (R & H) Ltd and W H Pim & Co's Arbitration, Re [1928] All ER Rep 763   *243*
Halsey v Wolfe [1915] 2 Ch 330   *376, 379*
Hamburg, The (1863) 2 Moore PC (ns) 289   *419*
Hammer & Barrow v Coca Cola [1962] NZLR 723   *233*
Hannan's Express Gold Mining and Development Co Ltd, Re, ex parte Carmichael [1896] 2 Ch 643   *473*
Harbutt's Plasticine v Wayne Tank & Pump Co Ltd [1970] 1 QB 447; [1970] 1 All ER 225   *120*
Hardy & Co v Hillerns & Fowler [1923] 2 KB 490   *97, 230, 233, 236*
Hargreave v Spink [1892] 1 QB 25   *178*
Harlingdon & Leinster Enterprises v Christopher Hull Fine Art [1990] 1 All ER 737   *66, 84*
Harmer v Armstrong [1934] Ch 65   *435*
Harper & Co v Vigers Brothers [1909] 2 KB 549   *434*
Harris v Wyre District Council [1989] 2 WLR 790; [1988] 1 All ER 691   *125*
Harrods Ltd v Lemon [1931] 2 KB 517   *455, 465*
Hartley v Hymans [1920] 3 KB 475   *52*
Hasell v Bagot Shakes & Lewis Ltd (1911) 13 CLR 374   *226*
Havering London Borough Council v Stevenson [1970] 3 All ER 609   *115*
Hawksley v Outram [1892] 3 Ch 359   *425*
Hayman v McLintock (1907) SC 936   *134*

Table of Cases

Head v Tattersall (1871) LR 7 Ex 7   *159*
Heald v Kenworthy (1855) 10 Exch 739   *442*
Healey v Howlett & Sons [1917] 1 KB 337   *135, 136, 157, 159*
Healings (Sales) Pty Ltd v Inglis Electrix Pty Ltd (1968) 42 ALJR 280   *48*
Heap v Motorists' Advisory Agency Ltd [1923] 1 KB 577   *185, 188, 192*
Hedley Byrne & Co Ltd v Heller & Partners Ltd [1964] AC 465; [1963] 2 All ER 575   *31, 35, 272, 319, 320, 463*
Heil v Hedges [1951] 1 TLR 512   *84*
Heilbutt v Hickson (1872) LR 7 CP 438   *235*
Helby v Matthews [1895] AC 471   *16, 197, 279, 282, 316, 325, 326, 344*
Hely-Hutchinson v Brayhead Ltd [1968] 1 QB 573; [1967] 3 All ER 98   *399, 400, 401, 403, 410*
Henderson & Co v Williams [1895] 1 QB 521   *169*
Hermione, The [1922] P 162   *461*
Hillas & Co v Arcos Ltd (1932) 147 LT 503   *7*
Hippisley v Knee Bros [1905] 1 KB 1   *455*
Hochster v De La Tour (1853) 2 E & B 678   *472*
Hodges (G T) & Sons v Hackbridge Park Residential Hotel Ltd [1940] 1 KB 404; [1939] 4 All ER 347   *454*
Hollier v Rambler Motors [1972] 2 QB 71   *108*
Holroyd v Marshall (1862) 10 HL Cas 191   *12*
Holwell Securities Ltd v Hughes [1974] 1 WLR 155; [1974] 1 All ER 161   *299*
Hongkong Fir Shipping Co Ltd v Kawasaki Kisen Kaisha Ltd [1962] QB 26; [1961] 1 All ER 474   *41, 42*
Hookway (F E) & Co v Alfred Isaacs & Son [1954] 1 Lloyd's Rep 491   *96*
Hop & Malt Exchange, Re, ex parte Briggs (1866) LR 1 Eq 483   *38*
Horn v Minister of Food [1948] 2 All ER 1036   *162*
Horner v Kingsley Clothing Co Ltd (1989) The Times 6 July   *258*
Horsfall v Thomas (1862) 1 H & C 90   *28*
Howard Marine & Dredging Co Ltd v A Ogden & Sons Ltd [1978] 1 QB 574; [1978] 2 All ER 1134   *37*
Howell v Coupland (1876) 1 QBD 258   *164*
Howes v Watson (1824) 2 B & C 243   *148*
Humble v Hunter (1848) 12 QB 310   *439*

Industrial Development Consultants Ltd v Cooley [1972] 1 WLR 443; [1972] 2 All ER 162   *464, 465*
Industries and General Mortgage Co Ltd v Lewis [1949] 2 All ER 573   *466*
Ingram v Little [1961] 1 QB 31; [1960] 3 All ER 332   *21, 171, 180, 440*
International Contract Co, Re (1871) 6 Ch App 525   *435*
Interfoto Picture Library v Stiletto Visual Programmes Ltd [1988] 2 WLR 615   *107*

Ireland v Livingstone (1872) LR 5 HL 395   *209, 401, 461*
Irvine & Co v Watson & Sons (1880) 5 QBD 414   *442*
Isaacs v Pardie (unreported)   *14*

Jackson v Chrysler Acceptances Ltd [1978] RTR 474   *245*
Jackson v Rotax Motors & Cycle Co Ltd [1910] 2 KB 937   *55, 56, 80, 81, 94, 97, 231, 240*
Jarvis v Swans Tours Ltd [1973] 1 QB 233; [1973] 1 All ER 71   *34*
Jeffcott v Andrews Motors Ltd [1960] NZLR 721   *201, 202*
Jend v Slade (1797) 2 Esp 571   *24*
Jerome v Bentley & Co [1952] 2 All ER 114   *168, 185, 411*
Johnson v Agnew [1980] AC 367; [1979] 1 All ER 883   *366*
Jones v Bowden (1813) 4 Taunt 84   *99*
Jones v Tarleton (1842) 9 M & W 674   *214*
Joseph v Lyons (1884) 15 QB 280   *207*

Karflex Ltd v Poole [1933] 2 KB 251   *45, 317, 325, 327*
Karlshamns Oljefabriker v Eastport Navigation Corp, The Elafi [1982] 1 All ER 208   *135*
Keighley Maxsted & Co v Durant [1901] AC 240   *413*
Kelly v Cooper [1992] 3 WLR 936   *465*
Kelner v Baxter (1866) LR 2 CP 174   *414, 433, 434*
Kemp v Falk (1882) 7 App Cas 573   *218, 219*
Kendall (Henry) & Sons Ltd v William Lillico & Sons Ltd [1969] 2 AC 31; [1968] 2 All ER 444   *76, 78, 89, 90, 92, 93, 108*
Kendall v Marshall, Stephens & Co (1883) 11 QBD 356   *217*
Keppell v Wheeler [1927] 1 KB 577   *461, 462*
Kidderminster Corporation v Hardwicke (1873) LR 9 Exch 13   *417*
Kings Norton Metal Co v Edridge (1897) 14 TLR 98   *21*
Kirkham v Attenborough [1897] 1 QB 201   *149*
Kleinwort Benson v Malaysian Mining Corporation [1989] 1 All ER 785   *19*
Kofi Sunkersette Obu v Strauss & Co [1951] AC 243   *453*
Kooragang Investments Pty Ltd v Richardson & Wrench Ltd [1982] AC 462; [1981] 3 All ER 65   *451*
Kordas v Stokes Seeds Ltd (1993) 96 DLR 129   *103*
Kronprinzessen Cecilie, The (1917) 33 TLR 292   *17*
Kruse v Seeley [1924] 1 Ch 136   *376, 379*
Kursell v Timber Operators & Contractors Ltd [1927] 1 KB 298   *9*
Kwei Tek Chao v British Traders and Shippers Ltd [1954] 2 QB 459; [1954] 1 All ER 779   *156, 235, 237, 449, 450*

L'Estrange v Graucob [1934] 2 KB 394   *103, 104*
Lage v Siemens Bros & Co Ltd (1932) 42 Ll LR 252   *457*

Table of Cases

Lagunas Nitrate Co *v* Lagunas Syndicate [1899] 2 Ch 392   *38*
Lally and Weller *v* George Bird (a firm) (1980) (unreported)   *113*
Lamb & Evans [1893] 1 Ch 218   *465*
Lambert *v* G & C Finance Corporation Ltd (1963) (unreported)   *203*
Lambert *v* Lewis [1982] AC 225; [1980] 2 WLR 299   *83, 160, 250*
Langmead *v* Thyer Rubber Co Ltd (1947) SR (SA) 29   *202*
Langton *v* Higgins (1859) 4 H & N 402   *137, 139*
Larner *v* Fawcett [1950] 2 All ER 727   *177*
Laurie & Morewood *v* John Dudin & Sons [1926] 1 KB 223   *134, 136*
Lavery *v* Purcell (1888) 39 Ch D 508   *10*
Lazenby Garages Ltd *v* Wright [1976] 1 WLR 459; [1976] 2 All ER 770   *227*
Leaf *v* International Galleries [1950] 2 KB 86; [1950] 1 All ER 693   *38, 241, 325*
Lee *v* Bayes (1856) 18 CB 599   *177*
Lee *v* Butler [1893] 2 QB 318   *197, 279*
Lee *v* Griffin (1861) 30 LJQB 272   *14*
Lee *v* Lee's Air Farming Ltd [1961] AC 12   *281*
Lee *v* York Coach and Marine [1977] RTR 35   *77*
Leigh & Sillivan Ltd *v* Aliakmon Shipping Co Ltd, The Aliakmon [1986] AC 785; [1986] 2 WLR 902   *470*
Lem *v* Barotto Sports Ltd (1977) 69 DLR   *86*
Lester *v* Balfour Williamson Merchant Shippers Ltd [1953] 2 QB 168; [1953] 1 All ER 1146   *435*
Levison *v* The Patent Steam Carpet Cleaning Co Ltd [1978] QB 69   *108, 111*
Levy *v* Goldhill Co [1917] 2 Ch 297   *474*
Levy *v* Green (1858) 8 E & B 575   *62*
Lewis *v* Averay [1972] 1 QB 198; [1971] 3 All ER 907   *21, 180*
Lickbarrow *v* Mason (1787) 2 Term Rep 63   *167, 171*
Lightburn *v* Belmont Sales Ltd (1969) 6 DLR (3d) 692   *238*
Liverpool City Council *v* Irwin [1977] AC 239 [1976] 2 All ER 39   *401*
Lloyd *v* Grace, Smith & Co [1912] AC 716   *448, 449*
Lloyds Bank *v* Bank of America [1938] 2 KB 147; [1938] 2 All ER 63   *190*
Lloyds & Scottish Finance *v* Williamson [1965] 1 WLR 404; [1965] 1 All ER 642   *191*
Logicrose *v* Southend United Football Club [1988] 1 WLR 1256   *467*
Lombard North Central plc *v* Butterworth [1987] 2 WLR 7; [1987] 1 All ER 267   *40, 330, 333*
Lombard Tricity Finance Ltd *v* Paton [1989] 1 All ER 918   *305*
London Wine Co, Re [1986] PCC 121   *134*
Long *v* Lloyd [1958] 1 WLR 753; [1958] 2 All ER 402   *38, 238, 241*
Lorymer *v* Smith (1822) 1 B & C 1   *97*
Lowther *v* Harris [1927] 1 KB 393   *185*
Luxor (Eastbourne) Ltd *v* Cooper [1941] AC 108; [1941] 1 All ER 33   *456, 471, 472*

Lyell v Kennedy (1899) 9 HLC 391   *413*
Lyle (B S) Ltd v Pearson and Medlycott [1941] 2 KB 391; [1941] 3 All ER 128   *377*
Lyons v May & Baker Ltd [1923] 1 KB 685   *209, 231*

McCann (John) & Co v Pow [1975] 1 All ER 129; [1974] 1 WLR 1643   *469*
McCutcheon v David McBrayne Ltd [1964] 1 WLR 125   *106, 108*
McDonald v Empire Garages (Blackburn) Ltd (1975) The Times 8 October   *92*
McRae v Commonwealth Disposals (1951) 84 CLR 377   *160*
Macaura v Northern Insurance Co [1925] AC 619   *281*
Magee v Pennine Insurance Co [1969] 2 QB 507; [1969] 2 All ER 891   *27*
Mahesan v Malaysia Government Officers' Co-Operative Housing Society Ltd [1979] AC 374; [1978] 2 All ER 405   *467*
Manchester Liners v Rea [1922] 2 AC 74   *88*
Maniffature Tessile Laviera Wooltex v Ashley [1979] 2 Lloyd's Rep 28   *239*
Maple Flock Co Ltd v Universal Furniture Products (Wembley) Ltd [1934] 1 KB 148   *57, 231*
Marcel (Furriers) Ltd v Tapper [1953] 1 WLR 49; [1953] 1 All ER 15   *15*
Mariola Marine Corporation v Lloyds Registry of Shipping, The Morning Watch [1990] 1 Lloyd's Rep 547   *31*
Market Overt, Case of (1596) 5 Co Rep 83b   *177*
Marshall v Green (1815) 1 CPD 35   *9*
Marten v Whale [1917] 2 KB 48   *199*
Martin-Baker Aircraft Co Ltd v Murison [1955] 2 QB 556; [1955] 2 All ER 722   *474*
Martineau v Kitching (1872) 2 QB 436   *148*
Mash & Murrell Ltd v Joseph I Emmanuel [1962] 1 WLR 16; [1961] 1 All ER 485 (reversed on its facts [1962] 1 WLR 16; [1962] 1 All ER 77n)   *160*
May & Butcher v R [1934] 2 KB 17   *6, 7*
Medway Oil & Storage Co Ltd v Silica Gel Corporation (1928) 33 Com Cas 195   *92*
Mehta v Sutton (1913) 108 LT 214   *186*
Mendelssohn v Normand [1970] 1 QB 177   *105*
Mercantile Bank of India Ltd v Central Bank of India Ltd [1938] AC 297   *168, 169*
Mercantile Credit Co Ltd v Cross [1965] 2 QB 205; [1965] 1 All ER 557   *339, 340*
Mercantile Credit Co Ltd v Hamblin [1965] 2 QB 242; [1964] 3 All ER 592   *172, 174, 302, 319*
Merchant Banking Co v Phoenix Bessemer Steel Ltd (1877) 5 Ch D 205   *211*
Mersoja v H Norman Pitt & Co Ltd (1989) The Times 31 January   *298*
Metropolitan Asylums Board Manager v Kingham & Sons (1890) 6 TLR 217   *416*

Microbeads A-G v Vinhurst Road Markings Ltd [1975] 1 WLR 218; [1975] 1 All ER 529   *48, 49*
Midland Bank v Reckitt [1933] AC 1   *426*
Mihalis Angelos, The [1971] 1 QB 164; [1970] 3 All ER 125   *25, 40*
Millar v Radford (1903) 19 TLR 575   *454*
Millars of Falkirk Ltd v Turpie (1976) SLT (Notes) 66   *84*
Miller v Race (1758) 1 Burr 452   *207*
Millett v Van Heeck [1921] 2 KB 369   *228*
Mitchell v Jones (1905) 24 NZLR 932   *193*
Mitchell (George) (Chesterhall) Ltd v Finney Lock Seeds Ltd [1983] 2 All ER 737   *103, 109, 110, 123, 131, 132*
Mitsui & Co v Flota Mercante Grancolombiana SA, The Guidad de Pasto, The Cuidad de Neiva [1989] 1 WLR 1145; [1989] 1 All ER 951   *154*
Molling v Dean & Son (1901) 18 TLR 217   *234*
Moore & Co and Landauer & Co, Re [1921] 2 KB 519   *62, 64, 67, 68*
Moorgate Mercantile Ltd v Finch & Reed [1962] 1 QB 701; [1962] 2 All ER 467   *176*
Moorgate Mercantile Co Ltd v Twitchings [1977] AC 890; [1976] 2 All ER 641   *172, 173, 174*
Mordaunt Bros v British Oil & Cake Mills Ltd [1910] 2 KB 502   *214*
Morgan v Russell & Sons [1909] 1 KB 357   *9*
Morison v Lockhart 1912 2 SLT 189   *145*
Mount v Jay & Jay Co Ltd [1960] 1 QB 159; [1959] 3 All ER 307   *134, 137, 200, 213, 214*
Mucklow v Mangles (1808) 1 Taunt 318   *137*
Muirhead v Industrial Tank Specialities Ltd [1985] 3 All ER 705   *251*
Muirhead and Turnbull v Dickson (1905) 7 F 686   *20*
Munro (Robert A) & Co Ltd v Meyer [1930] 2 KB 312   *57*
Munro v Willmott [1949] 2 KB 295; [1948] 2 All ER 983   *419*

Nanka Bruce v Commonwealth Trust Ltd [1926] AC 77   *147*
National Coal Board v Gamble [1959] 1 QB 11; [1958] 3 All ER 203   *138*
National Employers Mutual General Insurance Association Ltd v Jones [1988] 2 WLR 952; [1988] 2 All ER 425; [1987] 3 All ER 385   *188, 198, 203, 204*
National Pari-Mutual Association v R (1930) 47 TLR 110   *26*
National Westminster Bank plc v Morgan [1985] AC 686; [1985] 1 All ER 821   *381*
Naughton v O'Callaghan (1990) The Times 17 February   *36*
Navarro v Moregrand Ltd [1951] 2 TLR 674   *451*
Neilson v Stewart 1991 SLT 523   *19*
New Zealand Shipping Co Ltd v Satterthwaite (AM) & Co Ltd [1975] AC 154   *109, 111*

Newborne v Sensolid (Great Britain) Ltd [1954] 1 QB 45; [1953] 1 All ER 708
  434
Newsholme Bros v Road Transport and General Insurance Co Ltd [1929] 2 KB 356
  450
Newtons of Wembley Ltd v Williams [1965] 1 QB 560; [1964] 3 All ER 532   *181,
  196, 197, 198, 202, 203*
Niblett v Confectioners Materials [1921] 3 KB 387   *44, 48*
Nichol v Godts (1854) 10 Exch 191   *67*
Nicholson v Harper [1895] 2 Ch 414   *193*
Noblett v Hopkinson [1905] 2 KB 214   *140*
North West Securities Ltd v Alexander Breckon Ltd [1981] RTR 518   *300, 319*
Notts Patent Brick & Tile Co v Butler (1886) 16 QBD 778   *27*

Olds Discount v Krett [1940] 2 KB 117; [1940] 3 All ER 36   *194*
Ollett v Jordan [1918] 2 KB 41   *146*
Olley v Marlborough Court Hotel [1949] 1 KB 532   *107*
Oppenheimer v Attenborough [1908] 2 KB 221   *191*
Oppenheimer v Frazer & Wyatt [1907] 1 KB 50   *187*
Orion Insurance v Sphere Drake Insurance (1990) The Independent 11 February
  19
Oscar Chess Ltd v Williams [1957] 1 WLR 370; [1957] 1 All ER 325   *65*
Overbrooke Estates Ltd v Glencombe Properties Ltd [1974] 1 WLR 1335   *105*
Overstone Ltd v Shipway [1962] 1 WLR 117; [1962] 1 All ER 52   *331, 332, 333,
  335, 344, 348, 349, 350*

Pacific Motor Auctions Pty v Motor Credits Ltd [1965] AC 867; [1965] 2 All ER
  105   *194, 195, 199*
Panchaud Frères SA v Etablissements General Grain Co [1970] 1 Lloyd's Rep 53
  237
Panorama Developments (Guildford) Ltd v Fidelis Furnishing Fabrics Ltd [1971] 2
  QB 711; [1971] 3 All ER 16   *402*
Parker v Palmer (1821) 4 B & A 387   *95*
Parker v South Eastern Railway (1877) 2 CPD 416   *106*
Payne v Elsden (1900) 17 TLR 161   *4*
Pearson (S) & Son Ltd v Dublin Corporation [1907] AC 351   *29*
Pearson v Rose & Young [1951] 1 KB 275; [1950] 2 All ER 1027   *187, 188, 189,
  190, 203*
Peer v Humphrey (1835) 2 A & E 495   *177*
Perkins v Bell [1893] 1 QB 193   *97, 234*
Perlmutter v Beth David Hospital (1955) 123 NE 2d 792   *15*
Pfeiffer (E) Weinkellerei-Weineinkauf GmbH v Arbuthnot Factors [1988] 1 WLR
  150   *152*
Phillips v Brooks [1919] 2 KB 243   *180*

Photo Production Ltd v Securicor Transport Ltd [1980] AC 827; [1980] 1 All ER 556   *103, 109, 110, 113, 120, 122, 366*
Pickard v Sears (1837) 6 A & E 469   *171*
Pignataro v Gilroy [1919] 1 KB 459   *138, 142, 157*
Pletts v Campbell [1895] 2 QB 229   *143*
Plischke & Sohne GmbH v Allison Bros Ltd [1936] 2 All ER 1009   *217*
Pole v Leask (1863) 33 LJ Ch 155   *392*
Polenghi Bros v Dried Milk Co Ltd (1904) 92 LT 64   *97*
Polhill v Walter (1832) 3 B & Ad 114   *30, 445*
Poole v Smith's Car Sales [1962] 1 WLR 744; [1962] 2 All ER 482   *150*
Porter v General Guarantee Corporation Ltd [1982] RTR 384   *321*
Prager v Blatspiel, Stamp and Heacock Ltd [1924] 1 KB 566   *419, 421*
President of India v La Pintada Corporation [1985] AC 104; [1984] 2 All ER 773   *333*
Priest v Last [1903] 2 KB 148   *87*

R, Re (Enduring Power of Attorney) [1990] 2 WLR 1219   *430*
R v Carr-Briant [1943] KB 607; [1943] 2 All ER 156   *468*
R v McHugh [1977] RTR 1   *139*
R v Modupe (1991) The Times 27 Feburary   *301*
R v Secretary of State for Trade & Industry, ex parte First National Bank plc (1990) The Times 7 March   *298*
Rafaella, The [1985] 2 Lloyd's Rep 36   *408*
Raffles v Wichelhaus (1864) 2 H & C 906   *20*
Randall v Newsom (1876) 45 LJQB 364   *71*
Rasbora v JCL Marine Ltd [1977] 1 Lloyd's Rep 645   *115, 124*
Reading Trust Ltd v Spero [1930] 1 KB 492   *377, 379*
Reardon Smith Line v Hansen-Tangen [1976] 1 WLR 989; [1976] 3 All ER 570   *42, 64, 66, 68*
Reddell v Union Castle Mail SS Co (1915) 84 LJKB 360   *217*
Redgrave v Hurd (1881) 20 Ch D 1   *29*
Reese River Silver Mining Co v Smith (1869) LR 4 HL 64   *25*
Regent v Francesco of Jermyn Street Ltd [1981] 3 All ER 327   *58*
Reid v Commissioner for the Police for the Metropolis [1973] QB 551; [1973] 2 All ER 97   *179*
Reid v Macbeth [1904] AC 223   *141*
Reuter v Sala & Co (1879) 4 CPD 239   *56, 60*
Richardson, Spence and Company v Rowntree [1894] AC 217   *106*
Richmond Gate Property Co Ltd, Re [1965] 1 WLR 335; [1964] 3 All ER 936   *453*
Rickards (Charles) Ltd, v Oppenheim [1950] 1 KB 616; [1950] 1 All ER 420   *52, 272*

Riddiford v Warren (1901) 20 NZLR 572   *241*
Riley v Webb [1987] CCLR 65   *257*
Robertson (J S) Pty Ltd v Martin (1955-6) 94 CLR 30   *236*
Robinson v Graves [1935] 1 KB 579   *13, 14, 263*
Robinson v Mollett (1874) LR 7 HL 802   *402*
Roe v Minister of Health [1954] 2 QB 66   *15*
Rogers v Parish (Scarborough) Ltd [1987] 2 All ER 232   *76, 79, 80, 83*
Rohde v Thwaites (1827) 6 B & C 388   *138, 142*
Rolls Razor Ltd v Cox [1967] 1 QB 552; [1967] 1 All ER 397   *184, 459*
Rosenbaum v Belson [1900] 2 Ch 267   *401*
Rotherham MBC v Raysun [1988] CCLR 1   *257*
Rowland v Divall [1923] 2 KB 500   *5, 45, 46, 317*
Royscott Trust Ltd v Rogerson [1991] 3 WLR 57   *35*
Ruben (E & S) Ltd v Faire Bros Ltd [1949] 1 KB 254; [1949] 1 All ER 215   *96*

Sachs v Miklos [1948] 2 KB 23; [1948] 1 All ER 67   *176, 419*
Said v Butt [1920] 3 KB 497   *440, 441*
Sainsbury v Street [1972] 1 WLR 834; [1972] 3 All ER 1127   *162, 164*
Salford Corporation v Lever [1891] 1 QB 168   *466–467*
Saloman v Saloman & Co [1897] AC 22   *281*
Samuel v Newbold [1906] AC 461   *376, 378*
Samuels v Davis [1943] 1 KB 526; [1943] 2 All ER 3   *115, 272*
Santa Carina, The [1977] 1 Lloyd's Rep 478   *435, 436*
Saudi Crown, The [1986] 1 Lloyd's Rep 261   *450*
Saunders v Anglia Building Society [1971] AC 1004; [1970] 3 All ER 961   *105, 302*
Saunders v Pilcher [1949] 2 All ER 1097   *9*
Schmaltz v Avery (1851) 16 QB 655   *434*
Schneider v Heath (1813) 3 Camp 506   *26*
Scholefield v Templer (1859) 4 De G & J 429   *39*
Schuler AG v Wickman Machine Tool Sales Ltd [1974] AC 235   *40*
Scott v Hansor (1829) 1 Russ & M 128   *24*
Scruttons v Midland Silicones Ltd [1962] AC 446   *111*
Sealace Shipping Co Ltd v Oceanvoice Ltd, The Apecos M [1990] 1 Lloyd's Rep 82   *243, 245*
Sears Investment Trust Ltd v Lewis's Group Ltd [1992] TLR 459   *460*
Seddon v NE Salt Co [1905] 1 Ch 326   *241*
Shanklin Pier Ltd v Detel Products Ltd [1951] 2 KB 854; [1951] 2 All ER 471   *319*
Shaw v Metropolitan Police Commissioner [1987] 3 All ER 405   *166, 171*
Shearson Lehman Hutton Inc v I Maclaine Watson & Co Ltd (No 2) [1990] 3 All ER 723; [1990] 1 Lloyd's Rep 441   *243*

Shine v General Guarantee Corporation Ltd [1988] 1 All ER 911   *80, 318*
Shipton Anderson & Co Ltd v Weil Bros & Co [1912] 1 KB 574   *60*
Shipton Anderson & Co Ltd and Harrison Bros & Co Ltd, Re [1915] 3 KB 676   *151*
Shirlaw v Southern Foundries (1926) Ltd [1939] 2 KB 206; [1939] 2 All ER 113   *401*
Sims & Co v Midland Railway [1913] 1 KB 103   *175, 419, 420*
Singer Co (UK) Ltd v Tees & Hartlepool Port Authority [1988] 2 Lloyd's Rep 164   *126, 127*
Slater v Hoyle & Smith [1920] 2 KB 11   *245*
Smart Brothers Ltd v Holt [1929] 2 KB 303   *344, 345*
Smart v Sandars (1848) 5 CB 895   *474*
Smith v Bush [1989] 2 WLR 790; [1987] 3 All ER 179   *32, 125*
Smith v Chadwick (1884) 9 App Cas 187   *29*
Smith v Land & House Property Corporation (1884) 28 Ch D 7   *25*
Société des Industries Metallurgiques SA v Bronx Engineering Co Ltd [1975] Lloyd's Rep 336   *247*
Solle v Butcher [1950] 1 KB 671; [1949] 2 All ER 1107   *26*
Somes v British Empire Shipping Co (1860) 8 HLC 338   *212*
Sorrell v Finch [1977] AC 728; [1976] 2 All ER 371   *443*
South Western General Property Co Ltd v Marton (1982) 263 EG 1090   *127*
Southwark LBC v Charlesworth (1983) 147 JP 470   *257*
Southwell v Bowditch (1876) 1 CPD 374   *435*
Sovereign Leasing plc v Ali (1991) The Times 21 March   *367*
Spencer v Cosmos Air Holidays (1989) The Times 6 December   *111*
Spooner v Sandilands (1842) 1 Y & C 390   *474*
Springer v Great Western Railway [1921] 1 KB 257   *419, 420*
Spurling (J) v Bradshaw [1956] 1 WLR 461   *107*
Stadium Finance v Robbins Ltd [1962] 2 QB 664; [1962] 2 All ER 633   *189*
Staffs Motor Guarantee Ltd v British Wagon Co Ltd [1934] 2 KB 30   *187, 193, 194*
Stag Line Ltd v Tyne Ship Repair Group Ltd, The Zinnia [1984] 2 Lloyd's Rep 211   *126*
Stein, Forbes & Co Ltd v County Tailoring Co Ltd (1916) 86 LJKB 448   *138*
Stennet v Hancock and Peters [1939] 2 All ER 578   *251*
Sterns Ltd v Vickers Ltd [1923] 1 KB 28   *158*
Stevenson v Beverley Bentinck Ltd [1976] 1 WLR 483; [1976] 2 All ER 606   *205*
Stevenson v Nationwide Building Society (1984) 272 EG 663   *125*
Stewart Gill Ltd v Horatio Myer & Co Ltd [1992] 2 All ER 257   *109, 270*
Suisse Atlantique Société d'Armement Maritime SA v NV Rotterdamsche Kolen Centrale [1967] 1 AC 361; [1966] 2 All ER 61   *120*
Summers v Solomon (1857) 26 LJ QB 301   *473*

Swan, The [1968] 1 Lloyd's Rep 5   *435*
Syars v Jonas (1848) 2 Exch 111   *96*
Symmons (Peter) & Co v Cook (1981) 131 NLJ 758   *115*

Tai Hing Cotton Mill v Kamsing Knitting [1979] AC 91; [1978] 1 All ER 515
   243
Tailby v Official Receiver (1885) 13 App Cas 523   *12*
Tamplin v James (1880) 15 Ch D 215   *20*
Tanner v Christian (1855) 4 E & B 591   *427*
Tarling v Baxter (1827) 6 B & C 360   *145*
Tate v Crewdson [1938] Ch 869; [1938] 3 All ER 43   *355*
Tatung (UK) Ltd v Galex Telesure Ltd [1989] BCC 325   *152*
Taylor v Brewer (1813) 1 M & S 290   *453*
Taylor v Combined Buyers Ltd [1924] NZLR 627   *65*
Taylor v G E Railway Co [1901] 1 KB 774   *216*
Teheran-Europe v S T Belton Tractors Ltd [1968] 2 QB 545; [1968] 2 All ER 886
   88, 90, 437
Thacker v Hardy (1878) 4 QBD 685   *458*
Thomas Cheshire & Co v Vaughan Bros & Co [1920] 3 KB 240   *469*
Thompson Ltd v Robinson (Gunmakers) Ltd [1955] Ch 17   *226*
Thomson v LMS Railway [1930] 1 KB 40   *106*
Thorn v Commissioners of Public Works (1836) 32 Beav 490   *247*
Thorne & Co Ltd v Thomas Borthwick & Son (1956) SR (NSW) 81   *96*
Thornett & Fehr v Beers & Son [1919] 1 KB 486   *75*
Thornton v Shoe Lane Parking Ltd [1971] 2 QB 163   *107, 108*
Tiedemann and Ledermann Frères, Re [1899] 2 QB 66   *413*
Toulmin v Millar (1887) 12 App Cas 746   *454*
Tradax Export SA v European Grain [1983] 2 Lloyd's Rep 100   *67*
Tradax International SA v Goldschmidt SA [1977] 2 Lloyd's Rep 605   *237*
Turley v Bates (1863) 2 H & C 200   *147*
Turner v Mucklow (1862) 6 LT 690   *91*
Turner v Sampson (1911) 27 TLR 200   *186*
Turpin v Bilton (1843) 5 Man & G 455   *461*
Tye v Fynmore (1813) 3 Camp 462   *95*

UCB Leasing Ltd v Holtom [1987] CCLR 101   *325*
Underwood v Bank of Liverpool [1924] 1 KB 775   *281*
Underwood v Burgh Castle Brick & Cement Syndicate [1922] 1 KB 343   *10, 145, 146*
United City Merchants (Investments) Ltd v Royal Bank of Canada [1982] 2 WLR
   1039; [1982] 2 All ER 720   *450*
United Dominions Trusts Ltd v Ennis [1968] 1 QB 54; [1967] 2 All ER 345   *338, 339, 340, 347, 351*

United Dominions Trusts Ltd *v* Taylor [1980] SLJ 28   *322*
United Dominions Trusts Ltd *v* Western [1976] QB 513; [1975] 3 All ER 1017   *302*
Unity Finance Ltd *v* Woodcock [1963] 1 WLR 455; [1963] 2 All ER 270   *352, 353*
Universal Steam Navigation Co *v* McKelvie [1923] AC 492   *435*
Uxbridge Permanent Benefit Building Society *v* Pickard [1939] 2 KB 248; [1939] 2 All ER 344   *448, 449*

Vacwell Engineering Co Ltd *v* BDH Chemicals [1971] 1 QB 88; [1969] 3 All ER 1681 (appeal allowed by agreement [1971] 1 QB 111; [1970] 3 All ER 553n)   *93*
Valpy *v* Gibson (1847) 4 CB 837   *214*
Vantage Navigation Corporation *v* Suhail & Saud Bahwan Building Materials [1989] 1 Lloyd's Rep 138   *20*
Varley *v* Whipp [1900] 1 QB 513   *65, 68, 69*

Wadham Stringer Finance Ltd *v* Meaney [1981] 1 WLR 39; [1980] 3 All ER 789   *343, 344*
Wait, Re [1927] 1 Ch 606   *12, 140, 152, 241, 247*
Wait & James *v* Midland Bank (1926) 31 Comm Cas 172   *135, 137*
Waldron-Kelly *v* British Railways Board [1981] 3 CL 33   *126*
Walford *v* Miles [1992] 2 WLR 174   *19*
Walia *v* Michael Naughton Ltd [1985] 3 All ER 673   *425*
Walker *v* Boyle [1982] 1 WLR 495; [1982] 1 All ER 643   *126*
Walker, Winser & Hann, Re *v* Shaw & Co [1904] 2 KB 152   *95, 96*
Wallersteiner *v* Moir [1974] 1 WLR 991   *281*
Wallis Son & Wells *v* Pratt & Haynes [1911] AC 394; [1910] 2 KB 1003 at 1012   *39, 110*
Ward (R V) *v* Bignall [1967] 1 QB 534; [1967] 2 All ER 449   *143, 206, 221, 222*
Wardar's (Import & Export) *v* Norwood Ltd [1968] QB 663; [1968] 2 All ER 602   *140*
Warehousing and Forwarding Co of East Africa Ltd *v* Jafferali & Sons Ltd [1964] AC 1; [1963] 3 All ER 571   *417*
Warinco AG *v* Samor SPA [1977] 2 Lloyd's Rep 582   *231*
Warman *v* Southern Counties Car Finance Corporation Ltd [1949] 2 KB 576; [1949] 1 All ER 711   *317, 325, 327*
Warwickshire County Council *v* Johnson [1993] 2 WLR 1   *258*
Watson *v* Swann (1862) 11 CB BS 756   *413*
Watteau *v* Fenwick [1893] 1 QB 346   *421, 422, 423*
Watts *v* Spence [1976] Ch 165; [1975] 2 All ER 528   *34*
Way *v* Latilla [1937] 3 All ER 759   *452*
Weiner *v* Gill [1906] 2 KB 574   *149*
Weiner *v* Harris [1910] 1 KB 285   *149, 184*
Welch *v* Bank of England [1955] Ch 508; [1955] 1 All ER 811   *416*

Wertheim v Chicoutimi Pulp Co Ltd [1911] AC 301   *245*
West (HW) Ltd v McBlain [1950] NI 144   *46*
Western Credit Ltd v Alberry [1964] 1 WLR 945; [1964] 2 All ER 938   *352*
White v Garden (1851) 10 CB 919   *39*
Whitehorn Bros v Davison [1911] 1 KB 463   *182*
Wiehe v Dennis Bros (1913) 29 TLR 250   *158*
Wilensko Slaski Towarzystwo Drevno v Fenwick & Co Ltd [1938] 3 All ER 429   *60*
Williams v Agius [1914] AC 510   *242*
Willis v FMC Machinery & Chemicals (1976) 68 DLR   *86*
Wilson v Harper Son & Co [1908] 2 Ch 370   *455*
Wilson v Rickett Cockerell & Co Ltd [1954] 1 QB 598; [1954] 1 All ER 868   *73, 86*
Wimble & Sons v Rosenberg & Sons [1913] 3 KB 743   *59*
Wiskin v Terdich Bros [1928] Arg LR 242   *51*
With v O'Flanagan [1936] Ch 575; [1936] 1 All ER 727   *27*
Woodman v Photo-Trade Processing Ltd (1981) (unreported)   *125*
Woodstead Finance Ltd v Petrou [1986] BTLC 267   *379, 381*
Worcester Works Finance Ltd v Cooden Engineering Co Ltd [1972] 1 QB 210; [1971] 3 All ER 78   *187, 195, 199*
Workman Clark & Co Ltd v Lloyd Brazileno [1908] 1 KB 968   *224, 282*
Wormell v RHM Agricultural (East) Ltd [1987] 1 WLR 1091; [1986] 1 All ER 769   *73, 86*
Wren v Holt [1903] 1 KB 610   *98*

Yeoman Credit Ltd v Apps [1962] 2 QB 508; [1961] 2 All ER 281   *326*
Yeoman Credit Ltd v Latter [1961] 1 WLR 828; [1961] 2 All ER 294   *352*
Yeoman Credit Ltd v Waragowski [1961] 1 WLR 1124; [1961] 3 All ER 145   *331, 333*
Yonge v Toynbee [1910] 1 KB 215   *445, 472, 473*
Young (Thomas) & Sons Ltd v Hobson & Partners (1949) 65 TLR 365   *59*

Zagury v Furnell (1809) 2 Camp 240   *147*

Table of Statutes

Administration of Justice Act 1970
    s40   *341*
Auctions (Bidding Agreements) Act 1969 *22*
    s3   *22*

Banking Act 1979
    s38   *302*
Bankruptcy Act 1914
    s38(c)   *6*
    s38(3)   *164*
Bankruptcy and Deeds of Arrangement Act 1913
    s15   *175, 176*
Bills of Lading Act 1855
    s1   *134*
Bills of Sales Acts 1854–91   *278, 301*

Carriage By Air Act 1961   *130*
Companies Act 1985
    s36(4)   *414, 433*
    ss80–116   *281*
    ss190–197   *281*
    s395   *152*
    s396(1)   *152*
Consumer Credit Act 1974   *16, 22, 175, 176, 197, 204, 259, 268, 277, 279, 280, 281, 282, 283, 284, 286, 289, 293, 294, 298, 300, 303, 305, 307, 308, 312, 320, 323, 327, 328, 334, 343, 353, 354, 357, 360, 365, 377, 378, 382*
    s8   *281*
    s8(1)   *281, 282*
    s8(2)   *281, 284*
    s8(3)   *281*

Consumer Credit Act 1974 (*contd.*)
    s9(1)   *282*
    s9(3)   *282*
    s9(4)   *292, 384*
    s10   *285*
    s10(1)   *285, 288, 382, 383*
    s10(2)   *285, 384*
    s10(3)   *285, 383, 384*
    s11   *285*
    s11(1)   *286, 287, 288, 290, 382*
    s11(2)   *383*
    s11(3)   *286*
    s12   *285, 287, 288, 290, 311, 314, 321, 322, 323, 382, 385*
    s13   *285, 287, 383*
    s14   *383*
    s14(3)   *383*
    s16   *281, 283*
    s17(1)   *284*
    s17(2)   *383*
    s18   *289*
    s18(2)   *289*
    s19   *290, 292*
    s19(1)   *290, 291, 355, 385*
    s19(2)   *291*
    s19(3)   *291, 307*
    s19(4)   *291*
    s20(1)   *283, 292*
    s21(1)   *294*
    s22(1)   *295*
    s22(5)   *295*
    s23(3)   *315*
    s25(1)   *294*
    s25(2)   *295, 296*
    s32(1)   *297*
    s33   *297*

Consumer Credit Act 1974 (contd.)
- s39(1) 295, 296, 315
- s39(2) 295
- s40(1) 296
- s43 284
- s44 284
- s45 284
- s46 284, 299
- s47 284
- s48 284, 315
- s48(1) 315
- s48(2) 315
- s49 284
- s49(1) 315
- s49(2) 308, 315
- s50 284
- s51 284
- s56 284, 319, 320
- s56(2) 289, 310, 320, 321, 322
- s56(3) 320
- s56(4) 320
- s57 307, 309, 310
- s57(1) 306, 315
- s57(2) 307, 309
- s57(3) 306, 307
- s57(4) 307
- s60 284, 302, 353, 368,
- s61 284, 302, 368
- s61(1) 301, 302, 303, 368
- s62 284, 302, 305, 306, 368, 369, 372, 375
- s62(1) 303, 304, 383
- s62(2) 303, 304, 305
- s62(3) 306
- s63 284, 302, 305, 306, 368, 369, 372, 375
- s63(1) 303, 304, 305
- s63(2) 304, 305, 309, 310, 368, 383
- s63(3) 305
- s63(4) 383
- s63(5) 306

Consumer Credit Act 1974 (contd.)
- s64 284, 302, 368
- s64(1) 305, 309, 310, 354, 369
- s64(5) 306
- s65 284, 302
- s65(1) 303, 306, 365, 367
- s66 284
- s66(1) 386
- s66(2) 386
- s67 308, 309
- s68 308, 309
- s69 308, 310, 312
- s69(1) 310, 314
- s69(2) 313
- s69(5) 314
- s70 308
- s70(1) 310, 311, 312
- s70(2) 311
- s70(3) 311
- s70(4) 310
- s71 308, 314
- s71(1) 311
- s71(2) 311
- s71(3) 311
- s72 308, 313
- s72(1) 311, 312
- s72(2) 312
- s72(3) 313
- s72(4) 312, 313, 314
- s72(5) 312
- s72(6) 312
- s72(7) 312
- s72(8) 313
- s72(9) 313
- s72(11) 313
- s73 308, 313
- s73(2) 314
- s73(5) 314
- s73(6) 314
- s73(7) 314
- s74(1) 302
- s74(2) 284

Consumer Credit Act 1974 (*contd.*)
   s74(3)   *302*
   s74(3A)   *302*
   s75   *321, 322, 385*
   s75(1)   *321, 322, 323, 385*
   s75(2)   *385*
   s75(3)   *322, 385*
   s75(4)   *385*
   s75(5)   *385*
   s76   *329, 336, 359, 372*
   s76(1)   *329*
   s76(2)   *329*
   s76(3)   *329*
   s76(5)   *329*
   s77   *284*
   s77(1)   *328*
   s77(4)   *329*
   s78   *284*
   s78(1)   *328*
   s78(6)   *329*
   s79   *284*
   s81   *341*
   s82   *294*
   s82(1)   *384*
   s82(2)   *293*
   s82(3)   *294*
   s82(5)   *294*
   s82(6)   *294*
   s83(1)   *386*
   s84(1)   *386*
   s84(2)   *386*
   s84(3)   *386*
   s84(5)   *386*
   s85(1)   *384*
   s85(2)   *384*
   s86(1)   *359*
   s86(2)   *359*
   s86(5)   *360*
   s86(6)   *360*
   s87   *336*
   s87(1)   *335, 336, 342, 359, 366, 367, 385*

Consumer Credit Act 1974 (*contd.*)
   s87(2)   *385*
   s88(1)   *336*
   s89   *336*
   s90   *337, 339*
   s90(1)   *337*
   s90(2)   *337*
   s90(3)   *337*
   s90(5)   *337*
   s91   *338*
   s92(1)   *341*
   s92(3)   *341*
   s93   *333*
   s94   *285, 343, 357, 358*
   s95   *358*
   s97(1)   *357*
   s97(3)   *357*
   s98   *359, 372*
   s98(3)   *359*
   s99   *323, 360, 361, 364*
   s99(1)   *343, 360, 361*
   s99(4)   *360*
   s99(5)   *360*
   s100   *346*
   s100(1)   *361, 362, 363*
   s100(3)   *362*
   s100(4)   *363*
   s100(5)   *364*
   s102   *323*
   s102(2)   *323*
   s105   *353*
   s105(1)   *353*
   s105(4)   *353*
   s105(5)   *353*
   s105(7)   *354, 365*
   s106   *354*
   s107   *355*
   s108   *355*
   s111(1)   *355*
   s111(2)   *355, 365*
   s113(1)   *354, 374*
   s113(2)   *354*

Consumer Credit Act 1974 (contd.)
- s113(3) *354*
- s113(7) *355*
- s113(8) *355*
- s120 *176*
- s121 *176*
- s124 *365*
- s127 *306, 367*
- s127(1) *368*
- s127(2) *368*
- s127(3) *368*
- s127(4) *306, 369*
- s127(5) *368, 374*
- s129 *285, 372, 373*
- s129(1) *372*
- s129(2) *372, 373, 374*
- s130 *285*
- s130(1) *373*
- s130(4) *373*
- s130(5) *373*
- s130(6) *374*
- s131 *285, 370*
- s131(1) *371*
- s132 *285*
- s133 *285*
- s133(1) *370, 371*
- s133(3) *371*
- s133(4) *371*
- s133(5) *371*
- s133(6) *372*
- s134 *285*
- s135 *285*
- s135(1) *372, 374*
- s136 *285, 374, 378*
- s137 *285, 377*
- s137(1) *378*
- s137(2) *377*
- s138 *285, 377, 378, 379, 380, 381*
- s138(1) *378*
- s138(2) *379, 380*
- s138(3) *379, 380*

Consumer Credit Act 1974 (contd.)
- s138(4) *379, 380*
- s139 *285, 377*
- s139(1) *377*
- s139(2) *378*
- s139(5) *377*
- s140 *285, 377*
- s141 *367*
- s141(1) *367*
- s142 *375*
- s142(1) *375*
- s142(2) *375*
- s145(2) *296*
- s147(1) *296*
- s149(1) *296*
- s149(2) *296*
- s149(4) *296*
- s170(1) *280, 327, 329*
- s170(3) *280*
- s171(7) *378*
- s173(1) *280, 327, 343*
- s173(3) *339*
- s175 *323*
- s176(2) *310*
- s176(3) *310*
- s176(8) *310*
- s184(1) *292*
- s184(3) *288*
- s184(5) *288, 292*
- s185(5) *281*
- s187 *288*
- s187(1) *288*
- s187(2) *288*
- s187(3) *288*
- s187(4) *288*
- s189 *279, 294, 310*
- s189(1) *263, 281, 284, 327, 353, 365*
- Schedule 1 *296, 302, 303, 329*

Consumer Protection Acts 1961–71 *257*

Consumer Protection Act 1987 *249, 253, 254, 255*

Table of Statutes xxxv

Consumer Protection Act 1987 (*contd.*)
    s1(1)   *253*
    s1(2)   *253*
    s1(3)   *253*
    s2(1)   *252, 253*
    s2(2)   *252, 253*
    s2(3)   *252, 253*
    s2(4)   *252, 254*
    s3(1)   *254*
    s3(2)   *254*
    s4   *254*
    s4(1)   *255*
    s4(10)   *255*
    s5(7)   *252*
    s6(7)   *252*
    s7   *256*
    s10   *257*
    s13   *257*
    s14   *257*
    s39   *257*
    Part I   *16, 72, 249, 251, 252, 256*
    Part II   *257*
Consumer Safety Act 1978   *257*
County Courts Act 1984
    s15(1)   *367*
Criminal Justice Act 1982
    s67   *249*
Customs and Excise Act 1952   *176*

Enduring Powers of Attorney Act 1985   *428, 429, 430, 431*
    s1   *428, 429, 430*
    s1(1)   *129*
    s1(2)   *429*
    s1(3)   *430*
    s2   *428*
    s2(1)   *428*
    s2(2)   *428, 429*
    s2(3)   *429*
    s2(4)   *429*

Enduring Powers of Attorney Act 1985 (*contd.*)
    s2(5)   *429*
    s2(6)   *429*
    s2(7)   *428, 429*
    s2(8)   *429*
    s2(9)   *428, 429*
    s2(10)   *429*
    s2(11)   *429*
    s2(12)   *429*
    s2(13)   *429*
    s3   *430*
    s3(1)   *430*
    s3(2)   *430*
    s3(3)   *430*
    s3(4)   *430*
    s3(5)   *430*
    s8   *431*
    s8(2)   *431*
Factors Act 1889   *3, 165, 168, 182, 183, 184, 186, 189, 192*
    s1(1)   *183*
    s1(2)   *198*
    s1(4)   *50, 192, 195*
    s2   *185, 186, 187, 188, 190*
    s2(1)   *183, 193, 194, 202, 203*
    s2(2)   *190*
    s8   *192, 193, 194, 195, 196, 201, 202*
    s9   *192, 196, 197, 198, 199, 200, 201, 202, 203, 204, 213, 279*
Fair Trading Act 1973   *259*
    s2   *259*
    s14   *259*
    Part II   *171, 259*
    Part III   *259*
    Part IX   *260*
Food Act 1984   *258*
Frustrated Contracts Act 1943   *163*
    s2(5)   *163*

Hire Purchase Act 1964   *197, 205*
    s27   *204, 205, 206*
    s27(2)   *204, 205, 206*
    s27(3)   *206*
    s27(4)   *206*
    s27(6)   *206*
    s28   *204*
    s29   *204*
    s29(1)   *204, 206*
    s29(2)   *205*
    Part III   *204, 206, 328, 340*

Infants' Relief Act 1874   *414*
    s1   *399*
Innkeepers Act 1878
    s1   *176*
Interpretation Act 1978
    s5   *281*
    s6   *308*
    Schedule 1   *281*

Law of Property Act 1925
    s40   *8*
    s40(1)   *401*
    s74(3)   *427*
    s74(4)   *427*
Law of Property (Miscellaneous Provisions) Act 1989   *8, 9*
    s1   *431*
    s2   *8, 9, 22, 398*
Law Reform (Enforcement of Contract) Act 1954   *14*
Law Reform (Frustrated Contracts) Act 1943   *164*
Limitation Act 1980   *255*

Magistrates' Courts Act 1980
    s39(2)   *295, 296*
Marine Insurance Act 1906
    s86   *415*
Matrimonial Proceedings and Property Act 1970
    s41   *421*

Medicines Act 1968   *258*
Mental Health Act 1983
    Part VII   *429*
Merchant Shipping Act 1894   *22*
Merchant Shipping Act 1979   *130*
Misrepresentation Act 1967   *34, 35, 126, 232, 241*
    s1   *241*
    s2   *31, 34*
    s2(1)   *31, 32, 34, 35, 36, 37, 246*
    s2(2)   *32, 35, 36, 37, 246*
    s3   *37, 105, 120*
    s4(2)   *233*
Mock Auctions Act 1961   *259*
Money Lenders Act 1900   *375, 376, 377, 378, 380*
    s1   *378*
    s1(1)   *376*
Moneylenders Act 1927   *278, 375, 376, 377*
    s10   *376*

Powers of Attorney Act 1971   *424, 426*
    s1   *426*
    s1(1)   *424, 426*
    s1(2)   *426*
    s1(3)   *426*
    s2   *426*
    s3   *426*
    s4   *428*
    s4(1)   *428*
    s4(2)   *428*
    s5   *427, 429*
    s5(1)   *427*
    s5(2)   *427*
    s5(3)   *427*
    s5(4)   *427*
    s7   *427, 435*
    s7(1)   *427*
    s7(2)   *427*

Powers of Attorney Act 1971 *(contd.)*
    s7(3)   *427*
    s10   *424, 425*
    Schedule 1   *424*
Power of Criminal Courts Act 1973 *249*
Prevention of Corruption Act 1906
    s1   *467*
Prevention of Corruption Act 1916
    s1   *467*

Sale of Goods Act 1893   *3, 10, 70, 75, 87, 90, 146, 247, 264*
    s11(1)   *232*
    s55(4)   *124*
    s55(5)   *124*
Sale of Goods Act 1979   *xlii, 3, 4, 8, 9, 10, 12, 13, 14, 15, 16, 18, 40, 43, 54, 55, 63, 71, 72, 75, 100, 117, 119, 140, 145, 146, 147, 160, 162, 163, 166, 197, 219, 233, 241, 245, 248, 250, 256, 261, 262, 263, 269, 270, 278, 279, 316, 318, 324*
    s2(1)   *4, 6, 13, 197, 203*
    s2(4)   *5*
    s2(5)   *5*
    s3   *262*
    s4   *22*
    s4(1)   *22*
    s4(6)   *98*
    s5(1)   *10*
    s5(2)   *11*
    s5(3)   *11, 12*
    s6   *11, 160, 161, 162, 163*
    s7   *5, 11, 160, 161, 162, 163*
    s8   *6, 7, 16, 19*
    s8(1)   *6*
    s8(2)   *6, 7, 16, 19*
    s8(3)   *6*
    s9   *6, 7*
    s9(1)   *7, 203*
    s9(2)   *7*
    s10   *221*

Sale of Goods Act 1979 *(contd.)*
    s10(1)   *100*
    s11(1)   *146*
    s11(3)   *39, 40, 146*
    s11(4)   *56, 62, 232, 239, 240*
    s12   *47, 116, 206, 261, 316*
    s12(1)   *4, 43, 44, 45, 46, 47, 48*
    s12(2)   *43, 47, 48, 49, 318, 332*
    s12(3)   *4, 43, 47*
    s12(4)   *4*
    s12(5)   *4*
    s13   *40, 62, 63, 64, 65, 66, 67, 68, 69, 70, 94, 99, 116, 119, 156, 236, 261, 264, 268, 318, 325*
    s13(1)   *64, 66, 318*
    s13(2)   *64*
    s13(3)   *65*
    s14   *40, 63, 64, 69, 70, 72, 93, 94, 99, 116, 119, 156, 249, 261, 318, 325*
    s14(1)   *70, 88, 89, 92, 93*
    s14(2)   *59, 62, 71, 74, 76, 79, 80, 81, 82, 83, 84, 85, 89, 93, 94, 97, 98, 117, 245, 265*
    s14(3)   *71, 73, 79, 83, 86, 87, 88, 89, 90, 91, 92, 93, 94, 98, 99, 117, 265, 266*
    s14(4)   *99, 266*
    s14(5)   *71, 266*
    s14(6)   *75, 76, 82, 84, 265*
    s15   *63, 70, 94, 95, 98, 99, 116, 119, 261, 266, 318, 325*
    s15(1)   *94, 95, 98*
    s15(2)   *94, 95, 96, 97, 98, 99*
    s16   *134, 135*
    s17   *136, 143, 144, 147, 151, 153, 154, 155, 278, 360*
    s17(1)   *143*
    s17(2)   *143*
    s18   *49, 58, 135, 139, 141, 143, 144, 147, 149, 151, 155, 197, 278, 282, 327, 360*

Sale of Goods Act 1979 (*contd.*)
  s19 *139, 144, 151, 152, 155, 212*
  s19(1) *139, 151, 153*
  s19(2) *153, 154*
  s19(3) *154, 155, 200, 219*
  s20 *5, 140, 141, 158*
  s20(1) *157*
  s20(2) *158*
  s20(3) *158*
  s21 *166, 171*
  s21(1) *165, 166*
  s21(2) *149, 165, 166, 175, 182*
  s22 *177, 193, 327*
  s22(1) *177, 179*
  s23 *39, 179, 180, 181, 182, 193, 198, 202*
  s24 *187, 192, 193, 194, 195, 196, 220, 221*
  s25 *16, 169, 181, 196, 198, 200, 201, 202, 203, 204, 219, 327*
  s25(1) *134, 149, 151, 155, 181, 196, 212*
  s25(2) *327, 328, 341*
  s26 *183*
  s27 *50*
  s28 *100, 282*
  s29(2) *51, 97, 145*
  s29(3) *52*
  s29(5) *52*
  s29(6) *53*
  s30 *62*
  s30(1) *57, 58, 60, 164*
  s30(2) *61, 62*
  s30(3) *61*
  s30(4) *56, 61, 62, 240*
  s31 *53*
  s31(1) *53, 61*
  s31(2) *53, 54, 55, 57, 58, 240*
  s32(1) *49, 51, 216*
  s32(2) *57, 59*
  s32(3) *59*

Sale of Goods Act 1979 (*contd.*)
  s33 *59, 60, 160*
  s34 *101, 232, 233, 234, 324*
  s34(1) *97, 232*
  s34(2) *232*
  s35 *101, 155, 156, 232, 233, 234, 235, 236, 238, 324*
  s35(1) *232, 233*
  s36 *230, 231*
  s37 *225*
  s37(1) *225*
  s37(2) *225*
  s38 *206, 208, 210*
  s38(1) *182, 209*
  s38(2) *209*
  s39 *208, 210, 214*
  s39(1) *209, 210, 211, 214, 215*
  s39(2) *214*
  s40 *208*
  s41 *208, 210*
  s41(1) *211*
  s41(2) *211, 214*
  s42 *208, 210*
  s43 *208, 210*
  s43(1) *201, 212, 214*
  s44 *208, 214, 215*
  s45 *208, 214, 216*
  s45(1) *216, 218*
  s45(2) *217*
  s45(3) *216, 217*
  s45(4) *217*
  s45(6) *217*
  s45(7) *218*
  s46 *208, 214, 219*
  s46(1) *219*
  s46(2) *220*
  s46(3) *220*
  s46(4) *220*
  s47 *134, 155, 199, 208*
  s47(1) *200, 212, 213, 214*
  s47(2) *155, 199, 200, 212, 213, 214, 217, 218, 219*

Sale of Goods Act 1979 (*contd.*)
   s48   *208, 215, 220*
   s48(2)   *206, 220, 221*
   s48(3)   *206, 221, 222*
   s48(4)   *221, 222*
   s49   *101, 208, 282*
   s49(1)   *5, 101, 147, 223*
   s49(2)   *101, 223, 224*
   s50   *208, 226*
   s50(1)   *223*
   s50(2)   *225*
   s50(3)   *225, 226, 227, 228, 243*
   s51   *5, 242, 245, 246, 325*
   s51(1)   *12, 242*
   s51(2)   *242*
   s51(3)   *242, 243*
   s52   *5, 246, 247, 325*
   s52(1)   *246, 247*
   s52(2)   *246*
   s52(3)   *246*
   s53   *5, 242, 244, 246, 325*
   s53(1)   *242, 244*
   s53(2)   *242, 244*
   s53(3)   *242, 245*
   s54   *45, 225, 226, 243, 247, 325*
   s55   *269*
   s55(4)   *132*
   s57   *21*
   s57(1)   *21*
   s57(2)   *21, 146*
   s57(3)   *21*
   s57(4)   *22*
   s57(5)   *22*
   s59   *238*
   s61   *4*
   s61(1)   *4, 8, 11, 145, 262*
   s61(4)   *215*
   s61(5)   *145*
   s62   *182, 247*
   s62(2)   *4, 19*
   s62(4)   *4*
   Part III   *165*

Statute of Frauds 1677
   s4   *352, 398*

Supply of Goods and Services Act 1982   *13, 261, 262, 263, 266, 267, 272, 462*
   s1   *262*
   s1(1)   *262*
   s1(2)   *262, 263*
   s1(3)   *262, 263, 271*
   s1(4)   *265*
   s1(5)   *265, 266*
   s1(6)   *266*
   s1(7)   *266*
   s1(8)   *266*
   s2   *117, 262, 263, 264, 270*
   s2(1)   *263*
   s2(2)   *264*
   s2(3)   *263, 264*
   s2(4)   *264*
   s2(5)   *264*
   s3   *117, 262, 263, 264*
   s3(1)   *264*
   s3(2)   *264*
   s3(3)   *264*
   s3(4)   *264*
   s4   *117, 262, 263, 264, 265*
   s4(1)   *265*
   s4(2)   *265*
   s4(3)   *265*
   s4(7)   *266*
   s4(8)   *266*
   s4(9)   *265*
   s5   *117, 262, 263, 264, 266*
   s5(1)   *266*
   s5(2)   *266*
   s5(3)   *266*
   s5(4)   *266*
   s6   *262, 266, 267*
   s6(1)   *267*
   s6(2)   *267*
   s6(3)   *267, 271*
   s7   *117, 262, 266, 267, 270*

Supply of Goods and Services Act
1982 (*contd.*)
    s7(1)   *267*
    s7(2)   *267*
    s7(3)   *267*
    s8   *117, 262, 266*
    s8(1)   *268*
    s8(2)   *268*
    s8(3)   *268*
    s8(4)   *268*
    s9   *117, 262, 266, 268*
    s9(1)   *268*
    s9(2)   *268*
    s9(3)   *268*
    s9(4)   *268*
    s9(5)   *268, 269*
    s9(6)   *269*
    s9(9)   *268*
    s10   *117, 262, 266, 269*
    s10(1)   *269*
    s10(2)   *269*
    s10(3)   *269*
    s10(4)   *269*
    s11   *269*
    s11(1)   *269, 270*
    s11(2)   *269*
    s11(3)   *269*
    s12   *271*
    s12(1)   *271*
    s12(2)   *271*
    s12(3)   *271*
    s12(4)   *271*
    s12(5)   *271*
    s13   *262, 271, 272, 273, 462*
    s14   *262, 271, 272, 273, 462*
    s14(1)   *272*
    s14(2)   *272*
    s15   *262, 271, 273, 462*
    s15(1)   *273*
    s15(2)   *273*
    s16   *273*
    s16(1)   *273*

Supply of Goods and Services Act
1982 (*contd.*)
    s16(2)   *273*
    s16(3)   *273*
    s16(4)   *273*
    s17(2)   *270*
    s18(1)   *262, 265, 462*
    Part I   *114, 261, 267*
    Part II   *261, 271, 273*
    Part III   *270*
Supply of Goods (Implied Terms) Act
1973   *43, 47, 70, 75, 76, 82, 122, 123, 261, 267, 316, 324, 325*
    s8   *116, 267, 327*
    s8(1)   *316, 318, 325*
    s8(2)   *332*
    s9   *116, 119, 267*
    s9(1)   *318*
    s10   *116, 119, 267, 318*
    s10(2)   *318*
    s10(3)   *318*
    s11   *116, 119, 267, 318*
    s11(3)   *318*
    s12   *267*
    s14(2)   *324*
    s15(3)   *318*

Theft Act 1968   *138*
    s1(1)   *138*
Torts (Interference with Goods) Act
1977   *314*
    s3(2)   *363*
    s12   *176*
    s13   *176*
Trade Descriptions Act 1968   *113, 116, 249, 258*
    s1   *258*
    s2   *258*
Trading Stamps Act 1964   *259*
Trustee Act 1925
    s25   *429*
    s25(1)   *424*

Unfair Contract Terms Act 1977   3,
4, 47, 99, 102, 103, 109, 110, 111,
112, 115, 120, 123, 125, 127, 128,
130, 131, 132, 248, 250, 269, 270,
273, 280, 281, 327
   s1(2)   *112*
   s1(3)   *113, 117*
   s2   *112, 113, 117*
   s2(1)   *112, 116*
   s2(2)   *118, 125*
   s3   *69, 94, 112, 117, 118, 270, 273, 327*
   s3(2)   *118, 119, 128, 129*
   s4   *112, 117, 120, 125, 128*
   s5   *113, 117, 256*
   s5(1)   *116*
   s6   *69, 99, 113, 117, 119, 121, 122, 124, 128, 260, 270, 327*
   s6(1)   *47, 48, 49, 117*
   s6(2)   *116, 117*
   s6(3)   *117, 119, 122*
   s6(4)   *113, 117, 119*
   s7   *112, 113, 114, 117, 119, 121, 122, 270*
   s7(2)   *270*
   s7(3)   *119, 270*
   s7(3A)   *270*
   s7(4)   *119, 120, 270*
   s8   *37, 120*
   s9   *120*
   s10   *128, 129*
   s11   *69, 94, 99, 118, 121, 270*

Unfair Contract Terms Act 1977 (*contd.*)
   s11(c)   *37*
   s11(1)   *121, 126*
   s11(2)   *114*
   s11(3)   *121, 124*
   s11(4)   *122*
   s11(5)   *118, 120, 121*
   s12   *114, 115, 270, 324*
   s12(1)   *114, 117*
   s12(2)   *114*
   s12(3)   *114*
   s13   *113*
   s13(1)   *113, 114, 128*
   s13(2)   *114*
   s13(4)   *112*
   s14   *112, 121, 122*
   s26   *129*
   s27   *129*
   s27(2)   *129*
   s28   *129, 130*
   s28(2)   *130*
   s28(3)   *130*
   s29   *130*
   s29(2)   *130*
   s29(11)   *130*
   Part I   *130*
   Part III   *129*
   Schedule 2   *118, 121, 270*
Unsolicited Goods and Services Act 1971   *259–260*
Unsolicited Goods and Services Act 1975   *259–260*

Introduction

1 The problems of studying commercial law

2 Definitions

3 Historical development

4 Overlap with other legal topics

5 Methods of studying commercial law

1 Problems of studying commercial law

A number of problems arise in the study of most legal topics. In the case of commercial law the main problems are:

It is difficult to define the extent and scope of the subject. More will be said on this in the section on definitions (below) but merely to glance through a number of different authorities on 'Commercial Law' gives some idea of the extent of the problem.

For example some authorities would not include agency law at all, either considering it a topic in its own right, to be studied quite separately, or they would consider it a constituent part of contract law.

Continental authorities invariably treat company law as an element of commercial law, but here in England company law is quite rigidly separated from commercial. Some authorities include negotiable instruments, shipping law, and insurance, while others exclude them.

For many students their definition of the exact scope of the subject will depend on which syllabus they are studying. This is a realistic and sensible approach. Obviously it behoves the student to check precisely what is or is not included in his or her 'Commercial Law' syllabus. This book is largely intended for those studying for London University LLB, and to that extent it will reflect their syllabus. However, this is not to say that it will not be suitable for other syllabuses; but the student *must* verify, before commencing to study, just what the requirements of his own university, polytechnic or college are.

Secondly, commercial law is largely statute-based. Like most legal topics it is a mixture of common law and statute law. Unlike, shall we say, contract law, however, where the basic framework of the subject is provided by caselaw, commercial law is based on a number of major statutes.

This in itself is the source of the third problem. Commercial law is still very much a developing subject. Legislation - both primary and delegated legislation - is still being enacted. This means that quite frequently there is a dearth of interpretative case law. Although in some instances analogous case law may be used, often a particular question has simply never come before the courts. Thus, apart from academic speculation an ambiguous section or sections of a particular act will remain in doubt, until reviewed by the courts.

A further aspect is that certain areas in commercial law expand over a period of a few years to a point where they achieve a degree of importance which noone would have dreamed of earlier. A case in point is the Consumer Protection Act 1987, parts of which are only just beginning to be implemented. A few years ago consumer protection was, at best, just a footnote. Now it has expanded to a significant degree. Numerous new cases have been decided by the courts, and new authorities have appeared on the subject. It has, therefore, in effect become a complete new topic on its own.

Despite the fact that much commercial law is now incorporated into legislation it is not true to say that all the law on the subject is satisfactory.

In part this may be due to the interrelationship of legislation and caselaw as sources of law. Obviously, even where a statute appears late on the scene it often codifies and consolidates existing law, and early case law will remain relevant. Nevertheless, the use of cases to throw light on the meaning of statutory provisions is a very hit-and-miss affair. An ambiguous provision in a statute may remain unclarified for a considerable time, either because cases on the matter are contradictory or, more simply, because no case has yet arisen on that particular point of interpretation. For example, it is frequently remarked that the statutory definition of 'merchantable quality' as found in the Sale of Goods Act 1979 is highly unsatisfactory. This is in part due to bad drafting; but also arises to some extent because of infrequent case law on the subject and because of the contradictory nature of those cases which have been decided.

The Law Commission constantly reviews such weaknesses in the law (its function is not of course confined to commercial law). One of the problems facing a student of commercial law, however, is to remember that not every statute is perfectly drafted and interpreted.

2 Definitions

Professor Goode tells us that commercial law is 'that branch of law concerned with rights and duties arising from the supply of goods and services in the way of trade.'

This is, in fact, probably as close as one can get to defining the topic of commercial law as a whole. While one can consult the authorities and find the constituent areas defined - sale of goods, agency, export sales and so on - there is no single definition which is appropriate to all the different aspects. Indeed, as we have seen, no two authorities are in agreement as to exactly *what* the constituent areas of commercial law are. The one common thread that links all the different topics is that they are all in some way connected with business transactions. In any study of commercial law, sale of goods invariably takes priority over everything else. Most, if not all, the other topics that might be included in a study of commercial law are in some way relevant to sale of goods. Agency, for example, covers cases when the actual contract for sale of goods is negotiated by an agent on behalf of his principal. Export sales covers instances when the sale of goods involves some foreign element. Consumer credit concerns sales (and certain transactions analogous to sales) when the goods are not paid for immediately by the buyer, but are financed in such a way as to involve the buyer in credit transactions. In the first section of this book the law relating to sale of goods is defined and the scope of the major legislation, the Sale of Goods Act 1979, is defined. Similarly, in the sections that follow, on consumer credit and agency, the introductory chapter contains definitive material.

3   History

Commercial law is widely regarded as a modern phenomenon, yet it has its roots in the law merchant, 'lex mercatoria', one of the oldest branches of law. As early as the 10th and 11th centuries, statutes can be found relating to mercantile law, and some sort of customary law, governing dealings between merchants, presumably existed long before these statutory codifications began.

One intriguing factor is that even hundreds of years ago mercantile law was foreign rather than English in nature. The English mercantile courts of the time practised a distinct and unique blend of law reflecting international maritime and trading laws, and those courts were used as much by foreign merchant traders as native Englishmen. Special statutes enacted in the Middle Ages for the benefit of the merchants prescribed special rules for foreign merchants, including specially quick hearings for foreign traders who presumably might only be in England for a limited time.

Eventually the law merchant and the special merchants' law was absorbed into common law and into the common-law courts, but the heritage of the lex mercatoria lived on. Although the courts continued to apply ordinary English common law in the main, this was to some extent influenced by mercantile law in order to adapt to the special needs of the merchant. Slowly the two systems were merged into the body of law we know today as commercial law. By the time the Sale of Goods Act was enacted in 1893 it was able to provide that 'the rules of the *common law, including the law merchant* ... shall apply to contracts for sale of goods.' The two systems were finally fused.

In the 19th century the development of commercial law continued, but it began to lose the preoccupation mercantile law had had with international law. The period was that of the Industrial Revolution which saw a tremendous increase in domestic trade and consumption, and, of course, the steady expansion of the British Empire. England became more concerned to regulate dealings, not only between merchants but also between traders and consumers, both at home and abroad, and especially in the colonies.

We have seen that the law today is still developing. Much of the legislation enacted is of the 'framework' type, permitting delegated legislation to be issued by the relevant minister or public body. Consequently, not only is modern commercial law statute-based, but new regulations are also constantly appearing; and almost inevitably, as they appear they create problems of interpretation. Thus, new case law is created and becomes applicable.

4 Overlap with other topics

As with other similar topics, it is frequently disputed whether commercial law is a subject in its own right or simply a combination of bits and pieces from other areas of law. Certainly there is a very great deal of overlapping with other legal topics. Of course, to study commercial law successfully a student must have a good working knowledge of contract (see below). However, it should be borne in mind that an adequate appreciation of the subject also requires the student at various times to be familiar with conveyancing, land law, tort, and many topics.

Above all else two important aspects should be remembered about commercial law. First, it was until comparatively recently regarded simply as a part of the general study of contractual law. And secondly, foreign law is becoming increasingly important; in particular the rules of the EC are relevant to commercial law in a number of ways.

Commercial law and contract

So much of commercial law requires a good working knowledge of contract. We have seen (in para 2 above) that the standard definition of commercial law varies; but one common factor is an acknowledgement of the fact that it is primarily concerned with business transactions.

Most, if not all, business transactions are contractual in nature. While much of the new legislation adds additional detail to contractual law, only very rarely does it actually vary or change such law. Most commercial law legislation is of a codifying or consolidating type, rather than reformatory in nature. Consequently, much of the legislation on, for example, sale of goods is based on common law contractual rules.

Commercial law, international law and conflicts

Because many commercial transactions are of an international nature foreign law has always been of considerable importance. Conflict of laws is yet another of those legal topics which impinge to a considerable degree on commercial law!

Recently, however, a new trend has begun to creep into commercial law legislation, though it has not so far made its presence felt in many cases. Examination of statutes from the 1970s and 1980s will show that many of them are specifically worded in order to take into account EC law.

Finally, it should be noted that much of the new legislation transcends the civil/criminal division. Therefore, while most of the legislation is enacted to give effect to civil rights (particularly to consumers), quite frequently the same act will make provision for criminal sanctions to apply if a breach of the statute occurs. Obviously the criminal aspect of commercial law is not yet of primary importance. Nevertheless, it adds interest to the topic as a whole.

5 Methods of studying commercial law

For most students, commercial law is not a first year subject. More often it is a second or third year subject, and quite frequently only an optional one. For many students the study of commercial law is not even a part of a law degree course. However commercial law is a required topic of study for many other courses, from business studies to accountancy. Thus some students may come to commercial law not only without any background of contractual law but without indeed having studied any law at all.

To some extent those students who have no legal background at all are fortunate, since contract is one of those areas with which everyone comes into day-to-day contact. Everyone makes contracts all the time, for example buying anything from houses to the daily newspapers. However, do not let the sense of familiarity lull you into a sense of false security!

Although it has been said earlier that commercial law is largely statute-based, that does not mean there are no cases at all. In some areas - notably sale of goods, and agency - the potential volume of cases is enormous. Cases are still an extremely important source of commercial law and it is important that, from a very early stage, the student becomes used to reading as many cases as possible. To go through an entire year of commercial law without ever going near a law library is *not* a course of action ever to be recommended! Students who depend on textbook resumés of cases and who never read a case report themselves are at a considerable disadvantage. From reading as many cases as possible, right from the start of the course, it is possible to gain an insight into: how the courts reach their decisions; how judges interpret facts; and how they apply legal principles to those facts.

No casebook or textbook will give the student the sort of information to be found in a report. Although in a textbook the student may find some basic facts and the decision neatly documented, unless he reads the full report for himself he will *not* find out: whether the court was reluctant to reach its decision; or whether a dissenting judgment was of particular interest or importance; or what other cases the court considered or rejected.

Strictly speaking, it does not matter what cases the student reads, though obviously the majority of students will seek out the 'classics', that is, the cases of major importance in a particular area. However, any cases are useful reading. Working out what the courts took into account (or what they *should* perhaps have taken into account), will help to fix the topic in the memory and sharpen the student's perception of the subject.

At the same time it does no good to learn a few (or even a lot) of cases off by heart. This will only give a static view of contract. Nor is it wise to think that each case establishes one rule or law. Rather it is the relationship between a number of cases which may well be of importance. For only by careful and comprehensive study of a series of cases will the student begin to pick out patterns of conduct, and begin to be able to predict how the courts might react in similar cases in the future and how the law on the topic might progress.

Commercial law should never be studied in self-contained sections. Unfortunately, it often is! None of the rules relating to commercial law exist in a vacuum, and the student who is constantly revising and updating his notes in the light of what he learns as the course progresses will achieve a higher level of understanding of the topic as a whole.

The student should also note that different aspects may be studied at different levels of complexity. In part, this may depend on the exact syllabus content; that is, the more crowded the syllabus, the more superficial will be the level of study. But remember also that, for those on courses other than law degrees, the level may be fairly simplistic.

It is always helpful for the student to have a general idea of the rules of the subject to be studied before commencing the course, and to this end, an elementary book on the subject should be read first. There are several such books, but 'Sale of Goods and Consumer Credit' by AP Dobson, published by Sweet & Maxwell, is much recommended, except for the fact that it does not have a section on agency.

Sale of Goods

1

Scope of the Sale of Goods Act

1.1 Introduction

1.2 Scope of the SGA 1979: property in the goods

1.3 Sales and agreements to sell

1.4 Price

1.5 Categories of goods

1.6 Sale distinguished from other transactions

1.1 Introduction

The law relating to contracts for the sale of goods was first codified in the Sale of Goods Act 1893. The law is now contained in the Sale of Goods Act 1979 (SGA 1979), a consolidating statute which while repealing the 1893 Act largely re-enacts the pre-existing law. In addition to the SGA 1979 some other statutes such as the Factors Act 1889 and the Unfair Contract Terms Act 1977 are also relevant to the law of sale. It should also be noted that the 1893 Act and SGA 1979 have been the subject of statutory interpretation in the courts and there is a mass of decisions to which reference will be made in this book. Of rather less importance is the case law on sale prior to 1893.

The SGA 1979 is a consolidating statute and there is a presumption in construing it that no alteration of the previous law was intended. Recourse may be made to cases on the statutes which the SGA 1979 consolidates. The consolidated provisions of the SGA 1979 will frequently have first appeared in the 1893 Act which codified rather than consolidated. In interpreting a codifying statute Lord Herschell had the following observations to make in *Bank of England* v *Vagliano Brothers* [1891] AC 107:

> 'I think the proper course is in the first instance to examine the language of the statute and to ask what is its natural meaning, uninfluenced by any considerations derived from the previous state of the law, and not to start with inquiring how the law previously stood, and then, assuming that it was probably intended to leave it unaltered, to see if the words of the enactment will bear an interpretation in conformity with this view.
>
> If a statute, intended to embody in it a code of particular branch of the law, is to be treated in this fashion, it appears to me that its utility will be almost entirely destroyed, and the very object with which it was enacted will be frustrated. The purpose of such a statute surely was that on any point specifically dealt with by it, the law should be

ascertained by interpreting the language used instead of, as before, by roaming over a vast number of authorities to discover what the law was, extracting it by a minute critical examination of the prior decisions.'

As Lord Herschell himself recognised, earlier decisions may be consulted where the Act is ambiguous or a term has acquired a technical meaning which earlier cases may illustrate. It is also important to note that the SGA 1979 codifies only the special rules of law which are peculiar to the law of sale. The contract of sale is also subject to the general principles of contract and personal property. This is made clear by SGA 1979 s62(2) which states:

'The rules of the common law, including the law merchant, except in so far as they are inconsistent with the provisions of this Act, and in particular the rules relating to the law of principal and agent and the effect of fraud, misrepresentation, duress or coercion, mistake, or other invalidating cause, apply to contracts for the sale of goods.'

All references to section numbers in the text are to the SGA 1979 unless otherwise stated.

1.2 Scope of the SGA 1979: property in the goods

This is defined in s61(1). (*Note*: Section 61 is the general 'definitions section' of the SGA and as such will be referred to frequently.) Section 61(1) provides:

'Unless the context or subject matter otherwise require "the property" means the "general property" (ownership) in goods not merely a "special property".'

The 'general property' is the *ownership* of the goods. The various possible 'special properties' in the goods are not included. The Act therefore does not apply to contracts whereby an owner undertakes to transfer something less than ownership, for example the rights under a mortgage, pledge, hire or other bailment, or any transaction to provide security (see s62(4)). Nor does the Act apply where someone who does not have the ownership of the goods undertakes to transfer his own limited interest.

The SGA *will apply* to contracts whereby:

1. The contract or circumstances surrounding it show that the seller intends to transfer *only such title* as he or a third party *might have*. Section 12(3) expressly recognises such contracts. An example would be the sale by a finder of goods who discloses that he is selling only as a 'finder'. The warranties in s12(3), (4) and (5) as to 'such title as the seller might have' *cannot* be excluded. (The decision to the contrary in *Payne* v *Elsden* (1900) 17 TLR 161 has been reversed by the Unfair Contract Terms Act 1977).
2. A person with no title or defective title to property innocently or fraudulently contracts to pass absolute ownership. This is included because the seller here 'agrees to transfer the property'. In such cases the buyer will have an unexcluded breach of contract remedy under s12(1) since the seller will usually be unable to

pass ownership; the operation of this remedy is illustrated by *Rowland* v *Divall* [1923] 2 KB 500 (see below).

1.3 Sales and agreements to sell

These are two distinct types of transaction, but both are included in 'contracts of sale' in s2(1):

1. The contract is a 'sale' where, by the contract, the property in the goods passes to the buyer (s2(4)).
2. The contract is an 'agreement to sell' if the property is to pass at some future time or subject to some condition (s2(5)).

The distinctions between the two can be summarised as follows:

The sale
1. The contract is executed.
2. It creates rights *in rem* (ie rights against the property involved and not merely against the other party).
3. The buyer's remedies are damages pursuant to ss51 and 53, or perhaps in tort for wrongful interference with goods.
4. The seller's remedy is for the price (s49(1)).
5. The risk of loss lies with the buyer (s20).
6. The contract cannot be frustrated.

The agreement to sell
1. The contract is still executory.
2. It creates rights only *in personam*.
3. The buyer's remedies are damages for non-delivery under s51 (or in rare cases specific performance in s52 where damages are exceptionally an inadequate remedy).
4. The seller's remedy is damages for non-acceptance, under s50.
5. The risk of loss lies with the seller (s20).
6. The contract may be frustrated under s7.

The significance of the distinction is best illustrated by considering the position on the bankruptcy of another party before the performance of the contract.

On the seller's bankruptcy

In the case of an agreement to sell, the goods do not yet belong to the buyer, and the seller's trustee in bankruptcy can take them, leaving the buyer to prove in the bankruptcy of the seller.

In the case of a sale, the goods will already belong to the buyer and therefore the seller's trustee in bankruptcy cannot take the goods. This is however subject to the operation of the doctrine of 'reputed ownership'; by s38(c) of the Bankruptcy Act 1914, where the goods are in the 'possession, order or disposition' of a party in the course of his business or trade in such circumstances that they are in his reputed ownership then that party's trustee in bankruptcy can take them.

On the buyer's bankruptcy

With an agreement to sell, the seller can certainly retain the goods if they remain in his possession. If possession has passed to the buyer, then the 'reputed ownership' doctrine could operate in favour of the buyer's trustee in bankruptcy, letting him take the goods.

In the case of a sale, the buyer already has the property in the goods and should be able to take them. However if the seller has possession and has not yet been paid, he may have an 'unpaid seller's lien' over the goods (see Chapter 11: 'Real Remedies').

1.4 Price

Section 2(1) requires that the price is to be a 'money consideration'. This clearly excludes contracts of barter where goods are exchanged for other goods or services. The status of contracts where goods are exchanged for goods and money is unclear. This is discussed below at 1.6.

Sections 8 and 9 deal with the ascertainment of the price. Section 8 deals with both sales and agreements to sell while s9 applies only to agreements to sell. Section 8(1) states that:

> 'The price in a contract of sale may be fixed by the contract, or may be left to be fixed in a manner agreed by the contract, or may be determined by the course of dealing between the parties.'

Only if these methods do not result in a price being determined does s8(2) come into play and provide that 'the buyer must pay a reasonable price' which s8(3) says 'is a question of fact dependent on the circumstances of each particular case'.

In relation to the determination of the price under s8 most of the problems have concerned transactions where the price has not been specifically agreed but is left for determination at some later time. Price, however, is one of the most important elements of a contract of sale and vagueness on this point might well suggest that there has been no concluded contract. This was the case in *May & Butcher* v *R* [1934] 2 KB 17. The plaintiffs had entered into arrangements with the Controller of the Disposals Board to acquire surplus tentage. The terms of the arrangement were contained in a letter which stated that 'the price or prices to be paid :.. shall be agreed upon from time to time between the Commission and the purchasers as the quantities of the said old tentage become available for disposal'.

HELD (by the House of Lords): There was no contract because the agreement left vital matters still to be settled. The provision of what is now s8(2) of the Act was held not to be applicable because it applied only where there was silence and not, as here, where there was a reference to the fact that the parties were to agree but no mechanism for achieving that agreement was provided. It is to be noted that there was an arbitration clause among the terms of the arrangement but this was held not to be relevant to the determination of the price.

Courts are reluctant to hold void any provision that was intended to have legal effect and, where the determination of price is the difficult issue, have shown themselves prepared to find a solution. In *Hillas & Co v Arcos Ltd* (1932) 147 LT 503 the House of Lords found an option to buy timber was binding even though it did not specify the price. It was sufficient that it provided for the calculation of the price by reference to an official price list. Another example is provided by *Foley v Classique Coaches Ltd* [1934] 2 KB 1. Foley was the owner of a filling station and some land adjoining it. He sold the land to the defendants on condition that they should enter into an agreement to buy the fuel needed for their transport business from him. The defendants reneged on this arrangement and argued that it was unenforceable because it provided that fuel should be bought 'at a price agreed by the parties from time to time'.

HELD: The agreement was not void for uncertainty. The agreement was one which both parties clearly believed to be binding and had acted upon for some years. It was also significant that it contained an arbitration clause in a different form from that in the *May & Butcher* case which stated that it related to disputes as to 'the subject matter or construction of this agreement'. In the event the defendants were found liable to pay a reasonable price.

Section 9 applies only to agreements to sell and provides that in certain circumstances the price may be determined at a third party's valuation. It states:

> '(1) where there is an agreement to sell goods on the terms that the price is to be fixed by the valuation of a third party and such party cannot or does not make such valuation, the agreement is avoided; but if the goods or any part thereof have been delivered to and appropriated by the buyer he must pay a reasonable price for them.
> (2) where the third party is prevented from making the valuation by the fault of the seller or the buyer, the party not at fault may maintain an action for damages against the party at fault.'

Section 9 only applies where the third party who is to fix the price by valuation is *named* by the parties. Where the third party is so named then under s9(1) it seems that the contract will be avoided if the third party does not make the valuation subject only to the provisions of s9(2).

However, where the price is to be ascertained by a valuation by a third party who is not named by the parties it seems that the agreement will be for a sale at a reasonable price, according to s8.

Section 9(2) would cover a situation where the seller for example refused to allow the third party access to the goods in order to value them.

1.5 Categories of goods

There are several ways in which goods can be categorised for the purposes of the SGA 1979. In this section the meaning of the term 'goods' as used in the Act is discussed and then certain other methods of classifying goods will be discussed.

'Goods' subject to the Act

Section 61(1) provides:

> 'Goods includes all personal chattels other than things in action and money ... in particular 'goods' includes emblements, industrial growing crops and things attached to or forming part of the land which are agreed to be severed before the sale or under the contract of sale.'

Section 61(1) does not provide an exhaustive list of goods. It indicates that 'goods' includes all *personal chattels* as opposed to *real chattels* (such as leasehold land), except things in action and money.

'Things in action' includes debts, shares, patents, trademarks, cheques and equitable interests under trusts. The category can loosely be defined as property or rights to which a person is entitled but which cannot be reduced into *physical possession* and which therefore require to be enforced by a legal action.

Money is generally not 'goods', but a coin sold as a collector's item or as a curio would be 'goods'.

It is important to distinguish 'goods' from 'interests in land'

Several important consequences flow from this distinction:

1. Contracts for the sale of interests in land must now comply with s2 of the Law of Property (Miscellaneous Provisions) Act 1989. This requires such contracts to be in writing, and incorporating all the terms expressly agreed by the parties and signed by each party.
2. Contracts for the sale of interests in land made prior to 27 September 1989 are governed by the Law of Property Act 1925 s40 which provides that, if not in writing, there must be a written note or memorandum to serve as evidence of the contract.
3. There are now no special requirements as to formalities for contracts for the sale of goods.
4. The LP(MP)A 1989 provides that the written contract must contain 'all terms agreed on'. This means that the *price* must have been agreed; or some mode of calculation thereof (eg £x per acre). There is no similar requirement for sale of goods contracts (see Chapter 2.1 (below) as to consideration). Of course, like all contracts, a sale of goods contract that is too vague as to price *and other matters* may be void for uncertainty.
5. In a contract for the sale of an interest in land the property passes on completion, which is usually several weeks, at least, after the time of making the contract.

Additionally, property in such contracts can only pass by deed; whereas oral or even contracts by conduct can pass instant ownership in goods.

6. Under the rule in *Bain* v *Fothergill* (1874) LR 7 HL 158 it *used* to be the case that a disappointed purchaser in a contract for the sale of an interest in land could not get damages for the loss of a bargain. However, this rule has now been formally abolished, as of September 1989.
7. When a contract is for the sale of *land and goods* (eg the sale of a shop with all its stock and the two are not severable into different contracts), it is regarded as a sale of land or an interest in land and must comply with the LP(MP)A 1989 s2.
8. When the sale is for fixtures on the land it is regarded as being subject to LPA 1989. Difficulties arise in defining the term 'fixture'; *Morgan* v *Russell & Sons* [1909] 1 KB 357. The contract was for the sale of cinders and slag dumped on a piece of land. They had since become merged with the land and had been overgrown with grass and bushes. The buyer was to dig out the waste cinders and slag and remove it. The Court of Appeal held that this was a contract for sale of land because the slag had merged physically with the land. However, s61 states that 'goods' includes things 'to be severed before or under the contract of sale', which would appear to cover the slag in this case. *Morgan* v *Russell* should now be taken as doubtful authority.

Two categories require special consideration:

Growing crops
At common law two types of crop were distinguished:

1. *Fructus industriales*: crops requiring agricultural labour, planting, reaping, harvesting ... and maturing annually. Examples are corn and potatoes.
2. *Fructus naturales*: all other vegetable growths such as grass and trees.

At common law *fructus industriales* were always regarded as 'goods'. The position with *fructus naturales* was for a time confused, but a compromise was achieved in *Marshall* v *Green* (1815) 1 CPD 35. Here it was held that if the parties intended the crops to go on deriving benefit from the land before they were reaped then they were *land*, however if the crops were already mature and were left in the fields or trees purely for convenience of storage then they were goods.

After the 1979 Act there is probably no distinction between industrial and natural crops as long as the contract contemplates severance. The parties will almost inevitably contemplate severance unless it is a sale of *land with fruits on it*.

The SGA expressly includes industrial growing crops in the definition of 'goods'. In *Kursell* v *Timber Operators & Contractors Ltd* [1927] 1 KB 298 the contract was here for the sale of all the timber in a certain forest, to be cut over a period of 15 years. The Court of Appeal assumed this to be a contract for the sale of goods and applied the SGA.

In *Saunders* v *Pilcher* [1949] 2 All ER 1097 the contract was for the sale of a cherry orchard 'inclusive of this year's fruit crop'. The total price was £5,500. The buyer has inspected the land and crop, and in his own calculation had estimated that the crop would be worth £2,500 and the land £3,000. The Court of Appeal held that this was a contract for the sale of land carrying the fruit that happened to be on it. No separate price was fixed for the crop, and nothing in the contract required or contemplated severance. The seller was in no way concerned with what the buyer chose to do with the fruit after the sale. It is submitted that this result would remain unchanged by the SGA 1979. In effect therefore *fructus naturales* will be goods except where the contract does not contemplate severance.

A contract allowing one party to cultivate another's land could amount to a lease, and involve an interest in land in that sense.

Fixtures

Any contract for the sale of fixtures will almost certainly be for the sale of 'goods' provided the contract contemplates eventual severance.

Underwood v *Burgh Castle Brick & Cement* [1922] 1 KB 343 is one illustration. This case concerned a contract for the sale of a 30-ton engine which had sunk into its concrete base by its own weight. Under the contract it was to be severed and loaded onto a rail wagon. The Court of Appeal assumed it to be goods.

There is one inconsistent case: *Lavery* v *Purcell* (1888) 39 Ch D 508. A contract for sale of the materials comprising a building to be demolished was held to be a contract for the sale of land. This is a pre-1893 SG Act case and the judge was possibly too much impressed by the fact that the contract gave the seller a right for two months to remain on the land for the purpose of demolition, thinking this somehow to be an interest over land. The decision would *not* now be followed since the contract clearly contemplated severance.

Questions as to the classification of goods for the SGA

Five categories of goods are referred to in the SGA: specific, ascertained, unascertained, existing and future goods. Two preliminary points should be made. First, 'existing goods' and 'future goods' are deliberately contrasted in the Act but this distinction is rarely of importance. This classification is *distinct from* and *cuts across* the specific/ascertained/unascertained goods classifications. Secondly it should be emphasised that the categories of specific, ascertained and unascertained goods are *all mutually exclusive*.

Existing and future goods

All goods must be either existing or future.

Existing goods. These goods must be in existence somewhere and either owned or possessed by the seller at the time of the contract (s5(1)). They may be either specific or unascertained goods.

Future goods. These goods are defined in s61(1): 'Goods to be manufactured or acquired by the seller after the making of the contract of sale.' Future goods may therefore be:

1. Non-existent at the time of the contract. For example if they are to be manufactured or grown subsequently. These must be unascertained goods.
2. In existence at the time of the contract, but *not yet* owned or possessed by the seller. These can be specific or unascertained goods.

Schmithoff argues that future goods must always be *unascertained*. This would appear to be wrong: an example of a sale of *specific* future goods would be a contract for the sale of a specific painting which both the buyer and the seller know to belong to a third party. The painting is *specific* since it is 'identified and agreed upon at the time of the contract' (see below, and it is also future goods since it is not yet owned or possessed by the seller. The painting will still be specific future goods if the seller has previously agreed to buy it from the third party provided the property has not yet passed to the seller.

Both Goode and Lowe disagree with Schmithoff's view, and the latter points out that if the painting in the above example was destroyed after the contract between buyer and seller was made, then s7 which applies only to specific goods would operate to frustrate the contract.

Under s5(2) it is possible to contract to sell goods the acquisition of which depends on a contingency which may or may not happen. This would apply to a crop to be grown in a particular field or to a prize in a raffle *if* the seller wins it. An illustration is *Sainsbury* v *Street* [1972] 1 WLR 834; [1972] 3 All ER 1127 (a crop in a specific field).

By s5(3), property *cannot pass in future goods* while they are still future goods.

Specific, unascertained and ascertained goods

These distinctions are of far greater significance since they affect the passing of the property in the goods, and the provisions of sections 6 and 7 on impossibility of performance and frustration.

Specific goods. Section 61(1) defines 'specific goods' as: 'Goods identified and agreed upon at the time a contract of sale is made.' The goods must be *both identified and agreed on* by both parties at the time of the contract. If they are not *both* identified *and* agreed on at the time of the contract then they can only be *unascertained* goods. Such goods may later become 'ascertained goods' (below) but they *can never become specific goods*. Goods *cannot* be 'specific and ascertained': these are mutually exclusive.

A sale of 'all the coal now in my cellar' would be a sale of specific goods since the goods are identified and agreed on at the time of the contract.

The Act does not deal with the position where the form of the contract is one for unascertained goods yet in fact and in substance the goods are specific at the time of the contract. For example S contracts to sell 'one of the bottles of wine in my cellar' and in fact there is only one bottle in his cellar. Goode's view is that the Act takes specificity as a fact and that this would be a sale of specific goods. This is almost certainly correct.

With goods which are both specific and future, s5(3) still applies and the property cannot pass while the goods are still future.

Unascertained goods. These are not defined in the Act but are obviously goods defined only by description and *not* identified and agreed on at the time of the contract. They depend for their identification on some subsequent act of *appropriation*. By s16, the property *cannot pass in unascertained goods* until they become ascertained. Examples of unascertained goods are: '20 tons of wheat', or '50 bottles of Moet and Chandon champagne'.

Goode distinguishes two categories of unascertained goods:

1. 'Wholly unascertained goods': where the parties have not even designated a source of supply in their contract. For example a contract to supply '10 tons of grain'. Here the seller is free to supply the grain from any source so long as he meets the delivery date.
2. 'Partially identified goods': to which he applies the designation 'quasi-specific goods'.

Ascertained goods *must* therefore *have been unascertained goods at the time of the contract.*

In *Re Wait* [1927] 1 Ch 606 W contracted on 20 November to buy 1000 tons of wheat to be landed on the SS Challenger in Oregon in December. On 21 November W contracted to sell 500 out of that 1000 to X. On 21 December the 1000 tons were loaded and the property in them passed to W on the 6 February in accordance with the contract. However, on 1 February X had paid W the price for the 500 tons. Before the ship's arrival W became bankrupt and his trustee in bankruptcy obtained the shipping documents and claimed all 1000 tons. X obviously wanted to get 500 tons of wheat and not merely a dividend in the bankruptcy. Three issues were decided by the court:

1. The 500 tons at all times remained unascertained goods and therefore the property in them had not passed to X.
2. The court refused specific performance, claimed by X under s52(1), because s52(1) applies only to breaches of contracts to deliver 'specific or ascertained goods'. The goods here were neither specific nor ascertained.
3. X had further argued that following the equitable doctrine laid down in *Holroyd* v *Marshall* (1862) 10 HL Cas 191 and *Tailby* v *Official Receiver* (1885) 13 App Cas 523 (involving an agreement to transfer in good faith and for value) W in fact held the 500 tons on trust for him. This too was rejected by the court on the ground that it could only apply to a contract for identifiable future property. Lord Atkin added that the SGA was intended as a codification of the law on the

sale of goods and that in general equitable doctrines should not be brought into this case to make businessmen trustees for each other where there is no such intention.

1.6 Sale distinguished from other transactions

There are a number of transactions involving the transfer of goods which are in practical and economic terms often very similar to sale but which from a legal point of view are treated differently. Until recently these legal distinctions were often of some importance. However, recent changes in the law have considerably reduced their importance. In particular, the Supply of Goods and Services Act 1982, by implying terms as to quality and title in relation to contracts for the supply of goods which are modelled on those in the SGA 1979, has reduced the significance of these differences. Nevertheless, in some situations the fact that the supply of goods falls into a legal category other than that of sale can be of importance. For example, the time at which property in the goods passes may be different.

Contracts of barter or exchange

Where goods are transferred in exchange for other goods the transaction cannot be a sale; s2(1) states: 'A contract of sale of goods is a contract by which the seller transfers or agrees to transfer the property in goods to the buyer for a money consideration, called the price.' The contract of barter or exchange is governed by the common law and the Supply of Goods and Services Act 1982.

Where goods are transferred in exchange for other goods and money the legal significance of the transaction is not clear. A number of approaches to this problem of definition have been proposed. Professor Atiyah in his *Sale of Goods* (7th edn) suggests that the kind of test used in *Robinson* v *Graves* [1935] 1 KB 579 to distinguish contracts of sale from contracts for skill and labour may be appropriate. Using this test the answer depends on whether the money or the goods are the substantial consideration. Another possible approach for which support can be found in the cases is to say that it is sale if the parties have placed a value on the goods exchanged. This approach seems to have been adopted in *Aldridge* v *Johnson* (1857) 7 E & B 885. Aldridge agreed to transfer 32 bullocks valued at £192 to Knights and Knights agreed to transfer 100 quarters of barley valued at £215 to Aldridge. The difference of £23 was to be paid in cash.

HELD: this was a sale not barter.

A similar case is *Dawson (Clapham) Ltd* v *H & G Dutfield* [1936] 2 All ER 232. It would follow that if the parties have not placed a notional value on the goods subject to the transfer that the transaction should be classified as barter. This occurred in the Irish case of *Flynn* v *Mackin* [1974] IR 101. It had been arranged that a new Vauxhall Viva car would be supplied to a customer. The consideration was to be the customer's existing car and £250. No valuation was placed either on the new car or the car which was being traded in.

HELD: In view of the fact that no value had been put on the new car and the car to be traded in, this transaction was barter not sale.

Contracts for work and materials

The importance of this distinction is now much diminished. Until the Law Reform (Enforcement of Contract) Act 1954, written evidence was necessary for the sale of goods valued £10 or more. This requirement has now gone. A further important distinction lay in the fact that the implied terms contained in the SGA did not apply to contracts for work and materials although their equivalents existed at common law, and the ambit and operation of implied terms in such contracts was to a great extent uncertain. However the Supply of Goods and Services Act 1982 Part I now implies similar terms in contracts for work and materials.

The distinction should nevertheless be understood:

1. If the *substance* of the contract is the production of an article the ownership in which will be transferred for a price, although skill or labour is incidentally expended, then the contract will be a sale of goods. Examples are a furrier making a fur coat, an optician making a pair of spectacles or a dentist making false teeth.
2. Conversely if the *substance* of the contract is the exercise of labour or skill towards the production of some article, although incidentally the property in the materials employed passes to the person commissioning the work, then the contract will be for work and material. An example is an artist painting a portrait.

The above distinction was finally laid down in *Robinson v Graves* [1935] 1 KB 579 after a variety of prior cases laying down an even wider variety of tests. *Lee v Griffin* (1861) 30 LJQB 272 was one such case which seemed to decide that if a contract would ultimately result in the transfer of property in the goods then it must be sale of goods. *Robinson v Graves* itself concerned the commissioning of an artist to paint a portrait. The test laid down by the court was not (as had been suggested) a question of balancing the money value of the materials against the value of the work or skill used, but was a question of ascertaining the main purpose of the transaction in question. The Court of Appeal held that the purchaser here basically wanted the artist's skill and only incidentally ended up owning something. The SGA therefore did not apply.

Several other cases are illustrative.

Isaacs v Pardie (unreported). The court held that a shopkeeper commissioning an artist to paint a number of copies of a picture of a local beauty spot was sale of goods. The pictures here were the shopkeeper's stock-in-trade. The case shows that *Robinson v Graves* is not a general rule relating to all artists and pictures.

Marcel (Furriers) Ltd v *Tapper* [1953] 1 WLR 49; [1953] 1 All ER 15. A furrier contracted to make a mink coat from furs which he himself supplied but which were chosen by the customer. Notwithstanding the fact that the style was very unusual (the skins ran round and round, not up and down), the court held the transaction to be within the SGA and, *at that time*, unenforceable for want of written evidence.

Cammell Laird & Co Ltd v *Manganese Bronze & Brass Co Ltd* [1934] AC 402. The House of Lords held a contract to make ships' propellers to be sale of goods not work and materials.

Samuels v *Davis* [1943] 1 KB 526; [1943] 2 ALL ER 3. This case involved a dentist who agreed to make a set of false teeth for his client's wife. Since the result would have been the same at common law or under the SGA the court found it unnecessary to decide whether or not this was sale of goods, but expressed the view that it was inclined to think it to be a case of sale of goods.

In general where new materials or accessories are being attached or added to larger articles (for example, fitting a new carburettor to a car) then it will be work and materials.

There are some other slightly different situations where goods are supplied as an incident of the provisions of services where the contract is classified as one of services and not of sale. These are usually contracts for professional services such as those of solicitors, doctors or architects where what the client is paying for is essentially professional skill and advice and the fact that some tangible article is also provided is purely incidental.

An example is provided by *Grafton* v *Armitage* (1845) 135 ER 975. Grafton, an engineer, was commissioned by Armitage to devise a method of producing metal tubes which might be used in the production of a new type of lifebuoy which Armitage had designed. Grafton considered the problem and produced drawings from which he built a prototype which Armitage could inspect. Armitage refused to pay for this work.

HELD: that this was a contract for services not a contract of sale. It was never envisaged that the contract should result in the production of something which would be the subject of sale. It is interesting to note that in the course of argument Erle CJ referred to the position of an attorney who draws up a deed for a client. Clearly he considered that this would be a contract for services despite the fact that incidentally an object was also produced.

Contracts by doctors under which drugs are supplied are treated in the same way. *Roe* v *Minister of Health* [1954] 2 QB 66 is authority for the proposition that the fact that drugs are supplied in the course of treatment does not give rise to a contract of sale. Similarly, it seems likely that the provision of blood to a patient would be treated in the same way. There is no English authority on this point but, as Professor Atiyah states, it is highly likely that an English court would come to the same conclusion as the New York court in *Perlmutter* v *Beth David Hospital* (1955) 123 NE 2d 792. Perlmutter was injured as a result of a blood transfusion in the defendant hospital. The blood was infected with jaundice viruses which, according to the scientific evidence, could not be detected by any known tests. The account which was presented to the patient by the hospital showed that a separate charge was made for the blood.

HELD: there was not a sale of the blood. The patient was receiving a medical service to which the transfusion was merely incidental. It should be noted that in relation to legal liability for harm resulting from the provision of defective drugs or blood the situation may have been affected by Part I of the Consumer Protection Act 1987 which introduces strict liability for defective goods. (See Chapter 15.)

Hire purchase, conditional sale and credit sale agreements

Hire purchase agreements

These may loosely be defined as bailments of hire with options to purchase. Such agreements are in theory and in practice distinct from sale of goods. They were in fact first devised to avoid the pitfall in s25 SGA (see later 'Transfer of title by a non-owner') whereby a person with possession of goods with consent of the owner but without ownership could pass good title to the goods. The hirer in a hire-purchase agreement has not agreed to buy since he is not bound to exercise the option to buy and therefore falls outside the SGA (see *Helby* v *Matthews* [1895] AC 471).

The Consumer Credit Act 1974 has a variety of provisions governing hire purchase agreements where the total credit allowed does not exceed £5000 (soon to become £7500). These are obviously inapplicable to sale of goods contracts.

'Conditional sale' agreements

These are contracts for the sale of goods where the price is payable by *instalments* and the property is only to pass when certain specified conditions are fulfilled. The Consumer Credit Act 1974 in effect assimilates these in to hire-purchase agreements for credit under £5000, but the implied terms in conditional sales are still governed by the SGA.

'Credit-sale' agreements

These are contracts for the sale of goods where the price is payable by instalments but the property passes at once. These are governed by the SGA but in certain defined circumstances the Consumer Credit Act 1974 requires special formalities for these agreements.

Contracts involving interest in land (see above 1.5)

Sale and gift

The case of a gift in the normal sense of the word presents no problem. There is no consideration and so there is no possibility of a sale for as has been noted earlier the statutory definition of sale includes reference to a money consideration called the price. Problems can arise where so-called free gifts are offered as part of a commercial promotion. The leading case is *Esso Petroleum Ltd* v *Commissioners of Customs and Excise* [1976] 1 WLR 1. As part of a promotional scheme filling stations advertised 'free gifts' consisting of coins with pictures of members of England's 1966 World Cup squad. Anyone purchasing four gallons of petrol was entitled to one of these medallions. The liability of the petrol company to tax turned on the nature of this transaction.

HELD: this was not a contract of sale because the consideration for the contract to obtain the medallions was the motorist's contract to purchase four gallons of petrol not, as the statutory definition of sale requires, a money consideration. While there was agreement amongst the members of the House of Lords that this was not a contract of sale there was no agreement on what the legal nature of the transaction was. Two members thought that it was not a contract at all as there was not the requisite intention to enter into contractual relations; others thought that it was a collateral contract existing alongside the main contract to buy petrol.

Sale and agency

In some situations where one person is requested to obtain goods for another or he sells the goods of another it may be difficult to decide whether this is a contract under which the person supplying the goods does so as the agent of the other party or whether he does so on his own account. If the intermediary does so on his own account there is thus no privity between his supplier and the person to whom he sells the goods whereas if he is merely an agent of the person acquiring the goods there will be privity and legal action between the supplier to the agent and his principal will be possible. To determine the nature of the transaction it has been stated in *The Kronprinzessin Cecilie* (1917) 33 TLR 292 that the whole agreement must be looked at and that it is not conclusive that the terms 'sale' or 'agent' are used. If the supplier is entitled to sell at whatever price he chooses this will be strong evidence that he is not an agent. On the other hand a supplier who has to account to a supplier for the proceeds of transactions and provide details of customers will almost certainly be regarded as an agent.

Sale and bailment

A bailment is, to quote *Benjamin's Sale of Goods* (2nd edn) p42, 'a delivery of a thing by one person to another for a limited purpose upon the terms that the bailee will return the same thing to the bailor, or deliver it to someone in accordance with the bailor's instructions, after the purpose has been fulfilled.' In bailment the property in the goods is not intended to pass and does not pass on delivery. A case which turned on the distinction between bailment and sale is *Chapman Bros* v *Verco Bros & Co Ltd* [1933] 49 CLR 306. A farmer delivered wheat to millers and wheat merchants in bags similar to those of other farmers. Under the arrangement the company was required to buy and pay for the wheat on the request of the farmer. If no such request was made the company's obligation was to return an equal quantity of wheat of the same type. The contract referred to the company as storers.

HELD (by the Australian High Court): despite the reference to the company as storers this was a contract of sale as property passed to the company on delivery.

Credit and charge cards

Re Charge Card Services [1988] NLJ LR 201; [1988] 3 WLR 764. (The facts of this case are summarised on page 383.) The case demonstrates the difficulties sometimes found in classifying transactions surrounding the supply of goods. It appears that the Court of Appeal considers that a transaction when payment is made by means of a credit or charge card is a sale. It is difficult to see the logic of this in view of the fact that the SGA 1979 states that 'a contract of sale of goods is a contract by which the seller transfers or agrees to transfer the property in goods to the buyer for a *money consideration* called the price'. When a buyer uses a credit card, the goods are not transferred to him for a money consideration; it is the credit card company that eventually makes payment to the supplier. It is difficult to say what consideration the credit card holder furnishes, but it is not money.

2

Formation of the Contract and Formalities

2.1 Formation in general

2.2 Mistake

2.3 Auction sales

2.4 Formal requirements

2.1 Formation in general

Contracts of sale are, as was noted in chapter 1, subject to normal rules of the law of contract a fact underlined by s62(2). It follows that the general principles about formation of contract are relevant. It is necessary to show that there has been agreement, intention to create legal relations, and that there is consideration. Thus, in sale of goods' contracts, as with others, certainty and unambiguity are of paramount importance (see *Walford* v *Miles* [1992] 2 WLR 174 and *Neilson* v *Stewart* 1991 SLT 523). Also note that intention on the part of the parties to create legal relationships is more readily inferred in the commercial transactions typical of sale of goods.

The recent case of *Orion Insurance* v *Sphere Drake Insurance* (1990) The Independent 11 February shows that while it is not impossible to rebut the presumption that in commercial dealings there is automatically an intention on the part of both parties to create legal relations, the burden of proof required to rebut the presumption is very high. See for example, *Kleinwort Benson* v *Malaysian Mining Corporation* [1989] 1 All ER 785.

Consideration in sale of goods will always be in a particular form: on the one hand the provision of goods; on the other payment of a monetary consideration known as the price.

Section 8 SGA 1979 governs this question and in a normal situation this will be fixed or readily ascertainable. Occasionally the parties deal together so regularly that they do not need to refer specifically to the price; they know, from previous dealings, or the customs of their particular trade, how to calculate it. Section 8(2) provides that if for some reason this system breaks down, the contractual price may be determined by assessing what is 'reasonable'. For more detail on these points reference should be made to the general texts on the law of contract. Only in relation to auction sales does the Act deal with formation of contracts of sale and these are dealt with after a brief reference to the law of mistake in the next section.

2.2 Mistake

As with all contracts certain elements will vitiate a contract. For example, when misrepresentation occurs or mistake (see below) the contract may be rendered void or voidable. Similarly, commercial pressures amounting to duress will vitiate a contract. See *Atlas Express* v *Kafco* [1989] 1 All ER 647 and *Vantage Navigation Corpn* v *Suhail* [1989] 1 Lloyd's Rep 138.

As noted above one of the common law doctrines which is expressly stated to be applicable to sales contracts is mistake, a doctrine not without its difficulties in practical application. In some cases what is sometimes referred to as a question of mistake might more sensibly be treated as part of a discussion on whether there was ever a concluded agreement between the parties. In approaching this matter the courts take an objective approach. As Lord Dunedin, a Scottish judge said in *Muirhead and Turnbull* v *Dickson* (1905) 7 F 686: 'Commercial contracts cannot be arranged by what people think in their inmost mind. Commercial contracts are made according to what people say.'

The classic example of this approach in operation is *Tamplin* v *James* (1880) 15 Ch D 215 where the defendant agreed to buy premises under the mistaken belief that a particular field was included in the sale. It was quite clear from the details supplied by the vendor that the field was not for sale and there was no evidence that the vendor was aware of the purchaser's mistake. The Court of Appeal held that the purchaser was liable on the contract.

In rare cases it will not be possible, even applying this objective approach, to show that there was agreement. Such a case is *Raffles* v *Wichelhaus* (1864) 2 H & C 906. The seller agreed to sell and the purchaser agreed to buy a cargo of cotton stated to be *ex Peerless* from Bombay. In fact, there were two ships named *Peerless* sailing at slightly different times from Bombay and the seller had one ship in mind and the purchaser the other.

HELD: there was no contract and the buyer was not liable for refusing to accept the cargo arriving on the ship which the seller had in mind.

Difficulty has arisen in different circumstances where there have been mistakes about the identity of one of the parties to the contract. These cases usually result from a fraud perpetrated by someone, usually referred to in the law report as 'a rogue', and involve deciding which of two innocent parties should bear the loss occasioned by the fraud. The legal issue in dispute in these cases is usually whether the fraud that has been practised avoids the contract or merely renders it void. The significance of this is that the person who acquires title under the void contract cannot pass a good title; whereas a voidable contract allows a good title to be passed until steps are taken to avoid the contract. One way of deciding which category the transaction is in is to ask whether the mistake is to the identity of the other party or to his attributes. The former renders the contract void, the latter merely voidable. This seems to be the explanation of two similar cases *Cundy* v *Lindsay* (1878) 3 App Cas 459 and *Kings Norton Metal Co* v *Edridge* (1897) 14 TLR 98 where fraudulent statements were made by purchasers of goods about their identities. In the first the sellers thought that they were dealing with a reputable firm of whom they knew, whereas, in the second case, the sellers were content to deal with a firm of whom they had never heard and which, in fact, turned out to be a figment of the imagination of a rogue.

Where the parties are not dealing face to face (inter-praesentes) this identity/attributes distinction is not easy to reconcile with all the cases: and two relatively recent cases with very similar facts have been decided differently. In the first of these, *Ingram* v *Little* [1961] 1 QB 31 a rogue pretending to be a person of substance defrauded two elderly ladies over the sale of their car. The Court of Appeal held that the fraudulent statement as to identity rendered the contract void and so the third party who, in good faith, bought the car from the rogue did not get a good title. In a later case, *Lewis* v *Averay* [1971] 3 All ER 907, in very similar circumstances the Court of Appeal did not follow *Ingram* v *Little* and held that the contract was merely voidable.

The judgment of Steyn J in *Associated Japanese Bank (International) Ltd* v *Credit du Nord SA* [1988] 3 All ER 902 contains an illuminating discussion (albeit obiter) of the application of the law relating to common mistake.

2.3 Auction sales

Section 57 of the Act deals with auction sales. The first two subsections are declaratory of the common law. Subsection (1) states that 'where the goods are put up for sale by the auction in lots, each lot is prima facie deemed to be the subject of a separate contract of sale'. Subsection (2) provides that: 'A sale by auction is complete when the auctioneer announces its completion by the fall of the hammer, or in other customary manner: and until the announcement is made any bidder may retract his bid.' What this subsection does is to show that the bidder is making an offer for the goods which the auctioneer can accept. Consonant with general principles of contract formation the bidder can withdraw his offer at any time up to acceptance (ie the fall of the hammer).

The other subsections deal with the situation where the seller wishes to ensure that the goods are not sold below a minimum price. As subs(3) makes clear this can be done by giving notice that that the sale is subject to a reserve price being reached or that the seller has reserved the right to bid. Where the provisions of subs(3) have not been complied with but the seller or someone on his behalf does bid this is unlawful (subs(4)) and may be treated by the buyer as fraudulent according to subs(5).

It should be noted that the Auctions (Bidding Agreements) Act 1969 seeks to control bidding rings operated by dealers in order to obtain goods at lower prices. Section 3 of the Act provides that where agreements to refrain from bidding are operated the seller may avoid the contract and recover the goods or, in default, any loss he has suffered.

2.4 Formal requirements

There are now generally no formal requirements for contracts for the sale of goods. Section 4 SGA provides: '(1) Subject to this and any other Act, a contract of sale may be made in writing (either with or without seal), or by word of mouth, or partly in writing and partly by word of mouth, or may be implied from the conduct of the parties.'

However, certain statutes do impose the requirement that certain specified contracts of sale be in writing:

1. A contract for the sale of an *interest in land* will under s2 of the 1989 Law of Property (Miscellaneous Provisions) Act be unenforceable unless made in writing, incorporating all the terms agreed by the parties and signed by each party.
2. Conditional sale and credit sale agreements must be in writing and comply with a number of formal requirements under the Consumer Credit Act 1974.
3. A more minor example occurs under the Merchant Shipping Act 1894; the transfer of a British ship or a share therein must be in writing.

3

Types of Obligations Created

3.1 Introduction

3.2 Representations

3.3 Conditions and warranties

3.4 Innominate terms or intermediate stipulations

3.1 Introduction

In the case of all but the simplest transactions it is likely that there will be a process of bargaining during which various statements, oral and in writing, will be made. What is the legal significance of such statements? Should they turn out to be incorrect what is their effect and what remedies will the buyer have? These are the questions which are dealt with here. The traditional legal analysis is to distinguish between statements which are designated representations and those which are terms of the contract. Within the category of terms of the contract there was at one time a sharp dichotomy between conditions and warranties. However, more recently the courts have adopted a more flexible approach and while it may be possible to designate some terms as conditions or warranties in advance some terms must be regarded as 'innominate terms' or 'intermediate stipulations'.

In discussing the nature of the various statements made in the process of concluding a contract it is inevitable that there will be overlap with the remedies available should there be breach of an obligation. The discussion in this chapter will therefore anticipate that in the chapters on remedies.

3.2 Representations

> 'A representation is a statement of fact made by one party to the contract (the representor) to the other (the representee) which, while not forming a term of the contract is yet one of the reasons that induces the representee to enter into the contract.
> A misrepresentation is simply a representation that is untrue.'

This is how Cheshire and Fifoot define 'representation' and 'misrepresentation'. Note that the state of mind of the representor and his degree of carefulness are irrelevant to the classification of the representation as a misrepresentation. They are relevant however in determining the type of misrepresentation involved.

It is clear that a 'representation' means a statement of fact and not of intention or of opinion or of law. Moreover the statement must be of existing fact and must not relate to the future. This requirement has given rise to a great deal of case law, some of which is discussed below. A further problem relates to the question of whether silence can amount to a representation.

The misrepresentation must be one of fact

'Mere puffs'

'Mere puffs' are statements so vague that they have no effect in law or in equity. An example is *Dimmock* v *Hallett* (1866) LR 2 Ch App 21 where the description of land as 'fertile and improvable' was held to be merely salesman's talk. Treitel sees the distinction as one between indiscriminate praise and specific promises of verifiable facts.

There is no doubt a very fine distinction between some representations of fact and some mere puffs. Courts have in the past been indulgent to salesmen in this respect, tending to hold statements such as 'uncommonly rich water meadow' as mere puffs (*Scott* v *Hansor* (1829) 1 Russ & M 128).

If a statement purports to have support from facts and figures then the mere fact that it is expressed in a laudatory manner will not make it a mere puff.

Statements of opinion

Often a statement of opinion will be a 'mere puff'. Other statements of opinion will afford no relief if incorrect because they are not positive assertions of fact but merely statements of opinion or belief.

In *Bissett* v *Wilkinson* [1927] AC 177 the vendor of a farm in New Zealand asked how many sheep the farm could sustain. The land had never before been used as a sheep farm. The vendor's statement that it would support 2000 sheep was held to be a mere statement of opinion as to the capacity of the land. There was no action in misrepresentation where the opinion turned out to be erroneous.

In *Anderson* v *Pacific Fire & Marine Ins Co* (1872) LR 7 CP 65 an assertion that an anchorage was 'safe' was again held to be a mere statement of opinion.

The crucial factor is that in each case the maker of the statement had, to the knowledge of the other party, no personal knowledge of the facts on which it was based, so it can be understood that he could only state his own belief. The position would be otherwise if the purchaser had professed to have special knowledge or skill.

In certain cases an apparent statement of opinion will be held to involve a statement of fact:

1. Where the statement of opinion by implication involves a statement of fact. It is therefore a misrepresentation of fact for a person to assert that he holds an opinion which he does not in fact hold (see *Jend* v *Slade* (1797) 2 Esp 571).

2. Where the maker of the statement was in a position to know the true facts and it can be proved that the person concerned could not reasonably have held such a view as a result then there is a misrepresentation of fact.

In *Smith* v *Land & House Property Cpn* (1884) 28 Ch D 7 the vendor of a property described the sitting tenant as 'a most desirable tenant' where in fact the tenant was greatly in arrears with the rent. The defendants refused to complete the contract when they discovered this and the vendor sued for specific performance. The Court of Appeal held that the statement was not merely one of opinion but one of fact. This was an untrue assertion that nothing had happened to make the tenant other than a desirable one. The vendor was in a position to know the true facts: they were particularly within his knowledge so he could be taken to have represented that these facts existed.

The same consideration would apply to a shipowner who says that his ship is 'expected ready to load by a certain date'. He impliedly represents that he honestly holds that belief and that he does so on reasonable grounds (*The Mihalis Angelos* [1971] 1 QB 164; [1970] 3 All ER 125).

In certain circumstances an opinion may be stated as though it were a fact. For example, a layman using an expert's statement to back up his own opinions, putting them across as though they were facts: this will be a representation (*Reese River Silver Mining Co* v *Smith* (1869) LR 4 HL 64).

Representations or promises as to the future

A representation as to the future will not generally give rise to any liability unless it becomes a contractual term. Therefore a false statement as to future conduct will not found an action in misrepresentation.

However where a party makes a representation as to his future intention and at the time he made such statement he had no such intention, then this will be a misrepresentation. It is probably true to say that the courts tend to construe statements as relating to intention rather than to future conduct in order to give protection to the party induced into entering the contract.

In *Edgington* v *Fitzmaurice* (1888) 29 Ch D 459 certain company directors induced certain persons including the plaintiff to lend money to the company by means of a representation that the investments would be used to expand the company's business and premises. The money was in fact used to pay off pre-existing debts. In holding that the contract could be rescinded Bowen LJ said:

> 'There must be a mis-statement of existing fact; but the state of a man's mind is as much a fact as the state of his digestion. It is true that it is very difficult to prove what the state of a man's mind at a particular time is, but if it can be ascertained it is as much a fact as anything else.'

The directors were here making the representation that they had no intention of using the money in the manner stated.

Statements of law

There is no remedy for a misrepresentation of law. There is, however, some lack of clarity as to what in fact will amount to a representation of law and not of fact.

A representation as to the meaning of an Act of Parliament is clearly one of law (*National Pari-Mutual Assoc* v *R* (1930) 47 TLR 110). However, a representation as to the purported effect of a document may be one as to its contents or its meaning. If it is a representation of the contents then the representation is one of fact, but if the representation is as to the meaning of a document whose contents are known, this may be a representation of law.

Note that a representation as to the particular private rights of an individual in a particular situation is treated as one of fact (see for example, *Andre & Cie SA* v *Michel Blanc & Fils* [1979] 2 Lloyd's 427).

A representation that a common law rule or statutory rule applies to a known state of fact may be a representation either of fact or of law, apparently depending on the circumstances of the case. In *Solle* v *Butcher* [1950] 1 KB 671; [1949] 2 All ER 1107, a statement that the Rent Acts were applicable to a house because its 'identity' was erroneously believed to have been changed by works done. It was a misrepresentation of fact. The 'law' contained in the representation was correct it was only the facts (ie that the house had changed its identity) which were erroneous.

Silence amounting to misrepresentation

Bearing in mind the general maxim: 'caveat emptor' - let the buyer beware - the general rule is that mere silence does not amount to a misrepresentation. In its simplest form the tacit acquiescence in the self-deception of another will not be a misrepresentation. In particular in contracts of sale of goods there is no general duty to disclose facts material to the contract.

An example is *Fletcher* v *Knell* (1872) 42 LJQB 55, where it was held that a person applying for the post of governess is under no obligation to tell her prospective employers that she is a divorcee.

It should however be noted that a party may make a misrepresentation through his conduct - such as actively concealing defects in the goods (*Schneider* v *Heath* (1813) 3 Camp 506). Where a misrepresentation is made through conduct then a failure on behalf of the representor to clarify the other party's misapprehension will be a misrepresentation.

The general rule that silence does not amount to misrepresentation is subject to the following exceptions.

Where silence distorts a positive representation

This covers cases where the representor misleadingly tells only part of the story: if he is to make any representation at all it must be a full and frank statement and not a part story in which the part withheld makes that which is said false or misleading.

An example is *Notts Patent Brick & Tile Co* v *Butler* (1886) 16 QBD 778. Here a buyer of land asked the vendor's solicitor whether the land was the subject of any restrictive covenants. The reply was that he was not aware of any. He did not add that this was because he had not taken the trouble to read the relevant document.

Dimmock v *Hallett* (1866) LR 2 Ch App 21 is frequently cited in this context. Here the vendor of land stated that the farms involved were let but omitted to say that the tenants had given notice to quit. As it stood the statement was a misrepresentation.

Representation made false by later events

Where a representation is true when made but before the conclusion of the contract the representation to the maker's knowledge becomes false then he must disclose this fact.

In *With* v *O'Flanagan* [1936] Ch 575; [1936] 1 All ER 727 the parties were negotiating the sale of a doctor's practice which was represented to be worth £2000. Before completion the value was greatly reduced due to the incumbent doctor's illness. The non-disclosure of this fact was a misrepresentation.

A further example is *Davies* v *London & Provincial Marine Ins Co* (1878) 8 Ch D 469, where a company accepted a money deposit from the friends of one of its agents it had threatened to arrest even after it discovered that no felony had in fact been committed by the agent. This illustrates the proposition that this exception to the 'silence' rule extends to where a statement is false when made and is later discovered to be so by the maker.

Contracts uberrimae fidei

In certain types of contract known as contracts uberrimae fidei or contracts of the utmost good faith, there is a duty to disclose material facts. These tend to be contracts where one party is in a particularly strong position to know the material facts and the other is in a particularly weak position to have such knowledge. The main examples of such contracts are as follows.

Contracts of insurance. The assured in essence must disclose all such facts as would influence the judgment of a reasonable or prudent insurer. The case of *Magee* v *Pennine Insurance Co* [1969] 2 QB 507; [1969] 2 All ER 891 is illustrative in this context.

Family arrangements. For example, agreements between family members for settling disputes as to family property.

Contracts between parties in a fiduciary relationship

This will clearly apply where the relationship is such that the equitable doctrine of undue influence applies. The main fiduciary relationships will include solicitor and client, trustee and beneficiary, and bank manager and client. In these relationships the duty is not discharged by mere disclosure; there are more stringent obligations before any benefit may be taken from the contract. In other fiduciary situations, however, mere disclosure will be adequate: for example, between principal and agent, co-parties, and between a company and its promoters.

The representation must be material

A misrepresentation will usually be of no effect unless it is material, in other words it is a misrepresentation which would affect the judgment of a reasonable man in deciding whether or on what terms to enter the contract or one which would induce him to enter the contract in question without making such inquiries as he could otherwise make. For example, it is material in a contract involving a loan of money that the lender is notorious as a ruthless moneylender (*Gordon* v *Street* [1899] 2 QB 642).

Two exceptions are given to this rule:

1. If the misrepresentation is made fraudulently then materiality is irrelevant.
2. The contract may expressly provide that any or every representation is material.

The misrepresentation must have induced the contract

To found liability the misrepresentation must have induced the other party to enter the contract. In other words the person to whom the misrepresentation was made must have relied on it. There will therefore be no liability if the plaintiff is unaware that the representation has been made or if he is aware that it is untrue or if it did not in any way affect his judgment, or he relied on his own information.

Where the plaintiff is unaware of the existence of the misrepresentation
Horsfall v *Thomas* (1862) 1 H & C 90. This case involved the sale of a defective cannon. The seller had attempted to conceal the defect by use of a metal plug but the buyer never at any time examined the gun. It was held that the buyer's plea of misrepresentation must fail since he had never examined the gun and the concealment of the defect therefore could not have affected his mind.

A further example is *ex parte Biggs* (1859) 28 LJ Ch 50.

Where the plaintiff knows that the representation is untrue
Cheshire and Fifoot state that in such cases it must be clear that the plaintiff had actual and complete knowledge of the true facts, and the constructive or fragmentary knowledge is insufficient. Treitel however claims that the knowledge of an agent acting within the scope of his authority will suffice to bind the principal.

Where the representation does not affect the judgment of the representee
Attwood v *Small* (1838) 7 Cl & Fin 232. During negotiations for the sale of a number of mines the purchaser asked questions as to the capabilities of the property and the answers given by the vendor were untrue. However, the vendor's statements were verified by an experienced agent who had been appointed by the buyer to

investigate and had carried out an unhindered investigation. The statements were subsequently found to be untrue and the buyer sought rescission. The House of Lords held that rescission was not possible since the buyer had relied on his own report rather than the statements made by the seller.

Similarly in *Smith* v *Chadwick* (1884) 9 App Cas 187 the plaintiff admitted during cross-examination that he had not in fact been influenced by the misrepresentations in question (contained in a company prospectus) so the misrepresentation action failed.

Note, however, that a partial inducement will suffice, so if the representee is induced partly by the misrepresentation and partly by other factors then the misrepresentation action will lie (*Edgington* v *Fitzmaurice* (1888) 29 Ch D 459). There were in fact two inducements in this case. The plaintiff had been induced to invest in a company partly by a false statement in the prospectus and partly by his own incorrect belief that once he invested and became a debenture holder he would have a charge over the assets of the company. The action for misrepresentation succeeded.

The relevance of having an opportunity to test the accuracy of the representation
It is clear that with an innocent misrepresentation, if the representee in fact tests the accuracy of the representation even though he does not discover the truth then no action for misrepresentation will lie (see *Clarke* v *Mackintosh* (1862) 4 Giff 134). Treitel thinks the same rule applies in the case of negligent misrepresentation but not with fraudulent misrepresentation, and cites *S Pearson & Son Ltd* v *Dublin Cpn* [1907] AC 351 as authority.

A misrepresentation may still be actionable where the representee had, but did not take, the opportunity to test the truth of the representation. In *Redgrave* v *Hurd* (1881) 20 Ch D 1 the representee was here induced to buy a solicitor's practice by a misrepresentation, albeit innocent, as to the value of the practice. The representor gave the representee the opportunity of examining the accounts of the practice and such inspection would have revealed the truth of the matter but no examination was made. The action for rescission succeeded.

The categories of misrepresentation

The law now recognises three types of misrepresentation:

1. Fraudulent misrepresentation.
2. Negligent misrepresentation.
3. Innocent misrepresentation.

The differences lie in the state of mind of the representor. The significance of the distinctions is in the remedies which will be available in each category. It should be remembered that the law at one time did not distinguish negligent and innocent misrepresentation, often describing both as 'innocent misrepresentation', and some older cases should be considered only in the light of this change.

Fraudulent misrepresentation

Faced with a fraudulent misrepresentation the innocent party will be able either to affirm the contract and sue for damages for the tort of deceit or to rescind the contract and sue for damages for deceit (see below).

The leading case on the meaning of 'fraud' (or 'fraudulent') is *Derry* v *Peek* (1889) 14 App Cas 337 (see below). It should be noted, however, that the evidence of fraud must be clear and substantial before any claim in fraud is brought. The courts are reluctant to find fraud in the absence of very clear evidence. In addition, it is established that fraud must be specifically pleaded and proved: the court will not infer fraud from the circumstances (see *Belmont Finance* v *Williams Furniture (No 2)* [1980] 1 All ER 393).

In *Derry* v *Peek* (1889) 14 App Cas 337 a company was incorporated by private Act of Parliament which gave it the power to run trams by animal power or with the Board of Trade's consent, by steam or mechanical power. The company's directors issued a prospectus mentioning the company's 'right to use steam power' since they could foresee no problem in obtaining the Board of Trade's consent. The plaintiff sought shares in the company upon the faith of the statement in the prospectus, but the Board of Trade ultimately refused its consent.

The House of Lords held that the action in deceit must fail since it could not be said that the directors acted fraudulently. Lord Herschell states:

> 'The prospectus was inaccurate. But that is not the question. If the directors believed that the consent of the Board of Trade was practically concluded by the passing of the Act, has the plaintiff made out, which it was for him to do, that they have been guilty of a fraudulent misrepresentation?
>
> I think not. I cannot hold it proved as to any one of them that he knowingly made a false statement, or one which he did not believe to be true, or was careless whether what he stated was true or false. In short I think they honestly believed that what they asserted was true.'

The House of Lords judgments laid down the three cases where a fraud will exist in relation to a false statement:

1. Where a false statement is made with knowledge of its falsity.
2. Where a false statement is made without belief in its truth.
3. Where a false statement is made recklessly, not caring whether it is true or false.

Subsequent cases have laid down that a statement can be fraudulent even though made without a bad motive and without intention to cause loss.

In *Polhill* v *Walter* (1832) 3 B & Ad 114 an agent was held liable in deceit for accepting a bill of exchange on his principal's behalf knowing he had no authority to do so even though he believed his principal would ratify his actions.

Negligent misrepresentation

A misrepresentation will be made negligently if it is made carelessly and in breach of a duty owed by the representor to the representee to take reasonable care that the represention made is correct.

The remedies available to the innocent party are: to affirm the contract and claim damages under s2 MA; or to rescind the contract and claim damages under the same section (see below).

It had been thought after *Derry* v *Peek* that no action would lie for merely negligent words, especially where they only caused pecuniary loss. This idea was finally repudiated by the House of Lords in *Hedley Byrne* v *Heller & Partners Ltd* [1964] AC 465; [1963] 2 All ER 575, where it was held that an action would lie in tort in certain circumstances for negligent mis-statement. The plaintiffs here gave credit to another firm called Easipower Ltd having been induced to give such credit by a negligent reference provided by Easipower's bankers (the defendant). The plaintiff suffered loss when Easipower went into liquidation.

The House of Lords held on the facts that the plaintiff's action must fail since the reference had been given subject to a disclaimer, 'without responsibility', but the defendants could otherwise have been liable in negligence. The House of Lords made it clear that liability depends upon the existence of a 'special relationship' between plaintiff and defendant.

However, with the statutory liability for misrepresentation introduced by the MA, there is now no need to prove a 'special relationship' to found liability for negligent misrepresentation. It is simply necessary that the representor has induced the representee to make the contract by virtue of the misrepresentation. Section 2(1) MA provides:

> 'Where a person has entered into a contract after a misrepresentation has been made to him by another party thereto and as a result thereof he has suffered loss, then if the person making the representation would be liable to damages in respect thereof if the representation had been made fraudulently, he shall be so liable notwithstanding that the misrepresentation was not made fraudulently unless he proves that he had reasonable ground to believe and did believe up to the time the contract was made that the facts represented were true.'

Section 2(1) also has the effect of reversing the burden of proof. At common law the onus was on the representee to prove negligence but under s2(1) the representor will be liable unless he proves that he had reasonable grounds to believe and did believe up till the time of the contract that the facts represented were true. Note that the representor's actual means of knowledge are relevant: reasonable grounds for one man may not be reasonable grounds for another.

This reversal of the burden of proof is a second tactical advantage of pleading negligent (or, later, innocent) misrepresentation and claiming damages under s2(1). The onus shifts to the representor to show his reasonable belief. The first tactical advantage as above is that fraudulent misrepresentation is tactically very difficult to prove.

Section 2(1) applies also to innocent misrepresentation (below). Indeed the word 'negligent' is not mentioned in the section due to bad drafting and negligent misrepresentations are only included by clear implication.

The recent case of *Mariola Marine Corporation* v *Lloyd's Register of Shipping, The Morning Watch* [1990] 1 Lloyd's Rep 547 shows that the 'special relationship' question is still subject to scrutiny by the courts. In the sale of a ship, negligent misrepresentation occurred. The classification society, operated under the auspices of Lloyds Registry, had a survey carried out with a view to putting the yacht up for sale. The surveyor's report was negligently written and misleading. The ultimate purchasers alleged the boat had serious defects, which rendered it unseaworthy. The court held that a duty of care would only arise when:

1. there was a possibility of reliance;
2. there was a 'proximity' between plaintiff and defendant; and
3. it was fair and reasonable to impute forseeability to the defendants.

On the facts given, the court felt that item (2) did not apply here. Although there was a superficial resemblance to *Smith* v *Bush* [1987] 3 All ER 179, the close relationship did not exist here. The 'classification survey' was carried out without any particular purchaser in mind whereas in *Smith* the purchaser was known. Accordingly the court decided in favour of the defendant.

Innocent misrepresentation

An innocent misrepresentation is a misrepresentation made without fault on the part of the representor. The representor must believe in the truth of what he says, must have no intention of misleading the other party and must not be negligent in forming or conveying his belief.

At common law there was no remedy for innocent misrepresentation unless: the representation had become a term of the contract (where the action would be for breach of contract); or the representation amounted to a collateral warranty (ie an independent contract whereby the representor promises that the representation is true in return for the consideration which is the representee going ahead and entering the main contract).

In equity, however, the courts could order the rescission of the contract or perhaps specific performance.

Now the MA s2(1) provides the representee with an action in damages for innocent misrepresentation. Note too that under s2(2) MA the court has discretion to award damages in lieu of rescission.

Remedies for misrepresentation 1: remedies for fraudulent misrepresentation

The victim of a fraudulent misrepresentation has two alternatives:

1. He may affirm the contract and sue for damages in deceit.
2. He may rescind the contract and in addition claim damages for deceit.

Damages

The measure of damages when suing in the tort of deceit should be distinguished both from the contractual measure of damages and from the ordinary tortious measure. It is probably easiest at this early stage to explain the three measures of damages.

The contractual measure of damages. The object of damages for breach of contract is to put the injured party as nearly as may be possible in the position he would have been in had the contract been performed. It follows inter alia that loss of profits will generally be recoverable. The test of remoteness in contract damages involves a higher degree of probability than the test in tort, so the courts will more readily in contract than in tort hold certain items to be too remote. The relevant time for foreseeability to be measured is in contract at the time of the making of the contract.

The tortious measure of damages. The object of damages in tort is to put the injured party in the position he would have been in if the tort had not been committed. The test of remoteness in tort is foreseeability at the time of the breach of duty.

Damages for deceit: the measure of damages for fraud. It is clear that in damages for fraud the measure is not the ordinary tort measure. In fraud 'the defendant is bound to make reparation for all the actual damages directly flowing from the fraudulent inducement ... it does not lie in the mouth of the fraudulent person to say that the damage could not reasonably have been foreseen' (The Court of Appeal in *Doyle* v *Olby (Ironmongers)* [1969] 2 QB 158; [1969] 2 All ER 119). It appears therefore that the plaintiff in fraud is to be compensated for all the loss he has suffered with no test of remoteness of damage.

Doyle v *Olby* (supra) lays down that it is this third measure of damages which applies to fraudulent misrepresentations. This case involved the sale of a business where the vendor made misrepresentations as to its profitability: the buyer recovered inter alia damages for losses suffered in the course of running the business.

Rescission

All three types of misrepresentation make the contract voidable not void, so the contract is valid unless and until it is set aside by the representee. The representee has an election, therefore, to affirm or to rescind the contract.

In order to rescind the contract the representee must make it clear that he refuses to be bound by its provisions. The election must be unequivocal, and if made the contract is terminated ab initio (ie it is considered never to have existed).

As a general rule the decision to rescind must be communicated within a reasonable time to the representor. However, this rule has been given some flexibility particularly in the case of fraudulent misrepresentation by the case of *Car & Universal Finance Co Ltd* v *Caldwell* [1965] 1 QB 525; [1964] 1 All ER 290. Here the defendant had sold and delivered his car to a rogue who paid with a cheque which was subsequently dishonoured. The rogue inevitably had disappeared. The defendant contacted the police and the Automobile Association informing them of the situation. The rogue later sold the car to a motor dealer who sold it to the plaintiff who took it in good faith. The Court held that the defendant's action in telling the Automobile Association and the police were adequate to rescind the contract: he had made it clear he wished no longer to be bound by the contract. The contract was therefore avoided and no title vested in the plaintiffs.

It is thought by the editors of *Benjamin on Sale of Goods* that this 'exception' to the rule of communication in rescission cases extends to where the representor is innocently keeping out of the way, as well as where he is fraudulent.

Rescission in cases of fraudulent misrepresentation is subject to the general limitations on rescission outlined below.

Remedies for misrepresentation 2: remedies for negligent misrepresentation

The victim of a negligent misrepresentation has two alternative courses of action: he may affirm the contract and claim damages; or he may rescind the contract and claim damages.

The statutory right to damages of s2(1) MA has been set out above. This applies together with its reversal of the burden of proof to negligent misrepresentation.

Damages

The measure of damages in cases of negligent misrepresentation has been an area of much controversy. The wording of s2(1) is unclear on the point. 'So liable' in s2(1) might suggest that the negligent (or innocent) misrepresentor should be liable to the same extent in damages as in the tort of deceit/fraudulent misrepresentation, but this is not the position currently supported by the courts.

The view that damages under s2(1) should be measured like the tort of deceit is based on the so called 'fiction of fraud' which comes from the precise wording of s2(1): 'would be liable in damages ... had the misrepresentation been made fraudulently ... shall be so liable notwithstanding that it is not made fraudulently'. The fiction is rejected by Cheshire and Fifoot, and has not received much judicial support.

Another view is that the measure should be the contractual measure. This view was taken in the earliest cases after the MA 1967. In *Jarvis* v *Swans Tours Ltd* [1973] 1 QB 233; [1973] 1 All ER 71 Lord Denning MR said: 'it is not necessary to decide whether they were representations or warranties; because since the MA 1967 there is a remedy in damages for misrepresentation as well as breach of warranty'. In *Watts* v *Spence* [1976] Ch 165; [1975] 2 All ER 528, the plaintiff was induced to enter a house purchase contract by a representation of the defendant that he was the sole owner where in fact the house belonged to him and his wife. Graham J awarded damages for loss of a bargain under s2(1) MA.

It is submitted that in neither of these cases was the issue of the measure of damages fully argued. A better view is found in *Andre & Cie SA* v *Michel Blanc & Fils* [1979] 2 Lloyd's Rep 427, where the question of the measure of damages was fully considered by Ackner J. He held that the ordinary tortious measure was applicable.

Treitel is of the view that the damage should be the same as an action for deceit but does not draw the sharp distinctions made above between the ordinary tortious measure and damages for deceit.

It is submitted that the correct view is that damages under s2(1) should be measured according to the ordinary tortious measure.

Note that if the plaintiff sues in tort at common law for negligent mis-statement under *Hedley Byrne* and not under s2(1) MA the measure of damages is indisputably the ordinary tort measure (*Esso Petroleum Co Ltd* v *Mardon* [1976] QB 801; [1975] 1 All ER 203).

Rescission
Rescission is again available but subject to the limitations outlined below. The considerations outlined in 'Remedies for misrepresentation 1: Damages' (above) as regards the representee's election and the communication of rescission to the representator apply equally to negligent misrepresentation.

The MA s2(2) makes an important change in the law in this area. Under s2(2) the court now has a discretion in certain circumstances to award damages in lieu of rescission where the misrepresentation is not made fraudulently. Section 2(2) is discussed fully below under 'innocent misrepresentation' but note that it applies equally to negligent misrepresentations although it is less likely in the case of a negligent misrepresentation that the court will exercise its discretion in favour of the representor.

Remedies for misrepresentation 3: remedies for innocent misrepresentation

At common law there was no remedy for innocent misrepresentation unless the representation had contractual effect, in which case the action would be for a breach of that term. In equity, however, rescission or specific performance were both available.

Equity also devised a system of indemnity payments to compensate the representee for loss directly attributable to the innocent misrepresentation. It was difficult to distinguish between indemnity payments and damages, but the position has in any case been superseded by the MA 1967.

The statutory liability of s2(1) MA applies to innocent misrepresentations, giving the representee for the first time a right to damages. The measure of damages for innocent misrepresentation under s2(1) will be the same as that for negligent misrepresentation under the same subsection, namely the tortious measure of damages.

In *Royscott Trust Ltd* v *Rogerson* [1991] 3 WLR 57 it was held that the tortious measure of damage was the true one. In that case a car dealer agreed to sell a car on HP to a customer for a cash price of £7,600, of which the customer was to pay a deposit of £1,200. These amounts were mistakenly stated as £8,000 and £1,600 respectively to the finance company and all future transactions were based on these figures.

The customer paid part of the sum due to the finance company, but in 1987 he dishonestly sold the car, and later ceased to make any payments. The amount unpaid by that time was, the finance company claimed, £3,625. They based this figure on the difference between the amount repaid to them by the customer and the amount £6,400 which they had advanced to the car dealer. The figures supplied to the finance company, however, had been mistakenly set too high, and the finance company sued the car dealer for innocent misrepresentation and claimed damages under s2(1) of the Misrepresentation Act 1967.

The Court of Appeal held that the measure of damages recoverable under s2(1) of the MA 1967 was a tortious rather than contractual one. The finance company was entitled to recover damages in respect of all losses occurring as a natural consequence, including unforeseeable losses, subject to the normal rules on remoteness. It was in any event a foreseeable event that a customer buying a car on HP might dishonestly sell the car. The act by the customer was not a novus actus, the chain of causation was unbroken.

The car dealers were liable for innocent misrepresentation and the finance company could claim the £3,625 plus interest.

In *Naughton* v *O'Callaghan* (1990) The Times 17 February, the question of measure of damages arose. A racehorse was bought in reliance of its pedigree, which at a later date was discovered to be not as represented. The horse raced without success. The court held that since under s2(1) of MA the basic principle was that an award of damages should put the plaintiff in the position they would have been in had the representation not been made. Although the normal time for the assessment of damages was at the time of the breach, there was no absolute rule on this and the court had the power to fix such other dates as might be appropriate. In this case the situation was not quite the usual one, and the value of the horse fell, not because of a general fall in the market, but because of new information about its pedigree. At the same time some credit had to be given for goods retained. Accordingly the plaintiffs were entitled to recover the difference between the purchase price and the syndication share value of the horse when the misrepresentation became known.

The MA made a further important change in the law in this area. Under s2(2) the court has a discretion in the case of both a negligent or an innocent misrepresentation to award damages in lieu of rescission. Section 2(2) provides:

> 'Where a person has entered into a contract after a misrepresentation has been made to him otherwise than fraudulently, and he would be entitled by reason of the misrepresentation to rescind the contract, then, if it is claimed in any of the proceedings arising out of the contract that the contract ought to be or has been rescinded, the court or arbitrator may declare the contract subsisting and award damages in lieu of rescission, if it is of the opinion that it would be equitable to do so, having regard to the nature of the misrepresentation and the loss that would be caused by it if the contract were upheld, as well as to the loss that rescission would cause the other party.'

The court must therefore consider damages in lieu of rescission to be equitable before it may make such award.

For s2(2) to apply, the remedy of rescission must be available to the representee at the time of the action. If for any of the reasons set out below (see: Limits on the right to rescind) it has been lost then no damages award under s2(2) is possible.

In s2(2) rescission and damages are alternative remedies: the court cannot award both. Note that in the cases of fraudulent or negligent misrepresentation the court may award both damages and rescission.

The measure of damages under s2(2) is somewhat controversial. The section gives no clue as to the basis of assessment or as to the remoteness to be applied to an award under it. No conclusions are drawn by the commentators in this area. Perhaps the most which can be said is that the legislature almost certainly did not intend the contractual measure to apply, and that it would seem sensible to assimilate the measure in s2(2) to the measure in s2(1), namely the tortious measure of damages.

The Misrepresentation Act 1967 section 3

Section 3 MA as amended by s8 of the Unfair Contract Terms Act 1977 governs exclusion clauses which exclude liability for misrepresentation. Section 3 provides:

'If a contract contains a term which would exclude or restrict:
a) any liability to which a party to a contract may be subject by reason of any misrepresentation made by him before the contract was made; or
b) any remedy available to another party to the contract by reason of such a misrepresentation.
that term shall be of no effect except in so far as it satisfies the requirement of reasonableness as stated in s11(c) of the Unfair Contract Terms Act; and it is for those claiming that the term satisfies that requirement to show that it does.'

The Unfair Contract Terms Act made s3 MA subject to the reasonableness test of that Act (set out in the next chapter).

An illustration of the working of s3 is found in *Howard Marine & Dredging Co Ltd v A Ogden & Sons Ltd* [1978] QB 574; [1978] 2 All ER 1134, which involved a provision that 'the charterer's acceptance of handing over the vessel shall be conclusive evidence that they have examined the vessel and found her to be in all respects fit for the intended and contemplated use by the charterers'. The case turned on whether it was reasonable to allow reliance on this clause, but the test now after the UCTA would be whether the term was a reasonable one to insert in the contract.

Section 3 applies to all types of misrepresentation, but does not apply to terms of the contract, which are governed by the UCTA itself. Section 3 is intended to cover both clauses which exclude liability and clauses which restrict liability, but the precise ambit of s3 in either area is unclear. The divide between being a clause excluding and a clause defining liability is itself doubtful.

Limits on the right to rescind

Rescission is a drastic remedy and has consequently had some severe restrictions placed on its applicability. The right to rescind will be lost in the following circumstances: affirmation of the contract by the representee; lapse of time; restitutio in integrum no longer possible; third party rights.

Affirmation of the contract by the representee

Where the representee with full knowledge of the misrepresentation declares an intention to go on with the contract or does some other act from which such an intention may reasonably be inferred, then he will no longer be allowed to rescind the contract. This is probably the best explanation of *Long* v *Lloyd* [1958] 1 WLR 753; [1958] 2 All ER 402, involving a defective lorry which the plaintiff kept and used for some time before returning.

In *Re Hop & Malt Exchange Co, ex parte Briggs* (1866) LR 1 Eq 483, the representee who had bought shares on the strength of the misrepresentation subsequently and with knowledge of the misrepresentation tried to sell the shares. This was an affirmation.

Lapse of time

Lapse of time appears only to be relevant in so far as it amounts to evidence of affirmation. Indeed where the lapse of time is great it may be taken as conclusive evidence of an election to affirm the contract.

In *Leaf* v *International Galleries* [1950] 2 KB 86; [1950] 1 All ER 693, the court held that a contract for the sale of a painting could not be rescinded for misrepresentation when five years had passed between the sale and the discovery of the truth. It appears from this case that time 'lapses' even before the representee knew of the misrepresentation. The case also stretches the notion that lapse of time is only relevant as evidence of affirmation, since affirmation cannot occur until the representee knows the truth.

It is doubtful that lapse of time will apply to fraudulent misrepresentations (see *Armstrong* v *Jackson* [1917] 2 KB 822).

Restitutio in integrum no longer possible

Usually the party wishing to rescind a contract is required to restore to the other benefits that he obtained under the contract. In sale of goods, a buyer who wishes to rescind and receive the price must return the goods to the seller.

Clark v *Dickson* (1858) EB & E 148, involved some goods which had been consumed and some otherwise altered by the buyer.

However, provided substantial restitution can be made, rescission may be ordered on terms that the representee pay compensation for loss in value or deterioration of the goods (*Lagunas Nitrate Co* v *Lagunas Syndicate* [1899] 2 Ch 392).

Third party rights

Where third parties have acquired rights over the subject matter of the contract subsequent to the sale and these rights would be affected by rescission, then this could be a bar. The most obvious example is where goods obtained by fraud from the original owner have been sold on to an innocent third party. In these circumstances the contract of sale between the rogue and the owner is voidable only and where the rogue having bought the goods sells them to a third party in good faith for valuable consideration, then title passes to that third party (s23 SGA) and his rights cannot be defeated by the original owner. The title which the rogue obtained is valid until it has been voided.

White v *Garden* (1851) 10 CB 919 is an illustration. In this case the rogue persuaded Garden to sell him 50 tons of iron on the strength of a bill of exchange which appeared to have been accepted, but the acceptor was in fact fictitious. The rogue resold the iron to White. After delivering the iron to White, Garden realised the truth and repossessed it. White sued Garden for the goods and it was held that title had passed to him; the title had passed to the rogue under a contract that was at that time valid. Such title had been passed to White before Garden rescinded the contract.

If, to take a different example, a third party has given no consideration for his rights to goods or rights under a lease (*Scholefield* v *Templer* (1859) 4 De G & J 429) then rescission will still be possible to defeat those rights.

In the context of third party rights a rule has evolved relating to companies going into liquidation. In the normal case a person who is induced to become a shareholder by reason of a false representation can rescind the contract against the company, thereby recovering what he has paid. However, when the company has gone into liquidation, rescission would obviously prejudice the position of the company's creditors since the company's assets must be collected for distribution among them; so in these circumstances it is not possible to rescind such a contract.

3.3 Conditions and warranties

The term 'condition' is not defined by the SGA. The act merely lays down the effect of a breach of condition. Section 11(3) provides:

> 'Whether a stipulation in a contract of sale is a condition, the breach of which may give rise to a right to treat the contract as repudiated, or a warranty, the breach of which may give rise to a claim for damages but not to a right to reject the goods and treat the contract as repudiated, depends in each case on the construction of the contract and a stipulation may be a condition, though called a warranty in the contract.'

A condition is a central or important term of the contract. It is a term so essential to the contract that its non-fulfilment gives the innocent party a right to treat the contract as *repudiated* and usually to recover damages in addition. If the seller is in breach of the condition the buyer may reject the goods and decline to pay the price, or if he has already paid it he may recover it. The definition of 'condition' set out by Fletcher Moulton LJ in *Wallis* v *Pratt* [1910] 2 KB 1003 at 1012; affirmed [1911] AC 394 is frequently cited:

'An obligation which goes so directly to the substance of the contract, or in other words so essential to its very nature that its non-performance may fairly be considered by the other party as a substantial failure to perform the contract at all.'

'Warranty' is defined in s61:

'An agreement with reference to goods which are the subject of a contract of sale, but collateral to the main purpose of such contract, the breach of which gives rise to a claim for damages but not to a right to reject the goods and treat the contract as repudiated.'

Warranties are of less importance than conditions. They are not vital or fundamental terms and their breach will give rise only to a claim for damages and not a right to repudiate the contract.

In brief a condition is a major term of essential importance in the performance of the contract, whereas a warranty is a minor term.

Section 11(3) of the SGA does little more than state the problem: it does not give any guidance on deciding whether a particular term should be regarded as a condition or a warranty. It is generally agreed that there are four ways in which a term may be shown to be a condition. First, there are those terms which, to use the words of Fletcher Moulton LJ quoted above, go 'so directly to the substance of the contract' that their breach allows the other party to treat the contract as repudiated. Secondly, a statute may so designate the term as a condition. There are many examples in legislation but in the context of contracts of sale the implied terms about description and quality in ss 13 and 14 of the SGA which will be discussed in detail in chapter 5 provide excellent examples. It will be seen that these terms are stated by the Act to be conditions. Thirdly, and parallel to this statutory designation of a term as a condition, is the possibility that judicial decisions have clearly settled that a certain type of clause widely used in contracts is to be interpreted as a condition. A good example is an 'expected readiness to load' clause in a charterparty which in *The Mihalis Angelos* [1971] 1 QB 164 was said by the Court of Appeal to be a condition. Fourthly, it is possible for the parties themselves to attach the labels 'condition' and 'warranty' as they wish and to attempt to designate as a condition any term of a contract no matter how unimportant it might be. However, as the House of Lords pointed out in *Schuler AG v Wickman Machine Tool Sales Ltd* [1974] AC 235, the court will look at all the circumstances and the fact that the contract uses the word 'condition' will not necessarily be decisive if, in the context it is clear that the parties cannot have intended that breach should lead to the termination of the contract.

This aspect of the problem has recently been raised in the Court of Appeal in *Lombard North Central plc v Butterworth* [1987] 1 All ER 267. The defendant leased a computer from the plaintiffs for a period of five years on payment of an initial sum and 19 quarterly payments. The agreement gave the plaintiffs the right to terminate the agreement if the instalments were not paid punctually. It also contained a clause stating that punctual payment of the instalments was of the essence of the agreement. The first two payments were paid on time but after four further payments were made late the plaintiffs terminated the agreement, recovered possession of the computer and sold. They then claimed as damages the amount of the unpaid instalments under the agreement less an allowance to take account of early repayment and the amount realised on the sale of the computer. This claim was founded on the clause making payment of the essence. The plaintiffs argued that the terms of the contract showed that this clause was not intended to be elevated to such a degree of importance that breach would be regarded as repudiation of the contract.

HELD: The Court of Appeal agreed that the clause did have this effect and thus failure to make the payments punctually went to the root of the contract and entitled the plaintiffs to terminate the contract.

This seems to be a fairly extreme application of principle that the parties can designate any term a condition. There are dicta in *Financings Ltd* v *Baldock* [1963] 1 All ER 443 and by Lord Wilberforce in the House of Lords decision in *Bunge Corporation* v *Tradax SA* [1981] 2 All ER 513 to the effect that the commercial significance of punctual compliance with time stipulations must always be taken into account, so that where late payment is not repudiatory at common law the courts are not automatically bound to hold that a term declaring punctual payment to be of the essence is a condition.

3.4 Innominate terms or intermediate stipulations

It has now become necessary to distinguish a third type of contractual obligation, the innominate term or intermediate stipulation.

The category of 'innominate term' was established in the law of contract by a trio of cases:

***Hongkong Fir Shipping Co Ltd* v *Kawasaki Kisen Kaisha Ltd* [1962] QB 26; [1961] 1 All ER 474.** The Court of Appeal held the term in a charterparty to provide a ship 'in every way fitted for ordinary cargo service' to be an innominate term. This clause could not simply fall into the category of condition or of warranty. The court held that the remedies for a breach of such a term depend on the effect of the actual breach occurring. If it can be said that the breach deprives the other party of substantially the whole benefit he is entitled to get under the contract then the innocent party will be entitled to repudiate the contract. If not, his only remedy will be damages.

***Cehave NV* v *Bremer Handelgesellschaft, The Hansa Nord* [1976] QB 44; [1975] 3 All ER 739.** (A sale of goods case.) The contract was for the sale of citrus pulp pellets for use as cattle food, to be shipped 'in good condition'. The Court of Appeal held that the principle established in the *Hongkong Fir* case (that a term could be an innominate term being neither a condition nor a warranty) applied to sale of goods. On a true construction of the contract the term involved here was an innominate term.

Reardon Smith Line v Hansen-Tangen [1976] 1 WLR 989; [1976] 3 All ER 570. The House of Lords here approved the *Hongkong Fir* case thereby finally establishing the innominate term in the law of contract.

A term may be held to be an innominate term whenever it has not previously been designated by statute or previous judicial decision or by agreement of the parties as a condition (see *Bunge Corp* v *Tradax SA* [1981] 1 WLR 711; [1981] 2 All ER 513).

The consequences following upon such a breach will depend upon the nature of the breach itself and its effect. The *Hongkong Fir* case placed the emphasis firmly on the effect of the breach but subsequent cases have made it clear that the nature of the breach itself is still an important factor.

If the particular breach in question goes to the root of the contract even though not all breaches of that term would do so then the innocent party may repudiate. If however the particular breach is not so serious then damages will be the only remedy.

It is a fallacy to state that the condition/warranty approach represents the certain and fixed approach, whereas the innominate term approach represents the judiciary at its most flexible. Certainly it is difficult to predict just which approach the courts are going to take. Logically it would be sensible to assume that faced with such a choice the courts would opt for the condition/warranty dichotomy when the contract is one in common use, a standard form contract, when precision in terminology and classification may help *other* parties in the future. The more flexible innominate term might seem to be best employed in a non-standard individual one-off contract, which sets no particular pattern for the future. But, given the fact that in *Cehave NV* v *Bremer Handelsgesellschaft, The Hansa Nord* (supra), the House of Lords seemed prepared to apply something very much like the innominate-term approach to that archetypal standard form area, the sale of goods contract, it is apparent that this is not always the case.

4

Duties of the Seller I: Title, Delivery and Quantity

4.1 Introduction
4.2 Title
4.3 Delivery
4.4 Quantity

4.1 Introduction

In this chapter and the next the obligations of the seller are discussed. Most of the discussion turns on the meaning of the various terms implied by the SGA. In addition the Act deals with the concept of delivery and also has rules governing situations where the wrong quantity is delivered.

Remember that not all terms implied by the SGA are *conditions*. Look carefully at each section and subsection. Section 12(1) for example imposes an undertaking on the seller which is a condition, whereas the duties imposed by s12(2) are warranties.

4.2 Title

Section 12(1) SGA implies into contracts for the sale of goods an undertaking as to title. Section 12(2) implies undertakings as to freedom from encumbrances and quiet possession.

The seller's right to sell - s12(1)

Section 12(1) incorporating amendments made by the Supply of Goods (Implied Terms) Act 1973 provides:

> 'In a contract of sale, other than one to which subsection (3) below applies, there is an implied condition on the part of the seller that in the case of a sale, he has a *right to sell the goods*, and in the case of an agreement to sell, *he will have such a right at the time when the property is to pass*.'

This implied undertaking is a *condition* and like the other implied terms the liability imposed is strict and does not depend on any fault or knowledge of the seller.

The phrase 'a right to sell the goods' has given rise to some problems of interpretation. It is not vital that the seller actually has title to the goods. It will be sufficient that the seller sells with the consent of the party in whom title is vested; for example, where the seller sells as agent of the owner but appearing to be the principal in the transaction. Conversely, however, the fact that the seller actually has and actually transfers the property in the goods does not mean that a breach of s12(1) is impossible. Such a sale could infringe a trademark, patent or other proprietary interest and entitle the holder of the right in question to prohibit the sale.

In *Niblett* v *Confectioners Materials Co Ltd* [1921] 3 KB 387 S sold to B 1000 cases of condensed milk in tins which bore a label which infringed the trademark of Nestlés Condensed Milk Co. Nestlés complained and threatened legal action for the infringement. The tins were then detained at customs and the buyer was compelled to remove the labels in order to secure the release of the goods. The tins could then only be sold at a reduced price. The Court of Appeal held that the buyer was entitled to damages for breach of s12(1) by the seller, even though the seller had passed the property in the goods to the buyer. S was obliged not only to pass good title but also to ensure that the goods did not infringe the trademark of a third party so as to enable the third party to restrain the sale.

A 'right to sell' must further be contrasted with a power of sale. In certain cases where the seller does not have a right to sell the goods as against a third party he may still have a power to do so under one of the exceptions to the *nemo dat quod non habet* principle whereby a non-owner may pass to the buyer a good title (see Chapter 10, Transfer of title by a non-owner). In such cases most commentators agree that there is a technical breach of the s12(1) condition since vis-à-vis the true owner the disposition is unlawful. In such cases however the buyer will not be able to sue for damages for the breach since he has suffered no loss. The question of whether he will in these cases be able to rely on the breach to reject the goods remains unresolved there being no direct authority on the point. However, it seems to be the general view that the buyer cannot reject.

It has been suggested that in the *nemo dat* exception cases there is in fact no breach of s12(1). Atkins LJ put forward this view in *Niblett Ltd* v *Confectioner's Materials Co Ltd* (supra): 'It may be that the implied condition is not broken if the seller is able to pass to the purchaser a right to sell notwithstanding his own inability.' This suggestion is rejected by both Atiyah and Goode.

The editors of *Benjamin on Sale of Goods* however think that it is insufficient for a breach of s12(1) that the seller could be restrained by process of law from selling the goods. They suggest that *Niblett* does not lay down any general principle to the effect that there is a breach of s12(1) whenever the seller could be restrained by law from selling the goods, and that s12(1) does not extend to cases where the possession of the buyer could not be disturbed as where he has taken a good title under a *nemo dat* exception. Still less they argue should the buyer be entitled to reject on the grounds that the seller had no right to sell merely because the sale exposed the seller to a penalty in the criminal law as is often the case in the *nemo dat* exceptions. There is, therefore, some divergence of view on the interrelation of *nemo dat* and s12(1).

Where the seller's right to sell the goods is in some way doubtful then it is submitted that it should be up to the seller and not the buyer to substantiate that title. The buyer should not have to bear the difficulty and expense of proving he took a good title.

A breach of condition normally entitles the innocent party either to repudiate the contract and claim damages; or to claim damages for any loss suffered on the breach. With s12(1) where the breach consists of a failure by the seller to pass a good title to the goods there is a third possibility open to the buyer, established in the case of *Rowland* v *Divall* [1923] 2 KB 500. The buyer can here recover the full price of the goods, as being paid on a total failure of consideration, and the buyer will have had the free use of the goods up to the time he discovers the seller's breach of s12(1). The provisions of s54 should be noted in this context. Section 54 provides: 'Nothing in this Act affects the right of the buyer to recover money paid where the consideration for the payment of it has failed.'

The position is best illustrated by reference to the leading case: *Rowland* v *Divall* (supra). The buyer bought a car from the seller for £334 and proceeded to use it for four months. The buyer then discovered that the car had never belonged to the seller who had bought it in good faith from someone with no title. The car was claimed by the true owner so the buyer sued the seller seeking the return of the £334 purchase price. The Court of Appeal held that the buyer could recover the entire purchase price and that the seller could not set-off anything for the four months use by the buyer. There was a total failure of consideration and the buyer could therefore recover the whole of the price paid. Atkin LJ observed that the buyer had received no part of that which he contracted to receive, namely, the property and the right to possess, and the consideration had therefore totally failed.

Further cases are helpful in this context. In *Karflex Ltd* v *Poole* [1933] 2 KB 251, hire purchase was involved but the same principles were held to apply. The defendant had defaulted on his hire purchase payments and the plaintiff sued for possession. It transpired, however, that the plaintiff had no right to sell the goods so the defendant could recover his deposit and, had he paid any instalments, he could have recovered those also. The defendant in this case again had months of free use of the car in question.

In *Butterworth* v *Kingsway Motors Ltd* [1954] 1 WLR 1286; [1954] 2 All ER 694 a hire purchase finance company let a car to A on hire purchase. A mistakenly thought that she had a right to sell the car provided she continued to pay the hire purchase instalments, and she purported to sell it to B. The car passed through several hands and finally the defendant sold it to the plaintiff for £1,275. After the plaintiff had used the car for almost one year he received a notification from the finance company claiming the delivery up to them of the vehicle. The plaintiff therefore claimed from the defendant the whole purchase price (£1,275) for the breach of s12(1). Within a week, however, A paid the final instalment, so the title passed to her and this fed the defective titles of all subsequent purchasers.

It was held that the plaintiff could recover the whole purchase price of £1,275 for the defendant's breach of s12(1). Nothing done after the plaintiff had claimed this money could affect his right to it, so the 'feeding' of the plaintiff's title could be ignored. The market had in fact dropped and the car was by this time worth only £800; thus the plaintiff made a profit of £475.

If A had acquired title to the car and such title had passed to the plaintiff *before* he rejected the goods then it is submitted that there would not have been a total failure of consideration and it would not have been open to the plaintiff to recover the full purchase price. The plaintiff could however have sued in damages since he would for almost a year have been under the risk of repossession by the true owner.

No decision was reached in *Butterworth* on whether such a 'feeding' of the buyer's title could operate to prevent an action for total failure of consideration. Pearson J however considered that it would be an extraordinary position if the plaintiff should, where good title had already passed, seek to say 'there has been a total failure of consideration by the purchaser of this car, although here is the car in my possession and I am entitled to retain it against the world'. By contrast Sheil J in *West (HW) Ltd* v *McBlain* [1950] NI 144 rejected the proposition that the buyer's title could be fed so as to avoid an action for total failure of consideration. He stated that the subsequent acquisition by the seller of a good title could not affect the remedies of the buyer since 'you cannot revivify that which has never had life'.

The editors of *Benjamin* submit that despite difficulties with the strict wording of s12(1), no action for total failure of consideration but only for damages should lie in the above circumstances.

The general principle laid down in *Rowland* v *Divall* is undoubtedly unsatisfactory. The plaintiff in *Butterworth* had free use of the car for a year and in addition made a profit of £475. Atiyah puts forward certain hypothetical situations in which the absurdity of the principle is further illustrated. The real problem stems from the fact that *Rowland* v *Divall* operates even where the buyer in fact has the use and enjoyment of the goods free from the claims of third parties. The buyer should not be allowed to claim the price unless a third party has in fact made an adverse claim against him and even then consideration should be taken off the amount of actual uninterrupted enjoyment of the goods which he has had.

The Law Reform Commission 12th Report (1966 Cmnd Reports 2958) recommended that the buyer should not be able to recover the price in full with no allowance for the use of the goods he has had. The Law Commission considered the problem in its Working Paper No 65 (1975) where a number of proposals were made about the value of the unjust enrichment, but came to no conclusion. It returned to the problem in its report *Sale and Supply of Goods* (Law Com No 160, Cmnd 137 (1987)) and reached the following conclusion at p57:

'We have come to the conclusion that any reform of the law along the lines we previously considered would not be an improvement and indeed that problems of unjustified enrichment would not be solved by requiring the buyer of goods with defective title to make a money allowance in favour of another person who also does not have valid title to the goods. The problem in English law of the true owner being able to bring an action in conversion, claiming the full value of the goods, against either the seller or the buyer adds an extra layer of complexity to even the simplest solution. We do not believe that the introduction of complex provisions in this area would benefit either buyers or seller, and we therefore make no recommendation for change in the law governing the buyer's rights on termination of a contract due to the supplier having had no right to sell the goods at the time when the property was to pass.'

Two further points should be noted in relation to s12(1).

The time at which the s12(1) condition must be satisfied

In the case of a contract of sale the seller must have a right to sell at the time of the sale. It will be noted that there was a breach of s12(1) in *Butterworth* even though at the time of the litigation the property had vested in the plaintiff. In the case of an agreement to sell the seller must have a right to sell at the time when the property is to pass.

The exclusion of s12(1)

Prior to the Supply of Goods (Implied Terms) Act 1973 it was possible to contract out of the implied condition of title. The 1973 Act first precluded such exclusions and the situation is now governed by the Unfair Contract Terms Act 1977 (UCTA). Section 6(1) of the UCTA renders void any term of the contract of sale or of any other contract exempting the seller from all or any of the provisions of s12. This will therefore prevent the exclusion of the condition in s12(1) and also the warranties in s12(2) below.

Under s6(1)(a) UCTA 1977 liability for breaches of the obligations under s12 SGA cannot be excluded or restricted by reference to any contract term. This prohibition is not limited to 'business liability'. The condition implied by s12(1) will therefore be implied notwithstanding any contractual provision to the contrary.

Freedom from encumbrances and quiet possession

These are warranties implied by s12(2). Section 12(2) amalgamates with amendments the original ss 12(2) and 12(3). Section 12(2) provides that except where a limited interest is sold there is an implied warranty that:

'a) the goods are free and will remain free until the time when the property is to pass, from any *charge or encumbrance* not *disclosed* or *known* to the buyer before the contract is made; and
b) the buyer will enjoy quiet possession of the goods except in so far as it may be disturbed by the owner or other person entitled to the benefit of any charge or encumbrance so *disclosed* or *known*.'

The practical significance of s12(2)(a) (the implied warranty of freedom from undisclosed charges or encumbrances) is limited since in many cases the charge will be defeated by a sale to a purchaser without notice. A third party who is not in possession of the goods will only rarely therefore have an encumbrance which will bind the bona fide purchaser.

The buyer is not entitled to treat the contract as repudiated by reason of a breach of s12(2)(a) and can claim damages for breach of warranty only. The measure of damages for breach of s12(2)(a) will normally be the amount necessary to discharge the charge in question together with any legal costs paid and incurred in reasonably attempting to resist an adverse claim.

The warranty of quiet possession in s12(2)(b) continues to protect the buyer until he himself disposes of the goods. Again, a breach of s12(2)(b) does not entitle the buyer to repudiate the contract. The measure of damages for the breach will depend on the circumstances: for example if the buyer loses possession the measure will prima facie be the value of the goods at the time of losing possession together with any special damage suffered such as amounts spent in repairs or improvements by the buyer.

The warranty in s12(2)(a) unlike s12(1) will be broken by the mere existence of a charge or encumbrances over the goods and does not depend upon an actual enforcement of the charge or encumbrances by claim or demand on the part of a third party. It would seem that there is no breach of s12(2)(b) unless the buyer suffers some physical interference with his possession of the goods; however the editors of Benjamin point out that in *Niblett* v *Confectioners Materials* (supra) Atkin LJ considered that s12(2)(b) had been breached on the facts of that case since the buyers had to strip off the labels before they could assume possession of the goods, and in *Microbeads A-G* v *Vinhurst Road Markings Ltd* [1975] 1 WLR 218; [1975] 1 All ER 529, the Court of Appeal held that a breach had occurred upon a claim for infringement being made by the patentee of a patent over the goods.

Section 12(2) will protect the buyer against any wrongful disturbances of his possession by the seller himself (see *Healings (Sales) Pty Ltd* v *Inglis Electrix Pty Ltd* (1968) 42 ALJR 280). If the buyer's quiet possession is disturbed by a third party then it seems that he can rely on s12(2) only where that third party's interference is lawful. The law would be impractical if every seller warrants that no third party would ever interfere even unlawfully with the buyer's possession.

The prohibition in s6(1)(a) UCTA against exclusion or restriction of liability applies equally to liability arising under s12(2) as it does to liability under s12(1). Therefore, the implied terms of s12(2) will apply notwithstanding any contractual term to the contrary.

Two distinctions between the effects of s12(1) and s12(2) should be noted:

1. Time in the Limitation Acts runs against the buyer from the date of the sale under s12(1). Under s12(2) there is a continuing warranty of quiet possession so time runs against the buyer from the date his possession is disturbed.
2. The seller may in certain circumstances have a 'right to sell' under s12(1) and yet

may be unable to sell the goods free from a third party's right, as where a debtor sells goods which have already been 'seized' although not physically removed by a sheriff. Where such goods are sold the seller has a right to sell them but will sell subject to the rights of the sheriff. Where the buyer subsequently has to give the goods to the sheriff he would have a remedy in damages under s12(2) not s12(1).

Section 12(2)(a) as has been seen, is of limited practical importance. It has, however, been involved in one major case: *Microbeads A-G v Vinhurst Road Markings Ltd* (supra). Here the buyer's quiet possession was disturbed by the holder of a patent which was granted *after* the sale in question. There was no breach of s12(1) since at the time of the sale the seller had a right to sell. The buyer did recover under s12(2) however for disturbance of his possession.

4.3 Delivery

The duty of the seller to deliver the goods is not a distinct and isolated obligation but encompasses all the seller's obligations, express and implied, with respect to the goods. These will include the implied terms as to title, correspondence with description, merchantable quality and fitness for purpose as discussed in other chapters. The status of these implied terms as *conditions* will also be relevant to the buyer's right to reject, but when the buyer has *accepted* defective goods then the implied condition which has been broken becomes a mere warranty restricting the buyer to a remedy in damages. So the concept of delivery and indeed the question of acceptance are both related to the seller's obligations in general.

The term 'delivery' is defined in s61(1) SGA: 'A voluntary transfer of possession from one person to another.' This definition obviously does not confine 'delivery' to the transfer of physical possession. Both *actual* and *constructive* delivery will be included.

It should be noted that the fact of delivery may be significant for a variety of purposes, and what constitutes delivery for one purpose may not suffice as delivery for another purpose. For example delivery of the goods to a courier for transmission to the buyer is deemed to be delivery to the buyer within s32(1) and destroys the unpaid seller's lien and may in certain circumstances amount to an unconditional appropriation to pass property in s18 rule 5(2). However, such delivery does not amount to delivery to the buyer for the purpose of the rules relating to stoppage in transit. The transit continues until the courier subsequently delivers the goods to the buyer or wrongfully refuses to deliver.

The concept of delivery was, for example of importance in *Compagnie Commerciale Sucres et Denrées v C Czarnikow Ltd* [1990] 1 WLR 1337 when the question arose as to what was meant by 'ready for delivery'. In a mercantile contract for the sale of sugar (FOB) the sellers were to have the goods ready for delivery at any time within the contract period. The parties used the standardised conditions of the Sugar

Association which were incorporated into the contract. Despite repeated notifications and warnings the sellers failed to deliver the sugar.

HELD: 'Ready for delivery' meant ready to be loaded on board ship, as soon as the vessel was ready to load it. Failure to do this meant that the sellers were in breach of the contract and the buyers could treat the breach as terminating the contract.

In order to avoid a breach of the delivery obligation the seller must ensure not only conformity with the conditions outlined above and in the implied terms about title discussed above and those about quality discussed in Chapter 5 but also with any express requirements laid out in the contract itself. In particular delivery must be at the time and in the manner prescribed by the contract.

Section 27 provides: 'It is the duty of the seller to deliver the goods, and of the buyer to accept and pay for them, in accordance with the terms of the contract of sale.'

Methods of delivery

The 'voluntary transfer of possession' may be effected either by *actual delivery* or by *constructive delivery*. An actual delivery means that actual physical possession of the goods is transferred to the buyer or his agent. It is the commonest mode of delivery in domestic sales transactions. Constructive delivery means that *control* over the goods is transferred to the buyer without physical possession.

A variety of types of constructive delivery should be noted.

By transfer of document of title

Constructive delivery occurs where the seller who holds a document of title to the goods transfers that document to the buyer, thereby giving legal control of the goods themselves to the buyer. The buyer must take possession of the document and the document itself must indicate that the buyer's possession is authorised. The only common law document of title is the bill of lading, but there are a variety of statutory documents of title, such as delivery orders and warehouse warrants as set out in s1(4) Factors Act 1889.

By delivery of an object giving physical control of the goods

Benjamin refers to this as 'symbolic delivery'. The delivery of the keys to the premises in which the goods are stored would be an example of this particular type of constructive delivery. The view has been expressed that this is really a form of actual physical delivery, however it is traditionally treated as constructive delivery.

By attornment

A party here attorns to the buyer by lawfully acknowledging that goods which he previously held for himself or for the seller are now held for the buyer. This will occur:

1. where the seller still has possession of the goods and 'attorns' by acknowledging that he holds them as the buyer's bailee; or

2. where the goods are held by a third party (usually a warehouseman) to the order of the seller and that third party undertakes to the buyer to hold for the buyer, but only where the undertaking is lawful (ie authorised by the seller).

Where the buyer continues in possession in his own right
Where the goods were already in the buyer's possession as the seller's bailee before making the contract of sale, then upon the buyer becoming entitled to possession in his own right, under the contract or by consent of the seller, there is a notional delivery to the buyer by the seller.

By delivery to a carrier
This will usually constitute constructive delivery under s32(1). This is dealt with in greater detail below.

The place of delivery

Section 29(2) provides that in the absence of any express agreement to the contrary the place of delivery is the seller's place of business, if he has one and if not his residence, provided that, if the contract is for the sale of specific goods which to the knowledge of the parties when the contract is made are in some other place, that place is the place of delivery.

The place of delivery depends therefore primarily upon the terms of the contract. Only if there is no contractual provision do the provisions of s29(2) come into play. The seller may in the contract restrict his delivery burden by undertaking merely to hold the goods available for collection by the buyer or he could agree to deliver to the buyer's own premises. If, however, the contract is silent as to the place of delivery then s29(2) provides that this will be at the seller's place of business or residence. In this case it is therefore for the buyer to collect the goods and not for the seller to dispatch them.

The delivery point may be important for several reasons. Obviously it is relevant as to whether the seller has properly delivered the goods. It may indicate that the seller is not required to convey the goods beyond the delivery point or may indicate that the buyer must pay all expenses of conveying the goods beyond that point.

In modern business situations a 'contrary intention' in the contract will frequently be inferred from the circumstances of the case: for example, in *Wiskin* v *Terdich Bros Pty Ltd* [1928] Arg LR 242 the court held that the phrase 'please supply us with the following goods' signified that it was the seller's duty to send the goods to the buyer.

In practice few disputes arise as to the place of delivery which is usually obvious from the terms or circumstances of the contract.

The time of delivery

The basic rule is that the seller must tender delivery at the time stipulated in the contract. The buyer can reject a late tender if, but only if, the time is of the essence under the contract or, although not originally of the essence, it has been made so as the result of notice; or if more than a reasonable period has elapsed since the contractual delivery date. *Hartley* v *Hymans* [1920] 3 KB 475 held that the time of delivery is prima facie of the essence in commercial contracts.

Where the seller is bound under the terms of the contract to send the goods but no time for sending them is fixed, the seller is bound to send them within a reasonable time. Section 29(3) provides: 'Where under the contract of sale the seller is bound to send the goods to the buyer, but no time for sending them is fixed, the seller is bound to send them within a reasonable time.' Section 29(5) further provides: 'Demand or tender of delivery may be treated as ineffectual unless made at a reasonable hour; and what is a reasonable hour is a question of fact.'

What amounts to a 'reasonable hour' or reasonable time is therefore a question of fact. Failure to deliver in a reasonable time may amount to a breach of condition by the seller. In these circumstances the buyer may reject the goods although he may have suffered no loss. Wherever the seller fails to deliver on time and time is of the essence, or a reasonable time has expired, then the seller may reject even though he has suffered no damage.

In *Bowes* v *Shand* (1877) 2 App Cas 455 the court emphasised that the goods must be delivered within the stipulated time and that an early shipment or delivery will entitle the buyer to repudiate. In this case the agreement was to ship an amount of rice during March or April. The rice was shipped in February, and the House of Lords held that the buyers were entitled to reject the goods even though they had suffered no loss and even though the rice actually shipped was the same as that which should have been shipped in March or April.

The buyer may waive the condition relating to time of delivery. Modern cases do not seem to distinguish waiver and estoppel in these cases, and the waiver will bind the buyer even though made without consideration from the seller. The buyer is however entitled to make time once more of the essence after a first waiver, by giving the seller reasonable notice that he will not accept delivery after a certain date.

In *Charles Rickards Ltd* v *Oppenheim* [1950] 1 KB 616; [1950] 1 All ER 420 the agreement was for the supply of a Rolls Royce chassis to be ready by 20 March 1948 at the latest. The buyer after this date still pressed for delivery thereby impliedly waiving the condition as to time of delivery. Then on 29 June the buyer wrote to the plaintiff seller saying he could not accept delivery after 25 July. The buyer eventually refused to accept the car when delivered in October. The Court of Appeal held that he was entitled to reject the goods. The notice had again made time of the essence.

The expenses of delivery

At common law, unless otherwise agreed, the expenses of and incidental to the tender of delivery must be borne by the seller and the expenses of taking delivery by the buyer. By s29(6): 'Unless otherwise agreed, the expenses of and incidental to putting the goods into a deliverable state must be borne by the seller.'

Instalment deliveries

A problem often arises where delivery of goods is tendered by instalments as to the effect of the buyer's acceptance or rejection of one instalment on the duties of the parties to deliver or accept the remaining instalments.

For example the buyer may wrongfully reject one instalment. The question arises as to whether this unlawful rejection discharges the seller from his duty to tender all remaining instalments. Alternatively if the buyer accepts a defective instalment it must be determined whether this precludes him from rejecting subsequent instalments.

These situations are governed primarily by s31. Section 31 provides:

> '(1) Unless otherwise agreed, the buyer of goods is not bound to accept delivery of them by instalments.
> (2) Where there is a contract for the sale of goods to be delivered by stated instalments, which are to be separately paid for, and the seller makes defective deliveries in respect of one or more instalments, or the buyer neglects or refuses to take delivery of or pay for one or more instalments, it is a question in each case depending on the terms of the contract and the circumstances of the case whether the breach of contract is a repudiation of the whole contract or whether it is a severable breach giving rise to a claim for compensation but not to a right to treat the whole contract as repudiated.'

The buyer is therefore, in the absence of circumstances showing a contrary intention, entitled to insist on a single tender. Where several deliveries are tendered under the same contract then the seller will be in breach of s31(1) if the contract does not either expressly or by implication permit tender by instalments. There is in effect a presumption against instalment delivery.

In *Cobec Brazilian Trading and Warehousing Corp v Toepfer* [1983] 2 Lloyd's Rep 386 the contract was for 25 000 tons of certain specified commodities. One amount was to go to Seville and one amount to another Spanish port. The goods delivered to the second port were late and the buyer rejected all the goods. The seller argued that the use of separate bills of lading and two lots going to different destinations made the contract one of instalment delivery. (In the circumstances such a finding would have precluded the buyer from rejecting both deliveries).

The Court of Appeal held that on the facts this was one entire contract and one shipment of 25 000 tons. The mere fact that the 25 000 tons was going to different destinations did not oust the presumption of s31(1), and this was not a case of delivery by instalments.

It will be noted from this case that it is difficult to oust the s31(1) presumption against instalment delivery. In particular the mere fact that a shipment is to be split and tendered at two different ports does not make the case one of instalment delivery.

Section 31(2) deals with two important points arising where the contract *is* for delivery by instalments. It first sets out the one definite criterion given by the SGA for determining the situations in which a contract will be treated as severable (the distinction between *severable* and *non-severable* contracts is of great significance in this area). Where 'each instalment is to be separately paid for', ie each instalment is matched with a corresponding payment obligation on the part of the buyer, then this will normally but not necessarily be a severable contract. Section 31(2) secondly tells us how to determine when a buyer in a severable contract will be able to reject other good instalments where one or more deliveries are defective. These two points are discussed fully below.

In the area of instalment deliveries it is necessary to ascertain first whether tenders are being made under the same contract or under several separate contracts, and secondly where it is simply one contract whether that contract is severable or non-severable.

Single contract or separate contracts

The general rule is that where each tender is made under an entirely separate, self-contained contract then unless the parties have expressly or by implication agreed otherwise, a breach of one contract even amounting to a repudiation of that contract will not affect the right of the guilty party who has made defective deliveries under one contract to enforce the other contracts, unless the breach is such as to show that he is unwilling or unable to perform those contracts also.

The buyer in this position will therefore usually be unable to reject instalments tendered under different contracts even though tender by the seller under one or more contracts has been defective.

The criteria for determining whether one is dealing with one contract or several contracts are vague and uncertain. Ultimately the question is as to the intention of the parties. In attempting to ascertain such intention regard should be had to the documents used for the contract(s): if for example two separate order forms have been used or separate invoices tendered these may but do not necessarily point towards there being two contracts. The time at which the contract(s) are made may also be relevant: if the agreements are made simultaneously this may indicate one contract.

Is the contract severable or non-severable?

Once it has been ascertained that there is only one single contract providing for delivery by instalments, the effect of a breach by one party on the other's duties to perform depends on whether the obligation in the contract is *severable* or *non-severable*.

Under s31(2) a contract is severable (and s31(2) only applies) if the goods are to be delivered in instalments and the instalments are to be separately paid for. In other words each instalment delivery must be matched by a performance obligation on the part of the buyer to pay the price for that delivery. This provides the only definite criterion given by the SGA on what will point to a severable contract. Even so, a contract may it seems be severable in other situations:

In *Jackson* v *Rotax Motors & Cycle Co* [1910] 2 KB 937 a contract for the sale of some motor accessories was held to be severable purely because the contract specified 'deliveries as required'. This phrase was interpreted to mean that the goods would necessarily be delivered in instalments and it was assumed that this was enough to render it severable. It has been convincingly argued that this assumption is erroneous and that *any* contract in order to be severable must satisfy the requirement that the instalments are to be separately paid for. A further problem is that if the contract in *Jackson* did not provide that the instalments were to be separately paid for it seems that the other provisions of s31(2) would not apply to it. This would leave a rather awkward situation in which some *severable* contracts could fall outside the s31(2) provisions for determining the effect of defective deliveries.

Where an export contract provides that the seller is entitled to ship the goods in separate loads and that in such event each shipment is to be considered as a distinct contract, this has been held to give the seller the choice of treating the contract as a single contract by shipping in one load or as a severable contract by shipping in several loads.

One must distinguish the severability of an obligation from the mere right to spread its performance. The essential characteristic of severability is divisibility of performance on one side and consideration for each partial performance on the other, creating therefore a contract within a contract and making delivery of each individual instalment a separate self-contained part of the delivery obligation. If the seller has a right to tender the goods by instalments but the price is payable in a lump sum or in some other manner not fixed by reference to the separate individual instalments which must be tendered, the seller's delivery obligation, though it may be distributed over the number of instalments in question, is not divisible, for no part of it can be matched against any corresponding part of the price.

The consequences for the parties where the obligation is held to be non-severable or severable must now be considered along with the different results which will flow if each instalment is held to be a separate division or contract within the main contract.

Where the contract is non-severable

The following general propositions will apply in this case, except in so far as they are displaced expressly or impliedly by the contract:

1. The seller is in general not able to demand a part of the price against partial delivery unless the buyer elects to accept such delivery. In this latter case the buyer must pay for the goods accepted.
2. The acceptance by the buyer of an instalment of the goods constitutes an adoption of the contract as a whole and this in general precludes him from exercising a right he would otherwise have to reject the remaining instalments.

This proposition is governed by s11(4) SGA which provides as follows:

'Where a contract of sale is not severable, and the buyer has accepted the goods, or part of them, the breach of a condition to be fulfilled by the seller can only be treated as a breach of warranty, and not as a ground for rejecting the goods and treating the contract as repudiated, unless there is an express or implied term to that effect.'

Section 11(4) in relation to the buyer's right to reject is dealt with in detail in Chapter 13 under 'Remedies: the buyer's right to reject the goods'.

This second proposition is however subject to certain qualifications. In particular it will not apply (ie s11(4) will not apply) where s30(4) applies. Section 30(4) provides:

'Where the seller delivers to the buyer the goods he contracted to sell mixed with goods of a different description not included in the contract, the buyer may accept the goods which are in accordance with the contract and reject the rest, or he may reject the whole.'

Note that s30(4) only applies where the goods are mixed with goods of a different *description* not goods of defective *quality*.

The application of s30(4) is illustrated in *Ebrahim Dawood Ltd* v *Heath Ltd* [1961] 2 Lloyd's Rep 512. The seller here contracted to sell 50 tons of steel in a variety of lengths. The whole quantity was in fact delivered in six-foot lengths. The court held that the buyer under s30(4) could accept the part of the goods conforming with the contract and reject the rest. It was emphasised by the court that s30(4) is an exception to s11(4). Note that the buyer could under s30(4) alternatively have rejected all the goods. If the seller tenders an instalment of excessive quantity the buyer on his acceptance of the contract quantity can reject *the rest of that instalment*.

3. A breach by the seller with regard to part of the contract (any instalment) is treated like a breach of the whole and the buyer is prima facie entitled to reject all the goods. Here, the fact that the goods are delivered by instalments is really immaterial - the position is the same as if all the goods had been delivered at once (see *Jackson* v *Rotax Motors* (above)).
4. The buyer's improper rejection of an instalment properly tendered constitutes a repudiation of the entire contract (see *Reuter* v *Sala & Co* (1879) 4 CPD 239) and the seller may treat himself as discharged from further performance and sue for damages for non-acceptance.

Where the obligation is severable

The following rules of general application can be laid down:

1. The buyer's acceptance of one or more instalments does not as such debar him from rejecting subsequent defective instalments.
2. If the buyer improperly rejects one or more instalments or the seller improperly tenders or fails to tender delivery of one or more instalments, this will not *ipso*

facto constitute a repudiation of the contract as a whole but may do so in certain circumstances.

The provisions of s31(2) have been noted above. It sets out that in severable instalment contracts 'it is a question in each case depending on the terms of the contract and the circumstances of the case whether the breach of contract is a repudiation of the whole contract or whether it is a severable breach giving rise to a claim for compensation but not a right to treat the whole contract as repudiated'.

In effect, therefore, the right of the buyer to reject the whole of the goods where one or more instalments are defective and the right of the seller to treat the contract as repudiated where the buyer improperly rejects an instalment depend on the terms of the contract and the circumstances of the case.

In Goode's view a breach will amount to a repudiation of the whole contract either where it is done in circumstances in which an objective observer would perceive either an intention to repudiate or an inability to perform the contract as a whole, or where its effect is so substantial as to go *to the root of the contract*.

Lord Hewart in the leading case of *Maple Flock Co Ltd* v *Universal Furniture Products (Wembley) Ltd* [1934] 1 KB 148 laid down the main tests for whether a breach with regard to one instalment by either the buyer or the seller should be regarded as a breach of the entire contract:

1. First one should look to the seriousness of the breach itself.
2. Then assess the ratio quantitively which the breach bears to the contract as a whole.
3. Then assess the degree of probability or improbability that such a breach will be repeated.

On the facts the plaintiffs had contracted to sell 100 tons of rag flock to the defendants, delivery to be by three instalments per week of one and a half tons each. A sample from the sixteenth load showed it did not conform to government standards. The defendants had in the meantime taken delivery of four more loads, all satisfactory.

The Court of Appeal held on the above tests that the defendants were not entitled to repudiate the contract. The breach affected only one and a half tons out of 100 tons and it was improbable that the breach would recur.

This decision may be contrasted with a further case: *R A Munro & Co* v *Meyer* [1930] 2 KB 312. The contract was for 1500 tons of meat and bone meal, delivery to be by 125 tons a month. After more than 750 tons had been delivered and found to be defective, the buyer claimed to repudiate.

Wright J held: the buyer was entitled to repudiate. The breach was 'substantial and so serious and has continued so persistently'.

Something must now be said about the interrelation of s31(2) and s30(1), which in certain circumstances can appear to be mutually inconsistent. Section 30(1) deals with the situation where the seller makes a delivery of insufficient quantity. An example illustrates the problem. A purchaser agrees to buy 1500 tons of wheat by three instalments of 500 tons. On the first instalment the seller ships only 450 tons so the buyer rejects as he is entitled to do under s30(1). Assuming the breach is not so serious as to go to the root of the contract under s31(2), could the buyer now argue that since it is now impossible for the seller to complete performance according to the contract and still deliver the correct quantity, he (the buyer) can now treat the breach under s30(1) as a repudiation and treat himself as discharged from the contract? This problem now seems to have been settled by the case of *Regent OHG Aisenstadt* v *Francesco of Jermyn St Ltd* [1981] 3 All ER 327, where Roskill J stated:

> 'Where the nature of the misdelivery is the short delivery of one instalment so that the position is governed by the mutually inconsistent provisions of s30(1) and s31(2), then the more flexible provisions of s31(2) are to be applied in preference to s30(1).'

In effect therefore the buyer could not rely on s30(1) in these circumstances.

Delivery to a carrier

Section 32(1) provides:

> 'Where in pursuance of a contract of sale the seller is authorised or required to send the goods to the buyer, delivery of goods to a carrier (whether named by the buyer or not), for the purpose of transmission to the buyer is prima facie to be a delivery of the goods to the buyer.'

Note that delivery of the goods to the buyer's agent will transfer possession to the buyer *himself*. So s32(1) will only operate where the carrier is an *independent* carrier: if the carrier is agent of the seller then he still has possession, and if the carrier is the buyer's agent then the buyer himself is already deemed to have possession.

The effects of delivery to a carrier under s32(1) may be summarised as follows:

1. If the contract is for the sale of unascertained goods delivery to a carrier may well amount to an 'unconditional appropriation' under s18 rule 5(2). Whether it does or not depends in export contracts on whether the contract is CIF or FOB and perhaps on who nominates the carrier (or shipper). 'Unconditional appropriation' may pass property and risk to the buyer.
2. The buyer's right to examine and reject the goods will not be affected.
3. The unpaid seller will lose his lien but not his right of stoppage in transit. (See Chapter 11.)
4. When the seller delivers the goods to the carrier for transmission to the buyer, he usually makes this contract on behalf of the buyer. It is usually therefore the buyer who will be entitled to sue the carrier on the contract. Note, however, that in export sales, detailed rules govern this area.

Goods in transit

Where goods are sent from the seller to the buyer the question often arises as to who must bear the loss if any damage or deterioration occurs during transit.

It will be seen that the seller may be in breach of s14(2) (implied conditions of merchantable quality and fitness for purpose) if the goods fail to withstand a *normal* journey (see Chapter 5). Another relevant provision is s32(2):

> 'Unless otherwise authorised by the buyer the seller must make such contract with the carrier on behalf of the buyer as may be reasonable having regard to the nature of the goods and to other circumstances of the case. If the seller omits so to do, and the goods are lost or damaged in the course of transit, the buyer may decline to treat the delivery to the carrier as a delivery to himself, or may hold the seller responsible in damages.'

Therefore if the damage or deterioration is due to the seller having failed to make a reasonable contract of carriage, then he will be liable.

In *Thomas Young & Sons* v *Hobson & Partners* (1949) 65 TLR 365 the seller sold a very fragile engine to the buyer and sent it by railway 'at the owner's risk'. The seller could have sent it at the 'railway company's risk' for a greater fee, in which case the railway company would have handled the engine more carefully. The engine was damaged during the journey. It was held that the buyer could reject it because on the facts of the case the seller had made an unreasonable contract of carriage.

In all other cases the question is simply whether the *risk* has passed to the buyer, in which case he must bear the loss. If the risk has not so passed the loss will remain with the seller. Reference should be made to Chapter 9.

Two further SGA provisions may be relevant as regards risk in transit. First, the question of insurance is often relevant and in sea-transit situations where it is often for the buyer to insure the goods (such as FOB export contracts) the seller usually must give the buyer such notice and details relating to the goods as may enable the buyer to insure them. Otherwise they will be at the seller's risk. Section 32(3) provides:

> 'Unless otherwise agreed, where goods are sent by the seller to the buyer by a route involving sea transit, under circumstances in which it is usual to insure, the seller must give such notice to the buyer as may enable him to insure them during their sea transit, and if the seller fails to do so, the goods shall be deemed to be at his risk during such sea transit.'

In *Wimble & Sons* v *Rosenberg & Sons* [1913] 3 KB 743 the Court of Appeal said that s32(3) will be satisfied if either:

1. the buyer is already in possession of all the facts necessary for him to know in order to insure the goods (here, notice by the seller would be a redundant act); or
2. if such notice as is given to the buyer completes the buyer's knowledge so as to enable him to insure.

Note that s32(3) does not say that the seller will be in breach of contract if he does not give adequate notice, but only that the goods will be at his risk. So if the goods arrive safely the buyer will be obliged to pay.

Secondly, 33 provides:

> 'Where the seller of goods agrees to deliver them at his own risk at a place other than that where they are when sold, the buyer must, nevertheless, unless otherwise agreed, take any risk of deterioration in the goods *necessarily incident to the course of transit.*'

In these circumstances therefore the seller is only liable for deterioration or destruction not necessarily incidental to the course of transit. It seems that the words 'any risk of deterioration ... necessarily incident to the course of transit' must be confined to risks which would have arisen with any goods answering the contract description. Therefore a risk of deterioration which is only incidental to the course of transit because of the defective condition of the goods when transit commenced is not covered by s33, and in that respect the goods would still be all at the seller's risk.

Accepting of the goods by the buyer

This is dealt with in Chapter 13: 'Remedies of the Buyer I'.

4.4 Quantity

When the seller is obliged to dispatch the goods to the buyer he must send the correct quantity if he is not to be in breach of contract. In cases where it is for the buyer to take possession of the goods and not for the seller to dispatch them then the seller must have the correct quantity of goods available for the buyer to take.

The duty is a strict one and any failure in this respect entitles the buyer to reject the incorrect quantity delivered. This is subject only to the 'de minimis' rule: a deficiency or excess in quantity which is 'microscopic' (see *Arcos Ltd* v *Ronaasen* [1933] AC 470) and which is 'not capable of influencing the mind of the buyer' (see *Shipton Anderson & Co* v *Weil Bros & Co* [1912] 1 KB 574) will not entitle the buyer to reject the goods.

In *Shipton Anderson & Co* v *Weil Bros* an excess of 55 lb of wheat over and above agreed limit of 4950 tons was held to fall within the 'de minimis rule'. However, in *Wilensko Slaski Towarzystwo Drevno* v *Fenwick & Co Ltd* [1938] 3 All ER 429, under 1 per cent of the timber failed to comply with the contract requirements but the buyer was entitled to reject.

Insufficient delivery

Section 30(1) provides:

> 'Where the seller delivers to the buyer a quantity of goods less than he contracted to sell, the buyer may reject them, but if the buyer accepts the goods so delivered he must pay for them at the contract rate.'

The buyer in these circumstances has alternative courses of action. First, he can reject the insufficient quantity delivered and sue for any loss occasioned by the seller's breach (see *Borrowman* v *Drayton* (1876) 2 Ex D 15 and *Reuter* v *Sala* (1879) 4 CPD 239 for illustrations). Here if the price has already been paid it can be recovered as a payment made on a total failure of consideration. Secondly, he can retain the quantity delivered, paying for it at the contract rate and recover any part of the price which has been paid for the undelivered balance (see *Behrend v Produce Brokers' Co Ltd* [1920] 3 KB 530 below.) He can in addition claim damages for the breach.

If the seller makes delivery of a quantity of goods less than he contracted to sell he normally cannot excuse this by delivering the remainder at a later date because of the provisions of s31(1). Section 31(1) provides: 'Unless otherwise agreed the buyer of goods is not bound to accept delivery thereof by instalments.' The buyer is therefore entitled to the delivery of the whole of the goods at one and the same time unless the contract expressly allows the seller to deliver by instalments.

In *Behrend & Co Ltd v Produce Brokers' Co Ltd* [1920] 3 KB 530 the seller agreed to sell a quantity of cotton seed ex 'Port Inglis' in London. The ship discharged a small part of the cargo in London and then left for Hull where she discharged other goods. A fortnight later she returned to London to discharge the remaining cotton seed. It was held that the buyers were entitled to reject the later delivery and retain the earlier one.

Excessive delivery

The seller must not deliver too little, but he must also not deliver too much: Section 30(2) provides:

> 'Where the seller delivers to the buyer a quantity of goods larger than he contracted to sell, the buyer may accept the goods included in the contract and reject the rest, or he may reject the whole.'

Section 30(3) provides:

> 'Where the seller delivers to the buyer a quantity of goods larger than he contracted to sell and the buyer accepts the whole of the goods so delivered he must pay for them at the contract rate.'

If too much is tendered the buyer has the option of accepting the contract quantity and no more or rejecting all the goods.

Presumably the buyer could also take all the goods delivered since the tender by the seller amounts to a counter-offer which the buyer accepts by accepting the goods. This view is borne out by *Cunliffe v Harrison* (1851) 6 Exch 903. *Benjamin* agrees and states that the excess should be paid for at the contract rate. In such a case the buyer will be precluded from claiming damages for delivery of the wrong quantity.

Delivery of the contract goods mixed with goods of a different description.

Section 30(4) provides:

> 'Where the seller delivers to the buyer the goods he contracted to sell mixed with goods of a different description not included in the contract, the buyer may accept the goods which are in accordance with the contract and reject the rest, or he may reject the whole.'

An illustration of the operation of s30(4) is found in *Levy* v *Green* (1858) 8 E & B 575. Here the crockery ordered was sent but packed in a crate with crockery of a different pattern and easily distinguishable. In such a straightforward case it is, *Benjamin* argues, easy to see s30(4) as a simple application of s30(2): delivery of excess quantity. However where only the contract quantity is delivered some of the goods being of a different description it is necessary to rely on s30(4). As *Benjamin* observes the present authorities are clear that s30(4) applies not only to cases where the full contract goods are delivered mixed with other additional goods but also to cases where the contract amount only is delivered and it contains a mixture of goods of a different description (see *Re Moore & Co and Landauer & Co* [1921] 2 KB 519).

Where the contract goods are delivered but mixed with goods of *defective quality* as opposed to goods of a *different description*, s30(4) will not apply and the situation is governed by s11(4) and s14(2). An example would be where the contract is for Canadian wheat and the seller delivers Canadian wheat mixed with wheat defective in quality. (An example of mixing goods of a different description would be delivering Canadian mixed with American wheat.) The buyer will probably be able to reject the whole instalment under s14(2) (breach of the implied condition of merchantability) but his right to accept the conforming part and reject the rest will depend on the operation of s11(4) and whether the contract is 'severable' or 'non-severable'. The position is dealt with in full in Chapter 13. In the simplest case where one is dealing with one non-severable contract s11(4) will mean that the buyer cannot accept the conforming part and reject the rest since he is compelled in accepting some to treat the breach as a mere breach of warranty.

Benjamin suggests that 'mixed with' in s30(4) should really mean 'intermingled in such a way as to cause difficulty of separation'. However there is some authority, obiter in *Re Moore & Co and Landauer & Co* [1921] 2 KB 519, that 'mixed with' means only 'accompanied by' which would mean that difficulty of separation is irrelevant.

Generally

In all the circumstances dealt with in s30 the buyer is entitled to reject the whole of the goods. In substance, therefore, the seller commits a breach of condition by delivering the wrong quantity. There is an obvious parallel between the duties imposed by s30 and those imposed by s13 (the duty to deliver goods conforming with the contract description), indeed, s30 is in a sense simply an application of the duty to deliver goods corresponding with description as regards quantity (and, with s30(4), quality).

The Law Commission in its report *Sale and Supply of Goods* (Law Com No 160) Cmnd 137 (1987) recommended that the buyer's right to reject an excess should in all cases be preserved, but that where the non-consumer is delivered a wrong quantity of goods, and the shortfall or excess is so slight that it would be unreasonable to reject the whole, then he should be barred from so doing. This recommendation was not applied to consumers because it was believed that it was not a situation which consumers encounter in practice.

5

Duties of the Seller II: Quality

5.1 Introduction

5.2 Implied terms about description

5.3 Implied terms about quality: common factors

5.4 Implied terms about merchantable quality

5.5 Implied terms about fitness for purpose

5.6 Sales by sample

5.7 Other implied terms

5.1 Introduction

In this second chapter discussing the duties of the seller the emphasis is on the standard of quality which the seller must attain. Here again the terms implied by the SGA are important. Sections 13-15 set out terms about description and quality which in many cases must be complied with. As will be seen in Chapter 7 there is now limited scope for contracting out of these implied terms. In an important commercial transaction the contract may be specially drawn up, otherwise standard form contracts may be specially adapted to suit the particular needs of the parties. While the implied terms contained in the SGA are frequently, especially in consumer contracts, those governing the transaction it should not be forgotten that particularly in commercial contracts, the parties may have drafted their own express terms. In an important commercial transaction the contract may be specially drawn up, otherwise standard form contracts may be specially adapted to suit the particular needs of the parties. It is in these cases that the law relating to the classification of terms into conditions, warranties and innominate terms discussed in Chapter 3 becomes important in relation to the remedies which will be available on breach. It should be recalled, however, from Chapter 3, that, while the parties are within their rights to designate certain terms as conditions or warranties, the final analysis of whether the contract, as agreed, achieves the parties' objectives rests with the courts. The parties' own terminology is not necessarily conclusive.

5.2 Implied terms about description

Section 13 applies to all sales and is not limited to sales in the course of a business. 'Sales by description' has been interpreted in a wide sense and is thought by many to cover almost all sales. A more restrictive test has been laid down by two major cases as to which terms will actually form part of the contract 'description' once it has been ascertained that the contract is indeed a 'sale by description'. These cases are *Ashington Piggeries Ltd* v *Christopher Hill Ltd* [1972] AC 441; [1971] 1 All ER 847 and *Reardon Smith Line Ltd* v *Hansen-Tangen* [1976] 1 WLR 989; [1976] 3 All ER 570.

Section 13(1) and (2) provide as follows:

'(1) Where there is a contract for the sale of goods by description, there is an implied condition that the goods correspond with the description.
(2) If the sale is by sample, as well as by description, it is not sufficient that the bulk of the goods correspond with the sample if the goods do not also correspond with the description.'

As outlined by the editors of *Benjamin on Sale of Goods* there are effectively two types of breach of s13 which may occur. The first is failure to attain exact conformity with the full contractual description of the goods; for example, supplying the contract goods but packed in containers holding incorrect amounts, as in *Re Moore & Co and Landauer & Co* [1921] 2 KB 519 (see 5.2 below for full facts). No doctrine of 'substantial performance' operates here in marked contrast to the position under the general law of contract. The second is a total failure to perform the contract where the duty broken (ie to supply the contract goods) is so fundamental as hardly to need stating at all; for example, supplying a second-hand car where a new one was ordered.

The issues arising under s13 are as follows: a 'sale by description'; which terms are included in the 'Description'; breach of s13; the relationship between s13 and s14; the exclusion of s13.

A 'sale by description'

This phrase is not defined in the statute. Some basic principles may, however, be laid down. Essentially there will be a sale by description where descriptive words are used as terms of the contract, expressly or impliedly for the purpose of identifying or defining the goods, and are at least to some degree relied on by the buyer for that purpose.

First, the description in question must be a term of the contract and not a mere representation inducing the buyer to enter the contract. The courts do often in effect circumvent this requirement by finding that the descriptive words are in fact part of the contract where such a finding would appear to be doubtful.

It is unlikely that statements descriptive of the goods will amount only to 'mere puffs' and found no liability at all (see Chapter 3 'Misrepresentation'): they will be at least representations.

The view has been put forward that s13 in fact dispenses with the requirement that the description be a term of the contract, because where it is a contractual term the section performs the redundant function of declaring that it is an implied term that the seller comply with this express term. The generally accepted and (it is submitted) correct view is that s13 does not do away with this requirement. Salmond J held in *Taylor* v *Combined Buyers Ltd* [1924] NZLR 627 that s13 does not affect the traditional distinction between mere representations and terms of the contract, and in *Oscar Chess Ltd* v *Williams* [1957] 1 WLR 370; [1957] 1 All ER 325 it did not even occur to the court that the representation made about the car being 'a 1948 Morris' could conceivably be treated as part of the description unless the buyer first established that the statement was a term of the contract and not merely a representation.

Secondly, there must be a sale by description wherever the purchaser has not seen the goods but is relying on the description alone albeit the sale is one of specific goods. This was laid down by Channel J in *Varley* v *Whipp* [1900] 1 QB 513 where it was held that there was a sale by description where the seller met the buyer at Huddersfield and sold him an article described as a 'second hand self-binder reaping machine' which was at the time elsewhere. It follows (see below) that all sales of unascertained goods and most sales of future goods are sales by description.

Thirdly, a sale will often still be a sale by description when the contract is for specific goods and the buyer has seen and examined the goods.

Section 13(3) now provides that a sale of goods is not prevented from being a sale by description by reason only that, being exposed for sale or hire they are selected by the buyer. There could now perhaps only be a dispute in this area about whether a sale of an easily identifiable but undescribed article (such as a piece of fruit on a pile in a shop) is a sale by description.

Even before the new s13(3) it was clear that examination of the goods by the buyer did not prevent the sale being a sale by description. In *Beale* v *Taylor* [1967] 1 WLR 1193; [1967] 3 All ER 253, Beale read an advertisement offering for sale a 'Herald convertible, white, 1961'. B bought the car after he has seen and examined it. The car was in fact made of two parts which had been welded together and only one of the parts was from a 1961 model. The Court of Appeal held the words '1961 Herald' were part of the contractual description and since the buyer had bought by reference to that description he recovered damages under s13.

Atiyah remarks that in this case the Court of Appeal apparently came very close to disregarding the distinction between representations and contractual terms 'by giving a wide application to s13' and that s13 therefore makes it easier for a buyer to argue that a descriptive statement by a seller is a contractual term and not a mere representation.

This view is open to doubt particularly after the House of Lords decision in *Ashington Piggeries* v *Christopher Hill* (supra, but discussed more fully below) which appears to have made it more difficult for a buyer to maintain that a descriptive statement is in fact a term of the contract.

Fourthly, Atiyah observes that probably the only case of a sale not being by description is where the buyer makes it clear that he is buying a particular thing because of its unique qualities and that no other will do.

This statement is probably too general. In the House of Lords in *Ashington Piggeries Ltd* v *Christopher Hill Ltd* there are several statements to the effect that a 'description' and therefore a 'sale by description' will only exist where the descriptive words are used to *identify* the goods. It should be emphasised however that the House of Lords was dealing with the question (see below) as to which terms will be included in the description and was not concerned with any explanation of when 'sales by description' occur.

In the recent case of *Harlingdon & Leinster Enterprises* v *Christopher Hull Fine Art* [1990] 1 All ER 737 the question arose as to whether the sale of a picture by a named artist could be considered a sale by description. The court held that the fact that an artist had been attributed to the painting (incorrectly as it turned out) and a description of the painting published in the gallery's catalogue did not make it a sale by description within s13(1). In any case the plaintiff had not relied on the description, but had made his own examination and relied on his own assessment.

Fifthly, all contracts for the sale of unascertained goods are sales by description. As Benjamin's editors point out most sales of future goods will also be sales by description although the sale of a specific article seen and requested by the buyer which is in the hands of a third party and would require to be obtained by the seller is not.

Which terms will be included in the 'description'

Comments made by the House of Lords in *Ashington Piggeries* v *Christopher Hill* have had a profound effect on this area of the law. It is now the case that a term will only be part of the description if it is used to identify the goods.

In *Ashington Piggeries* herring meal was held to comply with its description as such even though it had become contaminated by a chemical reaction carried by perservatives added to it making it poisonous to mink. Had it been made poisonous to all animals, presumably the result would have been different.

The editors of Benjamin quote with approval a dictum of Lord Diplock stating that ultimately 'the key to s13 is identification'. This is borne out by the case of *Reardon Smith Line* v *Hansen-Tangen* (supra). In this case the contract was to provide a ship which was to be built, described in the charterparty as 'Japanese flag ... Newbuilding motor tank vessel to be constructed at Yard No 354 at Osaka.' The vessel as supplied was in fact built at Yard No 004 at Oshima. The buyer sought to reject the ship for a breach of s13. It was held by the House of Lords that on the facts 'Yard No 354 at Osaka' was not part of the contractual description and that the buyer must take the ship.

In this case Lord Wilberforce distinguished words which identify the goods, in the sense that they identify an essential part of the description of the goods, and words which merely provide the other party with an indication of where to find the goods. The latter will not readily come within the 'description' in s13.

A further requirement was laid down by Lord Wilberforce speaking for the majority of the Lords: that the term not only identify the goods but also that it form an essential element in the performance of the contract in order that it be part of the description. In determining this, Lord Wilberforce said, regard may be had to the commercial purpose of the contract and to the factual background against which the contract is made. This second requirement has attracted surprisingly little commentary from academic writers possibly because it is invariably found to be satisfied where the words of description are not merely words enabling the buyer to say 'those are my goods' such as 'No 354 Osaka', but instead fall into Lord Wilberforce's second category as outlined above.

Goode sees the whole problem as one of distinguishing between the identity of the goods and their mere attributes. The task he says is to ascertain what kind of goods were the subject of the contract (ie the essence of the bargain/the kind of article which is being offered). A suggested test is whether the descriptive statement is so crucial to the identity of the subject matter that its absence would make what is tendered something essentially different from the goods bargained for. Non-correspondence with a 'mere attribute' of the goods will not be a breach of s13 in Goode's view. The cases given below may serve to explain the meaning of 'description'. It is wrong though to place excessive reliance on decisions as to the effect of particular words or phrases since each case turns on the wording of the contract and the circumstances of the case.

'Long Staple Salem Cotton' was held to be part of the description in *Azemer* v *Casella* (1867) LR 2 CP 177, as was 'foreign refined rape oil' in *Nichol* v *Godts* (1854) 10 Exch 191. In particular circumstances the stipulated method of packing (*Re Moore & Co and Landauer & Co* (supra)) or shipment (*Bowes* v *Shand* (1877) 2 App Cas 455) or marking have been held to be the contract description. There are also examples where measurement and size, quantity, the place where the goods are said to be situated and the date of shipment have all been on the facts held to be part of the description. It is emphasised that this will not be so in every case.

One illustration is *Tradax Export SA* v *European Grain* [1983] 2 Lloyd's Rep 100 where the words 'Max 7.5 per cent fibre' although apparently words of quality were held to form part of the s13 description since they identified the goods and formed an essential element in the performance of the contract.

Finally, it should be noted that it is possible to prove a trade custom or normal commercial understanding to explain or qualify the meaning of a contractual description. In *Grenfell* v *E B Meyrowitz* [1936] 2 All ER 1313 evidence was allowed to show that at the time the description 'safety glass lenses' when applied to aviation goggles meant that they were made from laminated glass, so it was not a breach of s13 when the user was injured by a splinter from one of the goggles since they had exactly complied with description.

Breach of s13

Once s13 is found to apply, the duty it imposes is very strict and any slight deviation may and probably will amount to a breach of condition entitling the buyer to reject the goods. A seller in breach will probably only escape if the non-correspondence with description is 'microscopic' and comes under the '*de minimis*' principle. (This is explained below.)

It has been suggested that a breach of s13 could be a mere breach of warranty where the breach relates to a part of the description which is minor or ancillary. Were this to be the case the buyer in such circumstances could not reject the goods and would be confined to his action for damages. Atiyah is among those commentators who suggest that in certain cases a breach of s13 could be a mere breach of warranty; however, there seems to be little judicial support for the proposition. Some remarks of Lord Wilberforce in the *Reardon Smith Line* case do support Atiyah: these remarks are to the effect that certain parts of the contractual description may be 'innominate terms' or even mere warranties.

However in *Arcos Ltd v E A Ronaasen & Son* [1933] AC 470 (see below) it appears that the court could not conceive that a breach of s13 could be anything other than a breach of condition, and the *Re Moore & Co and Landauer & Co* decision supports *Arcos*.

Several of the leading cases illustrate the strict application of s13. In *Varley* v *Whipp* (supra) S agreed to sell a second-hand reaping machine which he described as 'new the previous year' and as 'hardly used at all'. The machine was in fact old and B refused to accept it or pay the price. It was held that this was a sale by description and the machine did not correspond with the description given. Following this breach of s13 the buyer could reject the goods.

In *Re Moore and Co Ltd and Landauer & Co* (supra) the agreement was for 3000 tins of Australian canned fruit packed in cases of 30 tins. When delivered it was discovered that half the cases contained only 24 tins although the total number of tins was still 3000. The market value was not affected. The Court of Appeal held that notwithstanding that there was no loss to the buyer, he could reject the whole consignment because of the breach of s13.

In *Arcos Ltd v E A Ronaasen & Son* (supra) B ordered a quantity of staves 1/2 inch thick. The seller was aware that the buyer wanted them to make cement barrels. When delivered, only 5 per cent conformed to the thickness requirement and the remainder were virtually all less than 9/16 inch thick. Even though it was found that the goods were commercially within the contract specification and were merchantable under that specification, the House of Lords held that the buyer was entitled to reject for a breach of s13. Lord Atkin observed that '1/2 inch does not mean about 1/2 inch. If the seller wants a margin he must and in my experience does stipulate for it'. This was not a case of a 'microscopic' deviation which could be ignored.

Implied terms about description 69

It may be concluded from the above two cases that the mere fact the buyer has suffered no damage does not prevent him rejecting the goods.

The relationship between s13 and s14

Section 14 implies conditions as to the quality and fitness of goods for a particular purpose. It is of course possible for goods to be of 'merchantable quality' and fit for their purpose within s14 and yet not correspond with their description under s13. This occured in *Arcos* v *Ronaasen & Son* (supra).

The converse of this is also possible, namely that where the goods do correspond with their description, this does not mean that they are necessarily of 'merchantable quality' or fit for their purpose.

The relation between s13 and s14 was discussed by the House of Lords in *Ashington Piggeries Ltd* v *Christopher Hill Ltd*, the detailed facts of which appear above. The herring meal which was the subject matter of the sale was contaminated with a substance which made it unsuitable for feeding to mink. It was, however, sold for use as mink food.

The House of Lords held:

1. The goods were still properly described as 'herring meal' and there was therefore no breach of s13.
2. There was however a breach of s14 since the goods were not of merchantable quality or fit for their purpose.

Note that a breach of s14 does not mean there must necessarily be a breach of s13. Not every statement relating to the quality or fitness of the goods will be part of the description.

The distinction between cases involving a breach of s13 and those involving a breach of s14 is often of practical importance since s13 sometimes applies where s14 does not, particularly where the goods are not sold in the course of a business (see *Varley* v *Whipp* (supra)).

The exclusion of s13

Section 13 as such can be excluded by agreement subject to ss3 and 6 of the Unfair Contract Terms Act 1977 (see Chapter 7). The effect of such exclusion is not as great as it might seem since it merely negates the implication by law of the condition of correspondence with description. Compliance will still be required with those parts of the contractual description which expressly identify the contract goods simply by virtue of the express contract as it stands.

The effect of s6 UCTA is essentially that any contract term excluding or restricting liability under s13 SGA is invalid against a person 'dealing as consumer', and against others is valid only so far as the exemption clause is reasonable under the criteria in s11 of the UCTA.

5.3 Implied terms about quality: common factors

Since the Sales of Goods Act 1893 terms about the quality of goods which the purchaser is entitled to expect have been set out in a statute. The relevant legislation is now the Sale of Goods Act 1979. Here we shall deal with the terms about merchantability and fitness for purpose and the terms implied in sales by sample. The term about description contained in s13 could also be said to be relevant but it has already been dealt with in 5.2.

It is made clear in the opening words of s14(1) that:

'Except as provided by this section and s15 ... and subject to any other enactment, there is no implied condition or warranty about the quality or fitness for any particular purpose of goods supplied under a contract of sale.'

Before analysing the two terms about quality set out in s14 certain points which are common to both should be noticed.

In the course of a business

An important feature to note is that the terms in s14 about merchantability and fitness for purpose apply only to sales 'in the course of a business'. These words were first inserted into the section by the Supply of Goods (Implied Terms) Act 1973. It had originally been suggested that the phrase should be 'by way of trade' but the Law Commission felt that such a phrase might lead to an excessively restrictive interpretation.

It was not envisaged that irregular or one-off sales would be included. As a result private sales, such as that of the person who buys privately, perhaps in response to a classified advertisement in a newspaper, has more limited protection than someone who purchases from a trader. The purchaser in a non-business sale, unless there is some express term about quality, has only the protection of the implied term about description. *Beale* v *Taylor* (supra) is a good example of this situation.

There will be some marginal cases where there may be doubt about the status of the transaction. It should be noted that s61 states that 'business' includes a profession and the activities of any government department or public authority. The phrase 'in the course of a business' appears in other statutes such as the Trade Descriptions Act 1968 where there seems to have been some uncertainty as to its interpretation. In *Davies* v *Sumner* [1984] 3 All ER 831 it was pointed out that business implied a degree of regularity and sporadic sales of pieces of equipment no longer needed by a business would not be regarded as being made in the course of the business. On the other hand, in *Corfield* v *Sevenways Garage Ltd* [1985] RTR 109 the Divisional Court seemed to place a wider meaning on the phrase. Mann LJ said:

'The word "business" standing by itself, is a word of great amplitude ...; almost any form of activity, apart from one pursued for pleasure or as a hobby, can be described as "business".'

In the same case Goff LJ added:

> 'A supplier may have more than one business. He may have a main line of business, and he may have a side-line business. Indeed, he may only indulge in that side-line business rarely. But, in such circumstances, goods supplied in the course of either part of his business will be supplied in the course of a trade or business. The mere fact that the transactions under the side-line were unusual would not be determinative of the matter.'

In *R & B Customs Brokers Co Ltd* v *United Dominions Trust* [1988] 1 All ER 847 the question of defining 'in the course of a business' arose. A company acquired a car, partly for business purposes, partly for private use by the directors. It was bought by the company with company money. Because the company was in the shipping business and had bought only one or two cars previously it was held not to be part of the company's normal day-to-day business.

Presumably, by analogy, should a surplus car or cars be sold in a similar situation, this would not be 'in the course of a business'.

This approach appears to be in line with that taken in tax cases where the similar phrase 'trade or business' has been given a wide meaning. It is submitted that this is the proper approach to its interpretation in the SGA as a matter of policy.

In accordance with current judicial interpretation of the phrase 'in the course of business' s14(2) and (3) will therefore not include irregular sales of items that might be said to constitute equipment rather than stock in trade. But in *Buchanan-Jardine* v *Hamlink* (1983) SLT 149 when the plaintiffs sold their farm and livestock, the court held that the entire sale was 'in the course of a business' within the meaning of the SGA 1979.

Less reputable traders have been well aware of the consequences of selling in the course of a business and it is not uncommon for such traders to attempt to mislead their customers by pretending to be private sellers. Such was the scale of the problem that it proved necessary, using the procedure under the now defunct Part II of the Fair Trading Act 1973, to make it a criminal offence to do this. The relevant legislation is the Business Advertisements (Disclosure) Order 1977.

A situation which occurs sometimes is that of a trader selling as agent of a private seller. One sometimes sees a car on the forecourt of a second-hand dealer with a notice stating that the car is being sold on behalf of a private customer. This situation is dealt with by s14(5) which states that:

> 'The preceding provisions of this section [about merchantability and fitness for purpose] apply to a sale by a person who in the course of a business is acting as agent for another as they apply to a sale by a principal in the course of a business and either the buyer knows that fact or reasonable steps are taken to bring it to the notice of the buyer before the contract is made.'

Liability is strict

It is clearly established that liability for quality under s14 is strict. As it was put in *Randall* v *Newsom* (1876) 45 LJQB 364 by Blackburn J:

'If there was a defect in fact, even though that defect was one which no reasonable skill or care could discover, the person supplying the article should nevertheless be responsible, the policy of the law being that in a case in which neither were to blame, he, and not the person to whom they were supplied, should be liable for the defect.'

A good example is *Frost* v *Aylesbury Dairy Co* [1905] 1 KB 608. The dairy had supplied Mr Frost and his family with milk which turned out to have been infected with typhoid germs. As a result his wife died. It was proved that the dairy's production methods were extremely careful and that the typhoid germs could only be detected by prolonged investigation.

HELD: that there was an implied term that the milk would be reasonably fit for consumption and it was irrelevant that the defect could not be discovered at the time of the sale.

The seller is liable

It is the seller who is liable under the Sale of Goods Act not the manufacturer except, of course, where the manufacturer has a contract with his customer. This means, for example, that in a consumer context it is the retailer who is the person to whom the consumer must normally look for redress if the goods do not prove to be satisfactory. It should be noted that the introduction of a measure of strict liability for defective products by Part I of the Consumer Protection Act 1987 has altered this situation and this is discussed in Chapter 15.

The terms are conditions

A further general point is that both the terms as to merchantability and fitness for purpose are designated conditions. This means that if they are breached the innocent party has the right to reject the goods. The innocent party may elect not to exercise this right but simply seek damages. The buyer's remedies are discussed in Chapters 13 and 14.

Goods to which s14 applies

The goods to which the terms about quality apply are not just the article specified in the contract but include the 'goods supplied under a contract of sale'. As a result the container in which the goods are supplied or the packaging and instructions are included as well as any foreign material erroneously supplied together with the goods contracted for.

In *Geddling* v *Marsh* [1920] 1 KB 668 Mrs Geddling, a shopkeeper, bought some bottles of mineral water from the defendant. If she returned the bottles she was paid 1p per bottle. As the result of a defect in one of the bottles it burst injuring Mrs Geddling and she sued the defendant for breach of the implied term that the goods should be reasonably fit for their purpose. The defendant argued that the mineral water was fit for its purpose and that the bottle, which was not, was not part of the goods supplied under the contract.

HELD: that the bottle was part of the goods supplied under the contract and it made no difference whether the bottle could be said to have been bailed to Mrs Geddling.

In *Wormell* v *RHM Agricultural (East) Ltd* [1987] 1 WLR 1091 a farmer bought weedkiller on the recommendation of the defendants and it was delivered in cans which had instructions for the use of the weedkiller printed on them. The farmer followed these instructions and as a result the weedkiller was completely ineffective against the weeds which he had hoped to destroy. He sued the suppliers for breach of the implied terms about quality.

HELD (High Court); that the misleading instructions on the cans made the weedkiller unfit for its purpose. 'Goods' for the purposes of the Sale of Goods Act included not just the weedkiller but also its packaging and instructions:

> 'All of these, it seems to me, are part of the goods. One must look at all of them as a whole ... By selling goods with such instructions the seller is warranting that the chemical, when used in accordance with those instructions, will be reasonably fit for its purpose ... If a retailer ... sells goods (that is the chemical together with its container and instructions) and those instructions make the goods not reasonably fit for their purpose, in my view there is a breach of s14(3) of the 1979 Act.'

On appeal (see [1987] 1 WLR 1091) the Court of Appeal reversed the decision of the High Court. However, this reversal was because they took a different view of the facts and came to the conclusion that the instructions were sufficiently clear. No doubt was cast on the principle that instructions are relevant in deciding whether goods are of merchantable quality or fit for their purpose. Indeed, there was no discussion of the issue in the judgments and no cases were referred to in them. Both the reasoned judgments delivered assume that principle to be correct.

Another aspect of the phrase 'goods supplied under a contract of sale' was explored in *Wilson* v *Rickett Cockerell & Co Ltd* [1954] 1 QB 598. Mr Wilson ordered a load of Coalite from the defendant. Unknown to either party the load contained not only Coalite but also a detonator which exploded in Mr Wilson's living room when placed on the fire.

HELD (Court of Appeal): that the goods delivered were not of merchantable quality. As Lord Denning put it, speaking of the words 'goods supplied under a contract of sale':

> 'In my opinion that means the goods delivered in purported pursuance of the contract. The section applies to all goods so delivered whether they conform to the contract or not: that is, in this case, to the whole consignment, including the offending piece, and not merely to the Coalite alone.'

The defendants had, somewhat ingeniously, argued that there was nothing wrong with the Coalite and that the detonator was not ordered under the contract. Lord Denning did not waste much time on that argument:

'Coal is not bought by the lump. It is bought by the sack or by the hundredweight or by the ton. The consignment is delivered as a whole and must be considered as a whole, not in bits. A sack of coal, which contains hidden in it a detonator, is not fit for burning and no sophistry should lead us to believe that it is fit.'

5.4 Implied terms about merchantable quality

This condition is set out in s14(2):

'Where the seller sells goods in the course of a business, there is an implied condition that the goods supplied under the contract are of merchantable quality, except that there is no such condition:
a) as regards defects specifically drawn to the buyer's attention before the contract is made; or
b) if the buyer examines the goods before the contract is made, as regards defects which that examination ought to reveal.'

The exceptions

Before looking at the core of this condition, the meaning of 'merchantable quality' it is necessary to consider the two situations in which the condition does not apply.

Defects specifically drawn to the buyer's attention
Not unreasonably a purchaser who has been told that certain things are wrong with goods which he then proceeds to buy with this knowledge cannot complain that the goods are not of merchantable quality. However, it is to be noted that the defects must be *specifically* drawn to his attention. This probably means that some general terms such as 'shop-soiled' or 'seconds' will not be sufficient.

Defects which that examination ought to reveal
Similarly if a buyer has examined his proposed purchase and noticed, or ought to have noticed, certain shortcomings in the article that he subsequently purchased it would be unreasonable to allow him to complain that the defect of which he was aware rendered the goods unmerchantable. Notice that the relevant examination is one made before the contract is made.

This qualification only applies where an examination is in fact made and it applies only to defects which 'that examination ought to reveal'. It seems reasonably clear that a purchaser who makes a cursory examination will not lose the protection of the merchantability condition if a more detailed examination would have revealed the defect. Take, for example, the common situation of the purchase of a second hand car. The buyer looks the car over in the showroom, examining the bodywork, the inside of the car and lifting the bonnet and observing that there is an engine but not road testing the car or even running the engine. Such a buyer will not be able to complain later of defects in the bodywork, but if the car should prove to have a mechanical defect such as a faulty clutch or brakes he will be able to attempt to argue that these defects render the car unmerchantable.

There had been some doubt about the interpretation of this proviso as a result of a High Court decision in *Thornett & Fehr* v *Beers & Son* [1919] 1 KB 486 where slightly different wording in the Sale of Goods Act 1893 was interpreted as if it read 'a reasonable examination' and a commercial buyer, who made a cursory examination of some glue which was not sufficient to have revealed a defect in the product, was, nevertheless, held to have lost the protection of the merchantability condition. This case may well have been wrongly decided as it seems inconsistent with an earlier Court of Appeal decision, *Bristol Tramways Co* v *Fiat Motors Ltd* [1910] 2 KB 831, which was not cited. In any event the present wording of the Sale of Goods Act 1979 which is slightly different and refers to 'defects which *that* examination ought to reveal' appears to leave no room for argument that it is only defects which the actual examination carried out by the buyer ought to have revealed which are relevant.

Merchantable quality

The term merchantable quality has exercised the courts on numerous occasions and the one thing that can confidently be said about it today is that it is widely regarded as being unsatisfactory especially in relation to consumer transactions. As the recent Law Commission report, *Sale and Supply of Goods* (Cm 137) observes:

> 'If the word "merchantable" has any real meaning today, it must strictly be a meaning which relates to "merchants" and trade; the word must be inappropriate in the context of a consumer transaction. The expression "merchantable quality" is, and always has been a commercial man's notion: this explains why the original Act [the Sale of Goods Act 1893] did not define it – commercial juries needed no direction on how to make the appropriate findings.'

To try to alleviate the problem of what the term means a definition was introduced by the Supply of Goods (Implied Terms) Act 1973 and is now set out in s14(6) of the Sale of Goods Act 1979. It reads as follows:

> 'Goods of any kind are of merchantable quality within the meaning of subs(2) above if they are as fit for the purpose or purposes for which goods of that kind are commonly bought as it is reasonable to expect having regard to any description applied to them, the price (if relevant) and all the other relevant circumstances.'

It is not altogether clear whether this definition is an attempt to re-state the pre-1973 law or whether it should be regarded as making a fresh start. Lord Denning in *Cehave NV* v *Bremer Handelsgesellschaft MbH, The Hansa Nord* [1976] QB 44 regarded it as the best description of merchantable quality even in relation to the pre-1973 law. (For a further discussion of this case, see below.)

Prior to 1973 there were two main approaches to the meaning of merchantability: the acceptability test and the usability test. The acceptability test was set out in a well-known passage from the judgment of Dixon J in the Australian High Court in *Australian Knitting Mills* v *Grant* (1933) 50 CLR 387 at 418:

> '[the goods] should be in such an actual state that a buyer fully acquainted with the facts and, therefore, knowing what hidden defects existed and not being limited to their apparent condition would buy them without abatement of the price obtainable for such goods if in reasonably sound order and condition and without special terms.'

The usability test can be illustrated by a quotation from the judgment of Lord Reid in *Henry Kendall & Sons Ltd* v *William Lillico & Sons Ltd* [1969] 2 AC 31 at 77:

> 'What subs(2) now means by "merchantable quality" is that the goods in the form in which they were tendered were of no use for any purpose for which goods which complied with the description under which these goods were sold would normally be used, and hence were not saleable under that description.'

Too much, perhaps should not be made of the fact that there seem to have been two tests propounded for, as the Law Commission Working Paper No 85, *Sale and Supply of Goods*, observes, 'the distinction between them was not clear-cut, and in several judgments both were referred to with approval'. In a recent Court of Appeal judgment in *M/S Aswan Engineering Establishment Co* v *Lupdine Ltd* [1987] 1 WLR 1 Lloyd LJ argued that Lord Reid in *Kendall* v *Lillico* had achieved a synthesis of the two definitions which Lloyd LJ summarised in his own words as follows:

> "To bring s14(2) into operation, a buyer had to show that the goods had been bought by description from a seller dealing in goods of that description. If so, then, subject to a proviso which is immaterial for present purposes, the goods were required to be of merchantable quality. In order to comply with that requirement, the goods did not have to be suitable for every purpose within a range of purposes for which goods were normally bought under that description. It was sufficient that they were suitable for one or more such purposes without abatement of price since, if they were, they were commercially saleable under that description.'

It should be noted that since 1973 the merchantability test has applied to goods whether or not sold by description and whether or not the seller dealt in goods of that description. It is sufficient that the sale was in the course of business.

There were some like Professor Goode in his *Commercial Law* (see p261) who suggested that the new statutory definition had changed the law by requiring that goods should be fit for *all* their normal purposes, whereas previously it was considered sufficient if the goods were suitable for any one normal purpose even though unfit for the others. It now seems clear, following the decision of the Court of Appeal in *Aswan Engineering Establishment Co* v *Lupdine Ltd* (supra), that where goods have more than one normal purpose they pass the merchantability test if they are fit for one of those purposes.

In *Rogers* v *Parish (Scarborough) Ltd* [1987] 2 All ER 232 Mustill LJ made a general comment on the use of the new definition of merchantable quality. He said at p235:

> 'In the course of argument before us our attention was drawn to various expressions of opinion in cases decided before the enactment of the 1973 legislation as to the precise significance of the term "merchantable quality". In my judgment this is not a practice to be encouraged. The 1973 Act was an amending Act and it cannot be assumed that the new

definition was included simply because the draftsman saw a convenient opportunity to reproduce in more felicitous and economical terms the gist of the speeches and judgments previously delivered. The language of s14(6) is clear and free from technicality, and it should be sufficient in the great majority of cases to enable the fact-finding judge to arrive at a decision without exploring the intricacies of the prior law.'

However, he did immediately add that the case before him was not 'one of those exceptional cases where it may be necessary to have recourse to the former decisions in order to give a full meaning to the words of s14(6)'. It therefore seems justifiable to consider some of these decisions below.

Before exploring some of the grey areas of the definition it will be useful to consider situations where goods can confidently be said not to pass the statutory test. Much emphasis is placed in the statutory definition on the fitness of the goods for their purpose or purposes. So a car which will not go, a hi-fi system which does not reproduce sound, a kettle which does not boil water and a refrigerator which does not keep its contents cold are not of merchantable quality. While there is no express reference to safety in the definition there is little doubt that an article which is unsafe is not of merchantable quality. In *Godley v Perry* [1960] 1 WLR 9 a toy catapult which fractured causing a child severe injuries was held not to be of merchantable quality. In *Lee v York Coach and Marine* [1977] RTR 35 the Court of Appeal held that a car which could not be driven lawfully and safely on the road was not of merchantable quality.

In *Bernstein v Pamson Motors (Golders Green) Ltd* [1987] 2 All ER 220 Mr Bernstein purchased a new Nissan Laurel car from the defendants for £8,000. Shortly afterwards when he was driving on a motorway he heard an unusual noise coming from the engine and pulled on to the hard shoulder. It proved impossible to restart the engine because, as later investigations revealed, the camshaft had seized in its housing when it had been starved of oil. Had not Mr Bernstein pulled off the motorway as soon as he heard the unusual noise from the engine there might have been a serious accident for the effect of a camshaft seizure is rather similar to the application of the brakes. Mr Bernstein purported to reject the car on the ground that it was not of merchantable quality.

HELD (High Court): that the car was not of merchantable quality. Much stress was placed on the fact that the purchaser of a new car is entitled to expect a car which is capable of being driven and being driven safely. To quote Rougier J:

> 'The two facts which have most influenced me in coming to my decision are first the safety consideration: I do not think it was by any means fanciful to suggest that when the camshaft began to seize up a situation of considerable potential danger had arisen. Second, I have been influenced by the extent and the area of the *potential damage* and consequently the risk that such damage might still exist. While I cannot go so far as [counsel for Mr Bernstein] in describing this breakdown as a catastrophic one, nevertheless it was, in my opinion, a major breakdown. Reverting to the language of the section, it is not reasonable for the buyer of a new car of this type and price to expect to sustain a major breakdown in the first 150 miles. Consequently I find that, at the time of the delivery of this car to the plaintiff, it was not of merchantable quality, still less was it fit for its purpose.'

It should be noted that Mr Bernstein's claim to be entitled to reject the car failed because he was deemed to have accepted the car. This aspect of the case is discussed in Chapter 13.

The goods will not be merchantable if they are only saleable at a 'substantial abatement of price', a test first laid down by Dixon J in *Australian Knitting Mills Ltd v Grant* (above and approved in *Kendall v Lillico* (supra). Two cases may be referred to as illustrations of this point.

In *Beecham & Co Pty Ltd v Francis Howard & Co Pty Ltd* [1921] VLR 428 B paid 80 shillings per 100 feet for spruce timber for making pianos. It later transpired that most of the timber was affected by dry rot which could not be observed on reasonable external examination. The timber was still fit for making boxes, one of the uses to which this type of timber was commonly put, but spruce timber for making boxes was worth only 30 shillings per 100 feet.

HELD: that the timber was not merchantable under its contract description: no buyer whether buying for manufacture or resale would accept this timber, its condition being known, without a substantial reduction in price.

This case may be contrasted with a later case in which there was no substantial abatement of price.

In *B S Brown & Son Ltd v Craikes Ltd* [1970] 1 WLR 750 cloth was bought for resale as dress material though this purpose was not intimated to the manufacturers. Although unsuitable for this purpose the cloth was suitable for industrial use and the price was appropriate to industrial use although rather high for dress fabric. The cloth was held to be merchantable. If the market value of the cloth had been as low as 10d per yard or even 15d as opposed to the 20d it was actually worth then presumably the cloth would have been unmerchantable (20d was the market price for industrial cloth).

As the statutory definition makes clear merchantability is related to the description applied to the goods. In this respect it is reflecting the earlier case law. Lord Reid in *Kendall v Lillico* (supra) had pointed out that goods would not be merchantable where they were 'no use for any purpose for which goods which complied with the description under which these goods were sold would normally be used'. This excludes the possibility that an article might be merchantable if saleable at any price and for any purpose for which such goods would normally be used.

Two cases are helpful in this context. In *Bartlett v Sydney Marcus Ltd* [1965] 1 WLR 1013; [1965] 2 All ER 753. B bought a second-hand car from S for £950. S (a car dealer) informed B that the clutch was defective and offered either to put it right and sell it for £975 or to leave it to the buyer to have it repaired and sell it for £950. B chose the latter option however the repair later cost £84. The Court of Appeal held that the car was of merchantable quality. A second-hand car could be of merchantable quality even though it was not as good as a new car and required some repairs. The 'contract description' was a second-hand car with a defective clutch and as such the car was merchantable. If a car was sold new with a defective clutch then that would be unmerchantable. However, the car in this sale was reasonably fit to be driven on the roads which in the circumstances was sufficient.

After stating that Lord Wright's previous test of whether the goods were of 'no use for any purpose for which such goods would normally be sold' covered only part of the case, Lord Denning stated:

'The article may be of some use though not entirely efficient use for the purpose. It may not be in perfect condition but yet it is in a usable condition. It is then, I think, merchantable.'

This case may be contrasted with a later decision in *Crowther* v *Shannon Motor Co* [1975] 1 WLR 30; [1975] 1 All ER 139. In B bought a second-hand Jaguar car from S for £390, it having at that time registered 82,165 miles. S described the car as being in excellent condition; however, three weeks later having driven it 2,300 miles the engine seized up completely and had to be replaced. The Court of Appeal held that while the buyer of a second-hand car should realise that defects might appear sooner or later so that minor repairs would be necessary, the replacement of an engine was totally different from a minor repair. The Court in fact found for the buyer on the ground of a breach of the implied condition of fitness for purpose (see below s14(3)) but it is submitted that there was probably a breach of s14(2) also in this case since the car was not merchantable under the contract description albeit that description was of a second-hand car.

The *Bartlett* case was considered in the context of a sale of a new car in *Bernstein* v *Pamson Motors (Golders Green) Ltd* (supra). Mr Bernstein bought a new car which had a serious engine fault, causing the whole engine to seize-up after only 140 miles driving. Rougier J held that the car was unmerchantable because the buyer of a new car should expect to get a car that was at least capable of being driven. He went on to set out four factors which he considered relevant in deciding whether a car would be merchantable: (1) can the defect be remedied easily; (2) on repair of the defect will the car be as good as new; (3) is the car of a type which the buyer can reasonably expect to be perfect in every way (eg a Rolls Royce); and (4) is there a collection of small defects which, taken together, amount to a serious defect? Rougier J's guidelines may be useful, but they appear to overlook one matter, which is that if it is held that despite the defect which exists the car is merchantable then the buyer will have no remedy unless he can prove that an express term has been broken.

Section 14(2) implies a condition, so any breach gives the right to reject, if there is no breach there is no remedy at all. It is certainly arguable that a buyer would expect a remedy if there is any defect, yet Rougier J appears to limit the circumstances in which he will be able to complain.

The answer to the problem is probably that which was given by the Court of Appeal in *Rogers* v *Parish (Scarborough) Ltd* (supra). The buyer bought a Range Rover which had defects in its engine and bodywork. The Court held on the facts that the defects rendered the car unmerchantable. In the course of giving judgment Mustill LJ said that simply because goods were repairable they were not therefore merchantable; he also said that a new car needs to be more than merely driveable in order to be merchantable. How much more is required depends on the car; some can be expected to be more comfortable than others, some can be expected to be more reliable than others, some can be expected to be easier to handle than others. Mustill LJ refuted the suggestion that a car with defects can be merchantable, but he accepted that something which counts as a defect in an expensive car may not do so in a cheaper car.

In two recent Court of Appeal decisions, *Rogers* v *Parish* has been applied. Both cases are curious in that, though the transactions concerned were hire purchase contracts, it was s14(2) of SGA 1979 which was regarded as the relevant quality standard.

In *Business Applications Specialists* v *Nationwide Credit Corporation Ltd* [1988] RTR 332 the appellant purchased a second-hand Mercedes motor car which was two-and-a-half years old and had travelled 37,000 miles for £14,850. After it had been driven a further 800 miles it broke down. The cause was burnt out valves, worn valve guide seals and worn valve guides in the cylinder head. Repairs cost £635. The County Court Judge had held that the car was merchantable on the basis that there was evidence that, despite its condition, the car was roadworthy.

HELD: The car was of merchantable quality but the County Court judge had reached the right conclusion for the wrong reasons. The correct test was not to ask if the car was roadworthy but to apply the test propounded in *Rogers* v *Parish*.

In *Shine* v *General Guarantee Corporation Ltd* [1988] 1 All ER 911 the plaintiff had purchased a specialised enthusiast's car at what he considered a fair price, second hand from the defendants who had described it as being in good condition. The plaintiff subsequently learnt that the car had been written off by an insurance company after having been submerged in water for 24 hours.

HELD: the trial judge had misdirected himself by considering that only the mechanical condition of the car was relevant to the issue of merchantability. Reference was made to *Rogers* v *Parish* and the fact that in assessing merchantability the mechanical condition of a vehicle was not necessarily the only characteristic to be taken into account. In this case the expectation of the purchaser of an enthusiast's car that he was getting a car that did not have the highly unsatisfactory history of this car was highly relevant. In the circumstances the car was not of merchantable quality.

Where part of the goods are unmerchantable

It may be the case that only part of a bulk of goods is unmerchantable and the rest is merchantable. However it has been held that the fact that part of the goods are merchantable does not help the seller and the buyer can reject all the goods for a breach of s14(2). In *Jackson* v *Rotax Motors & Cycle Co Ltd* [1910] 2 KB 937. P supplied motor horns to D. In one consignment however about 1/2 of the goods were slightly dented and scratched due to bad packing. D rejected the goods on grounds of unmerchantability. The Court of Appeal held that the buyer was entitled to reject the whole consignment.

The '*de minimis*' rule will of course apply in circumstances where the unmerchantable part of the goods is a 'microscopic' proportion.

Minor and cosmetic defects

One of the grey areas where the differing expectations of commercial and consumer buyers could be important is in relation to goods which work but have cosmetic or other minor defects. If, as has been argued in some cases, the test of merchantability is that of usability then the consumer might have to put up with minor defects. On the other hand, if one adopts an acceptability test as Dixon J did in the Australian High Court case of *Australian Knitting Mills* v *Grant* (1933) (supra) then a different conclusion may be reached. This dichotomy between a usability and an acceptability test may not actually exist especially in relation to consumer purchases. As pointed out above, even in commercial situations the Court of Appeal in *Aswan Engineering Establishment Co* v *Lupdine Ltd* (supra) has recently stated that the law prior to the introduction of the statutory definition was a synthesis of these two tests and that the definition merely sets out that common law position.

Certainly prior to the decision of the Court of Appeal in *The Hansa Nord* (supra) there was undisputed authority in *Jackson* v *Rotax* (supra) for the proposition that goods could be unmerchantable even though they could be made merchantable at very small cost and with very little trouble. It may be that this position has been changed by the *Hansa Nord* decision.

In *Cehave NV* v *Bremer Handelsgesellschaft, The Hansa Nord* (supra) a German seller agreed to sell 12,000 tons of US citrus pulp pellets to a Dutch buyer for £100,000, delivery to be at Rotterdam and shipment to be made in good condition. Having paid the price the buyer obtained the shipping documents and had the goods unloaded but then discovered that although the cargo in one hold was perfectly sound, part of the cargo in another hold was severely damaged through overheating. The buyer rejected the entire cargo and when the sellers refused to repay the price, the buyer obtained an order from the Rotterdam County Court for the sale of the cargo by agents of the Court. The entire cargo was sold for £32,000 to X who resold it to the original buyers at that price. The buyer therefore reacquired possession of the same goods he had previously contracted to buy and then rejected. He then used the pellets for precisely the same purpose he had contemplated in the original contract and so suffered absolutely no loss. The buyer had therefore without any detriment acquired the goods for £32,000 which should have cost him £100,000 but still claimed against the original sellers the return of the full price for a breach of s14(2).

The Court of Appeal held:

1. The stipulation in the contract that the goods were to be shipped 'in good condition' was not a condition but an innominate term, the breach of which here did not go to the root of the contract. The buyer was not therefore entitled to reject the whole cargo for the breach of that stipulation.
2. More importantly the court found the citrus pellets to be of merchantable quality even though part had been damaged at sea. As Roskill LJ stated the goods were 'far from perfect' but they did not have to be perfect to be of merchantable

quality: it sufficed that they remained saleable for the purpose for which they could normally be bought, even with some discount in the price. The pellets were bought for cattle food and were still usable as such.

The Court seems to have held here that goods with a trivial or minor defect, or goods of which some part is not up to the contract quality are not unmerchantable if the reasonable commercial man would consider that the proper way to deal with the situation was not to reject the goods but to get a discount off the price. As Goode points out this is an unpracticable position since the Court is not itself empowered to deal with the matter in this way. Either the goods are merchantable in which case there is no breach of s14(2) and therefore no remedy, or they are unmerchantable in which case the buyer has the right to reject. The court cannot hold the goods to be merchantable and also allow the buyer some discount off the price.

According to both Goode and Atiyah it is probably dangerous to read too much into the decision and Goode thinks it 'turns on its own particular facts, which were indeed extraordinary'.

The finding in the case that the goods were merchantable was probably influenced by the justice of the case which was firmly on the side of the seller. It is very unlikely that a court would hold newly manufactured consumer goods such as TVs, video recorders and cars to be merchantable if they are 'far from perfect'.

The Hansa Nord was decided after the introduction of the new statutory definition of 'merchantable quality' in s14(6). It has been suggested that the s14(6) definition by its wording has the effect of rendering goods merchantable (particularly manufactured or consumer goods) if they are suffering from some minor or perhaps cosmetic defect, and therefore deprives the buyer of his right to reject in such circumstances, as held in the *Hansa Nord*. This argument is based on the test given in the s14(6) definition: the test is as to what it is reasonable to expect these goods to be fit for. It is argued that the buyer should reasonably expect the goods to have some trivial defects.

The arguments against this view are strong:

1. The Supply of Goods (Implied) Terms Act 1973 was a consumer protection measure and should not without a clear indication be taken to have deprived the consumer of his main protection in this area.
2. If the definition did have this effect the buyer will not be able to reject the goods nor will he have a right to damages! As above, if the goods are merchantable there is no breach and no right to sue for damages.

The editors of *Benjamin* submit that where the defects are cosmetic or relate to minor items of ancillary equipment then these can when serious enough affect the fitness of the goods for their purpose and therefore the merchantable quality of the goods: for example, the buyer of a new product reasonably expects something that is not soiled or shoddy.

Durability

There is no express reference to durability in the statutory definition of merchantability and there is some confusion as to whether goods need prove to be durable. It has been stated in a number of cases, that the implied terms as to quality fall to be satisfied at the time of delivery and not at some later date. This still leaves scope to find that a product which does not work properly for very long is not of merchantable quality as the following case dealing with what is now s14(3) of the Act demonstrates. There is no difference in the principle between s14(2) and (3) on this point.

In *Crowther* v *Shannon* (supra) Mr Crowther bought a second-hand Jaguar car from the defendant motor dealers for £390. The car was eight years old and its odometer showed 82,165 miles. The salesman had described the car as being in excellent condition and said that as far as the mileage was concerned it was, for a Jaguar, 'hardly run in'. Three weeks after the car was purchased when it had been driven 2,300 miles the engine seized up completely and subsequent examination revealed that it had been in extremely bad condition and that it was necessary to replace it. The County Court judge had approached the case by asking what was a reasonable time for a car to function.

HELD: that the relevant time for determining whether the implied term was satisfied was the time of sale. However, the fact that the engine had seized up within a short time was evidence that the car was not fit for its purpose when it was sold.

In *Lambert* v *Lewis* [1982] AC 225 Lord Diplock appeared to go further than this in a case involving a farm trailer:

> 'The implied [term] ... is a continuing warranty that the goods will continue to be fit for that purpose for a reasonable time after delivery ... What is a reasonable time will depend on the nature of the goods but I would accept that in the case of the coupling the warranty was still continuing up to the date, some three to six months before the accident, when it first became known to the farmer that the handle of the locking mechanism was missing.'

It must be conceded that this statement is not supported by any authority and that there are rather more decisions which support the approach exemplified by *Crowther* v *Shannon*. For example in two recent Court of Appeal decisions, *Rogers* v *Parish* (supra) and *Bernstein* v *Pamson Motors Ltd* (supra) it is simply stated that the relevant time for assessing merchantability is the date of the contract.

Second-hand goods

Second-hand goods are required to comply with the merchantability standard just as new goods must. This does not mean that the buyer of second-hand goods is entitled to the same quality. The merchantability standard is a flexible one and the fact that the article was second-hand would be one of the factors to be taken into account when applying the statutory definition. As Lord Denning MR put it in *Bartlett* v *Sidney Marcus* (supra) in relation to a car:

> 'on the sale of a second-hand car, it is merchantable if it is in usable condition, even if not

perfect ... A buyer should realise that when he buys a second-hand car defects may appear sooner or later and, in the absence of an express warranty, he has no redress.'

Other aspects of merchantability

If it is assumed by both parties that the product will have to undergo some further process between being sold and being used the test of merchantability will be applied after this further process has been carried out.

In *Heil* v *Hedges* [1951] 1 TLR 512 the purchaser of some pork had been made ill by eating it after cooking it insufficiently.

HELD: the pork was not unmerchantable because if it had been properly cooked the poison which had been the cause of the illness would have been destroyed.

While most cases have been concerned with the 'usability' of goods, this is not always the case. In the case of *Harlingdon & Leinster Enterprises* v *Christopher Hull Fine Art* (supra) the question arose as to whether a forged painting could be described as 'of merchantable quality'. Though the painting was not by the artist to whom it was originally attributed, the court held that it still had aesthetic appeal and some (albeit lower) value and could, therefore, be said to be of merchantable quality and within s14(2) and (6) of SGA.

Exclusion of s14(2)

Where the buyer deals as a consumer any term purporting to exclude or restrict liability under s14(2) is void; and in other situations is subject to a reasonableness test.

Reform

There has been widespread concern about the appropriateness of merchantability as a standard of quality as has been noted earlier. This has been especially true in relation to consumer transactions and the decision in the Scottish case of *Millars of Falkirk Ltd* v *Turpie* (1976) SLT (Notes) 66 which appears to give a somewhat restricted interpretation to the concept of merchantability had much to do with pressure from consumer organisations which led to the government requesting the Law Commission to consider this issue and some related issues to do with the sale of goods. In their report, *Sale and Supply of Goods (Law Commission No 160)* (1987) the Law Commission recommends that the term 'merchantable' be replaced by 'acceptable quality'.

Goods would have to be of a quality acceptable to a reasonable person, bearing in mind the description of the goods, their price (if relevant), and all the other circumstances. The test of acceptable quality would require that the following circumstances should be considered where appropriate: the fitness of the goods for all their common purposes; their appearance and finish; their freedom from minor defects; their safety; and their durability. This reform is closely linked with the remedies available to the purchaser of goods which the report of the Law Commission also dealt with. That part of the report will be dealt with in Chapter 13.

5.5 Implied terms about fitness for purpose

Section 14(3) implies a condition that the goods be fit for any particular purpose which the buyer expressly or impliedly makes known to the seller. Section 14(3) replaces the original. As it now stands s14(3) provides as follows:

> 'Where the seller sells goods in the course of a business and the buyer, expressly or by implication, makes known:
> a) to the seller, or
> b) where the purchase price or part of it is payable by instalments and the goods were previously sold by a credit-broker to the seller, to that credit-broker;
> any particular purpose for which the goods are being bought, there is an implied condition that the goods supplied under the contract are reasonably fit for that purpose, whether or not that is a purpose for which such goods are commonly supplied except where the circumstances show that the buyer does not rely, or that it is unreasonable for him to rely, on the skill or judgment of the seller or credit-broker.'

The goods must be sold 'in the course of a business'

The words 'sells goods in the course of a business' exclude from s14(3) all private sales of goods. In this respect the operation of s14(3) is similar to that of s14(2) but different to that of s13. The meaning of 'in the course of a business' is discussed above under s14(2).

The practical effect of this will be that s14(3) will apply only to sales by dealers, manufacturers, wholesalers and retailers.

The condition extends to 'the goods supplied under the contract'

The implied condition of s14(3) extends to 'goods supplied under the contract' and so includes containers in which the goods sold are delivered. The new form of s14(3) confirms the two previous leading cases.

In *Geddling* v *Marsh* (supra) the facts are given above under 5.3 it was held here that the 'goods supplied under the contract of sale' included not only the mineral water which was the subject matter of the sale but also the bottles in which that water was contained. This was so even though the bottles remained at all times the property of the seller.

Benjamin notes that there may be cases where a container is something totally separate from the thing sold so that the quality of the goods is not affected by a defect in it. Hence in an old case *Gower* v *Van Dedalzen* (1837) 3 Bing NC 717 involving the sale of a cargo of oil it was held that the subject matter of that particular sale was merchantable though the oil was in fact delivered in unseasoned casks.

However, in the normal case s14(3) will also extend to foreign substances mixed with the goods when they are delivered, since they will be part of the 'goods supplied under the contract of sale'. *Wilson* v *Rickett Cockerell & Co Ltd* (supra) illustrates this (the facts are given above under 5.3 above). With reference to the phrase 'goods supplied under the contract' Denning LJ stated:

> 'that means the goods delivered in purported pursuance of the contract. The seller applies to all goods so delivered whether they conform to the contract or not ... including the offending piece ... The consignment is delivered as a whole and must be considered as a whole, not in bits.'

The Court of Appeal in this case held it to be irrelevant to the argument that there was nothing amiss with the coal *per se* and it was only the presence of the foreign substance which had caused the damage. This was because the offending article in question (a detonator) was part of the goods supplied under the contract.

The earlier case of *Duke* v *Jackson* (1921) SC 362 which came to the opposite decision on similar facts is generally regarded as wrong and the Court of Appeal refused to follow it in *Wilson* v *Rickett*.

The wording of the new s14(3) has put the matter beyond doubt: *Geddling* and *Wilson* represent the true law.

There is virtually no authority available to indicate whether or not instructions and labelling generally, either on the packaging or on the item for sale itself are to be 'of merchantable quality'. It is to be remembered that the mass production of complex goods has proliferated to a point where many goods simply *cannot* be used without instructions.

There are Canadian cases (*Willis* v *FMC Machinery & Chemicals* (1976) 68 DLR; *Lem* v *Barotto Sports Ltd* (1977) 69 DLR) which address this problem. In *Willis*, goods sold without warning labels as to possible dangers were not 'reasonably fit for sale'. In *Lem* a similar problem concerning a shotgun reloader, in which the brochure carried no warning as to potential dangers, was not similarly decided. Here the Canadian court decreed that lack of an adequate warning in the brochure did not render the whole gun 'not reasonably fit for sale'.

The only modern English case concerning instructions seems to be *Wormell* v *RHM Agriculture* [1987] 1 WLR 1091. Here the instructions on a can of herbicide were found to be ambiguous and misleading. No damage was done by the plaintiff's following the instructions, but the product proved totally ineffective. The court of first instance held that not only the herbicide, but the can and labelling were comprised in the 'goods' and these were not of merchantable quality. The Court of Appeal, however, reversed this. It is submitted that the first decision is preferable to that reached by the Court of Appeal.

'Expressly or by implication makes known to the seller any particular purpose for which the goods are being bought'

These words follow the provisions of the 1893 Act with only minor amendments. Cases under the former Act are therefore relevant.

Section 14(3) applies where the buyer expressly or by implication makes known to the seller or in certain circumstances a credit-broker any 'particular purpose' for which the goods are being bought.

Where the buyer wishes in a simple case to be supplied with something suitable for a special purpose his *request* may but need not itself be specific: for example, the seller may have notice of the purpose by extrinsic communications (see *Bristol Tramways Carriage Co* v *Fiat Motors Ltd* (supra)) or from the whole purpose of the contract (for example, a propeller being ordered for a specific ship under construction). Yet the particular purpose need not be a 'special' one: it can in the wording of the subsection be one for which goods of that kind are commonly bought.

In the context of s14(3) it is settled that the word 'particular' is opposed to 'general'. The purpose for which the goods are bought may therefore be a very general purpose; for example, food for eating or a car for driving.

Usually the buyer must make known a particular purpose for which he wants the goods, but in certain circumstances the seller's knowledge of the purpose is implied, as per Collins MR in *Priest* v *Last* [1903] 2 KB 148: 'where the sale is of goods which by the very description under which they are sold appear to be sold for a particular purpose.' The facts of *Priest* v *Last* were that B bought a hot water bottle from a chemist. B inquired of the seller whether the bottle would withstand boiling water, and was informed that it could withstand hot but not boiling water. B at no time stated the purpose for which he required the bottle. The bottle was used by B's wife in bed; however, it burst and scalded her. It was found as a fact that the bottle was not fit for use as a hot water bottle. It was held in the circumstances that although B had not specified or communicated the purpose for which he required the bottle, he had in fact used it for the usual and obvious purpose. The seller could therefore be taken to have known this obvious purpose. It was further held that on the facts the buyer had relied on the skill and judgment of the seller (see below: *Communication of the purpose*).

Decisions like *Priest* v *Last* in *Benjamin*'s view enhance the protection allowed to consumers by s14(3) and are expressly preserved in the new wording of the subsection.

Priest v *Last* is also the recognised authority for the rule that 'particular purpose' covers cases where the goods in question could be used for one conceivable purpose only. In such cases it will probably not be necessary for the buyer to communicate that purpose to the seller since the seller can generally be taken to know the purpose, as above. As *Benjamin* points out, where the description of the goods points to one purpose only, no further indication is required.

Of course, the position will be different where the particular purpose for which the buyer wants the goods is not obvious, or where, although the buyer has made known his particular purpose to the seller, there is some peculiarity about the purpose of which the seller remains unaware.

Two cases can be contrasted in this respect. In *Manchester Liners Ltd v Rea* [1922] 2 AC 74 coal was supplied by B to S for a specified ship, the *Manchester Importer*. The coal was unsuitable for that particular ship though it was suitable for other ships. The House of Lords held that the coal had to be suitable for that particular ship. Ships do, as Lord Greene observed, differ in type and requirements, and coal merchants are aware of this. So where a coal merchant undertakes to supply coal for a particular and specified ship he must supply coal suitable for that particular ship. It could not be said that the buyer's ship differed from any normal or standard type since there was no such type.

This is frequently contrasted with the case of *Griffiths v Peter Conway Ltd* [1939] 1 All ER 685. B contracted dermatitis from a tweed coat purchased from the seller. It was found as a fact that this buyer had unusually sensitive skin and that the coat would not have harmed a normal person. The buyer argued that she was within the old s14(1) (now s14(3)) since the coat was not fit for its obvious purpose (ie use by her). The Court of Appeal held that the case of *Manchester Liners* could be distinguished here. There was a peculiarity about the purpose for which the coat was required, of which the seller was wholly unaware. A normal person would not have been adversely affected by the coat. This decision finds support in the later case of *Teheran-Europe Co Ltd v S T Belton (Tractors) Ltd* [1968] 2 QB 545; [1968] 2 All ER 886 where it was stated that the seller is not presumed to know of unusual circumstances or sensitivity affecting fitness for the buyer's particular purpose.

The effect of those cases can be summarised as follows: where either the goods are required for a particular purpose which is not obvious to the seller or the goods are required for a particular purpose which the seller knows but there is some peculiarity about that purpose of which the seller is unaware, then the buyer must make clear to the seller the particular purpose or peculiarity involved.

The matter was considered by the House of Lords in *Ashington Piggeries Ltd v Christopher Hill Ltd* (supra). S sold herring meal to B for the purpose of processing it into animal feeding stuffs. The herring meal was contaminated with toxic material which made it very slightly harmful to most animals and fatal to mink. The House of Lords distinguished *Griffiths v Conway* calling it a 'highly specialised case'. In the present case, even if the mink belonging to the buyer in *Griffiths* had a peculiar or even abnormal susceptibility to the toxic material, there was still evidence that the material was harmful to other animals. In such a case, there was a breach of s14(1) (now s14(3)) since the goods were sold for the purpose of being made into animal feed. It is, however, unclear from the Lord's decision whether the feeding of the herring meal to mink in particular was itself a possible purpose which the parties both foresaw. The case would of course have had the same outcome had this been the case since the goods would certainly have been unfit for *that* purpose.

The 'particular purposes' for which the goods are bought may be manifold. There may be many uses to which those goods are ordinarily put, in which case these will all be purposes within s14(3) unless the buyer makes it clear he wants the goods for certain purposes only. This can obviously place a heavy burden on the seller in such cases, since the seller will be in breach of s14(3) if the goods although satisfactory and fit for a very wide range of uses are unfit for any one of the ordinary uses.

In *Henry Kendall & Sons* v *William Lillico & Sons Ltd* (supra) the buyer bought from the seller a quantity of Brazilian ground-nut extraction for the purposes of processing it into feeding stuffs for cattle and poultry. The extraction proved fatal to turkeys. It was held that the seller was in breach of s14(1) (now s14(3)) since the extraction was unfit for one of the given purposes (ie feeding to poultry). The fact that the extraction was harmless to cattle was irrelevant.

However, if the purpose to which the buyer puts the goods is in some way unforeseeable or abnormal then the seller will not be liable unless the buyer communicated that particular purpose to him.

Note also that in s14(3) it is not necessary to show that the goods are commonly supplied for the purpose in issue. Resale can be a 'particular purpose' in this context.

Communication of the purpose

If the goods are bought for some particular purpose of the buyer which is not their normal purpose or is more exactly defined than could normally be the case, then that purpose must be communicated expressly or impliedly to the seller for liability to arise under s14(3). Implied communication can be through related correspondence or an implication from the whole purpose of the contract.

In certain circumstances, set out clearly in s14(3), the communication can be made to a credit-broker.

The purpose must be indicated clearly and with sufficient detail particularly to enable the seller to make the goods fit for that purpose.

'Reasonably fit for that purpose'

Where s14(3) applies it is the duty of the seller to supply goods reasonably fit for the purpose in question. The standard to be achieved to be 'reasonably fit' is best illustrated by reference to the decided cases which are obviously still valid under the new s14(3).

In *Bristol Tramways Carriage Co Ltd* v *Fiat Motors Ltd* (supra) the buses ordered by B were to S's knowledge needed for passenger work in Bristol, a hilly city, and proved unsuitable for this. S was held liable.

Milk containing typhoid germs was not 'reasonably fit' (see *Frost* v *Aylesbury Dairy Co Ltd* (supra)). A plastic catapult which broke injuring the user's eye was not 'reasonably fit' (*Godley* v *Perry* (supra)). Many s14(3) cases will be concurrent breaches of s14(2).

The seller, however, does not warrant that the goods are totally suitable in every way: a second-hand car may be 'reasonably fit' even though it is known to require repairs (see *Bartlett* v *Sidney Marcus* (supra)). The seller also does not guarantee the goods against misuse by the buyer.

When dangerous substances are supplied they may not be fit for their purposes unless an appropriate warning accompanies them.

Reliance by the buyer on the seller's skill and judgment

The requirement in s14(3) of reliance on the seller's skill and judgment can be set out as follows. The condition in s14(3) will be implied unless (the seller proves that) the circumstances show that the buyer did not rely or that it was not reasonable for him to rely (substantially) on the seller's skill and judgment in supplying suitable goods.

It is clear from the wording of s14(3) that there is an initial onus on the buyer to show that he has made known the purpose for which the goods are bought. This is not a heavy onus. It will then be presumed that the buyer relied on the seller's skill and judgment unless that is positively disproved or the seller can show that the reliance was unreasonable.

Of course, if it can be shown that the seller at any time intimated to the buyer that he must not rely on the seller's skill and judgment, the subsection will normally be excluded.

The courts have always been ready, particularly in relation to consumer goods, to apply s14(3) in the buyer's favour. In such cases reliance is often obvious from the circumstances of the sale. There is an oft-quoted dictum of Lord Wright to this effect in *Grant* v *Australian Knitting Mills Ltd* [1936] AC 85:

> 'The reliance will seldom be express: it will usually arise by implication from the circumstances ... In purchases from a retailer the reliance will in general be inferred from the fact that a buyer goes to the shop in confidence that the tradesman has selected his stock with skill and judgment.'

Another useful dictum is that of Lord Wilberforce in *Henry Kendall & Sons* v *William Lillico & Sons Ltd* (supra): the mere fact that seller and buyer are members of the same commodity market is not in itself proof that the buyer does not rely on the seller's judgment, though it does tend to go against the inference of reliance.

Examples of cases where there was found to be no reliance appear in cases under the 1893 Act. In *Teheran-Europe Co Ltd* v *S T Belton Tractors Ltd* (supra), air compressors were sold in circumstances which gave the seller notice that they were for resale in Persia. It was held that the buyers relied on their own skill and judgment as to the suitability of the compressors for resale in Persia. The goods were sold for resale in the B's home market about which the buyer knew everything and the seller knew nothing. There could be no reliance on the seller's skill and judgment in such circumstances.

Benjamin suggests that the same may apply where the buyer knows the seller has only one commodity to supply and must be regarded as taking what he buys as it is (*Turner* v *Mucklow* (1862) 6 LT 690).

There are three further areas of importance under the question of reliance:

What will amount to unreasonable reliance?

If the buyer proves that the seller's reliance on him was unreasonable then he will not be liable under s14(3). The onus of proving unreasonableness is on the seller.

The mere fact that the buyer failed to take up an opportunity to examine the goods and, had he done so, he would have discovered their unsuitability for his purpose does not of itself make reliance on the seller's skill and judgment unreasonable. The decision not to examine the goods himself may obviously be made because of reliance on the seller.

Where the buyer has examined the goods and they contain faults which are apparent on examination and which should make the buyer aware that the goods are unsuitable, this *may* make reliance on the seller unreasonable. Such a result is not, however, inevitable.

If the buyer knows or ought to know that the seller has no experience or expertise in relation to the goods, or the seller disclaims such expertise then reliance is probably unreasonable.

Partial reliance on the seller

There may be a division of reliance: the buyer relying in part on himself and in part on the seller. In other words the buyer relies on his own skill and judgment on some aspects of the goods, and on the seller's as regards certain other aspects. In these cases it is necessary to determine whether the unsuitability of the goods arose out of an aspect in relation to which the buyer relied on the seller's skill and judgment. If this is the case then the implied condition of s14(3) will apply. However, if the unsuitability arose from an area in which the buyer relied on his own skill and judgment there will be no breach of s14(3).

If the goods are unfit for their purpose because of some feature within the buyer's area of expertise and in relation to which the buyer has relied on his own skill, then the seller will not be liable.

Ashington Piggeries Ltd v *Christopher Hill* (supra) (the facts are outlined above) concerned the supply of herring meal to be made into mink food. The herring meal was found to contain a toxic element which was fatal to mink. The House of Lords held (reversing the Court of Appeal) that Ashington Piggeries relied on their own skill or judgment to ensure that there was nothing in the formula for the feedstuff which made the food unsuitable for mink. They relied on the skill and judgment of Christopher Hill to obtain ingredients which did not contain a toxic rendering the mix unsafe for feeding to animals generally. Therefore, since Christopher Hill had failed to supply ingredients fit for the required purpose they were liable to

Ashington Piggeries. The unsuitability resulted from an area in which the buyer relied on the seller's judgment.

Benjamin agrees that this case is one of 'goods being made up for the buyer' to his specifications. In such cases there is no reliance as to the suitability of the end product but the seller must use materials or ingredients reasonably fit for their purpose. The liability in *Ashington* arose because one of the ingredients supplied was toxic.

The case reaffirmed the law as laid down in a previous case. In *Cammell Laird & Co v Manganese Bronze & Brass Co Ltd* [1934] AC 402, S agreed to construct two propellers for two of the buyer's ships. The propellers were to be made according to specifications laid down by the buyer, but certain matters including the thickness of the blades were to be left to the seller. One propeller was unsuitable due to defects in a matter not dealt with in the specifications. The House of Lords held that the seller was liable under s14(3) (at that time s14(1)) since in the area outside the buyer's specifications and directions, the buyer was inevitably relying on the skill and judgment of the seller.

Support for these decisions can be found in the more recent decision of *McDonald* v *Empire Garages (Blackburn) Ltd* (1975) The Times 8 October.

Note that the reliance must 'be such as to constitute a substantial and effective inducement which leads the buyer to agree to purchase the commodity' (*Medway Oil* v *Silica Gel Cpn* (1928) 33 Com Cas 195).

The time at which reliance is to be tested

It is generally agreed that reliance and the reasonableness thereof must be established as at the date of the contract.

Liability of the seller

Although the seller's duty is only to supply goods which are 'reasonably fit' not absolutely fit, the seller's liability under s14(3) is nonetheless very strict. It is not a defence to argue that the exercise of ordinary skill and care could not have discovered the defect. The seller will be liable even for latent defects which could not be discovered by any amount of diligence or care. The question of whether goods are reasonably fit for their known purpose is to be determined objectively: it does not depend on the degree of care which the seller may have exercised.

As Goode says, the fact that the implied condition is attracted by reliance on the seller's skill and judgment does not mean that the condition is satisfied by the exercise of all reasonable care and skill.

Lord Reid's dictum in *Henry Kendall* v *Lillico* is helpful in this context:

> 'By getting the seller to undertake to use his skill and judgment the buyer gets under s14 an assurance that the goods will be reasonably fit for his purpose and that covers not only defects which the seller ought to have detected but also defects which are latent in the sense that even the utmost skill and judgment on the part of the seller would not have detected them.'

These propositions are illustrated by the facts of *Frost* v *Aylesbury Dairy Co Ltd* (supra). S sold milk to B which was contaminated. The buyer's wife drank the milk and contracted typhoid and died. B sued under s14(1) (now s14(3)). S argued that had he exercised all reasonable care and skill he would not have been able to discover the defect and it could not be said therefore that the buyer relied on his skill and judgment on the non-contaminated nature of the goods. The Court of Appeal rejected the seller's argument. Under s14 the buyer gets an assurance extending to defects which are latent and undetectable even by the utmost care and skill on the seller's part.

The seller's obligation is nevertheless only to provide goods 'reasonably fit' for the known purpose. If the purpose in issue is stated in very broad terms and the goods are fit for most 'sub-purposes' or 'sub-uses' within that purpose but unfit for some obscure, improbable use then there may not be a breach of s14(3). This proposition found some support in the judgment of Lord Pearce in *Henry Kendall & Sons* v *William Lillico & Sons Ltd* (supra).

Whether or not there is a breach of s14(3) in the above circumstances will depend, according to Lord Pearce, on the 'rarity of the unsuitability' weighed against the gravity of its consequences. This approach was taken in a case decided in the same year. In *Vacwell Engineering Co Ltd* v *BDH Chemicals* [1971] 1 QB 88; [1969] 3 All ER 1681 (appeal allowed by agreement) [1971] 1 QB 111; [1970] 3 All ER 553n, S sold to B a chemical contained in glass ampoules. The purpose for which the chemical was required was a certain manufacturing process. The chemical was in itself fit for the manufacturing purpose but unknown to the buyer it tended to react violently on contact with water. During the manufacturing process one ampoule broke and the chemical then came into contact with water causing an explosion which destroyed all the goods and most of the buyer's factory. Rees J held that there was a breach of s14(3) since the goods were not reasonably fit for their purpose: the seller ought to have foreseen that the chemical might come into contact with water. The possibility of contact with water was not sufficiently small or obscure that such an unsuitability could be overlooked.

The time at which the goods must be reasonably fit

It is Atiyah's view that the goods must be fit for the same time as they are required to be merchantable under s14(2) and that the same considerations apply.

Benjamin does not see the position as being so clear cut although he recognises that there is support for Atiyah's view particularly in *Crowther* v *Shannon Motor Co* (supra). *Benjamin* notes that in CIF and FOB contracts the duty relates to the time of shipment. He concludes that it would be reasonable to say that the goods must be reasonably fit at the time of passing of property, or where property and risk are separated at the time of passing of the risk. However, the nature of the contract and surrounding circumstances could even indicate that the time of delivery is the relevant time (see *Jackson* v *Rotax Motors* (supra)). For further details on Export Sales contracts see *International Trade Textbook*, published by HLT Publications.

Relation between s14(2) and s14(3)

There is obviously a considerable overlap between these two subsections: in particular the requirement of being 'in the course of a business' applies to both, and the definition of merchantable quality' actually relates to 'fitness for purpose'.

The editors of *Benjamin* point out that two major practical differences remain:

1. Section 14(2) requires only that the goods be merchantable whereas s14(3) requires that they be reasonably fit for the purpose expressly or by implication made known. A higher standard can therefore be exacted by a buyer who makes his special purpose known, for the seller is then liable if the goods are not reasonably suitable for it, although they may be merchantable.
2. Section 14(3) is excluded where the circumstances show that the buyer does not rely or that it is unreasonable for him to rely on the seller's skill and judgment. There is no such limitation in s14(2) although that sub-section is itself limited in that it does not apply as regards defects drawn to the buyer's attention, nor when the buyer examines the goods, as regards defects which that examination ought to reveal.

Exclusion of s14(3)

See s3 of the Unfair Contract Terms Act 1977. Essentially under s6 of the UCTA any contract term excluding or restricting liability under s15 SGA is invalid against a person 'dealing as consumer' and against others is valid only in so far as the exemption clause is 'reasonable' within the criteria in s11 of the UCTA.

5.6 Sales by sample

Section 15 implies into contracts for sale by sample terms relating to the correspondence of the bulk of the goods with the sample provided. Section 15, like s13 but unlike s14, is not restricted to business sellers.

Section 15(1) and (2) provide as follows:

'(1) A contract of sale is a contract of sale by sample where there is an express or implied term to that effect in the contract.
(2) In the case of a contract for sale by sample there is an implied condition:
a) that the bulk will correspond with the sample in quality;
b) that the buyer will have a reasonable opportunity of comparing the bulk with the sample;
c) that the goods will be free from any defect rendering them unmerchantable, which would not be apparent on reasonable examination of the sample.'

The terms implied by s15(2) are conditions and their breach will entitle the buyer to repudiate the contract and reject the goods, and/or to sue for damages.

Section 15 will be analysed as follows: the meaning of 'sale by sample' s15(1), section 15(2)(a), section 15(2)(b), section 15(2)(c), section 15 applies whether or not the seller is selling 'in the course of a business', goods sold by description as well as by sample, exclusion of s15.

The meaning of 'sale by sample' s15(1)

Section 15(1) provides that a contract of sale is a contract of sale by sample 'where there is a term in the contract, express or implied, to that effect' This is obviously not of great assistance. 'Sale by sample' was given a case law definition in *Parker* v *Palmer* (1821) 4 B & A 387:

> 'A sale by sample is a sale whereby the seller expressly or impliedly promises that the goods sold should answer the description of a small parcel exhibited at the time of the sale.'

What is clear from s15(1) is that the mere fact a sample is exhibited during negotiations for a sale does not make it a sale by sample. Atiyah puts forward the view that the sample displayed in negotiations must be intended to form the contractual basis of comparison with the goods to be delivered. In other words there must be an intention that the sale be by sample. However, according to the editors of *Benjamin* it cannot be stated that actual intention to sell by sample is required, although they agree that the mere exhibition of a sample does not necessarily make the sale one by sample. They see the test as an objective one: the determination of the function of the sample. Frequently samples are displayed merely to give some indication of the nature of the goods offered. In other cases the seller represents that the bulk is like the sample. Only in the latter case will the sale be by sample. The difference between Atiyah's approach, seeking the subjective intention of the parties, and the approach taken in *Benjamin*, seeking the objective function of the sample probably leads to little practical difference in result.

In many cases a provision as to sample will be express, for example 'as per sample' appearing in the contract, as in *Re Walker, Winser & Hann* v *Shaw & Co* [1904] 2 KB 152, a case involving a sale of barley by sample.

The cases establish that purchases by consumers are less likely to be held to be 'by sample' than business purchases, and that where any buyer goes to examine the goods themselves after being shown a sample or where he requires of the seller an express warranty on the goods these are unlikely to be sales by sample.

Where a contract has been reduced into writing the parol evidence rule usually excludes any reference to extrinsic evidence to establish the existence of terms other than those in the written contract. Where a contract of sale has been so reduced to writing and in its written form contains no reference to any sample, evidence to establish that the sale was in fact by sample is usually excluded (see *Tye* v *Fynmore* (1813) 3 Camp 462). However, where the description of the goods used in the contract has no definite or effective meaning in the trade, then external evidence may be admitted to identify that description in accordance with a sample. (See for example *Cameron & Co v Slutzkin Pty Ltd* (1923) 32 CLR 81.)

Note, however, that in accordance with the established exceptions to the parol evidence rule, evidence could be adduced to prove a collateral contract that the goods are warranted to be equal to sample as in *Thorne & Co Ltd v Thomas Borthwick & Son* (1956) SR (NSW) 81, or to show trade usage that such sales are made by sample (*Syars v Jonas* (1848) 2 Exch. 111).

If the contract is made before the tender of a sample and the contract itself provides for such tender then several matters of interpretation arise. First, whether the seller is bound to tender a sample at all now the sale has been made. Second, whether the sample must comply with descriptive words in the contract (see *John Bowra & Son v Rodoma Canned Foods Ltd* [1967] 1 Lloyd's Rep 183). Third, whether the buyer has an unfettered right to reject the sample or whether he can only do so for good reason like non-compliance with description. All these are simply matters of interpretation of the contract.

Section 15(2)(a)

Section 15(2)(a) lays down that the bulk delivered must correspond in quality with the sample. In a sale by sample the seller will be in breach of s15(2)(a) where the bulk does not correspond with sample even where it could be made to correspond by a simple process (so held in *E & S Ruben Ltd v Faire Bros Ltd* [1949] 1 KB 254; [1949] 1 All ER 215). However, the buyer is only entitled under this sub-section to require the bulk to correspond with the sample as regards those qualities whether of the sample or of the bulk that would be apparent from the examination which is normal in the trade. This was made clear in the speech of Lord Macnaghten in *James Drummond & Sons v E H Van Ingen & Co* (1887) 12 App Cas 284:

> 'The sample speaks for itself. But it cannot be treated as saying more than such a sample would tell a merchant of the class to which the buyer belongs, using due care and diligence and appealing to it in the ordinary way and with the knowledge possessed by merchants of that class at the time.'

Therefore if, for example, the sample is only intended for visual examination there will be no breach of s15(2)(a) if the bulk does not correspond with that sample in other ways provided that in a normal visual examination it would appear so to correspond (see *F E Hookway & Co Ltd v Alfred Isaacs & Son* [1954] 1 Lloyd's Rep 491). There could in such circumstances be very great material differences between bulk and sample yet still the seller may not be in breach of s15(2)(a). Yet in other situations a test by touching or chemical analysis may be envisaged. Note that in any case evidence of trade usage and custom may be admitted as to what constitutes correspondence with sample (*Walker, Winser & Hann* (supra)).

If only part of the bulk does not correspond with sample then the buyer may reject or retain all the goods, but he cannot retain just those goods which correspond with sample and reject the rest unless the contract is severable (*Jackson* v *Rotax* (supra)).

Section 15(2)(b)

Section 15(2)(b) is in effect a specific application in the case of sales by sample of the general principle expressed in s34(1) regarding the buyer's right to examine the goods for the purpose of ascertaining whether they conform with the contract.

In contracts of sale by sample, as with other sales, the buyer is not deemed to have accepted the goods until he has had a reasonable opportunity of examining them. If, however, the buyer intimates to the seller that he is accepting the goods then he will be unable to reject the goods even if he has not yet had a reasonable opportunity for inspection (see *Hardy & Co* v *Hillerns & Fowler* [1923] 2 KB 490). Reference should be made to the operation of acceptance in general (see Chapter 13 below).

The buyer usually need not pay the price before he has had a reasonable opportunity to inspect the goods unless the contract expressly fixes a time for payment, but the payment does not prejudice the right to reject on later examination of the bulk (*Polenghi Bros* v *Dried Milk Co Ltd* (1904) 92 LT 64).

Note that the bulk should be compared with the sample at the place of delivery (s29(2)) unless otherwise stipulated in the contract. If the contract does so stipulate then delivery will not prejudice the right to reject on later examination of the goods: *Perkins* v *Bell* [1893] 1 QB 193. It should be emphasised that the place of examination will ultimately depend on the circumstances of the case. In *Lorymer* v *Smith* (1822) 1 B & C 1, a buyer in an FOB export contract was entitled to refuse to take delivery when the seller denied him an opportunity of examination prior to delivery.

Section 15(2)(c)

Section 15(2)(c) in effect excludes the implied condition that the goods shall be merchantable where the defect rendering them unmerchantable could have been discovered by reasonable examination of the sample. This applies whether or not it has in fact been examined. In s14(2) by contract the implied condition of merchantability is only excluded if an actual examination has been made. The practical difference is, therefore, that the seller in a sale by sample is entitled to assume that the buyer will examine the sample. If the buyer does not do so he will have no remedy for defects which he could have discovered by that examination.

As *Benjamin* points out, the Act speaks of a 'reasonable examination' and not of a 'practicable examination'. It is irrelevant that there are other practicable examinations of the goods which the buyer could carry out provided the examination he does make is reasonable. Thus in *Godley* v *Perry* (supra) the testing of a catapult by pulling the elastic was reasonable even though one can conceive of further ways of testing such goods.

A further point to note is that the buyer may reject goods which *do correspond* with sample *if latent defects* render them *unmerchantable* (ie defects which are not discoverable on reasonable examination). If the goods are unmerchantable by reason of *patent defects* (ie discoverable on reasonable examination) then the buyer has only himself to blame and will have no remedy under s15(1)(c) whether or not he examined the goods.

Much case law surrounds the question of what defects are discoverable by a reasonable examination. In *Wren* v *Holt* [1903] 1 KB 610. B purchased beer, which had been contaminated by arsenic, from S. It was held that the beer was unmerchantable but the defect was not (in s15) discoverable on a 'reasonable examination'.

In *Godley* v *Perry* (supra) S ran a toy shop, and displayed some plastic toy catapults in the shop window. B aged 6 saw them and purchased one. The catapult broke during normal use and injured the buyer in the eye. The relevant relationship was between S and his wholesaler from whom he had bought the catapult by sample and inspected it by pulling the elastic. It was held that S must succeed in his action against the wholesaler under s15(2)(c). The defect was not discoverable on a 'reasonable examination' since that phrase had to be understood according to the common sense standards of ordinary life. A reasonable examination in the circumstances would not involve taking the catapult to pieces, a process which might have revealed the defect.

A seller will sometimes be in breach of both s15(2)(a) and s15(2)(c). Note also that a clause excluding liability for 'all defects or faults' will not prevent there being a breach of s15(2)(a) where the goods do not correspond with sample. These two points are illustrated by a further case. In *Champanhac & Co* v *Waller & Co* [1948] 2 All ER 724 S sold to B a quantity of government-surplus goods. The contract stipulated that the goods were sold 'as sample taken away' and that 'it is distinctly understood that these are government-surplus goods and we will sell them with all faults and imperfections'. When delivered the goods had perished and were obviously unmerchantable. It was held:

1. This was a sale by sample and these goods did not correspond with sample. The exclusion clause had no effect where there was a breach of s15(2)(a) in non-correspondence with sample.
2. S was also in breach of s15(2)(c) since the defects in condition were not apparent when the buyer examined the sample at the time of the contract.

It is submitted that the interpretation of 'unmerchantable' in s15(2)(c) should be in accordance with the statutory definition given in s4(6) and that the omission of the word 'quality' makes no difference. This view is adopted by among others *Benjamin*.

Unlike s14(2) and s14(3), s15 applies whether or not the seller is selling 'in the course of a business'.

Goods sold by description as well as by sample

Where goods are sold by description as well as by sample then in accordance with ss13 and 15 the goods must correspond with description and with sample. If the goods are also sold in the course of a business, they must also be merchantable in s14. Section 15(2)(c) will still exclude liability however in respect of defects which should have been discovered on reasonable examination of the sample.

Exclusion of s15

See Chapter 7 and the Unfair Contract Terms Act 1977. Essentially under s6 UCTA any contract term excluding or restricting liability under s15 SGA is invalid against a person 'dealing as consumer' but against others is valid only so far as the exemption clause is 'reasonable' on the criteria in s11 of the UCTA.

5.7 Other implied terms

The only important category of implied terms still to be considered in that of terms annexed by trade usage.

Section 14(4) (replacing the old s14(3)) provides as follows: 'An implied condition or warranty about quality or fitness for a particular purpose may be annexed to a contract of sale by usage.' This subsection adds nothing to the pre-existing common law. In a transaction taking place in the context of a particular trade it is necessary to account the custom and usage of that trade in ascertaining the intention of the parties. Through that intention can be found a variety of conditions or warranties about quality or fitness for a particular purpose.

An old example is found in *Jones* v *Bowden* (1813) 4 Taunt 84 where evidence was admitted to show that in sales of pimento where the catalogue did not state that the goods were sea-water damaged, they were warranted to be free from such damage.

Another illustration which is frequently cited in this context is the case of *Peter Darlington Partners Ltd* v *Gosho Co Ltd* [1964] 1 Lloyd's Rep 149: P sold to D 50 tons of canary seed on a 'pure basis'. The custom of the trade dictated that there was no such thing as 100 per cent pure seed: the highest standard of purity was 98 per cent. D was not therefore entitled to reject the goods for an impurity of 2 per cent since the contract was governed by the trade custom.

6

Duties of the Buyer

6.1 Duty to pay

6.2 To take delivery

6.1 Duty to pay

It is the buyer's duty to pay for the goods in accordance with the terms of the contract of sale.

Section 28 provides that unless otherwise agreed, delivery of the goods and payment of the price are *concurrent conditions*, that is to say, the seller must be ready and willing to give possession of the goods to the buyer in exchange for the price and the buyer must be ready and willing to pay the price in exchange for possession of the goods.

Payment must usually be made at the seller's place of business, but the contract may provide otherwise. Several issues arise in the area of payment:

Time of payment

The seller is entitled to payment at the time expressly or impliedly laid down in the contract. However this statement requires qualification since any conditions precedent to the right to be paid which are prescribed by SGA or the contract must first be complied with. By s10(1) the time of payment is prima facie not of the essence, even in commercial sales. Like all provisions as to place or time of delivery this may, however, be changed expressly by the parties when the contract is first agreed.

Notice also that time may subsequently be made 'of the essence' by the simple means of serving a notice to that effect on the delaying party, provided a reasonable amount of time is given to comply (see *British & Commonwealth Holdings plc* v *Quadrex Holdings Inc* [1989] 3 WLR 723).

Payment and delivery: concurrent conditions

What s28 requires is not coincidence of performance of the delivery and payment obligations but coincidence of willingness to perform. So if the buyer sues the seller for non-delivery then the buyer need not prove actual payment to the seller but merely that he was *ready and willing to pay*. If the seller sues the buyer for non-acceptance then the seller need not prove that he has tendered delivery but merely that he was *ready and willing to deliver*.

The right to sue for the price.

Section 49 provides:

> '(1) Where, under a contract of sale, the property in the goods has passed to the buyer and he wrongfully neglects or refuses to pay for the goods according to the terms of the contract, the seller may maintain an action against him for the price of the goods.
> (2) Where, under a contract of sale, the price is payable on a day certain irrespective of delivery and the buyer wrongfully neglects or refuses to pay such price, the seller may maintain an action for the price, although the property in the goods has not passed and the goods have not been appropriated to the contract.'

It will be noted from this section that in order to maintain an action for the price the seller must show either that the property in the goods has passed to the buyer or that under the terms of the contract the price became payable on a day irrespective of delivery and that the delivery day has arrived.

6.2 To take delivery

Taking delivery

This is distinct from the duty to accept the goods. The taking of delivery is not as such an acceptance of the goods though it is usually the first step towards acceptance. In a variety of circumstances the the buyer can reject the goods even though he has previously taken delivery of them. The legal significance attached to the taking of delivery is quite different from that attached to acceptance. In taking delivery the buyer does no more than give up his right to treat the act of tender as ineffective as being made at the wrong time or place or in the wrong manner, and is not taken as showing the buyer's satisfaction with the goods. By contrast if the buyer accepts the goods then he will lose his right to reject them, even where the goods are manifestly defective.

Acceptance

The duty to accept conforming goods is merely a negative obligation: to refrain from rejecting the goods. Very often no positive act of acceptance will be necessary. Acceptance of the goods is governed by ss34 and 35 SGA; this is in practice an important area since the buyer loses his right to reject the goods if he accepts them or is deemed to have accepted them within the meaning of those two sections. Acceptance is dealt with fully under Chapter 13: 'Remedies of the buyer'.

7

Exclusion of Liability

7.1 Introduction

7.2 Judicial control: incorporation

7.3 Judicial control: interpretation

7.4 The Unfair Contract Terms Act 1977

7.5 Terms rendered void by the Act

7.6 Terms subject to the reasonableness test

7.7 The reasonableness test

7.8 Anti-avoidance provisions

7.9 Miscellaneous provisions

7.10 Conclusions

7.1 Introduction

It is not uncommon to find that a contract for the sale of goods is contained in the trader's standard form of contract. There are some good reasons for this. It is more efficient for the trader that he can use the same standard form each time rather than have to settle the terms of each transaction. In this there are advantages for purchasers in that costs are kept down. However, standard form contracts can be abused by traders and can be used to exclude the liability to which the trader would normally be subject. This can be particularly harsh where the supplier of the product or service is a monopoly or near monopoly supplier; or all the suppliers offer the same terms. As a result the courts, especially where consumers have been involved, have often been hostile to such clauses. The following extract from the Law Commissions' *Exemption Clauses: Second Report* puts the matter in perspective:

> 'We are in no doubt that in many cases they operate against the public interest and that the prevailing judicial attitude of suspicion, or indeed of hostility, to such clauses is well founded. All too often they are introduced in ways which result in the party affected by

them remaining ignorant of their presence or import until it is too late. That party, even if he knows of the exemption clause, will often be unable to appreciate what he may lose by accepting it. In any case he may not have sufficient bargaining strength to refuse to accept it. The result is that the risk of carelessness or of failure to achieve satisfactory standards of performance is thrown on to the party who is not responsible for it or who is unable to guard against it. Moreover, by excluding liability for such carelessness or failure the economic pressures to maintain high standards of performance are reduced.'

Lord Diplock defined an exemption or exclusion clause in *Photo Production Ltd* v *Securicor* [1980] AC 827 as 'one which modifies an obligation ... that would otherwise arise by implication of law'. These clauses can take many forms. In some cases there will be an outright attempt to exclude completely some liability such as the clause in the well-known case of *L'Estrange* v *Graucob* [1934] 2 KB 394 (for full facts see below) which stated that 'any express or implied condition, statement or warranty, statutory or otherwise, is hereby excluded'. Other clauses, usually referred to as limitation clauses, may not seek to prevent liability arising but instead will put a ceiling on the damages that are to be payable. For example, in *George Mitchell (Chesterhall) Ltd* v *Finney Lock Seeds Ltd* [1983] 2 All ER 737, which is discussed later, the seller limited his liability to the value of the goods. See, for instance, the recent Canadian case of *Kordas* v *Stokes Seeds Ltd* (1993) 96 DLR 129 in which the Ontario Court of Appeal decided that it was not unconscionable for a supplier of seeds to limit, by means of an exclusion clause, all liability to the value of the seed only. In addition, there are less obvious ways in which exemption clauses can be drafted. A contractual clause may make it a condition of obtaining compensation for breach that a claim is made within a certain time limit or clauses may discourage purchasers from exercising their rights such as one making clear that a deposit will be forfeited if the purchaser exercises his right of rejection.

The courts have attempted to control the use of exclusion clauses but it must be admitted that, despite the sometimes bold approaches of judges like Lord Denning to the problem, the problem necessitated legislative intervention. The most important, though not the only piece of legislation in this area, is the Unfair Contract Terms Act 1977. Before examining that Act in detail it is still important to consider the methods of judicial control. There are two reasons for this. First, the Unfair Contract Terms Act does not apply to all contracts; and secondly, where it does apply in some cases it says that an exemption clause may be relied on if it is fair and reasonable. In this latter case it makes sense to ask if common law might say either that the clause is not part of the contract or that it should be construed as not applying to the particular situation that has arisen. At common law in order for an exclusion clause to be binding, it must have been incorporated into the contract. The courts have evolved stringent tests to check whether the relevant clause is incorporated. The judiciary consider the topic under two broad headings: has the clause relied on been incorporated and, if so, as a matter of construction has it covered the problem now arising.

7.2 Judicial control: incorporation

Was the clause incorporated in the contract?

The first question to ask is: was the clause incorporated in the contract? This can be demonstrated either by showing that it is included in a document that the buyer has signed or that he has been given reasonable notice of it.

Incorporation by signature

Authority for the first proposition is to be found in *L'Estrange* v *Graucob* (supra). The plaintiff ran a cafe in Llandudno and was persuaded by a salesman to buy a cigarette slot machine from the defendants. The agreement stipulated that the plaintiff would pay by instalments and also contained exclusion clauses. She signed the agreement without reading it and it was found as a fact by the court that she had no knowledge of the contents of the agreement. The machine was faulty and the plaintiff purported to terminate the agreement. It was held that she could not do so because she was bound by the exclusion clause in the agreement which she had signed. As Scrutton LJ put it:

> 'In cases in which the contract is contained in a railway ticket or other unsigned document, it is necessary to prove that an alleged party was aware, or ought to have been aware, of its terms and conditions. These cases have no application when the document has been signed. When a document containing contractual terms is signed, then, in the absence of fraud, or, I will add, misrepresentation, the party signing it is bound, and it is wholly immaterial if he has read the document or not.'

As Scrutton LJ made clear there are circumstances in which the rule does not apply.

The effect of the clause has been misrepresented. In *Curtis* v *Chemical Cleaning and Dyeing Co Ltd* [1951] 1 KB 805, the plaintiff had taken her wedding dress to the defendants to be cleaned. She was asked by the assistant in the shop to sign a document which contained a condition excluding all liability on the party of the defendants for any damage to any article in their keeping. Before signing the document, the plaintiff asked why she was to do so and was told by the assistant that the defendants would not accept any responsibility for damage to the beads or sequins on the dress. The plaintiff did not read all of the document. When the dress returned there was a stain on the front of it which had not been there before.

HELD: Because the plaintiff's signature to the document had been obtained by an innocent misrepresentation the defendants were not entitled to rely on the exemption clause. Denning LJ said:

> 'In my opinion any behaviour, by words or conduct, is sufficient to be a misrepresentation if it is such as to mislead the other party about the existence or extent of the exemption. If it conveys a false impression, that is enough. If the false impression is created knowingly, it is a fraudulent misrepresentation; if it is created unwittingly, it is an innocent misrepresentation; but either is sufficient to disentitle the creator of it to the benefit of the exemption.'

It appears from *Overbrooke Estates Ltd* v *Glencombe Properties Ltd* [1974] 1 WLR 1335 that a trader could successfully avoid this result by exhibiting a notice or incorporating a term in the contract stating that its employees had no authority to add to or vary the terms of the agreement. Such a clause does not appear to be subject to s3 of the Misrepresentation Act 1967.

There has been an independent oral undertaking. In *Couchman* v *Hill* [1947] KB 554, the plaintiff, a farmer, purchased at an auction a heifer belonging to the defendant. He required an unserved heifer for service by his own bull and at the sale he asked both the defendant and the auctioneer whether they could confirm that the heifer was unserved. Both told him that this was the case. In fact she was found to be in calf and died as a result of carrying a calf at too young an age. The farmer's claim for breach of warranty was resisted by reference to clauses in the sale catalogue and the conditions of sale.

HELD: The exclusion clauses could not be relied upon because they were overridden by the oral promise.

This principle has also been applied in *Mendelssohn* v *Normand* [1970] 1 QB 177 and *J Evans and Son (Portsmouth) Ltd* v *Andrea Merzario Ltd* [1976] 1 WLR 1078.

Non est factum. If the consumer can show that the document which has been signed is radically different from that which he believed he was signing on the principles set out in *Saunders* v *Anglia Building Society* [1971] AC 1004, it will be possible to have the contract declared void.

Incorporation where no document is signed

Often the exclusion clause will be contained or referred to, not in a document that the purchaser has signed, but in an unsigned document which has been given to him or in a notice displayed on the trader's premises. Good examples are railway tickets or notices found in car parks. To determine whether such clauses are effective to exclude liability a number of questions must be considered: is the document contractual; has reasonably sufficient notice been given; when was the notice given; has the clause been incorporated by a course of dealing?

Is the document contractual? It must be shown that the document relied on as containing the exclusion clause is an integral part of the contract. It must be shown that the document was intended to have contractual force.

In *Chapleton* v *Barry Urban District Council* [1940] 1 KB 532 the plaintiff hired a deck chair from the defendants for three hours. He paid 2d and was given a ticket which he did not read. It contained an exemption clause which the defendants sought to rely on when the plaintiff was injured through their negligence.

HELD: The defendants could not rely on the exclusion clause printed on the ticket as it was merely a voucher or receipt which no one would expect to contain the terms of a contract. This approach has been approved by the House of Lords in *McCutcheon* v *David McBrayne Ltd* [1964] 1 WLR 125. The defendants operated steamers between the Scottish mainland and Hebridean islands. An oral contract was made with the plaintiff for the shipment of his car and on the voyage the car was lost as a result of the defendants' negligence. The defendants relied on exclusion clauses contained in 27 paragraphs of small print displayed both inside and outside their office. These terms were also printed on a risk note which customers usually signed, though, on this occasion, the plaintiff had not done so. The only document involved was a receipt for the freight paid stating that 'all goods were carried subject to the conditions set out in the notices.' Neither the plaintiff nor his agent who had made the contract had read the words on the notices or the receipt.

HELD: The receipt was not a contractual document and the exclusion clauses were not incorporated.

Has reasonably sufficient notice been given? It is not necessary to show that the exclusion clause has actually been brought to the attention of the consumer. The test as set out in *Parker* v *South Eastern Railway* (1877) 2 CPD 416 is whether the notice in all the circumstances of the case is reasonably sufficient. Each case depends on its own facts.

In *Richardson, Spence and Company* v *Rowntree* [1894] AC 217 the plaintiff had contracted with the defendants to travel from Philadelphia to Liverpool. On paying her fare she received a ticket containing a number of terms, one of which limited the defendants' liability to £100. The ticket was handed to her folded up and the terms were also partially obliterated. The jury found that the plaintiff knew there was writing on the ticket though she did not know that the writing contained terms of the contract.

HELD: that there was evidence on which the jury could come to the conclusion that sufficient notice had not been given of the terms.

In *Thomson* v *LMS Railway* [1930] 1 KB 40 the plaintiff, who was illiterate, purchased an excursion ticket. The ticket contained the words 'For conditions see back'; and on the back of the ticket were the words 'Issued subject to the company's timetables and notices and excursion and other bills.' Had she looked at the timetable, which she would have had to buy, she would have found amongst the conditions the following: 'Excursion tickets ... are issued subject to ... the condition that neither the holders nor any other person shall have any right of action against the company ... in respect of ... injury (fatal or otherwise), loss, damage or delay, however caused.' The plaintiff was injured as a result of the negligence of the defendants' employees.

HELD: The plaintiff was bound by the exclusion clause because the defendants had done enough to bring it to the attention of travellers and the fact that the plaintiff was illiterate was irrelevant.

It should be noted that if the defendant knows of some disability of the consumer the same result will not follow (see *Geier* v *Kujawa* [1970] 1 Lloyd's Rep 364).

Unusual terms. Where the exclusion clause is unusual in that type of contract the trader may have to show that he took special care to bring it to the attention of consumers. In *J Spurling v Bradshaw* [1956] 1 WLR 461 Denning LJ said, obiter, that 'the more unreasonable a clause is, the greater the notice which must be given of it. Some clauses which I have seen would need to be printed in red ink on the face of the document with a red hand pointing to it before the notice could be held to be sufficient.'

He expressed similar views in *Thornton v Shoe Lane Parking Ltd* [1971] 2 QB 163. The plaintiff drove his car into a car park. As he approached the car park there was a notice setting out the charges and stating that all cars were 'parked at owner's risk'. There was a barrier where motorists stopped, received a ticket from an automatic machine and then proceeded into the garage where their cars were automatically parked. The ticket stated the time of arrival and that it was to be presented when the car was claimed. In one corner in small print were the words 'issued subject to condition ... displayed on the premises' and on a pillar opposite the ticket machine a set of conditions was displayed, one of which said that the defendants were not liable for any injury to the customer while his car was on the premises. The plaintiff was injured through the negligence of the defendants.

HELD: in the circumstances the defendants had not given sufficient notice of the conditions. While the steps taken might have been sufficient to incorporate a more usual exemption clause they were inadequate to give notice of one which purported to exclude liability for personal injury.

In *Interfoto Picture Library v Stiletto* [1988] 2 WLR 615, the Court of Appeal refused to apply a clause contained in a delivery note on the ground that it contained highly unusual terms which were much to the disadvantage of the person to whom they were addressed without adequately drawing them to that person's attention. This rule has come to be called the 'red hand rule' because of the well known dicta of Denning LJ, as he then was in *Spurling v Bradshaw* [1956] 1 WLR 461. He said 'some clauses would need to be printed in red ink with a red hand pointing to it' before the notice could be held to be sufficient.

When was the notice given? It is well settled that an exclusion clause will only be effective if it is brought to the attention of the other party at or before the time when the contract is made.

In *Olley v Marlborough Court Hotel* [1949] 1 KB 532 the plaintiffs booked a room at an hotel. They then went to the room where there was a notice stating that 'The proprietors will not hold themselves responsible for articles lost or stolen unless handed to the manageress for safe custody.' While they were out some of their belongings were stolen from the room.

HELD: The defendants could not rely on the exclusion clause because it had not been incorporated in the contract with the plaintiffs which was completed before they went to their room.

Exactly when a contract has been concluded and what terms are thus incorporated can give rise to difficulties as *Thornton* v *Shoe Lane Parking Ltd* (above) demonstrates, as does *Levison* v *The Patent Steam Carpet Cleaning Co Ltd* [1978] QB 69. Mrs Levison telephoned the defendants to ask them to collect a valuable carpet for cleaning. They agreed to do this and when their employee called he asked Mrs Levison to sign a document containing exclusion clauses which she did. The carpet and another rug were taken away for cleaning and subsequently lost. One problem here is to determine when the contract was made. Was it on the telephone or only when the document was signed? Somewhat surprisingly the Court of Appeal did not regard the telephone conversation as giving rise to a contract. They decided that it was either the result of a course of dealing or it was concluded when the document was signed.

Has the clause been incorporated by a course of dealing? Where trader and customer have dealt with each other on a number of occasions it may be possible to argue that an exclusion clause is part of the contract even though on the critical occasion it was not referred to explicitly.

In *Henry Kendall and Sons* v *William Lillico and Sons Ltd* [1969] 2 AC 31 the parties had contracted on more than 100 occasions over the previous three years. On each occasion there had been a verbal contract and then the next day a 'sold note' containing exclusion clauses was sent. The recipients of the notes knew that there were conditions on them but did not know precisely what they were as they had not read them. When the suppliers broke their contract with the purchasers they relied on the exclusion clauses.

HELD: Because there had been a lengthy and consistent course of dealing it must be assumed that the purchasers by their conduct were accepting the conditions in the sold notes and, thus, the suppliers could rely on the exclusion clauses. It is not necessary, contrary to an obiter dictum of Lord Devlin in *McCutcheon* v *David McBrayne Ltd* (above), that the party against whom the clause is used does not know what those terms are, provided that he has had every opportunity to discover them.

In practice it is unlikely that incorporation by a course of dealing will succeed very often in a consumer context as it will be difficult to show that the dealing has been both sufficiently lengthy and consistent. There have been extremely few commercial cases where the argument has succeeded and no consumer cases. In *McCutcheon* v *McBrayne* (above) the shipping company failed because the course of dealing was not consistent. On some occasions the plaintiff had been asked to sign a risk note and on others he had not. In *Hollier* v *Rambler Motors* [1972] 2 QB 71 a garage were unable to show that their written conditions were incorporated in a contract with motorist who had left his car with them for servicing on only three or four occasions in the previous five years.

There is a fundamental criticism of the course of dealing theory because it runs counter to a basic principle of contract law that terms cannot unilaterally be introduced after the contract has been concluded. In the classic situation where the doctrine is argued a supplier has agreed to supply goods over the telephone. At that point there is a binding contract. When later some other document is introduced this ought theoretically to have no effect on the contractual position. Nevertheless, the courts do accept the possibility of incorporation in this way and one must assume that it is an example of the more expansive and less doctrinaire approach to contract formation of which Lord Scarman spoke in *New Zealand Shipping Co Ltd* v *Satterthwaite (AM) & Co Ltd* [1975] AC 154.

7.3 Judicial control: interpretation

Strict construction and the contra proferentem rule

The hostility of the judges to exclusion clauses has been well demonstrated in the lengths that they were sometimes prepared to go to interpret the clauses in ways favourable to the party against whom it was sought to use the clause. Lord Denning in his judgment in *George Mitchell (Chesterhall) Ltd* v *Finney Lock Seeds Ltd* (supra) referred to these efforts as 'gymnastic contortions'. With the enactment of the Unfair Contract Terms Act 1977 such methods are less necessary though it is not altogether clear what the relationship between the Act and the interpretation rules now is.

The burden of proof in satisfying a court that the exclusion clause is reasonable falls on the plaintiff. In *Stewart Gill* v *Horatio Myer & Co Ltd* [1992] 2 All ER 257, the Court of Appeal decided that by virtue of s13 of the Unfair Contract Terms Act 1977 a clause forbidding the withholding of sums by way of 'set-off' was prima facie unreasonable. Since the plaintiffs were unable to establish reasonableness within the meaning of s13, the clause was considered unreasonable and unenforceable.

In *Photo Production Ltd* v *Securicor Ltd* (supra) the House of Lords criticised the artificial methods of construction and in *Ailsa Craig Fishing Co Ltd* v *Malvern Shipping Co Ltd* [1983] 1 WLR 964 it was emphasised that in interpreting exclusion clauses the language should be given its ordinary and natural meaning. A distinction was drawn between limitation clauses which limit to a certain sum the liability of one party and exemption clauses which seek to remove entirely the legal liability of one party. Limitation clauses are not to be construed as strictly as exemption clauses. The *Ailsa Craig* case made it clear that limitation clauses were to be construed differently.

While it is difficult to see just *why* limitation clauses should be construed less rigidly than exclusion clauses the distinction has nevertheless been approved in *George Mitchell* v *Finney Lock Seeds* (supra).

Palmer (1982) 45 MLR 322 points out that some limitation clauses are so close to zero (1.8 per cent in *Ailsa Craig* and 0.33 per cent in *Finney Lock Seeds*) that they might almost be exclusion clauses anyway. Where this leaves that, admittedly small, number of contracts not subject to the Unfair Contract Terms Act is not discussed.

One suspects that without explicitly saying so the courts will be influenced by the new climate created by the Act and will in practice permit reliance on exemption clauses which they consider to be reasonable.

The construction rules must now be applied in the light of the observations of the House of Lords referred to above, but it seems likely that where the clause is clearly inapt to cover the situation that has occurred reliance on the clause will not be possible and that some of the earlier cases are still good law.

In *Wallis, Son & Wells v Pratt & Haynes* [1911] AC 394 a contract for the sale of seed contained a clause excluding all warranties. The buyer had ordered 'common English sainfoin' but had been sent 'giant sainfoin' which was of inferior quality.

HELD: The seller was unable to rely on the exclusion clause because it covered only breaches of warranty not breaches of condition and the breach of the implied term about description was such a term.

In *Andrews Bros (Bournemouth) Ltd v Singer & Co Ltd* [1934] 1 KB 17 the seller sold a new Singer car and in the contract included a clause excluding 'implied conditions and warranties'. What was delivered was not a new car.

HELD: The exclusion clause did not protect the seller because it applied to implied terms while the term that had been broken was an express term.

Whether a case like *Beck v Szymanowski & Co Ltd* [1924] AC 43, which would seem to be an excellent example of what Lord Denning called 'gymnastic contortions', is still good law must be open to doubt.

Fundamental breach

This doctrine has been declared dead by the courts but seems to be taking an interminable time to die. The emphasis of the House of Lords in the *Photo Production* case on the fact that the scope of an exemption clause is always a question of construction seems to make it clear that the doctrine has no role. In *George Mitchell (Chesterhall) Ltd v Finney Lock Seeds Ltd* (above) Lord Bridge criticised the reasoning of Kerr LJ in the Court of Appeal as coming 'dangerously near to reintroducing by the back door the doctrine of "fundamental breach" which this House in the *Photo Productions* case had so forcibly ejected by the front'.

Negligence

The strict approach to exemption clauses by the judges has been particularly clearly shown in relation to clauses seeking to exempt one party from the consequences of his own negligence. While the existence of the Unfair Contract Terms Act obviates to a large extent the need to rely on judicial techniques they are not redundant in this area for the reasons given above. It is, therefore, worth recalling that clear words are required to exclude liability for negligence and that where a party can be made liable on some ground other than negligence the clause will be construed as applying to that other ground. The rationale of this rule was explained by Lord Buckley in *Gillespie Bros Ltd* v *Roy Bowles Transport Ltd* [1973] QB 400:

> 'it is inherently improbable that one party to the contract should intend to absolve the other party from the consequences of the latter's own negligence. The intention to do so must therefore be made perfectly clear for otherwise the court will conclude that the exempted party was only to be free from liability in respect of damage occasioned by causes other than negligence for which he is answerable.'

Exclusion clauses and third parties

In *Scruttons Ltd* v *Midland Silicones Ltd* [1962] AC 446 it was held that an exemption clause in a contract could not protect a person who was not a party to the contract such as an employee of that party. *New Zealand Shipping Co Ltd* v *Satterthwaite (AM) & Co Ltd* (above) shows that this application of the privity rule can be circumvented by the employer contracting as the agent of his employees.

Spencer v Cosmos Air Holidays (1989)

The recent case of *Spencer* v *Cosmos Air Holidays* (1989) The Times 6 December shows that a party seeking to rely on exclusion clauses in the contract cannot simply decide on his own initiative that if the other party is (whether this is correct or not) to some extent guilty of misconduct also, then the exclusion clauses(s) in question will be more likely to apply.

The conduct of the other party is irrelevant so far as the validity and incorporation of exclusion clauses is concerned.

7.4 The Unfair Contract Terms Act 1977

The background to the Act

Despite the best efforts of the judiciary they were bound to achieve limited success because they were working within the confines of an approach which acknowledged the supremacy of freedom of contract which, as Lord Devlin put it, 'included the freedom to oppress'. Some judges, notably Lord Denning, were prepared to go outside this framework and discover a general power to apply a reasonableness test as he did in a series of cases culminating in *Levison* v *The Patent Steam Carpet Cleaning Co Ltd* (above); but he was a voice crying in the wilderness. Legislation was required and following reports from the Law Commissions and pressure from consumer organisations the Unfair Contract Terms Act 1977 was passed and came into force on 1 February 1978.

Scope of the Act

The title of the Act is somewhat confusing in that it both understates and overstates the scope of the Act. The act does not deal with all terms in all contracts which might be considered unfair. For example, if the price is thought to be unduly high or the delivery date is one that gives a lot of latitude to the supplier these would not come within the scope of the Act. On the other hand the title of the Act is too narrow in that it applies not just to contract terms but, as s2 which deals with negligence liability makes clear, also deals with notices attempting to restrict or exclude liability for negligence.

Contracts excluded

Certain contracts are not subject to the Act. Section 26 exempts 'international supply contracts', that is, contracts for the sale of goods or those under or in pursuance of which the possession or ownership of goods passes and are made by parties whose places of business or habitual residences are in different states. In addition, the goods must be carried from the territory of one state to the territory of another, or the acts of offer and acceptance must have taken place in the territory of another, or the acts of offer and acceptance have taken place in the territories of different states, or the goods are to be delivered in the territory of a state different from the state in whose territory those acts were done (s13(4)).

Certain other contracts are not controlled by the Act. Section 1(2) states that in relation to s2 (negligence liability), s3 (liability in contract), s4 (indemnity contracts), and s7 (miscellaneous contracts under which goods pass), certain contracts are outside the scope of the Act. Of these probably the most significant are contracts of insurance. The others, most of which are not relevant to sale contracts, are contracts relating to the sale of land; contracts concerning industrial and intellectual property; contracts relating to the formation or dissolution of a company or its constitution; and any contract relating to the creation or transfer of securities or rights or interests therein. Contracts of marine salvage or towage, charterparties of ships or hovercraft, and contracts for the carriage of goods by ship or hovercraft are covered by s2(1), but subject to the above such contracts are not affected by ss2, 3, 4 and 7 except in favour of a person dealing as a consumer. Sections 2(2), 3 and 4 do not apply, except in favour of a person dealing as a consumer, to contracts where goods are carried by ship or hovercraft where that means of carriage is specified to be used for part of the journey or it is not excluded as the means of carriage.

The Act is stated in s1(3) to apply, with one minor exception, to business liability. The term 'business' is defined in s14 to include 'a profession and the activities of any government department or local or public authority'. Beyond this there is no definition of 'business' in the Act. In the marginal cases which might arise it will be necessary to consider the interpretation which has been placed on this term in other contexts. There is an extensive case law on it in the context of revenue law where stress is laid on the regularity with which transactions take place and the profit motive. In *Davies* v *Sumner* [1984] 3 All ER 831 Lord Keith referred in interpreting the phrase 'in the course of a trade or business' in the Trade Descriptions Act 1968, to the necessity for some degree of regularity.

The meaning of business liability according to s1(3):

'is liability for breach of obligations or duties arising:
a) from things done or to be done by a person in the course of a business (whether his own business or another's); or
b) from the occupation of premises used for business purposes of the occupier.'

The one situation where the Act applies to non-business liability is set out in s6(4). This provides that even non-business sale and hire-purchase contracts are subject to the controls in the Act. This is not a very important exception because in such sales there are a few implied terms to exclude and it is, in any event, rare to find exclusion clauses.

At various points the Act speaks of excluding and restricting liability. Earlier reference was made to Lord Diplock's definition of an exclusion clause in *Photo Production Ltd* v *Securicor Ltd* (above) as 'one which excludes or modifies an obligation ... that would otherwise arise by implication of law'. Clearly the Act catches a wider range of exclusion clauses than this, for in s13 it states:

'To the extent that this Part of this Act prevents the exclusion or restriction of any liability it also prevents -
a) making the liability or its enforcement subject to restrictive or onerous conditions;
b) excluding or restricting any right or remedy in respect of the liability, or subjecting a person to any prejudice in consequence of his pursuing any such right or remedy;
c) excluding or restricting rules of evidence or procedure; and (to that extent) ss2 and 5 - 7 also prevent excluding or restricting liability by reference to terms and notices which exclude or restrict the relevant obligation or duty.'

These provisions are essentially anti-avoidance provisions. Paragraph a) deals with clauses such as that considered in *Lally and Weller* v *George Bird (a firm)* (1980) unreported which stated that: 'the contractors shall not be liable for any such claim unless the same is made within such three days'. Paragraph (b) would catch clauses which purported to limit the remedies open to a buyer who had purchased defective goods to replacement of the article. Paragraph (c) deals with the sort of clause which reverses the burden of proof or states that the report of the seller's expert shall be conclusive.

The final part of s13(1) is also of considerable importance and is by no means easy to interpret. The idea behind it is to prevent traders achieving by means of certain terms or notices which exclude a particular duty the same result as they might have tried to achieve by means of a more traditional exclusion clause. For example, a clause or notice stating that a fairground operator cannot accept any duty of care to those who choose to visit his premises has, so far as someone who visits his premises is concerned the same effect as the more traditional clause stating that no liability is accepted for death or injury howsoever caused. In one case the technique is to prevent the primary duty arising in the first place, and in the other, while implicitly acknowledging the existence of such a duty, to exclude it.

However, while one can sympathise with the intentions of the draftsman of this part of the Act there are some real difficulties. The problem is to distinguish between attempts to cut down unreasonably on the degree of liability which a trader should owe to a customer while at the same time not interfering in the ability of the trader to define exactly what he is prepared to sell.

In addition to the extended meaning given to exclusion clauses by s13(1) it is important to note that s13(2) states that: 'an agreement in writing to submit present or future differences to arbitration is not to be treated under this Part of this Act as excluding or restricting any liability'. This provision could be inimical to the interests of consumers as it provides a legitimate means for a trader to avoid being taken to the courts. If the form of arbitration is a satisfactory one this may not matter; but there are some arbitration schemes which do not seem especially useful to consumers.

One final point which it is worth repeating is that in s11(2) the common law rules relating to the incorporation of terms in a contract are expressly preserved. Where the Act makes void the use of a term this will not be of any relevance. But where the test for whether an exclusion clause may be relied on is the reasonableness test then it makes sense to attempt to show that it is not part of the contract instead of relying on the inevitably uncertain exercise of judicial discretion.

Dealing as a consumer

Before looking in detail at the types of contract clause controlled by the Act it is necessary to look at the meaning of the phrase 'dealing as a consumer' or some variant of it which is frequently used in the Act and is defined in s12.

> '1) A party to a contract "deals as a consumer" in relation to another party if:
> a) he neither makes the contract in the course of a business nor holds himself out as doing so; and
> b) the other party does make the contract in the course of a business; and
> c) in the case of a contract governed by the law of sale of goods or hire-purchase, or by s7 of this Act, the goods passing under or in pursuance of the contract are of a type ordinarily supplied for private use or consumption.
> 2) But on a sale by auction or by competitive tender the buyer is not in any circumstances to be regarded as dealing as a consumer.
> 3) Subject to this, it is for those claiming that a party does not deal as consumer to show that he does not.'

It is to be noted that a consumer is not just one who does not make the contract in the course of a business but one who not 'hold himself out as doing so'. The simplest case is that of the consumer who obtains a trade card to enable him to buy at discount terms from a wholesaler.

Within this definition are some grey areas. What are goods 'of a type ordinarily supplied for private use or consumption'? Most cases will present no difficulty, but what of building materials or building machinery? These are fairly readily available at DIY shops so it is likely that they would be regarded as consumer goods. Much will depend on the frequency with which the goods are available to those outside the trade.

Another problem which has been the subject of litigation is whether goods will be treated as bought in the course of a business simply because they have been bought for use in a business. Suppose, for example that a firm of solicitors buys a carpet for their offices. This is an article which is 'ordinarily supplied for private use or consumption' so everything turns on whether it is to be regarded as a purchase 'in the course of a business'. Professor Atiyah in *The Sale of Goods* (7th edn) argues that it should not. A purchase does not, he argues, cease to be a consumer purchase just because it is made by a business: it must be made in the course of a business in the sense that it must be for processing or resale in the course of the business.

This approach has recently been adopted by the Court of Appeal in *R & B Customs Brokers Co Ltd* v *United Dominions Trust Ltd* [1988] 1 All ER 847. R & B Customs Brokers Ltd was a private company whose only directors and shareholders were a Mr Bell and his wife. It had been in business for five or six years as shipping brokers and freight forwarding agents. Mr Bell purchased a car from the defendants and intended that it should be for personal and company use. The case turned on whether the plaintiff in this situation came within the definition of 'deals as a consumer' in s12 of the Act.

HELD: applying *Davies* v *Sumner* (supra) that where a transaction was only incidental to a business activity a degree of regularity was required before the transaction could be said to be an integral part of the business carried on and so entered into the course of that business. The car was only the second or third vehicle acquired by the plaintiffs and so there was not a sufficient degree of regularity capable of establishing that the contract was anything more than part of a consumer transaction.

A similar decision at first instance involving a partnership rather than a company is *Peter Symmons & Co* v *Cook* (1981) 131 NLJ 758. The plaintiffs were a firm of surveyors who purchased a used Rolls-Royce from the defendant. It appears that the car was bought in the firm's name and with its money but there was no evidence that they used the car in the course of their business.

HELD: that the sale was a consumer sale within the meaning of s12. The object of the Unfair Contract Terms Act was to try and prevent an unfair inequality of bargaining strength between two parties to a contract of sale and for a sale such as this to fall within the Act it would have to be shown that the buying of cars formed at least an integral part of the buyer's business or a necessary incidental thereto.

This case must be treated with some reserve as the cases on which the judge relied, *Rasbora* v *JCL Marine Ltd* [1977] 1 Lloyd's Rep 645 and *Havering London Borough Council* v *Stevenson* [1970] 3 All ER 609, are not really in point. In *Rasbora* the purchaser was a limited company but it was not a commercial enterprise; and the *Havering* case held that a car-hire company which periodically sold off some of its cars did so in the course of a business for the purposes of the Trade Descriptions Act although the sales were only incidental to its main business. It should also be noted that the judge stressed that the onus of proof was on the defendant and that he had produced little evidence on this point.

7.5 Terms rendered void by the Act

Any exclusion or restriction of liability will be wholly ineffective in the cases below.

Liability for personal injury or death

By s2(1) in cases of business liability a party cannot by any contract term or notice exclude or restrict his liability for death or personal injury resulting from negligence to any person whether that person deals as consumer or not.

Guarantees relating to consumer goods

Section 5 deals with contracts in which 'guarantees' are provided relating to goods of a type ordinarily supplied for private use or consumption. The main ambit of the section is contracts between manufacturers and their customers under manufacturers' guarantees.

Section 5(1) provides that in cases of business liability a party cannot by means of a guarantee exclude or restrict liability for loss or damage arising from defects in the goods while in 'consumer use' and resulting from the negligence of a person concerned in the manufacture or distribution of the goods.

'Consumer use' covers all cases where a party does not have the goods in his possession solely for the purpose of business (ie where any private purpose is involved).

Sale of goods and hire purchase contracts

It is provided in s6(1) that liability for breach of the implied undertakings as to title, implied into contracts for the sale of goods and the hire purchase of goods by the SGA 1979 s12 and the Supply of Goods (Implied Terms) Act 1973 s8 respectively, cannot be excluded or restricted by reference to any contract term. This is so whether or not the parties 'deal as consumer'.

Section 6(2) provides that exclusions of implied terms in the SGA ss13-15 and in the Supply of Goods (Implied Terms) Act 1973 ss9-11 as to correspondence of goods with description, their quality or fitness for a particular purpose or their correspondence with sample are ineffective as against a person 'dealing as consumer'. So in contracts for the sale of goods the implied terms of ss13-15 SGA discussed at length in Chapter 5 cannot be excluded against a party 'dealing as consumer'. Exclusions as against other parties depends on the test of reasonableness below.

The interrelation of s1(3) UCTA (which declares that ss2-7 of the Act apply only to 'business liability') and s6 has given rise to some difficulty. This is because s6(4) provides that the liabilities referred to under s6 are not just business liabilities but include 'those arising under any contract of sale of goods or hire purchase agreement'.

The effect of s6(4) seems to be as follows:

1. Section 6(1) will apply to all contracts for sale of goods or hire purchase, whether in respect of business liability or not, and so in a private sale the seller cannot exclude or limit liability for breach of the SGA s12 implied undertakings as to title.
2. Although s6(4) might suggest that an exclusion or restriction of liability for breach of the implied undertaking as to description and quality regulated by s6(2) should be equally ineffective even where they relate to private transactions, it is generally agreed that this is not the case. This is because s6(2) applies only 'against a person dealing as consumer' and a person can only deal as consumer where the other party 'does make the contract in the course of a business' - s12(1)(b). So in a private sale neither party deals as consumer and the s6(2) provisions cannot apply. However, the buyer in a private sale will be protected by the requirement of reasonableness laid down by s6(3) and discussed below. Note also in this context that by the SGA itself the implied conditions of merchantable quality (s14(2)) and fitness for a particular purpose (s14(3)) themselves only apply where the supplier of goods acts 'in the course of a business'. If no liability therefore arises under these subsections, in other words where the supplier is not acting in the course of a business, then no issue as to the exclusion of liability can arise.

Contracts within s7 for the supply of goods

Section 7 covers contracts of exchange, pledge, hire purchase and other contracts for the supply of goods, other than contracts of sale or hire purchase. The Supply of Goods and Services Act 1982 ss2-5, 7-10 first introduced implied terms as to title, correspondence with description, quality and fitness for a particular purpose and correspondence with description into these contracts.

These contracts divide into two categories as regards implied undertakings as to title. If the contract is one (such as exchange) whereby one party agrees to transfer the property in the goods to the other, then exclusions or restrictions on breach of implied terms as to title are wholly ineffective. Where, however, the contract is one whereby no property is transferred such as hire or pledge then exclusions of such liability are only subject to the requirement of reasonableness.

In all contracts under s7, as against a party dealing as consumer, liability cannot be excluded or restricted in respect of any breach of the implied undertakings as to correspondence with description, sample, or as to quality and fitness for a particular purpose.

Section 7 applies only to 'business liability'.

7.6 Terms subject to the reasonableness test

The second technique adopted by the Act is to make some terms subject to a test of reasonableness laid down in s11 and Schedule 2 of the Act. The Act imposes this requirement on exclusion clauses which are not regarded as being as unfair as those under 7.5, but which must nonetheless not be allowed to deprive the other of his protection in law except in so far as such deprivation is reasonable.

It is for the person alleging that a term (or notice) is reasonable to show that it is so (s11(5)). The following are terms made subject to the test:

Liability for loss or damage from negligence other than personal injury or death

Exclusions or restrictions of this type of liability are by s2(2) made subject to the test of reasonableness.

Contracts covered by s3

Section 3 is complex and gives rise to a number of problems of interpretation. It has been noted that s3 applies to two situations:

1. Where one party deals with another who 'deals as consumer';
2. Where one party deals with another on the latter's 'written standard terms of business'.

Section 3 applies only to business liability. It provides that a person who deals with a consumer or on his own written standard terms of business:

> 'cannot by reference to any contract term -
> a) when himself in breach of contract, exclude or restrict any liability of his in respect of the breach; or
> b) claim to be entitled:
> i) to render a contractual performance substantially different from that which was reasonably expected of him, or
> ii) in respect of the whole or any part of his contractual obligation, to render no performance at all ...
> except in so far as the term is reasonable.'

At first sight there appears to be a substantial overlap between s3(2)(a) and (b). However, it is generally accepted that s3(2)(a) applies as stated to situations where the party's default in performance actually amounts to a breach of the contract and s3(2)(b) applies where the default although of a type specified in s3(2)(b)(i) or (ii) does not actually amount to a breach. This view is adopted by, among others, Cheshire and Fifoot. Section 3(2)(b) is necessary to catch cleverly worded contracts in which acts which would otherwise be obvious breaches are stated to be non-breaches.

Cheshire and Fifoot note that s3(2)(b) may now catch many clauses which have never before been considered as exclusion clauses. The example quoted is of a machine-tool supplier providing in his standard conditions that payment terms should be 25 per cent with order and 75 per cent on delivery and that he should be under no obligation to start manufacture until the initial payment is made. Such a clause case may now be subject to the reasonableness test under s3(2)(b)(ii), although it would certainly pass that test.

Section 3(2)(b)(i) appears to create a dual test of reasonableness, involving a contractual performance 'substantially different from that which was reasonably expected' of a party. It might appear that delivery of a contractual performance substantially different from that reasonably expected could not be reasonable, but this is not so. For example the substitute performances could be better than the performance required by contract: such a performance would obviously be reasonable.

Sale of goods and hire purchase contracts

Where the buyer or hire purchaser deals otherwise than as consumer, then s6(3) applies the reasonableness requirement to any term in the contract of sale or hire purchase which excludes or restricts liability for breach of the statutory implied terms as to correspondence with description, as to quality or fitness for a particular purpose and as to correspondence with sample (these are implied into sales by the SGA ss13-15 and into hire purchase contracts by the Supply of Goods (Implied Terms) Act 1973 ss9-11).

By s6(4), s6 is not restricted to cases of 'business liability'; so terms in a private sale excluding liability for the implied terms in ss13-15 SGA will also be subject to the reasonableness requirement. Note, however, that the implied terms in the SGA as regards merchantable quality and fitness for a particular purpose only arise where the supplier 'acts in the course of a business' so if there is no implied term anyway (as in a wholly private sale), then there can be no liability to be excluded. A private seller could, of course, give an express undertaking as to merchantable quality or fitness of the goods and nothing in the Act prohibits the restriction of liability for breach of such an express undertaking.

Contracts falling under s7

Section 7(3) lays down a similar rule to that in s6(3) for contracts covered by s7 for breaches of similar statutory terms implied into these contracts. A difference is that s7 applies only to 'business liability' and its exclusion or restriction, whereas there is no such restriction in s6 because of s6(4).

A further category of terms made subject to the reasonableness test has been noted already. In contracts under s7 under which no property in goods is to be transferred any exclusion or restriction of liability for breach of an implied term as to title is by s7(4) made subject to the requirement of reasonableness. This will apply, for example, to contracts of hire or pledge. However, if property is to pass under the contract (as in a contract of exchange), then such exclusions on title are totally ineffective.

Section 7(4) again only applies to 'business liability', so the private supplier's rights to exclude liability on defective title are unaffected.

Contract terms falling within s4

Section 4 controls the operation of so-called indemnity clauses, whereby a businessman imposes an obligation on a consumer to indemnify himself or another person for the latter's negligence or breach of contract by subjecting the term to the requirement of reasonableness. The burden is on the party seeking to enforce the indemnity clause against the consumer to show that it is reasonable (s11(5)).

An example would be a car hire contract containing a promise by the hirer to indemnify the hire company for any loss caused by the driver's negligence.

Section 4 applies only to business liability, and applies only in favour of a consumer.

Liability for misrepresentation: s8

Section 8 UCTA amends s3 of the Misrepresentation Act 1967 to incorporate into the Misrepresentation Act (the MA) the requirement of reasonableness in the UCTA. Section 3 MA had originally applied a requirement of reasonableness to terms excluding or restricting liability for misrepresentation, but now these terms are made subject to the new statutory test of reasonableness in the UCTA s11 and Schedule 2.

Section 9

Section 9 does not strictly create a category of terms subject to the reasonableness test. Its object when passed was to abolish the rule in *Harbutt's Plasticine Ltd* v *Wayne Tank & Pump Co Ltd* [1970] 1 QB 447; [1970] 1 All ER 225. This case laid down that where a contract was discharged for a 'fundamental' breach, the guilty party could no longer rely on an exemption clause even if the breach occurs before the contract is discharged. Section 9 abolished this rule at least for contract terms to which the requirement of reasonableness applied, although the common law still applied to other contractual terms.

However, the common law rule of *Harbutt's Plasticine* has itself been changed as a result of two House of Lords cases: the *Suisse Atlantique Société d'Armement Maritime SA* v *NV Rotterdamsche Kolen Centrale* [1967] 1 AC 361; [1966] 2 All ER 61 and *Photo Production Ltd* v *Securicor Transport Ltd* (supra). The rule is now that a so-called fundamental breach or a breach going 'to the root of the contract' does not disallow the guilty party from relying on any exclusion clauses. The only question is as to whether as a matter of construction the parties could have intended that the party in breach should be entitled to rely on the clause in the situation in question. This is the same rule as has applied to terms which are subjected to the reasonableness test since 1977 because of s9.

7.7 The reasonableness test

The test of reasonableness in the Act is laid out in s11 and Schedule 2. To satisfy the test a term should be 'a fair and reasonable one to have been included, having regard to the circumstances which were, or ought reasonably to have been, known to or in the contemplation of the parties when the contract was made' (s11(1)). A non-contractual notice which is subject to the reasonableness test ought to be fair and reasonable 'having regard to all the circumstances obtaining when the liability arose' (s11(3)). This latter test will apply, for example, to a notice purporting to exclude liability for property damage caused by negligence or breach of the occupier's liability duty.

In contract cases the crucial time for the assessment of reasonableness is the time of formation of the contract, and in non-contractual cases it is the time of the proffering of the notice. One does not consider what has happened after the contract has been made.

Situations will vary from contract to contract, notice to notice, but there is nothing in the Act to make it possible for a party to be absolutely certain in advance that a particular contractual term or notice will be upheld.

A 'notice' in this context includes 'an announcement, whether or not in writing, and any other communication or pretended communication' (s14).

The requirement of reasonableness is to be satisfied by the party claiming that a contract term or notice is reasonable (s11(5)).

The Act states that when considering the test of reasonableness under ss6 and 7 of the Act, particular regard shall be had to the guidelines laid down in Schedule 2. It seems therefore that potentially two kinds of reasonableness may develop: one for ss6 and 7 and another for the other sections, but, in practice, notions about reasonableness developed in relation to one section will in fact influence the considerations of reasonableness in other sections. The 'guidelines' laid down in Schedule 2 will therefore inevitably be relevant under all considerations of reasonableness in the Act although not expressed to be so.

The 'guidelines' to be considered set out in Schedule 2 are as follows:

1. The strength of the bargaining positions of the parties relative to each other, taking into account (among other things) alternative means by which the customer's requirements could have been met.
2. Whether the customer received an inducement to agree to the term, or in accepting it had an opportunity of entering into a similar contract with other persons, but without having to accept a similar term.
3. Whether the customer knew or might reasonably have been expected to have known of the existence and extent of the term (having regard, among other things to any custom of the trade and any previous course of dealing between the parties).
4. Where the term excludes or restricts any relevant liability if some condition is not complied with, whether it was reasonable at the time of the contract to expect that compliance with that condition would be practicable.

5. Whether the goods were manufactured, processed or adapted to the special order of the customer.

With regard to limitation clauses, if a person seeks to restrict liability to a sum specified in a contract term or notice and the question arises as to whether it is reasonable, particular regard is to be had to the resources available to him in order to meet the liability should it arise and the availability of insurance cover (s11(4)). It seems to be the case that financial resources and the availability of insurance cover will also be considered in cases falling outside this last sub-section (ie in cases of exclusion, not limitation, of liability). There seems to be no reason why such considerations should not if relevant be taken into account: the House of Lords' reasoning in *Photo Production* v *Securicor Transport* suggests it is legitimate to take into account the fact that one party can more efficiently insure against the risk.

Section 11(4) itself was intended to meet the problem of consequential loss where the quantum is disproportionately large in relation to the amount which is involved in the contract and insurance cover is difficult to obtain. An example would be a manufacturer of burglar alarms who may be faced with a very large claim in the event of one of his alarms failing to work properly although the actual cost of installation of that alarm may have been very small in relation to the probable claim. Taken at face value, the sub-section seems to penalise prosperous businesses in that liability may well depend on whether the party liable is solvent or not, or on the size of his business.

In the context of s11(4) and the relevance of insurance cover, the Court of Appeal stated in *George Mitchell Ltd* v *Finney Lock Seeds Ltd* (supra) that a clause limiting the liability of a manufacturer for defects would normally not be reasonable if he could have insured against the liability without materially raising the price of the product.

The guidelines in (1) to (5) have been the subject of much academic commentary and, perhaps surprisingly, little litigation. Although stated to be relevant only to cases under ss6 and 7 it seems to be generally agreed that they will influence 'reasonableness' decisions in the other sections. It is difficult to see why the scope of the guidelines was restricted to ss6 and 7; in particular with guideline (1) one cannot see why the strength of the parties' bargaining positions is relevant only to contracts for the supply of goods and not to other contracts. Treitel points out the anomaly that the five guidelines apply where a seller delivers goods of the wrong quality (subjected to the reasonableness test by s6(3)) but not where he delivers goods of the wrong quantity (subjected to the reasonableness test by s3 if made on 'written standard terms of business').

Another odd feature of the guidelines is that it is not clear in whose favour guideline (5) stands. In other words, if goods are made to special order does that make it more reasonable or less reasonable to exclude or limit liability? Cheshire and Fifoot think either is possible depending on the circumstances of the case.

Turning to the case law, there has been remarkably little litigation on the reasonableness test and only one case has so far reached the House of Lords and that related to the earlier Supply of Goods (Implied Terms) Act 1973. However,

Lord Bridge in that case, *George Mitchell (Chesterhall) Ltd* v *Finney Lock Seeds Ltd* (above), made some comments of general importance on the reasonableness test and expressly said that his comments were relevant to the Unfair Contract Terms Act. He said:

> 'It would not be accurate to describe such a decision as an exercise of discretion. But a decision under [the Supply of Goods (Implied Terms) Act or the Unfair Contract Terms Act] will have this in common with the exercise of a discretion, that ... the court must entertain a whole range of considerations, put them in the scales on one side or the other and decide at the end of the day on which side the balance comes down. There will sometimes be room for a legitimate difference of judicial opinion as to what the answer should be, where it will be impossible to say that one view is demonstrably wrong and the other demonstrably right. It must follow, in my view, that, when asked to review such a decision on appeal, the appellate court should treat the original decision with the utmost respect and refrain from interference with it unless satisfied that it proceeded on some erroneous principle or was plainly and obviously wrong.'

In the *George Mitchell* case the plaintiffs had contracted on the defendants' standard form for the purchase of cabbage seed. When planted it turned out to be of very inferior quality and the plaintiffs sued for breach of contract including in their claim their loss of profit on the crop. The defendants relied on an exemption clause limiting their liability to the value of the seed. It was held by the House of Lords that the clause was not fair and reasonable because it was proved in evidence that it was the practice of the defendants to make *ex gratia* payments where there had been crop failure. It was also of importance that the defendants could have insured against this kind of loss; and that the standard terms had not been negotiated with any organisation representing potential purchasers.

A case which can usefully contrasted with *George Mitchell* and which also applied the test as found in the Supply of Goods (Implied Terms) Act is *R W Green Ltd* v *Cade Bros Farm* [1978] 1 Lloyd's Rep 602. The plaintiff seed potato merchants had been in regular dealings with the defendants who ran a farm. All contracts were for the sale of seed potatoes and were made on the standard conditions of the National Association of Seed Potato Merchants. It was the reasonableness of two of these conditions which was is issue in the case. These were:

1. that the buyer must notify the seller of any rejection claim or complaint within three days of the arrival of the seeds at their destination; and
2. that any claim for compensation against the seller should amount to a figure no greater than the contract price of the potatoes.

Twenty tons of seed potatoes delivered under one contract were found to be infected by a potato virus; so when sued for the price of the potatoes the defendant counterclaimed loss of profits for the virus. It was found that the virus was not discoverable by inspection at delivery. The defendant had not claimed within the three days specified in the contract.

Griffiths J held:

1. that the condition excluding liability where complaint was not made in three days was unreasonable; and
2. that the condition limiting liability to the contract price was reasonable.

It was held to be relevant that it would have been very difficult for the buyers to obtain seed potatoes on any other terms or conditions and that the conditions had been widely in operation for a long period and had been openly discussed between the National Association and the National Farmers Union. The judge concluded that guidelines (a) (accounting 'alternative means by which the customer's requirement could have been met') and (e) (whether the customer knew or ought reasonably to have known of the existence and extent of the term) went towards the terms being reasonable. However he held the three-day period for complaints to be unreasonable when applied to the present case since the defect in question was a virus not detectable by inspection; it was in these circumstances unreasonable to expect all complaints within three days of delivery.

The case also illustrates that it is perfectly possible for a particular term to be reasonable given one set of circumstances and unreasonable in regard to another set of circumstances.

Another case under the earlier Act is of some assistance. The facts of *Rasbora* v *JCL Marine Ltd* (supra) have already been given. This was a case under the 'reasonableness' requirement of the old SGA (1893) s55(4) and (5) under provisions which would now be covered by s6 UCTA. The court gave as an alternative ground for their decision in that case that the total exclusion of liability clause would not have passed the reasonableness test stating 'it is not fair or reasonable ... to allow reliance on a clause depriving the buyer of any remedy at all in circumstances where by fault of the seller the yacht had an electrical defect causing a total loss within 27 hours of delivery'. This decision might well be different today since under the UCTA test there is no account of such subsequent factors: the time for testing reasonableness is at the contract.

British Airways Board v *British Airports Authority* (1981) The Times 8 May is also helpful here. This case involved the conditions of use issued by the British Airports Authority to airline companies. These are not in fact contractual terms (the authority is obliged by statute to provide facilities) so the reasonableness test is slightly different. For contract terms the test is fairness and being in the reasonable contemplation of the parties at the contract, but for non-contractual terms, s11(3) UCTA provides: 'in relation to a notice not having contractual effect the requirement of reasonableness where it applies is that it must be shown to be fair and reasonable to allow reliance on the notice ... with regard to the circumstances obtaining when the liability arose.'

One condition laid down by the authority was that it should not be liable for loss or damage to any aircraft or property in it resulting from any act, neglect or default of the authority or its servants unless done 'with intent to cause damage or recklessly knowing such damage will probably result'. The condition was made subject to the reasonableness test by s2(2) UCTA. It was held to be reasonable to allow reliance on this condition because: the condition would contribute to keeping costs down; and it would free the authority from involvement in disputes about incidents, the facts of which would be to a large extent unknown to them.

It is worth noting another condition of the authority which was in issue in the case, to the effect that airline operators using the airports were to indemnify the authority in respect of liabilities incurred by the authority to third parties. The UCTA did not apply to this condition (the only relevant provision was s4 on Indemnity Clauses which applies only to consumer contracts: there was not even a contract here). The court, however, did consider whether the condition was reasonable, deciding it to be unreasonable, and on that ground it declared the condition ultra vires the authority.

The relevance of choice was an important issue in *Woodman* v *Photo-Trade Processing Ltd* (1981) (unreported) Exeter County Court. The plaintiff had taken photographs of a friend's wedding which he took to the defendants for processing. They failed to return most of the photographs and when sued relied on a clause in their contract limiting their liability to the replacement of the lost films with new ones. The clause was held not to satisfy the reasonableness test because it excluded liability for negligence as well as accident; the evidence showed that there was no alternative to the defendants' terms as all other processors used the same terms; and the loss could have been covered by insurance by the defendants.

On the other hand in *Stevenson* v *Nationwide Building Society* (1984) 272 EG 663 the plaintiff had purchased a property relying on the accuracy of a valuation report prepared for the defendant. The report was prepared negligently and the plaintiff sued the society for the loss occasioned to him. The society relied on a notice disclaiming liability. In the circumstances the notice was held to be fair and reasonable as required by the Unfair Contract Terms Act because it was made clear that the valuation report was a limited report and that at greater expense it was possible to obtain a much fuller survey. It was also relevant in this case that the plaintiff was an estate agent who was familar with the difference between a building society valuation and survey and their different costs.

This case needs to be read in the light of the more recent case of *Smith* v *Bush* [1989] 2 WLR 790; [1987] 3 All ER 179. The facts were very similar, except that the plaintiff was a potential housebuyer who had no special knowledge, unlike the plaintiff in *Stevenson* who was an estate agent.

This case, on appeal to the House of Lords was heard at the same time as that in *Harris* v *Wyre District Council* [1989] 2 WLR 790. A differently constituted Court of Appeal had held in that case that the person responsible for the survey report was not liable. However, the Court of Appeal had approached the problem in a different way, ruling that the disclaimer prevented liability arising in the first place, so the question of reasonableness never arose.

Both cases concerned the liability of valuers to the purchasers of houses for negligence in preparing valuation reports. Their relevance for the sale of goods lies in the approach of the House of Lords in applying the reasonableness test. It is to be noted that Lord Griffiths emphasised the importance of the fact that the purchaser had little bargaining power; that he had little alternative source of supply for the valuation service; and that the defendant was insured and able to meet the loss.

In *Singer Co (UK) Ltd* v *Tees and Hartlepool Port Authority* [1988] 2 Lloyds Reps 164 the High Court in applying the reasonableness test and finding an exclusion test to be reasonable took into account that the parties were of equal bargaining power; that insurance was readily available; and that the clause was one of limitation rather than total exclusion of liability.

In *Waldron-Kelly* v *British Railways Board* [1981] 3 CL 33 the plaintiff's suitcase was lost by British Rail who, in answer to his claim for compensation relied on a term in their conditions of carriage relating compensation to the weight of the goods and not their value. On this basis the compensation payable would have been £27 whereas the value of the contents of the suitcase was £320. This exclusion clause was held not to be fair or reasonable.

In *Stag Line* v *Tyne Ship Repair Group, The Zinnia* [1984] 2 Lloyd's Rep 211 this case, which concerned a contract for the repair of a ship, is notable for some pointers to the attitudes of the courts towards the reasonableness test. Staughton J stated that:

'I would have been tempted to hold that all the conditions are unfair and unreasonable for two reasons: first they are in such small print that one can barely read them; secondly the drafting is so convoluted and prolix that one almost needs an LLB to understand them.'

It should be stressed that these remarks were obiter but it is interesting that they should be made in the context of a commercial contract where it was held that the parties were of equal bargaining strength and, presumably, had persons with LLBs look over the contract. In the same case a clause which gave the plaintiff a remedy only if the ship was returned to the defendants' repair yard was held not to be reasonable as it could operate capriciously.

Two cases under the Misrepresentation Act 1967 are also instructive as exclusion of liability for misrepresentation is subject to the test of reasonableness set out in s11(1) of the Unfair Contract Terms Act.

In *Walker* v *Boyle* [1982] 1 WLR 495 the vendor of property innocently misrepresented that there were no disputes regarding boundaries. When the purchaser claimed rescission the vendor relied on condition 17(1) of the National Conditions of Sale which stated that 'no error, mis-statement or omission in any preliminary answer concerning the property ... shall annul the sale'. It was held that this term was unreasonable. The fact that it was a term of a widely used standard form did not save it; for while 'there are common-form clauses which have been evolved by negotiation between trade associations, associations of merchants or associations of growers or trade unions or other such bodies concerned to protect the rights of their members, which can be regarded as representing what consensus in the trade regards as reasonable ... the National Conditions of Sale are not the product of negotiation between such bodies'.

In *South Western General Property Co Ltd* v *Marton* (1982) 263 EG 1090 auction particulars described property as 'long leasehold building land' but failed to disclose that there were restrictions on development which, had he known of them, would have decided the purchaser not to buy. When the buyer refused to complete on the grounds of innocent misrepresentation and the plaintiff claimed for loss on resale the plaintiff relied on disclaimers in the catalogue stating that no representations were given with regard to the land, and that intending purchasers should satisfy themselves that the particulars in the catalogue were correct. The disclaimer failed to satisfy the reasonableness test. The matter which had been represented was of great importance to the purchaser and it was also significant that many potential purchasers attended auctions at short notice and would not have an opportunity to verify the particulars.

In *Singer Co (UK)* v *Tees & Hartlepool Port Authority* [1988] 2 Lloyd's Rep 164 damage caused to cargo during loading by the defendant port authority formed the basis of a claim by the plaintiff. The question arose as to whether the defendants could rely on general exclusion clauses contained in their standard form contract. The shipping note advising the plaintiff of loading details and supplied at the time of making the contract contained all the relevant terms and the clauses did not attempt to exclude liability for negligence altogether. The court held that, given all the circumstances, the clauses were reasonable in the light of the UCTA reasonableness test and the defendant could rely on them.

What seems to be clear from the statute and the few cases, none of which is directly in point, is that the courts do have a wide discretion in applying the reasonableness test. Sealy (1978) CLJ 15 argues that the provision of a reasonableness test is an abandonment of initiative by the law makers to the courts and that in principle the law should try to preserve certainty where possible. It is evident now that there has not been extensive litigation to sort out the uncertainties of the new statutory reasonableness test.

To an extent this is an area which does not readily lend itself to precise legal definitions so the provision of such a flexible test is understandable. The flexibility given could allow the court to reach just decisions on the fact but too much uncertainty in the context particularly of commercial contracts cannot be a good thing. The uncertainty does affect both sides, and it should really be the case in commercial sales at least that each party know exactly where he stands.

7.8 Anti-avoidance provisions

There are three means adopted by the Act to prevent the evasion of its provisions by use of ingeniously drafted contracts. The first of these has already been considered in 7.6 above: s4 on indemnity clauses.

An indemnity clause could in theory be used to avoid the effects of the UCTA by making one party indemnify the other for any liabilities which he is held to be under. Where for example the seller of goods inserts an indemnity clause in his contract with the buyer, whereby the buyer is to indemnify the seller against any legal liabilities in particular against claims by the buyer, then any action by the buyer against the seller is nullified. Such a clause operates very much like an exclusion clause. Section 4 now makes indemnity clauses subject to the reasonableness test and prevents exclusion of liability by avoiding the Act.

Two other possible ways of avoiding the UCTA are dealt with by the Act: evasion by use of secondary contracts; and evasion by use of choice of law clauses.

Evasion by use of secondary contracts

Section 10 provides:

> 'A person is not bound by any contract term prejudicing or taking away rights of his which arise under, or in connection with the performance of, another contract, so far as these rights extend to the enforcement of another's liability which this part of this Act prevents that other from excluding or restricting.'

Were it not for this section a party would be able to exclude liability by having the exclusionary term not in the principal contract itself but in another secondary contract.

One example which has been used in this context is a contract to buy a TV set with a related maintenance contract. The sale would clearly fall within s6 preventing exclusion of the SGA implied terms and any purported exclusion of the SGA implied terms and any purported exclusion in the maintenance contract relating to the main contract would under s10 not be binding.

A number of problems arise under s10 since it does not adopt the same terminology used in the rest of the Act. It refers to a contract term 'prejudicing or taking away rights' and not to one 'excluding or restricting liability'. The statutory definition of terms 'excluding or restricting liability' in s13(1) consequently will not apply to s10 and could leave it open to a different interpretation.

Another problem focused on by Treitel is that s10 may not apply to contract terms coming within s3(2)(b) (supra), that is, terms purporting 'to entitle a party to render a performance substantially different from that reasonably expected of him, or to render no performance at all'. This is because s10 refers to 'the enforcement of another's liability which ... this Act prevents the other from excluding or restricting', whereas s3(2)(b) does not deal with the exclusion or restriction of liability but with entitlements to render a performance substantially different. It might, however, be thought that the court would ignore the different in terminology and apply s10 to s3(2)(b).

It remains to be seen if the courts will exempt perfectly genuine renegotiations of contracts from the ambit of s10. In theory such a genuine renegotiation which happens to take away some rights in the first contract would be subject to s10, a position which was surely not intended.

Evasion by use of choice of law clauses

Another means of evading the Act would be to provide in a contract which would otherwise be subject to English law (and therefore to the UCTA) that it should be governed by the law of another country which has no equivalent to the UCTA. Section 27(2) provides that the UCTA will still have effect notwithstanding the existence of such a term where (either or both):

> 'a) the term appears to the court, or arbitrator or arbiter to have been imposed wholly or mainly for the purpose of enabling the party imposing it to evade the operation of this Act; or
> b) in the making of the contract one of the parties dealt as consumer, and he was then habitually resident in the UK, and the essential steps necessary for the making of the contract were taken there, whether by him or by others on his behalf.'

Under s27(2)(a) it should be noted that the term must be 'imposed' which suggests a deliberate, strong act. There also seems to be a need in s27(2)(a) to inquire into the motive of the party imposing the term, for this must be 'wholly or mainly for the purpose' of evading the Act. The motive will often be unclear.

Under s27(2)(b) the main question to be answered is as to what amounts to 'the essential steps'; does this mean all essential steps? Presumably it includes offer, acceptance and probably communication of acceptance.

7.9 Miscellaneous provisions

Part III of the Act

Part III of the Act contains a number of miscellaneous provisions which apply to the whole of the United Kingdom.

As we have seen already (7.4: Contracts excluded s26 exempts 'international supply contracts' from the provisions of the Act restricting exemption clauses. Section 27 dealing with evasion of the Act by use of a choice of law clause has already been discussed above (7.8). Briefly, the effect of s27(2) is that in commercial contracts, unless the choice of law clause appears to the court to have been inserted as an evasion device, the old law in exemption clauses will apply.

Section 28 makes temporary provision for contracts involving the sea carriage of passengers, where the provisions of the Athens Convention do not have the force of law in the United Kingdom in relation to the contract. Where the contract is not made in the United Kingdom and neither the place of departure nor the place of destination under it is in the United Kingdom, a person may exclude or restrict liability for loss or damage which could arise under the contract if the provisions of the Athens Convention had the force of law in relation to it (s28(2)). In any other case a person may exclude or restrict liability for that loss or damage in so far as such exclusion would have been effective had the contract been governed by the provisions of the convention or in such circumstances and to the extent prescribed by a term of the contract (s28(3)).

The Athens Convention is embodied in the Merchant Shipping Act 1979 but this Act is not yet in force. Section 28 was intended to cover this transitional period. The Convention itself provides that the carrier is liable for death or personal injury or loss of or damage to luggage caused during the course of carriage resulting from the fault or neglect of the carrier or his servants or agents acting in the scope of their employment, such fault or neglect being presumed until the contrary is proved. Liability is limited to certain amounts depending upon the loss or damage caused unless the act or omission causing it was done with intent to cause damage or recklessly.

Section 29 covers contractual provisions in the nature of exemption clauses allowed by United Kingdom legislation implementing international conventions. An example of such legislation is the Carriage by Air Act 1961. The Act does not affect contractual terms authorised or required by the express terms or necessarily implied by legislation or made in order to comply with an international agreement to which the UK is a party, if it is not more restrictive than the terms of the agreement (s29(11)). Also, a contract term is deemed to be reasonable for the purposes of Part I if it is incorporated or approved by, or incorporated pursuant to a decision or ruling of a 'competent authority' acting within its statutory jurisdiction or function where that authority is not a party to the contract (s29(2)).

7.10 Conclusions

Effect upon consumers

Until a greater body of case law on the interpretation of the Act has been laid down it is not possible fully to assess its significance. In theory at least the Act marks another advance in the development of greater consumer protection.

Thus the position of the consumer regarding claims for personal injury or death, or disputes arising from the use of standard form contracts, indemnity clauses, guarantees and for breaches of statutory implied conditions have been improved. This improvement has been more significant with regard to larger claims. This is possibly because the consumer in the case of a small claim probably thinks that the pursuance of the claim is not justified by the amount involved. Another factor is probably the uncertainty of success should the case come to litigation. So although the Act may secure more perfect justice for larger claims the overall effect for the consumer is less significant than might have been expected.

The UCTA must of course be seen in the context of the previous consumer protection legislation. The Act represents a continuation of the development of granting greater legal rights to the consumer. In general the most effective provisions have been those which are backed by criminal sanctions administered by public bodies. Such statutory provisions affect consumers at large and have a wider impact than the availability of rights which can only be enforced by individuals. However, it must be said that for the wide-reaching controls of the UCTA, criminal sanctions rather than civil ones enforceable by individuals would have been a draconian measure.

The courts for their part seem to be taking a wide view of the term 'consumer', making much of the UCTA protection available over a wide area. It should perhaps be said that the effect of the UCTA in this area has been 'behind the scenes' in forcing larger retailers to modify their standard term contracts for fear of multiple actions by consumers and loss of custom.

Effect upon businessmen

The problem now of the businessman is one of uncertainty about the way in which the court will apply the test of reasonableness. As regards terms made totally ineffective by the Act his position is clear, but as regards those subject to the reasonableness requirement there is much ambiguity and uncertainty, and there have been few decided cases to resolve the problems.

It is not yet clear whether the courts' approach is going to be to view exemption clauses in the context of the contract as a whole or in isolation to determine its reasonableness. It may be submitted that if a clause is viewed in the context of the whole contract then a more equitable result is likely to be reached, whereas if the clause is viewed in isolation then a false view of the contract is likely to be taken as undue emphasis will be given to one part of the agreement. The Act certainly does not stipulate that the court should look at the whole contract, and for some commercial and consumer agreements it seems to favour the approach of looking just at the term in question. It should be noted however that in *George Mitchell* v *Finney Lock Seeds* (supra), albeit under a different reasonableness test, the court did take some consideration of the clause in the context of the whole contract.

The impact of the Act has been perhaps less than expected. One reason for this is that where a clause is struck down in one context this does not necessarily mean that this will happen in another contract in differing circumstances. Those clauses subject to the reasonableness test are invalid only to the extent they are unreasonable, so the same clause may be valid in relation to one contract and invalid in relation to another contract.

In the commercial sphere the requirement of reasonableness now applies to a wider range of terms, especially those restricting or excluding liability for a failure on one part to fulfill his obligations under the contract. Now a businessman faced with what he sees as an unreasonable term may ignore it on the ground that the other party should not be able to rely on it. Nothing in the Act prevents unreasonable terms being put into contracts: the Act only nullifies their effect. Such a businessman does however take a risk unless the clause is manifestly unreasonable, and in addition he will not want to become involved in expensive litigation to prove his point.

Nevertheless it seems that today's contract draftsmen do bear the UCTA very much in mind and it can probably be said that the Act has eliminated most manifestly unreasonable contract terms at least in contracts drawn up by the major commercial concern. However, the uncertainty still surrounding the status of some common terms may prolong their usefulness. Certainly no one seems anxious to litigate about them.

The factor of insurance and who ought to or can most conveniently insure against the risk concerned will be an important factor in commercial contracts, much more so than in consumer contracts. This may greatly influence the 'reasonableness' of any particular clause.

Overall conclusions

The lack of case law in the years since the Act came into effect in many ways serves to prolong the uncertainties created by it, particularly with regard to the reasonableness test. On the other hand the Act is undoubtedly having a significant effect on the drafting of contracts in both the commercial and consumer fields.

The courts have not really attempted to lay down standard tests to be applied to contractual terms and notices, nor have they had much opportunity to do so. It is probably true to say that the uncertainty which consequently prevails is interfering to some extent with the calculations by businessman of their possible risks.

The best indication of the courts' approach to tests of reasonableness is probably given in *George Mitchell Ltd* v *Finney Lock Seeds Ltd* (supra) which dealt in fact with a different statutory reasonableness test (that in s55(4) SGA). The indications are that the court will consider a wide range of factors, including presumably those in the guidelines even when not expressly relevant, and that the decision will be made in a practical even pragmatic way.

The effect of the Act is probably greater than might appear from the case law surrounding it, or lack of such. Perhaps the true significance of the UCTA lies in the undoubted effect it has had on the draftsman of standard contracts, particularly those used by the larger institutions.

8

The Passing of Property

8.1 Introduction
8.2 Unascertained goods
8.3 Specific goods
8.4 Reservation of rights of disposal: s19
8.5 Acceptance: s39

8.1 Introduction

It can be important to ascertain the exact point at which property in the goods passes from seller to buyer. This is an important question for several reasons. A number of consequences may follow the passing of property of which the more important are:

1. Unless otherwise agreed the risk of accidental loss or damage to the goods passes to the buyer (the problems of risk will be examined in more detail in Chapter 9).
2. The passing of property gives the seller the right to sue for the price.
3. When property has passed the buyer can, quite legitimately, sell the goods to a third party, even though he may not yet have paid the seller.
4. If there is a difference between the passing of property and the physical taking of possession, then the person physically in possession of the goods may, despite the fact that he is not the lawful owner, pass good title to an innocent third party taking in good faith (for more on this, see Chapter 10).
5. If a seller becomes insolvent while the goods are still in his possession the only circumstances in which the buyer can claim the goods are if property has passed or, exceptionally, if the court grants specific performance (see Chapter 14).

Criteria as to when property passes depend largely on whether the goods are unascertained or specific; terminology which was discussed earlier in 1.5.

8.2 Unascertained goods

The basic rule relating to unascertained goods is laid down in s16 which states: 'Where there is a contract for the sale of unascertained goods no property in the goods is transferred to the buyer unless and until the goods are ascertained.'

In 1989 problems posed by s16 were examined in a report of the Law Commission (Working Paper No 112: 'Rights to Goods in Bulk') and almost simultaneously a report from the Scottish Law Commission (Discussion Paper No 83: 's16 of SGA and s1 of Bills of Lading Act 1855') appeared. Extensive re-drafting of s16 is suggested, though the two reports do not coincide on possible reforms.

The property will only pass when the goods are 'appropriated' to the contract or are ascertained by exhaustion as explained below. This basic, negative rule in s16 is illustrated by the following cases.

In *Hayman* v *McLintock* (1907) SC 936 S owned 420 sacks of flour stored in his warehouse. S agreed to sell 100 of the sacks to B who paid and obtained a delivery order addressed to H authorising the removal of the 100 sacks. B did not remove the bags but instead obtained a storage order from H (an attornment signifying that H held 100 sacks for B). At no point were 100 sacks separated or appropriated to the contract. S then went bankrupt and his trustee in bankruptcy claimed to be entitled to all 420 sacks.

HELD: The property in the goods remained with S. The goods were at all times unascertained.

In *Laurie & Morewood* v *John Dudin & Sons* [1926] 1 KB 223 the property was held not to have passed in 200 quarters of maize which was part of an undivided larger bulk stored in a warehouse. The property cannot pass in an unidentified part of a larger bulk.

In *Re London Wine Co* [1986] PCC 121 specific bottles in store were not segregated to the buyers. On insolvency it was held that property had not passed. The case of *The Gosforth* (1987) (unreported, Rotterdam Commercial Court) deals with unsegregated cargo on ships.

These cases and others illustrate that if a seller becomes insolvent the buyer of unascertained goods is, since no property has yet passed, to be regarded as an unsecured creditor without legal or equitable rights in a share of the bulk goods.

There are however at least three doubtful cases in which the property has magically been held to pass in unascertained goods.

One such case is *Mount* v *Jay & Jay Ltd* [1960] 1 QB 159; [1959] 3 All ER 307. B here obtained a document of title to the goods (a delivery order) which were held in a warehouse. B resold the goods using the delivery order (under s47 this can destroy the unpaid seller's lien - see Chapter 11) and it was held that property passed under s25(1) (see Chapter 11: sale by a person having agreed to buy goods and having possession of a document of title with consent). The goods however remained unascertained. *Mount* must be seen as illogical and exceptional on this point. Unascertained goods will usually become ascertained and the property pass when they are 'appropriated to the contract', a phrase which appears in Rule 5 of s18 and which is discussed below. Before considering Rule 5 it must be noted that the cases show that in some situations, usually when there are a series of sales from a large consignment, unascertained goods may become ascertained by 'exhaustion'.

In *Wait & James* v *Midland Bank* (1926) 31 Com Cas 172 the owners of a bulk quantity of wheat in a warehouse made three contracts with B agreeing to sell 350, 250 and 600 quarters of wheat respectively. B took delivery of 400 quarters, but the remaining 800 quarters were still unseparated. The owners then pledged the remainder of the wheat in the warehouse (ie the amount in excess of the 800 quarters already contracted for) to the Midland Bank. The quantity pledged to the bank was then sold and delivered to a third party.

HELD: The 800 quarters remaining must be the goods contained in the contract with B - they had been ascertained by exhaust. Ascertainment by exhaustion occurs when all other goods from the source specified in the contract are used for other purposes (for example to satisfy other contracts) leaving only the quantity of goods necessary to satisfy the buyer's contract.

Karlshamns Oljefabriker v *Eastport Navigation Co ('The Elafi')* [1982] 1 All ER 208 is a further example. Buyers in Hamburg, Rotterdam and in Sweden contracted to buy copra out of a bulk loaded in the Philippines. 22840 tons were loaded. The plaintiff Swedish buyers contracted at first for 6000 tons and later for a further 840 tons. A total of 16 000 tons were unloaded in Rotterdam and Hamburg, however some 1000 tons of the remaining bulk was then damaged because of the unseaworthiness of the ship. The question arose as to whether the plaintiffs could sue on the ground that their goods were damaged. The court used the principle of ascertainment by exhaustion, since the remaining 6840 tons was all destined for the plaintiffs.

More commonly it will be Rule 5 of s18 which will be relevant in deciding when the property in unascertained goods has passed. Section 18 Rule 5(1) provides:

'Where there is a contract for the sale of *unascertained* or *future* goods *by description*, and goods of that description and in a *deliverable state* are *unconditionally appropriated* to the contract, either by the seller with the assent of the buyer, or by the buyer with the assent of the seller, the property in the goods thereupon passes to the buyer; and the assent may be *express* or *implied*, and may be given either *before* or *after* the appropriation is made.'

Section 18 Rule 5(2) provides:

'Where in pursuance of the contract, the seller delivers the goods to the buyer or to a carrier or other bailee ... (whether named by the buyer or not) for the purpose of transmission to the buyer, and does *not reserve the right of disposal*, he is to be taken to have *unconditionally appropriated* the goods to the contract.'

As a preliminary point it will be noted that Rule 5, and in particular Rule 5(2), must be read subject to s16: no property will pass if the seller delivers the goods to a carrier still mixed with other goods (see *Healey* v *Howlett & Sons* below).

Rule 5 like the other rules in s18 is subject to a contrary intention appearing under s17. It must be emphasised that in all cases under Rule 5 the other party must assent to the appropriation by the other.

The meaning of 'unconditional appropriation'

The most difficult and controversial issue raised by Rule 5 is as to the meaning of 'unconditionally appropriated'. Rule 5(2) is in effect merely an example of one case of unconditional appropriation.

Reference must here be made to the vast case law in this area. Two preliminary points can, however, be made. First, note that what amounts to an unconditional appropriation in one kind of sale may not amount to such in another. Secondly, on the meaning of 'unconditional', it would seem that an appropriation is not unconditional if the seller only intends to let the buyer have the goods on payment of the price.

A precise definition of 'unconditional appropriation' is exceedingly difficult if not impossible. One can at least say from the decided cases that where an unidentified part of a bulk is sold there can be no unconditional appropriation until that part is severed from the rest.

In *Healey* v *Howlett & Sons* [1917] 1 KB 337 D ordered 20 boxes of mackerel from P. 190 boxes were despatched by P with instructions to the railway officials to set aside 20 boxes for D and the remaining boxes for two other consignees. The train was delayed at a point before the boxes were set aside and by the time the railway officials came to earmark them the fish had deteriorated badly. It was held that neither the property nor the risk had passed to D before the boxes were set aside. The boxes were consequently still at P's risk when they deteriorated.

In *Laurie & Morewood* v *John Dudin & Sons* (supra) the plaintiff buyers had contracted to buy 200 quarters of maize from the seller, the maize being held by the defendant warehouseman as part of a larger bulk. The plaintiffs obtained a delivery order and lodged it with the defendant. The plaintiffs did not pay so the seller stopped delivery, and the plaintiffs sued the warehouseman for detinue of the goods. The Court of Appeal held that there was no cause of action in this case since no property passed to the plaintiff. The goods remained at all times part of a bulk.

However, several cases must be considered in which the property seems mysteriously to have passed in an unidentified part of a bulk: for example, *Aldridge* v *Johnson* (1857) 7 E & B 885. The detailed facts of this case are given above in 1.6. The case involved the trading of a number of bullocks for 55 sacks of barley. The buyer sent 55 empty sacks to the seller to be filled with barley. The seller filled them but then, realising he was about to become bankrupt, he tipped the barley back into the original bulk. The buyer sued for the barley, and the court held that he was entitled to 55 sackfuls. The court seems to have held that property passed in unascertained goods.

A similar case is *Langton* v *Higgins* (1859) 4 H & N 402. The contract was for the sale of a quantity of peppermint oil at a price per lb. The buyer sent bottles to the seller for him to fill. The seller filled and labelled some bottles but then sold them to a third party. The buyer sued for the oil (there was obviously a conversion of the buyer's *bottles* but this was not in issue). The court held that the oil had been appropriated to the contract when the oil was put into the bottles and therefore the property had passed to the buyer.

Langton v *Higgins* goes against the authorities discussed below which held in effect that if the bulk is still under the seller's control then a mere mental or even physical separation by him where he is free to change his mind and choose different goods, as seems to have been the case in *Langton*, will not be an appropriation.

Aldridge and *Langton* were probably best explained by Pearson J in the leading case of *Carlos Federspiel* v *Charles Twigg & Co Ltd* [1957] 1 Lloyd's Rep 240. He stated that these were cases of *constructive delivery* to the buyer. The material fact in each case was that the containers into which the goods were placed belonged to the buyer. Had they been the seller's sacks or bottles then the property would not have passed.

The case of *Mount* v *Jay & Jay* (supra) has already been referred to. It is another case of property apparently passing in an unidentified part of a bulk and should be regarded as exceptional on this point.

A different problem arises with the case of *Wait & James* v *Midland Bank* (supra) (see above for facts). Roche J held that the property had passed in goods which in effect had become *ascertained by exhaustion*. Atiyah has raised the objection that what is necessary is an unconditional *act of appropriation* and not merely that the goods which are part of the bulk become ascertained.

If the bulk of the goods is still under the seller's control then a mere separation in the mind of the seller (ie he intends certain goods to go to a certain buyer) or even a physical separation in circumstances such that the seller can change his mind and allocate different goods will not amount to an unconditional appropriation. Therefore the performance by the seller of what would normally be recognised as acts of internal organisation, for example packaging and labelling the goods with the buyer's name, or segregating the goods in his (the seller's) own warehouse will not normally amount to appropriation. What the seller does while the goods are in his control is entirely his own affair and having provisionally allocated goods to the contract he can still change his mind and allocate different goods. Authority for these propositions is found in *Carlos Federspiel* v *Charles Twigg & Co* (above) per Pearson J, and in *Mucklow* v *Mangles* (1808) 1 Taunt 318.

The position will of course be different if the act of internal organisation performed by the seller is the one *specifically designated in the contract* as being *the act of appropriation*. In this case the performance of that designated act will be an appropriation, albeit the bulk is still under the seller's control.

If the seller physically separates the goods under his control *and* also informs the buyer that he has done so this is still probably inadequate to be an unconditional appropriation. However if in addition the buyer responds to the seller saying that he will come and collect the goods then a sufficient act of appropriation has probably occurred (*Rohde* v *Thwaites* (1827) 6 B & C 388).

The meaning of 'unconditional appropriation' has been considered by the courts on numerous occasions and it is probably easiest to grasp the meaning of the phrase by reference to the major cases. 'Unconditional' in this context is said by Benjamin to mean that the party appropriating must intend that the property shall pass by the appropriation if assented to by the other party, and not upon the occurence of some further event such as the payment or tender of the price. He cites *Godts* v *Rose* (1854) 17 CB 22 and *Stein, Forbes* v *County Tailoring Co* (1916) 86 LJKB 448 as support for this.

The meaning of 'unconditional appropriation' and what amounts to it is, as will be seen in the cases which follow, something of a flexible doctrine as applied to the facts of each case and leaves the courts some room for manoeuvre.

In *Pignataro* v *Gilroy* [1919] 1 KB 459 the seller sold to the buyer 140 bags of rice. The dispute concerned only 15 of the bags. These were held on the seller's premises, ready for delivery and the buyer was asked to collect the bags but a month passed before he decided to do so. In the meantime the bags had been stolen through no fault of the seller. The buyer sued for the return of the price he had paid on the 15 bags. It was held that since an unreasonable time had elapsed after the buyer was asked to collect, and because the buyer did not object to the seller appropriating those 15 bags to the contract, the buyer's assent to the appropriation would be implied and the property had therefore passed to the buyer at the time of the theft. (This may also have been a case of assent *in advance* because there had been a previous delivery order relating to the other 125 bags which had stated that the remaining 15 bags were ready at the seller's place of business. It may have been inferred from this that the buyer assented in advance to the appropriation of those 15 bags.)

Note *National Coal Board* v *Gamble* [1959] 1 QB 11; [1958] 3 All ER 203. (This is in fact a case under Rule 3 but the same considerations apply here.) The seller supplied coal as part of a bulk sale to a purchaser by loading it on to the buyer's lorry at a colliery. After loading the lorry was driven to a weighbridge so that the weight could be ascertained and a weight ticket issued as required by statute. It was held that the property did not pass until the coal had been weighed and the ticket given to and accepted by the buyer. The court was in no doubt that if too much had been loaded then the seller could have insisted on the excess being unloaded. Although not stated in the judgments the correct analysis must be that although the coal was appropriated to the contract when it was loaded onto the lorry, the appropriation was not unconditional until it was weighed and the weight ticket accepted by the buyer.

Edwards v *Ddin* [1976] 1 WLR 943; [1976] 3 All ER 705 was a criminal law case concerning a prosecution under the Theft Act 1968. The defendant having driven his car up to the pumps at a filling station requested the attendant to fill the tank. After this was done the defendant drove off without paying. He was charged with the theft of the petrol contrary to s1(1) of the Theft Act 1968. The prosecution case was that the property in the petrol had not yet passed to the defendant, arguing *inter alia* that the garage had reserved the right of disposal over the petrol under s19(1) SGA until the condition as to payment had been met. It was held that when the attendant delivered the petrol into the defendant's car, that was an unconditional appropriation with the assent of both parties. The property passed under s18 Rule 5(1) and (2) at that moment. Once the petrol was mixed with the petrol in the defendant's car the owner could not as a term of the contract of sale have reserved a right of disposal under s19 SGA. Nor could the court see how effect could be given to such a term. It followed that the offence here was not one of theft since the defendant had not 'appropriated property belonging to another' (a requirement of that offence): he already owned the petrol. In civil law the seller could of course have sued for the price but he could not detain the buyer's vehicle or attempt to drain out the petrol.

This decision was affirmed in *R v McHugh* [1977] RTR 1 where it was held that if the customer himself puts the petrol into the tank then the property passes at that moment: an unconditional appropriation with the assent of the seller.

The leading case now on the meaning of 'unconditional appropriation' is *Carlos Federspiel & Co v Charles Twigg & Co Ltd* (supra). The buyers in Costa Rica contracted to buy 85 bicycles from the sellers in England to be shipped in June 1953, the purchase price to be paid in advance. The bicycles were packed into crates bearing the seller's name and with the relevant shipping numbers, and the crates were registered for consignment and space reserved on board a named ship. Before the goods were actually shipped the sellers went into liquidation and the receiver refused to send the bicycles to the buyers. The buyer claimed that there had been an unconditional appropriation to which he (the buyer) had assented, and that the property had therefore passed to him. Pearson J held that the property in the bicycles had not passed to the buyer. The correspondence between the parties revealed an intention that the final act of appropriation should be the *shipment* of the goods which had not taken place. Up until that point the seller was free to choose other bikes. Pearson J reviewed the authorities and laid down five principles governing the appropriation of goods:

1. Section 18 Rule 5 is only one rule for ascertaining the intention of the parties as to the time at which the property in the goods is to pass to the buyer unless a different intention appears. Therefore the element of common intention must always be borne in mind. For an appropriation the parties must have had, or be reasonably supposed to have had an intention to attach the contract irrevocably to those goods so that those goods and no others are the subject of the sale and become the property of the buyer. A mere expectation of the seller that he will use certain goods in satisfaction of that contract is insufficient.

2. The appropriation is essentially made by agreement of the parties although in some cases the buyer's assent to the appropriation will be conferred in advance of the contract itself or otherwise.
3. An appropriation by the seller with the assent of the buyer may be said always to invoke an actual or constructive delivery. It is of course possible in the case of a constructive delivery that there is still an actual delivery to be made by the seller under the contract. In this context Pearson J cited *Aldridge* v *Johnson* (supra) and *Langton* v *Higgins* (supra). So if the seller retains possession after an actual or constructive delivery he does so as bailee for the buyer.
4. Use can be made of s20 SGA. Under this section ownership and risk are usually *associated*, so if it appears on the construction of the relevant documents that the goods are at all material times still at the seller's risk, then that is prima facie an indication that property has not passed to the buyer.
5. The appropriating act will usually but not necessarily be the last act to be performed by the *seller*. If for example the goods are placed by the seller onto the buyer's van or are left by the seller identified and in a position to be removed by the buyer, and in either of those situations the buyer is informed of the position and agrees to take the goods, that will be assent to an appropriation. If, however, there is a further act of some significance to be done by the seller that is prima facie evidence that the property probably will not pass until the final act is done.

Federspiel also made it clear that the equitable doctrine put forward in *Re Wait* [1927] 1 Ch 606 to effect the passing of the property otherwise than in the SGA had no application. It was assumed in the case that the only issues arose under the SGA and in particular Rule 5.

In *Noblett* v *Hopkinson* [1905] 2 KB 214, this unsatisfactory case involved a prosecution for selling alcohol outside licensed hours. The buyer had ordered the beer in question on a Saturday evening inside licensed hours and the appropriate quantity had been drawn off and put into five containers. On the Sunday morning the beer was delivered to the buyer. The seller was prosecuted, but to succeed the prosecution had to show that the property had not passed until the Sunday morning. The court held that a criminal offence had occurred. The reasoning of the respective judges differed: one judge apparently decided the case on the grounds of the absence of the buyer's assent to the appropriation on Saturday evening, and one judge apparently thought there was 'no complete appropriation' on the Saturday.

It is submitted that *Noblett* is wrongly decided and that no reliance should be placed on it. There was almost certainly a completed appropriation on the Saturday evening and the defendant seller was no longer the owner on the Sunday morning.

In *Wardar's (Import & Export) Ltd* v *Norwood Ltd* [1968] QB 663; [1968] 2 All ER 602 the seller sold to the buyer 600 cartons of frozen ox kidneys as part of the larger consignment of 1500 which were in cold storage in a third party's warehouse. The warehouseman subsequently wheeled 600 cartons onto the pavement outside ready for collection by the buyer. The buyer's carrier arrived and handed over the delivery order. It took some four hours to load all the cartons onto the buyer's vehicle and by that time much of the meat was thawing. The carrier did not switch on the refrigerating machinery in the vehicle until midway through loading and it did not become effective for three hours. On arrival at the buyer's premises in Glasgow the goods were found to be unfit for human consumption. The buyer claimed damages and the seller counterclaimed for the price. The Court of Appeal held that the property had passed to the buyer under s18 Rule 5(1) since there had been an unconditional appropriation of the goods to the contract. When the delivery order was handed over the property passed as soon as the goods were made available to the buyer. The warehouseman had selected the goods for the contract and had signified to the buyer that these were his goods. The risk of deterioration passed at that moment to the buyer under s20. The counterclaim therefore succeeded. It was not directly considered whether during the loading the warehouseman could have selected different cartons from those then on the pavement. Presumably the handing over of the delivery order was vital in this respect: it precluded the selection of any other cartons.

There is authority in *Badische Anilin und Soda Fabrik v Basle Chemical Works* [1898] AC 200 that goods sent by post are unconditionally appropriated when they are posted. This situation is discussed in detail below.

Shipbuilding contracts are sometimes given special consideration with regard to the question of appropriation. The general presumption laid down in *Reid v Macbeth* [1904] AC 223 was that property does not pass until the ship is completed. This will still be the case where the price is payable by instalments during the construction of the ship. It remains possible, however, to provide in the contract that the purchaser will be able to claim the property in those parts which when put together form the complete ship.

An illustration is *Re Blyth Shipbuilding Co* [1926] Ch 494. The seller agreed to build a ship for the buyer, the price to be paid by instalments as the work proceeded. It was agreed that on payment of the first instalment 'the vessel and all materials and things appropriated to her should thenceforth become and remain the absolute property of the purchaser'. The seller went bankrupt before the vessel was complete. Some worked and unworked material was lying about the yard at the relevant time. The Court of Appeal held the property in the incomplete ship had passed to the buyers but neither the worked or unworked materials had been sufficiently appropriated to pass the property.

Atiyah suggests that what is necessary to consitute an unconditional appropriation may vary according to the type of goods in question and the general circumstances of the case. For example, when goods are being manufactured by the seller, the courts will not readily infer that the materials have been appropriated since this might hamper the freedom of the seller to manufacture the goods as he thinks best. This consideration, Atiyah contends, does not apply in the case of goods to be grown by the seller. In such a case it could be held that the property in the goods, if sufficiently designated, passes as soon as they come into existence. So also where an unidentified part of a specified bulk is sold from the rest with the assent of the parties. These propositions are illustrated by *Aldridge* v *Johnson* and *Re Blyth Shipping Co* (supra).

Assent required for appropriation under Rule 5

Assent may be express or implied. An example of implied assent has been noted in *Pignataro* v *Gilroy* where assent was implied from a failure by the buyer to respond for a complete month.

Where the seller appropriates the goods the buyer's assent may be given prior to or subsequent to the act of appropriation. Property will pass on appropriation where the buyer has by express words previously assented to such appropriation by the seller or where he has done so by implication. *Benjamin* emphasises that the actual manner of appropriation must be approved by the buyer: this may for example be a delivery to a carrier or the issue of a notice of appropriation. Subsequent assent is illustrated in *Rohde* v *Thwaites* (supra) where the buyer ordered 20 hogsheads of sugar out of a bulk belonging to the seller. Four hogsheads were then filled up and appropriated by the seller who gave notice to the buyer to remove them which he promised to do. Property was held to have passed by this notice and promise.

Assent can, of course, be implied from conduct.

Difficulty may arise where the seller delivers the goods to an independent carrier for delivery in turn to the buyer. The situation usually discussed in this context is that where the goods are posted and the carrier is therefore the Post Office although the same considerations will apply wherever an independent carrier is involved. Where the buyer orders goods by post and the seller dispatches goods of that description to the buyer, Rule 5(2) states that here the seller is deemed to have unconditionally appropriated those goods to the contract; however, the Rule does not say that the buyer's assent is deemed to have been given. The buyer's assent must be found both to the appropriation *and* to the dispatch of the goods.

In this context there is a clear rule in commercial contracts that where the seller is to ship the goods to the buyer then it is assumed that the shipment will be an unconditional appropriation with the buyer's assent. Yet this rule although suitable in commercial contracts may give rise to difficulties in the case of *consumer* contracts. Where goods are ordered and dispatched by performance in a consumer contract it is as yet unsettled whether the posting passes the property from seller to buyer. Atiyah suggests that the dispatch of goods should not pass the property for if it did the goods would be at the buyer's risk whilst in the post and the buyer may even be unaware that the goods have been posted. Smith and Keenan are in agreement with this view. Lowe, however, tends towards the view that the buyer impliedly assents in advance to the seller's subsequent appropriation.

Atiyah concedes that the only authority in this area is unfavourable to his view. In *Badische Anilin und Soda Fabrik* v *Basle Chemical Works* (supra) the House of Lords held that the property in goods ordered and dispatched by post passed to the buyer on posting. Atiyah points out, however, that this case should not be regarded as decisive because this point was never disputed and the eventual decision turned on special provisions of patent law. Other cases which are not directly in point appear to lend some support to the opposite view: an example is *Pletts* v *Campbell* [1895] 2 QB 229.

8.3 Specific goods

In the case of specific goods it is ss17 and 18 of the SGA 1979 that are relevant in determining when the property passes. Section 17 which applies only to specific and ascertained goods states:

> '1) Where there is a contract for the sale of specific or ascertained goods the property in them is transferred to the buyer at such time as the parties to the contract intend it to be transferred.
> 2) For the purpose of ascertaining the intention of the parties regard shall be had to the terms of the contract, the conduct of the parties, and the circumstances of the case.'

An example is *Re Anchor Line* [1937] Ch 1; [1936] 2 All ER 941. B agreed to buy a dockside crane 'for a deferred purchase price of £4,000'. The arrangement here meant that B also paid a sum annually to S 'by way of depreciation and interest', such sums then being deducted from the total purchase price. B went into liquidation and S claimed the property in the goods. The Court of Appeal found an intention that property should remain with S until the full purchase price had been paid. Under the contract S was obviously receiving payment for 'depreciation' and this could only be the concern of the owner of the goods.

Most recently see *Davy Offshore Ltd* v *Emerald Field Contracting* [1992] 2 Lloyd's Rep 142, in which the Court of Appeal held that the contract showed the intentions of the parties quite clearly (that title was to pass after certain payments had been made). There was no need to utilise s18 or its Rules (see following) because under s17 the parties' intention was quite clear. The fact that the parties subsequently ran into delays which prevented payment being made as early as anticipated in no way altered their intention that title would pass on presentation of various documents to the bank in order to receive payment.

A further example of a s17 intention occurs in the purchase of items from supermarkets. Both parties obviously intend that the property should not pass until payment at the checkout.

In *Ward* v *Bignall* [1967] 1 QB 534; [1967] 2 All ER 449 Diplock LJ called s17 'the governing rule' in the passing of property. There are, however, dicta of Diplock and Sellers LJJ in this case which suggest that in modern times very little is necessary to give rise to the inference that the parties intend the property in specific goods to pass only on delivery or payment, thereby ousting s18. These dicta have caused some concern since they appear to bring uncertainty and unpredictability into the law: they would give the court what amounts to a discretion whether or not to find an intention existing under s17.

At least where s18 applies the law is certain. In all probability a court would only use the dicta where the result would otherwise be very harsh on the buyer (eg where he is uninsured).

It should be noted that in commercial contracts sellers frequently reserve title to the goods supplied and rights to products made from them, or to the proceeds of their resale to sub-buyers, until the price is paid in full. Such clauses are known as 'Romalpa clauses' after the leading case *Aluminium Industrie Vaasen BV* v *Romalpa Aluminium* [1976] 1 WLR 676; [1976] 2 All ER 552. These are in many ways examples of a s17 contrary intention, and are dealt with specifically in s19 SGA. They are dealt with in greater detail below under s19 (see para 8.4).

Where no intention can be found under s17 then resort must be had to the first four Rules of s18. Section 18 raises certain presumptions as to the intention of the parties, all of which are subject to a contrary intention appearing.

Rule 1

Rule 1 provides:

> 'Where there is an *unconditional contract* for the sale of *specific goods*, in a *deliverable state*, the property in the goods passes to the buyer *when the contract is made*, and it is immaterial whether the time of payment or the time of delivery, or both, be postponed.'

Where the conditions specified are fulfilled, then the property passes immediately on sale, notwithstanding the postponement of delivery and/or payment. The following conditions must be fulfilled.

It must be an 'unconditional contract'

This obviously does not mean that the contract must have no 'conditions' of any kind. The confusion in this area has in fact arisen through the abuse or over-use of the word 'condition' in the law.

The generally accepted view is that 'unconditional contract for sale' means no more than a contract of sale under which the passing of property to the buyer is not made the subject of any condition. In other words there is no condition holding up the passing of property.

Such a construction means that Rule 1 is not displaced by a condition subsequent, nor by a condition precedent if that is not a condition which suspends the contract as a whole or the passing of property but merely suspends the operation of other terms. Rule 1 will also be unaffected by the inclusion of 'conditions', the breach of which affect the parties' rights to terminate the contract (ie 'conditions' in contra-distinction to 'warranties'). However, a 'conditional sale agreement' in which the property is not to pass until payment or performance will be outside Rule 1.

A better phrase to have used in Rule 1 would have been '*a contract for the unconditional sale of goods*'.

The goods must be in a 'deliverable state'

Section 61(5) provides that goods are in a deliverable state when they are in such a state that the buyer would, under the contract, *be bound to take delivery of them*.

This would suggest that if the goods are in such a state that the buyer would be entitled to reject them (if, for example, they are not of merchantable quality) then Rule 1 would not apply. This would have the absurd result that in contracts for the sale of specific goods the property will never pass to the buyer on the making of the contract if the goods are defective. The courts have never held this to be the effect of s61(5). The better view is that the quality or condition of the goods should really be disregarded. What is important is that the seller should not have to do anything more to the goods before the buyer is obliged to take them. He should not, for example, have to bind copies of books, or dye the goods a certain colour, because such goods would not be ready for delivery. The test is really whether, on the assumption that the goods are what they purport to be, the seller has to do anything to them before the buyer must take them.

In the Scottish case of *Morison* v *Lockhart* 1912 2 SLT 189, it was held that, as long as something was attached to land it could not be in a deliverable state until severed. This has been applied in English law.

In *Underwood* v *Burgh Castle Brick & Cement Syndicate* [1922] 1 KB 343, the subject of the sale here was an engine weighing over 30 tons. It had sunk into its cement base by its own weight, and it was the seller's obligation under the contract to dismantle it and detach it from the floor. It was held that the engine was not in a deliverable state and the property in it could not yet pass.

It is worth noting at this stage the meaning of *'delivery'* in the SGA, although not strictly relevant to Rule 1. (*'Deliverable state' cannot* be construed with reference to the definition of 'delivery' in the Act). 'Delivery' is defined in s61(1) as *'the voluntary transfer of possession from one person to another'*. It is therefore not necessarily a handing over of any kind. By s29(2) the normal rule as to the place of delivery, subject to contrary intention, is that it should be at the seller's place of business if he has one, and failing this, his home. In other words it is for the buyer to collect and not for the seller to dispatch the goods.

Two cases are illustrative of the operation and importance of Rule 1 in general. First, *Tarling* v *Baxter* (1827) 6 B & C 360. (This case involved the equivalent common law rule which was later incorporated in the SGA.) The contract was for the sale of a stack of hay in a field, payment was to be one month later and the stack was not to be cut or taken away until payment. The stack was destroyed by fire shortly afterwards. (The stack was, of course, goods not land: see 1.5.) It was held that property in the goods had passed at the contract notwithstanding that payment and delivery had been postponed. The stack was in a deliverable state.

The result would be the same now under Rule 2. If the parties wish to oust Rule 1 when it would otherwise be applicable, they must do so at the time of the contract.

Second, in *Dennant* v *Skinner & Collom* [1948] 2 KB 164; [1948] 2 All ER 29 the buyer here attended a motor auction. His bid was accepted by the auctioneer and the hammer fell. By s57(2) a sale by auction is complete when the hammer falls. There was consequently a contract between buyer and seller. At the end of the auction the buyer offered the seller a cheque for the car but the seller was reluctant to accept this. They therefore 'agreed' that the buyer should have possession of the car but that the property should not pass until the cheque was cleared. (The seller would have had an unpaid seller's lien - see 'Remedies' - had he not given up possession of the car). The cheque was dishonoured, but the buyer had resold the car to C. The seller sued C for the car. It was held that when the hammer fell the property passed under Rule 1. The effect of the subsequent transaction was merely that the buyer persuaded the seller to give up his lien on the goods.

Finally it should be noted that in the SGA 1893 there was a notorious provision (s11(1)(c)) whereby the buyer lost his right to reject specific goods where the property in them had passed! Rule 1 with the property passing at the contract applies to many everyday contracts and according to this subsection there would be no right to reject the goods in such contracts. Section 11(1)(c) was thankfully repealed by the 1979 SGA, but its existence explains certain very odd decisions prior to 1979, in which Rule 1 was held not to apply simply to avoid the consequences of s11(1)(c). These cases are now only of historical interest. (An example is *Ollett* v *Jordan* [1918] 2 KB 41.)

Rule 2

Rule 2 provides:

> 'Where there is a contract for the sale of specific goods and the seller is bound to do something to the goods for the purpose of putting them into a deliverable state, the property does not pass until the thing is done, and the buyer has notice that it has been done.'

'Deliverable state' will of course have the same meaning as under Rule 1. The wording and operation of this rule is otherwise straightforward.

An illustration of the operation of Rule 2 is *Underwood* v *Burgh Castle Brick & Cement Syndicate* (supra). The facts are set out above. It was the seller's obligation under the contract to detach and dismantle the engine in question before it could be delivered. The situation therefore fell under Rule 2 and not Rule 1.

The Rule does not say that the seller must have given notice, merely that the buyer must *have notice*. The buyer may therefore be informed of the new position by a third party.

Rule 3

Rule 3 provides:

> 'Where there is a contract for the sale of specific goods, in a deliverable state, but the seller is bound to weigh, measure, test or do some other act or thing with reference to the goods, for the purpose of ascertaining the price, the property does not pass until the act or thing is done, and the buyer has notice that it has been done.'

The rationale behind the rule is that if the property were to pass in such a situation, then under s49(1) the seller's remedy would be for the price which would be unknown.

Rule 3 only applies where it is the seller who is to perform the act to ascertain the price. If the act is to be done by the buyer or by a third party then the case will fall under Rule 1. In addition Rule 3 only applies where the act is necessary to ascertain the price not where the act is necessary for some other purpose, a position which is curious since the ascertainment and payment of the price are not generally prerequisites for the passing of property.

As *Benjamin* points out it is odd that this rule should have found a place in English law which has never placed great weight on certainty of price.

The rule is of little practical importance. There are nevertheless three important cases dealing with its operation.

In *Zagury* v *Furnell* (1809) 2 Camp 240 the seller contracted to sell 289 specified bales of goat skins which were in a deliverable state at a price per dozen skins. It was unclear how many skins were in each bale, and it was for the seller to ascertain the price by counting the skins. Before counting, the skins were destroyed by fire. It was held that the property and the risk were still with the seller since the counting and therefore the ascertainment of the price had not yet taken place.

In *Turley* v *Bates* (1863) 2 H & C 200 the contract was for the sale of an entire heap of fire clay at 2s per ton to be loaded, removed and weighed by the buyer to ascertain the price. The court doubted that the common law equivalent to Rule 3 applied (the case was before the SGA) where the act to ascertain the price was to be performed by the buyer and not the seller but found an intention that the property should not pass in any case until the heap had been weighed. This intention would now fall under s17.

Nanka Bruce v *Commonwealth Trust Ltd* [1926] AC 77 concerned an agreement to sell cocoa at 90s per 60lbs. It was agreed that the buyer would resell the goods and that the sub-buyer would weigh them. It was held that the property in the goods passed from the seller to the buyer before the sub-buyer had weighed the goods. There are probably two reasons for this decision: first, it was not the seller who was bound to do the act in question, and second, the purpose of the act was not to ascertain the price but to enable the sub-buyer to ensure that he had received the correct amount under the contract.

As with the other rules under s18, Rule 3 is subject to a contrary intention being found in s17 (as in *Turley* v *Bates* above). Where the goods have been delivered to the buyer or where it has been acknowledged that they are held to the buyer's order (as in *Howes* v *Watson* (1824) 2 B & C 243) then the property may be held to have passed notwithstanding that the goods are still to be measured by the seller. The editors of *Benjamin* argue that if the parties provisionally fix a price for the goods, even though this is afterwards to be more accurately calculated by weighing by the seller, the inference is that they did not intend to suspend the passing of the property. They cite *Martineau* v *Kitching* (1872) 2 QB 436 in support of this argument. If this is the case it would seem that the presumption in Rule 3 can be rebutted without much difficulty.

The interrelation of Rules 2 and 3

If the goods are not in a deliverable state *and* the price is still to be ascertained by an act of the seller then the dilemma occurs of having to apply two apparently incompatible rules: Rule 2 requires that the goods are not in a deliverable state but Rule 3 requires that they be deliverable. The solution is that the rules should be applied consecutively:

1. If the price is in the course of things ascertained before the goods become deliverable then Rule 2 will govern the passing of property.
2. If the goods are made deliverable before the price is ascertained then Rule 3 will govern and the property can pass when the price is ascertained and the buyer has notice of that.

Rule 4

Where goods are delivered to the buyer 'on approval' or 'on sale or return' then the property passes as set out in Rule 4 (a) and (b) below.

The term 'on approval' is used where the question in the buyer's mind is as to the quality of the goods supplied or their suitability for his particular purpose. The label 'sale or return' is more appropriate where the question is one of quality (ie how many or how much of the goods does the buyer want).

No mention is made of the classes of goods to which this rule applies. It will in fact apply to specific goods and subsequently ascertained goods, but not to unascertained goods since the goods will be identified at least on delivery.

Rule 4 also applies initially to offers to sell where there is as yet no binding contract and the buyer can decide not to take the goods although such offers will become binding on the occurrence of one of the events in (a) and (b) below.

Property passes in the situations under Rule 4 as follows:

> '(a) when the buyer signifies his approval or acceptance to the seller or does any other act adopting the transaction.
> (b) If the buyer does not signify his approval or acceptance to the seller but retains the goods without giving notice of rejection, then, if a time has been fixed for the return of the goods, on the expiration of that time, and if no time has been fixed, on the expiration of a reasonable time.'

Rule 4(a)

'Act adopting the transaction'. The buyer adopts the transaction if *inter alia* he accepts offers for the goods; resells the goods (*Re Florence* (1879) 10 Ch D 591 and *Genn* v *Winkel* (1911) 28 TLR 483); pledges the goods (*Kirkham* v *Attenborough* [1897] 1 QB 201); or otherwise deals with the goods as though they were his own property. It should be noted that when the buyer adopts the transaction by resale then property passes to the sub-buyer through s18 Rule 4 and not under s25(1) (see 10.9). Since the buyer is selling his own goods he became owner as soon as he adopted the transaction with the original seller. Support for this is found in *Edwards* v *Vaughan* (1910) 26 TLR 545.

A clear example of the buyer adopting the transaction is found in *Kirkham* v *Attenborough* (supra). K the manufacturer of jewellery delivered certain pieces to W on sale or return. W then pledged them with a pawnbroker. K ultimately sued the pawnbroker for the return of the jewellery. It was held that W had adopted the transaction by pledging the goods so W was himself the owner of the goods when he pledged them. K therefore had no cause of action against the pawnbroker, and it was immaterial that W was guilty of a criminal offence.

As a result of this decision many traders who operated in the same manner as K ousted Rule 4 by use of a contrary intention. In *Weiner* v *Gill* [1906] 2 KB 574, W sold goods on sale or return stating that until the goods were 'settled for or charged' then the property in them should remain with the seller. The buyer pledged the goods to G, who W finally sued for the return of the goods. It was held that Rule 4 was ousted by an obvious contrary intention and no property had passed to G. W's action must therefore succeed.

A danger for the trader in these circumstances is that the provisions of s21(2)(a) on 'sale by a mercantile agent' may come into operation (see Chapter 10: The Transfer of Title by a Non-Owner). This will happen where the buyer is in fact an agent for sale of the seller with authority from him to sell and being bound to account to his principal the seller for the proceeds of such sale. In such circumstances the buyer may be able to pass a good title to any person to whom he in turn disposes of the goods notwithstanding he has no good title himself. The facts of *Weiner* v *Harris* [1910] 1 KB 285 illustrate that if the buyer is, for example, a travelling salesman, then he may be able to pass good title as a 'mercantile agent' in s21(2)(a) even where Rule 4 is excluded by contrary intention.

Where goods are delivered to the buyer on trial there is no authority as to whether a use of the goods which is more than that necessary for a fair test amounts to an adoption of the transaction by him. *Benjamin* sees the case as analogous to the 'acceptance' cases under s35 (see Chapter 13) and holds the view that an excessive use of the goods is an act from which the court would be entitled to infer an adoption.

A further situation which requires special consideration occurs where the buyer during the sale or return period himself disposes of the goods on sale or return to a third party. Suppose the buyer takes the goods on a seven-day sale or return basis from the seller and the *next day* delivers them in turn on a seven-day sale or return basis to a third party. In this situation he will have adopted the transaction with the seller since he can no longer return the goods to the seller within the seven days allowed. There would have been no adoption if the buyer had delivered the goods to the third party on the same day or for a period of less than seven days because in both these situations the buyer would still have been able to return the goods to the seller within the stipulated period. (For an illustration of this situation see *Genn* v *Winkel* (supra).)

Rule 4(b)
An illustration of the working of this situation is found in *Poole* v *Smith's Car Sales Ltd* [1962] 1 WLR 744; [1962] 2 All ER 482. S left his car with B essentially for storage, although B was authorised to sell if he could get £325 for it. (This agreement was held by the court to be effectively one of 'sale or return'.) After three months S demanded the return of the vehicle within three days, alternatively £325 realised by a sale of the vehicle. The car was only returned some weeks later and had been damaged by one of B's employees when using it for his own purposes. S refused to accept the car, suing instead for the £325. It was held that B had retained the car beyond a reasonable time and the property had passed under Rule 4(b). The seller could therefore sue for the price.

It is clear that the property will not pass under Rule 4(b) in goods delivered *unsolicited* with an offer to sell them. In addition, Rule 4(b) only applies where it is the *buyer* who retains the goods. In *Re Ferrier* [1944] Ch 295 antiques were delivered to X on a seven-day sale or return basis. Two days later they were seized by execution creditors of X (in this case actually by the sheriff) who retained them until the seven days had expired. X took no further action during the seven days. The seller then claimed the goods from the sheriff. It was held that the property had not passed under Rule 4(b): X had not 'retained' the goods for seven days under that rule, so the seller was still the owner and could recover the goods from the sheriff.

A further useful case in the context of Rule 4(b) is *Elphick* v *Barnes* (1880) 5 CPD 321. S supplied a horse to B on approval or return within eight days. The horse died during the eight days through the fault of neither party. S claimed that since B could not return the horse he must have bought it and sued for the price. It was held that property and risk remained with the seller who must bear the loss. S could not sue for the price.

If, however, the goods had been damaged by the fault of the buyer then it is possible that the seller could have refused to take back the damaged goods and the buyer would have been liable for the price (see Denman J obiter in *Elphick* v *Barnes*). The editors of *Benjamin* argue that in these circumstances the buyer should be permitted to return the goods but should be liable in damages for the loss sustained by the seller though not for the price.

8.4 Reservation of rights of disposal: s19

Section 19 sets out a variety of situations in which the seller in some way reserves a right of disposal over the goods.

Section 19(1)

Section 19(1) provides:

> 'Where there is a contract for the sale of specific goods or where goods are subsequently appropriated to the contract, the seller may, by the terms of the contract or appropriation, reserve the right of disposal of the goods until certain conditions are fulfilled; and in such a case, notwithstanding the delivery of the goods to the buyer, or to a carrier or other bailee ... for the purpose of transmission to the buyer, the property in the goods does not pass to the buyer until the conditions imposed by the seller are fulfilled.'

In the case of specific goods the seller must reserve the right of disposal at the time the contract is made (*Dennant* v *Skinner & Collom* (supra)). With subsequently ascertained goods it may be done either at the contract or at the time the goods are appropriated. Section 19(1) prevents the operation of s18 and holds up the passing of property until the stipulated conditions are fulfilled; it is in effect an example of a s17 intention, a contrary intention of the parties. It should be noted that the courts will readily find that the buyer does not acquire the property in the goods before delivery or in some cases even before payment. An example of this is *Re Shipton Anderson & Co Ltd and Harrison Bros & Co Ltd* [1915] 3 KB 676 where the contract term 'payment cash within seven days' was surprisingly held to delay the passing of property until the buyer paid and on payment received a delivery order.

The most common condition to be stipulated in contracts is a reservation of a right of disposal over the goods until the buyer pays the price. A buyer may still be able to resell the goods to a third party passing a good title under s25(1) (see Chapter 10) one case in which a non-owner is able to pass good title to the goods.

Section 19(1) has been used abundantly to protect the interests of the seller/supplier of the goods in the event of the buyer's bankruptcy. If the seller still has property in the goods or a right of disposal then he can claim the goods and will not be confined to claiming a dividend in the bankruptcy.

The leading case in this area is *Aluminium Industrie BV* v *Romalpa Aluminium Ltd* (supra).

Where a seller supplies raw materials to a manufacturer or goods to a wholesaler in circumstances where he is likely regularly to be shipping such goods to be processed or resold, a clause is commonly found stating that the property in the goods shall not pass until the manufacturer or wholesaler has paid in full. The seller may require payment for that particular delivery or even for all goods supplied by him to that buyer before the property is to pass.

The effect of such clauses was first considered by the Court of Appeal in the *Romalpa* case and the clauses became known as '*Romalpa* clauses'. The clause in question in the *Romalpa* case stated that the seller should be entitled to the proceeds of sale or resale of the goods supplied, and if the goods were in fact resold and the sub-buyer had not yet paid, then the seller should be entitled to the book-debt owed by the sub-buyer to the buyer. The Court of Appeal seemed to underestimate the significance of the case and held that the seller in fact retained ownership of the goods unsold by the buyer and was entitled to the proceeds of sale of goods the buyer had sold.

The *Romalpa* decision has been much criticised because it enables a seller to create a secret, unregisterable and unnotifiable form of security. Should the buyer become bankrupt before the seller is paid then the seller will reclaim the goods. However, the buyer's other creditors have no way of knowing that the property in such goods has actually remained with the seller and so they will be unfairly prejudiced, often receiving only a fraction of the dividend they could have expected on the bankruptcy since the buyer's assets (used to pay the dividend) will be reduced.

In *Re Bond Worth* [1980] Ch 228; [1979] 3 All ER 919 Slade J held that a clause similar to that in *Romalpa* only reserved equitable title to the seller and not legal title. The case turned on a construction of the clause in question. In *Borden (UK) Ltd* v *Scottish Timber Products Ltd* [1981] Ch 25; [1979]) 3 All ER 961, the court seems finally to have realised the dangers of the *Romalpa* decision. It was held that the attempted reservation of title was in effect a charge on the assets of the buyer company and unless it was registered under s395 of the Companies Act 1985 it would be void against the company's creditors and against the liquidator. This at least gives the company's other creditors a means of discovering which assets are the subject of s19 SGA reservations in title; however, it will not apply where the buyer is not a company.

A further criticism of the *Romalpa* case is that it introduces into commercial contracts the idea of *equitable tracing*: that a party may trace in equity into the proceeds of sale of property to which he has reserved title. This clearly goes against the policy statement of Lord Atkin in *Re Wait* (supra) that equitable doctrines should not be allowed to invade the law on sale of goods.

Two recent cases, *E Pfeiffer Weinkellerei-Weineinkauf GmbH* v *Arbuthnot Factors* [1988] 1 WLR 150 and *Tatung (UK) Ltd* v *Galex Telesure Ltd* [1989] BCC 325, provide a useful point of assessment of the current state of reservation of title clauses.

In *Pfeiffer* the court came to the conclusion that not only had a charge over book debts been created, but that such a charge was registrable under s396(1) of the Companies Act 1985. But, since the charge had *not* been registered, the defendant's claim must fail. *Pfeiffer* is extremely helpful in illuminating many of the key issues in the area of *Romalpa* clauses, but space precludes it being dealt with in full here.

In *Tatung* the contract actually made express provision for the interest that the plaintiffs were to have in the various stages of dealing with the goods. To this extent the court distinguished the case from *Aluminium Industrie* v *Romalpa Aluminium*. In *Tatung* the plaintiff's rights were contractual, in the original *Romalpa* case the court felt they arose from an application of equitable principles.

Note that the same judge, Phillips J, gave both judgments, and these should be read in full and in comparison with each other as well as with *Aluminium Industrie*.

A recent case, *Armour* v *Thyssen Edelstahlwerke AG* [1990] 3 WLR 810, gave some further insight into the attitude of the courts as to reservation of title. Though the contract was governed by Scottish law the House of Lords observed that similar statutory criteria would apply to contracts made under English law. The defendants sold and supplied steel strip to a third party. The third party went bankrupt and the question arose as to who had ownership of steel strip already delivered but not so far used. At the time of the Receiver's appointment the third party had a great deal of steel strip lying in its yards. Some had been cut into sheets, but the greater part was in the same condition as when delivered. None had been used in the manufacturing process. In the contract a clause purported to retain title against payment. No payment had yet been made.

HELD: By the terms of the contract the defendants had reserved the right of disposal of the steel strip until such time as payment had been made in full. By virtue of ss17 and 19(1) of the Sale of Goods Act 1979, therefore, the property in the goods did not pass to the third party until the conditions had been complied with. The defendants therefore remained the owners of the steel strip, despite the fact that it had been delivered.

Section 19(2)

Section 19(2) gives one situation concerned with goods sent by sea, in which a reservation of title will be presumed. Section 19(2) provides:

> 'Where goods are shipped, and by the bill of lading the goods are deliverable to the order of the seller or his agent, the seller is *prima facie* to be taken to reserve the right of disposal.'

If the bill of lading in a sale contract involving the shipment of goods is taken in the seller's name and not that of the buyer/consignee a reservation of title is presumed and the property will normally pass only when the bill of lading is transferred to the buyer and the price is paid or tendered. Conversely, if the bill of lading is taken in the buyer's name the property will often pass on shipment of the goods. Section 19(2) is of course subject to a contrary intention in s17 (it may be intended with a bill of lading taken in the seller's name that the property will pass on shipment) and the mere fact that a bill of lading is taken in the buyer's name does not mean the property must pass on shipment. For example, the seller may retain the bill of lading, an act which is probably inconsistent with an intention to pass the property immediately.

The two main types of contracts of sale involving the shipment of the goods are known as the FOB contract and the CIF contract. Briefly, FOB signifies 'free on board', that is, that the seller pays all expenses up to the point where the goods are placed on board the ship and the buyer bears the costs thereafter; CIF signifies that the price includes the 'cost, insurance and freight' and since the buyer pays these in the price, the seller is responsible for arranging shipment and insurance and paying the carrier. In the FOB contract the normal rule is that property and risk pass when the goods pass over the ship's rail inboard. With the CIF contract the risk normally passes on loading but the property does not. The recent case of *The Delfini* [1990] 1 Lloyd's Rep 252 shows that the statutory presumption that in CIF contracts passing of property will occur on transfer of shipping documents will not always apply. (See also *Enichem Anic SpA* v *Ampelos Shipping* (1989) The Times 11 August.) The effect of s19(2) in delaying the passing of property is therefore of greater significance in relation to the FOB contract, since with CIF contracts the property usually only passes when the shipping documents are presented and payment is made. However, it must be stressed that one must look to the exact terms of the particular FOB or CIF contract in question since the obligations imposed by each are not necessarily the same. The property in either ultimately passes when the parties intend it to pass (s17).

In *Mitsui & Co* v *Flota Mercante Grancolombiana SA* [1989] 1 All ER 951, [1989] 1 WLR 1145 an FOB contract the bill of lading stated that the goods were to be deliverable to the seller's order on part payment by the buyer. The goods were found to be damaged. The court held that the presumption was that property passed, when there was a reservation of rights by the seller, on payment of the *balance* by the buyer. Although more than 80 per cent of the total price had been paid by the buyer before shipment, because the seller reserved rights of disposal, property in the goods had not passed to the buyer.

Section 19(3)

Section 19(3) provides:

> 'Where the seller of goods draws on the buyer for the price and transmits the bill of exchange and bill of lading to the buyer together to secure acceptance or payment of the bill of exchange, the buyer is bound to return the bill of lading if he does not honour the bill of exchange, and if he wrongfully retains the bill of lading the property in the goods does not pass to him.'

This sub-section will apply to export/shipping contracts. The procedure in such contracts is often that the seller sends the bill of lading obtained from the shipper to the buyer together with a bill of exchange for the price drawn on the buyer. The buyer is then supposed to make himself primarily liable on the bill of exchange by writing 'accepted' on it. The effect of s19(3) is that if the buyer does not so accept the bill of exchange then the property in the goods will not pass. In effect the passing of property through the bill of lading is conditional upon the bill of exchange being honoured by the buyer. In such a case should the buyer send on the bill of lading or the goods to a sub-buyer, the buyer can be sued for wrongful interference with goods or for the price. If the buyer becomes bankrupt with the goods and bill of lading still in his possession without having accepted the bill of exchange, the seller can claim the goods since the property has not yet passed.

Section 19(3) however does not protect the seller where the circumstances are such that s25(1) SGA operates to allow the buyer as a non-owner to pass good title to a sub-buyer taking in good faith and for value. (See Chapter 10.)

Cahn v *Pockett's Bristol Channel Co Ltd* [1899] 1 QB 643 illustrates this proposition. The seller in England contracted to sell a quantity of copper to the buyer in Rotterdam, to be loaded on a ship at Swansea. The goods were shipped on the defendant's ship. In accordance with s19(3) the seller sent the bill of lading to the buyer together with a bill of exchange drawn on the buyer for the price. The buyer therefore obtained the bill of lading lawfully with the seller's consent but he failed to honour the bill of exchange, and therefore under s19(3) the property did not pass to him and he should have returned the bill of lading. However, the buyer resold the copper to a third party using the bill of lading, and the third party paid him in good faith. The buyer became insolvent and the seller attempted to exercise his right of stoppage in transit over the goods (see Chapter 13) before they reached the buyer by instructing the defendant carriers not to deliver. The third party sued the defendants for conversion of the property and needed therefore to show an immediate right to possess the goods. The third party argued, therefore, that he now owned the goods.

In addition to s19(3), two further subsections were involved in the decision: s47(2) and s25(1).

By s47(2), where a document of title (this includes a bill of lading) has been lawfully transferred to any person as buyer or owner of the goods and that person transfers the document to a person who takes it in good faith and for valuable consideration, then if the last-mentioned transfer was by way of sale the unpaid seller's rights of lien or stoppage in transit are defeated. (See Chapter 13 for a full discussion.) The conditions in s47(2) were fulfilled in this case, so the seller's right of stoppage was defeated.

However, s47 does not mention ownership. It was held that ownership had passed to the third party under s25(1) since the relevant conditions for transfer under that section were fulfilled: he had bought goods and had possession of a document of title to them taken in good faith without notice of the seller's rights. It appears that s25(1) will therefore prevail over the provisions of s19(3) enabling the non-owner in possession of the bill of lading to pass a good title if all other conditions are fulfilled.

8.5 Acceptance: s35

Section 35 is a 'longstop' provision. In any case where property does not pass under ss17-19 it must finally pass on 'acceptance' of the goods by the buyer within the meaning of s35. (See Chapter 13 for a full discussion of the meaning of 'acceptance'.)

Under s35 the buyer is deemed to have accepted the goods when, after he intimates to the seller that he has accepted them or when the goods have been delivered to him and he has had a reasonable opportunity to examine the goods, either:

1. he does any act in relation to the goods which is inconsistent with the ownership of the seller; or
2. after the lapse of a reasonable time he retains the goods without intimating to the seller that he has rejected them.

The buyer loses his right to reject the goods when he accepts them. The buyer does not lose his right to reject the goods merely because the property has passed. If the goods delivered in fact are of the wrong quantity or description or quality under the conditions stipulated in ss13-15, the property in the goods will revert to the seller. An illustration is *Kwei Tek Chao* v *British Traders and Shippers Ltd* [1954] 2 QB 459; [1954] 1 All ER 779.

9

Risk, Impossibility and Frustration

9.1 Risk

9.2 Antecedent impossibility and frustration

9.3 The seller's bankruptcy

9.1 Risk

In the previous chapter it was explained that one reason why it was important to show when the property in the goods passed was because this often determined at which parties' risks the goods were. In this chapter the question of risk is discussed together with the related questions of frustration and impossibility of performance.

The rules relating to risk decide which of the parties to the contract will bear the loss should the goods be accidentally damaged or destroyed. The general rule is that the risk passes with the property. This principle is sometimes referred to as *'res perit domino* (things perish to the disadvantage of the owner). So, if goods are lost while the risk is still on the seller the buyer is not liable to pay the price though the seller may be liable in damages for failure to deliver. Where the risk is on the buyer when the goods perish he must pay the price although the seller cannot deliver and would not be liable in damages for failure to deliver. The principle is embodied in SGA s20(1):

'Unless otherwise agreed, the goods remain at the seller's risk until the property in them is transferred to the buyer, but when the property in them is transferred to the buyer the goods are at the buyer's risk, whether delivery has been made or not.'

Examples of the general rule appear from many of the cases discussed in Chapter 8. *Healey* v *Howlett* [1917] 1 KB 337 and *Pignataro* v *Gilroy* [1919] 1 KB 459 are good examples.

Section 20(1)

As can be seen from s20(1), the general rule operates 'unless otherwise agreed'. Such contrary agreement may be by express stipulation; or implied by a trade custom.

In *Bovington & Morris* v *Dale & Co Ltd* (1902) 7 Com Cas 112 the seller delivered furs to the buyer on approval. They were stolen during the approval period.

The seller proved a well-established custom in the fur trade that goods on approval should be at the buyer's risk. The buyer was therefore liable to pay the price.

Section 20(2)

Under s20(2), where delivery has been *delayed through the fault of either buyer or seller* the goods will be at the *risk of the party at fault* as regards any loss which might not have occurred but for such fault. It follows that if for example the seller has been dilatory in the delivery of the goods, then they will be at his risk.

In *Demby Hamilton Ltd* v *Barden* [1949] 1 All ER 435 the buyer ordered by sample 30 tons of apple juice from the manufacturer, the seller. The contract provided for delivery to be weekly in casks of 6 or 12 cwts up to the quantity desired by the buyer. To ensure that the juice corresponded with sample the seller had to make all 30 tons at once. The buyer requested that the seller stop the deliveries after only a few weeks and never gave the instruction for them to recommence. The juice deteriorated.

HELD: The property had not passed to the buyer but the goods were at his *risk*, and he was liable for the deterioration (s20(2)).

The party at fault is, of course, only liable for loss which might not have occurred but for his fault, not for all losses.

Section 20(3)

Section 20(3) provides: 'Nothing in this section affects the duties or liabilities of either seller or buyer as a bailee or custodian of the goods of the other party.'

An illustration of this provision is *Wiehe* v *Dennis Bros* (1913) 29 TLR 250. A Shetland pony was sold, then bailed back to the seller to use it for a charitable collection at an Olympia show. Ultimately the bailee seller could not explain how the horse came to be damaged in his charge and so was liable under the rules of bailment.

Miscellaneous points arising under s20:

The risk passing before the property

In certain cases the *risk* can pass before the property. This may even take place in an unidentified portion of a larger bulk.

The celebrated case of *Sterns Ltd* v *Vickers Ltd* [1923] 1 KB 28 is an example. The buyer contracted to sell to the seller 120 000 gallons of white spirit which was stored in a tank (belonging to a third party bailee) containing 200 000 gallons. The 120 000 gallons was not separated. The seller gave to the buyer a delivery order for the spirit which the buyer in turn submitted to the bailee who accepted it. (This represents an *attornment* since the bailee thereby agreed to hold for the buyer not the seller.) All 200 000 gallons were then destroyed. The Court of Appeal held that the risk had passed to the buyer although the property remained in the seller.

The acceptance of the delivery order must have been crucial to the result of this case: it gave the buyer the immediate right to possess the goods. This would distinguish *Healey* v *Howlett* (Chapter 8) where there was no delivery order. The Court of Appeal in *Sterns* would (as considered below) have been in great difficulty if only a part of the 200 000 gallons had been destroyed: for example, 100 000 gallons. It was unclear *which* 120 000 gallons was at the buyer's risk. In such circumstances, how much of the 100 000 could be said to be the buyer's?

The exceptional nature of the *Sterns* case was emphasised by the House of Lords in *Comptoir d'Achat et de Vente* v *Luis de Ridder* [1949] AC 293; [1949] 1 All ER 269. Lord Normand commented:

> 'In those cases in which it has been held that the risk without the property has passed to the buyer it has been because the buyer rather than the seller was seen to have an immediate and practical interest in the goods, as for instance when he has an immediate right under the storekeeper's delivery warrant to the delivery of a portion of an undivided bulk in store, or an immediate right under several contracts with different persons to the whole of a bulk not yet appropriated to the several contracts.'

The risk remains with the seller

It is not easy to envisage circumstances where the risk remains in the seller after the property has passed, in the absence of an express agreement.

Head v *Tattersall* (1871) LR 7 Ex 7 is an example but it has been doubted whether this case has survived the SGA. Plaintiff bought a horse from the defendant who warranted that it had 'hunted with the Bicester Hounds' and who allowed the plaintiff a week to return it if it did not answer the description. The horse had an accident during that week and the plaintiff claimed to return it having discovered it had not hunted with the named hounds. Rather surprisingly it was held that the plaintiff could return the horse and recover the price. The risk was therefore on the seller, although the property had almost certainly passed to the buyer.

The case could (as Atiyah envisages) illustrate a broader principle that risk always remains with the seller where the buyer retains a right of rejection.

The passing of the risk in CIF and FOB contracts

The CIF Contract. This signifies that the price includes the cost of the goods, insurance and freight. Like the FOB contract, it is invariably used in export sales. Normally the *property* in a CIF contract passes only when the shipping documents are presented to the buyer but the *risk* passes as soon as the goods cross the ship's rail onto the ship.

The FOB Contract. This signifies that the goods will be put 'free on board' the ship and the costs from that moment lie with the buyer. *Property and risk* normally pass when the goods cross the ship's rail going on board.

Section 33 SGA

Section 33 SGA provides that where the seller of goods agrees to deliver them at his own risk at a place other than where they are sold, the buyer must still unless otherwise agreed take the risk of deterioration in the goods *necessarily incident to* the course of transit.

The risks referred to would appear to be only those risks which would have arisen with any goods answering the contract description. A risk of deterioration arising only because the goods were defective when shipped would not be included. Indeed, *Mash & Murrell Ltd* v *Joseph I Emmanuel* [1962] 1 WLR 16 suggests that the continuing nature of the warranty of merchantable quality to a large extent makes s33 redundant. In that case sellers in Cyprus sold potatoes under a CIF contract for shipment to Liverpool. The potatoes were sound when loaded in Cyprus but by the time the ship reached Liverpool they were rotten. It was held that the seller's warranty that the goods are of merchantable quality continues for a reasonable time after shipment in a CIF contract. The proposition that the warranty is a continuing one is not well settled but it has recently been re-stated by Lord Diplock in *Lambert* v *Lewis* [1982] AC 225 at 276 in the House of Lords.

9.2 Antecedent impossibility and frustration

The SGA, in addition to preserving the general rules of the common law as regards frustration and antecedent impossibility, contains two provisions, ss6 and 7, dealing in particular with the perishing of specific goods before the property in them has passed to the buyer.

Impossibility: s6

Section 6 is not strictly a rule about frustration but simply a statutory example of the equivalent common law rule rendering a contract void for antecedent impossibility. Section 6 provides that, unless otherwise agreed:

> 'Where there is a contract for the sale of specific goods, and the goods without the knowledge of the seller have *perished* at the time when the contract is made, the contract is void.'

An illustrative case is *Couturier* v *Hastie* (1856) 5 HL Cas 673. The defendant here was agent of the plaintiffs, and sold on their behalf a cargo of corn. However, before the date of that sale the cargo had already been sold lawfully by the ship's Master. The buyer repudiated, so the plaintiffs sued their defendant agent, who would be liable only if the purchasers would have been liable.

HELD: The defendant was not liable. The contract was avoided.

Section 6 will not apply to cases where the goods *have never existed*; it applies only where specific goods perish before the contract is made.

In *McRae* v *Commonwealth Disposals Commission* (1951) 84 CLR 377 the buyer contracted to buy a shipwrecked tanker purportedly lying on a specified reef off the Australian coast. The buyer incurred expenditure preparing his salvage expedition but it subsequently transpired that both the tanker and the reef were non-existent. The High Court of Australia held that the seller had warranted in the contract that there was a tanker at the position specified. He had warranted the existence of the goods and accordingly was liable to pay damages for breach of that warranty. Section 6 had no application in these circumstances since, although a sale was impossible there was nevertheless an agreement to sell, for the breach of which the party at risk was liable in damages.

A different result could have been reached by the court if it had found that the existence of the goods was an implied condition precedent to the liability of the parties - in which case the seller could have escaped liability.

In any case under s6 there could be an express or implied promise by the seller that the goods have not perished at the time of the contract, in which case he would be liable for breach of that promise if the goods had in fact perished at that time.

The meaning of 'perished'

The meaning of 'perished' in s6 has given rise to some difficulty and its interpretation is also relevant to s7. The question is does it apply only to the complete physical destruction of the goods or does it go further and included partial loss of the goods; or even perishing in a commercial sense.

The leading case in the area is *Barrow Lane & Ballard Ltd* v *Phillip Phillips & Co Ltd* [1929] 1 KB 574. Goode and Atiyah both hold the view, which is undoubtedly correct, that as regards the meaning of 'perish' this case is equally applicable to s7. The seller sold to the buyer a 'Lot' of 700 bags of ground nuts sitting on a specified wharf. Unknown to both parties, before the contract was made 109 bags had been stolen, and before collection a total of 400 bags had been stolen.

HELD: The contract was void because at the time of the contract there was no 'Lot' of 700 bags. It had already been reduced without fault of either party.

Some academic writers have used this case as authority for the proposition that if only *some* and not all of the goods have perished then the parties are released from their obligations. The counter-argument is, of course, that the subject of the *Barrow* contract of sale was the 'Lot' of 700 bags, and it was precisely that 'Lot' which had entirely ceased to exist as a 'Lot' of 700 bags. The mere fact that there remained a pile of some 591 bags on the wharf at the time of the contract was immaterial. If this second line of argument is followed, then presumably, had the goods been described simply as '700 bags of ground nuts' on the specified wharf and not as a 'Lot' of 700 bags, the goods would not have 'perished' by the time of the contract.

There have been several odd decisions on the meaning of 'perish' and it remains effectively undecided whether goods have perished if only part of them are destroyed. It is submitted that the better view is that such goods have perished, subject of course to the '*de minimis*' principle where the number having perished is 'microscopic'.

In *Sainsbury v Street* [1972] 1 WLR 834; [1972] 3 All ER 1127 it was suggested that where part only of the goods perish then the seller may be obliged to offer the remaining goods to the buyer but that the buyer may not be obliged to take them.

Although there are no cases decided under s6 on this point, it seems likely that 'perished' can also relate to the *quality* of the goods. If there has been a sufficiently serious deterioration in quality of some or all of the goods so that the goods as set out in the contract have *ceased to exist in a commercial sense* then those goods will have 'perished'.

Support for this view is found in several cases on freight and insurance law, of which *Asfar v Blundell* [1896] 1 QB 123 is one of the best known. A ship containing a cargo of dates sank but was subsequently salvaged. The dates while still having the appearance of dates were not of merchantable quality as dates and could not be sold as such. They could, however, still be used for distillation into spirits. Ultimately the cargo owners claimed under their insurance policy for a total loss of cargo.

HELD: The cargo owners should succeed. There was a total loss of dates in the commercial sense since they could no longer be sold as dates. As Esher MR put it:

> 'The ingenuity of the argument might commend itself to a body of chemists, but not to businessmen. We are dealing with dates as a subject matter of commerce; and it is contended that, although these dates were under water for two days, and when brought up were simply a mass of pulpy matters impregnated with sewage and in a state of fermentation, there had been no change in their nature, and they still were dates. There is a perfectly well known test which has for many years been applied to such cases as the present - that test is whether, as a matter of business, the nature of the thing has been altered.'

Against this view there are obiter remarks of Morris J in *Horn v Minister of Food* [1948] 2 All ER 1036 where it was held that potatoes which had so rotted as to be worthless had not perished within the meaning of s7. *Benjamin* appears to doubt the correctness of this view and Atiyah argues that it cannot be supported. It is clear that in all such cases the goods must be unsaleable under the contract description.

Finally, it should be noted that if part of the goods perish and the part of the contract relating to those goods is *severable*, then s6 or s7 will apply only to that part.

Frustration

Specific goods

Where it applies, frustration discharges both parties from their obligations under the contract whereas where there is no frustration but the risk rules applies one or other party bears the loss. The law relating to frustration of contracts for the sale of goods is somewhat complex and confused probably, as Atiyah suggests, because of the failure of the SGA to distinguish between different kinds of unascertained goods.

Section 7 provides:

> 'Where there is an agreement to sell specific goods, and subsequently the goods, without any fault on the part of the seller or the buyer, perish before the risk passes to the buyer, the agreement is thereby voided.'

The limitations on this section should be noted. Like s6 it applies only to agreements to sell *specific goods* and does not cover unascertained goods or even goods ascertained subsequent to the contract. It does not apply where there is an immediate sale but only where there is an 'agreement to sell' by which property will only pass to the buyer at a future date.

The perishing in s7 must take place *after* the contract is made but *before* risk passes. The fault of either party in the perishing, or an agreement between the parties to the contrary will exclude the application of s7. Similarly if the risk has already passed to the buyer then s7 is excluded and the buyer must bear the loss and pay the contract price.

The section only refers to goods 'perishing' though this is not the only way in which a contract can be frustrated. A contract could be frustrated if, for example, it became illegal to sell certain goods. Where s7 does not apply and the risk has not passed to the buyer then the common law rules of frustration may apply. (The common law rules themselves do not apply if either party is at fault.) A frustrating event at common law must destroy the whole basis of the contract.

The Frustrated Contracts Act 1943 does not apply to sales of specific goods which perish (see s2(5)(c) of that Act).

Atiyah submits that a contract cannot be frustrated *by perishing* other than under s7, which would mean that common law frustration in this area would have to be by events other than the *perishing* of the goods.

The frustration of contracts for the sale of unascertained goods

There is no provision in the SGA governing the frustration of contracts for unascertained goods. In dealing with this area, it is necessary to distinguish two types of unascertained goods.

Purely generic goods (ie goods coming from an unspecified source). An agreement to sell purely generic goods, such as '50 tons of wheat' or '10 bottles of red wine' probably cannot be frustrated by the perishing or destruction of the goods. It is no concern of the buyer's that the seller may have had a particular source in mind which happens to be destroyed after the contract is made.

For example, the seller contracts to sell to the buyer unascertained goods, identified by description: 'One copy of Treitel on the Law of Contract'. It may be that the seller expects to get the book from a particular source. Even if, as is unlikely this is the only source available at that time, then the bare fact that the seller's source has dried up will not absolve the seller. He will be liable for non-delivery. Note *Blackburn Bobbin Co* v *Allen & Sons* [1918] 1 KB 540: Per McCardie J: 'A bare and unqualified contract for the sale of unascertained goods will not unless most special facts compel the opposite be dissolved by the operation of frustration.'

Such contracts may however be frustrated by events other than perishing: *Re Badische Co Ltd* [1921] 2 Ch 331.

Goods which are part of a larger consignment. If the source of the goods has been specified in the contract, for example, 'a Bentley VI motor car from Smith's garage' or '100 tons of wheat from Jones' Mill' then there seems to be no reason why such contracts should not be frustrated at common law by perishing or otherwise.

For example, if a crop to be grown on a specified piece of land which is subject of a contract of sale fails to mature in the quantity contracted for then the seller should not be liable for the shortfall. The buyer can insist on delivery of what has matured, at the contract rate (s30(1)), or reject the same without liability. Authority for this can be found in *Howell* v *Coupland* (1876) 1 QBD 258 and *Sainsbury* v *Street* (supra).

It will be noted that in events other than perishing it will be difficult to persuade the court that the whole basis of the contract has been destroyed where the goods are unascertained.

NOTE: The Law Reform (Frustrated Contracts) Act 1943 applies to all contracts for the sale of unascertained goods. (It will also apply to contracts for the sale of specific goods which are frustrated by an event *other than* the perishing of the goods). This Act makes three main changes in the law of frustration in its application to these contracts:

1. It enables a party to recover any payments made under a frustrated contract even though there has only been a partial failure of consideration.
2. It enables the payee where he has incurred expenses for the purpose of performing the contract to retain all or part of a sum which would otherwise be reasonable as on a total failure of consideration.
3. It creates a particular exception to the 'rule in *Cutter* v *Powell* (1795) 6 Term Rep 320' relating to contracts where no part of the price is payable in advance. The details of this need not detain us here.

9.3 The seller's bankruptcy

The passing of the property will generally have an effect on the position of the buyer on the seller's bankruptcy. If the property in the goods has passed to the buyer, then the buyer may claim the goods unless they remain in the seller's 'reputed ownership' (see above and the Bankruptcy Act 1914 s38(3)); or the seller has an *unpaid seller's lien* or *right of stoppage in transit* over the goods (see Chapter 11).

10

The Transfer of Title by a Non-Owner

10.1 Introduction

10.2 Estoppel

10.3 Sale under common law or statutory powers of sale or under court order

10.4 Sale in market overt

10.5 Sale under a voidable title

10.6 Sale by an agent

10.7 Sale by a mercantile agent under the Factors Act 1889

10.8 Sale by a seller in possession

10.9 Sale by a buyer in possession

10.10 Motor vehicles subject to a hire purchase or conditional sale agreement

10.11 Sale by an unpaid seller exercising his statutory rights

10.12 Other miscellaneous exceptions to *nemo dat*

10.1 Introduction

The basic rule relating to the transfer of title to goods by a non-owner is often referred to by its Latin tag: *nemo dat quod non habet*. This means simply that no one can give a better title than he himself possesses. Transfer of title by a non-owner is dealt with in the second half of Part III of the Act. In this area the Act expressly confirms the *nemo dat* rule; s21(1) provides:

'Subject to this Act, where the goods are sold by a person who is not their owner, and who does not sell them under the authority or with the consent of the owner, the buyer acquires no better title to the goods than the seller had.'

At one time the only significant exception to the *nemo dat* rule was that of sale in market overt, but in response to the commercial and social demands of the times, further exceptions to the rule have been progressively introduced both by the common law and by statute. It is worth noting the dictum of Denning LJ in *Bishopsgate Motor*

Finance Cpn Ltd v *Transport Brakes Ltd* [1949] 1 KB 322; [1949] 1 All ER 37:

> 'In the development of our law two principles have striven for mastery. The first is for the protection of property: no-one can give a better title than he himself possesses. The second is for the protection of commercial transactions: the person who takes in good faith and for value without notice should get a good title. The first principle has held sway for a long time, but it has been modified by the common law itself and by statute so as to meet the needs of our own times.'

The question which tends to arise in *nemo dat* cases is as to which of two innocent parties is to suffer when a third has committed some kind of fraud. Invariably the third has stolen the goods from A and as a non-owner has sold them to B. An inflexible application of the *nemo dat* rule would mean that where the third's title is defective, then so is B's who took from him. The law however incorporates a variety of exceptions to the basic rule and the main ones appear in the SGA itself.

Although the situation is rare in practice, *nemo dat* also applies at common law to cases where an owner sells goods subject to some encumbrance or charge existing in favour of a third party.

The exceptions to *nemo dat* must now be considered. They are set out below.

10.2 Estoppel

This exception is embodied in the second part of s21(1):

> 'Subject to this Act, where goods are sold by a person who is not their owner ... the buyer acquires no better title to the goods than the seller had, unless the owner of the goods is by his conduct precluded from denying the seller's authority to sell.'

This subsection leaves the common law rules as to when the owner will be so precluded intact. Section 21 can only operate to pass title where there has been a sale, if the parties have made merely an ageement to sell then s21 will not pass title (see *Shaw* v *Metropolitan Police Commissioner* [1987] 3 All ER 405). The doctrine of estoppel operates in this context in the following situations:

1. Where the owner has by his words or conduct represented that the seller is in fact the true owner or has the owner's authority to sell the goods.
2. Where the owner has by his negligent failure to act allowed the seller to appear as the true owner or as having the owner's authority to sell.

In these situations the owner will be estopped from denying the truth of the representations made to the buyer, and the buyer will take a good title.

The treatment of estoppel is often sub-divided into estoppel by words, estoppel by conduct and estoppel by negligence. These distinctions are of some value in understanding the doctrine. The first two of these would come under 1(a) above, and the third under 1(b) above. The wording of s21(1) seems to imply that estoppel by words is really a type of estoppel by conduct but there would in any case be no real legal significance attached to the distinction between words or conduct estoppel. All these forms of estoppel involve a representation of some sort and it is submitted that estoppel 'by negligence' is merely a representation made by omission (eg omitting to correct a misrepresentation made by a third). However, for ease of reference, estoppel by conduct or words (ie situation (1) above) will be referred to as 'estoppel by representation' and estoppel by negligence (situation (2) above) will be referred to as such.

In any estoppel the party to whom the representation is made must act on it and alter his position. This is done in the present context when the representee buys the goods thereby altering his position. As *Benjamin* points out the estoppel is an unusual one in that it binds not only the true owner but confers a good title against all the world.

The origins of estoppel in this context are found in the oft-quoted dictum of Ashurst J in *Lickbarrow* v *Mason* (1787) 2 Term Rep 63, at page 70:

> 'We may lay it down as a broad general principle that whenever one of two innocent persons must suffer by the acts of a third, he who has enabled such third person to occasion the loss must sustain it.'

This dictum has been firmly rejected as being too wide. The undue width of the dictum is illustrated by the example of the householder who leaves his door open on leaving his house: this does not estop him from asserting his title against a thief who may steal from the house. The dictum is consequently now only relied on by despairing counsel who can find nothing else on which to base his claim to title. Indeed estoppel in general in this area is usually only pleaded as a last resort and is seldom successful.

The two species of estoppel outlined above will now be discussed in detail: estoppel by representation; and estoppel by negligence.

Estoppel by representation

A leading case in this area is *Farquharson Bros* v *J King & Co Ltd* [1902] AC 325. The appellants F Bros were timber merchants whose timber was bailed with a dock company at the latter's warehouse. The bailees were authorised to accept and act on the delivery orders signed by F Bros clerk. This clerk had authority to sign delivery orders for limited quantities of timber for certain listed customers only, but had no authority to sell the timber himself. The clerk fraudulently transferred some of the timber to himself under an assumed name by way of a delivery order to the bailees, and then sub-sold the timber to K Co, instructing the bailees by delivery order to deliver to them. F Bros then sued K Co in conversion. Matthews J whose decision was upheld by the House of Lords held that the defence of estoppel failed because K Co had not acted on any representation made by F Bros concerning the authority of the clerk. What was necessary was a representation by F Bros to K Co that the middleman (the clerk) was the owner.

It is by no means clear what acts in fact will definitely amount to an estoppel.

There are many cases stating what will not amount to estoppel and few which try to define what *will* be an estoppel. It is at least settled that the mere delivery of possession is not by itself sufficient to give rise to an estoppel even though possession was transferred with a view to sale and even though the owner was careless or negligent. What appears to be necessary is some words or conduct which in some way 'holds out' the third party as being the owner or having the authority to sell.

The dictum of Lord Wright in *Mercantile Bank of India Ltd* v *Central Bank of India Ltd* [1938] AC 297 is helpful: 'If estoppel by representation is to be invoked, there must be some act which positively misleads the third party beyond merely allowing a non-owner to have possession of the goods.'

It is submitted that the cases establish the following elements to be necessary for estoppel to operate:

1. Some knowledge of the proposed sale or disposition to the buyer or to the world at large must be present in the mind of the original owner.
2. There must be some kind of 'holding out' of the third party as being the owner or having authority to sell.
3. Carelessness or inactivity on the owner's part is unnecessary.
4. Simple delivery of possession is insufficient.
5. Nor does it make a difference if it turns out that the middleman is untrustworthy and the owner had doubts about him.

Benjamin notes that if the mere delivery of possession were adequate to raise an estoppel then any bailor would be estopped from denying his bailee's right to sell the goods and there would be no need at all for the Factors Act (see later). In *Benjamin*'s view the true owner must have so acted as to mislead the buyer into the belief that the seller was entitled to sell the goods, and the delivery of possession of the goods is therefore neither a necessary nor a sufficient condition to raise such an estoppel. Similarly the mere delivery by the true owner to another person of the possession of documents of title to goods docs not at common law estop him from asserting his title against one who has purchased the goods from that person (see below *Mercantile Bank of India* v *Central Bank of India*). Even though in one sense he could be said to have enabled the seller to represent that he was the owner by investing him with the documents necessary to appear as owner, it is clear that the delivery of possession of documents of title in itself has no greater effect than the delivery of possession of the goods themselves.

The following cases are illustrative of the general position. In *Jerome* v *Bentley* [1952] 2 All ER 114 T expressed interest in a diamond ring in J's shop priced at £550, saying he was considering it as a present for his mother. T had introduced himself as being a certain 'Major X'. T said he thought the ring to be more valuable than the £550 price and J agreed to give T the ring for him to sell within seven days for whatever price T could get, returning only £550 to J. T therefore obtained possession as agent and not as purchaser, and a written note of the transaction was taken. Eleven days later T offered to sell the ring to B. B asked whether T was the owner and T replied that he was and signed a note to that effect. J now claimed the ring from the buyer. It should be noted that T had no authority to sell after the expiry of seven days. Donovan J found that ownership had not passed to B since no *nemo dat* exception applied. There was no representation sufficient to raise an estoppel, nor under a further argued exception (see below) could T be seen as a mercantile agent since he was here acting only as a private individual.

Henderson & Co v *Williams* [1895] 1 QB 521 provides a good example of estoppel by words. O's goods were stored in a warehouse owned by W. F then fraudulently induced O to sell the goods to him: the contract was void for mistake. O instructed W to hold the goods to the order of F. F offered to sell the goods to H who being suspicious of the bona fides of F, made enquiries from W. W supplied H with a written statement that the goods were held to the order of F, and when this did not satisfy H, W endorsed it with a further statement that W now held the goods to H's order. H then bought the goods from F. On discovering the fraud O instructed W to detain the goods and indemnified him for so doing. The Court of Appeal held that both O and W were estopped from denying H's right to the goods. This was so in O's case because he represented that F was the owner of the goods by ordering W to transfer the goods in F's name. In W's case this was because he had attorned to H (so representing to him) that he held the goods to his order.

One case goes against the propositions laid out above on what is required to establish an estoppel. In *Commonwealth Trust Ltd* v *Akotey* [1926] AC 72 it appears to have been held here that the mere transfer of possession of a document was adequate to found an estoppel. Akotey, a cocoa grower in the Gulf Coast, consigned a number of bags of cocoa to a certain Mr Laing and sent him a consignment note. The two parties were negotiating the sale of this cocoa and no price had yet been agreed and no binding contract made (the *nemo dat* exception in s25 therefore could not come into play - see below). Laing sold the cocoa to the Commonwealth Trust and delivered the consignment note. He then died insolvent without having paid to Akotey the price received from the Commonwealth Trust. The Privy Council held that Akotey by sending the consignment note to Laing had 'clothed Laing with all the authority to sell the cocoa'.

This case is generally regarded as being wrongly decided. The mere transfer of possession of the goods themselves will not itself found an estoppel and it seems strange that the transfer of possession of a document relating to the goods should do so.

Akotey was rejected by the Privy Council itself in a later decision in *Mercantile Bank of India Ltd* v *Central Bank of India Ltd* (supra). The exporters of ground nuts had bought 35 consignments and obtained 35 consignment notes. They pledged these notes to the Central Bank in return for a loan. It was the Central Bank's practice when the goods relating to such notes arrived to collect them and store them with a bailee warehouse. When the goods arrived, however, the Central Bank handed back the consignment notes to the pledger (the exporter) so that he could collect the goods and place them in the bank's bailee warehouse. Instead of doing this the exporter pledged the documents to the Mercantile Bank and obtained a second loan. The Central Bank sued the Mercantile Bank for conversion, claiming that the middleman had no authority to dispose of the documents or goods as he had done, and had merely been the Central Bank's agent with authority *only to collect the goods*. The Mercantile Bank argued that the act of returning the consignment note to the pledger founded an estoppel, following the *Akotey* case. The Privy Council held that there was no estoppel. The possession of the consignment notes 'no more conveyed a representation that the merchants were entitled to dispose of the property than the actual possession of the goods themselves would have done'. Lord Wright expressly declined to follow *Akotey*.

In *Central Newbury Car Auctions* v *Unity Finance Ltd* (1957) 1 QB 371; [1956] 3 All ER 905, a rogue introducing himself as a 'Mr Cullis' offered to buy from Central Newbury CA a second-hand Morris car on hire purchase terms. He left his Hillman Minx car in part exchange which it transpired was also let on hire purchase. After filling in a hire purchase proposal form he was allowed to remove the car, together with its registration book in which the car appeared as registered under the name of 'Ashley'. The rogue sold the car to Unity Finance claiming to be Ashley and forging the appropriate signature. Central Newbury sued Unity Finance for the return of the car. Morris LJ in the majority of the Court of Appeal (Denning LJ dissenting) held that there was no estoppel and that Central Newbury CA were therefore entitled to recover the car. The registration book was not a document of title, in fact it contained a warning that the person under whose name the car is registered may not be the owner. Therefore it was not possible to say that Central Newbury CA had in any way represented the rogue as the owner or as having the owner's authority to sell. The mere delivery of possession of the car to the rogue was not itself sufficient to found an estoppel. Morris LJ added that there could only have been an estoppel if Unity Finance had shown that Central Newbury owed them a duty of care and that it had been breached. (Such a situation would come under 'Estoppel by negligence'.)

In *Eastern Distributors Ltd* v *Goldring* [1957] 2 QB 600; [1957] 2 All ER 525, the owner of a Bedford van, M, wanted to buy a Chrysler car from G, a car dealer, but was unable to pay the deposit. They agreed that M should sign proposal forms showing that G owned both vehicles and that M wanted them both on hire purchase. G submitted the forms to Eastern Distributors, a finance company, who accepted the proposal for the van but rejected the one for the car. When M was informed of this fact he assumed that the whole deal was off and did not pay the instalments to the finance company on the accepted hire purchase of the van. G then sold the van to Eastern Distributors. The Court of Appeal held: that by signing the proposal forms M had represented that G had the right to sell the van, and Eastern Distributors had altered their position in reliance on that representation; that M was therefore estopped from denying this; and accordingly that when G sold the van to Eastern Distributors they acquired a good title. According to Atiyah it seems odd that the case was not decided on the simpler ground that G had M's apparent authority to sell although in fact he exceeded such authority.

In *Shaw* v *Commissioner of Police (Natalegawa, claimant)* (supra), the claimant owned a car which he advertised for sale. He was contacted by L, who claimed to be interested in purchasing it on behalf of a client. L took delivery of the car and the claimant gave him a letter stating that 'This letter serves to certify that I ... have sold the Porsche 3.3 Turbo registration number NVS 958V to Mr Jonathan London ... and from the date shown below no longer have any legal responsibility connected with that car.' In dicta the Court of Appeal stated that this representation came within the principles in *Eastern Distributors Ltd* v *Goldring* (above) and was the clearest possible representation, intended to be relied on by the ultimate purchaser, that the claimant had transferred the ownership to L. However, s21 was held not be be relevant as there was no sale in this case, merely an agreement to sell.

Estoppel by negligence

The doctrine of estoppel by negligence is severely restricted by the need for a duty of care. The party who is alleging that it is the negligence of the true owner which has given the non-owner the apparent authority to sell must establish that the owner owed him a duty of care. Such a duty does not seem to exist where the owner of goods negligently loses them or facilitates their theft or other form of fraudulent disposition.

The difficulties of proving an estoppel by negligence are well set out by Benjamin who lists them as threefold. The buyer must establish:

1. that the true owner owed him a duty to be careful;
2. that in breach of that duty the true owner was negligent; and
3. that this negligence was the proximate or real cause of the buyer being induced to part with the purchase price of the goods to the seller.

The dictum of Ashurst J in *Lickbarrow* v *Mason* (supra) is particularly inappropriate in this context and has been dissented from more often than it has been followed.

There will be no duty of care where an owner of goods is induced to part with them to a buyer under a contract which is void for mistake no matter how negligent the owner may have been in allowing the buyer to take the goods. Examples are *Cundy* v *Lindsay* (1878) App Cas 459 and *Ingram* v *Little* [1961] 1 QB 31; [1960] 3 All ER 332.

The operation of estoppel by negligence is best illustrated by reference to the decided cases.

The case of *Pickard* v *Sears* (1837) 6 A & E 469 has been seen as one of estoppel by representation but it is submitted that it is best seen as an estoppel by negligence. The owner of certain machinery exercised a bill of sale in favour of Pickard and the ownership of the machinery therefore passed to Pickard subject to a right of redemption. The original owner then came into financial difficulties and his creditors obtained an order for the sale of his property by the sheriff. The machinery which was the subject of the Bill of Sale was seized and Pickard was subsequently told that the machinery was going to be sold. He discussed the sale with colleagues but failed to take any action. After the sale Pickard claimed that the machinery was his. It was held that Pickard was estopped from claiming the machinery. He had done nothing, knowing that his property was about to be wrongfully sold. It has been argued that in reality there was never a duty of care and that the decision was based on estoppel by representation not by negligence. The 'representation' was apparently established by Pickard passively acquiescing in the sale of his property by the sheriff, thereby holding out the sheriff as having a right to sell. It is submitted that the case is best seen as one of estoppel by negligence.

In *Mercantile Credit Co Ltd v Hamblin* [1965] 2 QB 242; [1964] 3 All ER 592, a duty of care was established but, on the facts, was found not to be broken. The defendant asked a dealer if she could get a loan on the security of her car. The dealer was apparently respectable and solvent. He gave her certain hire purchase forms to sign in blank which she signed thinking them to be some kind of mortgage transaction, but she retained possession of her car throughout. The dealer then gave her a blank cheque which he asked her to sign for the agreed figure when the scheme was finally completed. The dealer completed the hire purchase forms so as to constitute an offer by himself to sell the car to the M Credit Co Ltd (a finance company), and an offer by the defendant to take the car from M Credit Co Ltd on hire purchase terms. Without further consultation with the defendant the dealer forwarded the forms to M Credit Co Ltd which purported to accept both offers. The defendant repudiated the alleged agreement and M Credit Co Ltd claimed the car. The Court of Appeal held that the defendant was not bound by the agreement since she had not in fact authorised the dealer to make any offer to M Credit Co Ltd and was not estopped from denying that she had done so. The court did hold that the defendant owed a duty of care sufficient to raise an estoppel, but on the facts of the case she was not in breach of this duty: it was not unreasonable for her to have trusted this dealer.

In *Hamblin* the court treated the duty of care required in this area of estoppel as the same as that which arises in the ordinary law of negligence in both its nature and existence. There was a sufficient relationship or sufficient proximity between defendant and plaintiff that the defendant intended the document she was signing to be an offer, subject to certain conditions, to the plaintiff, and that she gave the documents to the dealer.

The House of Lords in *Moorgate* (below) apparently agreed that negligence in this area should be treated like negligence in the ordinary tortious meaning, save that any question of remoteness of damage will not arise.

The *Goldring* case was distinguished in *Hamblin* on the grounds that in that case M had expressly agreed that the dealer should make the representation to the finance company.

In *Coventry Shepperd & Co v Great Eastern Railway Co* (1883) 11 QBD 776 the defendant issued two delivery orders in respect of the same bulk of goods. This negligent act enabled the issuee to represent that the goods were in fact available, thereby raising an estoppel.

In *Moorgate Mercantile Co Ltd v Twitchings* [1977] AC 890; [1976] 2 All ER 641, the leading case on estoppel, both estoppel by negligence and estoppel by representation were unsuccessfully pleaded. This case is also notable because the majority of the House of Lords appears to have departed from *Hamblin* in apparently holding the negligence involved in estoppel by negligence to be different from that in the ordinary law of tort.

Twitchings centred around an organisation known as 'Hire-Purchase Information' (HPI). This body was set up by finance companies to prevent fraud in connection with hire purchase agreements, and most finance companies were members of HPI at the relevant time, together with many motor dealers as affiliated members. HPI kept a register of vehicles let on hire purchase: it was the practice of finance companies to inform HPI of any hire purchase agreement they entered into in relation to any vehicle, but at the relevant time it was not a condition of their membership that they do so. It should be noted of course that such registration was the whole purpose of membership and about 98 per cent of all hire purchase agreements on cars were so registered. The records kept by HPI were of great use to motor dealers as a means of checking whether a vehicle they were offered for sale was in fact subject to a hire purchase agreement. When he was offered a vehicle, a motor dealer would therefore contact HPI which would in reply to his enquiry issue a 'search voucher' under the express conditions:

1. that all information supplied was given to the best knowledge and belief of HPI according to the information contained in its records;
2. that HPI did not warrant or guarantee that it had a complete record of every vehicle which was the subject of a hire purchase agreement or that it had a complete and up-to-date record of those vehicles which had at one time been, but had subsequently ceased to be subject of a hire purchase agreement; and
3. that HPI did not accept liability for any action arising out of any information given.

The facts were that the plaintiffs (a finance company) let a car on hire purchase to X but omitted to register the agreement with HPI although it was a member. X offered the car for sale to the defendant who was a motor dealer and member of HPI. The defendant contacted HPI who informed him that the car was not registered with them and issued a 'search voucher' subsequently on the terms given above. The defendant bought the car, but when the plaintiffs discovered what had happened they sued the defendant in conversion.

The defendant contended that the plaintiffs were estopped from asserting their title to the car and put forward two arguments to this end:

1. There was an estoppel by representation. The defendant had to argue here that HPI gave the information as agent of the plaintiffs, and that since HPI had 'stated' that the car was not the subject of a hire purchase agreement, this representation estopped the plaintiffs.
2. There was an estoppel by negligence. The defendant argued that the plaintiffs were negligent in omitting to register the hire purchase agreement with HPI. This he argued gave rise to an estoppel by negligence and the plaintiffs could no longer assert their title.

The majority of the House of Lords rejected both the defendant's arguments and upheld the plaintiffs' claim.

Estoppel by representation was rejected for two reasons. The more obvious reason was simply that the statement made by HPI was *true*. HPI did *not* say that *there was no outstanding hire purchase agreement* in respect of the car; HPI merely stated that *there was no record of any such agreement on its files*. That statement was true. The Lords' second reason was that HPI did not act as agent of the plaintiffs: they were acting in their own capacity in quoting the information contained in their own records.

Estoppel by negligence was rejected on a more dubious reasoning. The majority of the Lords held that the plaintiffs were under no legal duty to the defendant to register or to take reasonable care in registering with HPI the hire purchase agreement in question. It was suggested by the Lords that if there had been a duty it would have been owed to the whole world, an impractical situation, but it is submitted that such a duty could have been confined to members of HPI. The Lords thought it important that smaller finance companies were not members of HPI and that the dealer here admitted that he was aware of this, so that the HPI information was not necessarily foolproof. Furthermore the relevant documents could be in the post going to HPI. A combination of these factors in the Lords' view meant that a dealer who bought a car after receiving a negative report from HPI was in any case to be regarded as taking a reasonable business risk. Thus the defendant could not plead that the plaintiffs were estopped by reason of their negligence from pursuing their claim.

Lords Wilberforce and Salmon dissented on this second point and thought that there was a duty of care owed by the finance company. This view is preferred by Atiyah who thinks that if the case had been approached as if it were a simple negligence action in tort then the court would probably have imposed a duty of care. In this respect the court departed from *Hamblin* which had associated negligence in this context with negligence in the ordinary law of tort. Of course, an ordinary negligence action would have produced other difficulties, such as the problem of whether an action lies for purely economic loss.

The rules of HPI have now been changed so members are now under an obligation to register agreements with it, so the particular decision in *Moorgate* will now only be relevant where a non-member of HPI is involved.

In conclusion it must be added that the doctrine of estoppel is very closely linked with the doctrine of the ostensible (or apparent) authority of an agent (discussed below). It is based on very similar principles and should be seen in this context. Indeed Goode deals with estoppel under 'apparent authority' and 'apparent ownership'.

10.3 Sale under common law or statutory powers of sale or under court order

Section 21(2)(b) provides:

> 'Nothing in this Act affects –
> (b) The validity of any contract of sale under any special common law or statutory power of sale, or under the order of a court of competent jurisdiction.'

This subsection preserves a variety of specialised legal situations in which a non-owner may pass a good title. It is only necessary to deal with the main examples, categorised as follows: common law powers; statutory powers; sale by order of the court.

Common law powers

At common law a pledgee has power to sell the goods pledged and in doing so give a good title to the purchaser. However, if the pledge is made under a 'regulated agreement' (ie taken by the provider of credit from a consumer) then the power will be governed by the Consumer Credit Act 1974 which has different provisions.

Another example would in theory be sale through 'agency of necessity' where the agent has no real authority to sell but sells in fact in circumstances rendering such disposition necessary. There is no English authority on sale through such agency but it was discussed by Scrutton LJ in *Sims* v *Midland Ry* [1913] 1 KB 103.

In this case a consignment of butter was loaded onto a train at Bristol. After only 14 miles the train was held up by a strike. It was a warm evening and the butter soon began to melt. The station master therefore sold it at a greatly reduced price. The case was decided on the terms of the actual contract of sale, but the court recognised that there was no reason why agency of necessity could not occur on land as well as at sea, as in the older cases.

Statutory powers

There is a variety of such statutory powers. The most important of these are:

A sheriff's power to seize and sell goods
The power of a sheriff to seize and sell goods under a writ of execution under section 15 of the Bankruptcy and Deeds of Arrangement Act 1913.

An illustration of the working of this power is *Curtis v Maloney* [1951] 1 KB 736; [1950] 2 All ER 982. Here goods held by a bailee were seized by a sheriff levying execution against the bailee's debts. The goods were sold by the sheriff and the owner argued that the sale was wrongful. It was held that the buyer acquired a good title even when the goods did not belong to the person against whom execution was issued and even where the buyer knew of the owner's existence. Following s15 of the Bankruptcy Act the former owner had no cause of action against the sheriff or the buyer but only against the execution creditors for the proceeds of sale.

This case is supported by *Dyal Singh v Kenyan Ins Ltd* [1954] AC 287; [1954] 1 All ER 847.

The power of an innkeeper to sell goods
The power of an innkeeper to sell goods upon which he has a lien under s1 of the Innkeepers Act 1878. These will be the goods of a guest whose bill is wholly or partly unpaid.

The powers of a bailee
The powers under the Torts (Interference with Goods) Act 1977. Section 12 confers power on a bailee to sell goods after due notice has been given in various circumstances specified in the 1977 Act. Where the bailee is unable to trace the bailor he may still be able to sell the goods subject to the Act's conditions. Sale here gives good title to the purchaser as against the bailor but not against the true owner if the bailor had no authority to bail the goods. The 1977 Act would now govern the position which occurred in *Sachs v Miklos* [1948] 2 KB 23; [1948] 1 All ER 67. In 1940 A arranged with B that B would store A's furniture gratuitously in B's house. By 1943 B was finding this arrangement inconvenient so he wrote to A three times but received no reply. In 1944 when there was obviously no demand for second hand furniture B sold A's furniture for £15. In 1946 A turned up and B explained the position and handed over the £15. In 1946 the furniture would have been worth £115, so A sued B for conversion, and the court found for A. Today the Torts (Interference with Goods) Act 1977 ss12 and 13 would govern the position and a bailee who cannot get instructions from the owner despite reasonable efforts would be allowed to sell and pass good title.

Powers relating to the pawning of goods
The powers under the Consumer Credit Act 1974 which relate to the pawning of goods: a pawn for under £15 can under s120 be forfeited when the redemption period ends, but there are special procedures in s121 for pawns exceeding £15.

Sale under the Customs and Excise Act 1952
In *Moorgate Mercantile v Finch & Reed* [1962] 1 QB 701; [1962] 2 All ER 467 a finance company let a car to F on hire purchase. The agreement included a provision that on any default on F's part the company would repossess the car. F

took the car to a garage for repairs and subsequently gave the garage authority to lend the car to R. R used the car for smuggling and the car was seized by customs officials and sold under the Customs and Excise Act. It was held that the buyer took good title under that Act.

Sale by order of the court

The court may under the Rules of the Supreme Court order the sale of goods. It must 'for any just and sufficient reason ... be desirable to have (the goods) sold at once'. Examples would be where the goods are perishable or where the market in these goods is falling.

In *Larner* v *Fawcett* [1950] 2 All ER 727 racehorse had been trained for a substantial period and bills almost equivalent to the value of the horse had mounted up for this training. The owner was therefore disinclined to collect the horse and pay the bill. The trainer sought and was granted a court order to sell the horse to pay the bill notwithstanding the objections of the owner.

10.4 Sale in market overt

This is an antiquated exception to *nemo dat* preserved by s22 of the SGA. Section 22(1) provides:

> 'Where goods are sold in market overt, according to the usage of the market, the buyer acquires a good title to the goods, provided he buys them in good faith and without notice of any defect or want of title on the part of the seller.'

It is generally agreed that this exception is out of date and should probably have been abolished in the Act.

Note that the market overt rule only protects a buyer who has bought in good faith and without notice of any defect or want of title on the part of the seller. It does not protect the seller (see *Peer* v *Humphrey* (1835) 2 A & E 495) or an auctioneer who sells the goods or any person who has previously converted the goods. The buyer in market overt acquires an absolute title to the goods.

'Market overt' – which applies only to sales and not to pledges – was defined by Jervis J in *Lee* v *Bayes* (1856) 18 CB 599 at page 601 as 'an open public and legally constituted market'. Such a market may be held under a *charter* or a *statute* or under a *long-standing custom*. The major example of a market established by long-standing custom is that a sale in every shop within the City of London will be in market overt for these purposes. This particular example was laid down in the case of *Market Overt* (1596) 5 Co Rep 83b. It is clear that sales in the City of London must be of goods which are within that shop's *usual trade*, and must be *completed* in a *shop open* to the public, by the shopkeeper (not *to* the shopkeeper).

Sales in other markets must be according to the custom of that particular market (the City of London custom, for example, is confined to shops). The market must be open and public not private, and the sale must be of goods usually sold in that market on a market day between the hours of sunrise and sunset. The sale need not be by a trader in the market provided sales by non-traders are part of that particular market's custom (note that the City of London custom includes only sales by shopkeepers).

The original idea behind market overt was that if goods were stolen, one would expect them to be sold in the local market, and in the olden days of single commodity traders one would know where to look for one's goods. So, if one did not bother to go and find them it was thought just that a buyer from the market should take a good title. However, now, in the days of easy transport and multi-commodity chain stores, the rationale of the rule has faded somewhat. For example, if Harrods were in the City of London it would be market overt for almost everything!

The Law Reform Committee 12th Report on 'Transfer of title to chattels' cited two conflicting views: one view urged that the rule be abolished and the other argued that it be rationalised and that any sale by retail or by auction should pass good title. Neither recommendation has been implemented.

The following cases illustrate some of the requirements of market overt sales in the City of London and in other markets.

Sale in the City of London must be in the public part of the shop. In *Hargreave* v *Spink* [1892] 1 QB 25 the sale took place in an upper room above a shop in the City of London into which customers were only allowed by special invitation of the shopkeeper. This was not market overt since it was not a sale in the public part of the shop. This case is not as has been suggested authority for the proposition that sales in the City must be on the shop's ground-floor!

The whole transaction must take place in the City. In sales in the City of London, the *whole* transaction must take place in the City, and it must be a sale *by* the shopkeeper not *to* him.

In *Crane* v *London Dock Co* (1864) 5 B & S 313 the shopkeeper owned two shops, one in the City of London and one outside. He agreed to buy stolen opium in the shop in the City but the goods were delivered to the shop outside the City. This was not market overt since part of the sale took place outside the City and it was a sale *to* the shopkeeper not *by* him.

The latter reasoning is illustrated again in *Ardath Tobacco Ltd* v *Ocker* (1930) 47 TLR 177.

Sales in the City must be in a shop. In *Clayton* v *Leroy* [1911] 2 KB 1031 the plaintiff bought an easily identifiable watch from the defendant jewellers. A number of years later the watch was stolen; the plaintiff informed the jewellers of this and asked them to look out for the watch. The watch was later sold to T in an auction room in the City of London and he resold it to B who took it to the defendant jewellers to ask if it was genuine. The jewellers recognised it and informed the plaintiff. When B was informed of the position he offered to return the watch to the plaintiff if the latter would pay him what he had paid for it. The plaintiff refused and issued a writ against the defendant jewellers maintaining that they were wrongfully detaining the watch. It was held that the sale to T had not been in market overt since it took place in an auction room in the City, not in a shop. B therefore had no good title and the plaintiff succeeded. (The Court of Appeal reversed this on a different ground.) Note that other markets could and do have customs whereby auctions rooms are market overt.

Sales in other markets must take place between sunrise and sunset. In Reid v Commissioner of Police of the Metropolis [1973] QB 551; [1973] 2 All ER 97 a stolen candelabra was sold to a purchaser taking in good faith at a market in Southwark. The sale took place during normal market hours (ie after 7 am) but before sunrise which was at 8.19 am on the day in question. The Court of Appeal held that the buyer was not entitled to the goods because the sale had been before sunrise. Only sales between sunrise and sunset were protected by s22(1).

The historic justification of this condition is presumably that the goods must be offered for sale at a time when everyone passing could see them and recognise them if they were the true owner!

Sales in markets outside the City must be according to the usual manner or custom of that particular market. In Bishopsgate Motor Finance Corporation v Transport Brakes Ltd (supra) the plaintiff let a car to B on hire purchase and gave to B the registration document with B's name on it. B took the car to Maidstone market to sell it. He failed to sell it by auction but later, while the car was parked in the market car-park a dealer approached B and bought the car. The question arose as to whether this was market overt. The Court of Appeal held that this was market overt since it was established by statute. It was customary in this market for individuals to sell goods privately provided an attempt had been made to sell by auction. Good title to the car had therefore passed.

The best solution to the anomalous exception of market overt might well be to expand the rule logically to cover all retail sales in shops, since one does expect to take good title when one buys goods from the shelf in a shop. Auction sales should be excluded from market overt.

10.5 Sale under a voidable title

Section 23 provides:

> 'When the seller of goods has a voidable title to them, but his title has not been voided at the time of the sale, the buyer acquires a good title to the goods, provided he buys them in good faith and without notice of the seller's defect of title.'

This section confirms the pre-existing common law rule that a person cannot void a voidable contract to the prejudice of rights acquired by a third party in good faith and for value. It is essential to distinguish contracts which are completely *void* and those which are merely *voidable* since s23 will only operate in the latter case.

Most cases in this area involve the purchase of goods by some fraud where the purchaser disposes of the goods before the seller voids the contract. Where the contract is so voidable then the third party who buys from the fraudulent purchaser will take a good title to the goods.

If, however, the contract is void (ie the fraud is such as to nullify the offer and acceptance and prevent a 'real' contract from coming into existence) then the fraudulent purchaser and the third party acquire no title. In such circumstances the ultimate purchaser will have to attempt to invoke another *nemo dat* exception.

The real distinction between void and voidable contracts, where the contract has been induced by fraud, lies in the intention of the original seller. Where he intends title to pass to the buyer then the contract will merely be voidable, but where he intends that title pass not to the buyer but to someone else then the contract will be void. It appears to be necessary to determine the seller's intention to distinguish two categories of case: first, contracts which are made where both parties are actually present, and secondly, contracts made 'at a distance'. The following cases illustrate this.

In *Lewis* v *Averay* [1972] 1 QB 198; [1971] 3 All ER 907, the Court of Appeal dealt with a 'face to face' contract. The buyer convinced A that he (B) was a certain 'X'. The question asked by the court was whether A meant to deal only with X or with the person actually in front of him. It laid down a presumption that if the parties deal face to face (ie they are both present) then the seller is to be taken to be dealing with the person in front of him, even if that person is not who the seller believes him to be. The contract was therefore merely voidable. This case followed *Phillips* v *Brooks Ltd* [1919] 2 KB 243.

In contrast to these cases is *Cundy* v *Lindsay* (1878) 3 App Cas 459. Here the parties negotiated by post. The seller had frequently dealt with a certain 'Blenkiron', but a buyer with a similar name set up in the same street. The seller assumed the buyer to be the same Blenkiron. It was held that the contract was void since the seller intended only to contract with the real Blenkiron.

The Law Reform Commission's 12th Report rightly states that this is a facile and unsatisfactory distinction. This finding is supported by the blatant injustice of *Ingram* v *Little* (supra). The Law Reform Commission recommendation that all such contracts be made voidable has not been implemented.

Where the contract is voidable and s23 therefore potentially applies, the defrauded party must, to retain his title, rescind the contract before the other party sells the goods. It was previously thought that this could only be done by communicating with the fraudulent party and notifying him of the rescission. This position has now been modified.

In *Car & Universal Finance Ltd* v *Caldwell* [1965] 1 QB 525; [1964] 1 All ER 290, a motor car was fraudulently purchased with a worthless cheque. The seller was unable to communicate with the rogue in question but did inform the police and the Automobile Association of the fraud. The rogue later resold the car. The Court of Appeal held that a seller can rescind the contract by evincing an intention to do so and taking all reasonably practicable steps open to him where he is not able to communicate with the fraudulent party. The seller in this case had succeeded in rescinding the contract before the resale by the rogue, so s23 did not apply. The court's decision is probably not confined to cases in which the fraudulent party is deliberately keeping out of the way although the court left this point open. *Benjamin*, however, is of the view that the rationale of the Court of Appeal's decision was that the rogue in this case deliberately intended to disappear and render it impossible for the seller to communicate with him or to recover the car. It would seem if this is the case that if the rogue is only innocently keeping out of the way then rescission would not be possible in the manner adopted in *Caldwell*. Many commentators go against *Benjamin* on this point.

Note that for s23 to operate the remedy of rescission must not for any reason have become barred. In particular the true owner must not have elected to affirm the contract, so losing his right to rescind. Once the true owner becomes aware of his right to rescind the mere lapse of time will not in itself amount to affirmation – he can keep his election open so long as he does not affirm by express words or unequivocal acts.

The *Caldwell* decision appeared to have greatly enhanced the protection afforded to the innocent seller in voidable contracts. The situation prior to *Caldwell* had meant there was little the innocent victim could do since he was unlikely to be able to find the rogue to communicate with him.

The Law Reform Commission's 12th Report recommendation that return to the old rule that only communication was adequate for rescission in order to protect the ultimate purchaser of the goods, was not implemented. However, the scope of *Caldwell* has now been greatly reduced, and in practice the decision is now defunct as a result of another Court of Appeal decision: *Newtons of Wembley Ltd* v *Williams* [1965] 1 QB 560; [1964] 3 All ER 532. (This case is dealt with in detail under 10.9: 'Sale by a buyer in possession'.) The Court of Appeal here did accept and follow *Caldwell* as regards methods of revocation. The rogue in question here had remained in possession of the car and subsequently sold it and the Court of Appeal held him to be a person who had 'bought or agreed to buy goods' within the meaning of s25(1) (see below). He therefore passed good title under *that* section. Therefore, by holding on to the goods and reselling them, as is usually the case, the fraudulent buyer can get round s23 and get into s25 and can pass good title under that latter section.

This decision has obviously greatly reduced the significance of s23.

Miscellaneous points arising under s23

There is no requirement for s23 that the party with a voidable title who is selling goods has possession of them.

If the original seller has not parted with possession to the rogue and he has not yet been paid, he will have an unpaid seller's lien on the goods (see Chapter 11) which will bind subsequent purchasers (s38(1)(b)).

In *Whitehorn Bros* v *Davison* [1911] 1 KB 463 the Court of Appeal held that the true owner bears the burden of proving that the buyer bought with notice or otherwise than in good faith. *Benjamin* notes that this ruling reverses the burden of proof which is applied in the case of most similar provisions and submits that it deserves reconsideration.

10.6 Sale by an agent

This should be distinguished from 'sale by a mercantile agent' (see below at 10.7).

Section 62 SGA expressly preserves the common law rules regarding principal and agent. Briefly, a sale by an agent will bind his principal if that agent had 'actual' or 'ostensible' authority to make the sale.

10.7 Sale by a mercantile agent under the Factors Act 1889

Section 21(2) of the SGA expressly preserves this exception to *nemo dat*. It provides:

'Nothing in this Act affects:
a) the provisions of the Factors Acts, or any enactment enabling the apparent owner of goods to dispose of them as if he were their true owner.'

The Factors Act 1889 (the FA) was passed to protect third parties dealing with professional or 'mercantile' agents who were acting in the ordinary course of their business as such agents. In this respect the FA is in effect a statutory extension of the common law rules on agency and on estoppel. If the agent has 'actual' or 'ostensible' authority to sell the goods then the principal (the owner) will be bound by that sale at common law, if the agent has no authority, actual or ostensible then at common law the sale cannot bind the owner. The FA, however, protects third parties in this latter situation, providing that the mere delivery of goods or the documents of title to goods to a 'mercantile agent' will subject to certain conditions be sufficient to enable that mercantile agent to pass good title to a purchaser with or without authority to sell the goods.

Section 2(1) of the Factors Act provides:

'Where a mercantile agent is, with the consent of the owner, in possession of goods or of the documents of title to goods, any sale, pledge, or other disposition of the goods, made by him when acting in the ordinary course of business of a mercantile agent, shall, subject to the provisions of this Act, be as valid as if he were expressly authorised by the owner of the goods to make the same; provided that the person taking under the disposition acts in good faith, and has not at the time of the disposition notice that the person making the disposition has not authority to make the same.'

This subsection raises several important issues as regards the definitions involved and as regards its application. These must be looked at in turn: the meaning of mercantile agent' for the purposes of the FA; if the party in question is a mercantile agent, then it is only his ostensible authority not his actual authority which matters; the mercantile agent must be in possession *as a mercantile agent* and not in some other capacity; the mercantile agent must be in possession *with the consent of the owner*; the disposition by the mercantile agent must be in the ordinary course of business; the purchaser or pledgee must prove he took in good faith and without notice of the agent's lack of authority; the meaning of 'document of title'.

The meaning of 'mercantile agent' for the purposes of the FA

The FA s1(1), reproduced in s26 SGA, provides:

> 'The expression "mercantile agent" shall mean a mercantile agent having in the customary course of his business as such agent, authority either to sell goods or to consign goods for the purpose of sale, or to buy goods or to raise money on the security of goods.'

It is often difficult to determine who will be a mercantile agent within this section. The question is ultimately one of substance and not of form, so the name or description applied to the agent will be of limited use only. Several propositions can be taken from the definition in the FA and from the case law surrounding it:

1. The agent must have a customary course of business.
2. He must have a usual authority to do the kind of things that sort of agent usually does. He need not be authorised by his principal for each specific thing he does provided it is within the kind of thing for which he has authority.
3. He must be an independent agent, not a mere employee or servant.
4. He will usually be acting in his own name for an undisclosed principal.
5. He may act for several principals or only for one, and he may be acting as mercantile agent on only one occasion: in other words there is no requirement that he act as mercantile agent in more than one transaction provided the other requirements of being such an agent are fulfilled.
6. He need not be one of a recognised kind or category of agent but he must act in the course of a business and not simply as a private individual who has no customary authority to sell or buy another's goods.
7. A mercantile agent unlike an ordinary broker will normally have possession of the goods. A broker normally brings two parties together to arrange a contract

between them: he rarely has possession. Note, however, that certain particular types of broker can also be mercantile agents.

Typical examples of mercantile agents are: a motor dealer selling motor cars, an art dealer buying and selling art pieces, and a variety of 'factors'. It should be noted that the mercantile agent is only a mercantile agent for the types of goods he usually deals in. This raises the interesting question of whether an auctioneer is a mercantile agent for any kind of goods. The concept of mercantile agent is best elucidated by reference to the decided cases:

In *Rolls Razor Ltd* v *Cox* [1967] 1 QB 552; [1967] 1 All ER 397, R Co was the manufacturer of washing machines. The agent in question was engaged to sell the machines door to door, yet by his contract he was not strictly an employee. The arrangement was that he had to pay to the company everything he received and he would then be paid a commission; he sold the machines in R Co's name. When R Co went into liquidation the agent claimed he had a 'factor's lien' over several machines still in his possession for his arrears of commission. In order to claim this lien, the agent had to show that he was a 'factor' (in this context the same as 'mercantile agent'). The Court of Appeal found that the agent was not a 'factor'. Lord Denning MR outlined the main characteristics of factors and found that the agent in the present case fell outside: he thought it to be crucial that this agent was entrusted with goods to sell in his principal's name and not in his own name. He was therefore only an agent, pure and simple, selling in his principal's name.

Wynn LJ indicated that the courts have in effect a 'general concept' of which agents will be mercantile agents in a general sense and within that category in which mercantile agents will be considered mercantile agents for the purposes of the Factors Act. This shows that some commercial agents who are generally thought of as 'mercantile agents' may not be so for the purposes of the FA where they do not satisfy the criteria laid down above.

The title which the contract gives to an agent is of little relevance. The question of whether someone is a mercantile agent is a question of substance and is not dependent upon his being labelled 'mercantile agent' in the contract (*Weiner* v *Harris* [1910] 1 KB 285). The evidence showed the agent in question, one Fisher, to be a travelling salesman, selling goods for his principal Weiner. The following characteristics of their relationship should be noted:

1. There was no intention that Fisher should buy the goods from Weiner: he was selling the goods for Weiner.
2. The contract between them provided that after a sale to a customer F should pay a fixed price to W and could keep anything obtained from the sale above that price.
3. A note was sent to F with each batch of goods sent by Weiner which stated that the goods were 'on approbation'. This phrase would normally signify that the goods were supplied on a 'sale or return' basis and would have made Fisher a mere agent.

The Court of Appeal held that it would not accept as conclusive the wording 'on approbation' on Weiner's notes (the phrase would normally signify that Fisher was not a mercantile agent): it was for the court to decide whether in all the circumstances of the case F was a mercantile agent. The court held on all the facts that Fisher was a mercantile agent selling goods and being paid on a type of 'commission' basis.

In *Lowther v Harris* [1927] 1 KB 393 Lowther was the owner of a number of antiques which were stored in a house. He agreed with X an antique dealer with a shop nearby that X would live in a flat in the house in question and from time to time he would sell some of the antiques for Lowther but only with Lowther's authority for each separate transaction. Among the antiques were two tapestries.

The first tapestry: X told Lowther that he had found a certain W who was willing to buy the first tapestry, and Lowther delivered that tapestry to X authorising him to sell it to W. W did not exist; X sold the tapestry to Harris. When Lowther claimed it from Harris the latter argued that he had purchased it in good faith from a mercantile agent (X). The Court of Appeal held that X was a mercantile agent. He was an antique dealer with a business and a habit of buying, selling, drawing cheques, etc, on his own account in relation to that business. As an antique dealer he had a customary course of business of selling antiques not only for himself but *for other people*. For s2 of the FA to operate the mercantile agent needs possession with the consent of the owner, but such consent was not vitiated by X's deceit (see The meaning of 'consent' (below)). Property in the first tapestry passed under this section. *The second tapestry*: X simply stole this tapestry and without Lowther's consent sold it to Harris. The court held that title could not pass in this tapestry under s2 FA since X did not have possession with Lowther's consent.

Harris is often cited as authority for the proposition that a person can be a mercantile agent for a single transaction. This argument must be treated with caution. A private individual who is a non-trader without a customary course of business of buying and selling, whatever item is in question, *cannot* be turned into a mercantile agent for a single transaction. If one private individual says to another 'Sell my watch for whatever you can get for it and keep £1 from the proceeds', then that does not turn the other into a mercantile agent. If, however, an agent is a trader with a customary course of business, although he acts only for *one principal* who keeps him busy, and although he may only act in one transaction, he can be a mercantile agent provided all other criteria are satisfied.

Note also *Jerome v Bentley* (supra). The facts of this case are given above under 10.2. Donovan J held that the rogue in question who had induced the owner to give him possession of the goods by a representation that he knew a buyer was not, without more, to be treated as a mercantile agent. He was not a member of any well-known class of agent let alone mercantile agent.

In *Heap v Motorists' Advisory Agency Ltd* [1923] 1 KB 577 the rogue here obtained possession of a car and disposed of it. After these events he temporarily got a job as a car salesman. One reason for holding that the disposal did not pass title was that he was not a mercantile agent at the time he obtained possession of and sold the car. At that time he was a private individual and not a trader.

In *Budberg* v *Jerwood* (1934) 51 TLR 99 a baroness delivered a necklace to a solicitor friend asking him to get offers for it. The solicitor while telling her that he was trying to obtain offers first pledged the necklace for a personal loan and then redeemed and sold it to Jerwood who took it in good faith. When sued for conversion Jerwood pleaded inter alia that the solicitor was a mercantile agent. The court apparently accepted this argument. This finding is at least dubious since it would be very odd if a solicitor had a customary course of business of buying and selling goods! The court did eventually decide in favour of the baroness since it held that although the solicitor was a mercantile agent he was not acting as such but only as a friend.

In *Mehta* v *Sutton* (1913) 108 LT 214, the question arose as to what was the customary course of business of a Paris pearl-broker. The court held this to be selling pearls but only after he had obtained the relevant invoice. The decision emphasises that the transaction in question must be within the actual customary course of business of the actual mercantile agent in question.

If the party in question is a mercantile agent, then it is only his ostensible authority not his actual authority which matters

Briefly, 'actual authority' is authority actually conferred on an agent either expressly by his principal or impliedly through custom or practice. 'Ostensible authority' is the authority of the agent as it appears to third parties, whether or not he *actually* possesses such authority.

In the context of s2 of the FA, actual restrictions placed on the authority of a mercantile agent are totally ineffective. It is only his ostensible authority which matters (ie his authority as it appears to third parties). It is therefore not possible to oust the FA by secret contrary restrictions in the contract between principal and agent. Of course, if the party buying from the agent knows of the restrictions, then he will not be in good faith and s2 FA will not operate for that reason.

The principle is best illustrated by reference to the case of *Turner* v *Sampson* (1911) 27 TLR 200. T delivered certain pictures to W, an art-dealer running his own gallery. W had previously sold pictures for T on commission. On this occasion T authorised W merely to get offers for the pictures and not to sell them before he had referred back to T. This was an actual restriction on W's authority. W sold the pictures to S without consulting T. It was held that S took a good title through s2 FA. It was only W's ostensible authority (ie his authority as it appeared to S) which was important and the private restriction imposed by T was inoperative.

The mercantile agent must be in possession as a mercantile agent and not in some other capacity

The purchaser from the mercantile agent will not be protected if the goods were entrusted to him for some purpose quite unconnected with his business as a mercantile agent: per Denning LJ in *Pearson v Rose & Young* [1951] 1 KB 275; [1950] 2 All ER 1027:

> 'The owner must consent to the agent having (the goods) for a purpose which is in some way or other connected with his business as a mercantile agent. It may not actually be for sale. It may be for display, or to get offers, or merely to put in his showroom, but there must be a consent to something of that kind before the owner can be deprived of his goods.'

Further dicta supporting Denning are found in *Oppenheimer v Frazer & Wyatt* [1907] 1 KB 50.

The FA s2 does not expressly lay down this requirement; it is a rule which the judiciary has interpolated, thinking it intolerable that a mercantile agent should get goods in a private capacity and be able to pass a good title to them. An example of the absurd position which would otherwise prevail would be a householder lending his lawnmower to a neighbour who happened to be a mercantile agent in such goods. That neighbour would, were there no requirement of taking as a mercantile agent, be able to sell and pass good title to the lawnmower.

In *Staffs Motor Guarantee Ltd v British Wagon Co Ltd* [1934] 2 KB 30 X ran a garage dealing in the sale of cars and lorries. He sold one lorry to a finance company and took it back immediately on hire purchase, paying the deposit out of the purchase price paid by the finance company. He therefore retained possession of the lorry but then wrongfully sold it to a third party. It was held that X was a mercantile agent and had possession with the consent of the owner, the finance company. However, good title did not pass by the FA s2 because X did not have possession of the lorry as a mercantile agent but as a hire purchaser from the finance company. This case was reaffirmed in *Astley Industrial Trust Ltd v Miller* [1968] 3 All ER 36.

Note that both these cases have been overruled on a different point (concerning possession in s24 SGA below) by *Worcester Works Finance Ltd v Cooden Engineering Co Ltd* [1972] 1 QB 210; [1971] 3 All ER 78.

The mercantile agent must be in possession with the consent of the owner

Two problems of definition arise under this requirement. These are as to the meaning of 'consent' and as to the meaning of 'owner' in the particular context of s2 FA.

The meaning of 'consent'

Considerable difficulty has been encountered in this area when dealing with the situation where a person is induced to part with goods as the result of a fraud or trick. In older cases which are no longer good law the courts discussed this problem in terms of the old criminal offence of 'larceny by trick' and held that in such cases the goods could not be said to be in the possession of the agent with the consent of the owner.

It was held in *Folkes* v *King* [1923] 1 KB 282 that a fraud or trick does not prevent a buyer from acquiring a good title under s2 FA. The Court of Appeal stated that the criminal law in this area was totally irrelevant. Criminal cases were concerned with what was in the mind of the rogue whereas the concern in civil cases was as to what was in the owner's mind. If the owner intended possession to pass to the person to whom he gave the goods then the mere fact that he would not have transferred possession had he known the man to be a rogue does *not vitiate consent*. Generally, consent obtained by a trick or a fraud is still therefore consent. On the question of the owner's consent, the case referred to above of *Heap* v *Motorists' Advisory Agency Ltd* (supra) is now wrong. (*Folkes* v *King* was at that time as yet unreported.) Lush LJ wrongly held that possession through larceny by trick meant the owner had not consented. The leading case in this area is now *Pearson* v *Rose & Young* (supra) which has recently been followed in *National Employers Mutual General Assurance Assoc Ltd* v *Jones* [1987] 3 All ER 385. (For further details as to this latter case see 10.9, below.)

In *Pearson* v *Rose & Young* (supra) the plaintiff delivered his car to a mercantile agent in order that the latter should obtain offers for it. The mercantile agent had no authority to sell the car. The agent obtained possession of the registration book by a trick in such circumstances that the owner clearly did not consent to parting with possession of it: while inspecting the book the agent asked the car owner to take his (the agent's) wife to hospital having feigned an emergency and kept the book. The agent then sold the car and handed over the registration book to the innocent purchaser. The Court of Appeal held:

1. The only question was as to whether the goods were in the mercantile agent's possession with the consent of the owner.
2. The question of whether the agent had committed larceny by trick to obtain possession was immaterial.
3. In this case the agent had possession of the car with the consent of the owner but his possession of the registration book was not with such consent.
4. A sale of a car without a registration book was not a sale 'in the ordinary course of business'. (See below: The disposition by the mercantile agent.)

For these reasons the court held that the innocent purchaser was not protected by s2 of the FA.

Pearson was the first case in which the registration book of a car was held to be of any significance. It is curious that all other goods should require no accompanying documents but that a car does, and for this reason the finding by the Court of Appeal that a car sale without a registration book is not 'in the ordinary course of business' has been criticised. The decision in *Pearson* is harsh on the innocent purchaser because, having the registration book, he had no grounds to be suspicious of the seller, whereas if the sale had been without the registration book, the buyer ought to have been suspicious. It seems therefore that a very prudent purchaser who has checked the registration book can still be caught out if it transpires that the party selling to him did not have possession of that book with consent. This position is odd since the intention behind the FA was to protect innocent purchasers. It has been cogently argued that the presence or absence of the registration book should go to the question of the good faith of the buyer and not to consent.

The Court of Appeal even went so far in *Pearson* as to suggest that a car without its registration book is not 'goods' and its sale therefore would not be 'sale of goods'! *Benjamin* argues that the decision of two members of the Court of Appeal, Denning LJ and Vaisey J, was based on this last ground, namely that the 'goods' in the case meant 'the car together with its registration book' and the agent was not in possession of both of those with the consent of the owner. Only the decision of the third member, Somervell LJ, was in *Benjamin*'s view based on the reasoning that the sale of a car without its registration book is not a sale in the ordinary course of business of a mercantile agent. It must be admitted that there is some ambiguity in the judgments of the Court of Appeal on these points.

The idea that a car without its registration book is not 'goods' was fortunately repudiated by the Court of Appeal itself in a further case, which, if *Benjamin*'s view on the reasoning adopted in *Pearson* is correct, must cast extreme doubt on that decision. In *Stadium Finance Ltd* v *Robbins* [1962] 2 QB 664; [1962] 2 All ER 633, a car-owner took his car to a garage for repairs but left the registration book by mistake in the locked glove-compartment in the car. The garage proprietor found the book and using it sold the car. The Court of Appeal held (leading judgment delivered by Willmer LJ):

1. A car without its registration book is 'goods'.
2. There was no consent here to possession of the registration book, it being in a locked compartment, and the sale was therefore not 'in the ordinary course of business' of a mercantile agent. Good title therefore did not pass to the innocent purchaser.

This second ground must be taken to be the true rationale of the *Pearson* decision.

However, even this reasoning has not escaped criticism, particularly by *Benjamin*. It is difficult, *Benjamin* submits, to see why the sale of a car with its registration documents should not be 'in the ordinary course of business' merely because the document has been obtained without the owner's consent. *Benjamin* submits that the only convincing ground on which it can be argued that the *Pearson* case was rightly decided is that, without the registration book, the owner did not consent to the agent being in possession of the car in his capacity as mercantile agent, but only as bailee. *Benjamin*'s view is not universally held, although an argument of considerable force.

Two further cases are of assistance in this area. First, in *Bentworth Finance Ltd* v

Lambert [1968] 1 QB 680; [1967] 2 All ER 810, the Court of Appeal stated that in an ordinary contract of sale of a motor vehicle it is an implied condition that the registration document will be provided either at the time of sale or within a reasonable time of the sale. If this is not done it will be grounds for rescinding the contract. This decision once more emphasises the significance of the registration document in car sales. The question now arises as to whether there can ever be a valid sale of a car in this context without the registration book.

Second, in *Astley Industrial Trust* v *Miller* (supra) the Court of Appeal in dealing with the sale of a new car would have accepted as a sufficient explanation of the absence of the registration book that it was with the County Council for the purpose of being registered and taxed. Were such an explanation to be given then good title could pass under s2 FA to the innocent purchaser without the registration book.

Note finally that s2(2) FA specifically lays down that the subsequent withdrawal of his consent by the seller (ie subsequent to the mercantile agent taking possession) does not prevent the operation of the Act.

The meaning of 'the owner'

The requirement in s2 FA that the consent be that of the 'owner' of the goods has also given rise to some difficulty. The 'owner' in s2 may in some cases apparently include a person with only a limited right over the goods.

In *Lloyds Bank* v *Bank of America* [1938] 2 KB 147; [1938] 2 All ER 63, the plaintiff, Lloyds Bank lent money to a mercantile agent on the security of certain Bills of Lading which he pledged with them. The documents were then released to the mercantile agent under a 'trust receipt' in order to enable the agent to sell the goods, holding the proceeds as trustee for the plaintiffs. The agent fraudulently pledged the documents with the Bank of America for an advance. Bank of America contended that they had the protection of s2 FA but the plaintiff argued that since the mercantile agent was himself the owner of the goods, it could not be said that he was in possession with the consent of the owner within the meaning of the Act. The Court of Appeal held in a judgment of Lord Greene MR that Lloyds Bank was here the *legal pledgee* and was as such the beneficiary of the proceeds of sale in equity, and that the mercantile agent was the legal and beneficial owner of the goods subject to the prior claims of Lloyds Bank. These two persons together constituted 'the owner' within the FA, and the goods were consequently in the possession of the mercantile agent with the owner's consent, since he was himself one of those two persons. Bank of America therefore acquired a good title under the Act as against Lloyds Bank.

The disposition by the mercantile agent must be 'in the ordinary course of business'

To claim the protection of s2 FA, the purchaser or pledgee must prove that the mercantile agent acted 'in the ordinary course of business' (see above, *Pearson* v *Rose*

& *Young* holding that the sale of a car with a registration book obtained without the owner's consent is not 'in the ordinary course of business'). This requirement cannot be taken too literally. What it means in effect is that the mercantile agent must act within the ordinary course of business of mercantile agents generally, and not necessarily of that particular mercantile agent.

The requirement was succinctly laid down by Buckley LJ in *Oppenheimer* v *Attenborough* [1908] 1 KB 221:

> 'acting in such a way as a mercantile agent would act, that is to say, within business hours, at a proper place of business, and in other respects in the ordinary way in which a mercantile agent would act, so that there is nothing to lead the pledgee (or purchaser) to suppose that anything is done wrong, or to give notice that the disposition is one which the mercantile agent has not authority for.'

It is not material that the agent entered into a transaction not normally sanctioned by the custom of the trade (unless possibly where the custom is so notorious that the third party could normally be taken to have knowledge of it, as where an auctioneer pledged goods entrusted to him for sale).

Oppenheimer v *Attenborough* (supra) is relevant here. The mercantile agent fraudulently obtained from a diamond merchant some diamonds which he then pledged with a pawnbroker. The agent was a diamond broker, and it was proved that diamond brokers did not usually pledge goods of this kind. It was nonetheless held that the act was in the ordinary course of business of a mercantile agent. The pawnbroker was therefore protected. The third party dealt with the mercantile agent as principal and did not know him to be an agent.

If a mercantile agent sells goods on the terms that the price is not to be paid directly to him but to one of his creditors, this may well be outside the ordinary course of business (see *Lloyds & Scottish Finance Ltd* v *Williamson* [1965] 1 WLR 404; [1965] 1 All ER 642). It is a question of fact in each particular case whether the agent has acted in the ordinary way in which a mercantile agent would act.

It must be emphasised that the requirement that the mercantile agent act in the ordinary course of business is distinct and separate from the requirement that the buyer take in good faith and without notice. It has been held that a buyer can be in good faith even though the sale is outside the ordinary course of business (see *Lloyds & Scottish Finance* (supra)). It follows that the dictum of Buckley LJ must be modified since he appears to envisage that a sale will only be outside the ordinary course of business in circumstances in which the buyer would have remarked on the agent's lack of authority.

There is perhaps little justification for having sale 'in the ordinary course of business' as a separate requirement as it would not appear that the owner would be adequately protected by the requirement that the buyer take in good faith without notice.

The purchaser (or pledgee) must prove that he took in good faith and without notice of the agent's lack of authority

The burden of proof here lies with the purchaser to prove he took in good faith and without notice that the sale was made without the owner's authority. This was laid down in *Heap* v *Motorists' Advisory Agency* (supra), the facts of which are given above. The court here, in holding in favour of the original owner, stated that it was not convinced of the purchaser's good faith.

The meaning of 'document of title'

Section 1(4) of the Factors Act provides:

> " 'Document of title" shall include any bill of lading, dock warrant, warehousekeeper's certificate, and warrant or order for the delivery of goods, and any other document used in the ordinary course of business as proof of the possession or control of goods, or authorising or purporting to authorise, either by endorsement or delivery the possessor of the document to transfer or receive goods thereby represented.'

A motor car registration book is not a document of title, although it is the best evidence of it (see *Central Newbury Car Auctions Ltd* v *Unity Finance Ltd* (supra)).

The Law Reform Commission's 12th Report recommended that there be no extension of this exception to *nemo dat*.

10.8 Sale by a seller in possession

This exception to *nemo dat* is contained in s8 of the FA 1889 which is reproduced with only a slight amendment in s24 SGA. The same is true of the next exception 'sale by a buyer in possession, 10.9' which is contained in s9 FA and in s25 SGA. It does indeed seem odd that there are two almost exactly parallel statutory provisions for these exceptions. It might have been better from a formal point of view if the SGA had repealed the relevant Factors Act provisions.

The Factors Act s8 provides as follows:

> 'Where a person, having sold goods, continues, or is, in possession of the goods or of the documents of title to the goods, the delivery or transfer by that person, or by a mercantile agent acting for him, of the goods or documents of title under any sale, pledge or other disposition thereof (or under any agreement for sale, pledge or other disposition thereof), to any person receiving the same in good faith and without notice of the previous sale, shall have the same effect as if the person making the delivery or transfer were expressly authorised by the owner of the goods to make the same.'

The words in parenthesis are not included in s24 SGA. References to the FA s8 should be read as applying equally to s24 SGA and vice-versa. They are in effect the same statutory provision.

Most of the requirements of this exception are self-evident or self-explanatory.

The section essentially deals with the seller who, after concluding a contract of sale with a buyer, remains in possession of the goods or document of title to those goods and then sells, pledges or otherwise disposes of the goods to a third party, obviously in breach of the contract with the original buyer. If the other conditions in s8 FA as to delivery of the goods or document of title and as to the good faith and absence of notice of the third party taking the goods are satisfied, then that disposition will have the same effect as if it were authorised by the owner of the goods. Note that the section does not say that the seller passes a good title but only that the transaction has the same effect as if the transfer were 'expressly authorised by the owner', a difference which could conceivably be of some significance.

Under s8 FA/s24 SGA it should be noted first that the property must have passed to the original buyer of the goods, otherwise the seller can still sell as owner of the goods, albeit in breach of the contract with the first buyer, and s8 is unnecessary. Secondly, the seller must *deliver the goods* or *transfer the documents of title* to a later buyer, pledgee or other taker who is in *good faith* and takes *without notice of the previous sale*. If there has been no delivery or transfer, s24 will not operate. This can be contrasted with the position under estoppel, under ss22 and 23 of the SGA and under s2(1) of the FA. In these cases the second buyer or taker of the goods is protected from the moment of sale and no delivery of goods or transfer of documents is necessary.

Section 8 FA goes further than s2(1) FA in one respect. It applies to a sale which is outside the ordinary course of business. A case which illustrates this point is *Nicholson* v *Harper* [1895] 2 Ch 414. X stored wine in Y's warehouse and then sold it to Z. Subsequently X executed a document whereby he pledged the wine to Y in return for a loan. At the time of delivery the wine no longer belonged to X who therefore had no right to pledge it. Furthermore, s8 was inapplicable because there had been no delivery from X to Y. Accordingly the pledge gave Y no rights at all.

The most important and controversial issue raised by s8 FA/s24 SGA is as to the meaning of the phrase 'continues, or is, in possession of the goods'.

The old authorities on this point laid down that it was not enough that the seller was simply in possession of the goods when he resold them, but that the third party claiming under this section must go further and show that the seller was in possession as seller, and not in some other capacity, for example as bailee. In *Mitchell* v *Jones* (1905) 24 NZ LR 932 (a decision from New Zealand), S here sold and delivered a horse to B but later S took it back as bailee for hire and subsequently sold it to a second buyer. It was held that the second buyer was not protected since the seller had not 'continued in possession' as seller; he had taken the horse back as bailee and not as seller.

This principle was applied in cases where there was no actual delivery or redelivery of the goods. In *Staffs Motor Guarantee Ltd* v *British Wagon Co Ltd* (for a full account of the facts see 10.7 above). S sold a lorry to a finance company and took it back on hire purchase. The vehicle at all times remained with the seller who then sold it to a second buyer. It was held that no good title passed to the second buyer under s8 FA since the seller no longer had possession *as a seller* at the time of the second sale. He was only in possession as bailee under a hire purchase agreement.

In *Olds Discount Co v Krett* [1940] 2 KB 117; [1940] 3 All ER 36, S sold a vehicle to a finance company but retained possession of it as the agent of the finance company. The finance company then let the vehicle on hire purchase to X and S delivered it to X. When X defaulted, S repossessed the vehicle as agent of the finance company, but then wrongfully disposed of it. It was held that no title passed under s8 FA. S no longer had possession as a seller but only as the agent of the finance company.

In *Eastern Distributors Ltd v Goldring*, in this case the Court of Appeal approved of the decision in *Staffs Motor Guarantee Ltd*.

However, the authority of the above decisions is now *very much in doubt* following two more recent decisions.

In *Pacific Motor Auctions Pty Ltd v Motor Credits Ltd* [1965] AC 867; [1965] 2 All ER 105, M Ltd who were dealers in motor vehicles sold a number of cars to the plaintiff under a 'display agreement'. Under this agreement, M Ltd remained in possession of the cars for display in their showrooms, and the plaintiffs paid 90 per cent of the price and authorised M Ltd to sell the cars as agents of the plaintiffs. After such a sale M Ltd would then have to account to the plaintiffs as owners. M Ltd got into financial difficulties so the plaintiffs revoked their authority to sell the vehicles. The defendants visited M Ltd after business hours and as creditors of M Ltd claimed some of the cars on display as security for the debts. M Ltd sold certain cars to the defendants (the defendants paid by a cheque which M Ltd was compelled to endorse back to the defendants) and it was agreed that the cars would be returned when M Ltd paid its debts. The defendants were aware of the display agreement and could not have assumed that M Ltd were owners, although they did believe that M Ltd had authority to sell. A number of the cars sold to the defendants belonged to the plaintiffs who sued for conversion.

The defendant put forward three arguments in his claim that he had title to the cars, all of which were rejected by the Australian Court of Appeal:

1. Estoppel did not operate: there was no duty of care owed by the plaintiffs nor was there an adequate representation that M Ltd were owners.
2. This could not be a sale by a mercantile agent under s2(1) FA since it was outside business hours and not therefore in the ordinary course of business.
3. Section 8 FA/s24 SGA did not operate since the seller did not have possession *as a seller* (following the earlier cases).

The Privy Council, however, reversed this traditional interpretation of s8 FA/s24 SGA and held that the defendant obtained a good title under the section of the New South Wales equivalent to s24 of our SGA. They rejected the old line of authorities as wrongly decided. The Privy Council in a judgment of Lord Pearce stated that the phrase 'continues or is in possession' referred only to the continuity of actual physical possession, regardless of any private transaction between the seller and the first buyer which might alter the legal title under which that possession was held. Accordingly, unless there is an actual transfer of physical possession away from the seller and back to him then the seller is to be treated as continuing in possession and as able to pass good title under s24. All that is required is that there be no delivery and redelivery to the seller, and the fact that M Ltd were now bailees of the cars did not break continuity of possession.

Decisions of the Privy Council are of course of only persuasive authority in the English Courts but the decision in *Pacific Motor Auctions* has now been followed by the Court of Appeal in *Worcester Works Finance Ltd v Cooden Engineering Co Ltd* (supra). This case is slightly unusual in that it deals with a 'disposition' other than a sale or pledge. The Court of Appeal in this regard held that 'disposition' was to be given a wide meaning: it covered any transfer of interest in the goods but not a mere transfer of possession.

The facts in *Worcester Finance* were that C sold and delivered a car to G who paid with a worthless cheque. G sold the car to a finance company, the plaintiffs, but retained possession of the car since he induced the finance company to let the car on hire purchase to his accomplice. The finance company bought from G in good faith. When the cheque from G to C was dishonoured C repossessed the car with G's consent. The finance company however sued C for the car.

The Court of Appeal held that s24 operated to protect C and give him a good title to the car. The court followed the decision in *Pacific Motor Auctions* and held that the phrase 'continues or is in possession' referred only to actual continuity of physical possession and there was no necessity that the seller be in possession 'as a seller'. In the present case therefore G had continued in possession of the car within the meaning of s24 SGA. The court further held that the repossession of the car by C constituted a 'disposition' by G, within the meaning of s24 in as much as it amounted to a rescission of the contract between C and G and therefore revested the property in C. The title which G temporarily had to the car must therefore it seems have been voidable. This finding enabled the court to hold G to be a 'seller in possession', having sold the goods first to the finance company and retained possession of them.

This decision must now be recognised as the law and the older cases should be regarded as wrongly decided. The case has been criticised because it uses a *nemo dat* exception to help the original careless owner when that exception was intended to help the innocent purchaser who in fact loses out. However, the decision has disposed of the unnecessary complication of having to decide what exactly is meant by 'possession as a seller' and has replaced it with the simply discernable criterion of whether or not the seller has remained in continuous physical possession.

'Document of title' in s8 FA/s24 SGA has the meaning defined in s1(4) Factors Act quoted above under 10.7.

Finally, it should be noted that where the seller wrongfully resells to a second buyer and passes a good title under s8 FA/s24 SGA, the first buyer can sue the seller either for wrongful interference with goods or for breach of contract for failure to deliver the goods.

10.9 Sale by a buyer in possession

This exception to the *nemo dat* principle is contained in two parallel statutory provisions: s25(1) SGA 1979 and in s9 Factors Act 1889:

> 'Where a person, having bought or agreed to buy goods, obtains with the consent of the seller possession of the goods or the documents of title to the goods, the delivery or transfer, by that person or by a mercantile agent acting for him, of the goods or the documents of title under any sale, pledge or other disposition therefore (or under any agreement for sale, pledge or other disposition thereof) to any person receiving the same in good faith and without notice of any lien or other right of the original seller in respect of the goods, shall have the same effect as if the person making the delivery or transfer were a mercantile agent in possession of the goods or documents of title with the consent of the owner.'

The words in parenthesis appear in s9 FA but not in s25(1) SGA. References to s9 FA should be read as applying equally to s25 SGA and vice-versa. They are in effect the same statutory provision.

Several issues of construction are raised by these somewhat complex sections: the meaning of 'a person having bought or agreed to buy goods'; what amounts to the consent of the seller; the requirement of possession of the goods; the relevance of documents of title; the requirements of good faith and absence of notice; the effect of s9 FA.

The meaning of 'a person having bought or agreed to buy goods'

The phrase 'a person having bought or agreed to buy' indicates that s9 FA applies whether or not the property in the goods has passed to the first buyer before the sale is made. (This is in contrast to s8 FA which applies only where the property has passed to the first buyer.)

It is difficult to see why a buyer who already owns the goods, the property having passed to him, requires statutory help to pass ownership on to another. It would seem, therefore, that s9 FA is superfluous and unnecessary in this situation, since such a buyer can sell the goods at common law by reason of his ownership. One possible explanation is that 'bought' in s9 includes 'voidably bought' and that a good title can pass from a buyer with a voidable title by virtue of s9 as well as by s23 SGA above. It was held in *Newtons of Wembley Ltd* v *Williams* [1965] 1 QB 560; [1964] 3 All ER 532 that these two sections do overlap and that in appropriate circumstances property could pass under either section from a buyer with voidable title. This argument of course would not explain why 'bought' was historically included in s9 since the draftsmen in 1889 could not have foreseen the *Newtons of Wembley* decision.

The phrase implies that there must be a 'contract of sale' within the meaning of the SGA: 'a contract under which the seller transfers or agrees to transfer the property in the goods to the buyer' (s2(1) SGA).

Section 9 FA originally proved to be a menace to traders supplying goods on credit by means of reserving ownership of the goods until the price was paid. This arrangement was held to be an 'agreement to sell' and s9 therefore applied, allowing the buyer who had possession but no title to pass good title to the goods.

Note *Lee* v *Butler* [1893] 2 QB 318. This case involved an agreement to 'hire' furniture, the consideration being £1 immediately and £90 after three months, the property in the goods to pass on the second payment. It was held that the buyer had bound herself to make the second payment and so this was an agreement to sell and s9 operated when she resold the goods. The 'hirer' therefore lost his title.

This decision precipitated the invention of hire purchase, under which the hirer is granted only an option to purchase, and so it is not a 'contract of sale' since there is no binding agreement to buy the goods. *Helby* v *Matthews* [1895] AC 471 decided that such hire purchase arrangements fall outside the ambit of s9 FA.

However, a person having possession under a *credit sale agreement* where the property has not passed will be able to pass a good title to an innocent third party under s9 since such person has 'bought or agreed to buy goods' within the meaning of the section.

A person in possession of goods under a *conditional sale agreement* (ie the transfer of property is conditional whether on payment or on the occurrence of some other event) in theory will also come within the ambit of s9 and will be able to give a good title to a third party. However, this general position has been greatly altered by the Hire Purchase Act 1964 which makes s9 FA inoperative in conditional sales provided they qualify as 'consumer credit agreements' under the Consumer Credit Act 1974. This means in effect that a buyer in possession under a conditional sale agreement will only be able to pass a good title under s9 if the total amount of credit *exceeds* £15,000 or if the buyer under the agreement is a corporation. This change is probably justified since it makes the law more consistent in its policy of assimilating hire purchase agreements and conditional sale agreements.

A person who buys goods on 'sale or return' has been held to come outside the provisions of s9 since he is not a person who has 'bought or agreed to buy goods'.

In *Edwards* v *Vaughan* (1910) 26 TLR 545 it was held here that when goods supplied on 'sale or return' are sold or pledged to the ultimate buyer, property passes not under s9 FA/s25 SGA but under s18 SGA Rule 4(b) as being an act adopting the transaction. (Section 18 SGA covers the normal rules for the passing of property: see above 8.2.)

Note that once it is established that the party in question is a 'person having bought or agreed to buy goods' then the disposal by him in s9 FA need not be by way of sale: it could be by pledge or other kind of disposition.

What amounts to the consent of the seller?

In order to pass title under this section the buyer must be in possession with the 'consent of the seller'. It is rather clumsy drafting for the Act to refer to 'the seller' in this context, because if A steals a car and then sells it to B and then B sells it to C, as far as the sale from B to C is concerned B had bought or agreed to buy the car (he bought it from A) and had possession of it with the consent of the person who had sold it to him. In fact it is necessary for the first person in the chain to have made a sale in order for s25 to work. Therefore, if A steals the car from X and then sells it to B, any sale by B cannot pass good title because the first person in the chain (X) did not sell (see *National Employers Mutual General Insurance Association Ltd* v *Jones* (above)). This assumes that 'seller' means 'owner', an assumption discussed below. In contrast, if A fraudulently induces X to sell him the car then the first person in the chain does make a sale and so s25 can operate. It makes no difference in such a case that A acted dishonestly, because he had X's consent to possession even though that consent was obtained by fraud (see *Du Jardin* v *Beadman Bros* [1952] 2 QB 712; [1952] 2 All ER 160). The withdrawal of consent by X when he discovers the fraud will not affect the operation of s25.

As a result of the decision of the Court of Appeal in *Newtons of Wembley Ltd* v *Williams* (supra), s25 now has a profound effect on the workings of s23 (supra, 10.5) dealing with sales by a person with voidable title. In the context of s23, *Car & Universal Finance* v *Caldwell* [1965] 1 QB 525; [1964] 1 All ER 290 had held that where a contract of sale was induced by fraud, the original owner could rescind it without communicating with the fraudulent party. The rogue's voidable title was therefore avoided. However, the Court of Appeal in *Newtons of Wembley* held that even after the contract had been avoided the rogue could still pass a good title to a third party, not under s23, but under s25. The rogue was literally a 'buyer in possession with the consent of the owner' and so s25 operated.

This decision has greatly limited the practical usefulness of the *Caldwell* case. That case had seemed to afford great protection to the original owner induced to part with his goods by fraud: he could rescind that voidable contract by taking all reasonable steps open to him in the circumstances, whether or not that involved communication to the buyer. Now, however, it is clear that such a fraudulent party can get round s23 and *Caldwell*'s case and into s25 thereby passing good title. *Newtons of Wembley* has been criticised as allowing fraudulent parties easily to dispose of goods improperly obtained.

The requirement of possession of the goods

Section 9 FA/s25 SGA will only protect a third party who has actually obtained possession of the goods or documents of title to the goods, and has not simply bought or agreed to buy them.

By s1(2) FA a buyer will be deemed to be in possession of goods or of documents of title to goods where the goods or documents of title are in his actual custody or are held by any other person subject to his control or for him or on his behalf. In *Capital & Counties Bank Ltd* v *Warriner* (1896) 12 TLR 216 the seller issued transfer notes to goods in favour of the buyer and sent them to a warehouseman. The warehouseman acknowledged receipt of the goods to the buyer and then issued delivery orders for the goods to the buyer who pledged these with an innocent pledgee. It was held that the pledgee was entitled to retain the goods. The buyer was in possession when he disposed of the goods.

It is generally thought (see in particular Atiyah on *Sale of Goods*) that the capacity in which the third party possesses the goods will not be relevant and that, by analogy with the *Pacific Motor Auctions* case and the *Worcester Finance* case, it is only his actual physical possession which matters. This view is supported by *Marten* v *Whale* [1917] 2 KB 48 in which s9 was applied even though the goods were temporarily loaned to the buyer who had conditionally agreed to buy them. (Note that many conditional sales agreements are now outside the scope of s9 FA).

The relevance of documents of title

Where the buyer has obtained documents of title to the goods with the seller's consent, as opposed to possession of the actual goods, he can still under s9 pass good title to a third party by delivery to him of the documents. Special attention should be drawn to the interrelation of s9 and two other SGA sections:

Section 47 of the SGA sets out the unpaid seller's rights of lien and stoppage in transit over the goods (see Chapter 11 for a full explanation). Briefly, these are the rights of an unpaid seller in certain circumstances either to retain the goods or to stop the carrier from delivering them to the buyer until the buyer has paid the price. Section 47(2) SGA deals with the loss of the unpaid seller's lien and right of stoppage.

Where the seller/owner still has possession or a carrier has possession of the goods *and* the documents of title then there is obviously no risk of s9 FA operating, and under s47 SGA his rights of lien or stoppage, if he is unpaid and the other requirements are satisfied, will also be intact. However, if the documents of title are transferred to the buyer and he uses those documents to resell the goods when the property has not yet passed to him then both s9 FA *and* s47(2) SGA defeating the seller's right of lien or stoppage may come into play. In such a situation the buyer will obviously be a buyer in possession of documents of title within s9 FA and that section may operate to pass title to a third party. However s9 does not mention lien or stoppage. These will be governed by s47(2) which provides:

> 'Where a document of title to the goods has been lawfully transferred to any person as buyer or owner of the goods, and that person transfers the document to a person who takes it in good faith and for valuable consideration, then -
> a) if the last mentioned transfer was by way of sale the unpaid seller's right of lien or stoppage in transit is defeated, and
> b) if the last mentioned transfer was made by way of pledge or other disposition for value,

the unpaid seller's right of lien ... or stoppage in transit can only be exercised subject to the rights of the transferee.'

So in this position the unpaid seller may also lose his right of lien or stoppage in transit under s47(2) as well as his title under s9 FA.

Note that s47(2) like s9 FA operates also where the buyer in possession of documents disposes of the goods otherwise then by sale. That sub-section, however, has no requirement of absence of notice of the third party taking the goods.

Both s9 FA/s25 SGA and s47 SGA will prevail over the provisions of s19(3) SGA. Section 19(3) relates to reservation of title by the seller: where s9 FA or s47 SGA operate they will take precedence over s19(3) SGA and the reservation of title by the seller will be defeated. (Section 19(3) is explained fully under 8.4 above. Briefly, it states that there is a deemed reservation of title by the seller where he sends the buyer a bill of lading with a bill of exchange drawn on the buyer and the buyer does not accept that bill of exchange. No property passes if he does not accept the bill.)

Two cases are helpful in this context. The first is *Cahn* v *Pockett's Bristol Channel Co Ltd* (supra). (This case is dealt with in detail under 8.4 above.) The Court of Appeal here held that an infringement of s19(3) by the buyers in transferring the bill of lading when they did not accept the bill of exchange did not deprive the plaintiffs of the protection of s47. Secondly, an interesting case is the context of the general interrelation of s47 and s9 FA is *Mount* v *Jay and Jay Co Ltd* [1960] 1 QB 159; [1959] 3 All ER 307. D Company Ltd owned 500 cartons of tinned peaches stored in X's warehouse. D Co Ltd contracted to sell 250 of the cartons to M in two lots of 100 and 150 respectively. M made it clear at the contract that he would not be able to pay D Co until he had resold the goods. D Co gave M two delivery orders addressed to X and M had them endorsed. At no point did X attorn to M so there was no constructive delivery of the goods to X. M subsold to Y and gave him delivery orders drawn up by himself (M), not by D Co. Eventually, Y paid M but M failed to pay D Co. It was held:

1. The D Co's right of lien as an unpaid seller was defeated by a sale in s47(1) (see Chapter 11) since the D Co was held to have consented to the sub-sale at the time of the contract.
2. Title to the goods passed to Y under s9 FA/s25 SGA.

In a comprehensive review of the law Salmon J contrasted s47(2) and s9 FA. He stated that for s47(2) to operate the same document must be handed from the original seller to the first buyer and then from that first buyer to the second buyer, since the subsection uses the words 'transfers *the document* to a person who takes it' Section 9 FA/s25 SGA, however, employs the phrase 'the delivery or transfer ... of *the documents* of title under any sale' and consequently Salmon J stated that under this section the document transferred from the original seller to the first buyer and the document transferred by the first buyer to the second buyer need not be the same document.

This distinction has been universally criticised. There was clearly no intention in the Act to attach any significance to the slight difference in wording, nor is there any reason in logic why there should be this difference between the sections.

The requirements of good faith and absence of notice

It is a requirement of s9 FA/s25 SGA that the third party take the goods 'in good faith and without notice of any lien or other right of the original seller in respect of the goods'.

Atiyah points out that it is difficult to see how the seller can have 'any lien or other right in respect of the goods' which are in the possession of the buyer with the consent of the seller. Under s43(1)(b) the unpaid seller loses his lien 'when the buyer or his agent lawfully obtains possession of the goods'. Thus if the buyer has obtained possession with the consent of the seller, according to Atiyah it seems to follow necessarily that he has lawfully obtained possession - even if such possession was obtained by a criminal offence like a fraud. Atiyah therefore submits that s9 is applicable irrespective of the capacity of the buyer who obtains possession of the goods provided it is with the consent of the owner. Such a buyer can accordingly pass a good title to an innocent third party free from the seller's claim.

In *Jeffcott* v *Andrews Motors Ltd* [1960] NZLR 721 it was held unnecessary to decide whether the seller's lien could survive where the buyer obtained possession by criminal fraud. The third party here was protected anyway by the terms of s9 FA. The seller's lien if it survived would be meaningless in such circumstances since it would give the seller no right to obtain possession of the goods *from* the third party.

Where the buyer has already bought the goods so that the property has passed to him, it is, Atiyah points out, also difficult to see of what 'other right of the original seller' the third party can have notice. Atiyah suggests that this clause cannot be operative where there has been non-payment of the price by the buyer to the knowledge of the third party, since it is a common business practice for a seller to be paid for goods before he himself has paid for them. Knowledge of these circumstances can hardly, if ever, amount to bad faith on the part of the third party (ie the sub-buyer). It certainly does not put him on inquiry. In any event this would seem not to be a right 'in respect of the goods' but a personal right in the contract of sale. On the above reasoning Atiyah contends that the requirement that the third party must receive the goods 'in good faith and without notice of any lien or other right of the original seller in respect of the goods' can generally only be applicable where the buyer does not have the property to the goods.

Goode agrees that it is difficult to see in what circumstances the seller could have a subsisting lien when he has voluntarily given possession of the goods to the buyer.

The effect of s9

There is a significant difference in wording between s9 and s8 FA with regard to their effect. Section 8 provides that a sale by a seller in possession shall 'have the same effect as if the person making the delivery or transfer were expressly authorised by the owner of the goods to make the same'. Section 9 provides that a sale by a buyer in possession shall have the same effect 'as if the person making the delivery or transfer were a mercantile agent in possession of the goods or documents of title with the consent of the owner'.

It had always been assumed until 1965 that both these phrases were to be taken as meaning that title passed to the third party. (This assumption almost certainly remains true for s8). It was assumed that the phrase used in s9 stating that the disposition was to take effect as if the person making the delivery or transfer were a mercantile agent in possession of the goods was simply an elliptical method of saying that the disposition should take effect as if the goods had been delivered by a mercantile agent *disposing of them in the ordinary course of business of a mercantile agent*. In other words it was thought that although the effect of the section was that of a sale by a mercantile agent in the ordinary course of a business, there was no need that the sale in the section *actually be* in the course of the business of each agent. This convenient interpretation of the section was adopted in Australia in *Langmead* v *Thyer Rubber Co Ltd* (1947) SR (SA) 29 and in New Zealand in *Jeffcott* v *Andrew Motors* (supra), but was unfortunately rejected by the Court of Appeal in *Newtons of Wembley Ltd* v *Williams* (supra).

In *Newtons of Wembley* a rogue bought a car with a worthless cheque and resold it to X while it was parked at the kerb in Warren Street in London. X resold the car to Y, who took it in good faith. When the cheque was dishonoured the original owner tried to avoid the contract by taking all practical steps under the principles in *Caldwell* (supra). It was held:

1. The contract had been avoided for the purposes of s23 SGA.
2. The rogue was however a 'person who had bought or agreed to buy goods' within the meaning of s25 SGA.
3. The first buyer (the rogue) was to be treated notionally as a mercantile agent and the court has then to determine from the given facts whether the sale would have been 'in the ordinary course of business of a mercantile agent' if he had in fact been a mercantile agent.
4. On the facts since used cars were frequently sold at the kerb in Warren Street in London, then this was enough to be 'in the ordinary course of business' for s25 SGA.
5. Title therefore passed to X under s25 SGA.

The Court of Appeal have adopted a very literal interpretation of s9 FA/s25 SGA in holding that a sale in that section must effectively comply with the requirements of s2(1) FA 1889 on sales by mercantile agents, namely, that the sale must actually be 'in the ordinary course of business of a mercantile agent'. However, although the sale must in some way be in the ordinary course of business for mercantile agents, the buyer in possession in s25 need not be a mercantile agent in the fullest sense as set out in s2(1) FA. In particular it appears from the *Newtons* decision that the sale need not be on business premises or within business hours.

Goode submits that this interpretation of s9 is erroneous and so drastically reduces its scope as to deprive the section of any rational policy basis.

It is unclear exactly which requirements of sale 'in the ordinary course of business of a mercantile agent' will apply to s25. It has been held in *Pearson* v *Rose & Young* and in *Lambert* v *G & C Finance Cpn Ltd* (unreported) (1963), the latter of which dealt with s25, that the sale of a car without its registration book is not 'in the ordinary case of business of a mercantile agent'. Presumably the absence of a car's registration book would therefore take a car sale outside s25.

Atiyah suggests that the *Newtons of Wembley* decision would not apply to a sale by a private person who is not a mercantile agent since the sale would almost certainly take place outside business premises. However, although the dicta of Pearson LJ are at times confusing, the facts and decision of the *Newtons* case were that title passed under s25 where the buyer in possession was a private individual and the sale took place outside business premises. Atiyah's view could only be justified if one regards the sale of second-hand cars in Warren Street, London as a very special case because of the custom in that street.

The approach adopted by the courts in Australia and New Zealand in the cases cited above is more acceptable and more realistic than that adopted in *Newtons*. Their approach is that s9 operates to validate as if the buyer in possession were a mercantile agent - it does not require that he should actually act as though he were a mercantile agent.

An aspect of s9 which has given rise to difficulty and academic speculation is its effect where the person who purports to sell is not the owner and does not have the authority of the owner to sell. The classic case is that of a car which is stolen and then transferred by a thief to an innocent purchaser who then resells to another innocent purchaser. Precisely this situation of a chain of sales following the theft of a car arose for the first time in a reported English case in *National Employers Mutual Assurance Co Ltd* v *Jones* (supra). As we have seen this case was decided by the majority of the Court of Appeal by holding that the person who obtained the car from the thief could not be a person in possession with the consent of the seller because a thief could not be a seller. This is because under s2(1) of the SGA, 'A contract of sale is a contract by which the seller transfers or agrees to transfer the property in goods to the buyer'. As a thief does not have the property in the goods he cannot come within this definition. The majority found support for their view in two Commonwealth decisions: *Elwin* v *O'Regan & Maxwell* [1971] NZLR 1124 NZ Sup Ct and *Brandon* v *Leckie* (1972) 29 DLR (3d) 663.

This section, read literally, does appear to validate the title of someone who buys in good faith and without notice of any lien or other right of the original seller. This argument can be supported by pointing out that the word 'seller' is used at beginning of s9(1) and the word 'owner' at the end; they cannot be intended to mean the same thing. In *National Employers Mutual General Insurance v Jones* (supra), the issue was whether the sections could operate to defeat the title of someone early in the chain of owners. Thieves had stolen a car and sold it to A who sold it to C (a car dealer) who sold it to D (another car dealer) who sold it to Jones. Jones claimed to have good title, both by virtue of s9 of FA and s25 SGA, thereby defeating the title of the owner from whom the thieves had stolen the car. The House of Lords rejected this argument and held that the two sections could defeat title only of an owner who had entrusted possession of his goods to a buyer. The sections were not meant to apply to cases when the goods were stolen from the original owner.

On policy grounds this decision is somewhat disappointing. It had been earlier mentioned (in the course of the appeal hearing) that, as pointed out by Lord Donovan in the 12th Report of the Law Reform Committee on Transfer of Title to Chattels (1966 Cmnd 2958), stolen goods are rarely recovered anyway and so innocent purchasers are rarely dispossessed. Also, since the original owner will presumably be protected by insurance, the innocent purchaser of stolen goods, if he cannot rely on ss25 SGA/9 FA, will have little chance of tracing the thief for redress.

10.10 Motor vehicles subject to a hire purchase or conditional sale agreement

Part III, ss27 to 29 of the Hire Purchase Act 1964 provides an important exception to the *nemo dat* rule. Part III which was amended by the Consumer Credit Act 1974 provides that a bona fide purchaser for value of a motor vehicle from a person in possession under a hire purchase agreement or a conditional sale obtains a good title. The purchaser must be a 'private purchaser' and not a 'trade or finance purchaser' and he may himself take the vehicle on hire purchase or conditional sale, in which case he will acquire the original owner's title on completing his payments and exercising his option to purchase.

The provisions of Part III are strictly limited to 'motor vehicles' meaning only mechanically propelled vehicles intended or adapted for use on roads to which the public has access: s29(1) of the 1964 Act.

A disposition to a private purchaser

Section 27(2) of the Hire Purchase Act 1964 provides that where the debtor, before the property in the vehicle has become vested in him under the hire purchase or conditional sale agreement, disposes of the vehicle to a private purchaser who takes in good faith and without notice of the agreement, then the disposition is to have effect as if the title of the creditor to the vehicle had been vested in the debtor immediately before the disposition. Two definitions are necessary to understand this sub-section.

'Disposition'

'Disposition' means any sale or contract of sale including a conditional sale agreement, any bailment under a hire purchase agreement and any transfer of the property in goods pursuant to a provision in a hire purchase agreement. It also includes transactions purporting to be dispositions in this context.

'Private purchaser'

This term is not defined by the Act: it effectively means a purchaser who is not a 'trade or finance' purchaser. This latter term is defined in s29(2) of the 1964 Act as a purchaser who, at the time of the disposition made to him, carries on a business which consists wholly or partly:

> '(i) of purchasing motor vehicles for the purpose of offering or exposing them for sale;
> (ii) of providing finance by purchasing motor vehicles for the purpose of bailing them under hire purchase agreements, or agreeing to sell them under conditional sale agreements.'

A 'trade or finance' purchaser will usually be either a finance company or a motor dealer. The fact that such a purchaser buys the goods for his own use does not alter his status as a trade or finance purchaser. 'Private purchaser' will include a body corporate provided it does not buy as a 'trade or finance purchaser'.

The case of *Stevenson v Beverley Bentinck Ltd* [1976] 1 WLR 483; [1976] 2 All ER 606 illustrates that it is the status of the purchaser as a private purchaser or as a trade or finance purchaser which determines whether or not he will be protected by s27(2). In this case a person having a part-time business in buying and selling cars in his spare time was held to be outside s27(2) even though he bought the particular car in question for his own use. The 1964 Act was, the Court of Appeal held, concerned with the status of a purchaser and not with the capacity in which he carried out the transaction.

The intention of the Act in making this distinction was presumably to protect members of the public who buy as consumers but not motor dealers or finance companies who can or should be able to look after themselves. If this is so the decision in *Stevenson* seems correct from the point of view of policy.

To acquire a title the private purchaser must take in good faith and without notice of the hire-purchase or conditional sale agreement to which the vehicle is subject. It is clear that for this purpose constructive notice will not be sufficient: the private purchaser must have actual notice to be deprived of the protection of s27(2).

The Court of Appeal further held in *Barker v Bell* [1971] 1 WLR 983; [1971] 2 All ER 867 that a purchaser does not have notice of a hire purchase agreement so as to defeat his title under s27 if, although he knew that the vehicle had been on hire purchase, he was led to believe that the hire purchase agreement had been settled.

The requirement of good faith is entirely separate from the requirement relating to notice. Therefore, if the buyer is, at the time of the disposition, aware of the defect in his seller's title, he still cannot claim the protection of s27 even though he was unaware of any hire-purchase agreement. The effect of s27(2) is that the private purchaser takes such title as the creditor had immediately before the disposition. It is, of course, possible that the hire purchase creditor had no title in which case the buyer will take none.

An interesting question raised by the Act is whether the buyer is obliged to accept a Part III title or whether he can repudiate the contract for a breach of the implied condition as to title in s12 SGA.

A disposition to a trade or finance purchaser

If the vehicle is disposed of to a trade or finance purchaser no title will pass. However, if the trade or finance purchaser then disposes of the vehicle to a private purchaser taking in good faith and without notice, then that private purchaser will take a good title (s27(3)). This only applies to a first private purchaser taking without notice: if the first private purchaser takes with notice, then there is no passage of title even though he may subsequently resell to a purchaser without notice.

If the hire purchaser disposes of the vehicle to a finance company which re-lets it under a new hire purchase agreement to a new hire purchaser then the latter will be protected by s29(1) and will take a good title once he has paid off the hire purchase instalments even though the true facts may have come to light before he exercises his option to purchase, provided those facts were unknown to him at the time when he entered the hire purchase agreement (see s27(4)). The finance company will remain liable to the original owner for wrongful interference with goods (s27(6)).

Note finally that in the normal case under the 1964 Act where the sale is to a private purchaser taking a good title, the original owner (usually a finance company) can still sue the hire purchaser for breach of contract or in tort for wrongful interference with goods.

10.11 Sale by an unpaid seller exercising his statutory rights

An 'unpaid seller' (see s38 SGA and 'Remedies' below) has certain statutory rights, even where the property has passed to the buyer, to enable him to recoup his losses. These rights include a right of resale under s48(3) after he has exercised either his right of lien or his right of stoppage in transit.

Under s48(2) SGA where an unpaid seller has exercised his right of lien or stoppage in transit and then resells the goods in accordance with that section, he will pass a good title to the second buyer. The best illustration of this is *R V Ward* v *Bignall* [1967] 1 QB 534; [1967] 2 All ER 449 which is set out in full in Chapter 11.

10.12 Other miscellaneous exceptions to *nemo dat*

These include: current coins of the realm; negotiable instruments (see *Miller* v *Race* (1758) 1 Burr 452); and sale by a legal owner, holding subject to equities, to a bona fide purchaser of a legal interest for value without notice (see *Joseph* v *Lyons* (1884) 15 QB 280).

11

Real Remedies

11.1 Introduction

11.2 The meaning of 'unpaid seller'

11.3 The unpaid seller's right of lien: ss39, 41, 42 and 43

11.4 The unpaid seller's right of stoppage in transit: ss39, 44, 45 and 46

11.5 The unpaid seller's right of resale: s48

11.1 Introduction

The seller's remedies in contracts for the sale of goods are dealt with in ss38-50 of the SGA. A seller may have both *real remedies* (ie rights and powers against the *goods*) and *personal remedies* (ie rights as against the *buyer*). It is the provisions regarding the real remedies which have given rise to the most difficulty and the most controversy.

Much of the confusion in the area of the seller's real remedies has been caused, as Atiyah points out, by a failure in the legislation to distinguish adequately between the separate situations which can exist in law between the seller and the buyer. These range from the position where the property has passed to the buyer and the goods have been delivered to him to that where there is merely an agreement to sell specific or even unascertained goods. However, from a practical point of view, most of the statutory ambiguities have been cleared up by the case law.

There are, in effect, three remedies which a seller may have against the goods: the right of *lien*, the right of *stoppage in transit* (or 'stoppage in transitu') and the right of *resale*. In practice the first two are often exercised as a preliminary to the resale of the goods since that is ultimately what the seller will want to do in order to realise his money or even profit on the goods.

However, these remedies themselves will only come into play when the buyer is in default in paying the price. In legal terms, they will be available only where the seller is an 'unpaid seller'. It is thus necessary to determine the meaning of the term 'unpaid seller'. The real remedies of the seller will therefore be discussed below.

11.2 The meaning of 'unpaid seller'

Section 38(1) SGA provides:

> 'The seller of goods is deemed to be an "unpaid seller" within the meaning of this Act
> a) When the whole of the price has not been paid or tendered
> b) When a bill of exchange or other negotiable instrument has been received as conditional payment and the condition on which it was received has not been fulfilled by reason of the dishonour of the instrument or otherwise.'

Section 38(1)(a) is somewhat misleading. It really covers situations where *any part* of the price has not been paid or tendered. In other words, a seller will still be an unpaid seller even when the buyer only has a small amount left to pay, even an insignificant amount. Also, the seller may be 'unpaid' even though he has sold goods on credit.

In addition, goods are now often sold on conditional payment. For example, in the case of payment by cheque, the cheque is usually taken conditionally upon it being honoured when presented, and if it is dishonoured the obligation to pay arises again. Acceptance of a cheque is only conditional payment unless the parties clearly intend that a dishonoured cheque will be adequate which obviously is very unlikely. It follows that if the cheque is dishonoured then the seller will be an 'unpaid seller'.

The meaning of 'seller' is explained in s38(2).

> '(2) In this part of the Act "seller" includes any person who is in the position of a seller, as, for instance, an agent of the seller to whom the bill of lading has been endorsed, or a consignor or agent who has himself paid (or is directly responsible for) the price.'

So if, for example, the seller sells goods through an agent and the agent has paid the price but has not been paid by the buyer, then that agent is entitled to exercise any of the rights of the unpaid seller (see *Ireland* v *Livingstone* (1872) LR 5 HL 395). A buyer who has paid for and then rejected goods is *not* an unpaid seller: *J L Lyons* v *May & Baker Ltd* [1923] 1 KB 685).

Where the seller is an unpaid seller, then even if the property in the goods has passed to the buyer he will, subject to the conditions laid down in the Act, have the remedies of lien (s39(1)(a)), stoppage in transit (s39(1)(b)) and resale (s39(1)(c)). Section 39(1) provides:

> 'Subject to this and any other Act, notwithstanding that the property in the goods may have passed to the buyer, the unpaid seller of goods, as such, has by implication of law–
> a) a lien on the goods or right to retain them for the price while he is in possession of them;
> b) in case of the insolvency of the buyer, a right of stopping the goods in transit after he has parted with the possession of them;
> c) a right of resale as limited by this Act.'

11.3 The unpaid seller's right of lien: ss39, 41, 42 and 43

The provisions of s39(1)(a) above should be noted.

Another major section with regard to the right of lien is s41, which provides:

'(1) Subject to this Act, the unpaid seller of goods who is in possession of them is entitled to retain possession of them until payment or tender of the price in the following cases, namely -
a) Where the goods have been sold without any stipulation as to credit;
b) Where the goods have been sold on credit, but the term of credit has expired;
c) Where the buyer becomes insolvent.'

The unpaid seller's right of lien is a right to retain the goods until the whole of the price has been paid or tendered (or the buyer's debt has been secured or satisfied). In practice, as *Benjamin* notes, the lien is often exercised as a preliminary to the resale of the goods. The exercise of the unpaid seller's lien does not strictly give the seller any property in the goods nor do liens in general give powers of resale, but the unpaid seller having exercised his lien is by statute given the power and right to resell the goods subject to certain conditions.

The unpaid seller's lien is not a general lien for all debts due from buyer to seller but only for payment for the goods presently in dispute. The advantage of the lien is obviously that when the buyer becomes bankrupt the seller is not treated equally with the general creditors; he receives preference by being able to retain the goods themselves. He will not like the other creditors be left simply to his dividend in the bankruptcy or liquidation.

The conditions necessary for the exercise of the lien must now be considered, followed by a discussion of the situations where the seller loses his lien.

The conditions necessary for the exercise of the unpaid seller's lien

Three conditions must be fulfilled for the seller to exercise the lien.

The seller must be an 'unpaid seller' within the meaning of s38

Certain problems arise here with regard to instalment contracts (see 4.3). Where there is *one contract* between the seller and the buyer allowing for delivery by instalments, then the seller can in general exercise his lien over *any part* of the goods if *any part* of the price is unpaid. He is not restricted to exercising the lien over those goods to which the unpaid part of the price relates. (See, for example, *ex parte Chalmers* (1873) 8 Ch App 289.)

The provisions of s42 should be noted here:

'Where an unpaid seller has made part delivery of the goods he may exercise his lien on the remainder, unless such part delivery has been made under such circumstances as to show an agreement to waive the lien.'

However, where there are a number of separate contracts between the seller and the buyer, each contract quantity to be separately paid for and delivered, then the seller cannot claim a lien over any part of the goods already paid for merely because payment for other goods in one of the other contracts is outstanding. (The position is obviously different if all the relevant goods fall under the same contract: see *Merchant Banking Co v Phoenix Bessemer Steel Ltd* (1877) 5 Ch D 205.)

The seller cannot claim the lien if the goods have been sold on credit
This requirement comes from s41(1)(a):

> '(1) Subject to this Act the unpaid seller of goods who is in possession of them is entitled to retain possession of them until payment or tender of the price in the following cases:
> (a) where the goods have been sold *without any stipulations as to credit*.'

The section does then provide for two exceptions to this rule, namely that the lien may still be claimed:

> '(b) Where the goods have been sold on credit but the term of credit has expired;
> (c) Where the buyer becomes insolvent.'

This first exception obviously covers cases where the buyer has not in the meantime during the credit period obtained possession of the goods. The second exception relates to insolvency and its meaning is dealt with fully under stoppage in transit.

The seller must be in possession of the goods
This requirement is expressed in s39(1)(a), the provision which in fact confers the right of lien: 'A lien on the goods or right to retain them for the price while he is in possession of them.' The term 'possession' is not used with consistency in the law and so there is inevitably some vagueness about what exactly it means in this particular context.

A problem arose where the seller delivered the goods to the buyer *as agent or bailee* of the seller. It was once held that this did not defeat the seller's lien but the general view is now that here the seller would lose the lien. However, some very limited element of control by the buyer would possibly not be inconsistent with the existence of the seller's right of lien.

The common law position with regard to the capacity in which the seller must have possession was changed by s41(2). At common law the seller needed to be in possession *as seller*, not as agent or bailee of the buyer. However, now under s41(2): 'the seller may exercise his lien notwithstanding he is in possession as agent, or bailee ... for the buyer.'

Note also that there may be no right of lien when the buyer has obtained *constructive possession* of the goods through the documents of title. Under s47(2) where the buyer has obtained the documents of title to the goods with the consent of the seller and resells to a party in good faith taking for valuable consideration, then the unpaid seller's right of lien or stoppage in transit will be defeated. (Section 47(2) is quoted in full under 'Loss of the lien'.)

The unpaid seller's lien is for the *price* and not for storage charges. It would seem to follow that the seller cannot claim a lien for such charges, however this point has never been finally decided. In *Somes v British Empire Shipping Co* (1860) 8 HLC 338 the House of Lords is generally thought to have laid down that the seller had no lien for storage charges under any circumstances, but in fact, as Atiyah points out, the Lords only decided that the seller cannot claim such a lien for charges arising as a result of the exercise by a seller of the unpaid seller's lien for the price. It is, however, difficult to argue that a court would allow a lien purely for storage charges in other circumstances.

Loss of the lien

The unpaid seller will lose his lien in any of the following circumstances: where the seller ceases to be an unpaid seller; where the seller delivers the goods to a carrier or other bailee for the purpose of transmission to the buyer without reserving the right of disposal of the goods: s43(1)(a); when the buyer or his agent lawfully obtains possession of the goods: s43(1)(b); sale or pledge by the buyer under s47(2); sale or other disposition by the buyer under s47(1); waiver of the lien by the seller: s43(1)(c).

Where the seller ceases to be an unpaid seller
This will occur when the whole of the price is paid or tendered. The seller, however, may retain possession until the time of payment or tender.

Where the seller delivers the goods to a carrier or other bailee
Where the seller delivers the goods to a carrier or other bailee for the purpose of transmission to the buyer without reserving the right of disposal of the goods: s43(1)(a). In this position the seller may still have the right of stoppage in transit, but it is nevertheless important to determine when the lien is lost since the right of lien is in some respects different from that of stoppage. For example, the seller can only stop the goods in transit if the buyer is insolvent, whereas there is no such stipulation in the seller's lien.

'Reservation of the right of disposal of the goods' should be taken here to have the same meaning as in s19 SGA (see 8.4).

When the buyer or his agent lawfully obtains possession of the goods: s43(1)(b)
'Lawfully' in this sense is generally taken to mean 'with the consent of the seller'. Therefore in this particular context it will not matter if possession is obtained as the result of a criminal offence like a fraud, provided the seller's consent is present. It is, of course, odd to describe such a position as 'lawful' but this is a necessary interpretation in order to make the section consistent with s25(1) SGA which deals with obtaining possession 'with the consent of the seller' (see 10.9).

Sale or pledge by the buyer under s47(2)

Where the buyer gets possession of the documents of title to the goods, the lien will probably be defeated under s47(2). Section 47(2) provides:

> 'Where a document of title to goods has been lawfully transferred to any person as buyer or owner of the goods, and that person transfers the document to a person who takes it in good faith and for valuable consideration, then -
> a) if the last-mentioned transfer was by way of sale the unpaid seller's right of lien ... or stoppage in transit is defeated, and
> b) if the last-mentioned transfer was made by way of pledge or other disposition for value, the unpaid seller's right of lien ... or stoppage in transit can only be exercised subject to the rights of the transferee.'

So under s47(2) where a document of title has been lawfully transferred to any person as buyer or owner of the goods and that person transfers the document to a person who takes it in good faith and for valuable consideration, then if the last-mentioned transfer was a sale, the unpaid seller's lien is defeated. If the last-mentioned transfer was a pledge then the lien is only exercisable subject to the pledgee's rights.

Section 47(2) has already been discussed at some length in 10.9. The main illustrations and discussions of this section are in *Cahn* v *Pockett's Bristol Channel Co* [1899] 1 QB 643 and in *Mount* v *Jay & Jay* [1960] 1 QB 159; [1959] 3 All ER 307. *Cahn* deals with stoppage in transit and is dealt with in that context.

In *Mount* v *Jay & Jay Co Ltd* (supra) (the facts are set out in full in 10.9) the agreement was for tinned peaches. The buyer made it clear at the time of contracting that he would not be able to pay the seller until he had resold the goods so the seller gave him the delivery order addressed to the owner of the warehouse where the goods were stored. There was no attornment by the warehousekeeper to the buyer, so constructive delivery never took place. The buyer instead subsold to Y using delivery orders *drawn out by himself* (not by the sellers). Y paid the buyer but the buyer did not pay the seller.

Salmon J reviewed the law in this area and stated that for s47(2) to operate (in contrast to s9 of the Factors Act) the same document must be handed from the original seller to the first buyer and then from that first buyer to the second buyer, since the subsection uses the words 'transfers the document to a person who takes'. Salmon J contrasted this position with that under s9 Factors Act, which he said operated also when a different document was used. The distinction has been criticised since there was clearly no intention in the Act to distinguish the two sections in this way. In dealing with s47(2) Salmon J therefore held that it did not operate in the present case since the buyer had not used the *same* document in the subsale to the second buyer. However, it was held that the right of lien was in fact defeated by a sale under s47(1) (below) since the seller was held to have consented to the sub-sale at the time of the contract. He clearly knew that the buyer could not pay him until he had resold the goods, and therefore clearly assented to the resale.

Sale or other disposition by the buyer under s47(1)
Section 47(1) provides:

> 'Subject to this Act, the unpaid seller's right of lien ... or stoppage in transit is not affected by any sale, or other disposition of the goods which the buyer may have made, unless the seller has assented to it.'

So if the buyer, not having possession of the goods, resells them and the seller assents to such sale, the sub-buyer will take free from the first seller's right of lien (or stoppage in transit, below).

An illustration of the workings of this subsection is found above in *Mount* v *Jay & Jay*. Note that the mere fact that the seller has been informed of a resale and has not objected to it does not amount to assent under s47 (see *Mordaunt Bros* v *British Oil & Cake Mills Ltd* [1910] 2 KB 502).

The proviso 'subject to this Act' in s47(1) refers to s47(2) in which the lien or stoppage may be lost by a disposition by the buyer notwithstanding that the seller does not consent.

Waiver of the lien by the seller - s43(1)(c)
There seems to be little general agreement and little helpful case law on what will in fact amount to waiver of the lien by the seller.

If, for example, the seller asks the buyer's permission to retain possession by way of a temporary loan this may amount to waiver notwithstanding s41(2) under which the seller may exercise the lien even if he is only in possession as the buyer's bailee or agent. Should the seller wrongly deal with the goods inconsistently with the buyer's rights this will probably amount to waiver (see *Jones* v *Tarleton* (1842) 9 M & W 674).

Note finally under lien that if the lien has been lost it is not regained merely because the seller regains possession (*Valpy* v *Gibson* (1847) 4 CB 837).

11.4 The unpaid seller's right of stoppage in transit: ss39, 44, 45 and 46

The unpaid seller's right of stoppage in transit (or stoppage 'in transitu') is first conferred by s39(1)(b) - see above 11.2 - and then fully laid down in s44. Section 44 provides:

> 'Subject to this Act, when the buyer of goods becomes insolvent, the unpaid seller who has parted with the possession of the goods has the right of stopping them in transit, that is to say, he may resume possession of the goods so long as they are in course of transit, and may retain them until payment or tender of the price.'

This is the right literally to stop goods in the course of transit, stopping them from reaching the buyer. Section 39(2) still applies and so it makes no difference that the property has passed to the buyer, stoppage will still apply. If the property is still with the seller then he will stop the goods by virtue of his ownership and the Act merely makes that stoppage rightful as against the buyer; where, however, the property has passed to the buyer, the Act here confers on the seller the power and the right to stop the goods.

The right of stoppage is only available when the buyer is *insolvent* (a requirement laid out in s39(1)(b) and in s44) and hence it can be seen as a just and fair mechanism for preventing goods which will not be paid for being applied to pay the debts of an insolvent buyer. In most cases, stoppage will elevate the seller to the effective position of being a 'secured creditor' with his goods as security, but this does not seem unduly harsh on the other creditors since the goods will not yet have reached the buyer. It will not have appeared to the other creditors, as it would have done if the goods had reached the buyer, that the goods were owned by the buyer and that they were available to pay his debts.

The use of banker's commercial credits and payment against documents in modern commercial transactions has substantially reduced the importance of stoppage, since the seller will retain control of the goods through documents until he is paid. Stoppage is now only of real importance in practice where goods are sold on credit.

As with the unpaid seller's lien, the exercise by the seller of the right of stoppage does not of itself rescind the contract of sale. It enables the seller to retake possession of the goods, retaining them until the price is paid or tendered. Section 48(c) makes this clear: '(1) Subject to this section, a contract of sale is not rescinded by the mere exercise by the unpaid seller of his right of lien ... or stoppage in transit.'

Conditions necessary for the exercise of the right of stoppage

There are four main conditions to be discussed in this context: the seller must be an 'unpaid seller' within the meaning of the Act; the buyer must be insolvent; the goods must be in the course of transit; the effect of sub-dealings by the buyer on the seller's right of stoppage.

The seller must be an unpaid seller within the meaning of the Act.
The meaning of 'unpaid seller' has already been discussed under 11.2 above.

The buyer must be insolvent.
A definition of 'insolvency' is provided by s61(4):

> 'A person is deemed to be insolvent within the meaning of this Act if he has either ceased to pay his debts in the ordinary course of business, or he cannot pay his debts as they become due, whether he has committed an act of bankruptcy or not.'

The seller is in a difficult position where there are merely rumours that the buyer is insolvent since it is far from clear whether this will be adequate for the exercise of the right of stoppage. If the seller wrongly exercises the stoppage right he leaves himself open to an action by the buyer. It is submitted that the buyer must actually be insolvent for stoppage to be rightly exercised.

The goods must be 'in the course of transit'.

The meaning of 'in the course of transit' has caused considerable problems. Thankfully s45 has now cleared up many of the ambiguities caused by previous judicial statements. Section 45(1) provides:

> 'Goods are deemed to be in the course of transit from the time when they are delivered to a carrier or other bailee ... for the purpose of transmission to the buyer, until the buyer, or his agent in that behalf takes delivery of them from the carrier or other bailee.'

Goods are in transit essentially when they have passed out of the possession of the seller into the possession of a carrier but have not yet reached the possession of the buyer. The concept of possession again poses problems.

The point where the transit commences is usually reasonably clear: it is when the independent carrier takes possession of them. However, if the carrier is the seller's own agent the question of stoppage never arises because the goods while in the possession of such agent are still sufficiently in the seller's possession to exercise the right of lien over them. For the question of the right of stoppage in transit to arise the carrier must be an *independent* contractor such as British Rail or an independent shipowner or shipping line who has possession of the goods on his own behalf *as carrier*.

Similarly, where the carrier is the buyer's agent, then transit never begins since the buyer already has possession of the goods.

The point where the transit ends is less easy to determine. The goods generally remain in transit while they are in the possession of the independent carrier, and 'transit' does not necessarily mean 'movement'. The goods could be sitting in a warehouse belonging to the carrier having arrived at their destination and still be 'in transit'.

Delivery to the buyer or his agent obviously ends transit. This position is complicated by the provisions of s32(1), stating that delivery to the carrier is prima facie deemed to be delivery to the buyer. This is in fact an example of one of the types of constructive delivery to the buyer which are inadequate to destroy stoppage. Certain types of constructive delivery will be adequate to end the right of stoppage but not the mere delivery to an independent carrier - otherwise there would be no such thing as 'transit' and stoppage could never arise!

Note under s45(3) a constructive delivery where the carrier *attorns* to the buyer as where the carrier agrees to hold the goods henceforth *for the buyer* will end the transit. Section 45(3) provides:

> 'If after arrival of the goods at the appointed destination the carrier or other bailee or custodier acknowledges to the buyer or his agent that he holds on his behalf and continues in possession as bailee or custodier for the buyer or his agent, the transit is at an end and it is immaterial that a further destination for the goods may have been indicated by the buyer.'

Such constructive delivery was probably adequate at common law also to end transit. In *Taylor* v *G E Railway Co* [1901] 1 KB 774, the goods had reached their destination which was a railway station. The station master informed the buyer of the arrival, the buyer asked the master to hold the goods for him and the master agreed.

It was held that transit had ended even though the buyer had not yet been to the station to take actual possession of the goods.

The question arises as to whether the transfer to the buyer of the documents of title to the goods will of itself be adequate to terminate the seller's right of stoppage. The view taken by Atiyah that this probably is not sufficient has been criticised.

Certainly if the buyer, having gained possession of the documents of title, goes on, using the documents, to sell the goods to a person taking in good faith and for valuable consideration, then stoppage will be lost under s47(2)(a) (as noted above under 11.2: Sale or pledge by the buyer). If the buyer pledges the goods, using the documents, to a person taking in good faith and for valuable consideration then the right of stoppage can only be exercised subject to the rights of the pledgee.

Where the carrier is a sea-carrier and the ship is chartered by the buyer for a voyage or fixed period then the Master will still be the servant of the shipowner and will not be the buyer's agent, so transit has not ended. Nor will transit have ended merely because it is the buyer who has given the instructions for the dispatch of the goods for all or part of the voyage (see *Kendall v Marshall, Stevens & Co* (1883) 11 QBD 356).

Two further situations must be distinguished. Where the goods pass through successive stages of transit from one independent carrier to another in pursuance of the contract or of directions given after the contract by the buyer to the seller, transit continues until they reach their ultimate destination (*Reddell v Union Castle Mail SS Co* (1915) 84 LJKB 360). However, where the buyer has requested delivery to be at a certain place and the goods have arrived there, transit will not continue merely because the buyer intends ultimately to give and even does give fresh directions to dispatch the goods elsewhere (see per Brett LJ in *Bethell & Co Ltd v Clark & Co Ltd* (1888) 20 QBD 615).

If the buyer intercepts the goods at some stage in the course of transit then the right of stoppage is lost. Section 45(2) provides: 'If the buyer or his agent in that behalf obtains delivery of the goods before their arrival at the appointed destination, the transit is at an end.' A case under this section is *Plischke & Sohne GmbH v Allison Bros Ltd* [1936] 2 All ER 1009. The seller contracted to deliver the goods free of charge to the buyer's London premises. The carrier in fact delivered the goods at a dock warehouse in accordance with instructions from the buyer. It was held that the right of stoppage was lost.

Where the carrier wrongfully refuses to deliver to the buyer, then stoppage is lost. Section 45(6) provides: 'Where the carrier or other bailee ... wrongfully refuses to deliver the goods to the buyer, or his agent in that behalf the transit is deemed to be at an end.' However, under s45(4) the transit is not at an end if the buyer rejects the goods. Section 45(4) provides: 'If the goods are rejected by the buyer, and the carrier or other bailee ... continues in possession of them, the transit is not deemed to be at an end, even if the seller has refused to receive them back.'

It seems to be unclear whether s45(4) takes precedence over s45(3) or vice-versa.

In other words, where the carrier attorns to the buyer saying he holds on his behalf but then the buyer rejects the goods, has transit ended? The better view is probably that transit continues and the attornment has no effect. Atiyah supports this view by reference to the common law position where attornment only transfers possession to the buyer on the assumption that he assents to such transfer, so transit will not have ended (*Bolton* v *Lancashire & Yorkshire Ry* (1866) LR 1 CP 431).

Finally under s45, the provisions of s45(7) should be noted:

> 'Where part delivery of the goods has been made to the buyer or his agent in that behalf, the remainder of the goods may be stopped in transit, unless such part delivery has been made under such circumstances as to show an agreement to give up possession of the whole of the goods.'

The significance of this subsection is that the right of stoppage like the right of lien may in general be exercised over part only of the goods where some other part has in fact been delivered.

The effect of subdealings by the buyer on the seller's right of stoppage.
This area has given rise to considerable difficulty. There are in effect two separate questions to be answered:

1. Is the sub-buyer or pledgee who takes from the buyer entitled to possession of the goods free from the seller's right of stoppage?
2. Assuming the sub-buyer or pledgee is so entitled, can the seller exercise his right of stoppage over the money paid by the sub-buyer in the case of a sale, or over the goods subject to the pledgee's rights in the case of a pledge?

With a pledge it is undisputed that the seller can still exercise his right of stoppage notwithstanding that the goods have been pledged; however, he can only do so subject to the rights of the pledgee (ie the seller can take the goods from the carrier only if he pays off the pledgee). Even if the pledgee sells the goods the seller is still entitled to claim the balance of the price from the pledgee. The authority for these propositions was *Kemp* v *Falk* (1882) 7 App Cas 573 but they are now incorporated in s47(2)(b), the wording of which is noted above under 11.3: Sale or pledge by the buyer. It states that 'if the last-mentioned transfer (by the buyer) was made by way of pledge ... the unpaid seller's right of lien ... or stoppage in transit can only be exercised subject to the rights of the transferee'. Note that the pledge must take in good faith and for valuable consideration to gain the protection of s47(2).

The position arising in the case of a sub-sale by the buyer has been the subject of a good deal of discussion by commentators, much of which over-complicates the law here. The situation must now be governed by s47(2)(a), which states quite clearly that if a document of title is transferred by the buyer by way of resale to a third party taking in good faith and for value, the unpaid seller's right of stoppage is defeated. Section 47(2) reads as follows:

'Where a document of title to goods has been lawfully transferred to any person as buyer or owner of the goods, and that person transfers the document to a person who takes it in good faith and for valuable consideration, then -
a) if the last mentioned transfer was by way of sale the unpaid seller's right of lien ... or stoppage in transit is defeated'.

Much discussion is devoted to the pre-SGA decision of *ex parte Golding Davies & Co Ltd* [1899] 13 Ch D 628. In this case the seller who had not been paid by the buyer claimed that he was entitled to intercept the money paid by the sub-buyer to the buyer. In effect he was claiming a right of stoppage over the money. The Court of Appeal held that the seller was entitled to do this.

Lord Selborne in *Kemp* v *Falk* (supra) thought *Golding* to be wrongly decided, and indeed the *Golding* decision is difficult to reconcile with the case of *Berndtson* v *Strang* (1868) 3 Ch App 588. Here the Court of Appeal had held that an unpaid seller has no right to the proceeds of an insurance policy covering the goods, in other words that his right was to stop *the goods* in whatever state they were and not to stop any monies involved.

It is submitted that these cases are only now of historical interest because of the express provisions of s47(2)(a) SGA set out above. No mention is made in the SGA of any possibility of transferring the stoppage right from the goods to the money, and the *Golding* case should be regarded as wrongly decided or overruled. A resale in the conditions laid down by s47(2) *will* end the seller's right of stoppage.

An illustration of the operation of s47(2) is found in *Cahn* v *Pockett's Bristol Channel Co Ltd* (supra) (the facts are set out in detail in 8.4). Briefly, the seller contracted to sell copper to a buyer in Rotterdam, to be loaded on a ship in Swansea. The bill of lading was transferred to the buyer who resold the copper using the bill to a third party who paid in good faith. The buyer became insolvent and the unpaid seller attempted to exercise his right of stoppage in transit over the goods before they reached the buyer. The case also involved s19(3) on reservation of title to the goods, and s25 on the transfer of property by a non-owning buyer in possession. It was held that good title did pass under s25 to the sub-buyer, and also that the seller had lost his right of lien under s47(2). The sub-buyer had bought in good faith and for valuable consideration, receiving transfer of a document of title.

The method of exercising the right of stoppage and the position as between vendor and carrier

Section 46 lays down the methods by which the seller can exercise his right of stoppage. The section also places the burden of redelivering the goods on the seller. Section 46 provides:

'(1) The unpaid seller may exercise his right of stoppage in transit either by taking actual possession of the goods, or by giving notice of his claim to the carrier or other bailee in whose possession the goods are.

> (2) The notice may be given either to the person in actual possession of the goods or to his principal.
> (3) If given to the principal, the notice is ineffective unless given at such time and under such circumstances that the principal, by the exercise of reasonable diligence, may communicate it to his servant or agent in time to prevent a delivery to the buyer.
> (4) When notice of stoppage in transit is given by the seller to the carrier, or other bailee ... in possession of the goods, he must redeliver the goods to, or according to the directions of, the seller; and the expenses of such redelivery must be borne by the seller.'

Obviously if the carrier has been sent a notice of stoppage and he then wrongly delivers the goods to the buyer then he will be liable to the seller for wrongful interference with goods.

The carrier's lien for any freight due will take priority over the seller's right of stoppage, and the carrier can refuse to redeliver the goods to the seller unless the seller first pays the freight. The same is not true of any general lien conferred on the seller by contract: the exercise of the right of stoppage postpones such a lien unless the seller was privy to the contract which conferred this lien.

The carrier is indeed in a strong position as against the unpaid seller who stops the goods in transit so far as the recovery of freight charges is concerned. He has first a positive action against the seller for the freight. Furthermore, after exercising the stoppage right, the unpaid seller is under a duty to give to the carrier instructions as to either the return or disposal of the goods.

In *Booth SS Co Ltd* v *Cargo Fleet Iron Co Ltd* [1916] 2 KB 570 the seller exercised his right of lien before the ship had reached its destination, telling the plaintiff carrier not to deliver to the buyer. The plaintiff asked for instructions on what to do with the goods but none were forthcoming. The defendants subsequently repudiated liability for the freight charges so the plaintiffs landed the goods at the original destination. The plaintiff sued for the freight. The Court of Appeal held the carrier to be entitled to damages representing the amount of the freight.

11.5 The unpaid seller's right of resale: s48

The most important provision governing resale by the seller is s48(2). It is this subsection which gives the unpaid seller the power to resell the goods after the exercise of the unpaid seller's right of lien or stoppage.

It should be emphasised at the outset that the question of the unpaid seller's statutory power of resale as laid down in s48(2) arises only after the exercise by him of the right of lien or the right of stoppage in transit. Section 48(2) provides:

> 'Where an unpaid seller who has exercised his right of lien or stoppage in transit resells the goods, the buyer acquires a good title to them as against the original buyer.'

It should be noted that the seller will have the power to resell the goods without need to resort to s48(2) if he still has the property in the goods or, even though the property has passed to the buyer, he is in possession within s24 SGA (supra). Section

48(2) presumably covers cases where the property has passed to the first buyer and the circumstances are not such that the seller could pass a good title under s24 SGA.

Section 48(2), like s24 confers a power of resale, in other words the ability to pass a good title; it does not confer on the seller a right to resell the goods. The court in *R V Ward Ltd* v *Bignall* (supra) contrasted this effect of s48(2) with that of s48(3) below which gives the seller the right to resell the goods.

The seller will, of course, be concerned as to whether he can resell the goods as of right as against the first buyer, as well as whether he has the power to pass a good title. First, the seller will be able to resell as of right in the initial contractual stages if his obligation to deliver has not yet crystallized into an obligation to deliver any specific goods. Secondly, if the buyer repudiates the contract then the seller can accept that repudiation and resell the goods if he so wishes, whether or not the property has passed to the buyer. (Rejection of the goods by the buyer is prima facie repudiation of the contract). If the seller does not accept the buyer's repudiation, he cannot resell the goods as of right unless such right is conferred by s48(3) or s48(4) below.

A third situation to be noted is that the seller may have a right of resale under s48(3). Section 48(3) provides:

> 'Where the goods are of a perishable nature, or where the unpaid seller gives notice to the buyer of his intention to resell, and the buyer does not within a reasonable time pay or tender the price, the unpaid seller may resell the goods and recover from the original buyer damages for any loss occasioned by his breach of contract.'

This is an important provision and requires some analysis. It deals with two situations: where the goods are perishable; and where the goods are not perishable. The subsection modifies the presumption as to the effect of the time of payment laid down in s10 SGA. Section 48(3) in effect makes time 'of the essence' in sales of perishables, allowing the seller to treat the contract as repudiated and to resell where the buyer has delayed unreasonably in paying for the goods. With non-perishables, notice to the buyer is required to make time of the essence; so only after such notice is given and the buyer has delayed unreasonably can the seller resell as of right. Note that the buyer could in either case be liable anyway in damages for the delay in payment.

A fourth situation to be noted is the right of resale in s48(4). Under s48(4) the seller has the right of resale on the default of the buyer if he has expressly reserved such a right in the original contract. Section 48(4) provides:

> 'Where the seller expressly reserves the right of resale in case the buyer should make default, and on the buyer making default re-sells the goods, the original contract of sale is rescinded, but without prejudice to any claim the seller may have for damages.'

When s48(3) and s48(4) are compared, it will be noted that whereas s48(4) expressly provides that a resale under that sub-section will rescind the contract, there is no parallel express provision in s48(3). In other words it is not clear whether a resale under s48(3) of perishables, or non-perishables after notice, will rescind the original contract of sale or not. This problem was first considered in *Gallagher* v *Shilcock* [1949] 2 KB 765; [1949] 1 All ER 921. The case involved the sale of a yacht. The buyer failed to pay and the seller resold it. Finnemore J contrasted the wording of s48(4) with s48(3) and held that resale by the seller under s48(3) did not rescind the original contract of sale. This decision is manifestly wrong in principle and has now been overruled. Where the seller resells even part of the contract goods under s48(3) then the original contract of sale must be rescinded since the seller is now incapable of performing that contract.

In *R V Ward Ltd* v *Bignall* (supra) the Court of Appeal overruled *Gallagher* v *Shilcock*. The details of *R V Ward* v *Bignall* (supra) are that the plaintiff seller contracted to sell two motor cars, a Zodiac and a Vanguard to the defendant buyer. The buyer repudiated, saying the age of the Vanguard had been misrepresented. The seller notified the buyer of his intention to resell if the buyer did not pay, but no payment was forthcoming. The seller finally resold the Vanguard but could not resell the Zodiac. He sued the buyer for the price of the Zodiac, his loss on the resale of the Vanguard and the expenses of reselling that car. The plaintiff seller argued that property had passed at the contract and that his resale under s48(3) had not rescinded the contract (as per *Gallagher* v *Shilcock*), and that the damages should therefore be the balance of the purchase price on the cars. The Court of Appeal held that the seller was not entitled to the price of the Zodiac, since the resale by him of the Vanguard under s48(3) had rescinded the contract. Such a resale by the buyer did rescind the contract and *Gallagher* was wrongly decided.

The court did not finally determine whether the property in the cars had ever passed to the buyer. If this was the case, then on rescission of the contract the property must have reverted to the seller, and the seller was therefore reselling as owner of the goods.

It should be added that had the court held otherwise (ie that there was no rescission and the property had indeed passed to the buyer), then the seller would have been reselling as agent of the buyer and would have had to account to him for profits on the resale! It would obviously be wrong to compel such a seller to account to a buyer who is actually in default.

The Court of Appeal explained the difference in wording of the two sub-sections on the ground that failure by the buyer to pay the price is not *per se* a breach justifying repudiation. However, once the seller has given notice to the buyer to pay up, time of payment is made of the essence and thereafter failure to pay amounts to a repudiation which the seller accepts by reselling the goods.

12

Personal Remedies of the Seller

12.1 Introduction

12.2 The action for the price of the goods sold

12.3 The action for damages for non-acceptance of the goods

12.1 Introduction

Two types of personal remedies may be available to the seller: the action for the price of the goods sold; and the action for damages for non-acceptance of the goods.

Section 49(1) and s50(1) lay down a rule of general application that it is an action for the price which is appropriate where the property in the goods has passed to the buyer, and an action for damages when the property has not passed. Section 49(1) provides:

> 'Where, under a contract of sale, the property in the goods has passed to the buyer, and the buyer wrongfully neglects or refuses to pay for the goods according to the terms of the contract, the seller may maintain an action against him for the price of the goods.'

Section 50(1) provides:

> 'Where the buyer wrongfully neglects or refuses to accept and pay for the goods, the seller may maintain an action against him for damages for non-acceptance.'

The question arises here as to the position when the property has passed to the buyer but the buyer has refused to accept the goods. Here it seems that the seller will have the choice of bringing an action for the price under s49(1) or for damages under s50(1).

12.2 The action for the price of the goods sold

This is generally available to the seller where the property in the goods has passed to the buyer. However, s49(2) provides one exceptional case in which the seller may sue for the price although the property in the goods has not yet passed. Section 49(2) provides:

'Where, under a contract of sale, the price is payable on a day certain irrespective of delivery, and the buyer wrongfully neglects or refuses to pay such price, the seller may maintain an action for the price, although the property in the goods has not passed, and the goods have not been appropriated to the contract.'

The price must be payable at a fixed time and irrespective of delivery. So if the price is payable before delivery the seller can still sue for the price if it has become due provided he does not treat the contract as repudiated. In such a situation the seller could not yet sue for damages for non-acceptance of the goods because the buyer may not yet have refused to accept them.

It is clear that a date for payment will be a 'day certain' within s49(2), whereas in an instalment contract that date is only ascertained by reference to the stage reached in performance by the seller. This was held to be so in *Workman Clark & Co Ltd v Lloyd Brazileno* [1908] 1 KB 968 where the contract was for the construction of a ship and the date of payment was ascertained according to the stage the construction had reached.

There are two main points of distinction between an action for the price and an action for damages for non-acceptance:

1. In financial terms, there will generally be a significant difference between the price of the goods, and damages for non-acceptance. The price is almost invariably the larger figure.
2. Where property has passed and the seller may sue for the price, he is not under a duty to mitigate his damage by reselling the goods or otherwise. Where, however, the property is still with the seller he must sue for damages and then he must mitigate.

These differences can place the seller in an unenviable position where either the goods have not yet been delivered and the buyer repudiates the contract; or the buyer has refused to take delivery. In either case the seller is uncertain as to whether the property in the goods has passed to the buyer. If he disclaims responsibility for the goods and sues for the price arguing that property has passed to the buyer, he may, if he is wrong and the property has not passed, have his damages reduced because of his failure to mitigate when obliged to do so. Conversely, if the seller mitigates by reselling the goods or attempting to do so and it transpires that the property had passed to the buyer, the court may treat the seller's acts as acceptance of the repudiation of contract by the buyer. Consequently, the property will revest in the seller and he will lose his action for the price.

As Atiyah points out, the seller's dilemma here is caused largely by the fact that the seller is entitled to sue for the price of the goods where the property has passed but the buyer has refused to take delivery. It should, Atiyah argues, be the balance of convenience which should determine where the responsibility lies for reselling the goods and not the passing of the property. In many cases that balance of convenience would mean that the seller should resell where delivery has not yet been made and accepted, but if the buyer for example refuses delivery in circumstances making it extremely difficult for the seller to make alternative arrangements to dispose of the goods the obligation ought to be on the buyer to resell, allowing the seller to sue for the price.

Note also that, in addition to the right to sue for the price or for non-acceptance damages, the seller may have the following two remedies:

1. The right under s54 to sue for *special damage* based on loss arising from special circumstances of which the parties were aware.
2. The right under s37 to claim for the cost of care and custody and any other loss incurred where the property has passed to the buyer and he neglects to take delivery of the goods.

Section 37 provides:

'(1) When the seller is ready and willing to deliver the goods, and requests the buyer to take delivery, and the buyer does not within a reasonable time after such request take delivery of the goods, he is liable to the seller for any loss occasioned by his neglect or refusal to take delivery, and also for a reasonable charge for the care and custody of the goods.
(2) Nothing in this section affects the rights of the seller when the neglect or refusal of the buyer to take delivery amounts to a repudiation of the contract.'

12.3 The action for damages for non-acceptance of the goods

This is the seller's remedy where the property in the goods has not passed to the buyer. It can also be used as an alternative to suing for the price where the property has passed but the buyer refuses to accept the goods. The seller in these circumstances is under a duty to mitigate his loss.

This topic will be dealt with as follows: the measure of damages: the general rule; displacement of the market price rule in s50(3); and where the market price rule applies.

The measure of damages: the general rule

Section 50(2) provides:

'The measure of damages is the estimated loss directly and naturally resulting, in the ordinary course of events, from the buyer's breach of contract.'

The method for calculating the loss directly and naturally resulting in the ordinary course of events from the buyer's breach is set out in s50(3):

'Where there is an available market for the goods in question the measure of damages is prima facie to be ascertained by the difference between the contract price and the market or current price at the time or times when the goods ought to have been accepted or (if no time was fixed for acceptance) at the time of the refusal to accept.'

In addition the seller may be able to claim special damages under s54 as above. The question of what amounts to an 'available market' in s50(3) has caused the courts some difficulty and there are very few cases on the point. In *Dunkirk Colliery* v *Lever* (1878) 9 Ch D 20 market was said to mean something in the nature of a fair or one of the specialist commodity markets such as the Cotton Exchange or the Baltic Exchange. As counsel pointed out in *Thompson Ltd* v *Robinson (Gunmakers) Ltd* (below), the meaning of the word must move with the time. In that case Upjohn J felt bound by the decision of the Court of Appeal in *Dunkirk Colliery* v *Lever* but it seems likely that his own definition of a market would now be adopted in relation to s50(3). He found that 'an "available market" merely means that the situation in the particular trade in the particular area was such that the particular goods could freely be sold, and that there was a demand sufficient to absorb readily all the goods that were thrust upon it, so that if a purchaser defaulted, the goods in question could readily be disposed of'.

If there is an available market at more than one place, the relevant place is prima facie the place at which the goods were to be delivered under the contract. In *Hasell* v *Bagot Shakes & Lewis Ltd* (1911) 13 CLR 374, delivery of Japanese superphosphate was to be at Adelaide. Therefore, the market price at Adelaide was taken.

Note, however, that where the buyer refuses to accept the goods, the question is as to where the seller should reasonably be expected to look for a new purchaser. The availability of markets for the goods may be diverse or very restricted depending on the circumstances of the case. An international shipper could well be expected to move the goods some distance from the delivery destination.

Displacement of the market price rule

Section 50 has been held to lay down a prima facie rule which can be displaced if it would not result in a correct assessment of damages resulting directly and naturally from the breach. The following cases are examples of the displacement of the rule.

In *Thompson Ltd* v *Robinson (Gunmakers) Ltd* [1955] Ch 17 the defendants contracted to purchase from the plaintiff car dealers a Vanguard car. Shortly afterwards they refused to take delivery of the car and the plaintiffs sued for the loss of profit on the transaction. It was proved in evidence that there was a considerable excess of supply of cars over the demand and the plaintiffs were unable to sell the car and had to return it to the company from which they had obtained it. The defendants argued that the market price rule in s50(3) should be applied.

HELD: That in the situation of the car market at the time it was inappropriate to apply the rule in s50(3). The seller had lost a sale and was entitled to the profit which he would have made if the buyer had gone through with the purchase.

From this case and *Charter* v *Sullivan* [1957] 2 QB 117 it seems that in relation to new manufactured goods the test is whether the seller has lost a sale. In *Charter* v *Sullivan* the facts were the same as in *Thompson Ltd* v *Robinson (Gunmakers) Ltd* except that the sellers could sell as many cars as they could obtain from the manufacturers. In this situation it was held by the Court of Appeal that they were entitled only to nominal damages.

The rule will not apply to unique goods. Here the damages will be the difference between the contract price and the price actually obtained in another sale. The seller cannot in such a case make more than one profit from the sale. Interestingly, second-hand cars have been held to fall into this category of unique goods.

In *Lazenby Garages Ltd v Wright* [1976] 1 WLR 459, Mr Wright agreed to buy a second-hand BMW for £1,670 from the plaintiffs. After talking over the matter with his wife he informed the plaintiffs that he would not be buying the car. They sold it a month later for £1,770. They sued Mr Wright for £345, the difference between the price that they had paid for the car and the price he had agreed to pay.

HELD: They were entitled only to nominal damages. Second-hand cars were unique in the sense that they were all different, those of the same year and model differing in mileage and condition. It could not be said that the sellers had lost a sale when the defendant reneged on the contract.

The effect of this seems to be that the court will not apply the prima facie rule in s50(3) when it is totally inconvenient, although Goode expresses the view that the s50(3) rule should not be readily displaced.

Where there is no market at all, or where the court holds that such market as there is does not amount to an 'available market' then s50(3) obviously does not apply. The measure of damages will then usually be the amount by which the contract price exceeds the value of the goods, and a useful indication of such value, though not conclusive, is the price at which the seller in fact resells the goods assuming the terms of the second sale to be similar to those of the original contract. Problems will arise in such situations in trying to ascertain the value of the breach but the court must make the best possible estimate based on the materials available to it.

Where the market-price rule of s50(3) applies

Where the market-price rule of s50(3) does apply, the measure of damages is under that subsection based on a notional sale by the seller on the market.

Where the seller has in fact resold the goods on the market at a price different from the market price, then certain problems can arise:

Resale by the seller at less than the market price

Here the seller will want to claim the difference between the original contract price and the resale price, rather than the market price.

If the seller resells at less than the market price almost immediately after non-acceptance by the buyer, then he will encounter difficulties in convincing the court that it was reasonable in the circumstances so to act. The obligation to mitigate must firstly be that the seller should resell at the market price. The seller could only recover here the full difference between the contract and actual resale price if he proves his acts to be reasonable. If, however, the seller holds onto the goods and then later resells at a price less than the market price, it may well be easier to establish that there were good reasons for so doing.

Resale by the seller at more than the market price
If the seller resells at more than the market price the buyer will wish to take advantage of this and claim that the damages should only be the difference between the contract and the resale prices. The seller will have the evidentiary problem of establishing that the market price was in fact lower than this resale price.

It would seem fair that the seller should keep the benefit of a sale above market price; however, this has not been finally settled in law. Indeed there seems to be a trend in these cases to deny recovery for an initial loss which is counter-balanced by a profit, so it is conceivable that the profit would be deducted from the damages (see especially dictum of the Court of Appeal in *Campbell Mostyn Ltd* v *Barnett Trading Co* [1954] 1 Lloyd's Rep 65, where on the facts the seller did not have to account for the profit in selling above the market price in his damages).

Where the market-price rule does apply, the question may arise as to the date on which the market price should be taken. In this regard the courts have at times strayed from the strict wording of s50(3). Where the buyer refuses to accept at the time in the contract when the goods should have been accepted, then s50(3) applies and the market price is taken at that time. If, however, no time has been fixed, the courts have tended still to take the market price when the goods should have been accepted thereby ignoring the last words of s50(3). Indeed in *Millett* v *Van Heeck* [1921] 2 KB 369 the Court of Appeal held the market price to be irrelevant when the buyer refuses to take delivery and his refusal is an anticipatory breach before the obligation falls due. The court here took the date when the goods should have been accepted. Presumably the court should make an estimate where the date on which the buyer should accept the goods has not yet arrived by the time of trial.

Where the market price rises between the date of the buyer's repudiation and the date when the goods should have been accepted, the relevant price is that prevailing at the latter date.

Where the market price falls between the date of repudiation by the buyer and the date when the goods should have been accepted, the outcome differs according to whether repudiation has been accepted or not. If it has, the seller must mitigate and sell at once on a falling market; if he fails to do so the buyer will not be liable for a greater loss. If the seller has declined to accept the repudiation, however, he need not resell at once and can resell on the delivery date, so his damages are assessed in that way.

13

Remedies of the Buyer I: the Right to Reject the Goods

13.1 Introduction

13.2 Time and method of rejecting the goods

13.3 The effects of rejection of the goods by the buyer

13.4 Instalment contracts

13.5 Situations in which the buyer loses the right to reject

13.6 Where the buyer accepts part of the goods: severable and non-severable contracts

13.1 Introduction

The main remedy available to the buyer on a breach of contract by the seller is to repudiate the contract and reject the goods. This remedy will of course primarily be available to the buyer when the seller's breach has gone 'to the root of the agreement'. This will be the case where the seller's breach is a breach of condition, or where the nature and consequences of the seller's breach of an innominate term are such as go 'to the root of the contract', as where, for example, the seller's breach has frustrated the commercial purpose of the contract.

In addition the buyer may reject the goods in two further situations:

1. Where he is permitted to do so by the express terms of the contract.
2. Where a right to reject is given by terms implied in fact or by usage of trade or a course of dealing between the parties.

13.2 Time and method of rejecting the goods

The goods cannot be rejected after they have been accepted by the buyer. What amounts to 'acceptance' is discussed below.

If there is time it is open to the seller who tenders goods that do not comply with the contract terms to make a fresh tender. This is what is known in American terminology as the right to cure. A good example is *Borrowman Phillips & Co* v *Frere & Hollis* (1878) 4 QBD 500. The plaintiffs contracted to supply to the defendants a quantity of maize and tendered a cargo on board a named vessel. However, they were unable to tender the shipping documents as required under the contract. An arbitrator agreed with the defendants that the tender was invalid whereupon the plaintiffs made a further tender of goods on board a different vessel together with the appropriate documents. The defendants refused this new tender arguing that the plaintiffs could not substitute other goods for those originally tendered. It was held that since the first tender did not irrevocably identify the contract goods and that since the defendants had rejected them the plaintiffs could tender another cargo complying with the contract, as they had in fact done. They were thus entitled to damages for non-acceptance.

The right to cure is possible in contracts for the sale of unascertained goods. Where the contract is for the sale of specific goods it is unlikely that cure will be possible. There are two reasons for this. If the cure is to take the form of tendering other goods, this cannot be done without the agreement of the buyer because the goods have been identified in the contract and the seller may not unilaterally change the contract goods. If cure takes the form of repair and the contract calls for new goods it may not be successful because, depending on the scale of the necessary repairs, it may not be possible to describe the repaired goods as new. However, where the goods are not new the doctrine of cure may be possible.

Rejection is performed by the buyer intimating to the seller unambiguously that he refuses to accept the goods. In rejecting the goods the buyer is not, unless the contract so provides, bound to return the goods to the seller. The buyer must hold the goods available for collection by the seller at the contractual place for examination (for example, per Bankes LJ in *Hardy & Co* v *Hillerns & Fowler* [1923] 2 KB 490, below).

Under s36 the buyer is not bound to return the goods to the seller. It is sufficient that he intimates to the seller that the goods are at the seller's disposal at the place of examination.

If goods reach the buyer's hands and he rejects them, intimating that rejection to the seller, he will be only an involuntary bailee of these goods. He will therefore only be liable for damage to those goods occurring when they are under his control that is caused by his own wilful default. In other words he must not deliberately damage the goods (although probably negligence on his part would suffice for liability in tort).

13.3 The effects of rejection of the goods by the buyer

Where the rejection is proper, the buyer having the right to reject, then the buyer can decline to pay the price or, if already paid, he can recover it as being paid on a total failure of consideration. The buyer may also maintain an action for damages for non-delivery (set out below). As stated above the buyer is not required to return the goods to the seller: s36. Section 36 provides:

> 'Unless otherwise agreed, where goods are delivered to the buyer, and he refuses to accept them having the right to do so, he is not bound to return them to the seller, but it is sufficient if he intimates to the seller that he refuses to accept them.'

Acceptance of the buyer's rejection by the seller revests in the seller any property which had passed to the buyer, and gives the seller the immediate right to possess.

It was held unambiguously in *Lyons & Co Ltd v May & Baker Ltd* [1923] 1 KB 685 that the buyer does not have a lien on the goods for the repayment of the purchase price.

It should be noted that after rejection of the goods by the buyer, if sufficient time still remains before the last date for delivery provided in the contract the seller may be able to tender a new load of goods before that time expires. This will not be so, however, in the general case where the buyer can treat a bad delivery as a breach of contract justifying repudiation by him (the buyer).

Where the buyer purports to reject the goods without being entitled to do so this will constitute a repudiation which the seller is entitled to accept as discharging the contract. Alternatively the seller can elect to keep the contract alive, in which case the purported rejection will be ineffective.

13.4 Instalment contracts

The position arising with regard to the buyer's right of rejection in a contract for the sale of goods by instalments where there is a breach by the seller with regard to one or more instalments has already been discussed at some length (see 4.3: Instalment deliveries).

It is perhaps best to summarise the position as follows:

1. Where the contract is 'non-severable' then the buyer may generally reject all the goods on a breach by the seller with regard to any one instalment delivery (*Jackson v Rotax Motors Ltd*).
2. If the contract is severable the right of the buyer to reject all the goods after one or more defective instalments depends on the terms of the contract and the circumstances of the case.

In particular, the court will have regard to the following factors:

1. The ratio quantitively which the breach bears to the contract as a whole.
2. The degree of probability or improbability that such a breach will be repeated (see *Maple Flock Co Ltd v Universal Furniture Products*).

One interesting case in this area discussed the position where *only one instalment is defective*. In *Warinco AG v Samor SPA* [1977] 2 Lloyd's Rep 582, the buyers rejected the first instalment of crude rape seed oil on the grounds of its colour. The seller rightly disputed the rejection and informed the buyer that the next instalment would be identical. Then the buyer objected to this and the seller therefore declined to send any more, arguing that the buyer had repudiated the contract. The Court of Appeal held that the seller had acted rightly in not sending the second instalment. The buyer had evinced an intention to abandon or refuse performance of the contract. Relevant factors to account included the degree of connection between one instalment and another and the proportion of the contract which had been affected.

The above is the position where the buyer is faced with defective instalment(s) and wishes to reject further instalments on that ground. The effect of the buyer's *acceptance* of any instalments on his right to reject further instalments must also be considered: it is dealt with in this context below in 13.6.

13.5 Situations in which the buyer loses the right to reject

This is an important area and has in the past given rise to some controversy. Where the buyer does lose the right to reject he will have to accept the goods and claim against the seller for damages.

It should be emphasised at the outset that the passing of property in the goods to the buyer *no longer affects the buyer's right to reject*. It was formerly the case that under the old s11(1) of the 1893 SGA that the buyer lost his right to reject when the property passed to him. However, the Misrepresentation Act 1967 amended this provision, and now the right to reject is lost *only by acceptance of the goods*.

Acceptance of the goods

The right to reject is now lost only by acceptance of the goods by the buyer. The SGA provisions on when the buyer will be deemed to have accepted the goods are in s34 and s35(1).

The provisions of s11(4) should also be noted at this stage. This sub-section provides in effect that where the buyer has accepted the goods then he will from that moment on be precluded from rejecting them whatever breach of contract has been committed by the seller. The buyer may, of course, still have one of the other remedies. Section 11(4) is considered in detail later.

The situations in which the buyer will be deemed to have accepted are set out in s34 and s35. Section 34 provides:

> '(1) Where goods are delivered to the buyer, and he has not previously examined them, he is not deemed to have accepted them until he has had a reasonable opportunity of examining them for the purpose of ascertaining whether they are in conformity with the contract.
> (2) Unless otherwise agreed, when the seller tenders delivery of the goods to the buyer, he is bound, on request, to afford the buyer a reasonable opportunity of examining the goods for the purpose of ascertaining whether they are in conformity with the contract.'

Section 35(1) provides:

> '(1) The buyer is deemed to have accepted the goods when he intimates to the seller that he has accepted them, or (except where s34 otherwise provides) when the goods have been delivered to him, and he does any act in relation to them which is inconsistent with the ownership of the seller, or when after the lapse of a reasonable time, he retains the goods without intimating to the seller that he has rejected them.'

It is obvious that a serious conflict may appear to arise between the provisions of s34 and s35. The buyer often does some act inconsistent with the ownership of the seller (s35) before he has had a reasonable opportunity of examining the goods (s34). In such a case, s34 says the buyer is not deemed to have accepted the goods and s35 says he is deemed to have accepted.

The original SGA provided no assistance in solving this conflict. The courts were left to answer the question and they in fact came to a very unsatisfactory conclusion.

In *Hardy & Co Ltd* v *Hillerns & Fowler* (supra) the Court of Appeal held that s35 took precedence over s34. Here the contract was for wheat to be shipped from South America to Hull. The ship arrived in Hull and three days later the buyer resold a part of the cargo and sent it off to the sub-buyer. Only two days after that did the buyer have his first opportunity to examine the goods and he found then that they did not conform to the contract. It was held that the buyer's act of sub-selling the goods was an act inconsistent with the ownership of the seller within s35. This section took precedence over s34 so the buyer lost the right to reject the goods.

This conclusion was evidently unfair and unsatisfactory and the Hardy decision was distinguished in New Zealand in *Hammer & Barrow* v *Coca Cola* [1962] NZLR 723.

Buyers frequently dispatch goods for sub-sale without having an opportunity until much later to examine them. In such a position the sub-buyer would still be able to reject the goods whereas the original buyer would not. Happily s4(2) of the Misrepresentation Act 1967 amended s35 SGA to make it clear that s34 is now the governing section. The Misrepresentation Act inserted the words '(except where s34 of this Act otherwise provides)' into s35.

To summarise the position the buyer is deemed to have accepted the goods and will therefore lose his right to reject in the following circumstances:

1. when he intimates to the seller that he has accepted them; or
2. (where he has had a reasonable opportunity to examine the goods and the goods have been delivered to him) the buyer does any act inconsistent with the ownership of the seller or when after the lapse of a reasonable time he retains the goods without intimating to the seller that he has rejected them.

It should be pointed out that the effect of the amendment of s35 is not wholly free from difficulty. Clearly the words in brackets do not apply to situations where the buyer intimates to the seller that he has accepted the goods. Equally clearly they do apply to situations where the buyer does an act inconsistent with the seller's ownership. What is not clear is whether they apply to the situation where the right to reject is lost after the lapse of a reasonable time. From the punctuation of the sub-section it would be perfectly possible to argue that they do not. However, Atiyah and Goode both take the view that neither of these methods of losing the right to reject is lost until the buyer has had a reasonable opportunity of examining the goods.

The view has been expressed that this amendment does not go far enough, and that the buyer should not lose the right to reject merely because he does an act inconsistent with the seller's ownership and has had the opportunity to examine the goods. It is Atiyah's view that in the case of an 'act inconsistent with the ownership of the seller' a buyer should only be deemed to have accepted the goods where he has in fact now made himself unable to restore the goods to the seller.

The buyer's problem here is, ultimately, that if the sub-buyer accepts the goods (or any part of them which has been sub-sold) then the buyer will be unable to restore the goods to the seller and therefore cannot reject.

It is now necessary to examine the wording of ss34 and 35 in greater detail to determine what will in fact amount to acceptance of the goods.

Section 34: what amounts to a reasonable opportunity to examine the goods

In determining whether the buyer has had a reasonable opportunity to examine the goods it is necessary to establish the place of examination under the contract, since until the goods have reached that place the buyer cannot be taken to have had the opportunity for examination contemplated by the contract.

Where the contract does not specify the place of examination then the presumption is that this is to take place at the delivery point designated by the contract (so held in *Perkins v Bell* [1893] 1 QB 193: prima facie the place of delivery is the place where the buyer ought to examine the goods). If the buyer chooses to redispatch the goods without examining them then he will have lost the right to reject.

This presumption will be rebutted, however, where the buyer is not entitled to take actual physical delivery at that point or where the place of delivery to the buyer is not a reasonable place to examine the goods. For example, in CIF contracts the place of examination is not that at which the documents are handed over but will be the port of arrival.

The above propositions with regard to the place of examination of goods are well illustrated in *Molling & Co v Dean & Son* (1901) 18 TLR 217. The defendants ordered 40 000 books to be made by the plaintiffs. The plaintiff sellers were aware that the books were intended for shipment and resale to a sub-buyer in the USA. The plaintiffs put the sub-buyer's imprint in the books and packed them for shipment to that sub-buyer. The defendants having taken delivery consigned the goods to the sub-buyers without examination. The sub-buyer rejected the goods. It was held that the defendants were in turn allowed to reject the goods and recover the cost of retransporting them back to England, since the proper place for inspection was here on delivery to the sub-buyers. The defendant buyer had not had a reasonable opportunity to examine the goods.

It is submitted that had the seller not known and had no reason to know that the goods were to be redispatched to a sub-buyer without examination, then the buyer would not have been able to reject since the place of examination would be the place of delivery to the buyer. The buyer would therefore have had a reasonable opportunity to examine the goods when they were delivered to him. It should be noted, however, that in many cases a sub-sale without examination especially in the case of goods loaded in containers will be foreseeable.

Section 35: Intimation of acceptance

This constitutes the most straightforward limb of s35. Problems sometimes arise in this context when acceptance notes are signed especially by consumer purchasers. If the note is no more than an acknowledgment that the goods have been delivered there is not likely to be any difficulty. If, however, they state that the buyer accepts the goods in terms of s35 of the SGA the position is not so clear. *Benjamin's Sale of Goods* 2nd edn (1981) para 918 takes the view that the right to reject is thereby lost. Atiyah thinks that it is very unlikely that a court would take this view. In their report Sale and Supply of Goods (1987 Cm) the Law Commission recommend that the law be amended in relation to consumer sales to make it clear that the right to reject is not lost in this situation.

Another problem which can arise here is that of the intimation of conditional acceptance. The position here is that a conditional acceptance will not be operative in s35 unless and until the condition is either satisfied or waived by the buyer (*Heilbutt* v *Hickson* (1872) LR 7 CP 438).

Section 35: The meaning of 'an act inconsistent with the ownership of the seller'

This category of deemed acceptance has been a source of some confusion.

There is, of course, a theoretical difficulty in s35, because it is a possible and indeed common situation for the property already to have passed to the buyer, especially after delivery of the goods. What is then the meaning of 'an act inconsistent with the ownership of the seller' when the property in the goods may already be with the buyer?

One explanation is that of Devlin J in *Kwei Tek Chao* v *British Traders and Shippers* [1954] 2 QB 459; [1954] 1 All ER 779 who states that where property passes to the buyer in circumstances where the buyer retains a right to reject, the passing of property is merely conditional. This solution has been criticised, in particular by Atiyah, for using a somewhat circular reasoning. Atiyah expands the proposition as follows: the seller has a reversionary interest in the goods in that he is entitled to the goods at the place and in the condition in which they are to be found when rejected; if the buyer then does something inconsistent with this he will lose the right to reject. There does here seem to be some element of arguing in a circle.

Goode's explanation is that s35 in effect is saying that where the property has passed to the buyer, if the buyer does an act which is inconsistent with the rejection of the goods (in other words, inconsistent with the revesting of the property in the seller), then he must be taken to have accepted them.

Whichever explanation is preferred, and they are perhaps irreconcilable, the problem remains as to what kind of act or what sort of use of the goods by the buyer will be sufficient to lose the rejection right. In reality 'act inconsistent with the ownership of the seller' has no fixed meaning and the court is really only able to decide whether the buyer should be allowed to reject according to the justice of the case.

However, the case law to date has at least established some acts which will be sufficient. Goode divides these into two groups: acts of affirmation and acts involving inability to restore the goods. This division is not universal and will not be adopted here.

All the acts under s35 will, of course, be subject to s34, so rejection will in any case not be lost until the buyer has had a reasonable opportunity to examine the goods.

Resale and delivery of the goods to a sub-buyer will be sufficient to lose the right to reject. An example is *Hardy & Co v Hillerns & Fowler* (supra), discussed above.

Another example comes from a New Zealand case, *Armaghdown Motors Ltd v Gray Motors Ltd* [1962] NZLR 5, in which G Ltd took to the plaintiffs' premises a car that they had recently bought and offered it to them for sale. In selling it they applied a description to it which was incorrect and were in breach of the equivalent of s13 of the SGA. The sale took place on 15 June but the plaintiffs did not discover the misdescription until 7 July when they received the vehicle's registration certificate. Four days later they registered the car in their own name and offered it for sale at their garage.

HELD: That as the defect was latent the plaintiffs were entitled to have the period from the date of sale until 7 July to discover the true position. However, their actions in registering the car in their own name and offering it for sale were acts inconsistent with the ownership of the seller and terminated their right to reject the car.

A mere sub-sale without delivery to the sub-buyer has never been held to suffice. The reasoning is almost certainly that a mere resale does not make the buyer unable to surrender the goods to the seller when he rejects the goods.

It was held in *J S Robertson Pty Ltd v Martin* (1955-6) 94 CLR 30, an Australian decision, that a claim by the buyer against the insurer in respect of damage to the goods is not an act inconsistent with the ownership of the seller.

Much academic discussion has been devoted to the question of what amount of use of the goods by the buyer will be sufficient to defeat rejection. The underlying principle is really that stated by Goode, that the buyer must be able to surrender the goods to the seller in the condition in which they were on arrival at the contractual place of examination. No doubt a slight change from that condition would be overlooked by the court but a substantial, prolonged or repeated use of the goods would probably be an act inconsistent with the ownership of the seller. Indeed Goode's principle of 'ability to restore the goods' solves the question of what happens when the buyer wishes to reject but a sub-buyer who already has possession does not: the buyer cannot reject since he will be unable to restore the goods to the seller.

In sales using documents the buyer has, subject to certain qualifications, two distinct rights of rejection. He has a right to reject *documents* not conforming with the contract and a separate right to reject goods not conforming with the contract. This view was expanded by Devlin J in *Kwei Tek Chao* case. As Devlin J pointed out the two rights of rejection are related. The right to reject the documents is governed by the same principles in s34 and s35 relating to opportunities to inspect and acts inconsistent with the seller's ownership, lapse of a reasonable time, and so forth.

In general the acceptance by the buyer of either the documents or the goods will not preclude rejection of the other. The qualifications for this rule are as follows:

1. If the goods arrive before the documents and the buyer accepts them, then he will have no separate right to reject the documents unless the documents disclose breaches of contract not ascertainable from inspection of the goods (see *Tradax International SA* v *Goldschmidt SA* [1977] 2 Lloyd's Rep 605).
2. If the buyer accepts the documents then generally if the breaches of contract relating to the documents and those relating to the goods are the same, there will be no separate right of rejection. In other words the buyer will not be able to reject the goods if their defects are the same as these in the documents. Note however that the defects in the documents must either be known by the buyer or be such that he ought to have seen them, had he inspected the documents properly (see *Panchaud Frères SA* v *Etablissements General Grain Co* [1970] Lloyd's Rep 53).
3. Certain dealings with the documents may affect the right to reject the goods. For example if the buyer resells and delivers the documents to a sub-buyer who does not reject the buyer will be unable to reject the goods.
4. Acceptance of the documents could, if he has paid, deprive the buyer of the right to reject the goods simply from a practical commercial point of view: rejection of the goods here would leave the buyer as an unsecured creditor, since he has no lien on the goods he has rejected.

A mortgage or pledge of the goods will be an act inconsistent with the ownership of the seller if it deprives the buyer of the ability to restore the goods to the seller.

Note finally that the buyer's right to reject may be varied or qualified by express agreement in the contract. The buyer who properly rejects goods must mitigate his damage according to the ordinary rules.

Section 35: Retention of the goods by the buyer after the lapse of a reasonable time

Under this third limb of s35 the buyer loses the right to reject where after the lapse of a reasonable time he retains the goods without intimating to the seller that he has rejected them. This part of s35 is also apparently subject to s34 so the buyer in such cases must have had a reasonable opportunity to examine the goods.

The question of what amounts to a 'reasonable time' has given rise to some difficulty. This is, of course, a question of fact as pointed out in SGA s59. The tendency at least in domestic sales is to hold that the right to reject is lost quite quickly, as in *Long* v *Lloyd* [1958] 1 WLR 753; [1958] 2 All ER 402. The time seems to be a matter of days rather than weeks or months. In *Bernstein* v *Pamson Motors (Golders Green) Ltd* [1987] 2 All ER 220 it was held that the use of a car for three weeks and for 140 miles led to acceptance. The important point was made that whether the buyer has had a reasonable time does not depend upon how long is required to discover the particular defect which exists. Rougier J said, 'a reasonable time means a reasonable time to examine and try out the goods in general terms'.

The effect that permitting or requesting that repairs be carried out on the defective goods will have on this aspect of rejection is not clear. Where the buyer requests that repairs be carried out it could be argued that he is doing an act inconsistent with the ownership of the seller. However, it could be argued in this case and more strongly where the seller offers to repair, that the buyer should not be prejudiced. Time taken in attempting repairs should not be counted in assessing a reasonable time. This was the attitude of a Canadian judge in *Lightburn* v *Belmont Sales Ltd* (1969) 6 DLR (3d) 692. The plaintiff had purchased a new car after being assured by the salesman that it would meet his requirements as to economy and reliability. In evidence it was shown that the car was totally unreliable, having been returned to the defendants on 17 occasions for repair. Eight months and eight thousand miles later, the plaintiff rejected the car and sued for breach of an implied term that the car was not fit for its purpose. The sellers argued that the right to reject had been lost through lapse of time. However, Ruttan J stated that:

> 'in the eight month period that he struggled with the car ... he was endeavouring to give it a reasonable chance to perform, and I do not agree that delay in finally repudiating his contract can be attributed to that period of time or the mileage that was covered. He was not acting as a capricious buyer who had repented the purchase and sought to get out of his contract at an early time on a frivolous basis ... I do not agree that he can be said to have accepted the car.'

and it was held that the buyer had the right to reject.

In export sales the position seems to be somewhat different. In *Manifatture Tessile Laviera Wooltex* v *Ashley* [1979] 2 Lloyd's Rep 28 it was held that the buyer was allowed as an ordinary matter of commerce to make sure that the goods were defective, and that to this end he was entitled to send samples of the cloths in question to experts for analysis. On the facts a delay of two months before intimation of rejection was held to be not unreasonable.

It is submitted that this *Wooltex* decision should be seen particularly in the context of export sales, although even in domestic sales a buyer could be entitled to send goods to be analysed if it is not readily ascertainable whether the goods are defective.

The time allowed to the buyer could be extended to allow, for example, a reasonable time in discussions with a sub-purchaser to discover whether the sub-purchaser himself intends to reject the goods.

Note that in all cases of rejection the buyer must be able to make restitution of the goods. The mere delivery of goods to a sub-purchaser will not lose the buyer's right to reject, but if the sub-purchaser does not in turn reject the goods then the buyer will be unable to reject for that reason: he will be unable to make restitution of the goods.

13.6 Where the buyer accepts part of the goods: severable and non-severable contracts

The question obviously arises as to whether a buyer who has accepted part of the goods particularly in an instalment contract can reject further conforming goods. The results differ according to whether the contract in question is severable or non-severable. The meanings of these two terms are discussed under 'Performance of the contract' (earlier).

The provisions of s11(4) are in issue here.

> 'Where a contract of sale is not severable, and the buyer has accepted the goods, or part of them, the breach of a condition to be fulfilled by the seller can only be treated as a breach of warranty, and not as a ground for rejecting the goods and treating the contract as repudiated, unless there is an express or implied term of the contract to that effect.'

Non-severable contracts

The wording of s11(4) is somewhat confusing with regard to the acceptance by the buyer of part of the goods and it is generally agreed that the effect of the sub-sale is as follows. Where the buyer has accepted the goods or where the contract of sale is *not severable* and the buyer has accepted part of the goods, then the right to reject the goods is lost. In other words where the contractual obligation is not severable, s11(4) means that acceptance of one or more instalments precludes rejection of other instalments. Therefore, in a non-severable contract s11(4) applies to the whole contract and the buyer cannot accept just part of the contract goods.

This position with regard to non-severable contracts is complicated by s30(4) which deals with the delivery by the seller of the goods he contracted to sell mixed with goods of a different description. It is now clear that s11(4) is subject to s30(4) (ie s30(4) is an exception to s11(4)), so in the circumstances specified in s30(4) and whether the contract is severable or non-severable the buyer will be able to reject part and accept part of the goods. (See above 4.3, discussing *Ebrahim Dawood Ltd* v *Heath Ltd* [1961] 2 Lloyd's Rep 512.)

Section 30(4) will not apply where the goods delivered are all of the contract description even though some of them are not of merchantable quality (*Aitken Campbell & Co* v *Boullen & Gatenby* (1908) SC 490). Nor will s30(4) apply where all the goods are of unmerchantable quality or fail to conform to the contract.

It is still open to the buyer in a non-severable contract to argue that his acceptance of one or more instalments was conditional on the good delivery of further instalments, but this will be difficult to prove in practice.

Severable contracts

If a contract is severable the buyer is entitled to reject goods not conforming to the contract and to accept the balance of the goods if he so wishes. This is the necessary implication of s11(4). Therefore, acceptance by him of any part of the goods will not prejudice his right to reject defective goods which are delivered subsequently.

Whether the delivery of one or more defective instalments *entitles* the buyer to reject further goods in such contracts depends on whether the breach by the seller in relation to the defective parts goes 'to the root of the contract' within s31(2). In a *non-severable* contract the seller will in this position be prima facie entitled to reject all the goods (*Jackson* v *Rotax Motors*).

Note that in all cases where the buyer loses his right to reject the goods, an action for damages usually survives.

14

Remedies of the Buyer II

14.1 Rescission for innocent misrepresentation

14.2 Damages for non-delivery

14.3 Damages for breach of condition or warranty: s53 SGA

14.4 Damages in tort

14.5 Damages for misrepresentation

14.6 Specific performance

14.7 Recovery of the price by the buyer

14.1 Rescission for innocent misrepresentation

It is not absolutely clear that the remedy of rescission for innocent misrepresentation has survived the passage of the SGA. In the New Zealand case of *Riddiford* v *Warren* (1901) 20 NZLR 572 the Court of Appeal held that this was not the case and that this remedy was not available in relation to contracts for the sale of goods. Dicta of Atkin LJ in *Re Wait* [1927] 1 Ch 606 also hint at this possibility. However, it is probably safe to say that rescission for innocent misrepresentation has survived the SGA. Certainly the Court of Appeal in *Leaf* v *International Galleries* [1950] 2 KB 86 and *Long* v *Lloyd* [1958] 1 WLR 753 believed that this was so. In those cases the remedy was not open to the buyer, but this was not on the basis that it was not available in a contract for the sale of goods but because the buyer had lost the right to claim it through delay.

This remedy is discussed in detail in Chapter 3 and it is enough to emphasise two points here relating to the Misrepresentation Act 1967. First, as a result of s1(a) it is immaterial whether the representation has become a term of the contract. And secondly, the rule in *Seddon* v *NE Salt Co* [1905] 1 Ch 326 to the effect that rescission was not available for innocent misrepresentation has been abolished by s1(b).

14.2 Damages for non-delivery

This is a species of damages for breach of contract. The buyer's action here is the same whether or not the property has passed to him. The buyer's action and the rules for the assessment of damages are set out in s51. Section 51 provides:

> '(1) Where the seller wrongfully neglects or refuses to deliver the goods to the buyer, the buyer may maintain an action against the seller for damages for non-delivery.
> (2) The measure of damages is the estimated loss directly and naturally resulting, in the ordinary course of events, from the seller's breach of contract.
> (3) Where there is an available market for the goods in question the measure of damages is prima facie to be ascertained by the difference between the contract price and the market or current price of the goods at the time or times when they ought to have been delivered or (if no time was fixed) then at the time of the refusal to deliver.'

This section lays down a market price rule which is apparently the same as that applicable when the seller sues for damages (see Chapter 12).

The case of *Esteve Trading Corporation* v *Agropec International, The Golden Rio* [1990] 2 Lloyd's Rep 273, though largely concerned with bankruptcy, contains a careful examination of the concept of 'market price' and contains, by analogy, useful guidelines. Under two contracts (FOB) for sale and shipment of soya beans, the plaintiffs (the buyers) had sold the goods on to a firm which while the goods were still afloat, went bankrupt. A clause in the contract provided that should any part in 'the circle' of buyers and sellers go bankrupt, the contract should immediately be closed out at a price 'then current for similar goods'. The buyers appealed the initial decision to fix the date for 'closing out' as at 28 July, the day of the act of bankruptcy.

HELD: The date should be fixed at the time the goods would have been traded, before the act of bankruptcy occurred and any public knowledge of it might depress the market. The difference between the market price at the time when they ought to have been delivered and the contract price puts the buyer in the position he would have been in if the goods had been delivered.

Where the buyer has arranged a sub-sale of the goods at a higher price than the contract price which he is no longer able to perform because of the seller's default, as a general rule the buyer cannot recover the loss of profits on the sub-sale, or the damages which he has had to pay to the sub-buyer.

In *Williams* v *Agius* [1914] AC 510 the seller sold coal to the buyer at 16s 3d per ton. The buyer resold the coal at 19s 6d per ton. The seller refused to deliver. At the date of refusal the market price had risen to 23s 6d per ton. The House of Lords held that in assessing damages for non-delivery the sub-contract should be ignored, so the buyer was entitled to the difference between 16s 3d and 23s 6d, in other words 7s 3d per ton.

If the buyer has arranged a sub-sale at a lower price than the contract price, that of itself does not displace the general market-price rule.

As with an action for damages by the seller, the words of s51(3) 'the time of the refusal to deliver' will be ignored where the breach is anticipatory. The market price will be taken at the date when the delivery might have been expected to be made (see *Tai Hing Cotton Mill* v *Kamsing Knitting* [1979] AC 91; [1978] 1 All ER 515).

Where the contract of sale expressly provides for a limited period of time during which delivery must be made the seller will not be in breach until the last day of that permitted period.

There are, however, certain cases in which the market price rule is displaced, for example, where there is no available market. *Coastal International Trading Ltd* v *Maroil* [1988] 1 Lloyd's Rep 92 provides an example of a situation where there was no available market. However, the buyer had already sold the cargo of oil and the price on the subsale, which was not shown to be in any way unreasonable, was accepted as providing an alternative to a price assessed on 'available market' criteria (see also *Sealace Shipping* v *Oceanvoice* below)

Shearson Lehman Hutton Inc v *I Maclaine Watson & Co Ltd* (No 2) [1990] 3 All ER 723; [1990] 1 Lloyd's Rep 441 discusses the concept of available market and the date at which the available market is to be assessed. The plaintiffs purchased tin from the defendants to the value of £70m for delivery in March 1986. The defendants then failed to deliver. The plaintiffs, in seeking damages, contended that damages should be assessed according to the 'available market' on 12 March 1986 – the day delivery had been scheduled. The defendants contended that there had to be a large pool of available purchasers for an 'available market' to exist and that this did not apply on that particular date.

HELD: In assessing damages under s50(3) of Sale of Goods Act 1979, a distinction should be made between cases where goods were really offered for sale, and cases such as the present one when no goods were ever delivered and the sale is therefore a notional or hypothetical one. If there is only a notional sale the day to be fixed for the available market should be (not necessarily the date of the breach) but a day on which a sufficient number of traders were ready to do business. This might have been shortly before or after 12 March. The assessment of damage would then be based on the difference between the present price, and the price the tin might have fetched if it had been *available* on 12 March, not necessarily *sold* on 12 March.

The buyer may be able to claim special damages under s54, based on loss arising from special circumstances of which the parties were aware. For example freight paid by the buyer even though the seller has not delivered. This section is in effect the second leg of the rule in *Hadley* v *Baxendale* for damages in a contract case. The first leg of that rule is represented by s51(3).

It has been seen above that damages in respect of a sub-sale are not normally awarded. Exceptionally, however, these may be recoverable, particularly if the parties must have contemplated a sub-sale of those particular goods. In *Re R & H Hall & W H Pim* [1928] All ER Rep 763, the seller sold a specific cargo of corn in a specific ship to the buyer at 51s 9d per quarter. The buyer resold at 56s 9d per quarter, but when the vessel arrived the market price had fallen to 53s 9d per quarter. The seller failed to deliver. The question was whether the measure of damages was the difference between the contract price and the resale price on the one hand, or the contract price and the market price at the date when the goods should have been delivered on the other. The House of Lords held that the former measure applied. The general principle of no recovery for the loss of a sub-sale was displaced by two factors:

1. The sale was for a specific cargo on a specific ship and it was the same cargo which had been resold.
2. The contract of sale by its terms actually provided for resale by the buyer.

Apparently both these requirements must be satisfied in order to displace the general principle. The mere contemplation of a sub-sale as a reasonable probability will not suffice (see *The Arpad* [1934] P 189).

Provided the conditions are fulfilled the buyer will probably be able to claim not only the loss of profits on sub-sales but also any damages he may have had to pay the sub-buyer in respect of that sub-buyer's loss of profits.

A buyer may be able to claim loss of profits on a sub-sale where although Atiyah's two criteria are not fulfilled, the seller is aware that the buyer is buying the goods to fulfil an already existing contract and knows therefore what the consequences of his failure to deliver will be. This proposition is supported by dicta but no decision has yet been made on such facts.

14.3 Damages for breach of condition or warranty: s53 SGA

Where the seller delivers the goods to the buyer, the buyer can sue under this head if the seller has committed a breach of warranty or a breach of condition which the buyer elects to or must treat as a breach of warranty.

Section 53 provides:

> '(1) Where there is a breach of warranty by the seller, or where the buyer elects (or is compelled) to treat any breach of condition on the part of the seller as a breach of warranty, the buyer is not by reason only of such breach of warranty entitled to reject the goods; but he may -
> a) Set up against the seller the breach of warranty in diminution or extinction of the price; or
> b) Maintain an action against the seller for damages for the breach of warranty.
> (2) The measure of damages for breach of warranty is the estimated loss directly and naturally resulting, in the ordinary course of events, from the breach of warranty.'

This section in effect imports most of the general princples of damages in the law of contract into this area.

Special attention should be paid to the case where the breach of warranty consists of a *late delivery*. Damages here are in general assessed as the difference between the value of the goods when they should have been delivered and the value at the time of actual delivery. However, the cases will differ according to whether the buyer is buying for resale or for his own use. The general rule above will apply in the former case, but in the latter the measure of damages will presumably be the cost of hiring a substitute for the delay period or of making do without.

An important case is *Wertheim v Chicoutimi Pulp Co Ltd* [1911] AC 301. In this controversial case the court awarded as damages the difference between the market price at the time when the goods ought to have been delivered and the actual resale price in a sub-sale. This case has attracted much criticism since the sub-sale in question was not especially contemplated. It may well turn on its own particular facts.

Where the breach of warranty is a defect in the quality of the goods then s53(3) will apply. Section 53(3) provides:

> 'In the case of breach of warranty of quality such loss is prima facie the difference between the value of the goods at the time of delivery to the buyer and the value they would have had if they had fulfilled the warranty.'

This measure will apply particularly to breaches of s14(2) SGA: the implied condition of merchantable quality.

Again the general rule is that sub-sales by the buyer are not accounted in the damages (see *Slater v Hoyle & Smith* [1920] 2 KB 11).

In any case under s53 consequential loss will be recoverable under normal contractual principles and are more likely to be associated with actions relating to defective goods. The value of the defective product may be trivial but a defect in it may cause very substantial physical injury. A tragic example is *Godley v Perry* [1960] 1 WLR 9. The plaintiff had purchased a toy catapult for a few pence from the defendant. Owing to a defect in it it shattered when used causing serious damage to the plaintiff's eye. His claim was one for damages for his physical injury and under this head he was awarded substantial damages.

It is a general principle of the law of damages in contract that damages will not be awarded for inconvenience or disappointment. While this holds good in relation to commercial contracts for the sale of goods it is now possible in consumer cases to obtain damages under this heading. An example is *Jackson v Chrysler Acceptances Ltd* [1978] RTR 474. The plaintiff bought a new car from the defendants informing them that he specifically wanted it to take his family abroad on holiday. On holiday the car broke down on several occasions substantially spoiling the holiday. Because the plaintiff had made it clear that the success of the holiday depended on the new car, it was held that the plaintiff was entitled to damages for the spoilt holiday in addition to damages for the defects in the car.

The recent case of *Sealace Shipping Co Ltd v Oceanvoice Ltd, The Apecos M* [1990] 1 Lloyd's Rep 82 makes it clear that buyer and seller may attempt to assert reliance on different sections of SGA 1979 in assessing damages. Here a contract for sale of a vessel provided that all spare parts, including a spare propeller, would become the property of the buyer, but the spare propeller was missing. The buyers claimed that s51 was the relevant section (damages for non-delivery) while the sellers relied on s53 (damages for defective delivery). Since there was no relevant 'available market' for spare propellers, the next best thing was to assess the value of the vessel with or without the spare propeller, and at the initial arbitration it was found that the value of the vessel would not be appreciably enhanced with a spare propeller. On appeal this measure of damages was held to be wrong. The court decided that s51 governed the case, that there was no breach of warranty and that to use s53 would be artificial. The buyers were entitled to claim the cost of the spare propeller, costs of transportation, and costs of its installation into the vessel. The measure of damages in the case of s51 for non-delivery was to ascertain the value of that which was not delivered, together with any consequences of non-delivery.

14.4 Damages in tort

If the buyer has an immediate right to possess the goods, an action may be brought (ie for interference with goods). In these cases the buyer cannot get a greater sum in damages in tort, and the action in tort is therefore rarely used. One advantage it could have is that it helps the buyer go against third parties who have damaged the goods or otherwise interferred with them provided he (the buyer) has the property in the goods.

The measure of damages in these cases is the ordinary tortious measure.

14.5 Damages for misrepresentation

These may be awarded under s2(1) or s2(2) Misrepresentation Act 1967. The court would usually award these under s2(2) if it thought rescission for misrepresentation inappropriate.

This remedy will obviously only be available where there has been an actionable misrepresentation by the seller (see 3.2).

14.6 Specific performance

Section 52 provides:

> '(1) In any action for breach of contract to deliver specific or ascertained goods the court may, if it thinks fit, on the plaintiff's application, by its judgment or decree direct that the contract shall be performed specifically, without giving the defendant the option of retaining the goods on payment of damages.
> (2) The plaintiff's application may be made at any time before judgment or decree.
> (3) The judgment or decree may be unconditional, or on such terms and conditions as to damages, payment of the price, and otherwise, as seems just to the court.'

The goods must be 'specific' within the meaning of s62 of the SGA: 'identified or agreed upon at the time the contract is made'. Provided the conditions for application of the section are present, s52 applies whether or not the property has passed.

Section 52 is a statutory application of the equitable remedy of specific performance and like that remedy it is discretionary as can be seen from the words of s52(1); 'the court may, if it thinks fit'. It will not be awarded where the goods are, to quote *Re Wait* supra, 'ordinary mercantile commodities' alternative supplies of which could be obtained in the market with, if necessary, damages based on any extra cost thus incurred. Prior to the SGA 1893 specific performance was only granted to compel sellers to transfer rare or unique articles such as china vases in *Falcke* v *Gray* (1859) 4 Drew 651 or particular stones from Old Westminster Bridge in *Thorn* v *Commissioners of Public Works* (1836) 32 Beav 490. An example of a commercial situation where the remedy has been ordered since the passage of the Act is *Behnke* v *Bede Shipping Co Ltd* [1927] 1 KB 649. In this case it was held that a ship was a specific chattel within the Act and that, in the circumstances it was appropriate to make an order because the ship 'was of peculiar and practically unique value' to the buyer and he required the vessel for immediate use. Damages would not in this case have been an adequate remedy.

However, some idea of the reluctance of the courts to use this remedy is to be gained from *Société des Industries Metallurgiques SA* v *Bronx Engineering Co Ltd* [1975] 1 Lloyd's Rep 336. There the remedy was refused in relation to a machine manufactured by the defendants although it weighed over 220 tons, cost £270,000 and could only be purchased in the market with a nine to twelve-month delivery date.

14.7 Recovery of the price by the buyer

This is governed by s54. Where the buyer has already paid the price he may recover it if the consideration has failed, as where the seller delivers goods which the buyer properly rejects.

15

Consumer Protection

15.1 Introduction
15.2 The Consumer Protection Act and product liability
15.3 Manufacturer's guarantees
15.4 Consumer Protection Act, Part II
15.5 Miscellaneous consumer protection statutes
15.6 Fair trading legislation

15.1 Introduction

The original SGA 1893 assumed that the typical transaction was a commercial sale where the parties were probably in a roughly equal bargaining postion. It took no account of what is usually referred to today as the consumer - the private individual buying for his own use, an individual who might contract now on a standard form which he has not read and which, if he were to read, he would not understand. In 1893 the consumer society with its mass marketing was a long way off, so it was not really surprising that the legislation took no explicit account of the consumer; though, of course, the legislation did help consumers to some extent in that it did set out clearly the rights of purchasers. The situation is very different today. Over the past thirty years consumers have become more conscious of their rights and more assertive. Organisations such as the Consumers' Association, publishers of *Which* magazine have become well established and the importance of consumers has been recognised by government in the setting up of organisations such as the Office of Fair Trading and the funding of the National Consumer Council.

It would therefore give an inaccurate picture of the law relating to sale if attention were not specifically paid to the position of the consumer buyer who is now given special treatment in a number of ways. This is what this chapter deals with. At least one important piece of legislation which gives extra protection has already been dealt with. That is the Unfair Contract Terms Act 1977 discussed in Chapter 7 which, it will be recalled, has a number of provisions specifically dealing with sales to consumers. In the next section the recent enactment of legislation making producers of products strictly liability to those injured as a result of a defect in the product is discussed. This is followed by a section on manufacturers' guarantees and one on various other statutes relevant to consumer sales. The final section deals with fair trading legislation.

Before looking at the substantive law it is important to note that it is not only consumers' rights that need to be considered but how these rights can be enforced. It is widely recognised that traditional court procedures are seriously inadequate for dealing with consumer disputes largely because they are expensive. To some extent this problem has been alleviated by the introduction of a small claims procedure in the County Court. In 1973 the County Court Rules were amended to permit claims for less than £1,000 to be dealt with by arbitration usually before the Registrar. Where less than £500 is involved the Registrar can order such arbitration even against the wishes of one of the parties. Another novel way in which a consumer might obtain compensation is by means of a compensation order under the Power of Criminal Courts Act 1973 (as amended by s67 of the Criminal Justice Act 1982). This permits a criminal court which convicts a person of any offence to order him to pay compensation for any personal injury, loss or damage arising from that offence. In Magistrates' Courts the maximum compensation that may be awarded is £1,000 but in the Crown Court there is no limit. In the context of sale the most likely use of this power is where there is a conviction of an offence against the Trade Descriptions Act 1968 discussed below.

15.2 The Consumer Protection Act and product liability

The Consumer Protection Act 1987 is a major piece of consumer legislation which contains several major innovations. At this point we are concerned only with the provisions of Part I which introduce a regime of strict liability for defective products.

To understand the reasons for the enactment of Part I of the Consumer Protection Act 1987 it is necessary to consider the law prior to its passage through Parliament and the history of attempts to change the law. The ability of someone injured by a defective product to recover compensation for loss suffered was riddled with anomalies. If the purchaser of the product was the one to suffer the injury recovery of compensation was fairly straightforward. An action in contract would lie against the seller based on breach of the implied terms about merchantability and fitness for purpose contained in s14 of the Sale of Goods Act 1979. The seller's liability was strict: the fact that he could not have discovered the defect was no defence. It is now clear that the seller may be liable although the goods were sold in a container or pre-packed and though the defect was discoverable only by carrying out detailed chemical tests. In *Ashington Piggeries Ltd* v *Christopher Hill Ltd* [1972] AC 441 the seller was liable under the Sale of Goods Act even though, in the words of Lord Diplock, 'in the then state of knowledge, scientific and commercial, no deliberate exercise of human skill or judgment could have prevented the meal from having its toxic effect upon mink. It was sheer bad luck.'

Contractual liability, where it existed, was the liability of the supplier, often a retailer, who may have sold the offending product in the manufacturer's sealed package. To some extent it could be said that legal liability was visited upon a not altogether appropriate person. It should be remembered that the supplier in his turn could sue in contract his supplier, and by this means a chain of actions might reach back to the manufacturer. This assumes that it was possible to identify the producer. In *Lambert* v *Lewis* [1982] AC 225 a distributor was unable to identify from his records the wholesaler from whom he had purchased the product and thus could not bring an action under the Sale of Goods Act. Another barrier to this indirect means of making the manufacturer liable may be the existence of an exclusion clause. While in consumer contracts it will not be possible, by virtue of the Unfair Contract Terms Act 1977, to exclude liability arising under the terms implied by the Sale of Goods Act 1979, it must be remembered that in non-consumer cases clauses excluding such liability will be valid provided that they are found to be fair and reasonable.

Where it is not open to the person injured by a defective product to sue the person who supplied him for any of the reasons set out in the previous paragraph it may be possible to sue the manufacturer. Such an action will have to be in tort, not contract. The classic example and, indeed the origin of the modern development of this area of law is *Donoghue* v *Stevenson* [1932] AC 562. Mrs Donoghue was taken by a friend to the Wellmeadow Café in Paisley and the friend purchased for her a bottle of ginger beer and some ice cream. The bottle was made of opaque glass and Mrs Donoghue had no reason to suspect that it contained anything but pure ginger beer. The proprietor of the café poured some of the ginger beer over the ice cream which was contained in a tumbler and Mrs Donoghue drank a little of it. Her friend then poured the rest of the contents of the bottle into the tumbler and at this point a decomposed snail emerged from the bottle. Mrs Donoghue suffered shock and contracted gastro-enteritis as a result. She did not sue the café proprietor. She had no contractual relation with him, so an action for breach of the implied term about merchantability was not possible. Neither was an action in negligence as there was no evidence that he had been careless in the selection of his stock and he had no possibility of examining the contents of a sealed, opaque bottle. There was no alternative but to sue Stevenson, the manufacturer of the ginger beer.

HELD: The principle propounded in this case, in its narrower form, is best put in the following passage from the judgment of Lord Atkin:

> 'a manufacturer of products, which he sells in such a form as to show that he intends them to reach the ultimate consumer in the form in which they left him with no reasonable possibility of intermediate examination, and with the knowledge that the absence of reasonable care in the preparation or putting up of the products will result in an injury to the consumer's life or property, owes a duty to the consumer to take that reasonable care.'

Since this momentous decision the principle has been extended to a great many other consumer situations and, of course, the wider principle in the case has had a great impact on the law of tort. The duty has been applied in a great many different circumstances. In *Stennet v Hancock and Peters* [1939] 2 All ER 578, to the owner of a garage who negligently repaired a vehicle with the result that a wheel came off and injured a passer-by.

However, the injured consumer must prove his case in the normal way in a tort action. As well as showing that he is owed a duty he must show that the injury was the result of breach of that duty and that damage resulted. Proving that the manufacturer has been at fault is often the most difficult part of the action. However, the principle enshrined in the maxim *res ipsa loquitur*, the facts speak for themselves, comes to the aid of the plaintiff. This might well have helped Mrs Donoghue as snails, decomposed or otherwise, are not supposed to be found in ginger beer bottles and suggest that the manufacturer has not taken sufficient care. An argument along these lines was successful in *Grant v Australian Knitting Mills Ltd* (above).

In addition to the problems of proof, the *Donoghue v Stevenson* principle does not permit recovery for damage to, or diminution in the value of, the defective product itself. It is by no means clear that what is usually referred to as pure financial loss, such as loss of profits flowing from a defect in a product, can be recovered unless that loss flows from damage caused by the defective product to other products as was the case in *Muirhead v Industrial Tank Specialities Ltd* [1985] 3 All ER 705.

In addition, serious harm can be caused by products put into the marketplace without any negligence. The classic case is the Thalidomide tragedy where many children were born with severe deformities to mothers who had taken a drug during pregnancy. At the time it was not known that this sort of drug could cause injury to a foetus and so it was not possible to prove negligence. Incidents of this sort led consumer organisations to campaign for the introduction of strict liability in tort for manufacturers along the lines of developments that had taken place in the United States of America. This was supported in a report by the Law Commissions, Liability for Defective Products, Cmnd 6831 (1977), and the Royal Commission on Civil Liability and Compensation for Personal Injury (the Pearson Commission). The issue was also taken up at European level by both the European Community and the Council of Europe. On 25 July 1985 the European Communities issued a Directive on Product Liability (No 85/374) and this has been implemented in the United Kingdom by Part I of the Consumer Protection Act 1987. Ironically, it almost certainly would not provide a remedy were a situation similar to the Thalidomide tragedy to recur.

While the official reports referred to in the previous paragraph were important in bringing about reform of the law relating to defective products the impact of American developments should not be overlooked. For many years American courts had been developing ways of circumventing the obstacles to recovery by individuals injured by defective products. The most innovative of these came in

1963 in the landmark judgment of the Chief Justice of California in *Greenman* v *Yuba Power Products Inc* (1962) 377 P (2d) 897. Greenman sued in respect of injuries received from a power tool manufactured by the defendants and bought from a retailer by his wife. His claim succeeded on the basis that there was a breach of an express warranty in the manufacturer's brochure. What is remarkable about the case is that the Court went on to say that 'the remedies of injured consumers ought not to be made to depend on the intricacies of the law of sale'. To quote Chief Justice Traynor:

> 'A manufacturer is strictly liable in tort when an article he places on the market, knowing that it is to be used without inspection for defects, proves to have a defect that causes injury to a human being.'

This principle has been adopted throughout the United States and is summarised in s402A of the American Law Institute's Restatement of Torts, second version.

The Act is described in detail below.

The key provision of the Consumer Protection Act: s2(1)

Section 2(1) provides:

> 'Subject to the following provisions of this Part, where any damage is caused wholly or partly by a defect in a product, every person to whom subsection (2) applies shall be liable for the damage.'

Section 6(7) makes clear that 'liability by virtue of this Part is to be treated as liability in tort for the purpose of any enactment conferring jurisdiction on any court with respect to any matter.' Section 5(7) makes clear that there is to be no liability for damage caused by a defect in a product which was supplied to any person by its producer before the coming into force of Part I of the Act.

Persons liable

For convenience it is usual to speak of product liability as the liability of the manufacturer but it should be remembered that the range of people liable is rather wider than this. Subsections (2)–(4) make this clear and the result is that the following are potentially liable (it is clear from this list that two or more persons may be jointly and severally liable):

1. *Producer*.
2. *Own branders*. This clumsy heading is used to sum up the group of persons who are liable by s2(2)(b): 'Any person who, by putting his name on the product or using a trade mark or other distinguishing mark in relation to the product, has held himself out to be the producer of the product.'

The most obvious relevance of this provision is to the trader who does not himself manufacture a product but has it produced by a manufacturer who puts the trader's name on it. This is common in supermarkets and the supermarket will be liable as if it had itself manufactured the goods.

3. *Importers.* To avoid the possibility of injured consumers having to bring actions in far off jurisdictions s2(2)(c) provides that the term producer includes: 'any person who has imported the product into a member State from a place outside the member States in order, in the course of any business of his, to supply it to another.'
4. *Others.* The heading is intended to cover the category comprised in s2(3). This provides that in certain circumstances, where damage has been caused by a defective product, any person who supplied the product to the person who suffered the damage, to the producer of any product in which the product is comprised or to any other person, can be liable. Liability arises in this situation if three conditions are fulfilled: the injured person must request the supplier to identify one or more of the persons listed in categories (1), (2) and (3) above; that request must be made within a reasonable time after the damage has occurred and at a time when it is not reasonably practicable for the person making the request to identify those persons; and the supplier must fail to supply the information requested within a reasonable time. An example of a situation where a supplier who would not normally be liable for the particular injury could find himself liable under the Consumer Protection Act 1987 would be a retailer whose goods have injured someone other than the purchaser. If the retailer cannot identify his supplier then under this provision he finds himself strictly liable.

The term 'producer' is defined in s1(1) to mean the manufacturer, one who abstracts or wins a substance (this would cover substances which are mined), and, in the cases of products which are not manufactured or abstracted, those who process a product. The example given in the Act is the processing of agricultural products.

'Product' is defined in s1(2) to mean:

'any goods or electricity and ... includes a product which is comprised in another product, whether by virtue of being a component part or raw material or otherwise.'

There is a proviso to the definition of goods that relates to components; it states that it is subject to s1(3), which is as follows:

'For the purposes of this Part a person who supplies any product in which products are comprised, whether by virtue of being component parts or raw materials or otherwise, shall not be treated by reason only of his supply of that product as supplying any of the products so comprised.'

It would seem that the producer of a product which incorporates some other firm's components is liable for those components in two situations. First, by virtue of s2(3) which is discussed above. Liability under that heading is only possible if it is the component that is defective and the producer fails to identify the supplier of the component. The second possibility is where the mere use of that component has rendered the product defective. In other words the producer of the finished product has selected an inappropriate component. If, for example, the producer of a car incorporated brakes supplied by another manufacturer which were not of the necessary strength to operate that car safely the car manufacturer would be liable. The brakes themselves could not be said to be defective: the problem has only arisen because they have been used in an inappropriate way.

However, remember that the 1987 Act does *not* apply to defective services. Liability for defective services remains still in the realms of tortious liability.

The Directive permits member States to exempt agricultural producers from the new strict liability regime. It has been decided to make such an exemption in the Act. Section 2(4) exempts the producers of game or agricultural produce 'if the only supply of the game or produce by that person to another was at a time when it had not undergone an industrial process.' What amounts to an industrial process seems likely to cause some difficulties. Is it an industrial process to wash potatoes or to put them in plastic bags for sale? Is the spraying of fruit trees an industrial process?

Defect

A key concept in the Act is that of 'defect' and this is defined in s3. The principal part of the definition is contained in s3(1):

> 'Subject to the following provisions of this section, there is a defect in a product for the purpose of this Part if the safety of the product is not such as persons generally are entitled to expect; and for those purposes "safety", in relation to a product, shall include safety with respect to products comprised in that product and safety in the context of risks of damage to property, as well as in the context of risks of death or personal injury.'

Subsection (2) then lists a number of circumstances which are to be taken into account in deciding what is the standard of safety that can be expected. These are as follows:

1. The manner in which, and purposes for which, the product has been marketed, its get-up, the use of any mark in relation to the product and any instructions for, or warnings with respect to, doing or refraining from doing anything with or in relation to the product.
2. What might reasonably be expected to be done with or in relation to the product.
3. The time when the product was supplied by its producer to another.

The fact that products produced after an injury has occurred have a greater level of safety may not be used to infer that earlier products were defective.

Defences

There are a number of defences open to the producer and these are set out in s4. It is a defence for a producer to show that:

1. The defect was attributable to compliance with a statutory requirement or Community obligation.
2. He did not supply the product or that he did so otherwise than in the course of business or without a view to profit.
3. The defect did not exist in the product when it was supplied.
4. In the case of component producers, the defect was a defect of the finished product which was wholly attributable to its design or to compliance by the component manufacturer with instructions given by the producer of the finished product.

He can also take advantage of the state of the art defence set out in s4(1)(e):

> 'that the state of scientific and technical knowledge at the relevant time was not such that a producer of products of the same description as the product in question might be expected to have discovered the defect if it had existed in his products while they were under his control.'

One difficulty that immediately becomes apparent is that the wording of s4(1)(e) appears to be considerably wider than the wording of the EC Directive. The legitimacy of s4(10(e) is under challenge in the European Court of Justice and may have to be reworded.

Damage

For the purposes of liability for defective products damage is defined in s5 to mean death or personal injury or any loss of or damage to any property including land. However, property does not include the product itself or any property which at the time it is lost or damaged is not of a description ordinarily intended for private use, occupation or consumption. So that actionable damage includes that to consumer property but not to business property. In the case of damage to property damages are only awardable where they exceed £275.

Time limits

The Limitation Act 1980 is amended by Schedule 1 of the Act and provides that product liability actions are extinguished ten years after the product was supplied by its manufacturer, importer or the person who put his own name on it. No action shall be brought three years after the later of the date on which the cause of action accrued and the date of knowledge of the injured person.

15.3 Manufacturer's guarantees

It is quite common especially in relation to cars and domestic appliances for the manufacturer to provide a guarantee. In the case of cars these are usually termed warranties. The manufacturer's guarantee consists of a written undertaking to the purchaser to make good a defective product by replacement or repair, or to give a refund, in the event of it proving to be defective within a stated period. In the case of cars and many domestic appliances this period is usually one year. Such a guarantee can be a very useful addition to the consumers' statutory rights. It avoids the problems surrounding the standard of quality which the consumer is entitled to expect under the Sale of Goods Act. As we have seen in Chapter 5 it is not altogether clear whether minor defects render goods unmerchantable and how far goods must prove to be durable. Indeed, guarantees are often used as a marketing ploy.

Despite their evident utility the legal status of guarantees is not entirely clear. Certainly by s7 of CPA 1987 no exclusion or limitation of liability clause can exclude or limit the 'strict' liability imposed by Part I of the Act. The difficulty is that it may not be easy to show that there is any contractual relationship between the consumer and the manufacturer because of the absence of consideration for the manufacturer's promise. The most difficult situation is where the information about the guarantee is contained in an envelope packed at the bottom of the box containing the article. This will only be opened after the goods have been purchased and taken home. It will be very difficult to fit this state of facts into the doctrine of consideration. Other cases may present less difficulty. Take the famous case of *Carlill* v *Carbolic Smoke Ball Company* [1893] 1 QB 256. There is was held that the consideration for the promise of the manufacturer was the purchase of the smokeball by the customer. Another problem which was discussed in that case was whether there was an offer as opposed to an invitation to treat. In view of the evidence of the statements made in the advertisements for the goods there was no difficulty in finding that there was a seriously meant offer albeit one which could be accepted in the somewhat unusual way of buying and using the product.

While one may expect manufacturers to be more careful than the manufacturers of the smokeball in making open-ended offers the principle of the *Carlill* case will probably cover many more common situations. It is common to see goods displayed with a ticket attached referring to the terms of a guarantee and in these circumstances it is probable that the manufacturer would incur contractual liability to the consumer.

To a large extent anxieties over the legal status of guarantees is irrelevant because it is highly unlikely that a manufacturer would ever renege on one. However, it is possible that were a firm to go into liquidation the liquidator would be forced to argue the point.

In the past there was considerable criticism of some so-called guarantees which took away much more than they offered the consumer. It was common practice for some guarantees to exclude liability for negligence. As we saw in Chapter 7 this is no longer possible as a result of s5 of the Unfair Contract Terms Act 1977.

15.4 Consumer Protection Act, Part II

Part II replaces provisions previously incorporated into the Consumer Protection Acts of 1961-71 and in the more recent Consumer Safety Act 1978. It does four main things.

First, it empowers the Secretary of State to make safety regulations governing the making and supplying of goods. Some regulations were made under earlier legislation and continue to be effective. Such regulations cover a wide variety of goods, ranging from composition of goods to colour coding of electric appliances. Such regulations may affect just a manufacturer or the whole possible range of 'producers' (see para 15.2(b) above). Non-compliance with such regulations is a criminal offence.

Secondly, ss13 and 14 allow quick action to be taken against those who market unsafe goods. Section 13 enables the Secretary of State to issue either:

1. a 'prohibition notice' preventing a trader on whom it is served from supplying goods considered unsafe; or
2. a 'notice to warn' requiring the trader on whom it is served to take specific steps to warn consumers about known risks in goods.

Section 14 allows local trading standards authorities to issue similar (but not the same) notices in specific circumstances.

Thirdly, s10 now makes it an offence to supply consumer goods which fail to comply with a general safety standard. Consumer goods are those 'which are ordinarily intended for private use or consumption' but they do not include food, water, growing crops, medicines and drugs, aircraft, and tobacco. Thus the ambit of s10 is considerably curtailed. The general safety requirement is that the goods must be 'reasonably safe' and the definition of 'unsafe' is very similar to that of 'defect' in 15.2(c) (above). The defence of 'due diligence' is available to anyone charged under s10 or under safety regulations generally. Section 39 defines this defence (see *Riley v Webb* [1987] CCLR 65 and *Rotherham MBC v Raysun* [1988] CCLR 1).

Fourthly, Part II of the CPA entitles a consumer to bring an action for damages against any supplier in breach of safety regulations for loss or damage suffered because of that breach. Note that both civil and criminal liability under Part II of the CPA attaches only to persons 'acting in the course of a business.' In *Southwark LBC v Charlesworth* [1983] 147 JP 470 the defendant was a cobbler who also sold second-hand goods. He sold, from his shop, an electric fire (previously used in his own home) which infringed safety regulations. He kept the proceeds of the second-hand sales separate from his shop accounts, but second-hand goods were displayed alongside other wares in his shoe-repair shop. On balance, therefore, the court decided that this was a sale 'in the course of a business'. The decision might, however, have been different had the sales of odd second-hand goods been less frequent or had the shopkeeper displayed a notice making it clear that the goods were not part of his normal business stock in trade.

The recent case of *Warwickshire County Council* v *Johnson* [1993] 2 WLR 1 concerned the phrase 'in the course of any business of his' in the context of the Consumer Protection Act 1987. The House of Lords ruled that this must mean a business of which the defendant is the owner, or who has a controlling interest. In the case in question, the appellant was branch manager of an electrical goods shop. It was held that Johnson could not be said to be acting 'in the course of any business of his'.

15.5 Miscellaneous consumer protection statutes

Food and drugs legislation

In addition to the consumer safety legislation there is quite a lot of legislation sanctioned by criminal penalties which plays an important part in ensuring that the quality of goods is satisfactory. Under the Food Act 1984 the quality and composition of food is controlled. The detailed control of the composition of food is found in a mass of subordinate legislation made principally under powers conferred under the Act. Similarly the Medicines Act 1968 deals with the quality of drugs.

Trade Descriptions Act 1968

The Trade Descriptions Act 1968 is another consumer protection measure which uses the criminal law to achieve its aims. Section 1 of the Act creates the offences of applying in the course of a trade or business a false trade description to goods, or supplying or offering to supply goods to which a false description is applied. 'Trade description' is very widely defined in s2 to cover such things as quantity, size, gauge, method of manufacture, composition, fitness for purpose, strength, behaviour, accuracy, the results of tests, the place and date of manufacture and the history of goods. A false trade description is one that is false to a material degree and includes one that is misleading.

In *Horner* v *Kingsley Clothing Co Ltd* (1989) The Times 6 July the defendants sold sweat-shirts with the logo 'Marc O Polo' on the front. This name was the registered trade mark of a British distributor of expensive garments which included sweat-shirts. While the goods sold by the defendants were not exactly of the normal style and fabric of true Marc O Polo sweat-shirts, the name was clearly meant to mislead the average consumer. The court held that since the use of a registered trade mark was clearly meant to be misleading, whether the deception was or was not successful was irrelevant. The prosecution was successful under the Trades Description Act.

15.6 Fair trading legislation

The Fair Trading Act 1973

The Office of Fair Trading and the post of Director General of Fair Trading created by the Fair Trading Act 1973 have been among the most important steps in consumer protection in the country. Put briefly, the role of the Director General of Fair Trading is to keep a continuing watch on developments which are likely to damage the consumer's economic interests. The Director General, who holds office for a five-year period, can, as the present Director General Sir Gordon Borrie has on two occasions, be reappointed. The scope of the Director General's functions is set out in s2 of the Fair Trading Act. Broadly speaking, he is required to keep himself informed about commercial activities carried on in the United Kingdom relating to the production and supply of goods and supply of services. He requires this information in order to become aware of practices which may adversely affect the interests of consumers with respect to their economic interests or their interests with respect to health, safety or other matters. The fact that the Office of Fair Trading combines consumer protection and competition policy functions is one of its strengths as competition policy has a considerable role to play in protecting the consumer.

In addition to these general functions the Fair Trading and other legislation give the Director General certain more specific functions. For example, s14 of the Fair Trading Act permits him to refer to the Consumer Protection Advisory Committee practices which are considered adversely to affect the economic interests of consumers.

This function is now in abeyance as the government did not reappoint the members of the committee when their terms of office expired. Its existence is referred to because the procedure under Part II of the Fair Trading Act of which it was a part did result in some significant pieces of consumer protection legislation which will be referred to below.

Under Part III of the Fair Trading Act the Director General has important powers enabling him to obtain assurances from traders who persistently indulge in courses of conduct which are detrimental to consumers' interests.

One of the most important innovations in the Consumer Credit Act 1974 was the creation of a licensing system for those involved, in any way, in the credit industry. It is one of the Director General's most important functions to operate the licensing system which is discussed in more detail in the section of this book dealing with consumer credit.

Other statutes regulating trading practices

There are a number of statutes which regulate trading practices which could be conducted in a manner inimical to the interests of consumers. Two examples are the Mock Auctions Act 1961 and the Trading Stamps Act 1964. The Unsolicited Goods and Services Acts 1971 and 1975 deal with inertia selling; and Part XI of the Fair Trading Act regulates pyramid selling schemes. The Mail Order Transactions (Information) Order 1976 SI 1976 No 1812 requires sellers by mail order to furnish information to potential customers about their true name and registered place of business; and the Business Advertisements (Disclosure) Order 1977 SI No 1918 requires businesses to make clear in their advertisements that sales are in the course of a business. This is an attempt to control those who seek to evade the extra legal liability of business sellers by, for example, placing classified advertisements in newspapers as if they were private sellers. The Consumer Transactions (Restriction on Statements) Order 1976 SI No 1813 makes it a criminal offence for a trader to use terms which are void by virtue of s6 of the Unfair Contract Terms Act 1977.

The Package Travel, Package Holidays and Package Tours Regulations 1992, implementing an EC Directive of the same name, apply to all package holidays sold in the UK as from 1 January 1993. These regulations (SI 1992 No 3288) are highly prescriptive in nature. Primarily they formalise good practice, that is they regulate the form of brochures and pre-contract information and the content and form of contracts. Surcharges may be allowed only in certain circumstances. Protection for consumers is secured in a number of ways by constraining the terms on which the parties deal and imposing a wide number of obligatory terms and conditions.

16

The Supply of Goods and Services Act 1982

16.1 Introduction

16.2 Contracts for the transfer of goods which are not sale of goods contracts

16.3 Contracts of hire

16.4 Contracts to supply services

16.1 Introduction

The Sale of Goods Act 1979 and the Supply of Goods (Implied Terms) Act 1973 cover, as we have seen, sale and hire purchase agreements. Prior to the introduction of the Supply of Goods and Services Act the supply of services and some transfers of property in goods outside the then current statutory control were covered by the common law. To remedy the lacunae and embody the law as a code, the Supply of Goods and Services Act was passed and received Royal Assent on the 13 July 1982. The Act is divided into two major parts; Part I governing the supply of goods and in particular covering contracts for the transfer of property in goods and contracts for the hire of goods; Part II is exclusively concerned with the supply of services.

It should be clearly understood that the contracts covered by the Supply of Goods and Services Act 1982, although often economically similar in their effects to contracts of sale, are legally different in character. It is necessary to distinguish between sale of goods contracts and non-sale of goods contracts for a number of purely practical reasons.

Firstly, although the 1982 Act is based largely on SGA 1979, the reverse is not true. The sections in SGA cover more ground by far. For example, the Supply of Goods and Services Act covers only ss12-15 of SGA. There are no statutory concepts such as the doctrine of 'acceptance'; nor are there statutory rules as to passing of property and risk.

Secondly, the law related to non-sale of goods contracts is, despite the 1982 Act, still largely a matter of common law. There is very little case law casting light on statutory provisions. The piecemeal way in which the legislation has evolved often makes it difficult to see the subject in its proper perspective.

Before reading the remaining parts of this chapter it may be helpful to remember that all the provisions of the 1982 Act really amount to three separate sets of terms to be implied into different types of contracts.

The first set of terms (ss2-5) apply to contracts other than sale of goods or hire purchase (see 16.2 for details). They cover rights as to title, description and merchantability generally and are largely analogous to similar implied terms in the SGA.

The second set of terms (ss6-10) (see 16.3 for details) apply to contracts of hire, other than hire purchase agreements. Again the intention is to imply terms analogous to those of the SGA as to the general quality of the goods hired.

The third set of terms (ss13-15) is implied into any contract 'for services', whether or not in providing such services the supplier also supplies certain goods (see 16.4 for more detail.) These are not, and cannot by their nature be, totally analogous to SGA. However, they cover 'quality' in general terms, inasmuch as this can ever relate to supply of services.

16.2 Contracts for the transfer of goods which are not sale of goods contracts

Section 1 provides:

'1(1) In this Act a "contract for the transfer of goods" means a contract under which one person transfers or agrees to transfer to another the property in goods, other than an excepted contract.
(2) For the purposes of this section an excepted contract means any of the following:
a) a contract of sale of goods;
b) a hire purchase agreement;
c) a contract under which the property in goods is (or is to be) transferred in exchange for trading stamps or their redemption;
d) a transfer or agreement to transfer which is made by deed and for which there is no consideration other than presumed consideration imported by the deed;
e) a contract intended to operate by way of mortgage, pledge, charge or other security.
(3) For the purposes of this Act a contract is a contract for the transfer of goods whether or not services are also provided or to be provided under the contract, and (subject to subsection (2) above) whatever is the nature of the consideration for the transfer or agreement to transfer.'

Section 1(1) includes contracts where property is transferred or it is to be transferred on the fulfilment of a condition.

'Property' is defined in s18(1) of the 1982 Act as 'the general property in [goods] ... and not merely a special property'. This reflects the definition in s61(1) of the Sale of Goods Act 1979; general property broadly meaning ownership.

By s1(2) of the 1982 Act certain contracts are excepted from the operation of the Act:

1. Sale of Goods. The 1979 Statute governs the sale of goods and transactions within that statute are not within the scope of the 1982 legislation.
2. Hire purchase agreements. Hire purchase agreements as defined in s189(1) of the Consumer Credit Act 1974 are ouside the ambit of the section.

The other excepted contracts under s1(2)(c)(d) and (e) are less important for the purpose of this course.

Agreements within the 1982 Act

Section 1(3) of the 1982 Act is an important provision, stating that a contract which transfers property as defined in the Act remains within the Act whether or not services are also provided or to be provided under the contract. The second limb of s1(3) brings within the ambit of the statute contracts regardless of whether the consideration is money consideration or otherwise. Accordingly, barter and exchange contracts which fall outside the 1979 Act are covered by the 1982 Act.

For example, the case of *Esso Petroleum Co Ltd* v *Commissioners of Customs and Excise* [1976] 1 WLR 1; [1976] 1 All ER 117 where medallions were given to buyers of a certain quantity of petrol, although not all sale of goods, would be a transfer of property for the purposes of the 1982 Act.

More importantly, contracts for skill and labour or work and materials are within the 1982 Act if general property in goods passes. In *Robinson* v *Graves* [1935] 1 KB 579, a contract for an artist to paint a portrait was a contract for skill and labour not one for the supply of goods. The 1982 Act would now cover that contract. Consequently, contracts under which goods and services are supplied, in so far as the essence of the contract is one for service and labour, will be subject to the 1982 Act. Contracts for the installation of central heating, plumbing and electrics will normally be within this part of the 1982 Act if property in goods passes.

Note that the essence of the contract must not be for the passing of property in goods (where the Sale of Goods Act 1979 will govern).

The Implied Conditions and Warranties

All contracts within the scope of s1 of the Act have implied into them the conditions and warranties stipulated in ss2, 3, 4 and 5 of the 1982 Act. The distinction between condition and warranties has already been covered in depth and students are referred back to the relevant parts of the course material.

Title

Section 2 of the 1982 Act provides:

> '(1) In a contract for the transfer of goods, other than one to which subsection (3) below applies, there is an implied condition on the part of the transferor that in the case of a

transfer of the property in the goods he has a right to transfer the property and in the case of an agreement to transfer the property in the goods he will have such a right at the time when the property is to be transferred.

(2) In a contract for the transfer of goods, other than one to which subsection (3) below applies, there is also an implied warranty that:

a) the goods are free and will remain free until the time when the property is to be transferred, from any charge or encumbrance not disclosed or known to the transferee before the contract is made and;

b) the transferee will enjoy quiet possession of the goods except so far as it may be disturbed by the owner or other person entitled to the benefit of any charge or encumbrance so disclosed or known.

(3) This subsection applies to a contract for the transfer of goods in the case of which there appears from the contract or is to be inferred from its circumstances an intention that the transferer should transfer only such title as he or a third person may have.

(4) In a contract to which subsection (3) above applies there is an implied warranty that all charges or encumbrances known to the transferor and not known to the transferee have been disclosed to the transferee before the contract is made.

(5) In a contract to which subsection (3) above applies there is also an implied warranty that none of the following will disturb the transferee's quiet possession of the goods, namely:

a) the transferor;

b) in a case where the parties to the contract intend that the transferor should transfer only such title as a third person may have, that person;

c) anyone claiming through or under the transferor or that third person otherwise than under a charge or encumbrance disclosed or known to the transferee before the contract is made.'

Section 2 of the 1982 Act is identical to s12 of the 1979 Act save in so far as it applies to the transfer rather than the sale of goods. Both sections contain one condition and two warranties.

Correspondence with description

By s3 the 1982 Act provides:

'(1) This section applies where, under a contract for the transfer of goods, the transferor transfers or agrees to transfer the property in goods by description.

(2) In such a case there is an implied condition that the goods will correspond with the description.

(3) If the transferor transfers or agrees to transfer the property in the goods by sample as well as by description it is not sufficient that the bulk of the goods corresponds with the sample of the goods if the goods do not also correspond with the description.

(4) A contract is not prevented from falling within subsection (1) above by reason only that, being exposed for supply, the goods are selected by the transferee.'

Section 3 of the 1982 Act is adapted from s13 of the 1979 Act. The case law relevant to the development of that provision and the decisions upon the old 1893 Sale of Goods Act are applicable mutatis mutandi.

Merchantable quality

Section 4 of the 1982 Act provides:

'(1) Except as provided by this section and section 5 below and subject to the provisions of any other enactment, there is no implied condition or warranty about the quality or fitness for any particular purpose of goods supplied under a contract for the transfer of goods.

(2) Where, under such a contract, the transferor transfers the property in goods in the course of a business, there is (subject to subsection (3) below) an implied condition that the goods supplied under the contract are of merchantable quality.

(3) There is no such condition as is mentioned in subsection (2) above:

a) as regards defects specifically drawn to the transferee's attention before the contract is made; or

b) if the transferee examines the goods before the contract is made, as regards defects which that examination ought to reveal.

(9) Goods of any kind are of merchantable quality within the meaning of subsection (2) above if they are as fit for the purpose or purposes for which goods of that kind are commonly supplied as it is reasonable to expect having regard to any description applied to them, the price (if relevant) and all the other relevant circumstances.'

Section 18(1) defines 'business' as including 'a profession and the activities of any government department or local or public authority'. 'Quality' as defined in s18(1) includes the 'state or condition' of goods.

In all respects s4(2), (3) and (9) mirror s14(2), (3) and (6) of the Sale of Goods Act 1979. The cases discussed under s14 should be referred to by the student.

Note the following points:

1. For this condition to be implied into the contract the transfer must transfer property in the course of business.
2. As R G Lawson points out in his Practical Guide to the Act, 'The implied condition as to merchantable quality refers to the goods supplied "under" the contract of transfer, thus encompassing more than just the goods, the property in which is to pass pursuant to the contract.

For instance, if a firm installs central heating fired by oil, any oil provided by the contractors will have to meet the requirement as to merchantable quality even though it is not provided as part of the agreement but as part of an initial test to determine the satisfactory working of the equipment.'

Fitness for purpose

Section 4 of the 1982 Act provides

'1(4) Subsection (5) below applies where, under a contract for the transfer of goods, the transferor transfers the property in goods to the course of a business and the transferee, expressly or by implication, makes known:

a) to the transferor, or;

b) where the consideration or part of the consideration for the transfer is a sum payable by

instalments and the goods were previously sold by a credit-broker to the transferor, to that credit-broker;
any particular purpose for which the goods are being acquired.
(5) In that case there is (subject to subsection (6) below) an implied condition that the goods supplied under the contract are reasonably fit for that purpose, whether or not that is a purpose for which such goods are commonly supplied.
(6) Subsection (5) above does not apply where the circumstances show that the transferee does not rely, or that it is unreasonable for him to rely, on the skill or judgment of the transferor or credit-broker.
(7) An implied condition or warranty about quality or fitness for a particular purpose may be annexed by usage to a contract for the transfer of goods.
(8) The preceding provisions of this section apply to a transfer by a person who in the course of a business is acting as agent for another as they apply to a transfer by a principal in the course of a business, except where that other is not transferring in the course of a business and either the transferee knows that fact or reasonable steps are taken to bring it to the transferee's notice before the contract concerned is made.'

Again the 1982 Act follows the provisions of s14(3) of the 1979 Act. Compare s4(7) with s14(4) of the 1979 Act. Section 4(8) corresponds with s14(5) of the 1979 Act (see *Peter Darlington Partners Ltd* v *Gosho Co Ltd* [1964] 1 Lloyd's Rep 149).

Transfer by sample

Section 15 of the Sale of Goods Act 1979 is the basis upon which s5 of the 1982 Act was drafted. Section 5 provides:

'(1) This section applies where, under a contract for the transfer of goods, the transferor transfers or agrees to transfer the property in the goods by reference to a sample.
(2) In such a case there is an implied condition:
a) that the bulk will correspond with the sample in quality; and
b) that the transferee will have a reasonable opportunity of comparing the bulk with the sample; and
c) that the goods will be free from any defect, rendering them unmerchantable, which would not be apparent on reasonable examination of the sample.
(3) In subsection (2)(c) above "unmerchantable" is to be construed in accordance with section 4(9) above.
(4) For the purposes of this section a transferor transfers or agrees to transfer the property in goods by reference to a sample where there is an express or implied term to that effect in the contract concerned.'

16.3   Contracts of hire

Prior to the 1982 Act simple hire or leasing agreements were outside the scope of the statutory implied terms appertaining to hire purchase, conditional sale or ordinary sale contracts.

Sections 6 to 10 of the 1982 Act introduce the regime mutatis mutandi to hire agreements. Section 6 defines the contracts concerned as follows:

'(1) In this Act a "contract for the hire of goods" means a contract under which one person bails or agrees to bail goods to another by way of hire, other than an expected contract.
(2) For the purposes of this section an excepted contract means any of the following:
a) a hire purchase agreement;
b) a contract under which goods are (or are to be) bailed in exchange for trading stamps on their redemption.
(3) For the purposes of this Act a contract is a contract for the hire of goods whether or not services are also provided or to be provided under the contract, and (subject to subsection (2) above) whatever is the nature of the consideration for the bailment or agreement to bail by way of hire.'

Hire purchase agreements are, of course, excluded from the operation of the 1982 Act, being governed already by the Supply of Goods (Implied Terms) Act 1973. (See in particular ss8 to 12.)

Note that although services may be provided under the hire contract as well as the goods, the provisions of this part of Part I of the 1982 Act still apply. For example the contract for a hire of a car may include charges in respect of maintenance which the hirer is obliged to undertake with the owner.

A contract for the hire of goods encompasses contracts where goods are bailed by way of hire (eg the delivery of goods by one to another without title in the goods being transferred). The bailee therefore must have possession of the goods before the 1982 Act applies. Hire or leasing agreements are accordingly the main categories of agreement falling within s6 of the 1982 Act.

In every contract within the scope of s6 the following warranties and conditions are implied.

The right to transfer possession

Section 7 of the 1982 Act provides:

'(1) In a contract for the hire of goods there is an implied condition on the part of the bailor that in the case of a bailment he has a right to transfer possession of the goods by way of hire for the period of the bailment and in the case of an agreement to bail he will have such a right at the time of the bailment.
(2) In a contract for the hire of goods there is also an implied warranty that the bailee will enjoy quiet possession of the goods for the period of the bailment except so far as the possession may be disturbed by the owner or other person entitled to the benefit or any charge or encumbrance disclosed or known to the bailee before the contract is made.
(3) The preceding provisions of this section do not affect the right of the bailor to repossess the goods under an express or implied term of the contract.'

Note the following points:

1. Section 7(1): the bailor must have a right to transfer possession (he need not be the owner of the goods).
2. Section 7(2): the warranty follows the analogous provision in the 1982 Act. However, there is no statutory warranty that goods are free from any undisclosed

charge or encumbrance.
3. Hire agreements may be regulated agreements within the Consumer Credit Act 1974, and, if so, either the free and voluntary consent of the bailee must be given at the times the bailor wishes to repossess or the order of the court is required.

Section 8 provides:

'(1) This section applies where, under a contract for the hire of goods, the bailor bails or agrees to bail the goods by description.
(2) In such a case there is an implied condition that the goods will correspond with the description.
(3) If under the contract the bailor bails or agrees to bail the goods by reference to a sample as well as a description it is not sufficient that the bulk of the goods corresponds with the sample if the goods do not also correspond with the description.
(4) A contract is not prevented from falling within subsection (1) above by reason only that, being exposed for supply, the goods are selected by the bailee.'

The section is analogous to the 1979 Act s13.

Merchantable quality

Section 9 of the 1982 Act provides:

'(1) Except as provided by this section and s10 below and subject to the provisions of any other enactment, there is no implied condition or warranty about the quality or fitness for any particular purpose of goods bailed under a contract for the hire of goods.
(2) Where, under such a contract, the bailor bails goods in the course of a business, there is (subject to subsection (3) below) an implied condition that the goods supplied under the contract are of merchantable quality.
(3) There is no such condition as is mentioned in subsection (2) above:
a) as regards defects specifically drawn to the bailee's attention before the contract is made; or
b) if the bailee examines the goods before the contract is made, as regards defects which that examination ought to reveal.
(9) Goods of any kind are of merchantable quality within the meaning of subsection (2) above if they are as fit for the purpose or purposes for which goods of that kind are commonly supplied as it is reasonable to expect having regard to any description applied to them, the consideration for the bailment (if relevant) and all the other relevant circumstances.'

See discussion above.

Fitness for purpose

By s9 the 1982 Act provides:

'(4) Subsection (5) below applies where, under a contract for the hire of goods, the bailor bails goods in the course of a business and the bailee, expressly or by implication, makes known:

a) to the bailor in the course of negotiations conducted by him in relation to the making of the contract, or
b) to a credit-broker in the course of negotiations conducted by that broker in relation to goods sold by him to the bailor before forming the subject matter of the contract;
any particular purpose for which the goods are being bailed.
(5) In that case there is (subject to subsection (6) below) an implied condition that the goods supplied under the contract are reasonably fit for that purpose, whether or not that is a purpose for which such goods are commonly supplied.
(6) Subsection (5) above does not apply where the circumstances show that the bailee does not rely, or that it is unreasonable for him to rely, on the skill or judgment of the bailor or credit-broker.'

These provisions again follow the Sale of Goods Act 1979 model. The only difference is the noticeable inclusion of the words 'in the course of negotiation'. It is doubted whether this adds anything to the interpretation of this section as compared to the previous statutory wording.

Hire by sample

Section 10 of the 1982 Act provides:

'(1) This section applies where, under a contract for the hire of goods, the bailor bails or agrees to bail the goods by reference to a sample.
(2) In such a case there is an implied condition:
a) that the bulk will correspond with the sample in quality; and
b) that the bailee will have a reasonable opportunity of comparing the bulk with the sample; and
c) that the goods will be free from any defect, rendering them unmerchantable, which would not be apparent on reasonable examination of the sample.
(3) In subsection (2)(c) above 'unmerchantable' is to be construed in accordance with section 9(9) above.
(4) For the purposes of this section a bailor bails or agrees to bail goods by reference to a sample where there is an express or implied term to that effect in the contract concerned.'

Exclusion of liability

The basic rule, which reflects s55 of the 1979 Act is confirmed in s11 of the 1982 Act. By s11 the Act provides:

'(1) Where a right, duty or liability would arise under a contract for the transfer of goods or a contract for the hire of goods by implication of law, it may (subject to subsection (2) below and the 1977 Act) be negatived or varied by express agreement, or by the course of dealing between the parties, or by such usage as binds both parties to the contract.
(2) An express condition or warranty does not negative a condition or warranty implied by the preceding provisions of this Act unless inconsistent with it.
(3) Nothing in the preceding provisions of this Act prejudices the operation of any other enactment or any rule of law whereby any condition or warranty (other than one relating to quality or fitness) is to be implied in a contract for the transfer of goods or a contract for the hire of goods.'

The Unfair Contract Terms Act 1977 is expressly referred to in s11(1) of the 1982 Act and the referment provision of that Act is s7. Section 7 UCTA controls attempts to exclude liability where the possession or ownership of goods passed under or in pursuance of a contract not governed by the law of sale of goods and hire purchase.

As to exclusion clauses in contracts for supply of goods and services see *Stewart Gill Ltd* v *Horatio Myer & Co Ltd* [1992] 2 All ER 257 (see section 7.3).

To Title

Unlike s6 of UCTA 1977, however, s7 permits the exclusion of terms (if any) as to title, save in so far as the reasonableness test is satisfied. In Hire Purchase and Sale of Goods Act cases, s6 expressly forbids the exclusion of terms as to title.

Section 17(2) of Part III of the 1982 Act, however, adds a new s7(3A) to UCTA 1977, providing:

'(2) The following subsection shall be inserted after s7(3) of the 1977 Act:
"(3A) Liability for breach of the obligations arising under s2 of the Supply of Goods and Services Act 1982 (implied terms about title etc in certain contracts for the transfer of the property in goods) cannot be excluded or restricted by reference to any such term."
(3) In consequence of subsection (2) above, in section 7(4) of the 1977 Act, after "cannot" there shall be inserted "(in a case to which subsection (3A) above does not apply)".'

Although s2 of the 1982 Act is covered, the test of reasonableness must still be applied in relation to hire contracts and s7 of the 1982 Act.

Furthermore, the Consumer Transactions (Restrictions on Statements) Order 1976 (SI 1976 No 1813) which makes it unlawful to attempt to exclude terms implied by the Sale of Goods Act 1979 does not apply to s7 UCTA exclusions.

Correspondence with description, merchantable quality and fitness for purpose

Section 7(2) UCTA only deals with consumer contracts as defined in s12 UCTA (see back to course materials). In respect of contracts falling within s7(2), and the implied terms as to correspondence with description or sample, merchantable quality and fitness for purposes, terms cannot be excluded or restricted by contract.

In respect of non-consumer contracts s7(3) UCTA permits exclusion or restriction of the implied terms in so far as the clause is reasonable.

Note the following points:

1. Section 3 UCTA, which applies as is relevant to contracts within the 1982 Act.
2. For what is reasonable see s11 and schedule 2 of UCTA and the discussion above.

16.4 Contracts to supply services

The contracts concerned

By s12 the 1982 Act provides:

> '(1) In this Act a "contract for the supply of a service" means, subject to subsection (2) below, a contract under which a person ("the supplier") agrees to carry out a service.'

In *Cronin (Trading as Cronin Driving School)* v *Customs and Excise Commissioners* [1991] STC 333 it was made clear that services supplied on a 'franchise' system came within the definition.

> '(2) For the purposes of this Act, a contract of employment or apprenticeship is not a contract for the supply of a service.
> (3) Subject to subsection (2) above, a contract is a contract for the supply of a service for the purposes of this Act whether or not goods are also:
> a) transferred or to be transferred; or
> b) bailed or to be bailed by way of hire
> under a contract, and whatever is the nature of the consideration for which the service is to be carried out.
> (4) The Secretary of State may by order provide that one or more of ss13 to 15 below shall not apply to services of a description specified in the order, and such an order may make different provision for different circumstances.
> (5) The power to make an order under subsection (4) above shall be exercisable by statutory instrument subject to annulment in pursuance of a resolution of either House of Parliament.'

Note that by subsection (3) contracts for the supply of a service are still governed by Part II of the Act notwithstanding that goods are transferred or to be transferred under the contract or that goods are bailed by way of hire. A hire purchase agreement which involves the provision of a service, although unusual, would be governed by Part II of the 1982 Act.

Note also that services provided by builders, architects, surveyors, estate agents, barbers, etc, are all within Part II, as are services provided by lawyers. The latter category may be exempted from the operation of the Act by the Secretary of State who is empowered to do so by subsection (4) of s12. Remember that a contract may come within s1(3) or s6(3) as well as s12(3) of the 1982 Act.

Section 12(2) of the 1982 Act expressly excludes a contract of employment or apprenticeship from the provisions.

Implied term about care and skill

Section 13 of the 1982 Act provides:

> 'In a contract for the supply of a service where the supplier is acting in the course of a business, there is an implied term that the supplier will carry out the service with reasonable care and skill.'

Section 13 merely enacts the common law. In the important case of *Greaves & Co (Contractors) Ltd* v *Baynham Meikle and Partners* [1975] 1 WLR 1095; [1975] 3 All ER 99 Lord Denning in the Court of Appeal considered that:

> 'The law does not usually imply a warranty that the professional man will achieve the desired result, but only a term that he will use reasonable care and skill. The surgeon does not warrant that he will cure the patient. Nor does the solicitor warrant that he will win the case. But, when a dentist agrees to make a set of false teeth for a patient, there is an implied warranty that they will fit his gums: see *Samuels* v *Davis* [1943] 1 KB 526; [1943] 2 All ER 3.'

He went on:

> 'It seems to me that in the contractual employment of a professional man, whether it is a medical man, a lawyer, or an accountant, an architect or an engineer, his duty is to use reasonable care and skill in the course of his employment.'

Note that s13 of the 1982 Act only implies terms into a *contract*. Where no contract exists reliance will have to be had on the tortious principles enunciated in *Hedley Byrne & Co Ltd* v *Heller & Partners Ltd* [1964] AC 465; [1963] 2 All ER 575.

Implied term about time for performance

Section 14 of the 1982 Act provides:

> '(1) Where, under a contract for the supply of a service by a supplier acting in the course of a business, the time for the service to be carried out is not fixed by the contract, left to be fixed in a manner agreed by the contract or determined by the course of dealing between the parties, there is an implied term that the supplier will carry out the service within a reasonable time.
> (2) What is a reasonable time is a question of fact.'

This is also a codification of the common law (see *Charles Rickards Ltd* v *Oppenheim* [1950] 1 KB 616; [1950] 1 All ER 420).

Note that the section does not state whether the term is a condition or warranty. That must be inferred from whether the parties intend time to be of the essence. In most commercial contracts time is of the essence, and therefore a condition. If, however, a commercial contract did not stipulate dates, it could be argued that the parties could not have intended time to be of prime consideration.

As to time of performance note also the recent case of *Bass plc* v *Customs and Excise Commissioners* (1991) (unreported) in which a hotelier guaranteed a reservation, keeping a room free until a specified time. When the customer failed to show, he charged for the room but did not add VAT. Customs and Excise assessed the hotelier on the basis that VAT should have been charged, because the contract was for the supply of a room, regardless of whether the customer used it or not. The hotelier appealed. It was held that the appeal would be allowed; VAT should not be chargeable. Although the reservation was a contract in itself, it was not a contract as defined by the Supply of Goods and Services Act 1982. Such a contract of supply would not be completed until the customer arrived and took up his reservation. Where a customer failed to arrive there could be no supply of goods and services.

Implied term about consideration

Section 15 of the 1982 Act provides:

> '(1) Where, under a contract for the supply of a service, the consideration for the service is not determined by the contract, left to be determined in a manner agreed by the contract or determined by the course of dealing between the parties, there is an implied term that the party contracting with the supplier will pay a reasonable charge.
> (2) What is a reasonable charge is a question of fact.'

Note that only if consideration is not agreed prior or concurrent with the entering into the contract does s15 apply. Quotations given by a tradesman are fixed price contracts, and are not variable upwards or downwards. Section 15 does not apply. Estimates, however, are just that and if the final charge exceeds the estimate, the receiver of the services is bound only to pay a reasonable price.

Exclusion of implied terms

Section 16 of the 1982 Act provides:

> '(1) Where a right, duty or liability would arise under a contract for the supply of a service by virtue of this part of this Act, it may (subject to subsection (2) below and the 1977 Act) be negatived or varied by express agreement, or by the course of dealing between the parties, or by such usage as binds both parties to the contract.
> (2) An express term does not negative a term implied by this Part of this Act unless inconsistent with it.
> (3) Nothing in this Part of this Act prejudices:
> a) any rule of law which imposes on the supplier a duty stricter than that imposed by ss13 or 14 above; or
> b) subject to paragraph (a) above, any rule of law whereby any term not inconsistent with this Part of this Act is to be implied in a contract for the supply of a service.
> (4) This Part of this Act has effect subject to any other enactment which defines or restricts the rights, duties or liabilities arising in connection with a service of any description.'

Section 16 is self-explanatory. Note that s3 UCTA is the provision which concerns Part II of the 1982 Act.

Consumer Credit

1

Introduction

1.1 Introduction

1.2 Definitions

1.3 Multiple agreements

1.4 Linked transactions

1.5 Total charge for credit

1.6 Variation of agreements

1.7 Licensing

1.1 Introduction

General introduction

The Consumer Credit Act 1974 (referred to hereafter as the Act) controls the working of contracts under which individuals are given credit. In this book we are concerned with contracts which allow people to buy goods, but there any many other types of contract controlled by the 1974 Act. In outline, there are two common ways in which credit can be given to someone to allow him to buy goods: either he may be lent money with which he buys them; or he may be supplied with the goods on condition that he pays for them in instalments.

He may be given a loan which must be repaid at a specified rate per month or per week; or he may be allowed an overdraft, which means he can write cheques or draw cash from his bank account even though he does not have money in the account. Obviously the bank will want to make a profit from such arrangements, so it will charge him interest on the amount borrowed.

The purchase of goods by paying in instalments allows the buyer to use the goods before he has paid for them in full. Many shops would like to allow customers to buy goods by instalments, but cannot afford to pay their own suppliers and wait months or perhaps years to recoup the money from the customer. The normal practice, therefore, is that the shop will sell the goods to a finance company which will enter into a separate contract with the customer allowing him to pay in instalments. In this way the shop gets its money from the finance company and the buyer is still able to pay in instalments, although he pays the finance company and not the shop. The three most common credit transactions which operate in this way are hire purchase, credit sale and conditional sale. We will look at these contracts in some detail in the pages which follow, but a brief definition is necessary here. A hire purchase contract is one by which the customer agrees to hire goods for a period of time and has an option to buy them - he is not bound to buy them but he may do so if he chooses. A conditional sale is a sale of goods where the buyer pays in instalments and property passes to him on the happening of a stipulated event (normally the payment of the last instalment). A credit sale is a sale of goods where the price is paid in instalments but the passing of property is determined according to the normal rules in ss17 and 18 of the Sale of Goods Act 1979.

Hire purchase

Probably the most common of these types of contract is the hire purchase contract. These contracts are not contracts of sale because the customer does not bind himself to buy. Instead he agrees to hire the goods for a period of time after which he may buy them for a nominal fee.

The working of the modern hire purchase contract was described in graphic terms by Lord Denning in *Bridge* v *Campbell Discount Co Ltd* [1962] AC 600; [1962] 1 All ER 385:

> 'It is in effect, though not in law, a mortgage of goods. Just as a man who buys land may raise part of the price by a mortgage of it, so, also, a man who buys goods may raise part of the price by hire purchase of them. And just as the old mortgage of land was not what it appeared to be, so, also, the modern hire purchase of goods is not what it seems to be ... Take this present transaction. If you were to strip it of the legal trappings in which it has been dressed and see it in its native simplicity, you would discover that the appellant agreed to buy a car from a dealer for £405 but he could only find £105 towards it. So he borrowed the other £300 from a finance house and got them to pay it to the dealer, and he gave the finance house a charge on the car as security for repayment. But if you tried to express the transaction in those simple terms you would soon fall into troubles of all sorts under the Bills of Sale Acts, the Sale of Goods Act, and the Moneylenders Acts. In order to avoid these legal obstacles, the finance house has to discard the role of a lender of money on security and it has become an owner of goods who lets them out on hire. So it buys the goods from the dealer and lets them out on hire to the appellant. The appellant has to discard the role of a man who has agreed to buy goods, and he has to become a man who takes them on hire with only an option to purchase. And when these new roles have been assumed, the finance house is not a moneylender but a hire purchase company free from the trammels of the Moneylenders Acts. So you arrive at the modern hire purchase transaction whereby (i) the dealer sells the goods to a finance house for cash; and (ii) the finance house lets them out on hire to a hirer in return for rentals which are so calculated as to ensure that the finance house is eventually repaid the cash with interest; and (iii) when the finance house is repaid, the hirer has the option of purchasing the car for a nominal sum. The dealer is the intermediary who arranges it all. The finance house supplies him with the printed forms, and he gets them signed. In the result, the finance

house buys a car it has never seen, and lets it to a hirer it has never met, and the dealer seemingly drops out.'

In fact there are two types of hire purchase contract. In one, the customer binds himself to pay hire charges over a certain period of time and at the end of that period he has an option whether to buy. For example, the customer may promise to pay 24 monthly instalments of £250 with the right to pay a further £2 at the end of the 24 months; if he pays the £2 he becomes the owner of the goods, but if he does not pay he should return the goods to the finance company. In the other type, the customer agrees to pay hire charges over a certain period of time and the contract provides that at the end of that period the customer will become the owner, but the contract contains a clause allowing the customer to back-out at any time and return the goods. Neither of these types of hire purchase contract is a sale of goods, because a contract of sale is one under which the customer promises that he will buy; yet in the hire purchase contracts the customer is never bound to buy. In the first type he has to pay the final fee before he becomes the owner and he has an entirely free choice whether he pays it or not. In the second type the buyer may back-out of the contract and therefore is not bound to buy. In contrast to hire purchase, credit sales and conditional sales are sales of goods, and the Sale of Goods Act 1979 applies to them in the same way as it does to normal cash sales, save for one or two special rules which we will examine in due course.

The 1974 Act

Hire purchase, credit sale and conditional sale contracts are all recognised by the Consumer Credit Act 1974 as contracts under which the customer is provided with credit; but they were not invented by the Act, they are contracts which have been recognised by the common law for many years. For example, in *Lee* v *Butler* [1893] 2 QB 318 the buyer under a conditional sale contract was held to be a person who had bought or agreed to buy goods, so as to be able to pass title under s9 of the Factors Act 1889; but in *Helby* v *Matthews* [1895] AC 471 the House of Lords held that the second type of hire purchase contract set out above was not a contract of sale because the customer could back out at any time by returning the goods. The Act defines these instalment contracts in s189, the relevant parts of which read as follows:

' "conditional sale agreement" means an agreement for the sale of goods under which the purchase price or part of it is payable in instalments, and the property in the goods is to remain in the seller (notwithstanding that the buyer is to be in possession of the goods) until such conditions as to the payment of instalments or otherwise as may be specified in the agreement are fulfilled;
"credit sale agreement" means an agreement for the sale of goods, under which the purchase price or part of it is payable in instalments, but which is not a conditional sale agreement;

"Hire purchase agreement" means an agreement, other than a conditional sale agreement, under which:

a) goods are bailed in return for periodical payments by the person to whom they are bailed, and

b) the property in the goods will pass to that person if the terms of the agreement are complied with and one or more of the following occurs:
- the exercise of an option to purchase by that person,
- the doing of any other specified act by any part to the agreement,
- the happening of any other specified event.'

These statutory definitions are no different to the common law definitions which are given above.

The Act contains a detailed code of consumer credit law and contains its own definitions and concepts, designed to ensure that it is clear. Undoubtedly the Act is a very good piece of draftsmanship, but like all statutes it creates problems as well as solving them. We deal with many of the most important definitions in section 1.2 of this chapter, but three must be set out here. The person who has been described as the customer above is known as the debtor because he received credit and has to repay it; the person who gives the debtor credit is the creditor (the creditor is almost always a company); and the person (if any) who supplies goods to the debtor is known as the supplier. These definitions may appear obvious, but they do contain at least one potential trap for the unwary. Where goods are sold by a shop to a finance company and the finance company then sells them to the debtor, the finance company is both supplier and creditor. The importance of remembering this will be seen in Chapter 3, where we explain the debtor's remedies if something goes wrong.

Those agreements which are governed by the Act are known as regulated consumer credit agreements; or regulated agreements, for short. We will define regulated agreements in section 1.2 below.

In order to try to ensure that creditors comply with their statutory obligations towards debtors, failure to comply with certain obligations is made a criminal offence. It is not necessary in this book to deal with these in any detail, because the only sanction is a criminal one, the debtor may not also sue for breach of statutory duty (s170(1)).

Where appropriate the debtor may apply for an injunction either requiring the creditor to comply with a duty or to prevent him from breaching one (s170(3)). This is rarely done, for two reasons. Firstly, debtors are unlikely to consult solicitors until after a breach has occurred, by which time it is usually too late; and secondly, there is often an effective sanction within the Act for breach of a creditor's duty. In many instances the credit agreement will be unenforceable without a court order if the creditor is in breach, and sometimes the agreement becomes wholly unenforceable.

Further general protection is given to the debtor by s173(1), which prevents credit contracts fom excluding provisions of the Act which are for the protection of the debtor. This operates in the same way as the most important provisions of the Unfair Contract Terms Act 1977, and will be looked at in more detail in Chapter 3.

1.2 Definitions

Regulated agreements

Definitions within s8

The policy of the Act is to control consumer credit agreements only. It does not apply to credit provided to commercial organisations. There is no Commercial Credit Act, so commercial credit is subject to the common law and certain other Acts, such as (where appropriate) the Unfair Contract Terms Act 1977. The definition of the type of agreement covered by the Act is contained in s8, which provides:

> '(1) A personal credit agreement is an agreement between an individual ("the debtor") and any other person ("the creditor") by which the creditor provides the debtor with credit of any amount.
> (2) A consumer credit agreement is a personal credit agreement by which the creditor provides the debtor with credit not exceeding £15,000.
> (3) A consumer credit agreement is a regulated agreement within the meaning of this Act if it is not an agreement (an "exempt agreement") specified in or under s16.'

'Individuals'

It is rather curious that the Act uses the word 'individual' to describe one of the necessary qualities of a debtor, because as well as individual men and women, groups of people working as a partnership and a human being who applies for credit along with a company count as individuals (this definition appears twice in the Act see ss189(1) and 185(5)).

The only entity which does not count as an individual is a limited company or a group of limited companies which apply for credit jointly (s189(1)). In English law a company is generally treated as though it were a separate person from those who set it up (*Saloman* v *Saloman & Co* [1897] AC 22), those who manage it (*Macaura* v *Northern Insurance Co* [1925] AC 619), those who own shares in it (*Underwood* v *Bank of Liverpool* [1924] 1 KB 775), those who work for it (*Lee* v *Lee's Air Farming Ltd* [1961] AC 12) and those who take the profits from it (*Wallersteiner* v *Moir* [1974] 1 WLR 991).

But it is important to note that a company is a 'person' not an 'individual' ('Person' includes a body of persons corporate or unincorporate see Interpretation Act 1978 s5 and Sch I). If a company wishes to raise money it can do so in various ways, the most important of which are regulated closely by the Companies Act 1985 (Companies Act 1985 ss80-116 (shares) and ss190-197 (debentures)) and case law (see Farrar's Company Law Chapters 13 and 18). Therefore there was no need to bring agreements made between finance houses and companies within the regulation of the 1974 Act. The Crowther Committee recommended that a separate Act should deal with commercial credit transactions, but, to date, no such legislation has been passed.

Once a human being or a group of human beings joins with the company in obtaining credit, however, the 1974 Act does apply. Therefore, an agreement is regulated if credit is being given to one or more human beings whether he or they act alone or in conjunction with a company or companies. The only debtor who is not an 'individual' is a limited company which obtains credit for itself, or along with other limited companies.

Although the debtor must be an individual, there is no such limitation on the creditor. It would, of course, be absurd for the Act to regulate only those credit agreements which are made between individuals and individuals, because the vast majority of credit contracts which need to be regulated are made between individuals and large finance companies. Section 8(1) accordingly says that a personal credit agreement is an agreement between an individual and any other person.

'Credit'

The Act only controls contracts by which a debtor is given 'credit'. Credit is defined in s9(1) as including 'a cash loan, and any other form of financial accommodation'. Unfortunately no explanation is given of the meaning of 'financial accommodation'. Goode has commented that the essence of financial accommodation is the deferment of a debt (Consumer Credit Legislation para 442). But this only helps us in so far as we are able to define when a debt is deferred. It is clear that overdrafts and sales of goods to be paid for in instalments over a number of months, are covered by s9(1); but there may be difficult cases. For example, there may be a sale where the price is to be paid within one month of the goods being delivered. In such a case the essence of the contract is that it is a cash sale and therefore there is a duty to pay, but the performance of that duty is delayed.

One of the main areas of dealing in goods which the Act regulates is hire purchase agreements. We have already seen that in a hire purchase contract the debtor hires goods and is not obliged to buy them unless he wishes to do so at the end of the agreed period of hire. The hire payments are, in theory at least, periodic payments for use of the goods and cannot be seen to be an immediate debt which is being paid in instalments (*Helby* v *Matthews* [1895] AC 471).

In conditional sale and credit sale agreements, on the other hand, there is deferment of a debt, because the agreement by the debtor that he will buy creates an immediate liability for the price which is being put off until some time in the future. Normally payment and delivery are concurrent conditions (Sale of Goods Act 1979 s28). In a credit sale the agreement is that property will pass in accordance with the normal rules in s18 of the Sale of Goods Act 1979 and a failure to pay on time may allow the seller to sue immediately for the whole of the outstanding price under s49 of that Act (see *Workman Clark & Co* v *Lloyd Brazileno* [1908] 1 KB 968). In conditional sales, however, a failure to pay may allow the seller to repossess the goods, because they still belong to him, rather than sue for the agreed price (see further Chapter 4 below). To avoid any doubt, s9(3) expressly provides that hire purchase agreements involve the provision of credit by the finance company to the hirer. The Act will only regulate an agreement if the amount of credit advanced does not exceed £15,000. Originally the figure was £5,000, but this was increased to £15,000 on 20 May 1985 (Consumer Credit (Increase of Monetary Limits) Order 1983). Under the now repealed Hire Purchase Acts, agreements were regulated provided the total price of goods supplied under the contract did not exceed a certain figure. The Consumer Credit Act, however, looks at the amount of credit which is advanced, not at the total price of any goods involved. So, for example, if Mr D wishes to buy a new car costing £20,000 and he places a £6,000 deposit and is allowed to pay the remaining part of the price in instalments, he is being given credit for £14,000 and the agreement will be within the financial limits of the Act.

The example just given does not make any mention of interest. In the real world interest-free credit is a great rarity and usually indicates a seller who is so desperate to show up well against his competitors that he is prepared to allow payment over a period without penalising the buyer for not paying in one lump sum. Where interest is charged, however, the amount of credit advanced is not affected.

The creditor may receive a benefit other than interest. The Act is concerned not just with how much interest is charged, but also with any other payments the debtor has to make. In other words it looks for what s20(1) refers to as 'the true costs to the debtor of the credit'; this true cost is known as the total charge for credit. The Consumer Credit (Total Charge for Credit) Regulations 1980 define how the total charge for credit is to be calculated. We will look at these regulations in more detail in section 1.5 below.

Exemptions

Once it has been established that there is a consumer credit agreement in which the amount of credit does not exceed £15,000, the only thing which can prevent it being regulated is if it falls within the category of exempt agreements. Exempt agreements are defined in the Consumer Credit (Exempt Agreements) (No 2) Order 1985, made under s16. The Consumer Credit (Exempt Agreements) Order 1989 which came into force 19 June 1989 consolidates the 1985 Order, but there are few major changes. There are five categories of such agreements, of which three fall within the discussion in this book. (The fourth category is certain consumer hire agreements (Art 6) and the fifth relates to consumer credit agreements secured on land (see Art 2)).

Firstly, low-cost agreements, where the rate of interest charged is low. In fact, it is not just interest which is taken into account in the calculations. Everything which falls within the total charge for credit can be looked upon as interest and, therefore, when the rate of interest charged is investigated those items must be included. This is done by calculating the rate of the total charge for credit. It is beyond the scope of this book to give all relevant formulae, they are contained in Regs 6-18 of the Consumer Credit (Total Charge for Credit) Regulations 1980. The rate of interest against which the rate of total charge for credit must be measured is the higher of

13 per cent and 1 per cent above the highest base rate of any of the major high street banks (Consumer Credit (Exempt Agreements) (No 2) Order Art 4).

Secondly, certain agreements where the number of payments to be made does not exceed four (Art 3. Only debtor-creditor-supplier agreements are affected by this Article, see below: Classification of agreements. There is one special case where the relevant number is one, see Art 3(1)(a)(ii). This is where the debtor is given a charge card and must settle his indebtedness to the charge card company at the end of the month, like American Express. Hire purchase and conditional sale agreements are never exempt, however, even if the number of repayments is small (Art 3(2)).

Thirdly, certain international trade contracts where the debtor is given credit in the course of his business (Art 5). Many such agreements will not be regulated however, because the debtor will be a company.

An agreement is not exempt where the amount of credit exceeds £15,000, because where that financial limit is exceeded, the agreement is not a consumer credit agreement at all, by virtue of the definition of such agreements in s8(2) (see section 1.2 above). Nevertheless, the effect of the financial limit being exceeded is the same as if the agreement were exempt.

There are two categories of agreement which are exempt from certain aspects of the Act, but which are treated like ordinary regulated agreements for other purposes. These are small agreements and non-commercial agreements.

Small agreements are regulated agreements under which credit not exceeding £50 is provided (s17(1)). Hire purchase and conditional sale contracts are never small agreements, even if the amount of credit does not exceed £50 (s17(1)(a)). The only practical effect of an agreement being a small agreement is that the detailed provisions about formation of the contract do not apply, but even this limitation is only applicable to certain small agreements (s74(2)). But s56 (see below: Negotiations) applies to all regulated agreements, small or not.

Non-commercial agreements are consumer credit or consumer hire agreements made by the creditor otherwise than in the course of a business (s189(1)). 'Business' has a very wide definition, and many contracts which would appear at first sight to be made not in the course of business are in fact business agreements and subject to the full rigours of regulation. In practice many people who borrow on a relatively informal basis are given the protection of the Act but are unaware of it. It is important to note that the agreement must be a 'consumer credit agreement' within the definition in s8(2). Again, agreements are not prevented from being regulated simply because they are non-commercial, but the important provisions of the Act which regulate the formation of agreements and the giving of information to the debtor during the currency of the agreement do not apply to them.

The Act controls regulated agreements by prescribing stringent rules in relation to advertising (s43-47; see also ss48-51 in relation to canvassing), formation of the contract (ss60-66) and information which must be given to the debtor in the course of the agreement so that he is in a position to see what his liabilities are from time to time (ss77-79). In addition, the remedies that the creditor would have at common law are subject to various rights in the debtor to ask the Court for relief by having the agreement varied (ss129-140) and the debtor has a statutory right to settle his liability early if he wishes (s94).

The classification of agreements

All regulated agreements must be further defined, in accordance with ss10, 11, 12 and 13 of the Act. In these sections there are three pairs of definitions: (1) running account credit and fixed sum credit; (2) restricted use credit and unrestricted use credit; and (3) debtor-creditor-supplier credit and debtor-creditor credit (more commonly known as DCS and DC, respectively). Every regulated agreement is classified in three parts - one part from each of the three pairs. For example, hire purchase agreements are classified as fixed sum, restricted use, DCS agreements.

Running account credit or fixed sum credit

Running account credit is provided where the debtor is enabled to obtain cash, goods or services up to a certain credit limit (s10(1)(a)). For example, if the debtor is given an overdraft facility on his bank account he may draw from his account up to an agreed maximum figure; of course, he is not obliged to use the full amount of credit available and he may make payments into his account in order to reduce the overdraft. Similarly, if a debtor is given a Barclaycard or Access card, he may draw cash or may purchase goods or services up to pre-determined maximum value and may pay back the cost over a period of time. The essence of running account credit is that the debtor is given a facility which he may use if he wishes and for which he pays interest only if he chooses to use it - if you have an Access card you are not obliged to use it and if you agree with your bank that you may overdraw on your current account you are not obliged to do so but you may if you wish: the facility is there for your convenience.

There may be times when the debtor exceeds his credit limit, but this will not usually affect the regulation of the agreement under which he is given the credit facility. For example, a debtor may have an overdraft limit of £15,000 but may be allowed to exceed this temporarily. As long as he is only allowed to exceed it temporarily the agreement by which he is given the overdraft will still be regulated (s10(2)). Similarly, if there is no formal limit on the overdraft but the debtor is not able to overdraw by more than £15,000, the agreement will still be regulated (s10(3)(b)(i)) and if the limit exceeds £15,000 but it is probable that no more than £15,000 will be drawn, the agreement is also regulated (s10(3)(b)(iii)).

All credit which is not running account credit is fixed sum credit (s10(1)(b)). Therefore, if a debtor is given a bank loan which attracts interest from the day it is given, whether or not the money lent is in fact used, he receives fixed sum credit. Also, if the debtor buys goods under a conditional sale or credit sale agreement or if he hires goods under a hire purchase agreement, he is given fixed sum credit.

Restricted or unrestricted use credit

The difference between restricted and unrestricted use credit is simple to define, although for various reasons the Act's wording is rather complicated. Unrestricted use credit is provided where the debtor is given money which he has the power to use as he pleases. Restricted use credit is provided where the debtor does not have control over the money which is advanced to him. This has the rather strange result that a credit agreement which appears to be for a restricted purpose may actually be an agreement for unrestricted use credit. For example, the debtor may be given a bank loan specifically for use in buying a car, but may withdraw the money from the bank and spend it on something else. He may be in breach of his agreement with the bank by not buying the car, but because he had the power to actually get his hands on the money the agreement would be for unrestricted use credit (s11(3)).

Section 11(1) sets out three types of restricted-use credit agreement:

> '(a) to finance a transaction between the debtor and the creditor, whether forming part of that agreement or not, or
> (b) to finance a transaction between the debtor and a person (the "supplier") other than the creditor, or
> (c) to refinance any existing indebtedness of the debtor's, whether to the creditor or another person.'

The reason for this division is that certain provisions of the Act apply to agreements which fall within one of the clauses but not to those within the others. The meaning of the three clauses is quite straightforward, although the distinction between restricted-use and unrestricted-use agreements set out above must be remembered. Clause (a) covers agreements where the debtor obtains goods or services from the creditor and pays for them over a period of time: for example, hire purchase or conditional sale contracts. Clause (b) covers agreements where the debtor buys goods or services from someone other than the creditor, and the creditor pays that supplier directly. If the debtor is given the money and has to pass it on to the supplier, the agreement is unrestricted-use because of s11(3). A common example of this type of restricted-use agreement is where the debtor uses his Barclaycard to buy goods - he buys goods from the shop (the supplier) and the supplier is paid directly by Barclaycard. Clause (c) covers agreements where the debtor borrows money from a creditor in order to pay-off existing debts, and the creditor pays the money directly to the person to whom the debtor owes that existing debt. Again, if the debtor is given the money and is trusted to pass it on, the agreement is for unrestricted-use credit because of s11(3).

Debtor-creditor-supplier (DCS) and debtor-creditor (DC) credits

The final classification is between DCS and DC agreements. The difference between these classifications is sometimes explained as the difference between connected lending and unconnected lending. Where the creditor and supplier are connected, the agreement is DCS. Where they are unconnected, or where there is no supplier but a simple loan of money, the agreement is DC. Section 12 defines DCS agreements and s13, DC. It is important to remember the way in which ss12 and 13 are drafted, because they do not have numbered sub-sections. The drafting of these sections is complicated by the need to distinguish between those cases where the creditor and supplier are connected and those where they are not. This distinction is drawn by asking whether there are 'pre-existing arrangements' between them and whether the credit is advanced in 'contemplation of future arrangements' between them. The meaning of these terms will be examined after s12 and 13 have been set out (see below: Further classifications).

Section 12 provides that the following types of agreement are DCS:

'(a) a restricted-use credit agreement which falls within s11(1)(a), or
(b) a restricted-use credit agreement which falls within s11(1)(b) and is made by the creditor under pre-existing arrangements, or in contemplation of future arrangements, between himself and the supplier, or
(c) an unrestricted-use credit agreement which is made by the creditor under pre-existing arrangements between himself and a person (the supplier) other than the debtor in the knowledge that the credit is to be used to finance a transaction between the debtor and the supplier.'

It will be remembered that agreements within s11(1)(a) are those where the debtor is given credit in order to finance a transaction between himself and the creditor. In such cases, because the creditor is also the supplier of any goods or services which are provided, there is the clearest possible connection between creditor and supplier. There is clearly no need to investigate whether there are any pre-existing arrangements.

Section 13 provides that the following types of agreement are DC:

'(a) a restricted-use credit agreement which falls within s11(1)(b) but is not made by the creditor under pre-existing arrangements, or in contemplation of future arrangements, between himself and the supplier, or
(b) a restricted-use credit agreement which falls within s11(1)(c), or
(c) an unrestricted-use credit agreement which is not made by the creditor under pre-existing arrangements between himself and a person (the "supplier") other than the debtor in the knowledge that the credit is to be used to finance a transaction between the debtor and the supplier.'

In the same way that s12(a) defines as DCS those cases where there could not possibly be a closer connection between creditor and supplier, so s13(b) defines as DC agreements for the refinancing of the debtor's debts, because there is no supplier in such cases. Between them, ss12 and 13 cover all regulated consumer credit agreements. As has been said already, it can be seen that ss12(a) and 13(b) state the obvious in relation to ss11(1)(a) and 11(1)(c). Sections 12(b) and 13(a) classify exhaustively all agreements which fall within s11(1)(b); as do ss12(c) and 13(c) in relation to unrestricted use credit agreements.

Further classifications: pre-existing and future arrangements

The definitions of pre-existing arrangements and future arrangements are contained in s187 and are somewhat elliptical. An agreement is entered into under pre-existing arrangements if it is entered into 'in accordance with, or in furtherance of, arrangements previously made' between the creditor and the supplier (s187(1) and (4)). In other words there are pre-existing arrangements where arrangements were made between the creditor and the supplier prior to the making of the regulated consumer credit agreement between creditor and debtor. Similarly, a consumer credit agreement is made in contemplation of future arrangements between the creditor and the supplier where it is made 'in the expectation that arrangements will subsequently be made between' the creditor and the supplier (s187(2) and (4)).

Section 187 does, however, extend the definition of these arrangements a little, by including arrangements made between: (1) the creditor and the supplier's associate; or (2) the creditor's associate and the supplier; or (3) the creditor's associate and the supplier's associate. A company is the 'associate' of another company if they are under common control (s184(3)). A person is an individual's 'associate' if he is that individual's spouse or relative or is the relative of the individual's spouse (s184(1)). For the meaning of relative, see s184(5), which is discussed in more detail at section 1.4 below.

In most cases it is clear whether there are pre-existing arrangements between the creditor and the supplier. An obvious example arises where a credit card is used - the shop cannot take payment by credit card unless it has been supplied with the necessary forms by the credit card company; in other words the shop cannot take such payment unless it has pre-existing arrangements with the credit card company. Similarly, if a garage advertises that it can arrange finance with a particular finance company, and has a stock of hire purchase forms in order to allow the debtor to make a hire purchase contract, there is the clearest possible evidence of pre-existing arrangements between the garage and the finance company.

Future arrangements may be more difficult to detect. For example, if the debtor wishes to borrow money to buy a car and the creditor agrees to pay the supplier directly, there will not be future arrangements if all that is envisaged is that arrangements will be made specifically to allow that single direct payment to be made (s187(3)). In other words, for there to be relevant arrangements between the creditor and the supplier, there must be a degree of permanence to whatever arrangements are made.

Hire purchase, credit sale and conditional sale contracts are always classified as fixed-sum (s10(1)(b)), restricted-use (s11(1)(a)), DCS (s12(a)) agreements. It is impossible for them to be classified in any other way.

Negotiations

In the vast majority of cases hire purchase, conditional sale and credit sale agreements are negotiated by the debtor with a shop or garage which has the goods he wants. The shop or garage is not the supplier of the goods because, as we have seen, they are sold to the finance company which then supplies them to the debtor. But the shop or garage is the only body with which the debtor negotiates direct.

Section 56(2) provides that a negotiator is the agent of the creditor. The definition of 'negotiation' is explained in Chapter 3, but for present purposes it means anyone who negotiates the credit agreement with the debtor, even if the negotiation only amounts to handing him a proposal form.

1.3 Multiple agreements

The classification of agreements as defined above is inadequate to explain properly the working of some types of credit contract, because it assumes that the contract is always classified in the same way. But, some credit agreements have more than one function. For example, if an Access card is used at a bank to withdraw cash, the transaction is DC and unrestricted use because there is no supply of goods or services and the debtor gets his hands on money; whereas if the card is used in a shop to buy goods the transaction is DCS and restricted use. Agreements which have a dual function, or more than two functions, are known as multiple agreements and are covered by s18.

There are three types of multiple agreement within s18: agreements which fall within more than one category; agreements which are partly within one category and partly within another; and agreements which are partly within one category and partly outside the Act altogether. Indeed there can be agreements which fall partly within one category, partly within another and partly outside the Act.

We have already seen that Access cards fall within two categories. Barclaycards are similar in operation except that when used as cheque guarantee cards they fall outside the Act because no credit is advanced. Nowadays there are many bank cards with similar dual functions.

The important part of the multiple agreement rules is in s18(2) which makes clear that a transaction entered into by the debtor must be broken down into its component parts and each part classified and considered separately. For example, if a customer goes into a shop and agrees to take a freezer on hire purchase at a total price of £250 and also buys £80 of frozen food, he makes two separate transactions; the hire purchase contract is regulated but the purchase of food is not (although it may in certain circumstances amount to a linked transaction: see section 1.4 below). Even if he pays £100 by a single cheque to pay for the food and puts down an initial payment of £20 on the freezer, the agreements made must be treated separately.

Hire purchase, conditional sale and credit sale agreements are not multiple agreements. Although they have two elements, the supply of goods to the debtor and the provision of credit to the debtor, the two are part of the same contract. Also, the Act's classification of such agreements involves consideration of the supply of goods element: in other words we cannot separate the supply of goods from the provision of credit because the classification of these agreements as restricted use under s11(1)(a) and DCS under s12(a) is only possible because there is a supply of goods.

1.4 Linked transactions

Linked transactions are contracts made by the debtor or a relative of his which are ancillary to a consumer credit agreement. The most obvious examples are contracts of insurance taken out at the insistence of the creditor when a car is taken on hire purchase. There are so many different examples of linked transaction that it is not possible for the Act to set out a list of such contracts, instead it defines three types of linked transaction in s19.

Section 19(1)(a)

The first is in s19(1)(a), and is transactions entered into in compliance with a term of the consumer credit agreement, which is known for the purposes of this section as the principal agreement. This is, perhaps, the most common type of linked transaction and covers contracts which are entered into because the principal agreement requires them to be entered into. For example, where it is a term of a hire purchase contract for a car that the debtor insures it.

Section 19(1)(b)

The second is in s19(1)(b). This covers transactions which are to be financed by DCS agreements. For example, if there is a loan to the debtor from a finance company to which he was introduced by the garage from which he then buys the car, there would be two separate contracts - the loan and the sale - and the sale would be a linked transaction in relation to the loan. Hire purchase, conditional sale and credit sale agreements cannot come within s19(1)(b), because there is no separate supply of goods. In other words, the supply of the goods and the giving of credit are all part of the same transaction, and s19(1) expressly provides that a transaction cannot be a linked transaction if it forms part of the principal agreement.

Section 19(1)(c)

The most complicated linked transactions provisions are in s19(1)(c). Linked transactions within this section are sometimes referred to as suggested linked transactions, because they are transactions entered into at the suggestion of the creditor, or a person who is represented by a negotiator, or some other person who knows of the existence of the regulated agreement or contemplates that the regulated agreement may be made (s19(2)). But not all transactions entered into at the suggestion of such a party will be linked transactions. The transaction must be made for one of three purposes:

1. To induce the creditor to enter into the principal agreement.
2. For another purpose related to the principal agreement.
3. For a purpose related to a transaction which is financed or to be financed by the principal agreement where the principal agreement is for restricted use credit.

The first of these three purposes is quite straightforward. If the creditor is prepared to sell a car to the debtor on conditional sale, but wishes him to insure the car, he may suggest to the debtor that a policy is taken out. If it is a term of the conditional sale agreement that insurance should be taken out then the insurance policy is a linked transaction within s19(1)(a), but if it is only suggested to the debtor it is linked within s19(1)(c)(i). The other party to the linked transaction would be the insurance company, not the creditor, but that does not matter so long as the person who suggests that the linked transaction be made is one of the people listed in s19(2).

The second purpose is not so simple. It certainly covers most insurance policies which provide for the repayment of the credit in the event of the debtor's incapacity to do so. A further purpose related to the principal agreement may arise if the debtor takes a new telephone on hire purchase and at the suggestion of the creditor or the telephone shop he makes a contract with British Telecom for a new telephone line to be installed to his house. Perhaps it would also apply if the debtor takes a car on hire purchase but cannot drive; if the creditor or negotiator suggests that the debtor takes driving lessons and a contract for driving lessons is then made that could be seen as a contract made for a purpose related to the principal agreement. It may also apply where a debtor takes a freezer on hire purchase and the shop with whom he negotiates suggests that he buys food to put in the freezer.

It is the third purpose which is the most difficult to define, because it is far from clear when a transaction is made for a purpose related to a transaction which is financed by a restricted use agreement. One example could arise where the debtor buys a car from a supplier who is paid direct by the creditor, the debtor repaying the creditor in instalments. If the supplier suggests to the debtor that he also buys a radio for the car, the purchase of the radio is clearly related to the purchase of the car and that purchase is what is financed by the principal agreement.

A linked transaction within paragraph a), b) or c) of s19(1) which is made prior to the making of the principal agreement will take no effect until the principal agreement is made (s19(3)). If the principal agreement is not made, therefore, the linked transaction will be of no effect. The Consumer Credit (Linked Transactions) (Exemptions) Regulations 1983, made pursuant to s19(4) exclude insurance contracts, contracts guaranteeing goods, deposit accounts and current accounts from the effect of s19(3). Such linked transactions will, therefore, be fully effective both by and against the debtor even if the principal agreement is not made.

Introduction

There is nothing to stop a linked transaction being a regulated consumer credit agreement: for example, if the debtor takes a car on hire purchase and, at the dealer's suggestion, also takes a stereo system on conditional sale. Where this happens each regulated agreement is a linked transaction in relation to the other.

Transactions need not be made by the debtor himself to count as linked transactions, because s19 applies to transactions made by the debtor or a relative of his. This is a necessary rules otherwise creditors or suppliers could avoid the linked transactions rules by requiring some other member of the debtor's family to insure goods supplied or enter into some other contract to their benefit. The debtor's relatives for these purposes are his brother, sister, aunt, uncle, nephew, niece, lineal ancestor or lineal descendent (s184(5)). This is a very wide definition and includes any parent, grandparent, great grandparent, etc, as well as any child, grandchild, great grandchild, etc; it includes illegitimate children, step-children and adopted children. It does not include the debtor's cousin or his cousin's children. Furthermore, by s184(1), it includes the debtor's spouse or former spouse and any relative of his spouse or former spouse. it does not include people who live together unless they are reputed to be married.

1.5 Total charge for credit

Additional charges

Because of the complex arrangements which can be made between creditors and debtors, it would be too simple for the Act merely to provide that the amount of interest charged shall be ignored when calculating the amount of credit. For example, C Ltd may sell a car to Mr D for £20,000 plus £1,000 interest, of which a deposit of £6,000 is paid immediately, and may in addition require him to take out one year's insurance on the car (at a cost of, say, £1,000) and to enter into a contract to have it serviced by C Ltd for five years at £300 per year. C Ltd could argue that the total package it is offering costs £23,500 (£20,000 for the car, £1,000 interest, £1,000 for insurance and £1,500 for servicing) so that when the interest and deposit are deducted the amount of credit is £16,500, which is above the maximum the Act will regulate.

Some additional charges are perfectly bona fide, but some can be a form of disguised interest, forcing the debtor to pay for additional services which he does not really want and may not need. In order to avoid such manoeuvres, s9(4) provides that any item within the 'total charge for credit' shall be ignored when working out how much credit is being advanced. Regulations made under s20(1) draw a distinction between charges which are made under bona fide transactions, and those which are disguised interest charges (Consumer Credit (Total Charge for Credit) Regulations 1980). The Consumer Credit (Total Charge for Credit and Rebate on Early Settlement) (Amendment) Regulations 1989 became operative 30

June 1989. They amend the 1980 regulations by requiring the inclusion in the total charge for credit of any fees payable by the debtor for brokerage arrangements. This relates to brokerage commission charges levied for both actual and prospective consumer credit agreements.

Charges not included

The Regulations work in two stages. At the first stage all charges payable by the debtor or a relative of his, whether they are said to be interest or not, are included in the total charge for credit (Reg 4, naturally the principal sum which is being advanced is not included, only 'charges' which are payable on top). In other words, it is presumed that every payment which the debtor has to make over and above repaying the amount of money 'borrowed', is interest on that sum. The second stage is that certain specific charges are then removed from the total charge for credit, so that only those charges which are true interest or disguised interest remain (Regs 3 & 5).

There are, in fact, many charges which are not included in the total charge for credit: for example, sums which are payable on breach by the debtor (Regs 5(1)(a) and 5(1)(b)), premiums on insurance policies entered into before the consumer credit agreement was entered into (Reg 5(1)(g)), premiums payable on a motor insurance policy (Reg 5(1)(h)), premiums under a life assurance policy where the insurance money will go towards paying the creditor what he is owed (Reg 5(1)(i)), bank charges which are payable when an account is overdrawn or in excess of the agreed overdraft limit (Reg 5(1)(f)), and charges for essential maintenance works on the goods which are being bought on credit terms (Regs 5(1)(e) and 5(2)).

To return to the example given above, the motor insurance premium on the car being bought by Mr D will not, therefore, count as part of the total charge for credit, but the maintenance contract will because it is not for essential maintenance but is payable in each of the first five years whether the car needs servicing or not. In the above example, then, the total charge for credit includes the £15,000 payable for the maintenance contract, but not the £1,000 insurance premium; making the amount of credit:

£23,500   -   £1,000   -   £6,000   -   £1,500   =   £15,000.
(Total)   (Interest)   (Deposit)   (Charge)   (Credit)

So the agreement falls within the Act's financial limits.

1.6 Variation of agreements

For various reasons the parties may wish to vary the terms of a regulated agreement so as to cater for changes in circumstances: for example, the debtor may lose his job and wish to pay smaller instalments over a longer period. If there is a variation the Act provides in s82(2) that the effect of this is to rescind the earlier agreement and replace it by the new agreement on the varied terms. The new agreement is known as a modifying agreement.

If the original agreement was regulated but the modifying agreement would not be if it stood by itself, the modifying agreement is treated as a regulated agreement unless it is for running account credit (s82(3)). Therefore, if the debtor is given a bank loan of £12,000 and then negotiates a further loan to be combined with the first for a further £10,000, the total amount of credit being provided is £22,000 and therefore the modifying agreement would appear to be unregulated; but because the original agreement was regulated, so the new one is treated as regulated.

Often the debtor has the right to cancel a regulated agreement within the seven days following the day it was made. We will examine the details of cancellation in section 2.4 below, but it is necessary to say something about it here. If an agreement is cancellable, the time during which the debtor may cancel is known as the 'cooling-off period'. During this time the debtor may, by written notice, extinguish the agreement completely. There are some instances in which parts of the agreement remain enforceable (see 2.4 below), but generally cancellation results in the agreement being treated as though it had never been made. The Act allows a modifying agreement to be cancelled in some circumstances, but not always.

It is possible that the original agreement was varied within the cooling-off period. If this happens the modifying agreement is cancellable but only for as long as the original agreement would have remained cancellable had it continued to exist (s82(5)). Where the original agreement was not cancellable, or where it was cancellable but the cooling-off period has expired, the modifying agreement is not cancellable (s82(6)). At first sight, this is a rather surprising provision because there could be cases where the original agreement was not regulated at all but the modifying agreement is both regulated and, on the face of it, cancellable. It may be that s82(6) is only meant to apply where the original agreement was a regulated agreement, but the words of s82 do not seem to confine its operation to agreements which modify regulated agreements, so it is probably the case that s82(6) applies to all modifying agreements whether the original agreement was cancellable or not and whether it was regulated or not.

1.7 Licensing

An important protection given to the public is the requirement in s21(1) that a licence is needed if a person wishes to carry on a consumer credit business. A consumer credit business means, simply, a business under which regulated consumer credit is provided (s189). It is for the Director General of Fair Trading to decide whom to license and the granting of licences is not a matter of pure formality because the applicant must satisfy the Director General that he is a fit and proper person to hold a licence (s25(1)). In many ways the licensing of consumer credit businesses is similar to the licensing of premises for the consumption of alcohol, save that liquor licences are granted to individual people whereas consumer credit licences are granted to businesses in their business names. A register is kept of licences currently in force.

In deciding whether to grant a licence the Director General must take into account all relevant circumstances, including whether the applicant or any employee, agent or associate of his has committed offences of fraud, or has breached any requirements of the Act, or has practised racial or sexual discrimination, or has engaged in deceitful or oppressive business activities (s25(2)). Where the applicant is a company the Director General must also take into account whether the controller of the company or any associate or his has acted in any of the ways set out in s25(2). This is of particular importance because it prevents unsuitable people obtaining licences by hiding behind the name of a company.

Forms of licence

There are two types of licence, namely the standard licence and the group licence (s22(1)). A standard licence allows a named person (including a named company) to carry on such activities as are described in the licence. A group licence is rather more flexible because it allows the Director General to license several different people to carry on consumer credit businesses without all of those people having to apply for separate licences. Naturally the purpose of a group licence is to allow people who are in fact working as a group to obtain one licence between them. Of course, the Director will investigate the suitability to hold a licence of each of the people involved, and the licence only authorises the named people to carry on the business.

If a standard licence is granted to a partnership or company, it will allow the partnership or company to carry on a consumer credit business without the individual employees having to be licensed. But there are many situations in which it is convenient for separate companies within the same group to be covered by a group licence in the name of a holding company. Group licences can only be issued where it appears to the Director General that the public interest is better served by issue of such a licence than by requiring the individual members of the group to be licensed separately (s22(5)).

Failure to obtain a licence

Anyone who carries on a consumer credit business without a licence commits an offence (s39(1)). Similarly, a person who is allowed under a standard licence to conduct a consumer credit business under a particular name but carries on such a business under a different name, commits an offence (s39(2)). Both offences are punishable on trial in the Magistrates' Court with a maximum fine of £2,000 (Magistrates' Courts Act 1980 s39(2)); or, if tried in the Crown Court, with a maximum penalty of two years imprisonment or an unlimited fine or both

(Consumer Credit Act 1974, Schedule 1). These criminal penalties do not of themselves help the debtor who is given credit by an unlicensed creditor, but s40(1) makes the agreement unenforceable against the debtor unless an order is obtained from the Director General allowing enforcement. In deciding whether to make such an order the Director General must ask how far, if at all, debtors have been prejudiced by the creditor being unlicensed, whether a licence would have been likely to have been granted if it had been applied for and the degree to which the creditor is to blame for not applying (s40(1)). This allows the necessary flexibility to protect debtors where they need protection but to uphold agreements where the creditor has acted fairly throughout and has simply overlooked the need for a licence.

A person is not precluded from applying for a licence if he has committed an offence under the Act, although it is something which is required to be considered by the Director General under s25(2). Therefore an unlicensed creditor may still be granted a licence even if he has been prosecuted and fined for carrying on his business without one.

In addition to the requirement in relation to creditors, persons who act as credit brokers must also be licensed (s147(1)). In fact there are various other activities which must be licensed and which are known collectively as ancillary credit businesses. Of the ancillary credit businesses, we are only concerned with credit brokers in this book. A credit broker is someone who effects introductions of potential debtors to persons who carry on consumer credit businesses (s145(2)). This includes shops and garages who introduce customers to finance companies.

Effect on agreements

If a credit broker is not licensed, any agreement made as a result of the introduction is unenforceable against the debtor unless the Director General orders that it is enforceable (s149(1)). The Act requires that the creditor applies to the Director General for such an order (s149(2)), and again the Director General should consider the extent to which the debtor was prejudiced by the credit broker being unlicensed and the degree to which the creditor was to blame (s149(4)). The credit broker commits an offence by acting in that capacity when unlicensed (ss39(1) and 147(1)) and is liable to the same penalty as is an unlicensed creditor (Magistrates' Courts Act 1980 s39(2) and Consumer Credit Act 1974 Schedule 1).

Duration of licences

Standard licences operate for 10 years from the date stated on the licence which must not be earlier than the date of issue (Consumer Credit (Period of Standard Licence) Regulations 1975). The Director General has power to revoke or suspend a licence where the creditor or credit broker commits an offence. This is not a general power exercisable at the Director General's will, but is only available where he would refuse to renew the licence if it ran out (s32(1)). In other words, if something happens, such as the commission of an offence under any consumer protection legislation, and the Director General feels that he would not renew the licence of the creditor or credit broker who commits the offence if it expired, he may suspend or revoke the licence. But before doing so he must give the licensee the opportunity to make representations. The creditor or credit broker may apply for a suspension to be lifted (s33); and if his licence has been revoked he may apply for a new one, although the revocation will militate against it being granted.

2

Formation of the Contract

2.1 Advertisements

2.2 Making the contract

2.3 Formalities

2.4 Withdrawal

2.5 Cancellation

2.6 Canvassing

2.1 Advertisements

Bear in mind that, such is the degree of protection given by the law to consumers, the Consumer Credit Act 1974 permits regulations to be made by the Secretary of State as to the form and content of advertisements for loans.

For example the Consumer Credit (Advertisements) Regulations 1989 require advertisement for loans secured by way of a mortgage or charge on the debtor's home to carry on the face of the advertisement the following warning: 'Your home is at risk if you do not keep up repayments on a mortgage or other loan secured on it.'

In *R* v *Secretary of State for Trade & Industry, ex parte First National Bank plc* [1990] The Times 7 March a bank sought a declaration that such a warning was ultra vires the Consumer Credit Act 1974 s44. The bank held that such requirements were unfair since there were no similar provisions for unsecured loans. The Court of Appeal affirmed the decision of the court of first instance that such a requirement was neither unfair nor unreasonable and not ultra vires the Act of 1974. The exact status of a contract made in circumstances in which the preliminary advertising material contravenes consumer credit regulations was not at issue. Certainly it seems likely that in considering whether a bargain is 'unconscionable' (see Chapter 6) the courts would take this into account.

In *Mersoja* v *H Norman Pitt Ltd* (1989) The Times 31 January an advertisement for Renault cars placed by a garage in sundry newspapers and displayed at their sale room clearly stated that the APR was 0 per cent. The complainant, a trading standards officer, visited the garage and asked about the offer. It transpired that the 'trade-in deal' was to be adjusted downwards in order to allow the garage to recover the cost of financing the deal. The trade-in deal offered on the complainant's car was £250–350 less than he would otherwise receive if he paid cash or arranged his own finance. Both the Consumer Credit Act 1974 s46 and the Consumer Credit (Advertisements) Regulations 1989 provide that no advertisement shall be false or misleading when offering credit. If it is misleading an offence has been committed.

It was found that the lower trade-in value was indeed a way of exerting a hidden charge on what was supposed to be free credit. Therefore an offence had clearly been committed. There is still, however, no direct ruling by any court as to the potential status of any contract made as a result of such an advertisement.

2.2 Making the contract

Offer and acceptance

The Act does not specifically state that consumer credit agreements have to be contracts, but by their nature they are. Normal rules of offer and acceptance and consideration apply. The reader should be familiar with the rules of offer and acceptance, so only a brief resumé will appear here.

We will see below that, generally, regulated agreements must be made in writing in order to be enforceable against the debtor. At common law there is no such requirement for simple contracts and there is nothing to stop a contract for the provision of credit being made orally or partly orally and partly in writing. In practice, however, there are two ways in which the contract may be made. Both methods of formation require a written offer and acceptance. In both the debtor is given a standard form which contains details of the credit being advanced, including where appropriate details of goods being supplied to him. If the form has already been signed by the creditor (which inevitably means a human agent where the creditor is a company), it is the creditor who makes an offer and by his signature the debtor accepts that offer. Alternatively the debtor may sign the form which is then submitted to the creditor who counter-signs it; in such a case the debtor makes the offer which is accepted by the creditor. It is this latter method of creation which is the more common, although the former is far from unknown. In the latter situation the form is known as a proposal form because the debtor signs it and thereby makes a proposal (the offer) to the creditor.

The contract is made when acceptance is complete, which means when the offeror has notice of it unless the postal acceptance rule applies. The postal acceptance rule says that where it is reasonable to post the acceptance, it is effective as soon as it is put in the post box or handed to a postman who has authority to collect letters. It is arguable that the postal acceptance rule should not apply to regulated agreements because it would create manifest absurdity or inconvenience for the debtor to be bound by something he has not seen (*Holwell Securities Ltd* v *Hughes* [1974] 1 WLR 155; [1974] 1 All ER 161).

At common law a shop or garage which negotiates a hire purchase contract is the agent of the creditor for the purpose of receiving notice of revocation if the debtor decides he does not wish to enter the contract (*Financings Ltd v Stimson* [1962] 1 WLR 1184; [1962] 3 All ER 386). It seems that the shop or garage is also the creditor's agent for the purpose of accepting or rejecting the debtor's offer (*North West Securities Ltd v Alexander Breckon Ltd* [1981] RTR 518), although the proposal form itself may provide that only the creditor may accept or reject the offer and if it does so this common law agency does not arise.

In the vast majority of cases it will not matter how the contract is made, but the interpretation of certain sections of the Act may depend on the proper construction of the offer and acceptance rules. In particular the debtor is often entitled to receive a copy of the agreement within the seven days following its making. This means within the seven days following the acceptance, so it is necessary to know when the offer is accepted. This right to receive copies of documents will be discussed further in section 2.3 below.

It is thought to be extremely unlikely that any judge could be persuaded to hold that the contract was made in any way other than the two set out above, although in theory it may be arguable in some cases that oral agreement is reached and the written form merely puts into writing the oral contract.

Professor Guest (*The Law of Hire Purchase*, page 157) has suggested that proposal forms are properly seen as invitations to treat and that it is the creditor who makes the offer if he accepts the proposal. It is thought that this view is not correct because the debtor is not treated as having a right to refuse to complete once the proposal has been signed and sent back to him. There is a statutory right to cancel in some cases (see section 2.5 below), which is clearly envisaged as giving the debtor a right which he does not possess at common law. If he had the option to reject an offer from the finance company there would be no need to give him an additional right to cancel which, if anything, is more restrictive than the right to reject an offer, because the right to cancel can be lost by passage of time whereas the debtor's silence could not constitute acceptance at common law (*Felthouse v Bindley* (1863) New Rep 401). We will therefore assume that in all cases the contract is made by written offer and acceptance in one or other of the two ways set out above.

Deposits

The debtor is frequently asked to pay a deposit and to submit that to the creditor along with the signed proposal form. If the creditor refuses the proposal the debtor is entitled to the return of the deposit because it was paid on the understanding that it would be returned if no contract came about (*Branwhite v Worcester Works Finance Ltd* [1969] 1 AC 552; [1968] 3 All ER 104). In theory it is possible for a creditor to demand a non-returnable deposit as a condition of considering proposals, but unless such a demand appears clearly on the face of the proposal form any deposit will be refundable.

Regulated agreements

There can be two added complications where goods are supplied under the regulated agreement. Firstly, the formation of the regulated agreement may depend upon a shop or garage selling the goods to the creditor; and secondly, the debtor is sometimes allowed possession and use of the goods before the contract is made.

If the formation of the regulated agreement is dependent on the sale of goods to the creditor, the failure of that sale to take place will inevitably mean that the regulated agreement is not made. The normal practice is for the debtor to sign the proposal form which is sent by the shop or garage to the creditor along with an offer from that shop or garage to sell the goods to the creditor. Once the creditor has checked the creditworthiness of the debtor it will either reject both offers or accept both.

In such cases the debtor is often required to declare that he has no interest in the goods. The purpose of this is to avoid the provisions of the Bills of Sale Acts 1854 - 1891. If someone (A) sells goods to another (B) and then leases them back on hire purchase, a written agreement to that effect must be registered in order to be enforceable. The document evidencing such a transaction is a bill of sale and its true nature is that A is lent a lump sum which he repays in instalments and the loan is secured by the transfer of ownership of the goods to B. If A makes all repayments he gets back ownership of the goods, but if he does not make all repayments he forfeits ownership. If, however, A (a debtor) has declared that he has no interest in goods which are sold to B (a creditor) by a third party (a shop or garage), B can sue him on this declaration if it turns out that he was the owner and the hire purchase agreement is unenforceable.

If the debtor is given possession of goods before the regulated agreement is made, he is a bailee of them and will be obliged to take reasonable care of them and return them to their true owner if the contract is not made.

Other aspects of formation

As to the legal effect of an improperly executed agreement, whether liability exists thereunder, see *R v Modupe* (1991) The Times 27 February. M in making a HP agreement for a Mercedes 190E car gave a false name and address, and was convicted of evading a liability by deception. The agreement was improperly executed. The person filling in the details failed to add the total amount payable in cash and balance payable. Section 61(1) of the 1974 Consumer Credit Act provided that a regulated agreement was not properly executed unless the document contained all the prescribed terms and also conformed to the Consumer Credit (Agreements) Regulations 1983, para 11, in Schedule 1 of which required information as to the total amount payable. It was suggested that there could be no liability under such an agreement.

The House of Lords disagreed. The fact that the agreement was not properly executed and enforceable only by order of a court, did not mean there was no existing liability. There was liability, albeit it would be necessary for an aggrieved creditor to seek a court order to enforce the agreement.

Finally, on the common law aspects of formation, if the debtor signs a proposal form in which various details are left blank, and trusts the creditor or shop owner to fill in the correct details, he runs the risk of letting himself in for a contract on terms he does not want. If the shop owner fills in a higher total price than the debtor expects and the creditor accepts this offer, he will not be able to argue that the contract is void for mistake because it is his own fault for not ensuring that the document signed was complete (*United Dominions Trusts Ltd* v *Western* [1976] QB 513; [1975] 3 All ER 1017, following *Saunders* v *Anglia Building Society* [1971] AC 1004; [1970] 3 All ER 961). There may be exceptional circumstances in which the debtor is not bound by a document signed in blank, although it is clear from *Mercantile Credit Co Ltd* v *Hamblin* [1965] 2 QB 242; [1964] 3 All ER 592 that the facts must be quite exceptional.

2.3 Formalities

Form of agreement

The Act does not alter the common law rules on formation of contracts, but it does provide for the debtor to receive documents from which he is able to consider the effect of what he has signed. The relevant provisions are in ss60 to 65 and fall into two parts, regulations about the form in which the consumer credit contract must be made and regulations about documents the debtor should be given. Section 74(1)(b) excludes agreements by which debtors are allowed to overdraw on current bank accounts from the need for the formalities requirements to be complied with. By s74(3) that exclusion only applies where the Director General of Fair Trading has made a determination that particular banks are exempt. However, s38 of the Banking Act 1979 added a new sub-section (s74(3A)) to the 1974 Act, so that the Director must determine that the main banks are exempt from having to comply with ss60-64. The Director General made such a determination in General Notice No 29.

The rules about the form of the contract are simple in principle but very detailed. Section 60 allows for regulations to be made prescribing the form and content of documents embodying regulated agreements, and s61(1) requires the document to contain all of the terms of the agreement other than implied terms. In other words it is not open to the creditor to argue that there was express oral agreement which overrides the written terms. The regulations are the Consumer Credit (Agreements) Regulations 1983 and their general effect is to require the document which the debtor signs to be legible (reg 6) and also to state all relevant information about how the agreement operates (Schedule 1).

The information which must be presented on the documents, according to Schedule 1 is as follows: (i) The form must have a heading which sets out the nature of the agreement, for example 'Hire Purchase Agreement regulated by the Consumer Credit Act 1974'; (ii) it must name the parties and give their postal addresses; (iii) if it is a DCS restricted use agreement it must describe the goods being supplied and the cash price; (iv) obviously it must state the amount of credit being provided; (v) the amount of any deposit which the debtor pays; (vi) the total charge for credit; (vii) the total amount payable; (viii) the amounts and times of repayments; (ix) the APR; (x) any security given by the debtor; and (xi) if it is a running-account agreement the credit limit must also be stated.

If the agreement is not in the prescribed form or is not signed by both creditor and debtor or is not readily legible when presented to the debtor, it is improperly executed (s61(1)) and cannot be enforced by the creditor without a court order allowing its enforcement (s65(1)).

Copies of documents

Immediate entitlement to copies

When the debtor signs a proposal form or an agreement which has already been signed by the creditor, he is, with one exception, always entitled to a copy of what he signs 'there and then'. If the agreement is handed personally to the debtor and he signed it before the creditor he is entitled to a copy by virtue of s62(1) and if the creditor has already signed it a copy must be provided by virtue of s63(1). Similarly, if the agreement is sent to the debtor for his signature, he must also be sent a copy so that he can sign and send back the agreement but keep the copy for himself (s62(2)).

Exceptions to the rule

The exceptional case when the debtor is not entitled to a copy is where the agreement is neither presented personally to him for his signature nor sent to him. This would happen if the debtor picks up a proposal form from a pile of them in the negotiator's office. In such a case ss62(1) and 63(1) would not apply and the debtor would not be entitled to a copy of the form there and then when he signs it.

If, for example, the debtor's wife is handed the form and asked to pass it on to him, when she hands it to him s62(1) or 63(1) applies and a copy must therefore be delivered to him there and then when he signs it. This could cause problems because he may sign it at home when the creditor is not present and it would not be possible for the creditor or negotiator to deliver a copy to him 'there and then'. This problem also arises if the debtor himself is handed the form but takes it away to consider it and signs it when the creditor or negotiator is not present. It would not be good enough for him to be given two forms to take away, because the Act requires the copy to be handed to him there and then when he signs it and the second form would have been handed to him too early.

Additional copies

In addition to usually being entitled to a copy of the agreement when he signs it, if it was not executed when he signed it (that is, if s62(1) applies) he is entitled to receive a copy of the executed agreement within the seven days following the making of the agreement (s63(2)). It is important to note that the time when this copy must be delivered to the debtor is within the seven days following the making of the agreement, not within the seven days following its execution. The agreement will be executed when both debtor and creditor have signed it, but it will only be made when the debtor's offer has been accepted. As we have seen this may only be on postage of the copy to the debtor or on its actual receipt by him.

As we shall see below, in some cases the copy which is required to be given to the debtor by s63(2) must be posted. In such cases it is not necessary that it arrives within seven days, merely that it is posted then.

According to s62(1) the debtor is entitled to receive a copy of the unexecuted agreement and under ss63(1) and (2) he is entitled to receive a copy of the executed agreement. This is rather misleading because it seems to suggest that he must be presented with an exact copy of what he has signed showing his signature and, where the agreement is executed, the signature of the creditor. But the Consumer Credit (Cancellation Notices and Copies of Agreements) Regulations 1983, Reg 3(2) states that the signatures may be omitted from the copies. Therefore, the debtor is not necessarily entitled to a photocopy or carbon copy of what he signs. It will suffice to give him an unsigned copy of the form which he signed, provided of course that it contains the same terms. In practice the copy handed to the debtor will often be either a photocopy or a carbon copy. These days it is common for the debtor to be handed a form for signature made from special chemically treated paper which has the effect of a carbon copy when the top copy is written on by ball point pen but does not actually involve sheets of carbon paper.

Where the debtor is not entitled to a copy there and then because the agreement was not handed to him personally for signature, he will nonetheless be entitled to a copy of the executed agreement within the seven days following the making of it (s63(2)). There is, therefore, no case in which the debtor is not entitled to a copy of the executed agreement and the only effect of s62(1) is that he is also entitled to a copy of the unexecuted agreement in cases within that subsection.

Other documents

In all cases, whether the debtor receives a copy by virtue of s62(1), 62(2), 63(1) or 63(2), he is also entitled to a copy of any document referred to in the regulated agreement. This normally means documents by which the debtor or someone else gives security; for example if a man and woman who live together are joint debtors under a conditional sale contract by which they buy a car, the creditor may require one of them to deposit a building society book and signed withdrawal slip so that if they do not pay the instalments the creditor may withdraw money from the building society. A copy of the security agreement must be delivered to both debtors along with the s62 or s63 copies.

The normal method of delivery of copies of documents is by either handing them directly to the debtor or by sending them by post. Where it must be delivered there and then the only practicable method of delivery is by handing it over in person. Copies which must be delivered by virtue of s63(2) are usually sent by post and if the agreement is cancellable (as to which see section 2.4 below) the s63(2) copy must be sent by post (s63(3)). Documents sent by post will only be delivered if they actually arrive. The rules which say that a document served by first-class post is served on the second working day after postage, and if sent by second-class post, the fifth working day after postage, do not apply where a document must be 'delivered' rather than 'served'.

Notices of cancellation rights

We will see below that some regulated agreements are cancellable by the debtor. Where this is the case every copy of the executed or unexecuted agreement which is delivered to the debtor must contain a box setting out that he had the right to cancel (s64(1)(a)). In cases where the debtor is not entitled to a copy of the executed agreement within the seven days following its making, he is entitled to receive a separate notice of his cancellation righs within those seven days (s64(1)(b)).

This means that in the case of cancellable agreements the debtor is always entitled to a notice of his right to cancel within the seven days following the making of the contract. So, in cases within ss62(2) or 63(1) where the agreement is executed when the debtor signs it, he is given an extra reminder of his right to cancel.

Variation

Lombard Tricity Finance Ltd v *Paton* [1989] 1 All ER 918. In an agreement regulated by the Consumer Credit Act 1974 the defendant entered into a credit agreement with the plaintiff finance company to finance a loan to buy a computer.

A box on the face of the agreement stated that the rate of interest payable on the credit balance was 'subject to variation by the creditor from time to time'.

The question arose as to whether such variation was permissible. In considering this the Court of Appeal decided that it was lawful for the finance company to vary the rate of interest unilaterally. The Consumer Credit (Agreements) Regulations 1983 [Reg 2 Sch 1 para 19] which govern the form and content of consumer credit agreements do not make it unlawful for a finance company to make such a provision. Nor does either the 1974 Act or the 1983 Regulations require a lender to state the circumstances under which the rate of interest might be varied; nor to state that the lender had an absolute discretion to vary. The clause permitting unilateral variation of the interest rate was therefore allowed to stand.

Formation of the Contract

Effect of non-compliance

If the debtor is not given a copy to which he is entitled under s62, the agreement is not properly executed (s62(3)). The same applies to breaches of the s63 requirements (s63(5)) and to failure to serve the second copy of notice of cancellation rights (s64(5)).

If the agreement is not properly executed it cannot be enforced without a court order (s65(1)). The order made is known as an enforcement order (s127), and we will look at these in detail in Chapter 6, below. In cases where ss62 or 63 has been breached the court may not make an enforcement order unless the creditor gives the debtor the correct copy of the agreement before proceedings are instituted (s127(4)(a)). This allows the creditor to remedy his failure to comply with the Act. But no remedy is possible if the notice of cancellation rights required by s64(1)(b) was not delivered because s127(4)(b) prevents the court from making an enforcement order in such a case under any circumstances.

2.4 Withdrawal

Change of heart by the debtor before formation of contract

If a person makes an offer but changes his mind before acceptance of it, he is entitled at common law to revoke the offer by informing the offeree of his decision to revoke. If the offer has been accepted then the contract is made and there is no right to withdraw, save that if both parties are happy to simply rescind the contract then they may do so. In order to revoke an offer it is necessary for the offeror to communicate the decision to revoke to the offeree. There is no postal revocation rule. Clearly the requirement of communication is satisfied if the offeror informs a properly authorised agent of the offeree of the revocation. In addition *Dickinson* v *Dodds* (1876) 2 Ch D 463 holds that revocation of an offer is effective if the offeree is informed by anyone of the offeror's intention to revoke, whether or not the informant is authorised to do so.

The Act does not vary these rules in so far as they apply to the revocation of an offer, although it does give the debtor a right to cancel a regulated agreement after formation in some circumstances. We will look at cancellation in section 2.4 below.

Where an offer has been made but not yet accepted, as where a person signs a proposal form and submits it to a finance company for consideration, that offer may be revoked at any time before acceptance. The terminology of the Act is not entirely satisfactory in such cases. Section 57(1) allows withdrawal from what is called a prospective regulated agreement. But if all that has happened is that an offer has been made, there is no agreement yet. Section 57(3) mentions the creditor and debtor, but if no agreement has been made there is no creditor or debtor there is simply a proposal from a person to a finance company. This criticism is not entirely fair, because the use of 'creditor' and 'debtor' is not in any way confusing, and the definitions of creditor and debtor in s189 include prospective creditors and debtors.

Change of heart by creditor before formation of contract

In addition to allowing the debtor to revoke his proposal, s57 also allows a creditor who has made an offer to revoke it. In practice a creditor is unlikely to make an offer to provide credit unless he has first checked the creditworthiness of the debtor, so the chance of him ever wishing to revoke his offer is slim.

In order to withdraw all the offeror has to do is give notice to the offeree. The notice need not be in writing and it may be expressed in any way; it will be effective provided it indicates the intention to withdraw (s57(2)).

Various people are the agents of the creditor for the purpose of receiving notice of withdrawal. An obvious example is a credit broker or supplier who is a negotiator in antecedent negotiations (s57(3)(a)); this includes shopkeepers who act as negotiators in hire purchase transactions. But, rather strangely, anyone who in the course of his business acted on behalf of the debtor in the course of any negotiations is also treated as the creditor's agent (s57(3)(b)). The reason why the Act provides that such a negotiator is the creditor's agent is that, because the debtor is negotiating through that person the most obvious way for him to revoke his offer is by telling his negotiator.

Section 19(3) states that a linked transaction entered into before the making of the regulated consumer credit agreement has no effect until such time as the regulated agreement is made. Therefore, if a linked transaction is agreed upon and then the debtor withdraws his offer to make a regulated agreement, the linked transaction never takes effect.

The general rules about the effect of withdrawal are contained in s57(4) which provides that withdrawal has the same effect as cancellation. We look at cancellation in the next section, but in outline the position is that on cancellation the debtor has to give back anything he has received and is entitled to receive back anything he has given to the creditor. The picture in relation to linked transactions following withdrawal, therefore, is that the linked transaction does not take effect and all parties must give back anything they have received.

2.5 Cancellation

Cancellable agreements

Once a regulated consumer credit agreement is made it is, at common law, fully binding on both parties. We have seen that a failure to comply with the formalities provisions may mean that it is improperly executed and unenforceable against the debtor, but this does not mean there is no contract and if in fact it is performed it will be fully effective. Of course, at common law a party to a contract may not unilaterally withdraw from it just because he changes his mind, yet under the Act some regulated agreements are cancellable by the debtor. The rules are in ss67 to 73.

Conditions for a regulated agreement to be cancelled

Section 67 lays down four conditions to be fulfilled for a regulated agreement to be cancellable.

Firstly, the antecedent negotiations must have contained oral representations. There is no requirement that these representations should take any particular form; so, to take an extreme example, if a representative from a finance company calls on the debtor and says 'I am John Smith from the finance company' and nothing else is said before the debtor signs the proposal form, there have been oral representations. In reality the reason for this requirement is that where a regulated agreement is made wholly by correspondence there is no likelihood of the debtor having been pressurised into it by a pushy salesman, whereas once they meet face to face that risk is present and the debtor may need protection. It should be noted that the use of the plural 'representations' includes a single representation (Interpretation Act 1978, s6(c)).

The second requirement is that the oral representations must have been made by the negotiator when in the presence of the debtor. This is a rather difficult requirement to define and explain because it would appear not to cover telephone calls, yet considerable pressure may be put on the debtor over the telephone. But it would appear to cover representations made when the debtor is present even though they are not made to him and are not intended to be heard by him. For example, if the debtor enters a garage and while waiting outside the sales office overhears a telephone call in which the salesman tells another customer that a particular make of car is extremely reliable, and the debtor relying in part on what he has heard subsequently takes such a car on hire purchase; it is hard to see what mischief the debtor is being protected against. Furthermore, there is no requirement that the representations should relate to the credit agreement. So, to use the last example again, the representation made is that the car is extremely reliable. This may be true and there is no reason why the debtor should be allowed to cancel the hire purchase contract as a result of it; but all that s67 requires is that there are representations.

The third requirement is that the oral representations must be made by a negotiator or someone acting as a negotiator or on his behalf. Clearly it would be unfair to allow the debtor to cancel because of something said by someone for whom the creditor cannot be properly held responsible.

The final requirement is that the unexecuted agreement was signed by the debtor at premises other than those on which the creditor or negotiator conducts a business whether permanently or temporarily, or on which a party to a linked transaction (other than the debtor or his relative) carries on a business. In other words, if the agreement is signed by the debtor off trade premises (to use a phrase from s49(2)), it may be cancellable. The mischief here is, apparently, that a debtor who signs an agreement on the business premises of the creditor or negotiator may feel pressurised by the unfamiliar surroundings, yet if he signs it at home or at his business premises he will be able to consider it more calmly and carefully.

The reference to the debtor signing the unexecuted agreement is peculiar because it is not possible for him to sign anything else. Even if it has been signed by the creditor first, it is only executed once the debtor has signed it and while he is signing it it is still unexecuted. It is unclear whether this aspect of s67 is meant to confine cancellability to agreements which were signed first by the debtor.

There is a further provision in s67 which restricts the cancellability of regulated agreements which are secured on land, but these are outside the scope of this book.

When to cancel

A cancellable agreement is cancellable during what is known as the 'cooling-off period'. This period starts when the debtor signs the unexecuted agreement and ends at the end of the fifth day following the day on which he receives his second notice of cancellation rights (s68). If the agreement is signed first by the debtor he is entitled to a copy of what he has signed there and then and to a copy of the executed agreement within the seven days following the making of the agreement. In such cases the notice of cancellation rights must appear upon the face of the agreement in the box headed 'Your Right to Cancel' and the copy of the executed agreement must be accompanied by a form which the debtor should fill in if he wishes to cancel (Consumer Credit (Cancellation Notices and Copies of Documents) Regulations 1983, Reg 5).

If the agreement becomes executed when the debtor signed it he is entitled to a copy there and then and must be sent a copy of the notice of cancellation rights within the seven days following the making of the agreement. That notice must not be a copy of the whole agreement, but must be on a single sheet of paper and must be accompanied by a cancellation form (Reg 6).

Until the agreement is executed the debtor may withdraw under the power in s57, but even if he says he is cancelling when in fact he is withdrawing, his withdrawal will be effective by virtue of s57(2).

Because the cooling-off period ends at the end of the fifth day following receipt of the second notice of cancellation rights, if that notice is not sent or is sent late the agreement is indefinitely cancellable. This is the result of the wording of s68(a) which says that the cooling-off period ends at 'the end of the fifth day following the day on which (the debtor) received a copy under s63(2) or a notice under s64(1)(b)'. If the copy or notice is served late it is not a copy under s63(2) or a notice under s64(1)(b), because those sections only apply to documents which are served in time. The creditor cannot make good his failure to serve a document on time by serving it late - if it is not served on time it is not served at all.

This can have a drastic effect on the creditor because the consequences of cancellation are that the debtor gets back everything he has paid (see below: How to cancel). Where the agreement is indefinitely cancellable it seems possible for the debtor to have use of goods supplied under a hire purchase, conditional sale or credit sale agreement for many months and then cancel and get back all his money. Whether this effect was intended by the draftsman is not known. If, however, the agreement is fully performed by the debtor it will be discharged and there will be nothing for him to cancel. So, if he was not served with the proper documents according to s63(2) or s64(1)(b), but he pays everything under the agreement, he will not then be able to cancel.

How to cancel

Cancellation must be in writing. This is not apparent from s69 which merely says that 'a notice of cancellation' must be served. But s189 defines notice as meaning 'notice in writing', and any doubt on this is cleared up by comparing s69 with s57 which expressly allows notice of withdrawal to be 'written or oral'. No particular form of words is required provided the debtor makes clear his intention to cancel, and it is not necessary for the debtor to use any cancellation form which the creditor has given him (s69(1)).

Notice of cancellation must be served on the creditor or any person specified by the creditor as being his agent for the purpose of receiving a notice of cancellation or on anyone else who is the creditor's agent (s69(1)). It does not matter in what capacity the person is the creditor's agent. In particular it is not necessary for the creditor to have nominated him as a person on whom notice of cancellation may be served. Perhaps the most important agent is the negotiator; he is the creditor's agent during negotiations by virtue of s56(2) and so a debtor may serve notice on him. This, of course, includes the dealer with whom the debtor first comes into contact.

Service can be effected by actually handing over the notice (s176(8)), or by sending it by post to him, properly stamped and addressed, or by leaving it at his proper address (s176(2)). A person's proper address is his last known address. It is the knowledge of the server which matters (s176(3)).

Effect of cancellation: recovery of money

The first effect of cancellation is to cancel the regulated agreement and any linked transaction and also to withdraw any offer the debtor or his relative may have made to enter into a linked transaction (s69(1)).

The general principle is that on cancellation both the debtor and creditor should be put back into the position they were in before the regulated agreement was made, because on cancellation a regulated agreement is treated as though it had never been entered into (s70(4)). Therefore, the debtor gets back any money he has paid (s70(1)(a)); he is also released from any obligation to pay any more, whether it should have been paid at some time before cancellation or would only have become payable in the future (s70(1)(b)). In cases within s12(b) the supplier is a separate person from the creditor but is paid by the creditor direct. If the creditor has already paid the supplier and then the debtor withdraws from the regulated agreement, the creditor is entitled to get back what he has paid (s70(1)(c)).

The debtor is entitled to recover money he has paid from the person to whom it was originally paid (s70(3)). In many hire purchase, conditional sale or credit sale cases this may be the dealer and not the creditor. It seems that if the dealer does not have the money, the debtor may not be entitled to recover it from the creditor direct; save that since the dealer will have received the money as the creditor's agent it could be argued that the creditor is the proper person from whom it should be claimed. If the agreement fell within s12(b) the creditor and supplier are jointly and severally liable to repay the debtor (s70(3)).

These rules on the repayment of money apply to money paid under a linked transaction as they do to money paid under a regulated agreement, and they apply to money paid by a relative of the debtor as they apply to money paid by the debtor himself (s70(1)).

There are special rules to deal with cases other than hire purchase, conditional sale and credit sale. Where the agreement is for credit other than DCS restricted use credit the cancellation of the agreement does not give rise to it being totally eliminated. In such cases the agreement continues in force so far as it relates to the repayment of credit and the payment of interest (s71(1)). What this means is that the cancellation of the agreement merely cancels the duty of the debtor to pay anything other than interest. This is a particularly important provision in relation to loans because if the debtor has actually been given money he must be under an obligation to repay it.

In all cases other than hire purchase, conditonal sale and credit sale the debtor must pay interest if he fails to repay the whole of the credit within one month of cancellation (s71(2)). If he has repaid some of the credit advanced by the expiry of the month then he only has to pay interest on that part of the credit which he has not repaid (s71(2)). Also, if he has not repaid all of the credit within the month he is not liable to repay it unless the creditor requests repayment in writing, setting out how much is payable (s71(3)).

Effect of cancellation: goods and work

Duty to restore

The normal rule is that the debtor must restore goods to the supplier on cancellation (s72(1)). There are two exceptions to this in s70(2)).

1. The first is that if the agreement is hire purchase, conditional sale or credit sale and finances the doing of work or the supplying of goods to meet an emergency, the effect of cancellation is to translate the credit agreement into an agreement to

pay cash for the work or goods. In other words, instead of paying in instalments the debtor becomes liable to pay the price of the work or goods immediately; but, of course, he does not have to pay anything other than the cash price. This has the effect where goods are supplied of turning the contract into one of sale even if it was originally hire purchase.
2. The second special case arises where, prior to service of the notice of cancellation, goods supplied have been incorporated into land or other goods by the act of the debtor or his relative. An example of this would be where the debtor is supplied with kitchen units which he builds and fits into his house prior to cancellation. This case gives rise to a problem: what happens if it is the creditor who incorporates goods into the debtor's land?

If the debtor makes a contract to take a fitted kitchen on hire purchase and the creditor is responsible for installing it, it is hard to look upon that installation as being done 'by the act of the debtor or his relative'. It is artificial to say that the creditor acts as the debtor's agent when installing the kitchen. He is not the debtor's agent at all, the kitchen will be installed because part of what the debtor bargains for and agrees to pay for is the work of installation. The result in such a case seems to be that the debtor does not have to pay for the kitchen (because of s70(1)) and does not have to return the goods (because they are no longer 'the goods supplied' but have become fixtures). This is a ridiculous result because contracts for the supply of fitted kitchens are very often made on hire purchase terms. But the words of the Act seem to allow the debtor to keep the kitchen without paying for it. It seems likely that the courts will find the debtor liable to pay a reasonable sum for the goods which have become incorporated into his land, but this would be contrary to s69.

In almost all other cases where goods are supplied prior to cancellation of a hire purchase, conditional sale or credit sale agreement, the debtor is under a duty to restore them to the creditor (s72(4)). This duty extends to goods supplied under a linked transaction provided the regulated agreement was hire purchase, conditional sale or credit sale (s72(1)). Because the agreement has been cancelled it is no longer appropriate to refer to the debtor as the debtor, so he is known as the possessor and the supplier is known as the other party (s72(2)(a)).

The duty to restore is not a duty to redeliver the goods, but a duty to make them available for collection from his premises following a written request from the other party (s72(5)). He may redeliver them without such a request if he wishes and if he delivers them to any person on whom he could have served a notice of cancellation or sends them to such a person, he will have effected redelivery (s72(6)). Naturally he is under a duty to take reasonable care to see that the goods are not damaged in transit and are actually received (s72(7)). But his duty in this respect is only to take reasonable care and he will satisfy the duty by packing the goods in a reasonable manner and using any reputable carrier, including the Post Office.

Duty of care
While the possessor has possession of goods he is under a duty to take reasonable care of them (s72(4)). He is also deemed to have been under that duty since he first obtained possession (s72(3)). This duty is a statutory duty and its breach gives rise to liability in tort for breach of statutory duty even though it may also amount to negligence at common law (s72(11)).

The duty of care after cancellation does not last indefinitely. It ceases after 21 days unless the possessor has received a written request to restore the goods and has not complied with it, in which case the duty lasts until the goods are restored to the other party (s72(8)). It is not known what duty, if any, the possessor owes after the expiry of the 21 day period. It is thought that his duty is to refrain from wilfully damaging the goods.

The provisions of s72 do not apply to perishable goods, goods which by their nature are consumed by use and which are in fact consumed prior to cancellation, goods supplied to meet an emergency or goods which before cancellation had become incorporated in any land or thing (s72(9)). This subsection makes sense at first reading because its effect is that if goods cannot be restored to the other party, they do not have to be restored. But do they have to be paid for? We have seen that in relation to goods supplied to meet an emergency and goods which are incorporated into land or some other thing by the act of the debtor, the debtor becomes under a duty to pay for them on cancellation (s69(2)).

But that duty is not extended to perishable goods or goods which are consumed or goods which are incorporated by the act of someone other than the debtor. It would seem peculiar that someone should be able to make a contract for the supply of, say, coal on hire purchase, burn the coal, cancel the agreement and not have to pay the cash price for it. As stated above, it is thought that the courts would impose an obligation to pay because cancellation is a right which the debtor can exercise even without a breach by the creditor or supplier and it would be thoroughly unjust for him not to have to pay. To date there is no reported authority on the point.

Effect of cancellation: part exchange

It is common for people who take a car on hire purchase, conditional sale or credit sale to give their old car in part-exchange. Of course, it should not be thought that part-exchange transactions are restricted to cars, but they are the most common example. Normally the part-exchange goods are retained by the negotiator who pays the creditor for them. If the regulated agreement is cancelled it may not be possible for those goods to be returned to the debtor, so special rules are laid down in s73.

Unless within ten days following cancellation (including the date of cancellation) the part-exchange goods are returned to the debtor in condition substantially as good as when they were delivered to the negotiator, the debtor is entitled to be paid a sum of money by the negotiator (s73(2)); if the agreement fell within s12(b) the creditor and negotiator are jointly and severally liable to pay that sum. The sum of money is known as the part-exchange allowance.

Often a value for part-exchange goods will have been agreed during negotiations, and if it was that figure is the part-exchange allowance (s73(7)(a)). But if it was not, the part-exchange allowance is a reasonable sum (s73(7)(b)). The debtor has a lien over goods supplied to him under the regulated agreement to secure the return of the part-exchange goods or the payment of the part-exchange allowance (s73(5)). This means that he may retain possession of the goods until he is given the part-exchange goods or the part-exchange allowance. The duty to restore goods in s72(4) is subject to this lien. The lien is a possessory lien only, it does not entitle the debtor to sell the goods supplied to him and to take a sum equal to the part-exchange out of the proceeds of sale. If he did sell the goods he would be liable for the tort of wrongful interference (Torts (Interference with Goods) Act 1977).

Once the debtor is given the part-exchange goods or paid the part-exchange allowance his lien is discharged and his duty to restore the goods supplied under the regulated agreement is itself restored. If he is paid the part-exchange allowance, any rights of ownership he may have had in the part-exchange goods pass to the negotiator (s73(6)), and this is the case even if it is the creditor who pays the debtor the allowance.

Effects of cancellation: linked transactions

The normal effect of cancellation of the regulated agreement is that linked transactions, including prospective linked transactions, are also cancelled (s69(1)). By s69(5) regulations may be made to exclude some linked transactions from the normal effect of cancellation. The relevant regulations are the Consumer Credit (Linked Transactions) (Exemptions) Regulations 1983. The important class of such linked transactions is insurance contracts (Reg 2(2)(a)).

Contracts of insurance are exempted from cancellation because the debtor may get the benefit of the insurance policy even if the regulated agreement is cancelled. For example, if the debtor is required to take out a policy of life insurance in order to ensure that money will be available if he dies to repay the credit advanced to him; that policy will remain to the debtor's benefit even though the regulated agreement is cancelled and this is particularly so if the regulated agreement is covered by s71.

Some contracts of insurance, however, are more directly related to the regulated agreement: for example, insurance of a car which has been taken on hire purchase. There can be no possible benefit to the debtor from that policy once he has cancelled, because the car is no longer at his risk. However, since he will no longer have an insurable interest in the car, so the policy will cease to have effect anyway. But, since it was not treated as though it never existed, if the debtor has already had cause to make a claim under it, that claim will survive cancellation of the regulated agreement.

Withdrawal

It should be remembered that because of s57(1), these effects of cancellation are also the effects of withdrawal. Some of them cannot arise on withdrawal, however, because by definition the regulated agreement would not have been made.

It is quite possible for the debtor to be given the goods as soon as he signs the agreement, even if the agreement must be countersigned by the creditor before it is executed. Because of this the rules on restoring goods and on part-exchange goods can apply on withdrawal as they do on cancellation.

2.6 Canvassing

The detailed regulation by the Act of advertising is outside the scope of this book, but something must be said about canvassing. Canvassing is the soliciting of individuals for the purpose of getting them to enter into regulated agreements (s48(1)). But not all soliciting counts as canvassing. If there has been a prior request for the solicitor to visit the debtor, the solicitation carried out is not canvassing (s48(1)(b)), but the request must be in writing (s49(2)). Also canvassing can only take place on what under the Hire Purchase Acts were known as 'trade premises'. This phrase is not used in the general definition of canvassing in s48, but s48(2) makes clear that canvassing can only take place at premises on which the creditor, the supplier, the canvasser or the debtor carries on a business, whether permanently or temporarily. If the premises are business premises then the solicitation does not count as canvassing.

A particular evil which the Act tries to control is door-to-door selling of loans because there are a great many people of limited means who could be persuaded by unscrupulous creditors to take loans at exorbitant rates of interest. Therefore it is an offence to canvass debtor-creditor credit 'off trade premises' (s49(1)). Presumably the use of the phrase 'off trade premises' relates back to s48(2). The offence is punishable in the Magistrates' Court with a maximum fine of £2,000 and in the Crown Court with an unlimited fine and/or up to one year's imprisonment.

The canvassing of other types of credit will also be an offence unless the canvasser is licensed (s39(1)). Therefore DCS credit, like hire purchase, may be canvassed only by those who are licensed to do so. That a licence may allow this is implicit in s23(3).

3

The Creditor's Obligations

3.1 Implied terms

3.2 Debtor's remedies

3.3 Transfer of ownership

3.4 Information

3.1 Implied terms

Introduction

Both conditional sales and credit sales are sales of goods and therefore the creditor's obligations to provide goods of a certain quality are governed by the Sale of Goods Act 1979 (see above: Chapters 4 and 5 of Sale of Goods). There is one special provision in relation to the doctrine of acceptance in conditional sale contracts; this will be examined in section 3.2 (below).

Hire purchase contracts are not sales of goods (*Helby* v *Matthews* [1895] AC 471) and therefore are not governed by the Sale of Goods Act 1979, but similar implied terms are contained within the Supply of Goods (Implied Terms) Act 1973. The working of these terms is not exactly the same as those under the 1979 Act although for some purposes they are identical in their effect.

Title

We have seen that the effect of s12 of the 1979 Act is that the seller of goods is in breach of condition if he does not have the right to sell at the time ownership is to pass. If the contract is a sale he must have that right at the time the contract is made, if it is an agreement to sell he must have the right at the time the agreement to sell is translated into a sale.

Section 8(1)(a) of the 1973 Act provides that it is an implied condition of hire purchase contracts that the owner (creditor) will have the right to sell the goods at the time when the property is to pass. This appears to allow a creditor to let goods which he does not own, and which he has no right to let, on hire purchase provided he becomes the owner by the time the final instalment is paid. In fact that is not the case because the Act only deals with the position if the contract is successfully completed, it does not deal with the time during which the goods are being hired.

At common law there is an implied term that the creditor must have the right to sell throughout. In *Warman* v *Southern Counties Car Finance Corporation Ltd* [1949] 2 KB 576; [1949] 1 All ER 711 the debtor (Warman) paid all the instalments under a hire purchase contract for a car, but then the true owner of the car, London Finance Corporation, claimed it from the debtor who agreed to give up possession. The debtor then sued to recover all payments from the creditor, the creditor counterclaimed arguing that although they had not been able to give the debtor title at the end of the day they had been able to give him possession and that that is what the hire payments were paid for. Finnemore J held that for two reasons the finance company had no right to retain anything for the debtor's use of the car. Firstly, the whole purpose of the hire charges being paid was so that the debtor could become the owner at the end of the day; they were not simple hire payments in return for use. Because the debtor never became the owner so the main purpose for which the hire payments were made failed and it could not properly be said that he had received what he had paid for. Secondly, the effect of the creditor's counterclaim was that they were claiming to be entitled to money for letting the London Finance Corporation's goods. No one has the right to let goods which are not his unless he is authorised to do so by the true owner and, therefore, he cannot claim to be entitled to any money for having let those goods.

Rather surprisingly *Rowland* v *Divall* [1923] 2 KB 500 was not cited to Finnemore J, although his judgment is entirely consistent with the Court of Appeal's decision in that case. The only case which was cited was *Karflex Ltd* v *Poole* [1933] 2 KB 251 in which the debtor failed to make all repayments, following which the car was repossessed and the creditor sued for damages. The debtor counterclaimed for the return of all money he had paid on the ground that the creditor was never the owner of the car. The King's Bench Divisional Court held that the debtor could recover all payments he had made because the whole contract was conditional on the creditor being the owner throughout. Goddard J said, obiter, that he was not deciding the position where the creditor honestly believed that he was the owner. It was this point which Finnemore J in *Warman* decided in favour of the debtor.

Atkin LJ's dictum in *Rowland* v *Divall*, that there is a total failure of consideration if the buyer under a sale contract does not get ownership, cannot directly be applied to hire purchase cases because the instalments the debtor pays are for use. But, as was made clear in *Karflex Ltd* v *Poole* and *Warman* v *Southern Counties Car Finance Corporation Ltd*, the debtor is nevertheless paying for not only use of the goods but also the contingent right to become their owner if he continues paying, and therefore there is a total failure of consideration if he never has use coupled with that contingent right.

The implied term that the creditor should be owner throughout was expressly declared by Goddard J in *Karflex Ltd* v *Poole* to be a condition not a warranty.

Therefore the debtor under a hire purchase contract will always be entitled to bring the contract to an end if he discovers that the creditor never had the right to hire the goods to him.

Although there is no authority on the point, it is likely that the creditor will be able to remedy any defect in his title by buying the goods from the true owner before the debtor brings the contract to an end, following the dicta of Pearson J in *Butterworth* v *Kingsway Motors Ltd* [1954] 1 WLR 1286; [1954] 2 All ER 694 (see above Chapter 4 Sale of Goods). If the debtor does bring the contract to an end before the creditor perfects his title, however, the creditor will be obliged to refund all money paid.

In addition to the condition implied by s8(1)(a), there are also implied warranties that the goods are free from encumbrances and that the creditor will not interfere with the debtor's quiet possession (s8(1)(b)). These operate in the same way as the implied warranties in s12(2) of the Sale of Goods Act 1979.

Description and sample

Section 9(1) of the 1973 Act implies a condition identical in effect to that in s13(1) of the 1979 Act. There is no reason to suppose that this section will ever need to be construed differently to s13.

Section 9(1) also provides that where a letting on hire purchase is by reference to sample and description the goods must match not only the sample but also the description. Furthermore, the general rules in s15 of the 1979 Act about sales by sample are reproduced in s11 of the 1973 Act for lettings by sample on hire purchase.

Quality

Section 10 of the 1973 Act contains provisions implying conditions of merchantable quality and fitness for purpose into hire purchase contracts. The wording is effectively the same as that in s14 of the 1979 Act. As with the 1979 Act it is subsection 2 which deals with merchantable quality, and subsection 3 with fitness for the debtor's particular purpose. Because most hire purchase contracts are negotiated by shops or garages in their capacity as credit brokers, it is provided in s11(3) that the debtor makes known his particular purpose sufficiently if he makes it known to the credit broker. The definition of merchantable quality is the same as in sale cases and is found in s15(3).

There are cases where judges have applied the Sale of Goods Act implied conditions on quality to hire purchase cases (see, for example, the Court of Appeal's recent decision in *Shine* v *General Guarantee Corporation Ltd* [1988] 1 All ER 911); although this is clearly incorrect, it cannot affect the result save that the doctrine of acceptance does not apply to hire purchase (see section 3.2 below).

3.2 Debtor's remedies

Position of the dealer at common law

Because most hire purchase contracts are entered into as a result of the debtor visiting a shop or garage and negotiating only with the dealer, it is necessary to make the creditor responsible for the acts of the dealer if the debtor is to be fully protected. If a dealer makes a misrepresentation to the debtor which induces him into taking goods on hire purchse, that will not allow the debtor to sue the creditor unless the dealer is the creditor's agent, because usually the dealer himself does not make a contract with the debtor.

There are statutory rules creating such an agency in s56 of the 1974 Act, but at common law the dealer is not always the agent of the creditor. In *Branwhite* v *Worcester Works Finance Ltd* (supra) the House of Lords held, by a majority of 3 to 2, that the dealer was not the agent of the finance company when receiving payment of a deposit from the debtor. This case did not lay down any general rule because the House approved a dictum from Pearson LJ in *Mercantile Credit Co* v *Hamblin* (supra) that whether the dealer is the creditor's agent is a matter of fact to be decided from case to case. Indeed it will be remembered that in *Financings Ltd* v *Stimson* (supra) and *North West Securities Ltd* v *Alexander Breckon Ltd* (supra) the dealer was held to be the creditor's agent.

If the dealer is the creditor's agent when making representations to the debtor then there is no difficulty in holding the creditor responsible for any representations which turn out to be false. But sometimes the dealer may be personally liable for misrepresentations made. If the relationship between debtor and dealer falls within *Hedley Byrne & Co Ltd* v *Heller & Partners Ltd* [1964] AC 465; [1963] 2 All ER 575 then he may be liable for the tort of negligent misstatement. It is unlikely that the relationship of dealer and debtor is covered by the *Hedley Byrne* rule in the vast majority of cases. A more appropriate way to hold the dealer personally responsible for his false statements is by finding a contract between him and the debtor.

In *Andrews* v *Hopkinson* [1957] 1 QB 229; [1956] 3 All ER 422 a debtor took a car on hire purchase after being told by the dealer, 'It's a good little bus. I would stake my life on it. You will have no trouble with it.' The car broke down shortly after delivery and the debtor sued the dealer for damages. McNair J held that the representation amounted to a promise from the dealer that the car was of merchantable quality and that the promise became binding on him once it was acted on by the debtor entering into the hire purchase contract. McNair J followed *Shanklin Pier Ltd* v *Detel Products Ltd* [1951] 2 KB 854; [1951] 2 All ER 471, holding in effect that the dealer had said, 'If you take the car on hire purchase from the creditor, I promise that it is merchantable.' Like any other unilateral offer, once it was acted on in the way prescribed it made the offeror liable in damages if the result he promised did not materialise.

It does not appear from the reports of this case why the debtor did not sue the creditor for breach of the implied condition of merchantability. Whether or not the dealer had made the false statement about the quality of the car the debtor was entitled to receive a car of merchantable quality. Nevertheless, the decision is good law on the relationship between debtor and dealer, although there are probably very few cases where it is more advantageous to sue the dealer than the creditor.

Andrews v *Hopkinson* is also authority that a motor dealer who is directly responsible for the supply of a car to a debtor can be liable in negligence if the goods are dangerous. Of course, the law of negligence has developed considerably since 1956, but it would not deprive a debtor of a remedy in negligence where carelessness can be proved because the existence of a duty of care could not seriously be disputed.

Position of the negotiator under the Act

The 1974 Act does not impose any direct liability on the dealer for false statements or promises he may make to the debtor; therefore, if an action is to be maintained against him it will be necessary to rely on either *Hedley Byrne & Co Ltd* v *Heller & Partners Ltd* or *Andrews* v *Hopkinson*. But the Act does create an agency relationship between the dealer and the creditor.

The relevant section is s56. In general terms the purpose of s56 is to make the creditor liable for statements made by: (1) himself, or (2) a shop or garage which sells goods to the creditor which the creditor then lets on hire purchase or sells on conditional sale or credit sale to the debtor, or (3) a supplier who sells goods to the debtor under a contract which is financed by a DCS agreement within s12(b) or (c). The person who conducts negotiations is the negotiator. So far in this chapter he has been referred to as the dealer.

By virtue of s56(4), antecedent negotiations start when the negotiator and the debtor first enter into communication, which includes when the debtor reads an advertisement published by the negotiator. Section 56(4) also provides that any representation made by the negotiator and any dealings between himself and the debtor amount to antecedent negotiations. What this means is that any communications between the two are antecedent negotiations, whether they are directly or indirectly related to the credit agreement and even if they are nothing to do with the credit agreement.

If the creditor is also the negotiator he cannot possibly seek to avoid responsibility for misrepresentations otherwise than by an exclusion clause. If the negotiator is someone other than the creditor, the creditor is responsible for his acts because s56(2) states that the negotiator is deemed to be the agent of the creditor even if he also acts in his own capacity. It is necessary for s56(2) to make the negotiator the creditor's agent because, as we have seen, *Branwhite* v *Worcester Works Finance Ltd* holds that the negotiator is not always the creditor's agent at common law.

Any clause in a regulated agreement which attempts to evade the effect of s56(2) by stating that the negotiator is not the creditor's agent is void (s56(3)). But it is only that clause which is void, not the whole contract.

Creditor's liability

Because the negotiator is the creditor's agent, the debtor will have a remedy against the creditor if the negotiator makes a misrepresentation which induces the debtor into the regulated agreement. It does not matter whether the misrepresentation is about the credit agreement or about the goods supplied, provided it is a representation of present fact.

Where the regulated agreement involves a supply of goods from the creditor to the debtor, any defect in the goods or failure of them to match their description gives the debtor a direct contractual remedy against the creditor. This covers hire purchase, conditional sale and credit sale. He does not take the goods under a contract with the negotiator, but under a contract with the creditor. Therefore, his remedy for breach is exerciseable against the creditor. If the creditor has made a misrepresentation the debtor's remedy, again, is exerciseable directly against the creditor; and if it is the negotiator who has made a misrepresentation he has done so as the creditor's agent, so, yet again, the debtor's remedy lies against the creditor. The creditor's responsibility for the acts of the negotiator arises by virtue of s56(2) only, no other provision of the Act is relevant.

Other credit agreements are different. If the debtor is given a loan to enable him to buy a car, he makes two separate contracts - a credit contract with the creditor and a contract of sale with the supplier. If the credit contract is DCS within s12(b) or (c), the supplier is a negotiator and, although the contract to buy the car is made between supplier and debtor, the creditor will nonetheless be responsible for misrepresentations made during the course of negotiations because of s56(2). But this is of little use to the debtor if the goods turn out to be defective. The fact that the negotiator is the creditor's agent during negotiations does not of itself mean that the negotiator is the creditor's agent when he sells the goods to the debtor. For example, if the debtor goes into a garage and buys a car using a loan which he has obtained because of pre-existing arrangements between the garage owner (supplier) and the finance company (creditor), the loan will be DCS within s12(b), but the contract of sale is a separate agreement made between the debtor and the supplier only.

In such cases the debtor may have a remedy against the creditor if the goods are defective because of s75. This provides, in s75(1), that where a debtor under a DCS agreement within s12(b) or 12(c) has a claim against the supplier for breach of contract or misrepresentation, he has a 'like claim' against the creditor. It is important to note that s75 is only applicable where the credit agreement falls within s12(b) or 12(c). In *Porter v General Guarantee Corporation Ltd* [1982] RTR 384 it was held that s75 applied to a hire purchase contract. This is simply wrong; hire purchase is DCS under s12(a) not under s12(b) or (c).

Section 75 can only be used if the cash price of each item of goods about which complaint is made is more than £100 and less than £30,000 (s75(3)). This is primarily designed to prevent a person who buys goods using a credit card from suing the credit card company when something goes wrong with goods of a small value. His proper remedy is against the shop which sold the goods.

There are certain difficulties of interpretation of s75(1), particularly because of the use of 'like claim' to describe the remedy of the debtor against the creditor. A few examples should illustrate the way s75(1) works and the difficulties of construction.

There is little by way of decided cases to throw any light or construction, although in the much criticised *UDT* v *Taylor* (1980) SLJ 28 a Sheriff's Court took the view that, if a debtor is entitled to rescind the supply contract, he is also entitled to rescind the credit contract. The two contracts in the eyes of the court came within the ambit of 'like claims'. However, most authorities incline to the view that 'like claim' refers to monetary claims only.

So for example, if the debtor takes out a loan which falls within s12(b) or s12(c) on 3 January in order to buy a car, following a misrepresentation made to him about the car by the negotiator on 30 December, and then buys the car, he may wish to rescind the sale contract. In such a case the taking of the loan is also induced by the misrepresentation because it was made before the loan was taken. If the debtor wishes to rescind the loan contract he may do so by virtue of s56(2); but it seems he may also do so by virtue of s75(1). He has a right of rescission against the supplier and a 'like claim' against the creditor. There is nothing wrong with allowing rescission of the loan contract because it was induced by a misrepresentation, and the debtor is not made any better off by s75(1) because he is fully protected by s56(2).

If the debtor takes out the loan on 3 January and the supplier makes a misrepresentation about the car on 10 January, and the debtor then buys the car from the supplier, a remedy open to the debtor against the supplier is to seek rescission of the sale contract. If he does rescind the sale contract, is he also entitled to rescind the credit contract on the ground that he is given a 'like claim' against the creditor by s75(1)? It seems that this must be the result of s75(1), and there are strong arguments in its favour. If the debtor is obtaining the loan in order to make a particular purchase it makes sense to allow the loan to be rescinded if the sale contract is rescinded; otherwise the debtor is left having to repay a loan which he may no longer need. On the other hand, the loan contract was made properly, it was not induced by the misrepresentation, and it is arguable that it is not fair to the creditor to allow the loan to be rescinded. There is no authority to help on this point.

If the debtor buys a car on 1 February, agreeing to pay for it by a number of monthly instalments and is then introduced to a creditor who advances a loan on 3 February to allow him to raise the money to pay the supplier, the sale contract will be concluded before the credit agreement is made. If the car turns out to be unmerchantable he may sue for damages. Is it fair to allow him to claim those damages from the creditor when the sale was complete and the breach had occurred before the creditor ever came on the scene? Again he has a claim against the supplier, and provided the loan agreement falls within s12(b) or 12(c) he has a 'like claim' against the creditor. It is strongly arguable that the debtor should be restricted to suing the supplier only, but there seems no way around s75(1) because it does not say the breach about which the debtor sues should take place only after the credit agreement is made.

The last example raises a further problem. If the debtor rejects the car, thereby discharging the sale contract, is he also entitled to discharge the credit contract? Again, since he only takes the loan in order to pay for the car it makes sense to allow him to bring the loan to an end if he rejects the car. But the creditor is still being held responsible for a breach which occurred before he had any involvement with the debtor.

The answer to the argument that s75(1) can act unfairly against the creditor is that under s75(2) he is given a right to be indemnified by the supplier. In other words, if the creditor is sued and has to pay damages he can recover those damages from the supplier as well as his costs. If the creditor loses in any other way, for example by losing the right to interest if the loan agreement is rescinded or discharged, he may claim this loss from the supplier as well - his right to an indemnity is a right to a full indemnity.

Debtor rescinding

If the debtor has the right to rescind the credit agreement he may do so by informing the creditor directly or by informing the negotiator or by informing any person who acted on behalf of the debtor in negotiations, provided in this final case that the person concerned acted in the course of a business. Each of these people is the agent of the creditor for the purpose of receiving notice of rescission (s102). The person who is informed of the decision to rescind is under a duty to communicate that fact to the creditor forthwith (s175), but the rescission will be effective from the time the agent is informed.

No particular form of words is necessary in order to make rescission effective, provided the debtor makes clear his intention. If he does rescind the credit contract, it is treated as though it had never been made. Therefore, if the debtor has received money he must repay it and if he has made any payments to the creditor these must be repaid.

The Act does not define rescission fully. It is understood to refer to rescission for misrepresentation only, but 'rescission' is also used by some judges, and by Professor Treitel (*The Law of Contract* 7th edn pp574–631) to refer to the bringing to an end of a contract following breach. Section 102(2) tells us that rescission does not include cancelling the agreement or terminating it early under the special powers in s99 which allow the debtor to buy his way out of an agreement (see Chapter 5, below).

Rejection of goods

Where the debtor takes goods on credit sale and there is a breach of condition by the seller, the right to reject is governed by ss34 and 35 of the Sale of Goods Act 1979 (see above Chapter 13 of Sale of Goods). The Sale of Goods Act doctrine of acceptance does not, however, apply to certain conditional sales or to either regulated or unregulated hire purchase contracts.

Conditional sales in which the debtor deals as consumer within the definition in s12 of the Unfair Contract Terms Act 1977 are treated like hire purchase contracts for the purpose of the debtor's remedy for breach of condition (Supply of Goods (Implied Terms) Act 1973, s14(2)). The debtor will deal as consumer where the creditor acts in the course of a business, the debtor acts otherwise than in the course of a business and the goods supplied are of a type ordinarily supplied for private use or consumption (Unfair Contract Terms Act 1977, s12). This will not apply to all regulated conditional sales because in some the debtor will not act as consumer. If he does not act as consumer his right to reject is governed by the Sale of Goods Act rules.

Although the doctrine of acceptance does not apply to hire purchase or conditional sale contracts in which the debtor deals as consumer, there is a rule which prevents rejection of goods where the agreement has been affirmed following a breach. In effect the right to reject goods for breach of contract is treated in the same way as the right to rescind for misrepresentation. The law in this area has not been fully formulated, because there are few reported cases from which the rules can be extracted.

The leading case is *Farnworth Finance Facilities Ltd* v *Attryde* [1970] 1 WLR 1053; [1970] 2 All ER 774. The debtor took a motor cycle on hire purchase from Farnworth Finance Facilities Ltd, the creditor. It broke down after a few days and he took it back to the shop which had sold it to Farnworth Finance. The shop could not mend it so it was taken to the manufacturers. They tried twice to mend it but it still did not work. He then wrote to the creditor saying he was rejecting the motor cycle because he could not use it and it had been a troublesome burden ever since he got it. This rejection took place on 23 November 1964, the debtor having taken delivery on 11 July 1964. The Court of Appeal held that the motor cycle was unmerchantable and unfit for the debtor's purpose (there were no statutory rules governing the required quality of goods under hire purchase contracts, but there was ample authority for the implication of terms relating to merchantable quality, etc, at common law).

It was held that the right to reject the motor cycle could only be lost if the contract had been affirmed by the debtor. Lord Denning MR said:

> 'A man only affirms a contract when he knows of the defects and by his conduct elects to go on with the contract despite them. In this case the [debtor] complained from the beginning about the defects and sent the machine back for them to be remedied. He did not elect to accept it unless they were remedied.'

Not only does affirmation require a decision by the debtor to go on with the contract following defects becoming apparent, it also requires the debtor to have full knowledge of all defects. In *Farnworth Finance Facilities Ltd* v *Attryde* some defects only appeared weeks after delivery. If the motor cycle had seemed to be perfectly merchantable on delivery, but later broke down due to defects which existed on delivery but were not discovered until later it seems that the debtor may still reject. If the analogy between affirmation after breach by the creditor and affirmation after misrepresentation is a true analogy, there must come a time when the debtor has had the goods for so long that he will not be entitled to reject them, even though a latent defect which was present on delivery only appeared long afterwards (*Leaf* v *International Galleries* [1950] 2 KB 86; [1950] 1 All ER 693).

It had always been thought that, in hire purchase contracts, if the debtor affirmed the contract and the goods remained unfit or in some other way in breach of a condition of the contract after affirmation, then the debtor's right of rejection was resurrected. It is clear after *UCB Leasing Ltd* v *Holtom* [1987] CCLR 101 that this is not so. Once a debtor affirms a contract, he loses for good his right to reject. If he attempts to reject he himself will be guilty of a repudiatory breach.

In *UCB Leasing*, for the whole of the time the debtor had a car, it suffered persistent electrical problems. In purporting, after using the car for some time, to exercise the right of rejection, the court held that this was no longer available to her. Sued by the creditor for wrongful rejection, the defendant was held able to counterclaim and the sum awarded to the debtor included a substantial amount for inconvenience and distress.

Damages

The debtor's right to damages for breach of any of the implied terms discussed above is not subject to any special statutory rules. If the agreement is a conditional sale or credit sale the rules in ss51 to 54 of the Sale of Goods Act 1979 apply (see section 1.4 above). But if it is hire purchase the common law alone applies because the Supply of Goods (Implied Terms) Act 1973 does not deal with damages.

Breach of s8(1) of the 1973 Act (creditor not having the right to sell) amounts to a total failure of consideration by the creditor, so the debtor is entitled to get back all money he has paid (*Warman* v *Southern Counties Car Finance Corporation Ltd*, *Karflex Ltd* v *Poole*). In addition he will be able to recover for any other losses he has suffered, provided they are not too remote.

Breach of any of the other implied terms will allow the debtor to sue for damages to compensate him for the effects of the breach. In general terms the same principles apply as apply to a buyer who has received goods in breach of the terms implied by s13 to 15 of the 1979 Act. But in one important respect the debtor under a hire purchase contract is in a different position. If he rejects the goods he may still be liable to pay for the use which he has enjoyed. *Helby* v *Matthews* (supra) holds that the instalments paid by the debtor are hire payments in the eyes of the law. There are dicta in many cases which recognise that the reality of a hire purchase contract is that the debtor is paying in instalments in order to become owner at the end of the day, and that the amount which he has to pay usually exceeds what is a reasonable charge for use alone. But, no case can go behind *Helby* v *Matthews* and say that the debtor's payments are not in law payments for use (see Lord Denning's dicta from *Bridge* v *Campbell Discount Co Ltd* at the beginning of Chapter 1). Therefore, if the debtor has had use of the goods, he must pay for that use.

However, if the goods are defective in some way the fact that his use of them is thereby impaired can be reflected in damages. In *Yeoman Credit Ltd* v *Apps* [1962] 2 QB 508; [1961] 2 All ER 281 the Court of Appeal held that a debtor under a hire purchase contract who had had use of a car for five months had to pay the instalments which were due in those months, but that he could claim damages to reflect the fact that the use he had had was impaired by defects in the car. The total he had to pay was almost £185, but he was awarded £100 in damages because that was the amount required to put right the defects. There was no argument advanced that the debtor was entitled to any other measure of damages.

A different approach was adopted by the Court of Appeal in *Charterhouse Credit Co Ltd* v *Tolly* [1963] 2 QB 683; [1963] 2 All ER 432 in which the car broke down after two journeys. The debtor elected to affirm the contract but did not pay the instalments and the creditor terminated the agreement and sued for arrears. The Court held that the arrears had to be paid but that the debtor was entitled to damages because of the seriously defective nature of the car. The total amount due to the creditor up to the time the agreement was terminated was just over £137, but the debtor was held to be entitled to damages of £132. The Court held that the debtor was entitled to the full amount of his hire payments in damages save for £5 because for all but two short journeys the car was useless. In other words, the use he had was valued at £5. In *Yeoman Credit Ltd* v *Apps* the Court held that the proper measure of damages was the amount it would have taken to put the car right, but in *Charterhouse Credit Co Ltd* v *Tolly* this was held not to be the proper measure because, as Upjohn LJ said, the proper measure of damages is the debtor's 'loss on the transaction'. In this case the debtor's loss on the transaction was the loss of use while the car was off the road and since he was paying for use it follows that the amount of the hire payments is what he loses by not having use.

The debtor in *Farnworth Finance Facilities Ltd* v *Attryde* did not have to pay anything for use, because the Court of Appeal held that the trouble to which he was put by the motor cycle persistently breaking down was so great that the overall benefit to him was nil. A better solution would have been for the debtor to pay for the use he did have, but to be awarded additional damages for distress and inconvenience.

Exclusion clauses

The seller of goods under conditional sale or credit sale agreements is in the same position as a seller under a cash sale if he wishes to rely upon an exclusion clause. The relevant rules are explained in Chapter 7 of Sale of Goods (above). The supplier under a hire purchase contract is in a similar position. Section 6 of the Unfair Contract Terms Act 1977 applies to hire purchase contracts as it does to sales of goods.

The Unfair Contract Terms Act 1977 does not need to regulate the position of a creditor who tries to exclude his liability for breach of his obligations under the Consumer Credit Act 1974. Instead s173(1) states that a term in a regulated agreement is void if and to the extent that it is inconsistent with a provision of the Act which is for the protection of the debtor. This does not make the whole agreement void, merely that part of it which attempts to deprive the debtor of the protection given to him by the 1974 Act.

It is probably the case that s3 of the Unfair Contract Terms Act 1977 applies so as to require terms attempting to deprive the debtor of the 1974 Act's protection to satisfy the test of reasonableness. But, of course, s170(1) of the 1974 Act takes precedence.

3.3 Transfer of ownership

We have already seen that if the creditor fails to transfer ownership to the debtor because of a defect in his title, the debtor is fully protected by s8 of the Supply of Goods (Implied Terms) Act 1973 and the decisions in the *Warman* and *Karflex* cases. Nevertheless it is important to consider when the debtor becomes the owner of goods because this may affect his liability to people to whom he sells them.

By definition a debtor under a credit sale agreement obtains ownership as if he were a cash buyer (s189(1)). The rules in s18 of the Sale of Goods Act 1979 apply (see Chapter 8 of Sale of Goods, above). The passing of ownership to the debtor may be delayed for various reasons, perhaps because the goods are unascertained and need to be unconditionally appropriated to the contract, but the fact that he pays in instalments will make no difference to the application of s18.

Conditional sale agreements contain express provisions that ownership will only pass to the debtor once certain conditions are fulfilled. The most common of these is that the price must be paid in full. At common law conditional sales fall within s25 of the 1979 Act and the debtor is in the position of any other buyer who takes goods subject to a reservation of ownership to the seller pending payment. His position is governed by the rules in the '*Romalpa* clauses' (see *Four Point Garage Ltd* v *Carter* [1985] 3 All ER 12).

But, a debtor under a regulated conditional sale agreement will have no right to sell the goods until he has become their owner. If he does so he will not pass good title to the purchaser unless the sale is in market overt (s22, Sale of Goods Act 1979). He cannot come within s25 of the 1979 Act, because s25(2) expressly stipulates that a debtor under a regulated conditional sale agreement is not a person who has 'bought or agreed to buy goods'. This is consistent with the policy of the Consumer Credit Act 1974 to treat regulated conditional sales and regulated hire purchase contracts the same.

If the debtor takes a motor car under a hire purchase or regulated conditional sale agreement he may be able to pass title by virtue of Part III of the Hire Purchase Act 1964 (see Chapter 10 of Sale of Goods, above). But with this exception, and that of sales in market overt, it seems that the debtor will not normally be able to pass good title no matter how bona fide the purchaser.

One matter which has not yet come before the courts is the position of a debtor under a regulated conditional sale who obtains the goods for resale in the course of his business. His agreement can be regulated even though he acts in a business capacity, because the 1974 Act applies unless the debtor is a company or a group of companies.

It is quite possible, and indeed it is very common, for the debtor under a regulated agreement to be a partnership or a sole trader. Despite s25(2) of the 1979 Act, it may be that in such cases the debtor has implied authority to sell the goods in the course of his business in the same way that the buyer in *Clough Mills Ltd* v *Martin* [1985] 1 WLR 111; [1984] 3 All ER 982 was held to have implied authority. Whether the debtor has this authority is a matter to be determined from case to case and the terms of the agreement must be examined to see whether they determine the point. But if in a particular case the debtor does have implied authority to sell then he may pass ownership by virtue of that authority and s25(2) will be irrelevant.

The debtor under a hire purchase contract will become the owner of the goods only when the agreement has been fully performed. Whether the hire purchase contract provides for an option fee to be paid at the end of the hire period, or provides for ownership to pass once all instalments are paid but giving the debtor the right to terminate the hiring at any time, makes no difference. By definition it is not possible for the debtor to have to pay any money after he has become the owner. In many of hire purchase agreements made these days there is an option fee payable, but the creditor does not require it to be paid. In other words, provided the debtor makes all of the hire payments the creditor will waive the right to insist on the option fee being paid and the debtor will be treated as though he has paid it.

3.4 Information

Information required

The Act imposes an obligation on the creditor to provide the debtor with information about the agreement. The debtor is entitled to: (1) a copy of the executed agreement and any other document referred to in it; (2) details of how much he has paid to the creditor; (3) details of how much is due but unpaid; and (4) how much is to be paid in the future. The information need not be given on demand but must be given if the debtor pays the creditor 50p and makes his request in writing. This information must be given whether the agreement is fixed sum (s77(1)) or running account (s78(1)). The information must be given within the 12 days following receipt of the written request (Consumer Credit (Prescribed Periods for Giving Information) Regulations 1983, Reg 2).

Failure to supply information

The failure of the creditor to supply information within 12 days has the effect that he is not entitled to enforce the agreement until such time as he does supply it and if his default continues for one month he commits an offence (ss77(4) and 78(6)). The offence is triable in the magistrates' court only and is punishable by a fine of up to £1,000 (Schedule 1). The debtor is not entitled to sue for damages, his only protection if the creditor breaches his duties is that the agreement is unenforceable until the duty is complied with (s170(1)).

We will see in section 4.2 (below) that if the creditor wishes to take certain action on breach by the debtor he must serve a default notice first. A similar requirement exists if the creditor wishes to take certain actions when the debtor is not in breach. Regulated agreements often contain terms which allow the creditor to recover possession of the goods even though the debtor is not in breach. For example, the creditor may wish to do so on the bankruptcy of the debtor. The creditor does not have any right to repossess unless either the debtor is in breach or there is a term allowing him to do so, but if there is such a term he must first serve a notice on the debtor informing him of his intention to enforce such a term (s76(1)).

Section 76(1) applies not only where the creditor intends to repossess the goods, but also if he intends to demand early payment of any sum or treat any right of the debtor as terminated, restricted or deferred. If the agreement is for a loan which is repayable on demand there would be no need for the creditor to service a s76 notice first, because when he demands repayment the creditor is not bringing the loan to an end early - it is only if the creditor is cutting short the normal duration of the credit that s76 applies (s76(2)). Therefore, if the agreement provides for the loan to be repaid in monthly instalments, but also provides that the creditor shall be entitled to demand payment of all amounts outstanding if the debtor loses his job the duration of the contract is being shortened and a notice must be served.

The notice must be in the prescribed form (s76(3)), which is laid down in the Consumer Credit (Enforcement, Default and Termination Notices) Regulations 1983. The regulations are detailed, but in outline they require the notice to state that it is served pursuant to s76, identify the agreement under which it is served and the term of that agreement which is being enforced, and inform the debtor of any right that he may have to go to court (eg to ask for extra time to pay). We will look at the right of the debtor when faced with a s76 in section 6.2, below.

Regulation 2(9), which is made pursuant to s76(5), provides that s76 does not apply to non-commercial agreements in relation to which no security has been provided. Normal regulated hire purchase, conditional sale and credit sale agreements are commercial agreements and therefore s76 applies.

4

Default by the Debtor

4.1 Breach of contract

4.2 Default notices

4.3 Repossession

4.4 Acceleration clauses

4.5 Minimum payment clauses

4.6 Security

4.1 Breach of contract

The duty to pay

The debtor's most important duty under a regulated agreement is to repay the credit which has been provided and also the total charge for credit. His obligation to pay is fundamental to the contract, but his obligation to pay at the times stipulated is not always particularly important provided that he eventually pays the total amount due.

In recent years it has become common practice for finance companies to stipulate that it is 'of the essence' of the contract that payments are made on time. If the agreement says this, then failure to pay on time will be a breach of condition and the finance company will be entitled to bring the contract to an end (*Lombard North Central plc* v *Butterworth* [1987] 2 WLR 7; [1987] 1 All ER 267). Such express terms have a drastic consequence in terms of the damages he must pay for his breach (see below: Damages for late or non-payment).

Mere failure to pay will not entitle the creditor to repossess unless the breach by the debtor is very serious. But it is frequently the case that the contract expressly allows the creditor to terminate the agreement and repossess the goods on *any* breach by the debtor. We will see below that a clause like this is valid but that the creditor will only be able to claim such instalments as are in arrears if he decides to terminate by virtue of it (*Financings Ltd* v *Baldock* [1963] 2 QB 104; [1963] 1 All ER 443). In all cases where the creditor has repossessed the goods and claims monetary compensation from the debtor, the position of the parties must be approached in two stages. Firstly, it must be ascertained whether the creditor was entitled to repossess, and secondly, it must be asked what damages the debtor must pay, if any, for his failure to pay in accordance with the agreement.

Repossession for late payment or non-payment

At common law the duty to pay on time is an innominate term of the contract. In other words it is only if the effect of the breach goes to the root of the contract that the creditor would be entitled to treat the contract as discharged. It is a matter of fact to be determined from case to case whether the debtor's failure to pay is so serious as to go to the root of the contract; little guidance can be found in the cases although some are of a little assistance. The question to be asked is whether the debtor has shown that he is unwilling any longer to be bound by the contract.

In *Yeoman Credit Ltd* v *Waragowski* [1961] 1 WLR 1124; [1961] 3 All ER 145 the total hire purchase price of a car was just over £434, made up of a deposit of £72, 36 monthly instalments of just over £10 and a £1 option fee. The debtor paid the deposit but none of the instalments. After six months the creditor repossessed the car. The Court of Appeal held that by his persistent failure to pay the debtor had shown that he was not willing to perform the contract and, therefore, that the creditor was entitled to repossess. The breach by the debtor had gone on for so long that it was sufficiently serious to amount to a repudiation of the contract.

Similarly in *Overstone Ltd* v *Shipway* [1962] 1 WLR 117; [1962] 1 All ER 52 the total hire purchase price was a little more than £452 payable by a deposit of £73 and 36 monthly instalments of almost £10.55. The debtor paid the deposit but none of the instalments. After four months the creditor repossessed. The Court of Appeal held that the debtor's breach was a repudiation of the contract, but applied a slightly different test to that applied in *Yeoman Credit Ltd* v *Waragowski*. In the *Waragowski* case the court asked whether the debtor had shown that he was unwilling to perform the contract. In *Overstone Ltd* v *Shipway* the question asked was whether it was reasonable for the creditor to repossess. This difference is probably only another way of saying the same thing, but if there is a conflict between the cases it was held in *Financings Ltd* v *Baldock* (supra) and *Brady* v *St Margaret's Trust Ltd* [1963] 2 QB 494; [1963] 2 All ER 175 that the *Waragowski* test is the correct one.

On the other hand, in *Financings Ltd* v *Baldock* the debtor paid the deposit of £100 but none of the monthly instalments of £28 and a few pence. When two of the 24 instalments were outstanding the creditor repossessed, claiming that the debtor's breach was a repudiation of the contract. The Court of Appeal held that the breach was not so serious as to show that the debtor did not intend to be bound by the contract and therefore that the breach was non-repudiatory. *Yeoman Credit Ltd* v *Waragowski* and *Overstone Ltd* v *Shipway* were distinguished because the debtor's default was considerably more serious than in *Financings Ltd* v *Baldock*.

Because agreements usually contain a provision allowing the creditor to terminate the agreement and repossess the goods upon any breach by the debtor, it does not matter in such cases whether the breach is repudiatory or not, the goods can be repossessed anyway (subject to what is said in section 4.3 below). If there is no such clause, the wrongful repossession by the creditor will be a conversion because the debtor's right to possession would be wrongfully interfered with. It would also be a breach of contract. If the agreement is conditional sale or credit sale it is the warranty implied by s12(2)(b) of the Sale of Goods Act 1979 which is breached and if it is hire purchase it is the equivalent warranty implied by s8(2)(b) of the Supply of Goods (Implied Terms) Act 1973. The damages payable to the debtor would have to compensate him for losing possession. In hire purchase contracts because he pays for use he would be entitled to damages equivalent to the hire he has paid and also a sum for inconvenience.

Damages for late payment or non-payment

Repudiatory breach

If the debtor's breach is repudiatory and the creditor repossesses the goods the debtor will have to compensate the creditor not just for outstanding instalments, but also for the loss of the future benefits of the contract. A repudiatory breach by definition is one which is so serious that it indicates an unwillingness to go on with the contract. As was explained by the Court of Appeal in *Overstone Ltd* v *Shipway* the only reasonable thing for the creditor to do where the debtor has shown that he is not willing to pay is to repossess the goods. Once he has repossessed he will not receive future instalments under the agreement. But it will be the debtor's serious breach which has forced the creditor to lose those future instalments and therefore the debtor will have to compensate for their loss.

Non-repudiatory breach

If, on the other hand, the debtor's breach is non-repudiatory, as in *Financings Ltd* v *Baldock*, the creditor is not forced to repossess. A non-repudiatory breach is one which does not show that the debtor is unwilling to pay in the future. In other words, if the creditor leaves the debtor in possession he is likely to receive the future instalments. Therefore, if the creditor chooses to repossess it is that choice which deprives him of the future instalments, not the breach by the debtor.

In the event of a non-repudiatory breach the creditor's only entitlement is to those instalments which should have been paid by the date of repossession. In *Financings Ltd* v *Baldock* the Court of Appeal held that, because the debtor's breach was non-repudiatory, only the two outstanding instalments could be recovered. Strictly speaking these instalments are recoverable as debts due to the creditor, not as damages, but this matters little and if the creditor sues for damages he will be able to recover the outstanding instalments.

Interest

Interest is recoverable on instalments paid late only if the agreement provides for it to be paid. There is no right at common law to interest on debts paid late (*President of India* v *La Pintada Corporation* [1985] AC 104; [1984] 2 All ER 773). It is normal practice for regulated agreements to stipulate that interest is payable if an instalment is delayed. The rate of interest charged must not exceed the rate of interest charged on the credit advanced under the agreement (s93(a)).

Measure of damages

In the event of a repudiatory breach by the debtor the amount of damages due is the sum required to put the creditor in the position he would be in if the contract were performed properly. This does not necessarily entitle him to end up with a sum equivalent to the total price, however, because in hire purchase contracts the option fee is included in the total price but it cannot be sued for because it is entirely at the discretion of the debtor whether the option to buy is exercised. Part of the total price may have been paid already: for example, the deposit and maybe one or more instalments. Also, under the agreement the creditor would receive payment in instalments over a period of time (in *Waragowski* and *Shipway* the period was three years). Therefore, if he is to receive damages before the end of that period the amount of damages should be reduced slightly to reflect that he is getting the money early. In addition, instalments already due by the date of repossession are recoverable as debts due and not as damages. Finally, because the creditor has repossessed he is able to resell the goods; this is something which he would not be able to do if the debtor performed properly because the debtor would have them. In the end the amount due to the creditor is calculated according to the following formula: Total Price minus the aggregate of Deposit Paid, Instalments Paid, Instalments Due, Resale Value and Rebate of Interest for Early Payment.

In *Yeoman Credit Ltd* v *Waragowski* the Court of Appeal applied this formula but did not give a rebate for early payment. In *Overstone Ltd* v *Shipway* however the Court did give such a rebate, and to the extent that *Yeoman Credit Ltd* v *Waragowski* failed to give such a rebate it is wrongly decided.

The most recent case in this field, *Lombard North Central plc* v *Butterworth* (supra), gives rise to an enormous loophole in consumer protection in hire purchase cases. The contract was one of hire, not hire purchase, but the applicable law is identical. The total sum which the creditor would have received if the contract had run its full course was £11,681, payable by a deposit of £584.05 and 19 quarterly instalments of the same amount. The debtor paid the first two instalments on time, the next three were paid late and when the sixth was six weeks overdue the creditor terminated the agreement. There was a clause allowing the creditor to terminate on any breach by the debtor; there was also a clause saying that punctual payment was of the essence of the contract. The Court of Appeal held that because the phrase 'of the essence' was used, so punctual payment was a condition of the contract and any failure to pay promptly was a repudiatory breach. The creditor was therefore entitled to recover not only the outstanding instalment but also the total amount of hire payments, minus £172.88 which had been raised on resale of the goods and a rebate for early payment. This case gives cause for concern because the Court of Appeal recognised that the breach by the debtor would not have been repudiatory in the absence of the clause making punctual payment 'of the essence'. In other words, simply by using the phrase 'of the essence' the creditor became entitled to damages far in excess of what he would get at common law.

The creditor's position on a repudiatory breach by the debtor, therefore, is that he may recover outstanding instalments because they are debts due to him and he may also recover damages for loss of the future benefits of the contract. A rebate must be given if the creditor receives payment of damages earlier than he would have received the instalments under the contract. Although there are provisions allowing the debtor to ask for more time to pay (see Chapter 6 below), nothing in the Consumer Credit Act 1974 changes the common law rules on damages payable for failure to pay.

The duty to take care of the goods

The debtor will be under a duty to take care of goods supplied to him under a hire purchase or conditional sale agreement. This duty will not arise if he has goods under a credit sale because the goods will be his. The 1974 Act does not impose the duty, but it is always an express term of the contract that care must be taken. Indeed, even at common law, a duty to take reasonable care is thought to arise from the debtor's position as a bailee. There is no authority on this point in relation to hire purchase contracts, but as Wild points out (*The Law of Hire Purchase*, 2nd edn pp61-2) the position of the debtor is the same as that of a hirer of goods and there is ample authority that a hirer owes such a duty (*Dean* v *Keate* (1811) 3 Camp 4).

Arguably the debtor under a conditional sale only owes a duty of care if he fails to complete the contract because he would then have to redeliver the goods in the condition in which he received them save for fair wear and tear. But the end result in such a case is that if he has failed to take reasonable care they will not be in the necessary condition and he will be liable.

The contract will normally require the debtor to use the goods for their normal purposes only and to keep them in his own custody or control. Failure to comply with these duties will give rise to liability in contract, but as will be seen in the next paragraph the loss to the creditor may be nil.

A failure to take reasonable care of the goods may be of no concern to the creditor at all, provided the debtor pays the instalments as and when they fall due and there is no reported case in which a creditor has claimed damages from a debtor for damaging goods which later became his. Indeed, there would only rarely be any point in such an action being taken because if the debtor pays for the goods the creditor loses nothing by them being damaged. If, on the other hand, the debtor commits a repudiatory breach by non-payment and the creditor repossesses the damaged goods, their loss of value caused by the damage will mean that the resale price is less than it would otherwise be and the debtor would have to pay more damages according to the formula in *Overstone Ltd* v *Shipway*.

The only time when the creditor would have an interest in suing for damage done would be where there has been a non-repudiatory breach by the debtor and the creditor has elected to terminate the contract, because in such a case the creditor will, prima facie, only be able to claim outstanding instalments. In *Brady* v *St Margaret's Trust Ltd* (supra) exactly that happened. The creditor recovered the outstanding instalments, following *Financings Ltd* v *Baldock*, and also damages which reflected the extent to which the car's value after repossession was lower than it would have been had it been looked after properly.

4.2 Default notices

When a default notice must be served

When the debtor is in breach the creditor may wish to sue for damages or to sue for instalments which have not been paid. He may also wish to terminate the contract and repossess the goods. If he merely wishes to sue for damages or for outstanding instalments he may do this without giving the debtor any formal notification. But if he wishes to take any of the steps specified in s87(1), he must serve a default notice first. Section 87(1) covers cases where the creditor wishes:

'a) to terminate the agreement, or
b) to demand earlier payment of any sum, or
c) to recover possession of any goods ..., or
d) to treat any right conferred on the debtor ... by the agreement as terminated, restricted or deferred, or
e) to enforce any security.'

Termination of the agreement in s87(1)(a) means treating it as discharged for breach of condition or bringing it to an end by virtue of an express power to do that on the debtor committing any breach (as in *Financings Ltd* v *Baldock*). It does not include rescinding the agreement for misrepresentation.

Demanding earlier payments refers to terms which are normally described as acceleration clauses. These are terms which say that the whole of the credit must be repaid immediately on the debtor committing a breach. We will consider acceleration clauses separately in section 4.4 below. As to the question of whether a debtor in default can legitimately claim any rebate for early settlement (which is usual in the case of accelerated payments), see *Forward Trust* v *Whymark* (section 5.1 below).

Recovering possession of goods also raises special problems because in some circumstances the creditor must not only serve a default notice, but also obtain a court order before being entitled to recover possession. A default notice will be required whether or not the agreement specifically provides for repossession on breach by the debtor.

Treating rights of the debtor as terminated, restricted or deferred includes preventing the debtor under a hire purchase contract from paying the outstanding balance and the option fee until he has remedied his breach.

The default notice

A default notice must be in the form prescribed by the Consumer Credit (Enforcement, Default and Termination Notices) Regulations 1983 (s88(1)). It must say that it is a default notice served under s87 and contain details of the agreement, the parties, the term which is being enforced and what the creditor intends to do.

Furthermore, s88(1) requires the notice to specify the breach and, if capable of remedy, what must be done to remedy it. If it is not capable of remedy, the notice must specify a sum of money which must be paid to the creditor to compensate for the breach. If the debtor takes the remedial action set out in the notice, his breach is treated as not having occurred (s89).

Once seven days have elapsed after the service of the notice and the debtor has not remedied his breach the creditor will be entitled to take any of the steps specified in s87(1). But if he wishes to demand earlier payment the mere service of the notice and the passing of seven days will not be enough to make the demand effective, he has to actually make the demand after the seven days have elapsed.

Non-default notices

In section 3.4 above, we saw that the creditor must serve a notice on the debtor if he wishes to demand earlier payment, recover possession of goods or treat any right of the debtor as terminated, restricted or deferred, otherwise than because of a breach by the debtor. If a notice is served on the debtor pursuant to s76 a seven-day period must elapse before he may take the action specified in the notice.

But notices served by virtue of s76 are different to default notices in that they do not contain a statement of what the debtor has to do to remedy the position. Because the debtor will not be in breach when served with a s76 notice so there can be no question of him remedying any breach and, accordingly, s89 does not apply.

Professor Goode has shown that a s76 notice can be served where there has been a breach, provided the term which entitles the creditor to repossess does not depend upon a breach being committed (Consumer Credit Legislation, para III.77). For example, the agreement may allow the creditor to repossess if the debtor loses his job (which of itself would not be a breach), but it may be a breach for the debtor to deliberately put himself in the position where he cannot pay the instalments due. Therefore, if he leaves his job voluntarily he may be in breach, but the reason the creditor will want to repossess is not because of the breach but because he has lost his job.

4.3 Repossession

Protected goods

It should be stressed that, as will be seen below, these provisions only apply to regulated conditional sale and hire purchase agreements.

There are few cases where the creditor may wish to repossess when the debtor is not in breach; by far the most common cause of wishing to repossess is that the debtor has failed to pay the instalments on time. We have seen already that a default notice must be served before the creditor can become entitled to repossess, but there is a further provision of the Act applicable in some cases when the debtor is in breach.

Whether the breach by the debtor is repudiatory or not the creditor may have the right to repossess because of an express clause allowing repossession on any breach. Where the debtor is in breach, the goods still belong to the creditor and the debtor has paid one-third or more of the total price, the goods are protected goods and may not be repossessed without a court order (s90(1)). Because of the requirement that the creditor must still be the owner of the goods, s90 can only apply to hire purchase and conditional sale contracts and not to credit sales.

If an installation charge had to be paid by the debtor, the goods will be protected only if a sum equivalent at least to the installation fee plus one third of the remainder of the total price has been paid (s90(2)).

In addition, there is a provision applicable where the debtor has not paid one-third of the total price under the agreement but did pay more than one-third of the total price under a previous agreement. If there was a previous regulated hire purchase or conditional sale agreement between the same creditor and debtor relating to the same goods and the debtor paid one-third or more of the total price under that agreement, the goods under the new agreement are protected (s90(3)). The new agreement need not be a modifying agreement but in many instances it will be.

Goods cannot be protected if the debtor has terminated the agreement even if the conditions in s90(1) are fulfilled (s90(5)). This subsection is necessary because the debtor's right to terminate is not dependent upon him not having breached the contract and in many cases the best way for him to act if he is in breach is to terminate the agreement. Termination by the debtor can arise in two ways, either by the exercise of a right to terminate or by the debtor discharging the contract following a breach of condition by the creditor. The debtor does not, however, terminate the contract by breaching a condition himself. If the creditor chooses to do so he may discharge the contract following a repudiatory breach by the debtor, but in such cases it is the creditor who terminates the contract, not the debtor (*FC Finance Ltd* v *Francis* (1970) 114 SJ 568).

It is for the creditor to prove that the debtor has terminated the agreement and the onus is a heavy one. The House of Lords held in *Bridge* v *Campbell Discount Co Ltd* [1962] AC 600; [1962] 1 All ER 385 that a debtor does not terminate the agreement by stating that he could not pay any more due to unforeseen circumstances. In that case there was an option to terminate in writing, but when the debtor lost his job and wrote to the creditor saying he would not be able to pay any more he did not refer to the contractual clause and therefore it was held that he was not exercising the right to terminate.

The Court of Appeal followed *Bridge* v *Campbell Discount Co Ltd* in *United Dominions Trust Ltd* v *Ennis* [1968] 1 QB 54; [1967] 2 All ER 345 in which the debtor telephoned the creditor saying he could not pay and wrote a letter, which was dictated to him by an agent of the creditor, saying he wished to terminate the agreement. Because he did not apply his mind to whether he was terminating, the Court of Appeal held that he was not electing to terminate. The Court of Appeal recently followed *United Dominions Trust Ltd* v *Ennis* in *Chartered Trust plc* v *Pitcher* (1987) The Times 13 February. The debtor wrote to the creditor because his wife had been told by the creditor's Default Controller that if he did not write and terminate the agreement the creditor would have to repossess the goods, which would be more expensive for him. Kerr LJ reviewed the authorities (*Bridge* v *Campbell Discount Co Ltd*, *United Dominions Trust Ltd* v *Ennis* and *FC Finance Ltd* v *Francis*) and said:

> 'Three principles can be derived from these cases. First, an agreement to terminate a hiring involves the exercise by the hirer of a contractual option, viz to terminate his remaining rights and obligations under the agreement ... Secondly, any doubt or ambiguity about the hirer's intention so to exercise this option should be resolved in his favour. Thirdly, any contractual provision dealing with the method of termination must be strictly construed and complied with before such termination will be said to have occurred.'

We will look at some of these cases in more detail in section 4.5 below.

Effect of protection

Court orders

If goods are protected they may not be repossessed without a court order. If the creditor does repossess without first obtaining a court order he must repay to the debtor all money paid under the agreement and if the agreement has not already been discharged it is discharged (s91). Clearly this is a severe penalty and it is all the more severe because the creditor cannot cure a wrongful repossession by redelivering goods which he has wrongfully taken (*Capital Finance Co Ltd* v *Bray* [1964] 1 WLR 323; [1964] 1 All ER 603). This is so even if the original repossession was a simple error.

Abandonment

Not all repossession is prevented without a court order because s90 says that the creditor shall not 'recover possession of the goods from the debtor'. If the goods have been abandoned by the debtor the creditor can repossess them because that repossession will not be 'from the debtor'. Once again the case law is weighted against the creditor, in that it is difficult to prove that goods have been abandoned. In *Bentinck Ltd* v *Cromwell Engineering Co* [1971] 1 QB 324; [1971] 1 All ER 33 the debtor was involved in a collision in which the car he was driving and which he held under a hire purchase agreement was severely damaged. He left it at a garage. When approached by the finance company he gave a false telephone number and disappeared. The finance company traced the car nine months after the collision and repossessed it. The Court of Appeal held that the car had been abandoned and therefore that the creditor had not recovered possession from the debtor. Lord Denning MR said:

> 'The abandonment, to entitle the finance company to retake possession, must be abandonment of all rights to the car so as to evince quite clearly that the hirer no longer has any interest in it.'

By contrast, in *FC Finance Ltd* v *Francis* the repossession of a car from a garage which had it with the debtor's consent in order to repair it was a repossession from the debtor because the garage held the goods as his agent.

Consent by debtor

An alternative way in which possession may be taken without the need for a court order is by consent of the debtor. Section 173(3) recognises that a debtor is entitled to waive a provision of the Act which is designed to protect him, but it is also clear that he will only be held to have waived that protection if he makes an informed decision to waive. The first authority on this point would probably not be followed today. In *Mercantile Credit Co Ltd* v *Cross* [1965] 2 QB 205; [1965] 1 All ER 557 the debtor was in arrears and the creditor wrote to him informing him that the hire purchase agreement was ended and that he no longer held the goods with the creditor's consent. The debtor's wife telephoned the creditor and was told to deliver the goods to a local shop; this was done. The Court of Appeal held that the debtor had given up possession of the goods voluntarily and, therefore, that the creditor had not enforced a right to possession against him.

A better approach to this problem is that adopted in *United Dominions Trust Ltd* v *Ennis* which, it will be remembered, held that a debtor only consents to giving up protection afforded him by statute if he has full knowledge of his rights. Undoubtedly the debtor in *Mercantile Credit Co Ltd* v *Cross* did not know of his rights and therefore did not truly consent to losing possession. Of particular importance in this area is the knowledge of the debtor of his right to apply to the court for more time to pay (see Chapter 6 below). If he knows of that right but still consents to handing back the goods, he can hardly argue that the repossession is wrongful, but if he does not understand the full protection given to him by the Act any repossession will be wrongful.

The level of knowledge required is full knowledge of his statutory protection. Against this, in the *Cross* case Willmer LJ said:

> 'What is said is that a hirer's consent has to be looked at as though it were in the nature of a waiver or acquiescence, and therefore is of no effect unless it is given with full knowledge of the legal rights of the party whose consent is in question. It seems to me that that is going much too far. I agree ... that consent has to be a free and voluntary consent, and I am disposed to agree that it must be an informed consent. Here the fact is that the hirer has been informed, in language about as simple as could be devised, of exactly what his rights are, and what the rights of the owner of the goods are. If a hirer chooses not to read what the notice required to be inserted in his hire purchase agreement says, he himself is, to my mind, the only sufferer. It cannot be said that if, having failed to ascertain what his rights are, he then gives a consent which he might not otherwise have given, his consent is any the less a real consent.'

The Court of Appeal was not referred to *Bridge* v *Campbell Discount Co Ltd* in which Lord Denning said of the debtor:

> 'His conduct should be interpreted on the assumption that he would do that which is the least burdensome to him, rather than that which is the most profitable to the finance company.'

Also, in *United Dominions Trust Ltd* v *Ennis* Lord Denning MR said of the option to terminate the agreement:

> 'a hirer is not to be taken to exercise such an option unless he does so consciously, knowing of the consequences, and avowedly in exercise of the option. If this were not so, the document would be an absolute trap set to catch him. Not one hirer in a thousand reads these small printed clauses. Even if he did, he would not understand them.'

And in *Chartered Trust plc* v *Pitcher* the dicta of Willmer LJ cited above were said not to be definitive. The proper view is that of Lord Denning whose opinion recognised that the whole point of imposing stringent conditions if the creditor repossesses protected goods without a court order is to ensure that debtors do not lose, unknowingly, the right to apply for extra time to pay. This point will be illustrated further in section 4.5 because it arises in connection with minimum payment clauses.

Repossession from third parties

Although no court order is needed to repossess from a third party to whom the debtor has sold the goods or who has possession after abandonment, the effect of the *nemo dat* rules must not be forgotten. Of particular importance is the position of a private purchaser of a motor vehicle under Part III of the Hire Purchase Act 1964 (see Chapter 10 of Sale of Goods, above).

Part III will vest the creditor's title in the private purchaser who buys in good faith and without notice of the credit agreement whether or not the credit agreement is regulated. But it only applies where the credit agreement is hire purchase or conditional sale. If it is credit sale the debtor will be the owner and will pass good title by virtue of that ownership. Even if there is a clause in the credit sale agreement requiring him not to sell, a sale will be effective to pass title because the clause will create a personal duty owed by debtor to creditor but does not affect the debtor's title.

Debtors under regulated conditional sale agreements are not persons who have 'bought or agreed to buy goods' and therefore cannot pass title by virtue of s25 of the Sale of Goods Act 1979 (s25(2))

Additional protection

In addition to the repossession of protected goods allowing the debtor to recover all sums he has paid, without having to give any credit for use which he has received of the goods, s92(1) says that the creditor may not enter the debtor's premises in order to repossess goods. This provision applies whether or not the goods are protected and its breach is an actionable breach of statutory duty (s92(3)).

Furthermore, it is an offence for a creditor to harass a debtor, and threats to repossess may amount to harassment (Administration of Justice Act 1970, s40). The debtor is not given a right to sue for damages if this offence is committed, but whether or not goods are protected the criminal sanction can apply against the creditor.

Apportionment of payments

Where the debtor has more than one regulated agreement with the creditor and cannot afford to pay the full instalment due under each agreement, he has the right to choose how much of any payment made goes towards each (s81). This right can be significant where not all of the goods supplied to the debtor are protected goods.

For example, Mr D takes a car and a washing machine on hire purchase. The total price of the car is £9,501 payable by a deposit of £500 and 15 monthly instalments of £600, with a £1 option fee. The total price of the washing machine is £441 made up of a deposit of £20 and 14 monthly instalments of £30 with a £1 option fee. He pays the instalments for the first four months but then finds himself in difficulties and can pay only £63 in total in the fifth month. The total amount which he has to pay to make the car protected goods is £3,167 and for the washing machine it is £147. After four months he would have paid in total £2,900 towards the car and £140 towards the washing machine. If he had to pay towards the contracts in proportion to their respective monthly payments he would have to pay £60 for the car and £3 for the washing machine, and neither of them would be protected. But, because he can apportion the payment as he wishes, he may pay £55 for the car and £8 for the washing machine, thereby ensuring that the washing machine becomes protected goods.

Even where the goods are not protected the debtor will be entitled to apply to the court for extra time in which to pay. Often the creditor will start proceedings and the claim for extra time can be raised as a defence. The orders for which the debtor can apply are discussed in Chapter 6.

Relief against forfeiture

Relief against forfeiture lies within the power of the courts but they will not always grant it, (see, for example, *Goker* v *NWS Bank plc* (1990) The Times 23 May).

In *Goker* v *NWS Bank plc* the plaintiff negotiated a contract to buy a car from a car dealer, to whom he paid cash. He financed the transaction by taking out a loan with the defendant bank. He failed to keep up the instalments and the defendants repossessed the car. The plaintiff obtained an injunction to restrain the defendants from disposing of the car.

HELD: While, as a matter of law a court did have the power to grant relief against forfeiture, this was a jurisdiction to be exercised only in the most exceptional cases, and where it seemed likely that the debtor might be able to keep up the payments again, given a 'period of grace'. Since grave doubts applied to this hirer's ability to pay in the future, the court would not grant him relief against forfeiture. The injunction was lifted.

4.4 Acceleration clauses

Conditional sale and credit sale

Conditional sale and credit sale agreements frequently contain a clause stipulating that on breach by the debtor the whole of the outstanding price becomes payable. Such clauses are commonly known as acceleration clauses because they accelerate the rate at which the debtor has to pay the creditor. They are not objectionable in principle because by the very nature of the contract the debtor binds himself to pay for the goods.

Where the debtor wishes to enforce an acceleration clause he must serve a default notice because he is demanding earlier payment of a sum due (s87(1)(b)).

Because acceleration clauses operate on breach by the debtor it is important that the creditor does not fall foul of the rule against penalties. This rule, which will be examined in more detail in section 4.5 below, prevents a creditor from enforcing a clause which requires the debtor to pay a sum of money on breach which is not a genuine pre-estimate of the creditor's loss. If the debtor breaches and is required to pay the full amount of the total price immediately, this will allow the creditor to make a profit out of the breach because it will give him immediately a sum of money which, if the contract is performed properly, he can only get in instalments over a period of time. In other words, if the debtor did not breach the contract he would pay the total price in instalments, but if he breaches it he has to pay the total price immediately. The debtor gets his money earlier and therefore could invest it until the end of the contract period and make an extra profit. To avoid this it is necessary for the acceleration clause to provide for a rebate.

We will see in Chapter 5 that by s94 the debtor under a regulated agreement may pay the outstanding price early and that if he does so there is a statutory formula setting out the rebate he must be allowed. When working out what rebate should be given when an acceleration clause comes into effect, the same formula will be applied. There is nothing in the Act which stipulates this, but the reason for giving a rebate is the same whether the creditor makes early payment voluntarily or because an acceleration clause says so.

The debtor under a hire purchase or conditional sale has an additional right. He may back out of the agreement by giving notice to any person entitled to receive payment (s99(1)). Sometimes he has to pay the creditor if he wishes to terminate. This form of termination is different to early settlement under s94 because the debtor does not pay the full price and get property in the goods, he backs-out before property vests in him (see section 5.3). This right to terminate is exercisable at any time before the final payment falls due. The High Court has held that acceleration payments do not deprive the debtor of this right to terminate and therefore are not void under s173(1).

The argument for acceleration clauses being void is that under the agreement as it originally stands the debtor must pay over a period of time and may terminate at any time until that period has expired. But under the acceleration clause he must pay the outstanding balance immediately and therefore does not have until the end of the contract period in which to decide whether to terminate.

An example will show this argument. Say the original contract was made in January 1987 and that the debtor had to make payments over three years, with the last payment due in December 1989. If in January 1988 he breaches the contract and the acceleration clause is invoked, the full outstanding balance minus the rebate is payable immediately. If the debtor pays that balance immediately the agreement will be discharged because there is nothing further for either party to do. Therefore, after January 1988 the debtor would not be able to terminate the agreement, because there will be no agreement left to terminate. And the result of this is that the debtor is deprived of a right given to him by the Act - to terminate the agreement at any time until December 1989.

In *Wadham Stringer Finance Ltd* v *Meaney* [1981] 1 WLR 39; [1980] 3 All ER 789, Woolf J held that an acceleration clause did not deprive the debtor of his statutory right to terminate. The reason for this is that the Act allows the debtor to terminate 'at any time before the final payment ... falls due'. But it is for the agreement to state when payments fall due. And if there is an acceleration clause one effect of it is to bring forward the time when the final payment falls due. In other words the right of the debtor to terminate the agreement only lasts for as long as the agreement lasts and if the acceleration clause says it comes to a close sooner than it would otherwise do, then that is quite proper.

Hire purchase

Acceleration clauses cause few problems in conditional and credit sale agreements because the debtor is bound to pay the full price for the goods; and it cannot prejudice him to any substantial degree to have to pay it sooner rather than later. But in hire purchase the debtor never promises to pay for ownership of the goods, he only promises to hire. We saw in Chapter 1 that there are two types of hire purchase contract; in one the debtor promises to hire the goods over a period of time and has an option whether or not to buy, and in the other he agrees to hire them over a period of time but has the right to bring an end to the hiring at any time. If he does not put an end to it he becomes the owner on paying the final instalment.

If the second type contains an acceleration clause its effect will be to demand that the debtor buys the goods, because the whole of the outstanding hire will become payable, including the last instalment, and on the last instalment being paid the debtor will become the owner. This effectively converts a contract which was recognised in *Helby* v *Matthews* as being one of hire, into one of sale. Of course, the vast majority of hire purchase contracts end by the hirer buying the goods, but this is because of his decision to do so, it is not forced on him against his will. Nevertheless, the reasoning of Woolf J in *Wadham Stringer Finance Ltd* v *Meaney* applies in this situation as it does to conditional sales - if the contract says that the final instalment is due early when the debtor is in breach, then the final instalment is indeed due then. However, because the payments are for hire of the goods, the effect of the debtor's breach will be that he has to pay what can be an enormous amount of money as a final hire payment.

There is an additional difficulty with hire purchase contracts of the first type. The option fee is payable at the election of the debtor, the creditor does not have the right to demand it. Therefore, if there is an acceleration clause, it may bring forward the time when the debtor has to pay for hire of the goods but it cannot make the debtor the owner because that can only happen as a result of his decision to pay the option fee. Because the clause cannot invoke the option to purchase, so the debtor will have either to exercise that option or return the goods. If the debtor exercises the option then the acceleration clause will cause him no prejudice provided it allows a rebate for early payment. But if he does not exercise it, the true effect of this is to force the debtor to not only pay any hire payments due for use he has received but also to pay substantial damages. This is the result of the immutable principle that the instalments due under a hire purchase contract are payments for hire of the goods. So, where the debtor has to pay all outstanding instalments he is paying not only for the use he has received but also for future use which he will not receive. On this basis the acceleration clause is a penalty clause and is unenforceable. What the court must do is ask what loss the debtor has actually caused - in other words it must be asked whether it is an *Overstone Ltd* v *Shipway* case or a *Financings Ltd* v *Baldock* case and the creditor's remedy will be calculated according to the rules in those cases (see section 4.1 above). The way around this difficulty is to use a *Smart* v *Holt* clause.

Smart v Holt Clauses

Creditors frequently give themselves a wider range of remedies by inserting clauses which say that on breach by the debtor the creditor may either (1) without notice terminate the hiring and repossess the goods or (2) terminate the agreement totally by written notice but without prejudice to existing rights. A clause giving the creditor these alternative rights was upheld in *Smart Brothers Ltd* v *Holt* [1929] 2 KB 303.

The purpose of such clauses is to ensure that third parties who may be able to seize the debtor's goods could not seize the goods let to him on hire purchase because they would not be his goods in any way - he would not even be allowed to retain possession of them. They are particularly designed to prevent landlords seizing the goods from tenants who had not paid rent.

Because a default notice must now be served before the creditor is entitled to terminate a regulated agreement, a *Smart* v *Holt* clause cannot operate to treat the right of the debtor to keep the goods as terminated automatically - termination of that right can only occur once the seven-day period after service of the default notice has expired. Nevertheless, a *Smart* v *Holt* clause can assist the creditor because it gives him rights he might not otherwise have.

4.5 Minimum payment clauses

The penalty rule

When a party is in breach of contract he is liable to pay damages to the other party. Damages are meant to compensate for the actual effects of the breach and any clause in a contract which provides for more than fair compensation to be paid is liable to be struck down as a penalty. If it is struck down, damages must still be paid but at a level which is proper compensation only.

The conventional view is that the penalty rule is applicable only to terms of a contract which set out an amount of damages to be paid on breach. If the money is to be paid on an event which is not a breach of contract, the penalty rule does not apply. The problem for the court is how to apply two conflicting principles. On the one hand the court will not investigate the adequacy of the consideration and therefore will not investigate whether a party has to pay an unreasonable amount of money under the contract in order to receive a benefit from the other party, but on the other hand it will allow relief in equity from a term which imposes an unreasonable obligation to pay excessive damages if the contract is breached. At common law, careful drafting of a credit contract may be able to ensure that a creditor can make a large profit by relying on the first of these principles, without running any risk of the second having any application.

For example, if the parties wanted to they could incorporate a clause which says that if England win a test match against the West Indies the debtor must pay £1,000 to the creditor. The money is not payable on a breach of contract, because the debtor does not promise that England will not win, he simply agrees to pay a sum of money if they do win. The payment of the money on the happening of the agreed condition is all part of the credit bargain – it is part of the consideration and the courts cannot investigate whether it is a good bargain or a bad bargain.

On the other hand, if the parties said that if the debtor pays any two consecutive instalments late he is liable to pay £1,000, the penalty rule would apply. The reason it would apply is simple – the event on which the money is payable is a breach of contract.

It is hard to see what difference there is between the two examples given. They each stipulate for £1,000 to be paid by the debtor on the happening of a stated event, and in each case the debtor gets nothing in return for his money.

Lord Denning said frequently that the penalty rule applies to any contractual stipulation that money should be paid on the happening of an agreed event, whether or not that event is a breach of contract. But, as we shall see, his view does not represent the law.

Termination by the debtor

One consequence of the rejection of Lord Denning's view is that the penalty rule does not apply to clauses which stipulate that the debtor may terminate the contract provided he buys his way out by paying a certain sum of money. The principle behind the law as it stands at present is that under normal contract rules a party is not entitled to back out of a contract once he has made it. But, he may buy his way out by giving the other party whatever he wants in return for being released from the agreement. It is, of course, very common for managers and directors of companies to be bought out of their contracts by the payment of a 'golden handshake', and when footballers are 'bought' by a club the price paid represents the cost of buying the player out of his existing contract. There can be no question of golden handshakes being struck down as inequitable or the transfer of footballers from club to club being seen to be anything other than perfectly legitimate transactions. And it follows from such cases where, after the contract is made, the parties are free to negotiate whatever terms they like as being the price for getting out of an unwanted bargain, that they can stipulate in the contract itself that one or other of them can buy his way out by paying a sum of money. We will see in Chapter 5 that the amount which can be claimed from the debtor as the price of terminating the contract is limited by s100 of the 1974 Act. But for the moment we must examine the common law.

The main reason why finance companies wish to stipulate that money is payable on the debtor terminating the agreement is that the goods which are repossessed may have fallen in value and the creditor wishes to ensure that the cost of depreciation is paid by the debtor.

In *Associated Distributors Ltd* v *Hall* [1938] 2 KB 83; [1938] 1 All ER 511 the debtor took a bicycle on hire purchase, the agreement was to run for 53 weeks. By clause 5 he was entitled to terminate the agreement at any time and by clause 7 he then had to make a payment so as to make up the total amount paid to one-half of the total hire purchase price. Termination after half or more had been paid would be free of charge, but if less had been paid he would have to make a single payment to make the total paid up to half. It was conceded by his counsel that the option had been exercised so as to bring clause 7 into effect, but the argument was advanced that the penalty rule applied. The Court of Appeal held that the penalty rule did not apply. Slesser LJ said,

'This is a case where the hirer has elected to terminate the hiring. He has exercised an option, and the terms on which he may exercise the option are those set out in clause 7. The question, therefore, whether these payments constitute liquidated damages or penalty does not arise in the present case for determination.'

Associated Distributors Ltd v *Hall* was said to be wrongly decided by Lord Denning and Lord Devlin in *Bridge* v *Campbell Discount Co Ltd* (supra), but Viscount Simonds and Lord Morton said it was correct. The fifth Law Lord, Lord Radcliffe, passed no opinion on the question.

In principle, despite what is said at the beginning of this section, *Associated Distributors Ltd* v *Hall* can be challenged. The payment in that case was expressed to be recompense for depreciation. Arguably, if the debtor is really being asked to pay for depreciation the clause ought to reflect the true amount by which the goods have depreciated. If it does not reflect that true value it can be rectified, provided it is clear that the parties intended the clause to give genuine recompense for depreciation, in the same way that any clause which is inaccurately expressed can be rectified to reflect the true intention of the parties. If, on the other hand, it is not meant to give recompense for depreciation but merely to set the price which is payable by the debtor on exercising the right to terminate, it should say so.

Today *Associated Distributors Ltd* v *Hall* would be decided differently because of the presumption in *Bridge* v *Campbell Discount Ltd* and *United Dominions Trust* v *Ennis* (supra) that the acts of the debtor should be construed in the manner most favourable to him. We have seen this principle in relation to the giving by the debtor of consent to protected goods being repossessed. It is equally applicable where the question is not whether he is consenting to protected goods being repossessed, but whether he is exercising an expensive right to terminate or acting in some way which leaves him open to liability for a smaller sum.

The decision in *Associated Distributors Ltd* v *Hall* rests on the incorrect contention that the debtor had elected to terminate the agreement. We will investigate this aspect of the case later (see below: The important presumption).

Payments on breach

There can be no doubt that the penalty rule applies to clauses which require the debtor to pay a particular sum on breach of the contract. We saw in section 4.1 that breach by the debtor can be either repudiatory or non-repudiatory; that is, it can either go to the root or not go to the root. If it is repudiatory: the creditor is entitled to compensation for the loss of the whole transaction (*Overstone Ltd v Shipway*); if it is non-repudiatory, the creditor is always entitled to claim arrears and if there is an express term allowing him to terminate the agreement he may do so, but he will get no more than the arrears (*Financings Ltd v Baldock*). Therefore, in order for a clause providing for money to be paid on breach to be valid it must differentiate between repudiatory and non-repudiatory breaches and must set out the appropriate sums to be paid on each type of breach. It is not possible for the creditor to argue that a rough-and-ready calculation should be accepted as agreed damages because the court is able to calculate the proper amount of damages payable according to the formulae in the *Shipway* and *Baldock* cases.

The term stipulating the quantum of damages which is most frequently found in a conditional sale or hire purchase agreement is the so-called minimum payments clause. It is a clause providing that the debtor should make-up the amounts paid already to one-half or two-thirds or all of the total price. In *Cooden Engineering Co Ltd v Stanford* [1953] 1 QB 86; [1952] 2 All ER 915 it was held by the Court of Appeal that the debtor had committed a repudiatory breach by consistent default in payment. The minimum payments clause provided for the debtor to pay the whole of the outstanding balance of the total price and also all costs and expenses of the creditor caused by the breach. It was held that this clause was a penalty because it provided for the same sum to be paid whether breach was trivial or serious. This was an application of *Dunlop Pneumatic Tyre Co Ltd v New Garage and Motor Co Ltd* [1915] AC 79. The clause was not an accurate reflection of the loss to the creditor, but this was not crucial because the penalty rule applies whenever a clause could be anything other than a genuine pre-estimate of the creditor's loss and the clause could not possibly be correct on every occasion there was a breach; on that ground alone it would be a penalty.

The House of Lords approved *Cooden Engineering Ltd v Stanford* in *Bridge v Campbell Discount Co Ltd*. In that case the debtor committed a repudiatory breach by writing to the creditor, saying that he would not be able to complete the payments. A clause providing that he should make up the amount paid to two-thirds of the total price was held to be penal. Two approaches are evident from the speeches. Lords Morton and Radcliffe said it was a penalty because it did not accurately reflect the loss to the creditor by the breach which had occurred. They held that the true loss is the amount of damages which would be payable if there were no express clause. Lords Denning and Devlin held that the true loss was the amount by which the car had depreciated between its delivery to the hirer and its repossession by the creditor. The clause did not accurately calculate depreciation, despite claiming to do so, and therefore was not a genuine pre-estimate of loss. Viscount Simonds agreed with both views. It will be seen later that the view of Lords Morton and Radcliffe is the correct one (see below: Compensation for depreciation).

Compensation for depreciation

Much confusion in this area is caused by clauses which attempt to allow the creditor to be compensated for depreciation. The clause in *Bridge* v *Campbell Discount Co Ltd* was in this form and, as has been seen above, Lords Denning and Devlin held that it was penal because it did not accurately reflect the extent of depreciation. Originally minimum payments clauses were expressed in terms of being compensation for depreciation because that was felt to provide a way around the penalty rule. Eventually the cases reached the stage that it was assumed that a creditor is entitled to be compensated for depreciation when in fact no such right exists.

When the debtor is in breach the creditor is entitled to be put into the position he would have been in had the contract been performed. But, if the creditor himself is responsible for part of his loss he may not recover that part in damages from the debtor. That is why *Financings Ltd* v *Baldock* was decided as it was. The non-repudiatory breach by the debtor did not cause the creditor to have to repossess and therefore the creditor could not recover for those losses which would have been avoided if he had not repossessed. In other words he could not get compensation for the loss of the future hire payments because he had caused them to be lost by his decision to terminate the agreement and repossess.

The amount of damages to which the creditor is entitled is well settled. The measure is as defined in *Overstone Ltd* v *Shipway* if the breach is repudiatory and as defined in *Financings Ltd* v *Baldock* if non-repudiatory.

In *Anglo-Auto Finance Co Ltd* v *James* [1963] 1 WLR 1042; [1963] 3 All ER 566 the minimum payments clause allowed the creditor to recover the total hire purchase price minus instalments already paid. The Court of Appeal held this to be a penalty because the breach was non-repudiatory and *Financings Ltd* v *Baldock* sets out the amount recoverable on such a breach. There was no argument whether the breach was repudiatory or non-repudiatory, but it seems to have been conceded that it was the latter. Even had the breach been repudiatory the clause would be an inaccurate reflection of the creditor's loss because it did not give a rebate for early payment. The importance of the decision, however, is that it recognises, as did Lords Morton and Radcliffe in *Bridge* v *Campbell Discount Co Ltd* and the Court of Appeal in *Cooden Engineering Ltd* v *Stanford*, that a clause will be a penalty unless it reflects the common law rules on damages for breach of a hire purchase contract.

Similarly in *Capital Finance Co Ltd* v *Donati* (1977) 121 SJ 270, the clause gave the correct formula for repudiatory breach (ie the *Overstone Ltd* v *Shipway* formula), but the clause applied whether the breach was repudiatory or non-repudiatory and therefore was a penalty.

A clause which provides for the creditor to be compensated for depreciation will also fall foul of the penalty rule (save for the exceptional case discussed in the next paragraph). If the breach is non-repudiatory, the only loss to the creditor is that he has not received the outstanding instalments. Whether the goods have depreciated, and if so by how much, is completely irrelevant because the loss of the creditor is fixed: it is the amount of outstanding instalments. But, if the breach is repudiatory the creditor gives the debtor credit for the resale value and where the goods have depreciated the amount of this credit is less than where they have not. The creditor's loss is fully compensated by the *Overstone Ltd* v *Shipway* measure of damages; the greater the depreciation the less he obtains on resale and the more the debtor has to pay in damages. Again the extent of depreciation is, of itself, irrelevant.

In one case only will a clause providing for a depreciation payment be upheld. This is where the only thing being claimed by the creditor is loss for depreciation following a repudiatory breach. In other words, it is where the creditor does not make a full claim for damages but is prepared to cut his losses by claiming the loss of capital value of the goods: for example, where the debtor fails to pay and the creditor repossesses and claims in damages the difference between the original cash price and the value raised on resale. If there is any possibility of this figure exceeding the damages awardable at common law, the clause will be a penalty. This rules out a depreciation claim following a non-repudiatory breach because it may allow the creditor to claim a sum larger than the outstanding instalment(s).

The reason that Lords Denning and Devlin were wrong in *Bridge* v *Campbell Discount Ltd* to say that the minimum payment clause was a penalty because it did not accurately reflect depreciation was because the amount of depreciation could have exceeded the *Overstone Ltd* v *Shipway* measure of damages and, therefore, if the creditor recovered the amount of depreciation his damages would exceed what the common law allowed.

The important presumption

We saw in section 4.1 that the courts will presume that the debtor acts in the way which will do him least financial harm. In *Bridge* v *Campbell Discount Co Ltd* the debtor wrote to the creditor saying:

> 'Owing to unforeseen personal circumstances I am very sorry but I will not be able to pay any more payments on the [car]. Will you please let me know when and where I will have to return the car. I am very sorry regarding this but I have no alternative.'

The House of Lords held the sending of this letter to be a repudiatory breach by the debtor. It was not an exercise of the option to terminate because the contract said that to terminate the debtor had to return the car to the creditor and he actually returned it to the garage with whom he had negotiated. Also termination would have cost him more than breach and, following the presumption, this meant that he must have been refusing to perform and therefore was in breach.

In *United Dominions Trust Ltd* v *Ennis* the debtor wrote to the creditor saying:

> 'I am writing to inform you I wish to terminate my agreement with you as I find I cannot fulfil the terms stated. Please find enclosed the keys of the car and also the log book.'

The Court of Appeal held that the case was indistinguishable from *Bridge* v *Campbell Discount Co Ltd* and that the debtor was in breach. In relation to the general presumption, Lord Denning MR said:

> 'a hirer is not to be taken to exercise such an option unless he does so consciously, knowing of the consequences, and avowedly in exercise of the option. If this were not so, the document would be an absolute trap set to catch him. Not one hirer in a thousand reads these small printed clauses. Even if he did he would not understand them. When he returns the car, he naturally assumes that is an end of the hiring and, in consequence, an end of the instalments. He should not be bound to make in addition this tremendous payment - as the price of termination - unless he knows what he is doing. In order to bind him to it, knowledge of it must be brought home to him in fact so as to amount to a new agreement by him to pay the sum.'

The presumption is clearly laid down that the acts of the debtor will be construed in the way which gives rise to the lowest financial liability. It is in relation to this only that *Associated Distributors Ltd* v *Hall* can be properly criticised. It was conceded that the debtor was terminating the agreement. But his liability would have been lower had he been seen to be in breach rather than terminating, so the concession was wrongly made. In this way the apparent harshness of the decision is abrogated and the fears of Lord Denning in *Bridge* v *Campbell Discount Co Ltd* about the *Hall* case are without foundation:

> 'Let no one mistake the injustice of this. It means that equity commits itself to this absurd paradox: it will grant relief to a man who breaks his contract but will penalise the man who keeps it.'

4.6 Security

Security at common law

The whole purpose of a hire purchase transaction is to allow the creditor security for the credit he advances. This was recognised by Lord Denning in the passage from *Bridge* v *Campbell Discount Co Ltd* cited in Chapter 1. A creditor who advances credit runs the risk of not being repaid. It can be said that he does not need any security because he can sue if he is not paid. But this does not take into account that in the vast majority of cases where the debtor is in breach he has failed to pay because he does not have enough money, and so to sue him would be pointless; if he cannot pay the instalments he will not be able to pay the damages. Therefore, a creditor wishes to ensure, so far as is possible, that there is a way for him to receive payment even if the debtor cannot manage it himself. The retention of ownership in the goods pending payment is one way of doing this, but even that does not give the creditor full protection because by repossessing and reselling the goods he will not necessarily raise the full amount of money outstanding from the debtor.

Therefore, creditors frequently want either a third party or the debtor himself to give additional security. Common examples are a bank requiring the deposit of a building society book and a withdrawal slip so that it can withdraw money from the building society account if the debtor does not pay.

Alternatively, a third party may undertake to pay if the debtor fails to do so. There are many different ways in which security can be given but we will deal with only two, guarantees and indemnities. In addition, we are predominantly concerned with security given by someone other than the debtor.

A guarantee is an undertaking by a third party, (the guarantor), that he will pay the creditor if the debtor is in breach of the agreement. The guarantor's liability depends upon the debtor breaching the agreement. Where, for example, the debtor exercises an option to terminate the agreement early, he will not be in breach and the creditor would not have a claim against the guarantor.

An indemnity is an undertaking by a third party (the indemnor) to cover any loss the creditor may make whether or not the debtor is in breach. Therefore, if the debtor exercises his option to terminate the agreement early, the indemnor will have to compensate the creditor for the loss of the future instalments which the debtor will not now pay.

The importance of the distinction between a guarantee and an indemnity is twofold. Firstly a contract of guarantee must be evidenced in writing (Statute of Frauds 1677, s4), otherwise it is unenforceable. Secondly, because a guarantee is only enforceable where the debtor is in breach, if the credit agreement is unenforceable against the debtor the guarantee will also be unenforceable against the surety.

It is necessary to look at the substance of the security agreement to see whether it is a guarantee or an indemnity. The security agreement in *Unity Finance Ltd* v *Woodcock* [1963] 1 WLR 455; [1963] 2 All ER 270 was called an indemnity by the parties, but the liability of the surety depended on the debtor defaulting and therefore it was a guarantee. In the earlier case of *Yeoman Credit Ltd* v *Latter* [1961] 1 WLR 828; [1961] 2 All ER 294, however, the liability of the surety was to reimburse the creditor if, at the end of the day, the creditor did not recover the full price from the debtor. The debtor was an infant and the credit agreement was unenforceable against him. But, because the surety had agreed to reimburse the creditor no matter why the full price was not paid by the debtor, so the contract was an indemnity.

Yeoman Credit Ltd v *Latter* was distinguished in *Western Credit Ltd* v *Alberry* [1964] 1 WLR 945; [1964] 2 All ER 938 in which the surety agreement was described as a guarantee but said that the surety would indemnify the creditor against any loss arising from the 'act default or negligence' of the debtor. The agreement was held by the Court of Appeal to be a guarantee, not an indemnity because the acts upon which the surety had to 'indemnify' the creditor were breaches of contract.

Recourse agreements

Finance companies have little use for goods which are repossessed or which are returned by the debtor on the termination of the agreement and they do not like losing money financing hire purchase contracts which are really designed for the benefit of debtor and dealer. It is, therefore, common for a contract to be made between the creditor and dealer under which the dealer agrees to reimburse the creditor for any losses which may be suffered as a result of the debtor not paying the full price. These contracts are known as recourse agreements. Often one aspect of a recourse agreement is that the dealer will buy the goods back from the creditor.

A recourse agreement is a security agreement even though the security is not provided by the debtor. Therefore, the distinction between guarantees and indemnities is important because it determines the liability of the dealer. *Unity Finance Ltd* v *Woodcock* involved a recourse agreement which was construed to be a guarantee. By contrast in *Goulston Finance Co Ltd* v *Clark* [1967] 2 QB 493; [1967] 1 All ER 61 the dealer agreed to indemnify the creditor 'against any losses that you may suffer by reason of the fact that the hirer ... for any cause whatsoever does not pay the amounts which he would if he completed his agreement by exercising the option to purchase'. The Court of Appeal held this to be an indemnity and to entitle the creditor to recover from the dealer everything that would have been due under the contract even though the debtor's breach was non-repudiatory.

Security under the Act

Securities are only regulated by the Act if they are provided by the debtor or at his request (s189(1)). Therefore, recourse agreements are not affected. The Act regulates security agreements in two ways. Firstly, it lays down formal requirements for the making of securities, and secondly, it links the liability of the surety to the liability of the debtor. We are concerned primarily with the rules applicable to sureties other than the debtor because the Consumer Credit (Agreements) Regulations 1983, made under s60, cover not only the regulated agreement itself but also any security given by the debtor. Regulation 2(8) provides, simply, 'Documents embodying regulated consumer credit agreements shall embody any security provided in relation to the regulated agreement by the debtor.' In other words, the regulated agreement and the security will both be contained within the same document.

The formality rules in relation to sureties other than the debtor are in s105 and the Consumer Credit (Guarantees and Indemnities) Regulations 1983. The main requirements are:

The security agreement must be in writing (s105(1)). The document must be signed by the surety, contain all of its terms save for implied terms, its terms must be readily legible, and the surety must be given a copy of it when he is given the original for signature (s105(4)). The surety must also be given a copy of the regulated agreement. If he provides the security after or at the same time as the regulated agreement is made, he should be given a copy of the regulated agreement when he provides the security (s105(5)(a)). If, on the other hand, he provides the security before the regulated agreement is made, he should be given a copy of it within seven days after it is made (s105(5)(b)).

The Regulations lay down the necessary form of the security document in Regulation 3 and the Schedule to the Regulations. It must contain a heading which says whether it is a guarantee or an indemnity and that it is subject to the Act, give the name and address of both creditor and debtor and also the postal address of the surety. In addition, the surety's rights must be set out in general terms (see below).

If these formalities are not complied with, the security agreement is not properly executed and can be enforced only on order of the court (s105(7)). In addition, if the regulated agreement cannot be enforced otherwise than by order of the court the same applies to the security agreement, even if it has been properly executed (s113(2)). On cancellation by the debtor or discharge of the agreement by repossession of protected goods, the security is treated as never having effect (s113(3) and 106). Therefore, if the surety has paid the creditor any money or has deposited any property with him, it must be returned, and if the creditor has registered a charge over any property of the surety the entry in the register must be removed (s106).

Also, if the position is reached when the regulated agreement cannot ever be enforced, the security is again treated as never having effect (s113(3) and 106). This could happen by the court refusing to allow a creditor to enforce where he has failed to comply with his obligations under the Act, or by the court granting the debtor a declaration that the agreement cannot be enforced because of the creditor's failure to comply (as to which see Chapter 6 below), or by the security being provided in anticipation of the making of the regulated agreement and that agreement is never made (including where the debtor withdraws after making his proposal to the creditor). We saw in Chapter 2 that the failure of the creditor to provide a copy of the notice of cancellation rights in a case under s64(1)(b) prevents the court from granting the creditor permission to enforce (known as an Enforcement Order). That is the sort of case in which the debtor may apply for a declaration that the regulated agreement is wholly unenforceable, and the declaration will make the security unenforceable as well.

In addition to the formality requirements, the Act limits the extent to which a security can be enforced. The general rule is in s113(1).

> 'Where a security is provided in relation to an actual or prospective regulated agreement, the security shall not be enforced so as to benefit the creditor ... directly or indirectly, to an extent greater (whether as respects the amount of any payment or the time or manner of its being made) than would be the case if the security were not provided and any obligations of the debtor ... under or in relation to the agreement were carried out to the extent (if any) to which they would be enforced under this Act.'

The key phrase is 'an extent greater ... than if the security were not provided'. This means that all securities provided are treated as guarantees. The liability of the surety is no greater than that of the debtor. If the events which have happened do not entitle the creditor to claim anything from the debtor, the same limit applies to the surety. There is one exception, in the case of debtors who are minors. In such cases it is presumed that the debtor is an adult and the liability of the surety is the liability that the adult debtor would have (s113(7)).

To provide a consistent approach to all aspects of the regulated agreement, security agreements made to secure the performance of a linked transaction are also only enforceable to the extent that the linked transaction is enforceable (s113(8)). It should be noted that security agreements are not themselves linked transactions, because s19(1) expressly excludes them.

Information

A surety is entitled to receive information about the regulated agreement in the same way as the debtor. Under s107 a surety to a fixed-sum regulated agreement may obtain copies of the regulated agreement and the security agreement and a statement of the present state of the debtor's account on making a request in writing and paying 50 pence. The same applies to running account credit by virtue of s108.

Of more practical importance is the duty of the creditor to serve a default notice on the surety as well as the debtor (s111(1)). Failure to do this makes the security unenforceable except by order of the court (s111(2)). This does not affect the enforceability of the regulated agreement, however.

Rights of surety against debtor

The Act does not regulate the relationship between sureties and debtors. At common law, a guarantor who has had to honour the debtor's liabilities steps into the creditor's shoes by virtue of the principles of subrogation (*Tate* v *Crewdson* [1938] Ch 869 [1938] 3 All ER 43). In the same way that an insurance company takes over the right of an injured motorist once it has paid him under his policy, so a guarantor who pays the creditor takes over the rights of that creditor. This right arises only where it is expressly agreed between debtor and guarantor or where it can be implied, and this will only be the case if the debtor has requested the guarantor to act as a surety (*Re a Debtor (No 627 of 1936)* [1937] Ch 156; [1937] 1 All ER 1).

The principle of subrogation will not help an indemnor who has had to reimburse the creditor even though the debtor is not in breach. Such a surety will only be able to recover his losses from the debtor if there is a separate agreement between himself and the debtor to that effect. It is rare for a debtor under a regulated agreement to agree to indemnify a surety because, in the main, sureties are other individuals who secure the debtor's liability without ever thinking that they will be called upon to pay anything. Even dealers who are required by the creditor to enter into a recourse agreement do not make a separate agreement with the debtor allowing for their losses to be recoverable from him.

In the vast majority of cases involving regulated consumer credit agreements, a surety will only be called upon by the creditor if the debtor is unable to pay. It goes without saying that a surety's rights against the debtor are not worth pursuing if the debtor has no money.

5

Termination

5.1 Early settlement

5.2 Creditor terminating

5.3 Debtor terminating

5.4 Termination, breach and settlement

5.1 Early settlement

A debtor under any regulated consumer credit agreement is entitled to settle his liability early. The creditor cannot complain if this is done because he gets the credit repaid. He will not get all of the total charge for credit, however, because the debtor is entitled to a rebate for early settlement. The principle behind the right to settle early is simple. It can only be to the advantage of the debtor to pay back the credit advance and, provided the creditor does not make a loss on the transaction, he can have no legitimate objection to this being done. If the debtor wishes to exercise this right he should write to the creditor asking how much he must pay in order to be released from the agreement and the creditor must tell him (s97(1)). If the creditor does not reply with the information within seven working days of the request being received, the agreement is unenforceable until he does reply and if the failure continues for one month he commits an offence (s97(3)).

The right to settle early is given by s94 and is exercised by giving the creditor notice in writing and paying the sum required to settle the indebtedness. No particular form of words need be used. Early settlement has the effect of completing the transaction. So, if it is a conditional sale, property will pass to the debtor automatically on his paying the creditor. Where the agreement is hire purchase the debtor should exercise the option to buy, if there is one, at the same time as making payment.

Section 95 provides that the debtor is entitled to a rebate for settling early and for regulations to be made to allow the calculation of the rebate.

In *Forward Trust* v *Whymark* [1989] 3 WLR 1229 the defendant obtained from the plaintiff finance company a personal loan repayable over ten years. The agreement was a regulated consumer credit agreement to which the provisions of the Consumer Credit Act 1974 and the Consumer Credit (Rebate on Early Settlement) Regulations 1983 applied (see below). Within two years the defendant had defaulted.

The plaintiffs claimed and entered judgment for the full amount outstanding. The defendant applied to pay the amount in instalments; in the first instance the Registrar set aside the judgment on the grounds of the defendant's entitlement to a rebate under ss94–95 of the Consumer Credit Act for early settlement. On hearing the appeal from the plaintiffs the Court of Appeal held that ss94–95 regarding rebates for early settlement were clearly meant to apply only when the debtor intended to pay the full amount of his indebtedness before the time fixed for expiry of the agreement; and that on a true construction of the Act and the Regulations it did not apply to default cases. Judgment was entered for the plaintiffs for the full amount outstanding and the matter remitted to the County Court for a determination of the defendant's application to pay in instalments.

The relevant regulations (referred to above) are the Consumer Credit (Rebate on Early Settlement) Regulations 1983. Naturally the debtor must repay the credit advance in full. The rebate is of the part of the total charge for credit which would be payable if the agreement continued but is no longer payable because it is terminated. There are complex formulae in the regulations for calculation of the rebate, and various methods of computation are used depending on the type of credit agreement. For example, there is a difference between the way the rebate is calculated for repayment of a cash loan which was originally designed to be repaid as a single lump sum with interest and the method used in hire purchase and conditional agreements.

It is beyond the scope of this book to examine the arithmetical details of these formulae in any detail. The formula used to calculate the rebate due for early settlement of a hire purchase, credit sale and conditional sale contracts is known as the 'Rule of 78' (see Schedule 2 to the Regulations). It works in three stages (note that for hire purchase it may be necessary to pay the option fee as well).

Stage 1

The number of instalments due to be paid in the future is calculated. The date for assessing this figure is not the date on which the debtor gives notice of his intention to settle early but is a date either two months or one month after that date. It will be two months after if the agreement was meant to last for five years or less, and one month if it was meant to last for more than five years (Reg. 5). This figure is given the letter 'm' in the formula below.

Stage 2

The total number of instalments to be paid under the agreement is calculated. Any initial payment should be ignored and, therefore, the figure represents the number of periodical payments only. This figure is given the letter 'n' in the formula.

Stage 3

The figures are applied to the following formula:

$$\frac{m(m+1)}{n(n+1)} \times \text{Total Charge for Credit} = \text{Rebate}$$

5.2 Creditor terminating

The creditor is only entitled to terminate the agreement if either the debtor has committed a repudiatory breach or the agreement contains a clause which allows termination in certain defined circumstances. We saw in Chapter 4 that it is common for creditors to be entitled to terminate the agreement whenever the debtor is in breach, whether that breach is repudiatory or non-repudiatory. But it is also common for the creditor to be entitled to terminate on the bankruptcy of the debtor.

Where the event which causes the creditor to decide to terminate is a breach of contract, a default notice must be served before the agreement can be terminated (s87(1)). But where the event is something other than a breach a default notice cannot be served because there is no default. Instead a notice must be served pursuant to s98. A s98 notice is concerned with terminating the agreement only. Any other act, like repossession, can only be done following service of a s76 notice. But s76 specifically applies only where the creditor wishes to repossess, demand earlier payment or treat any right of the debtor as terminated, restricted or deferred; and this is not wide enough to cover termination of the whole contract. That is why s98 termination notices are required.

A termination notice must be in the form prescribed by the Consumer Credit (Enforcement), Default and Termination Notices) Regulations 1983, and is ineffective if it is not in the prescribed form (s98(3)). It must state that it is served pursuant to s98 and must contain the following information: a description of the agreement which is sufficient to identify it, the names and addresses of the creditor and debtor, the term which entitles the creditor to terminate, what he intends to do following termination and what sum, if any, is payable by the debtor on termination (see Reg 2(3) and Schedule 3). In addition it must state that the debtor is entitled to apply to the court for more time to pay any sum due.

There is a further limitation on the creditor's right to terminate on the death of the debtor. That right only exists at all if the agreement specifically allows it, and even then it cannot be done if the agreement is fully secured (s86(1)). There is no point in the creditor terminating the agreement on the debtor's death if it is fully secured, because he can enforce it fully against the surety. An agreement which is not fully secured can only be terminated on death of the debtor if there is an order of the court allowing termination (s86(2)). The same limitation applies where the creditor does not wish to terminate the agreement but merely to demand earlier payment, or repossess the goods, or treat any right of the debtor as terminated, restricted or deferred.

The need to obtain a court order applies not only where the creditor relies on a term of the agreement allowing him to terminate following the debtor's death, but also where he is allowed to terminate it at will but chooses to exercise this power following the death of the debtor (s86(6)(b)).

In order to avoid unnecessary applications to the court there is one specific exception to the need to obtain a court order. This arises where the creditor wishes to enforce a term whereby sums due under the agreement are payable on the debtor's death out of a life assurance policy (s86(5)). Naturally this only applies if the policy was on the life of the debtor himself.

5.3 Debtor terminating

When termination allowed

In addition to the right to settle the agreement early the debtor also has the right to terminate it early. The difference between early settlement and termination is that early settlement involves the debtor paying off the whole of his outstanding indebtedness whereas termination allows him to back out without completing his obligations. Unlike the right of early settlement, the right to terminate is limited to debtors under hire purchase and conditional sale agreements. Both of these types of contract involve the debtor in paying for goods in instalments and, usually, only becoming their owner if he completes the agreement. A debtor who is unable to complete the agreement may wish to cut his losses by bringing to an end his duty to pay the instalments.

Of course, a conditional sale may provide for property to pass to the debtor before all payments are due. This will not preclude him from terminating unless he has transferred the property in them to someone else (for example by selling them), in which case the right to terminate is lost (s99(4)). But, if property has vested in the debtor he may terminate under s99 and if he does, property will re-vest in the person who was the owner immediately before him (s99(5)). In the vast majority of cases this will be the creditor.

Under a credit sale the debtor gets ownership in the goods from the beginning (subject to ss17 and 18 of the Sale of Goods Act 1979) and it would be absurd for him to be able to stop paying yet keep the goods. Similarly, a debtor who obtains a cash loan must repay it, so termination would be inappropriate. This does not mean that the debtor under a credit sale is not entitled to come to an arrangement with the creditor allowing him to give back the goods in return for the discharge of his duty to make any further payments; but any settlement on those or similar terms must be negotiated by the parties and are not subject to the Act's regulation.

The right to terminate can be exercised at any time before the final payment is due (s99(1)). We saw in Chapter 4 that acceleration clauses can bring forward the date when the final payment is due. But in the absence of such a clause the final payment will be due at the end of the period set for instalments to be paid. It is not necessary for there to be any express clause allowing termination, because s99 specifically allows termination. The debtor's position, therefore, is different to that of the creditor, who has no right to terminate unless the agreement specifically allows it or the debtor commits a repudiatory breach.

How to terminate

The right to terminate pursuant to s99 must be exercised by giving notice in writing to any person who is authorised to receive payment under the agreement (s99(1)). Although the Act does not specifically cover the point there can be no doubt that oral notice will be sufficient if that is what the agreement allows or if the creditor treats it as effective notice. It follows from this that notice to anyone not authorised to receive payment may also be effective if the agreement, or the conduct of the creditor, allows it. As with notice of withdrawal, cancellation or early settlement, no particular form of words need be used. The persons entitled to receive payment will be stated in the agreement and such persons may or may not include the dealer.

In addition to giving notice, the debtor may have to pay a sum of money to the creditor. The Court of Appeal in *Associated Distributors Ltd* v *Hall* (see above: section 4.5) held that a sum stipulated in an agreement as being payable on exercise of an option to terminate a hire purchase agreement is not subject to the rule against penalties. The Act reduces the effect of this decision by providing in s100(1) that the maximum the debtor will ever have to pay in order to be able to terminate is the amount by which one half of the total price exceeds the aggregate of payments already made and payments already due. In other words, the most the debtor will have to pay is a sum to make up the total amount payable to one-half of the total price (but see below). If he has already paid half or more of the total price, he may terminate without having to pay anything.

The sum required to bring payments made up to one-half of the total price is not always due. There are three situations in which less is payable.

1. Where the agreement does not provide for the payment of any sum on termination, no sum is payable (s100(1)). This does not just cover cases where the agreement contains a clause saying that the debtor may terminate for free. It also covers cases where the agreement is silent. So, if the agreement does not specifically allow termination by the debtor and, therefore, does not specify a figure as being payable on termination, the debtor may terminate because of s99 and is not liable to pay anything.
2. The second case where less than the sum required to make up to half the total price is payable is where the agreement does lay down a figure, but this figure is less than the statutory figure (s100(1)). For example, if it says the debtor may terminate by making payments up to one-third of the total price.

3. The third case is covered by s100(3) which says: 'If in any action the court is satisfied that a sum less than the amount specified in subsection (1) would be equal to the loss sustained by the creditor in consequence of the termination of the agreement by the debtor, the court may make an order for the payment of that sum in lieu of the amount specified in subsection (1).'

Strictly speaking, subs(3) only applies 'In any action', in other words where there is a case before the court. But any claim by the creditor to be entitled to more than the debtor is offering, or any claim by the debtor for a declaration that he does not have to make payments up to one-half will suffice for this purpose. So, in effect, subs(3) applies to limit the amount payable by the debtor whether the matter is before the court or not. The court is given a discretion by subs(3), but it is unlikely that the court will ever allow the creditor to make a profit out of termination, so subs (3) should be looked upon as laying down a mandatory rule and not a discretionary one.

It is not clear how the 'loss sustained by the creditor in consequence of the termination' is to be calculated. There is no definition of it in the Act. If the debtor does not terminate it, the agreement will normally continue and the creditor will be entitled to the total price or, where appropriate in hire purchase cases, the total price minus the option fee. But the creditor will only make a loss if he fails to recover the cash price of the goods; if he merely fails to receive the total charge for credit he has not made a loss, he has merely failed to make a profit. Nevertheless, it is unrealistic to construe 'loss' very narrowly and the proper way to approach subs(3) is to assume that the creditor will receive the total price and to see whether he receives less than that following termination. Any costs to the creditor as a result of the debtor's termination should also be taken into account. There are often administrative costs involved because major finance companies employ people who deal exclusively with terminations.

It is certainly envisaged by subs(3) that the effect of termination will be to cause the creditor a loss, so what must be done is to see how much the creditor would receive if the agreement were not terminated. In all cases he is entitled to the payments already made and any which are due but not yet paid. So s100(3) is concerned with the difference between: (1) the amount already paid plus the amount in arrear, and (2) what the creditor gets if the debtor terminates without paying any money at all.

The cases where the creditor does not make a loss, or makes a smaller loss than the amount of money the debtor would have to pay to make up his payments to one-half of the total price, would include cases where the goods have increased in value so that when the debtor terminates and hands the goods back the creditor can sell them and raise a sum larger than the cash price under the regulated agreement. But s100(3) would apply to all other cases where the creditor can reduce his loss to under one-half of the total price by reselling the goods, it is not strictly necessary for them to have increased in value.

For example, the total conditional sale price of a car is £9,000. The debtor has already paid £3,000. The maximum he will have to pay is £1,500 because that is what is required to make up payments to £4,500, which is one half of the total price. The creditor's maximum loss is £6,000, which represents that part of the total price not yet paid. If the creditor can sell the car following repossession for £5,000, the debtor only has to pay £1,000 more, because that is what is required to make the creditor's total receipts up to £6,000 (which is the creditor's loss). If it can be sold for £5,750 the debtor only has to pay £250. But if it can be sold for £6,000 or more, the debtor does not have to pay anything.

A further instance of the creditor making a lower loss than envisaged by s100(1) would occur where the creditor has breached, or would in the future breach, the agreement in some way so that the debtor would have had the right to sue him. If the agreement were not terminated and the debtor did sue, the creditor may receive the total price but he would not make as large a profit as if he did not have to pay damages.

To continue the example used above, if the car is resold for £5,000 but it was defective when delivered to the debtor and he could have recovered, say, £250 in damages, the creditor will be entitled not to £1,000 but to £750. It is hard to imagine any case in which the creditor will not be able to sell the goods and raise something, even if it is not a very large sum, and therefore the full amount in s100(1) may only rarely be payable. Further, if the debtor failed to take reasonable care of the goods so that they are worth less when repossessed than they should be worth, the amount to be paid under s100(1) must be increased to take into account the damage done to them (s100(4)). So, if the car has not been looked after properly and as a result is worth £500 less than it should be the figure under s100(1) is not £1,500 but £2,000. The only effect of subs(4) is to increase the maximum amount payable under subs(1). It does not prevent subs(3) from applying. So if the car when repossessed is sold for £5,000 the creditor can still recover £1,000. Of course, had it been looked after properly it might have been possible to sell it for £5,500, so the result of the debtor's failure to take reasonable care is that the creditor has made a greater loss than would otherwise have been the case.

The goods

Once the debtor has terminated the agreement he is no longer entitled to retain possession of the goods. If he fails to deliver them to the creditor when asked he will commit an act of conversion. The duty to deliver the goods goes no further than a duty to make them available for collection (*Capital Finance Co Ltd* v *Bray* [1964] 1 WLR 323; [1964] 1 All ER 603).

The creditor has a choice of remedies open to him on conversion. He may sue for: (1) the delivery up to him of the goods plus damages for consequential loss; or (2) their value; or (3) their delivery and damages or their value at the debtor's option (s3(2), Torts (Interference With Goods) Act 1977). Their value is to be calculated at the time they should have been handed back (*Belvoir Finance Co Ltd* v *Stapleton* [1971] 1 QB 210; [1970] 3 All ER 664).

Section 100(5) of the 1974 Act provides that the court shall order delivery-up of the goods if the creditor sues for possession, without giving the debtor the option of paying their value. This is designed to prevent the debtor from making a profit by keeping the goods after termination and paying their value, where the result of this is that he pays less than he would have paid had the agreement not been terminated.

5.4 Termination, breach and settlement

The debtor has three ways of extracting himself from a regulated consumer credit agreement which he cannot afford. He could terminate the agreement (if it is HP or conditional sale), breach it seriously, or settle his liabilities early. No matter which course is adopted, he is likely to have to pay something to the creditor.

We have seen in Chapter 4 that there is a presumption that the debtor acts in the way which costs him least. But this presumption is probably only applicable where he has acted equivocally. If it is clear that he is acting in one of the three ways stated above, then that is how his conduct must be construed, even if it is not the cheapest method of release from the contract.

For example, if the debtor writes to the creditor and expressly says that he is terminating under the power in s99 of the Consumer Credit Act 1974 there will be no scope for his letter to be construed as anything other than an election to terminate. Similarly, if he writes saying that he refuses to pay because the goods are of no use to him, this will be a repudiatory breach unless he can prove that the goods were not of merchantable quality or were not fit for his particular purpose.

Debtors often get into trouble by refusing to pay instalments due under hire purchase contracts because they are not happy with the way in which the goods are performing. Unless the creditor is in breach of condition the result of the debtor refusing to pay will be that he himself will be in breach. It is usually impossible in such cases to argue that the debtor is doing anything other than breaching the agreement, because it will be clear from the terms of his letter that he does not want to back out of the agreement completely, but merely intends to withhold payment until the goods are repaired. Unfortunately, a debtor does not have this right. He should continue paying and claim compensation for the loss he incurs through the problems encountered with the goods.

Where the debtor is sued for failing to pay, and he argues in his defence that the goods did not perform properly, he will have a counterclaim to the creditor's claim for outstanding instalments. But it is a counterclaim and not a set-off. In other words the debtor is not able to say that he was not obliged to pay; although he can make his own claim, separate to that of the creditor, in which he can claim damages for loss of use.

6

Judicial Control

6.1 Enforcement orders
6.2 The debtor's protection
6.3 Extortionate credit bargains

6.1 Enforcement orders

Enforcement

We have seen that in some circumstances the creditor is not allowed to enforce a regulated agreement unless he first obtains an order of the court. Not surprisingly, the order which he applies for is known as an enforcement order. Not all orders which the creditor may need are enforcement orders, however, because s189(1) defines enforcement orders as orders required by virtue of s65(1) (improperly executed agreements), s105(7) (improperly executed securities) and s111(2) (failure to serve copy of notice on surety). In addition there is a provision which is not relevant to this book whereby the taking of a negotiable instrument from a surety must be done in a particular way; if this is not done properly an enforcement order is necessary before the creditor can enforce against the debtor (see s124). Any other order which the Act requires the creditor to obtain is not an enforcement order.

There is no definition in the Act of what amounts to enforcement of a regulated agreement. In principle there are four things the creditor may try to do. Firstly, he may claim sums which the debtor ought to have paid but has not paid. Secondly, he may claim to be entitled to damages for the debtor's breach of the agreement. Thirdly, he may seek repossession of goods supplied by him to the debtor. And fourthly, he may seek to discharge the contract because of the debtor's breach.

The first claim is without doubt an enforcement of the agreement. The claim is that sums have become due but have not been paid and the creditor is claiming to enforce his right to receive that money. The creditor's action is not for damages in such cases but is for a debt which has fallen due (*Financings Ltd* v *Baldock* (supra)).

The second claim is not for sums due under the agreement but for damages which are sums due because the agreement has been breached. Damages are due whenever the debtor breaches the agreement. But normally the only breach by the debtor is that he does not pay on time. As we saw in the previous paragraph the creditor's claim for arrears is a claim for a debt, not a claim for damages. However, the debtor can be in breach in other ways, for example by damaging goods supplied under a hire purchase or conditional sale contract. It is likely that such claims for damages will be ruled to be enforcements of the regulated agreement under which the goods were supplied, because what the creditor is doing is claiming that he is entitled to damages by virtue of the agreement having been breached. In other words, he has to rely on the terms of the agreement to establish his right to damages and there is the clearest authority that a claim for damages arises by virtue of the contract which is breached (*Photo Production Ltd* v *Securicor Transport Ltd* [1980] AC 827; [1980] 1 All ER 556).

The third claim is in the same position as the second. In order to claim to be entitled to repossess the goods the creditor will have to show that the terms of the contract allow him to do so. Therefore, a claim for possession is also an enforcement of the agreement. It should be remembered, of course, that where the goods are protected goods (see section 4.3 above) the creditor will need a court order whether or not he needs an enforcement order. It follows from this that where the agreement is improperly executed and the goods are protected the creditor must obtain both an enforcement order and an order entitling him to repossess.

The fourth claim is different in nature to the others because the creditor need not go to court to discharge the contract. In the three other claims if the debtor does not pay or does not return the goods the creditor must go to court for an order in his favour. But the contract will be discharged at common law by the creditor giving the debtor notice that the agreement is discharged. It will be necessary for the debtor to have committed a repudiatory breach of the contract before the creditor will be entitled to discharge the contract, but provided such a breach has occurred it will be discharged as soon as the debtor has notice (*Johnson* v *Agnew* [1980] AC 367; [1979] 1 All ER 883).

We will see in section 6.2 below that in some circumstances the debtor can apply to the court for more time to pay; so if his only breach was a failure to pay sums due to the creditor the court can bring back to life a contract which has been discharged at common law. This does not, however, affect the general principle of common law that a contract is discharged following a breach of condition or a serious breach of an innominate term as soon as the creditor gives notice of his decision to discharge it. At common law the court has no part to play and if the debtor refuses to accept that the contract is discharged this will have no effect. It is therefore unlikely that a decision by the creditor to discharge a contract because of the debtor's breach will be seen to be an enforcement of the contract and therefore no enforcement order need be applied for.

It must not be overlooked that the creditor must serve a default notice on the debtor before he can become entitled to do any of the things listed in s87(1)(a)-(e) (see section 4.2 above). The service of a default notice is not itself an enforcement of the agreement, because s87(1) provides that a default notice must be served before the creditor is entitled to terminate the agreement, demand earlier payment, etc. So the default notice must be served first and when it has expired the creditor may, for example, terminate the agreement. But if an enforcement order is required the default notice can be served first and only if the debtor does not remedy his breach will there be any need to go on to apply for an enforcement order.

Making the application

Application for an enforcement order is made by virtue of the section which requires the creditor to obtain such an order. So, for example, if the agreement is improperly executed it is s65(1) which requires an enforcement order. Section 127 determines how the court should approach such applications, but it does not of itself enable the application to be made.

The county court has jurisdiction to determine any action which is taken to enforce a regulated agreement, a security or a linked transaction (Consumer Credit Act 1974 s141(1)). This is so even if the amount in dispute is greater than that court's usual jurisdictional limit of £5,000. An action by a debtor is not caught by s141, so it should be taken in either the county court or the High Court, depending upon whether the amount involved is in excess of £5,000 (County Courts Act 1984, s15(1)).

See *Sovereign Leasing plc* v *Ali* (1991) The Times 21 March. The Consumer Credit Act 1974 s141 provides that jurisdiction to hear and determine 'actions brought by a creditor or owner to enforce a regulated agreement or any security relating to it' is as follows: the county court 'shall have jurisdiction to hear any such action' and 'where an action is ... brought in the High Court that ought to have been brought in the county court it ... shall be transferred to the county court.'

Two actions to enforce regulated agreements were brought by a finance company in the High Court. They were struck out as improperly brought. The finance company appealed against the striking out of the actions.

The appeal was allowed. The court had no power to dismiss the actions as an abuse of process. The legislation dictated quite clearly that actions started incorrectly in the High Court had to be transferred to the county court; there was no jurisdiction to strike out the actions as improperly brought.

The form of application is laid down in CCR O.13 r1(2) and simply requires the creditor to state that he wishes to apply for an enforcement order and also to state which section of the Act entitles him to do so. Alternatively, where the creditor is suing for some relief as well as applying for an enforcement order he may include his application for the order in his Particulars of Claim (O.49 r4(9)). He must always set out the circumstances which make it necessary for him to apply for an enforcement order (O.49 r4(10)).

Unless the application is combined with a claim, it will be heard by the registrar

(O.13 r1(6)). In all cases if the amount in dispute is not more than £500 it will automatically be referred to arbitration and will be heard by the registrar (CCR 19 r2(3)). Appeal from the registrar lies to the judge (O.13 r1(1)).

The court's powers

The presumption is that the court should allow the creditor to enforce the agreement because s127(1) says 'the court shall dismiss the application if, but ... only if, it considers it just to do so'. The section contains many limitations to this presumption. In deciding whether it would be just to allow or refuse the application the court must have regard to the prejudice caused (which in practical terms means the prejudice caused to the debtor) and the degree of culpability for that prejudice (in other words the extent to which the creditor is at fault) (s127(1)(i)). The court must also have regard to its power to suspend the operation of an enforcement notice, or to make it conditional on the creditor doing something (for example, serving any document which it has not yet served), or to vary the regulated agreement (s127(1)(ii), and see section 6.2 below).

If the debtor has suffered prejudice but the court feels that the creditor ought to be able to enforce the agreement anyway, it can order that the sums payable by the debtor be reduced or extinguished so as to compensate him for that prejudice (s127(2)). For example, if the creditor served the s63(2) copy of the agreement late this may have had the effect of leaving the debtor unaware whether the creditor was agreeing to his proposal. The worry or anxiety caused is a prejudice to the debtor and the court may reduce the amount payable by the debtor to compensate him for it.

There are special provisions applying to the most common type of application for an enforcement order, which is where the creditor has not complied with ss60-64 of the Act. If s61(1)(a) is not complied with, that is if a document in the proper form has not been signed by both debtor and creditor, the court has no power to grant an enforcement order unless a document containing all the terms required by the Act and the relevant Regulations has been signed by the debtor (s127(3)). The purpose of this rule is to ensure that creditors allow the debtor to sign a written agreement, in other words it rules out the enforcement of oral regulated agreements.

This rule is of particular application where the debtor has signed a contract but, in breach of s61(1)(b), it does not contain all of the terms of the agreement. Provided it contains the terms which Parliament requires it to contain, an enforcement order can be made. The creditor cannot get around s127(3) by serving the debtor with a copy of the terms of the agreement, because what is required is that the debtor has signed a document, and if he refuses to sign or if the creditor fails to ask him to sign, the court has no power to enforce the agreement. In appropriate cases the court can order that the regulated agreement is enforceable only to the extent of the terms on the document signed by the debtor. So if the debtor signs a document which does not contain all the terms of the contract, the court can order that only the terms on the document actually signed are enforceable (s127(5)).

Breach by the creditor of his duties under ss62 and 63 to give the debtor copies of a cancellable agreement do not prevent an enforcement order being made provided a copy of the executed agreement and any document referred to in it is given to the debtor before the commencement of proceedings in which the enforcement order is applied for (s127(4)(a)). This covers cases where there has been a failure to serve one or more of the copies at all, and it also covers cases where service was late. If the correct documents were served slightly late the court will have little hesitation in allowing the creditor to enforce. Also if the debtor has received a s63 copy late it is not necessary for another copy of the executed agreement to be served before the creditor applies for an enforcement order. But failure to serve the documents at all can cause the debtor considerable problems because he will be deprived of information about his rights, particularly of his right to cancel, which is contained in the documents. It is therefore essential that a copy of the executed agreement is served before the creditor makes his application for an enforcement order. Proceedings commence on the issue of a Summons or the issue of a Notice of Application. Therefore the creditor must not issue the Summons or Notice and then serve the copy of the executed agreement otherwise he will be refused an enforcement order and will have to make a second application later.

By s127(4)(b), where s64(1) has not been complied with (giving the debtor copies of notices of cancellation rights) the court may not make an enforcement order. There are no ways around this for the creditor. Section 127(4)(b) says that where s64(1) was not complied with no enforcement order can be made, but the position is not as simple as this would indicate because some breaches of s64(1) can be remedied. The Consumer Credit (Cancellation Notices and Copies of Documents) Regulations 1983 Reg 5(1) requires a s62 or 63 copy to contain a box which tells the debtor of his right to cancel. Therefore, if there is a breach of s62 or s63 there is necessarily a breach of s64(1)(a). But s127(4)(a) says that breach of ss62 and 63 can be remedied and this must mean that breach of s64(1)(a) can be remedied also.

Regulation 6 of the Cancellation Notices and Copies of Documents Regulations requires a s64(1)(b) notice to be on a single piece of paper. The remedying of a breach of s62 or 63 cannot put right a breach of s64(1)(b). Therefore s127(4)(b) can only apply to breaches of s64(1)(b).

Performance of unenforceable agreements

Unenforceable agreements are not void, but they will not be enforced by the courts. Therefore, if they are performed by both parties in whole or in part, that performance will be effective. For example, if a hire purchase agreement is unenforceable but the debtor pays some hire charges and uses the goods, he will not be entitled to recover the hire payments. It follows from this that if he pays the total price he will become their owner.

Further, unenforceable agreements may be enforced by the debtor against the creditor. So, breaches by the creditor allow the debtor to sue for damages. If the debtor does sue, that does not amount to a waiver of the unenforceability of the agreement, so the creditor will not be entitled to counterclaim unless he first obtains an enforcement order.

In cases where (1) the debtor has possession of the goods under a hire purchase or conditional sale agreement but does not pay the sums due from him, and (2) the court has no power to allow enforcement of the agreement, the creditor will not necessarily be left without a remedy because the law of conversion may be able to help him. We have seen already that the right to discharge the contract for breach by the debtor is not subject to the creditor first obtaining an enforcement order. So if the creditor does discharge the agreement and serves a demand for the return of the goods, he will have a right to immediate possession which he can enforce. He will be able to enforce his right to possession because that exists by virtue of the debtor's right to possess having been revoked and not by virtue of the unenforceable contract. In other words he does not enforce the agreement by asserting his right to possession.

Supplementary orders

A bare enforcement order is often inadequate to do justice to the creditor or debtor. For example, the creditor under a hire purchase or conditional sale agreement may prove that the goods are in danger or that the debtor is in serious breach and the contract has been discharged. Therefore the court has additional powers to deal with these situations.

Protection Orders

By s131 it may make a protection order requiring the goods to be protected from damage or depreciation pending the hearing of any dispute between the creditor and the debtor. This is of especial importance where the debtor is unlikely to be able to pay damages and the creditor wishes to ensure that once they are repossessed the goods can be resold for as high a price as possible so as to keep his losses to a minimum. Protection orders can be made at any time provided there are proceedings under way, and in principle application can be made for a protection order even before application is made for an enforcement order. The order made can give directions about the custody of the goods and can restrict or prohibit their use.

Return Orders

Furthermore, by s133(1)(i) the court may make a return order requiring the goods to be returned to the creditor. Return orders can be made in hire purchase and conditional sale cases when application is made for an enforcement order, or where the debtor applies for a time order (see section 6.2 below), or where the creditor is taking action to repossess. It is only in extreme cases that a return order will be made where the creditor's only other application is for an enforcement order because by its nature an enforcement order is a preliminary step allowing the creditor to go on to sue the debtor, and at that preliminary stage it will rarely be possible for the court to determine that the goods should be returned. But if the creditor can establish an overwhelming case for the return of the goods, it will save time and money to grant a return order without further ado.

Transfer Orders

Sometimes it is not right to make a return order requiring all goods to be returned to the creditor, so a partial return order, known as a transfer order, can be made (s133(1)(ii)). A transfer order is appropriate where there are several different goods covered by the hire purchase or conditional sale contract and the debtor has paid up part of the total price. In principle there would be nothing wrong where the total price is, say, £10,000 for two identical cars and the debtor has paid £5,000 to allow him to keep one car and make him return the other. But transfer orders are not quite as simple as that. It is necessary for the debtor to have paid up (1) the part of the total price attributable to certain of the goods, and (2) at least one-third of the unpaid balance of the total price (s133(3)). The example given can illustrate this:

1. Total price is £10,000 for 2 identical cars. Therefore, £5,000 is attributable to each car. If the debtor (D) has paid £5,000 and at least one-third of the outstanding balance, the court may allow him to keep one car.
2. If D has paid in total £6,000, the outstanding balance is £4,000. The amount paid up is the part of the total price attributable to one car (£5,000) plus £1,000. £1,000 is less than one-third of £4,000; so D will not be allowed to keep a car.
3. If D has paid in total £6,500, the outstanding balance is £3,500. The amount paid up is the part of the total price attributable to one car (£5,000) plus £1,500. £1,500 is more than one-third of £3,500; so the court may allow D to keep one car.

The court has a discretion whether or not to make a transfer order, but it is likely to make one where the amount paid up is sufficient. The transfer order will order that ownership of the paid up goods be transferred to the debtor, and the other goods be returned to the creditor.

Return and transfer orders deprive the debtor of at least some of the goods and mean that money paid by him has returned no lasting benefit. It is always possible that the debtor may be able to raise the outstanding balance owed to the creditor from another source. If this is possible and the debtor does pay the balance of the total price before the creditor actually regains physical possession of the goods, the debtor will be entitled to claim all of the goods (s133(4)). The reason he will be entitled to claim them is that the creditor's title will vest in him as from the time he pays the outstanding balance (s133(5)).

Problems sometimes arise when debtors refuse to hand back goods despite having been ordered to by a return or transfer order. Normally the debtor will be given time in which to return them, although there is no legal requirement for him to be given time. If that time elapses and he has still not returned them, or if no time limit was imposed and he fails to return them within a reasonable time, the creditor may apply for the court to revoke the order and order the debtor to pay the outstanding balance (s133(6)). It will rarely be in the creditor's interest to do this because he will only apply for a return order if he feels the debtor will not be good for the money. However, the power is there for use where appropriate.

An alternative course for the creditor is to sue in conversion because the effect of a return order or transfer order is to give him an immediate right to possession as from the date when the goods should be given back to him. It will be of no advantage to the creditor to sue in conversion, however, because judgment will be either for the return of the goods (which is what the return or transfer order requires anyway) or damages (which will not be more than the outstanding balance).

Any order, whether enforcement, return or transfer, may be made conditional on the doing of some act by either the creditor or the debtor, or can be suspended for a certain time or until a particular act occurs (s135(1)). It is extremely common for the court to suspend return and transfer orders and we will consider this in more detail once the debtor's position has been considered.

6.2 The debtor's protection

Time orders

We have seen already that applications for enforcement orders are subject to various limitations designed to protect the debtor: for example, the need to serve a copy of the executed agreement if there has been a breach of s62 or 63. More general protection is given to the debtor by s129 which allows him to apply for a time order.

In the vast majority of cases the only breach by the debtor will be a failure to pay or late payment. The court has power under s129(2)(a) to reschedule the payments due from the debtor and/or a surety. The power is not limited in any way, so the court can in effect rewrite the contract so far as it relates to the times when and the amounts in which payment is due.

A debtor may not apply for a time order unless (1) the creditor has applied for an enforcement order, or (2) he has been served with a default notice, or (3) he has been served with a s76 or s98 notice, or (4) the creditor has taken action to enforce the agreement or recover possession of the goods (s129(1)). This has the effect that an application for a time order is a defensive application - it is made in defence to the creditor's act.

Even where the debtor's breach is other than the non-payment of money he may apply for a time order, but in such cases he will ask for time to remedy his breach (s129(2)(b)). So, for example, if the debtor has damaged the goods and has been served with a default notice requiring him to repair them within a certain time, he may ask for more time to carry out the repairs than the creditor has given him. The debtor's first application in such cases ought to be to the creditor, because he may be given more time if he asks for it. But if the creditor stands by the time limit in the default notice then application should be made to the court. It is not a legal requirement that he approaches the creditor first, but he may waste costs by going to court when the creditor is content to allow more time.

The court must have regard to the means of the debtor and any surety before deciding whether to reschedule the payments due (s129(2)(a)). But if the debtor makes an offer to the creditor to repay in smaller instalments over a longer period and the creditor accepts that offer, the court can simply 'rubber-stamp' that agreement without investigating the debtor's means (s130(1)).

Note, however, *First National Bank* v *Syed* [1991] 2 All ER 250 in which the Court of Appeal made it clear that in awarding or withholding a time order under s129, the court should have regard not only as to the debtor's protection, but to the interests of the creditor.

It was shown in section 6.1 that the creditor may discharge the contract at common law without having to apply for an enforcement order. It is, of course, also the case that he may discharge the contract where he does not need to apply for an enforcement order. The debtor's right to apply for a time order is not limited to the time during which the contract exists at common law. For example, it may happen that the creditor serves a default notice and then on its expiry serves notice that the contract is discharged, and the debtor only visits a solicitor after all this has happened. Although the common law says the contract no longer exists, provided the debtor under a hire purchase or conditional sale agreement is in possession of the goods he is treated as having possession of them under the agreement for the purposes of an application for a time order (s130(4)). And if he complies with the terms of the time order and pays off the total price, he will become the owner of the goods.

In cases other than hire purchase or conditional sale the Act does not specifically state that the agreement is deemed to remain in force even though it has been discharged. But s129 does not limit applications for time orders to cases where the contract does still exist, so it is safe to assume that the discharge of an agreement is no handicap to the debtor applying for more time to pay.

A similar rule applies where the time order relates to the remedying of a breach rather than the payment of money. So long as the debtor complies with the terms of the time order the creditor may not take any action against him (s130(5)(a) and (b)). And if he successfully remedies the breach in the way directed by the time order the breach will be treated as though it never occurred (s130(5)(c)).

Suspended and conditional orders

The individual orders which can be made are all concerned with breaches of either the provisions of the Act or the terms of the regulated agreement. It therefore makes sense to clear up all breaches at one court hearing, if possible. The court can do this by making a combination of orders and making them conditional on each other or suspending the operation of one or more of them. The power to make orders conditional or suspended is contained in s135(1).

In the most common case which comes before the county court the debtor has failed to pay on time and the creditor asks for a return order, while the debtor asks for a time order. Subject, of course, to whether it is appropriate to make both orders, the judges often make a return order and a time order and say that the return order only operates if the debtor fails to comply with the time order. In other words there is a suspended return order. If the debtor cannot keep up payments once they are rescheduled he may apply to vary the time order (s130(6)) and if he does so the court can again reschedule the payments and again say that the return order is to operate only if the debtor does not comply with the time order.

Where the creditor's application is for an enforcement order the court may grant it on condition that he remedies his breach first. For example, if the reason why an enforcement order is needed is that the agreement signed by the debtor did not include all of the terms of the regulated agreement, the court may order that the agreement can be enforced once the debtor is supplied with a document which does contain all of those terms.

Overall the county court judge has an extremely wide discretion to make such orders as will allow both creditor and debtor to be treated fairly. Although finance companies can generally expect little sympathy if they have not done what they ought to have done, that does not necessarily mean that the debtor should get something for nothing. Provided he is not treated unfairly the court is always likely to allow full enforcement of an agreement, albeit that to ensure fairness to the debtor it is often necessary to make orders in favour of the creditor conditional on the creditor putting right what he has done wrong.

Amendment of agreements

When making any order the court may also order that the regulated agreement itself be amended (s136). This is useful where some terms are said to be unenforceable (s127(5)) or the payments are rescheduled (s129(2)(a)). The amended agreement will then set out exactly what each party has to do and they will not have to look at the original agreement and also one or more court orders in order to see where they stand.

Amendment can also be made of a security agreement, because if the debtor's duty to pay is altered the surety's duty will similarly be altered. This is an inevitable consequence of the rule in s113(1) that a security agreement is only enforceable to the extent, 'whether as respects the amount of any payment or the time or manner of its being made', that the regulated agreement can be enforced.

Declarations

The court may make a declaration that the creditor may not act in a way that requires an enforcement order. This is only possible where the court dismisses an application for an enforcement order or where an interested party applies for such a declaration (s142(1)). The court will only make such a declaration where it decides that the creditor should not be allowed to apply for an enforcement order in the future, because the effect of the declaration is to prevent an application being made in the future (s142(1)). Sometimes a creditor's application will be dismissed on technical grounds, for example where a provision of the County Court Rules has not been complied with, or where it is made prematurely such as where the creditor was in breach of s62 or 63 and did not give the debtor a copy of the executed agreement before commencing proceedings. In such cases the court can make a declaration that the creditor cannot do the thing he needs an enforcement order for (s142(1)(b)), but will only do so if it is clear that no enforcement order will be granted even if the technicality is put right.

By s142(2) the court may also make a declaration that an agreement has been cancelled or terminated by virtue of the creditor's wrongful repossession of protected goods. The purpose of such a declaration is to prevent litigation in the future, because the declaration will effectively prevent the creditor from suing under the agreement.

Section 142 is necessary because the county court may only make a declaration where either it concerns land or it is a relief asked for in the course of proceedings in which other relief, usually damages, is sought (*De Vries* v *Smallridge* [1928] 1 KB 482).

6.3 Extortionate credit bargains

The Moneylenders Acts 1900 and 1927

Prior to 1900 the Courts of Chancery gave debtors relief against forfeiture of their goods in only very few cases. The body of authorities was immense but the relief given was severely restricted, in that it was available only where there was fraud or the contract concerned an estate in remainder: for example, if there was a settlement of land to A for life remainder to B and B put up his estate in remainder as security for a loan; equity protected B whether he was the original settlor (in which case B was a reversioner) or was a separate person to the settlor (in which case B was a remainderman). This limited the jurisdiction of equity to relieve against forfeiture in normal money-lending agreements for the simple reason that many other categories of borrower put up security when borrowing money on quite extortionate terms and had no opportunity to ask for relief when they failed to pay, even if their breach was very minor. The Courts of Chancery were not prepared to step in simply because the rate of interest charged was high because 'the Chancery mends no man's bargain'.

The position was remedied to a great extent by s1(1) of the Moneylenders Act 1900 which, so far as is relevant, read:

> 'Where proceedings are taken in any court by a moneylender for the recovery of any money lent ... or the enforcement of any agreement or security ... and there is evidence which satisfies the court that the interest charged in respect of the sum actually lent is excessive ... and that ... the transaction is harsh and unconscionable ... the court may reopen the transaction ... and may ... relieve the person sued from payment of any sum in excess of the sum adjudged by the court to be fairly due ...'

For the first time this allowed the courts to look primarily at the rate of interest as the determining feature of whether relief would be given. It is noteworthy that s1(1) required the rate of interest to be excessive and also required the transaction to be harsh and unconscionable. In *Re A Debtor* [1903] 1 KB 705 the Court of Appeal held that an excessive rate of interest can itself render a transaction harsh and unconscionable.

The House of Lords agreed with this view in *Samuel* v *Newbold* [1906] AC 461 in which moneylenders operated by giving loans at interest rates of up to 104 per cent per annum. Default in any one payment made all future payments including all future interest immediately payable, which increased the rate of interest for the year in which default occurred up to 418 per cent. It was necessary to investigate the risk being undertaken by the lender, but on the facts proved the rate of interest was clearly excessive. Lord Loreburn LC and Lord James said that there was a presumption where the rate of interest was very high that the agreement was harsh and unconscionable and that it was for the lender to prove to the contrary. Lord MacNaughten said that whether an agreement is harsh or unconscionable depends upon whether it is 'in accordance with the ordinary rules of fair dealing'.

Of particular importance was the degree of security to the lender, so in *Charringtons Ltd* v *Smith* [1906] 1 KB 79 Channell J held that an unsecured loan of £150 with a rate of interest of 75 per cent if the debtor defaulted was not harsh and unconscionable because there was no security and the debtor went into the contract with his eyes open. In *Halsey* v *Wolfe* [1915] 2 Ch 330 Joyce J held that a bargain was harsh and unconscionable where the lender said that the risk undertaken was a 'fair average risk' but the rates of interest charged on two loans were 72 per cent and 120 per cent respectively. Joyce J allowed 15 per cent interest. Similarly in *Kruse* v *Seeley* [1924] 1 Ch 136, Eve J held that a rate of $82\frac{1}{2}$ per cent per annum which increased to a maximum of 150 per cent on default was excessive because the borrower deposited furniture worth nearly six times the amount of the loan as security. He also allowed 15 per cent interest.

The 1900 Act did not lay down any particular rate of interest as being 'excessive'. But that step was taken by s10 of the Moneylenders Act 1927. Between 1900 and 1927 the judges experienced considerable difficulty in deciding whether a particular rate was excessive, and there were many cases involving similar rates where the judges took different views. So the 1927 Act provided that if the rate was over 48 per cent per annum there was a presumption of unconscionability. It was then for the lender to prove that the rate was a fair rate to charge in all the circumstances of the case. The only effect of s10 was to provide a clear presumption in favour of reopening the contract where the rate of interest was over 48 per cent per annum; it did not say what rate should be charged because that depended on all the circumstances of the case. The Court of Appeal cut down the contract rate from 150 per cent to 48 per cent in *BS Lyle Ltd* v *Pearson and Medlycott* [1941] 2 KB 391; [1941] 3 All ER 128. The court did not say that the statutory figure of 48 per cent was always acceptable, but it was accepted by the borrower that 48 per cent was reasonable so that rate was charged. There was nothing in this case to show unconscionability other than the high rate of interest. By contrast, in the earlier case of *Reading Trust Ltd* v *Spero* [1930] 1 KB 492 the Court of Appeal upheld a contract in which a rate between 80 per cent and 96 per cent was charged. The borrower originally borrowed at 60 per cent. He could have obtained a loan at a lower rate from a bank but chose to go to a moneylender instead. He needed more money, so he borrowed from another moneylender at 80 per cent to 92 per cent and then took the third and final loan from Reading Trust Ltd at 80 per cent to 96 per cent. The borrower was a businessman who knew what he was doing, he gave no security and the loans were for short periods. The court held that the rate charged was not excessive, following *Charringtons Ltd* v *Smith*.

The Consumer Credit Act 1974: jurisdiction

The Moneylenders Acts 1900 and 1927 were repealed by the Consumer Credit Act 1974. In their place are the provisions of ss137-140. The control of extortionate credit in the 1974 Act applies to all credit arrangements, whether or not they are regulated (s140). The Act talks of extortionate credit bargains rather than extortionate credit agreements. The reason for this is that when deciding whether to reopen a credit agreement the court must consider it in context, so it is relevant to investigate not just the agreement under which credit is advanced but also any linked transactions and any other credit agreements which are in any way connected: for instance, where there is a series of loans to the same debtor by the same creditor (s137(2)).

The court's jurisdiction is extremely wide. The debtor or any surety may apply (1) in the course of an action being taken by the creditor against either of them, or (2) by an application which stands by itself, or (3) in any other proceedings where the amount paid or payable under the credit agreement is relevant (s139(1)). This third class of application would arise where the creditor is sued for not paying other bills and he says that he could not pay because of the credit agreement. It would normally be necessary to make the creditor a party to the case if he is not already a party. The application must be made to the county court if the agreement is regulated (unless the point is raised in the course of a case in the High Court) and must also be made in the county court even if the agreement is not regulated provided the amount of credit provided is not more than the county court limit, presently £5,000 (s139(5)).

All the debtor need do is allege that the credit bargain is extortionate, because once that allegation has been made it will be for the creditor to prove that it is not (s171(7)). If it finds a credit bargain to be extortionate the court's powers are wide. Section 137(1) reads: 'If the court finds a credit bargain extortionate it may reopen the credit agreement so as to do justice between the parties.'

The powers of the court are more comprehensively defined in s139(2) which provides that it may:

'(a) direct accounts to be taken ... between any persons,
(b) set aside the whole or part of any obligation imposed on the debtor or a surety ...
(c) require the creditor to repay the whole or part of any sum paid ... by the debtor or a surety, whether paid to the creditor or to any other person,
(d) direct the returns to the surety of any property provided for the purpose of the security, or
(e) alter the terms of the credit agreement or any security instrument.'

Section 139(2)(e) provides a power the court already has by virtue of s136.

The most important aspects of the court's powers are in s139(2)(b), (c) and (e), which between them provide that the court may rewrite the credit agreement and alter the parties' financial positions so as to put them in the position they would have been in had the agreement not been extortionate from the beginning.

The Consumer Credit Act 1974: general

Unlike the Moneylenders Act 1900, the Consumer Credit Act 1974 lays down a list of factors which the court should take into account when deciding whether a credit bargain is extortionate. There are two principal factors to consider. Firstly, does the debtor or any relative of his have to make payments which are grossly exorbitant (s138(1)(a)) and secondly, does the credit bargain otherwise grossly contravene ordinary principles of fair dealing (s138(1)(b))? Only one of these factors need be proved in any case, although it may be that both are satisfied sometimes.

It can be seen from s138(1) that the basic formula of s1 of the 1900 Act is used. In that Act the two questions were whether interest charged was excessive and whether the agreement was otherwise harsh and unconscionable, under the 1974 Act they are whether the sums payable are grossly exorbitant and whether the agreement grossly contravenes ordinary principles of fair dealing. It can also be seen that the second test in the 1974 Act bears a great similarity to how Lord MacNaughten described the proper approach to the 1900 Act in *Samuel* v *Newbold*.

Grossly exorbitant payments

Section 138 lists the factors the court must consider when deciding whether to reopen an agreement. But its drafting does not draw a clear distinction between grossly exorbitant payments and gross contraventions of ordinary principles of fair dealing.

It is obvious that extremely high rates of interest will always be an important consideration for the court. That the prevailing rates at the time the agreement was made should be considered is made clear by s138(2)(a). But it is not clear to what extent factors personal to the debtor are relevant. For instance, is it relevant whether the debtor can afford to repay at the rate demanded by the agreement?

The answer seems to be that all factors listed in s138 must be considered, whether the challenge to the agreement is that it requires exorbitant payments to be made, or that it contravenes ordinary principles of fair dealing. In other words, requiring the debtor or his relative to make exorbitant payments is just one example of contravention of ordinary principles of fair dealing. Various factors must be considered in relation to the debtor and in relation to the creditor (s138(2)(b)), as well as what s138(2)(c) describes rather obliquely as 'any other relevant considerations'.

If the only challenge made by the debtor is that the rate of interest (that is, the APR) is exorbitantly high, the court will look to see whether the rate charged was an open market rate for the type of loan in question. We will investigate this matter below.

Principles of fair dealing

The relevant factors in relation to the debtor are his age, experience, business capacity and state of health, as well as whether he was under financial pressure and if so the nature of that pressure (s138(3)). In cases like *Reading Trust Ltd* v *Spero* and *Charringtons Ltd* v *Smith* where the debtor goes into the agreement with his eyes open, he can hardly complain about the terms of the contract unless he was under such pressure as to make it unfair to hold him to the contract. Mr Spero, for example, needed money for his business but gave no satisfactory explanation why he did not seek it from the bank. Therefore, to use the language of s138(3)(b), the pressure he was under was not of such a nature that it justified reopening the bargain he had made.

The relevant factors in relation to the creditor are the degree of risk accepted having regard to the value of any security provided, his relationship to the debtor and 'whether or not a colourable cash price was quoted for any goods or services included in the credit bargain' (s138(4)). A colourable cash price is a cash price which is artificially inflated so as to disguise the true rate of the total charge for credit. For example, if a washing machine of a particular type normally costs £300 the creditor may let it on hire purchase with a cash price of £400 and £50 in credit charges. In reality the agreement has a cash price of £300 and credit charges of £150, figures which change the complexion of the agreement considerably.

Again the old cases are useful illustrations. In *Halsey* v *Wolfe* and *Kruse* v *Seeley* the provision of security meant that the creditor could not justify charging extremely high rates of interest. Recently, in *Woodstead Finance Ltd* v *Petrou* [1986] BTLC 267 the debtor was in severe difficulties with a bank loan so he went to the creditor and borrowed £25,000 over 6 months at an annual rate of 42 per cent. He gave no security other than his wife's guarantee, and she was in an equally poor financial position, he had a bad record of repayment and there was evidence before the court that short-term loans to people in his position were charged at about 42 per cent. The Court of Appeal held that the agreement should not be reopened.

In *Coldunell Ltd* v *Gallon* [1986] QB 1184; [1986] 1 All ER 429 the Court of Appeal held that the creditor had discharged the burden on him by proving that the agreement made to lend £20,000 over 6 months secured by a charge over the debtor's home was at a normal market rate of interest. It was argued for the debtor that the agreement was tainted by undue influence because the debtor's son had undoubtedly put great pressure on him to secure a loan which was obtained to help the son pay business liabilities. This argument failed because the son was not the creditor's agent for any purpose and therefore any undue influence applied by the son was not the creditor's responsibility.

The most comprehensive review to date of s138 was conducted by Edward Nugee QC sitting as a deputy High Court Judge in *Davies* v *Directloans Ltd* [1986] 1 WLR 823; [1986] 2 All ER 783. The plaintiffs, Mr Davies and Miss Hedley-Cheney wished to buy a house but had difficulty raising a mortgage because they both had irregular incomes. They entered into an arrangement to buy a house whereby they were lent the purchase price at what they were told was a high rate of interest, but they represented a high risk to the creditor. Edward Nugee QC investigated the factors listed in s138(2), (3) and (4) one by one and found on the facts that the plaintiffs had been fully and impartially advised throughout, that they appreciated the full effect of the agreement and that they were not put under any unfair pressure. He also held that the rate of interest charged was a normal commercial rate for the type of loan made. Counsel for the plaintiffs had submitted that the proper rate of interest to charge the plaintiffs was 18 per cent whereas the APR was 21.6 per cent. It was held that even if counsel's submission was correct the difference was not so large as to make 21.6 per cent grossly exorbitant. Therefore the agreement was not reopened.

Three points from *Davies* v *Directloans Ltd* are significant. Firstly, the rate of interest which must be investigated and compared to market rates at the time credit is advanced is the APR. Secondly, the rate of payment will only be grossly exorbitant if it exceeds 'ordinary or proper bounds'. And thirdly, it was said that the words of s138 must be considered as they appear in the Act and that it is not permissible to go to cases decided under the Moneylenders Act 1900 for guidance on how to approach the question whether the credit bargain is extortionate.

The relevance of undue influence

In *Davies* v *Directloans Ltd* there was no question of undue influence having been exerted on the debtors. But Edward Nugee QC said that in all cases the factors listed in s138 are the only relevant factors to be taken into account when deciding whether to reopen an agreement. Section 138(3)(a) and (b) and 4(b) set out matters which are of relevance to allegations of undue influence. But it is not clear whether it is necessary to establish undue influence in order to reopen a bargain in which the rate of payments is not grossly exorbitant.

In *Woodstead Finance Ltd* v *Petrou* the Court of Appeal treated arguments on undue influence and exorbitant payments as separate arguments and did not directly consider whether pressure applied to debtors which is less than undue influence can amount to unfair dealing. But in *Coldunell Ltd* v *Gallon* (which predates *Woodstead Finance Ltd* v *Petrou*) a differently constituted Court of Appeal held that once it was shown that no undue influence was exerted by the creditor there was no argument for the agreement grossly contravening ordinary principles of fair dealing. Lord Denning MR in *Avon Finance Co Ltd* v *Bridger* [1985] 2 All ER 281 suggested that pressure falling short of undue influence could amount to conduct grossly contravening ordinary principles of fair dealing, but the point did not directly arise for decision in that case.

The difficulty with undue influence is that it requires proof of either a relationship between the parties from which undue influence can be presumed provided the contract is manifestly to the disadvantage of the debtor, or a relationship where there is no presumption of undue influence but where the creditor 'took advantage' of the weak position of the debtor and imposed a contract manifestly to the debtor's disadvantage (*National Westminster Bank plc* v *Morgan* [1985] AC 686; [1985] 1 All ER 821). Even the apparent relaxation of the strict rules in *National Westminster Bank plc* v *Morgan* by the Court of Appeal in *Goldsworthy* v *Brickell* [1987] 1 All ER 853 so that 'domination' of the debtor by the creditor need not be proved, does not allow it to be said that the doctrine of undue influence can be invoked in other than the most extreme cases.

Section 138 does not say that either the payments required of the debtor or his relative must be grossly exorbitant or there must be undue influence, but it is hard to avoid such a reading of s138 given the way the courts have approached allegations of contraventions of ordinary principles of fair dealing.

7

Credit Cards

7.1 The agreement
7.2 The goods
7.3 Loss and misuse

7.1 The agreement

Classification

In Chapter 1 we saw that the 1974 Act classifies regulated agreements as (1) either fixed sum or running account, (2) either restricted use or unrestricted use and (3) either debtor-creditor or debtor-creditor-supplier. We also saw that there can be agreements, known as multiple agreements, where the agreement fits into different classifications in different circumstances. The most important multiple agreements are agreements concerning credit cards.

A credit card can be used either to obtain goods and services or to obtain cash. Furthermore, Barclaycards can be used as cheque guarantee cards by customers with accounts at Barclays Bank plc. The use of a credit card as a cheque guarantee card does not involve the provision of credit, because all that happens is that the card is used as evidence of the identity of the person writing the cheque and as a guarantee of payment provided the amount of the cheque does not exceed £50, (or £250 with some newer cards).

Credit cards involve the provision of credit in two ways. Firstly, when the debtor is given the card he is given a facility which he may use, and secondly, when he uses the card he is given credit to the extent of the price of the goods or services obtained or the amount of cash drawn.

Use of a credit card to obtain goods or services involves the provision to the card holder of fixed sum (s10(1)(b)), restricted use (s11(1)(b)), debtor-creditor-supplier (s12(b)) credit. There are three separate contracts made. Firstly, the finance company (creditor) and the shop (supplier) arrange for customers of the shop to be able to use the credit card. This involves the creditor giving the supplier credit card slips and a machine by which transactions involving credit cards can be properly documented and the customer (debtor) given a receipt to show what he has spent.

Secondly, the creditor and debtor enter into an agreement by which the debtor is given the card and entitled to use it up to a pre-determined level, the credit limit. Thirdly, the debtor and the supplier make a contract of sale whereby the supplier supplies the debtor with the goods and the debtor pays for them. This contract is a sale under which the debtor is liable to pay the supplier, although the payment is actually made by the creditor. Dicta in cases such as *Alan & Co Ltd v El Nasr Export & Import Co* [1972] 2 All ER 127 had always indicated that it is perfectly possible for a seller to agree to accept payment from a third party, and furthermore to accept the risk of that party's (in)solvency when the time for payment comes.

However, it was not until *Re Charge Card Services* that this issue was directly considered in the context of credit cards. In *Re Charge Card Services Ltd* [1988] NLJ LR 201; [1988] 3 WLR 764 the Court of Appeal held that the debtor's liability to pay the supplier is settled completely as soon as the supplier accepts the credit card as payment. In that case the creditor went into liquidation leaving some suppliers unpaid. The court held that once a supplier has accepted payment by credit card the debtor has paid the supplier in full; in other words, payment by credit card is absolute and not conditional, and therefore money recovered by the liquidator of the creditor from debtors did not represent money owed by the debtor to the supplier.

If a credit card is used to obtain money there are only two parties, the creditor who advances the cash and the debtor who receives it. The agreement made is for fixed sum (s10(1)(b)), unrestricted use (s11(2)), debtor-creditor (s13(c)) credit.

In addition to these classifications, credit cards also fall within s14 because they are credit tokens. Section 14(3) provides that whenever the debtor uses his credit card he is provided with credit. This subsection is necessary because it would not otherwise be clear whether each purchase or drawing of cash is a separate provision of credit.

But just because each use of the card involves the provision of credit does not mean that each use should be looked at separately to assess whether the agreement is regulated. Section 10(3)(a) provides that primarily it is the credit limit which determines whether the agreement is regulated, although the agreement can still be regulated where the limit is in excess of £15,000. Also, the use of a credit card for purchases under £50 does not involve the debtor in a small agreement, because it is the credit limit which determines regulation (s17(2)).

Formalities

On making a contract for a credit card the debtor is not entitled to copies of the agreement in the same way as any other debtor. He is entitled to a s62(1) copy (provided, of course, s62(1) applies in the circumstances of the case). But he need not be given a s63(2) copy within the seven days following the making of the agreement if he is given a copy of the executed agreement when he receives the card (s63(4)).

But credit cards are issued for limited periods only and when a replacement is sent the debtor must also be sent a copy of the executed agreement and any document referred to in it (s85(1)). Failure of the creditor to give the debtor a copy of the executed agreement on renewal prevents him from being entitled to enforce the agreement against the debtor until he does give him the copy (s85(2)(a)). And if default continues for a month he commits an offence (s85(2)(b)).

Although the debtor is given credit each time he uses his credit card he is not entitled to copies of the agreement on each use because he does not make a separate regulated consumer credit agreement; he merely uses the facility available to him under the agreement whereby he obtained the card.

The rate of interest charged by credit card companies fluctuates. This is only permitted where the credit card contract contains a provision allowing it, but the contracts always do allow it. Variation of the rate is only effective once the debtor has been given notice of it (s82(1)).

The credit limit

The most popular credit cards such as Access and Barclaycard can be used by the debtor up to a predetermined credit limit (s10(2)). The limit can be increased or reduced by agreement and provided it does not exceed £15,000 any alteration will not affect the regulation of the agreement by the Act. Even if the limit is more than £15,000 the agreement will be regulated provided that it is likely that the debtor will not actually receive more than £15,000 of credit (s10(3)(b)(iii)).

In some circumstances a debtor may exceed his credit limit. This will almost inevitably be a breach of the contract by which he obtained the card but there will be no loss to the creditor provided he pays off his debt when asked to do so. If the effect of exceeding the credit limit is that the debtor also obtains in total more than £15,000 of credit, the agreement will still be regulated as long as the credit limit does not exceed £15,000 (s10(3)(a)).

In order to ascertain how much credit has been advanced to the debtor it is important to remember that interest charges are not themselves credit (s9(4)). So, for example, if the debtor's credit limit is £15,000 and in the first month of using the card he buys goods to the value of £14,800 he has obtained only £14,800 of credit. If he fails to pay on time he will incur interest. An interest rate of 2 per cent per month will render him liable to £296 interest. When this is added to the amount of credit (£14,800) the total bill to the debtor is £15,096. But he has not obtained more than £15,000 of credit because the £296 is not credit but is part of the total charge for credit.

Repayment

The normal contractual duty of a credit card holder is to pay at least 5 per cent of the outstanding balance each month. Where the balance is £5 or less he will usually be obliged to pay off the whole of the balance. This obligation to make monthly payments is a contractual requirement but is not required by the Act. From December 1973 until April 1978 there was a formal request to the companies operating Access and Barclaycards from the Chancellor of the Exchequer that minimum monthly payments of 15 per cent of the balance or £6 whichever was the higher should be required. But in April 1978 that request lapsed and there is no statutory or other control on the credit card companies in this report.

Default by a credit card holder is no different to default by any other debtor. The creditor is only allowed to terminate the agreement or call in the outstanding balance unless a default notice is served (s87(1)). But the creditor may restrict or defer the right to draw credit until the debtor has remedied his breach (s87(2)). Credit card companies will normally only stop a debtor using his credit card if either default continues for more than one month or the debtor is in excess of his credit limit.

7.2 The goods

A debtor who buys goods using a credit card has the full protection of the Sale of Goods Act 1979. The contract of sale is a linked transaction within s19(1)(b). It is made with the supplier only, not with the creditor, but in some circumstances the debtor has rights against the creditor as well.

Section 75(1) of the 1974 Act provides that in cases involving debtor-creditor-supplier credit within s12(b) or (c), where the debtor has a claim against the supplier for misrepresentation or breach of contract he has a like claim against the creditor. This only applies where the debtor's claim relates to goods of a cash price between £100 and £30,000 (s75(3)). The cash price limits apply per item about which complaint is made. So if the debtor buys goods totalling £150 but only has complaint about certain of those goods costing, say, £70, he cannot invoke s75 and is limited to an action against the supplier.

Before *Re Charge Card Services Ltd* there was no clear authority that the debtor buys the goods from the shop when he uses a credit card. It was certainly arguable that the shop sells the goods to the credit card company which then sells them to the debtor. But it is now clear beyond any dispute that the debtor buys from the shop. This does not mean that the debtor must claim against the supplier before he can invoke s75 against the creditor. Nor is it necessary to join both supplier and creditor as parties. The debtor can choose to sue the creditor only or the supplier only. If he sues the creditor only, the creditor may join the supplier because he has a right to be indemnified by the supplier (s75(2) and (5)). It is normal practice for the debtor to sue both supplier and creditor if he is in any doubt about the ability of the supplier to pay damages due. Bringing the creditor in from the beginning can also have the effect of applying pressure on the supplier to settle in order to avoid embarrassment.

The debtor is not precluded from suing the creditor by the fact that he may have exceeded his credit limit when making the purchase about which he is suing (s75(4)).

7.3 Loss and misuse

Credit cards remain the property of the creditor at all times. But this does not absolve the debtor from having to take reasonable care of the card. Misuse of the card by the debtor or anyone acting as his agent or who has possession of the card with his consent is the debtor's responsibility (ss83(1) and 84(2)). But where the debtor is not at fault (eg where the card has been stolen) he is protected from having to reimburse the creditor in full for misuse by a third person.

But the debtor is not wholly immune. He can be liable for up to £50 of misuse which occurs after he loses possession of it (s84(1)). But he is not liable for any losses incurred after he has given the creditor oral or written notice of the loss of the card (s84(3)). Oral notice must be confirmed in writing within seven days and written notice is effective from the time it is received not the time it is sent (s84(5)). These rules render the debtor liable for up to £50 whether or not he knows the card has been lost or stolen. His liability will not arise, however, until such time as he has signed the card or signed a receipt for it or used it for the first time (s66(1) and (2)).

Agency

1

Introduction

1.1 Agency defined

1.2 The creation of agency

1.3 The consent model revisited

1.4 A general principle?

1.1 Agency defined

Auctioneers, estate agents, travel agents, mercantile agents, brokers, solicitors and barristers are just a few of the many people described as agents who may act on our behalf in the ordinary course of life. It may be useful at the beginning of our discussion of agency to attempt a definition of the common factor which brings them all into the category 'agent' or, indeed, it may be useful to ask whether they are all properly called agents. The courts have only very rarely attempted to define the agency relationship though they have an occasion pronounced on what agency was not. See, for example, the recent case of *Comet Group plc* v *British Sky Broadcasting* [1991] TLR 211 in which the court held promotional contracts to be quite distinct from agency.

Fridman (in Fridman's *Law of Agency*) stresses that the effect of someone being an agent is that he affects the legal rights of his principal, and he works backwards from this conclusion to suggest the following definition:

> 'Agency is the relationship that exists between two persons when one, called the agent, is considered in law to represent the other, called the principal, in such a way as to be able to affect the principal's legal position in respect of strangers to the relationship by the making of contracts or the disposition of property.'

This is a useful starting point in that it focuses attention on the most important aspect of an agent's position - that he can make contracts which bind someone else. This is a major exception to the doctrine of privity of contract and a definition of the agency relationship which recognises this can never be strongly criticised. The major problem with Fridman's definition, however, is that he states the effect of the relationship without indicating when the courts will hold that the relationship has arisen. In other words he tells us what an agent has power to do, but does not tell us what we should look for when investigating whether someone is an agent. Perhaps a more accurate criticism (and a more fair one since Fridman makes it clear that he only offers his definition tentatively) is that Fridman does not give us a principle or rationale behind the agency relationship; he does not tell us why there is agency in a given case, merely what the effect of the agency is.

Bowstead (in Bowstead on *Agency*) does attempt to give a general basis for deciding when someone is to be treated as the agent of another; he suggests that agency is:

> 'The relationship which results from the manifestation of consent, by one person to another, that the other shall act on his behalf and subject to his control, and consent by the other so to act'.

This is what we will refer to as 'the consent model'; the argument is that agency arises because principal and agent consent to the relationship arising. The analysis of Bowstead is essentially contractual, it asserts that one person is an agent because he consents to being an agent and because the principal consents to have the agent act on his behalf. It is not, though, a purely contractual analysis in that there is no need to establish an intention to create legal relations. A parent who sends a child to the shops with money to buy a loaf of bread consents to the child being an agent and the child consents to being an agent, but there is no way in which the courts would ever say there is a contract between them.

The consent model finds favour with the writers of the major textbooks on contract, but this is not altogether surprising since they look at agency in the context of a full treatment of contract law. Subtle differences can be seen between the three leading students' textbooks. Treitel (in Treitel, *The Law of Contract*) says:

> 'Agency is the relationship which arises when one person, called the principal, authorises another, called the agent, to act on his behalf, and the other agrees to do so. Generally the relationship arises out of an agreement between principal and agent'.

Here Treitel uses the consent model in so far as he lays emphasis on agency arising by agreement – of course, the essence of agreement is the consent of the two parties to the agreement – but he is of the view that even when there is no agreement there is still a principal who can be seen to vest authority in the agent.

Cheshire and Fifoot (in Cheshire and Fifoot's *Law of Contract*) also analyse agency in terms of the vesting of authority, but they do not openly say that this must be with consent of the agent:

> ' "Agency" is a comprehensive word which is used to describe the relationship that arises when one man is appointed to act as the representative of another'.

This varies slightly from Treitel's view in so far as Cheshire and Fifoot seem to look upon the position of an agent as an office to which someone may be appointed, which could be misleading if it is taken to mean that formality is required for the creation of agency. It is thought that Cheshire and Fifoot merely lay emphasis on the fact that the agent has the power (they call it authority) to act as the representative of another. Again there is no discussion in their definition of any principle which can be applied to find out whether someone is an agent, apart from looking for an appointment as agent. Their definition fits the consent model to a degree because it suggests that the principal must consent to the agent acting as agent – if he did not give that consent then he would not make an appointment; but they do not say that the agent must consent, any more than does Treitel.

In Anson's *Law of Contract*, agency is looked on as arising by way of the vesting of authority in the agent by the principal, but unlike Cheshire and Fifoot, Anson does not indicate that the position of an agent is an office to which one must be appointed:

> 'Although as a general rule one man cannot by contract with another confer rights or impose liabilities upon a third party, yet he may represent or act on behalf of another, with that other's authority, for the purpose of bringing him into legal relations with a third party. The relationship thus constituted is called Agency'.

Unlike Fridman, the contract writers look at the rationale behind the creation of agency, not just at the effect of agency. Anson says that an agent must act with the authority of the principal, and this is very similar to Bowstead's consent model.

The result of the above is that we can see four points of importance:

1. An agent is someone who acts with the consent/authority of a principal (Bowstead; Treitel; Cheshire and Fifoot; Anson).
2. The agent himself has to consent to acting in that way (Bowstead).
3. The effect of agency is that the agent can affect the legal right and liabilities of the principal (Fridman; Anson).
4. The effect of agency is that the agent represents the principal (Bowstead; Treitel; Cheshire and Fifoot).

Points (1) and (2) are not necessarily mutually exclusive, but there may be a difference in that Fridman and Anson would not consider someone to be an agent if, say, he merely passed on an informal invitation to dinner on behalf of a host to a guest, whereas it would seem that the writers cited in support of principle (4) would consider the messenger to be an agent.

In addition to the textbooks mentioned above, there is a considerable body of literature in periodicals defining agency. Of particular interest are articles by Dowrick ('The relationship of principal and agent' (1954) 17 MLR 24) and Reynolds ('Agency: theory and practice' (1978) 94 LQR 224). Dowrick stressed the fact that a true agent is one who affects the legal position of the principal. He would not consider the messenger who passed on the invitation to dinner as an agent. A useful catch-phrase from Dowrick's article is that agency is a 'power-liability relationship'. As Dowrick put it:

> 'The essential characteristic of an agent is that he is invested with a legal power to alter his principal's legal relations with third persons: the principal is under a correlative

liability to have his legal relations altered ... This power-liability relation is the essence of the relationship of principal and agent'.

This is further explained on the following page of the article:

'A power-liability relation is one of the fundamental legal relations. Agency is but one of the numerous kinds of power-liability relations recognised in our legal system. The distinctive feature of the agency power-liability relation is that the power of the one party to alter the legal relations of the other party is a reproduction of the power possessed by the latter to alter his own legal position'.

Dowrick's point here is twofold. Firstly, he makes the point also made in Fridman's definition, that the only true agent is one who affects the legal position of the principal. Secondly, he asserts that it is a special relationship because the agent can only do what the principal could himself do. Therefore, if the principal does not have legal capacity, then the act of the agent on his behalf cannot be effective.

Reynolds, who is the editor of Bowstead, has stressed the unfortunate use of 'agency' to describe relationships which do not possess the power-liability structure. He used the example of the estate agent who in most cases just makes intoductions and does not negotiate contracts on behalf of purchaser or vendor. The main difficulty caused by describing people such as estate agents as 'agents' is that the relationship of principal and agent involves certain rights and duties between the principal and agent, which are not present between estate agents and potential vendors or purchasers. Reynolds also argues that it is too simple to say that the agent represents the principal, because this does not explain the cases (discussed in Chapter 4 below) where the agent is personally liable upon a contract which he has made as agent. If the agent is just the principal's representative, he argues, then the agent would drop out of things altogether, leaving all problems and disputes to be sorted out between principal and third party.

These two articles merit careful reading by the student of agency, but it is suggested that this is done once the remainder of this section of the book has been read, because they both discuss in some detail aspects of the agency relationship which we have not yet mentioned in any detail.

It has already been stated that the courts have rarely attempted to define the nature of the agency relationship. Two dicta are, however, so forcefully made that they should be examined. In *Pole* v *Leask* (1863) 33 LJ Ch 155 Lord Cranworth said:

'No one can become the agent of another person except by the will of that person'.

This was echoed in *Garnac Grain* v *Faure & Fairclough* [1966] AC 1130n; [1967] 2 All ER 353 by Lord Pearson:

'The relationship of principal and agent can only be established by consent of the principal and the agent. They will be held to have consented if they have agreed to what in law amounts to such a relationship, even if they do not recognise it themselves and even if they have professed to disclaim it...The consent must, however, have been given by each of them, either expressly or by implication from their words and conduct.'

The difference between Lord Cranworth and Lord Pearson (with whom, incidentally, all their Lordships agreed) is that Lord Cranworth did not state a requirement of the agent having to consent to being agent, but this does not undermine the clear terms in which he asserted that the principal must consent. He seemed to have in mind cases where the agent had voluntarily acted as agent, so the consent of the agent would be there anyway.

To understand the problem with the consent model it is necessary to say something about the ways in which agency can be created. These are covered in detail in Chapter 2, but will be mentioned briefly here.

1.2 The creation of agency

There are four ways in which an agency can arise. Two different matters must be appreciated before they are looked at. Firstly, when we talk of the creation of agency we may be discussing cases where a person who is not an agent at all is made an agent; and secondly, we may be discussing cases in which an existing agent who has limited powers is given greater powers. For example, if Mr P owns a shop and employs Miss A as a shop assistant, there is a creation of agency where there was none before. If after a while he promotes Miss A to the position of manageress of the shop he is giving her extra powers. In both cases there is a creation of agency; the promotion to manageress builds on an existing agency, but is still the creation of a new agency because the relationship between Mr P and Miss A has been altered.

The first way in which agency can be created is by express creation. This is commonly the result of contract: for example, the making of the employment contract between Mr P as the employer and Miss A as the employee.

Secondly, there is creation by estoppel. For example, if Miss A is employed with instructions to sell only shoes from the shop department, but Mr P tells Mrs T, a customer, that Miss A is also authorised to sell handbags, then Mr P will be estopped from denying that a sale of a handbag by Miss A to Mrs T is binding on his business. Mr P made a representation to Mrs T which she relied on by making the purchase; the fact that Miss A had been told only to sell shoes does not prevent Mrs T from establishing an estoppel against Mr P.

Thirdly, there can be creation by ratification. For example, Miss A knows that she is only empowered to sell shoes, but sees that Mrs T wants to buy a handbag and as there is no assistant in the handbag department, sells Mrs T a handbag and tells Mr P that she has done this; then, if Mr P says that he is content with what she has done he will be seen to have validated her action. This giving of approval to acts which were originally done without authority is known as ratification and the matter will be treated by the courts as though Miss A had authority to sell a handbag to Mrs T all along.

4. Fourthly, there is creation by operation of law. For example, if a carrier is entrusted with property and there is an imminent danger to that property in such circumstances that the carrier cannot contact the owner to ask what he should do, then the carrier will be an agent of necessity. The law will hold that acts done in such emergencies in protection of the owner's interests are done with the authority of the owner.

1.3 The consent model revisited

How does the consent model fit in with the four ways of creating agency? There is no problem with the case of express creation. In the example given it is clear that both Mr P and Miss A consent to her being employed, and the acts which she does within the authority given to her will bind Mr P because he has given his consent. The third party who buys shoes had made a contract with Mr P because Miss A was acting within the scope of her authority when she made the sale. It could be said that Miss A was Mr P when she made the sale, she was his alter ego.

However, agency by estoppel does not arise because of any agreement between Mr P and Miss A. It arises because of the representation from Mr P to Mrs T. It is submitted that it is most artificial to say that Mr P and Miss A consented to Miss A having the power to sell handbags, because no such consent was ever shown. It does not matter what arrangement was agreed between Mr P and Miss A; even if he had expressly told her never to sell handbags, the sale to Mrs T would be binding on Mr P because of the position between Mr P and Mrs T. The consent model does not fit agency by estoppel.

When dealing with cases of ratification the law presumes that authority had been given all along. The ratification is an act done between Mr P and Miss A, it is somewhat artificial to say that they consented to her being an agent for the sale of handbags because 'consent' indicates a prior agreement; perhaps 'assent' would be a more appropriate word to describe why the sale is effective. But, because the law looks on the ratification as though authority had been given all along, so this case can be fitted within the consent model. Lord Pearson said that agency will arise when the parties have 'agreed to what in law is such a relationship', and this fits cases of ratification – the ratification of Miss A's act is part of the relationship between Mr P and Miss A, and once they have entered into this relationship the law deems that consent was given to her acting in this way from the beginning.

Agency of necessity can also be fitted into the consent model, but not without a little deviousness. It can be said that when goods are entrusted to a carrier both he and the owner of the goods know that if an emergency arises it may be necessary to take steps to protect the goods; it follows from this that they both consent to these steps being taken. The argument really revolves around the presumption that everyone is presumed to know the law. Given that both the carrier and the owner are presumed to know that agency of necessity may arise, so it can be said that they consent to such agency. Again there is a degree of artificiality in this because, of course, neither of them really applies his mind to the problem. But if they did apply their minds to the question of what is to happen in an emergency, the law will say that they would agree to an agency of necessity arising and in this way there is presumed consent to agency of necessity arising.

The consent model, therefore, is useful to explain many agency relationships, but is not a satisfactory explanation of agency by estoppel – that does not arise because of the consent of principal and agent; it arises because of the relationship between principal and third party. To argue that both principal and agent consent to the application of an estoppel if the principal makes a representation to the third party is unsatisfactory in cases where there are specific instructions to the agent not to act in a certain way.

1.4 A general principle?

We have seen above that agency can arise because of the consent of principal and agent, and that it can arise because the principal has represented to the third party that the agent has authority. It is not realistic to treat these cases as being subject to any general principle governing the creation of agency; but the relationship between principal and agent will be regulated by the same rules regardless of the manner of creation of the agency, so it is perhaps not surprising that there is sometimes said to be a general rule about how agency is created.

In paragraph 1.1 above, we saw four rules which have been suggested by writers. In the books and articles which consider the point there is a uniform view that only someone with the power to alter the legal position of the principal is truly an agent; others may effect introductions between principal and third party but they are not agents unless they are themselves instrumental in affecting (or effecting) the legal relationship between the principal and third party. The importance of this is that there is a clear line of authority holding that agents owe certain fiduciary duties to their principals, whereas those who are not agents do not hold these duties unless the special facts of each case gives rise to them. Therefore, it can be confidently stated that a person is only an agent if he affects or effects the legal relationship between principal and third party, and it follows from this that a definition of when agency will be held to exist should include a statement that agency only exists if the position of the agent is such that he can affect or effect the legal relationship between principal and third party.

Further, if we are to define when a principal/agent relationship will be found to exist between two people, we can state two tests: firstly, agency can arise because of the arrangements made between the principal and the agent, and secondly, agency can arise where someone (the principal) is estopped from denying that someone else is his agent. The first of these tests investigates the express and implied agreement between principal and agent; the second is concerned with the position between principal and third party and operates wholly independently of the arrangements made between principal and agent. It is quite possible to have both tests satisfied. For example, Mr P employs Miss A in his shop to sell shoes, and he telephones Mrs T telling her that Miss A is his sales assistant and is able to sell shoes. If Mrs T then relies on the telephone call and goes to the shop where Miss A sells her a pair of shoes, then there is express creation of agency between Mr P and Miss A. There is also a representation from Mr P to Mrs T which is relied on by Mrs T. In such cases no problem arises from overlap between creation and creation by estoppel, but the use of terminology can be confusing.

As will be shown below, the acts of an agent bind the principal if they are within the agent's 'authority'. Where there is an overlap of methods of creation of agency, sometimes the courts will refer to actual authority - which is what arises when there is express creation of agency - and sometimes they will talk of apparent or ostensible authority - which is what arises when agency is created by estoppel. Despite this difficulty (which is looked at in more detail in Chapter 2 below), the rules on creation are fairly clear.

The result of all this is that we can find three rules about creation and nature of agency:

1. An agent is someone who is in a position to affect or effect legal relations between another person (the principal) and one or more third parties. Agency is a power/liability relationship where the agent has power to affect or effect his principal's legal position and the principal is under liability to have his legal position changed by the acts of the agent.
2. An agent may be put in that position because he and the principal have expressly or impliedly agreed to it, this is the case when agency is created expressly or by ratification or by operation of law; it gives rise to actual authority.
3. An agent may be put in that position because the principal has made a representation to the third party that the agent is an agent with certain authority and the third party has acted upon this representation. This is the case when agency is created by estoppel; it gives rise to apparent or ostensible authority.

2

The Creation of Authority

2.1 Introduction

2.2 Creation by agreement

2.3 Creation by estoppel

2.4 Creation by ratification

2.5 Creation by operation of law

2.6 Usual authority

2.1 Introduction

In this chapter we will look at the various ways in which agency can be created. These have already been mentioned briefly in Chapter 1, above, in section 1.2, where we talked of express creation, creation by estoppel, creation by ratification and creation by operation of law. In this chapter we will call 'express creation' creation by agreement because there can also be implied creation. Many of the books call 'creation by agreement' 'creation by contract', though that is not always an appropriate description because a contract as such is not necessary in every case. One example of creation of agency by agreement is the granting of a power of attorney - a formal grant of authority by deed - and this will be dealt with separately in Chapter 3 below, because the rules relating to it are of little importance to other examples of creation by agreement.

Some of the books separate discussion of the creation of agency from discussion of the scope of an agent's authority. It is not proposed to do that here. It is felt that the two are so inextricably mixed that it would be misleading if the rules relating to authority were not seen in the context in which the agency is created. Therefore, we will examine the ways in which agency can be created and the extent of the agency created by each of them.

There are difficulties of terminology here, but that adopted in this book is:

1. *Actual authority*. The authority which is given to an agent when he is created agent by agreement. Its scope is to be determined by construing the agreement by which he is appointed. It falls into express actual authority - the authority

expressly stated to be possessed by the agent in the agreement itself; and implied actual authority – the authority which is not expressly said to exist but which is implied.
2. *Apparent authority*. The authority which an agent has when the creation of agency is by estoppel.
3. *Usual authority*. This can be actual or apparent and will be considered separately at the end of the chapter after aspects of it are considered in relation to actual and apparent authority.

2.2 Creation by agreement

Introduction

It is often inappropriate to talk of the creation of agency by contract, because many of the features required for there to be a binding contract are not necessary for the creation of an agency. In the previous chapter we gave the example of a parent asking a child to go to the shops, which would not be a binding contract because of the absence of intention to create legal relations, but it is clear that this would not prevent the child being the parent's agent.

The similarities between creation of agency by agreement and the normal rules on the making of contracts are great, however. No formality is required for someone to be created an agent. In the same way that a simple contract can be made orally, so can the creation of agency. But, if an agent is to execute a deed on behalf of his principal, then the agency itself must be created by deed, and such a deed is called power of attorney (for details of this see Chapter 3 below).

This rule, that an agent who is to execute a deed on behalf of his principal must himself be appointed by deed, is best explained by looking at the distinction between simple contracts and covenants.

A simple contract is one made otherwise than by deed; formalities are not required unless laid down by statute (for example the Law of Property (Miscellaneous Provisions) Act 1989 s2, or s4 of the Statute of Frauds 1677).

A covenant is a contract made by deed. The distinction between the two has been in English law ever since the courts first allowed enforcement of contract in the fourteenth century, and it is not surprising that it has permeated agency law so that an agent may sign a memorandum even if he was not created agent in writing, because the signing of a memorandum is just a statutory formality in the making of a simple contract.

It must not be thought that agencies are not usually created by contract, however, because they are. The point being made here is simply that a contract as such is not necessary. If creation is by contract, then we must apply normal contractual rules of capacity. For example, if a child is created an agent by contract we must ask whether the child has the requisite capacity. There is an important distinction to be drawn at this stage. The child who is an agent requires us to separate two rules in relation to contractual capacity. On the one hand we must ask whether the child is competent to make a contract of agency; on the other hand we must not forget that if the child acts as agent and contracts with a third party on behalf of the principal, it is the principal's capacity which will determine the enforceability of the contract made by the child with the third party. So, if a child is sent to the shops by his mother to buy a cookery book, it does not matter that the cookery book is not necessary goods so far as the child is concerned (so as to come within s1 of the Infants' Relief Act 1874), because when the child acts as agent the contract to buy the book is the mother's contract and it is her capacity to buy the book that matters.

Implied creation of agency

In the same way that a contract can arise by implication, so can an agency. This is quite rare, however; the normal role for implication is in the discovery of the implied terms of the agency agreement, but occasionally the agency itself can be implied. In *Hely-Hutchinson* v *Brayhead Ltd* [1968] 1 QB 573; [1967] 3 All ER 98, the chairman of a company acted as its managing director even though he had never formally been appointed to that job. He made various contracts on behalf of the company which were honoured, and the board of directors had full knowledge that he had assumed the position. He agreed that the company would act as guarantor of various debts for a third party and the question arose whether these guarantees were enforceable against the company. The Court of Appeal held that the guarantees did bind the company because despite the fact that the chairman was not formally appointed as managing director he had acted in that capacity with the acquiescence of the company and so was impliedly given the authority which a managing director would normally have. It was clear that in his capacity as chairman he did not have the authority to bind the company by guarantees, so the implication of agency was vital to the decision in the case. There was a further matter relating to whether the chairman had breached fiduciary duties which he owed to the company, but nothing revolved around that in the end.

In the *Hutchinson* case Lord Denning MR was of the opinion that there was implied agency and also that there was agency by estoppel. The two are not inconsistent (see 1.4 above) but Lord Denning has been criticised for not separating them clearly enough. Lord Wilberforce said that we must always look to all aspects of the relationship between the parties concerned to see if one of them has been appointed the agent of the other. In this case the acquiescence of the company to the acts of the chairman would have led the reasonable man to believe that the chairman was acting as managing director with the company's approval, so there was an implied creation of agency. Lord Wilberforce went on to say that because he had found a creation of agency by implied agreement, it was not necessary to look for creation by estoppel, clearly showing that he felt that if there is an overlap between creation by agreement and creation by estoppel, it is the agreement which is the true creator of the agency. The third judge, Lord Pearson, agreed that there was creation by implied agreement and he also agreed that creation by agreement and creation by estoppel are not mutually exclusive - it is quite possible for the facts of a particular case to show both an agreement between principal and agent and also a representation by principal to third party.

The distinction which has already been noted between the question of whether someone is an agent and the question of the scope of his authority is of importance in the realm of creating agency by implication. In *Biggar* v *Rock Life Insurance Co* [1902] 1 KB 516 an agent acting for an insurance company filled in a form on behalf of a customer. It was held that when he assumed this task, he was acting as the agent of the customer, not as agent of the insurance company. The customer's argument that because the agent had not filled in the form with the answers which he (the customer) had given, he could not have been the customer's agent, was held to be misconceived. It did not matter that the agent had filled in the form with incorrect answers, when he was filling in the form he did so on behalf of his principal, the customer; whether he did so correctly was something to be considered in answering the question whether the acts of the agent were within the scope of his authority.

The authority created

Actual authority

When agency is created by agreement the agent possesses 'actual' authority. The scope of this authority is to be discovered by construing the agreement by which the agency is created. So, in *Hely-Hutchinson* v *Brayhead Ltd*, it was implied actual authority which the Court of Appeal held to exist. If there is express creation of agency, then there will be express actual authority to do those things specifically mentioned in the agreement and implied actual authority to do those things which it can be implied the agreement allows.

Implied actual authority

Implied actual authority arising out of the creation of agency by contract is discovered by applying normal contractual rules about implying terms. After all, if an agency is created by contract then it is to the contract that we must look to find its terms and there is no reason to look upon it as anything other than a normal contract. Indeed, in *Freeman & Lockyer* v *Buckhurst Park Properties (Mangal) Ltd* [1964] 2 QB 480; [1964] 1 All ER 630, Diplock LJ said that these normal rules of construction should be applied to all agreements creating agency, whether amounting to a contract or not. At common law, terms are implied into contracts where there is a commonly arising relationship between the parties and it is necessary to imply a term to make sense of that relationship (*Liverpool City Council* v *Irwin* [1977] AC 239; [1976] 2 All ER 39). Terms are also implied where the contract is not workable without some term being added and the common intention of the parties that certain terms should be in their agreement can be ascertained (*Shirlaw* v *Southern Foundries (1926) Ltd* [1939] 2 KB 206; [1939] 2 All ER 113).

The terms implied into contracts of agency can be either of these two kinds. For example, in *Rosenbaum* v *Belson* [1900] 2 Ch 267 an agent appointed to make a binding contract to buy a house had implied authority to sign a memorandum for the purpose of s40(1) of the Law of Property Act 1925. A special problem arises where it is not clear what the express terms of the agreement mean. In *Ireland* v *Livingstone* (1872) LR 5 HL 395 the House of Lords held that where a document by which an agent is appointed is ambiguous, then provided the agent acts in good faith and adopts a reasonable construction of that document, he will be acting within his actual authority. This is just a standard example of the rules of construction of contracts generally. Today the courts are less willing to hold that the interpretation of a document by an agent is reasonable, because he could usually communicate with his principal in order to find out what the document means. The point here is not really any different from that in *Ireland* v *Livingstone*: in that case it was reasonable for the agent to interpret the document himself because communication with the principal was not reasonably possible. In *European Asian Bank AG* v *Punjab and Sind Bank (NZ)* [1983] 1 WLR 642; [1983] 2 All ER 508, the Court of Appeal refused to allow the sellers' bank to rely on ambiguities in a documentary credit as giving it the right to negotiate the credit. *Ireland* v *Livingstone* was distinguished because the sellers' bank was not an agent, but Robert Goff LJ appeared to be of the view that the case should now be applied in the light of modern means of communication, so that if there is a patent ambiguity in an agent's instructions he should check with his principal.

Usual authority

When an agent carries out a job which normally carries with it certain powers, then all the normal powers which go with that job will be given to the agent unless the parties have expressly excluded them. For example, in *Hely-Hutchinson* v *Brayhead Ltd* Lord Denning said that if a board of directors appoints one of their number to be managing director, then he will have all the powers that a managing director normally has, unless some express limit is put on his powers. Fridman has separated what is in this book called implied authority into implied and usual authority. His argument is that implied authority arises from the agreement of the parties and usual authority arises from someone being appointed to a job which customarily carries with it certain powers, and he would include Lord Denning's example of the managing director within usual authority rather than implied authority. The view taken in this book is that these are not in fact different concepts at all. If an agent is appointed to a job which carries with it customary powers then it is not unrealistic to say that the parties intend the agent to possess those usual powers unless they expressly provide to the contrary. Admittedly this means that in appropriate cases we are faced with authority which is properly described as 'implied usual actual authority', but, awkard though this phrase may be, it is an accurate reflection of the position.

In some cases there can be problems in discovering whether there is a body of 'usual' powers which a particular agent will possess. It must not be thought that whether or not there are usual powers associated with a certain job does not change with time. In *Barnett, Hoares & Co* v *South London Tramways Co* (1887) 18 QBD 815 a company secretary was said to be 'a mere servant; his position is that he is to do what he is told and no person can assume that he has any authority to represent anything at all'. In *Panorama Developments (Guildford) Ltd* v *Fidelis Furnishing Fabrics Ltd* [1971] 2 QB 711; [1971] 3 All ER 16, the Court of Appeal held this to be outdated because a company secretary now has an established position of importance within the company and therefore has implied usual authority to do any act in the normal administration of the company. In that case the making of a contract to hire cars was within the secretary's authority. The court held the authority of the secretary to have arisen by estoppel, but that matters little; it was a clear recognition that certain jobs will be looked upon by the courts as carrying with them certain usual powers.

In *British Bank of the Middle East* v *Sun Life Assurance Co of Canada (UK) Ltd* [1983] 2 Lloyd's Rep 9, the House of Lords stated that a branch manager of an insurance company which had branches all over the United Kingdom did not have implied usual authority to bind the company by various contracts because there was no well-established practice relating to the powers of such a branch manager. It was made clear that whether implied usual authority arises is a matter of investigating the facts of each case. We will return to this case when looking at apparent authority.

The question of usual authority arises most frequently when an agent has been given specific instructions not to make certain contracts, but in excess of his actual authority he does attempt to make such a contract on behalf of his principal. This gives rise to a problem of apparent authority and will be discussed below.

In some cases it may be desired to attempt to imply a term into an agency agreement by relying on a custom. This is most often the case where the agent acts within a particular trade which has well-established divisions of powers. No custom can imply a term into an agency unless the custom itself is reasonable. In *Robinson* v *Mollett* (1874) LR 7 HL 802 there was a trade custom which allowed agents employed on the London tallow market to buy in their own name in order to satisfy the orders of several principals. This was held to be unreasonable because it was fundamentally inconsistent with the principal/agent relationship. The difficulty of establishing authority by trade custom is illustrated by the following definiton of what is required before a 'usage' will be recognised by the courts; in *Cunliffe-Owen* v *Teather & Greenwood* [1967] 1 WLR 1421; [1967] 3 All ER 561, Ungoed-Thomas LJ said:

> ' "Usage" as a practice which the court will recognise is a mixed question of fact and law. For the practice to amount to such a recognised usage, it must be certain, in the sense that the practice is clearly established; it must be notorious, in the sense that it is so well known in the market in which it is alleged to exist that those who conduct business in that market contract with the usage as an implied term, and it must be reasonable. The burden lies on those alleging usage to establish it.'

This was not an agency case, it was concerned with dealings on the Stock Exchange, but the principal stated is one of the general common law and applies equally to agencies as it did to the Stock Exchange.

2.3 Creation by estoppel

Introduction

We have already seen that agency can arise by estoppel where there is a representation made by the principal to the third party that the agent has authority to undertake certain acts on behalf of that principal. Lord Wilberforce noted in *Hely-Hutchinson* v *Brayhead Ltd* that when actual authority is found there is no need to investigate whether there was also a representation of authority made by the principal; in other words if there is creation by agreement then it is that agreement which must be looked to as the foundation of the agency. But, it was also made clear, by all three judges, that if the scope of actual authority is not wide enough to encompass the acts done by the agent, then it is necessary to look for estoppel. This was a recognition that creation of agency by estoppel does not just allow an agency to be imposed where there was none before, it also allows the scope of an existing agency relationship to be extended.

The creation of agency by estoppel requires three criteria to be satisfied: firstly, there must be a representation by the principal; secondly, that representation must be relied on; and thirdly, the third party who deals with the agent must not know that the agent is acting without authority.

The authority created

When agency is created by estoppel it gives rise to 'apparent' or 'ostensible' authority. These terms are used interchangeably, though at times commentators have criticised the fact that two words are used to describe the same concept. Lord Denning in *Hely-Hutchinson* described it as the 'the authority of an agent as it appears to others'.

Apparent authority does not arise unless he third party is led to believe that the agent is an agent. For example, P entrusts A with a book and asks him to sell it at a second-hand bookshop. The owner of the bookshop, T, notices P's name inside the book and is suspicious, so he telephones P and asks why someone else has his book. If P says to T that he has entrusted A with the book to sell on his behalf, then A would appear to be an agent. On the other hand, if P says to T that he has sold the book to A, then A does not appear to T to be an agent at all, he appears to be the owner, and apparent authority does not arise. This does not mean, of course, that A's sale of the book is not effective, because P is estopped from denying that A was the owner; but the estoppel in such a case is not because of the doctrine of apparent authority it is because of the doctrine of apparent ownership.

The doctrine of apparent ownership is an estoppel which arises against a person who has held out another as being the owner of property. A third party who deals with this apparent owner can prevent the representor from denying that this apparent owner was the owner.

The leading cases

No estoppel can arise against someone unless he has made a representation which has been relied upon. The representation upon which the estoppel of apparent authority is based can be by words or conduct in other words it can be expressed or implied. The general principle was stated by Diplock LJ in *Freeman and Lockyer* v *Buckhurst Park Properties (Mangal) Ltd* (supra), and has been restated recently in *Armagas* v *Mundogas, The Ocean Frost* [1986] AC 717; [1986] 2 All ER 385 in the House of Lords.

In *Freeman & Lockyer* v *Buckhurst Park Properties (Mangal) Ltd* a director of a company acted as managing director although there had been no appointment to that office. The company's articles of association (the rules laying down how the company should operate) allowed the board of directors to appoint a managing director, but the minutes of board meeting showed that no such appointment had been made. This ruled out actual authority. The director employed a firm of architects, but the company refused to honour his contract holding that it fell outside the director's authority. The Court of Appeal held that there was apparent authority because the board knew that he had acted as managing director and acquiesced in his so doing, therefore, it was held, they held him out as having the authority of a managing director. Willmer LJ discussed a point of company law, which need not be discussed here, and concluded his judgment with a very short paragraph in which he stated that if a director acts as managing director to the knowledge of the board, then he is held out by the board, and therefore by the company, as being the managing director and therefore as having the authority that a managing director would normally have. Pearson LJ agreed, the basis for his judgment being that the director had held himself out as being managing diretor and the company had acquiesced in this. This meant, as Pearson LJ put it, 'the company is considered to have made the representation, or caused it to be made, or at any rate to be responsible for it'. The approach of Pearson LJ in this case was repeated by Lord Pearson, as he had by then become, in *Hely-Hutchinson* v *Brayhead Ltd*, and is the subject of more detailed treatment below.

The third judge in *Freeman & Lockyer* was Diplock LJ whose judgment has become the classic work on the subject of apparent authority. The following passages from the judgment are of such importance that they merit quotation in full. When Diplock LJ referred to 'the contractor' he meant the third party who tries to enforce the act of the agent against the principal:

> 'An "actual" authority is a legal relationship between principal and agent created by a consensual agreement to which they alone are parties. Its scope is to be ascertained by applying ordinary principles of construction of contracts, including any proper implication from the express words used, the usages of the trade, or the course of business between the parties. To this agreement the contractor is a stranger; he may be totally ignorant of the absence of any authority on the part of the agent. Nevertheless, if the agent does enter into a contract pursuant to the "actual" authority, it does create contractual rights and liabilities between the principal and the contractor. It may be that this rule relating to 'undisclosed principals', which is peculiar to English Law, can be rationalised as avoiding circuity of action, for the principle could in equity compel the agent to lend his name in an action to enforce the contract against the contractor, and would, at common law be liable to indemnify the agent in respect of the performance of the obligations assumed by agent under the contract.
>
> 'An "apparent" or "ostensible" authority, on the other hand, is a legal relationship between the principal and the contractor created by the representation, made by the principal to the contractor, intended to be and in fact acted on by the contractor, that the agent has authority to enter on behalf of the principal into a contract of a kind within the scope of the 'apparent' authority, so as to render the principal liable to perform any obligations imposed on him by such contract. To the relationship so created the agent is a stranger. He need not be (although he generally is) aware of the existence of the representation. The representation, when acted on by the contractor by entering into a contract with the agent, operates as an estoppel, preventing the principal from asssserting that he is not bound by the contract. It is irrelevant whether the agent had actual authority to enter into the contract.'

Later in his judgment Diplock LJ stated the form the representation may take:

> 'The commonest form of representation by a principal creating an "apparent" authority of an agent is by conduct, viz, by permitting the agent to act in the management or conduct of the principal's business. Thus, if in the case of a company the board of directors who have "actual" authority to manage the company's business permit the agent to act in the management or conduct of the company's business, they thereby represent to all persons dealing with such agent that he has authority to enter on behalf or the corporation into contracts of a kind which an agent authorised to do acts of the kind which he is in fact permitted to do normally enters into the ordinary course of such business. *Prima facie* it falls within the "actual" authority of the board of directors, and the company is estopped from denying to anyone who has entered into a contract with the agent in reliance on such "apparent" authority that the agent had authority to contract on behalf of the company.'

It can be seen that Diplock LJ drew the distinction between actual and apparent authority which is adopted in this book and stressed that it is necessary for there to be a representation relied on by the third party before there can be an estoppel. It is worth noting that Diplock LJ showed that cases of agency created by estoppel depend not on the relationship between principal and agent, but on the relationship between principal and third party; this is worth bearing in mind when considering the point made in section 1.3 above, about the inapplicabiity of the consent model to such agencies.

In *Armagas* v *Mundogas, The Ocean Frost,* a shipping company, Mundogas, owned a vessel, the *Ocean Frost*, which it wished to sell, It was proposed to sell the ship to Armagas. Armagas could not raise the full price, and said that they would only buy it if Mundogas agreed to hire it from them for three years at a suitable rate of hire. Mundogas were only prepared to hire it for one year. Mundogas's chartering manager, Magelssen, then signed a three-year charterparty (as contracts to hire ships are known) saying that he was doing so on behalf of Mundogas. This was part of a fraud which he was perpetrating on Mundogas with the assistance of Mr Johannesen, a ship broker. The fraud aspect of the case is examined in a later chapter. The question for the House of Lords was whether the three-year charterparty was binding on Mundogas. Armagas argued that because Magelssen was the chartering manager, he had authority to charter ships under three-year charters and that therefore Mundogas were bound. Lord Keith, with whom the other law lords agreed, held that Magelssen had neither actual nor apparent authority. He drew a distinction between 'ostensible general authority' and 'ostensible specific authority', a distinction which corresponds with a distinction which has been drawn in some books between general and special agents. Lord Keith said:

'Ostensible authority comes about where the principal, by words or conduct, has represented that the agent has the requisite actual authority, and the party dealing with the agent has entered into a contract with him in reliance on that representation. The principal in these circumstances is estopped from denying that actual authority existed. In the commonly encountered case, the ostensible authority is general in character, arising when the principal has placed the agent in a position which in the outside world is generally regarded as carrying authority to enter into transactions of the kind in question. Ostensible general authority may also arise where the agent has had a course of dealing with a particular contractor and the principal has acquiesced in this course of dealing and honoured transactions arising out of it. Ostensible general authority can, however, never arise where the contractor knows that the agent's authority is limited so as to exclude entering into transactions of the type in question, and so cannot have relied on any contrary representation by principal.

It is possible to envisage circumstances which might give rise to a case of ostensible specific authority to enter into a particular transaction, but such cases must be very rare and unusual. Ex hypothesi the contractor knows that the agent has not general authority to enter into the transaction as was the position here. The principal might conceivably inform the contractor that, in relation to a transaction which to the contractor's knowledge required the specific approval of the principal, he could rely on the agent to enter into the transaction only if such approval had been given. In such a situation, if the agent entered into the transaction without approval, the principal might be estopped from denying that it had been given. But it is very difficult to envisage circumstances in which the estoppel could arise from conduct only in relation to a one-off transaction such as this one was.'

The position set out by Lord Keith had been recognised in many previous cases, but never expressed so clearly. We have already seen in *British Bank of the Middle East v Sun Life Assurance Co of Canada (UK) Ltd* that there was no general ostensible authority because the position of branch manager did not have sufficiently clearly defined powers. On the other hand, in *Freeman & Lockyer* there was a general ostensible authority because the man who was acting managing director had a position which did carry with it well-defined powers. Such decisions depend so much on the facts of the case that it is fruitless to give too many examples.

What Lord Keith referred to as 'ostensible general authority' has been called 'usual authority'. We saw above that in the realm of actual authority there is usual authority when someone is properly appointed to a job which carries with it usual powers. The position in such a case is that if Mr A is appointed managing director of P Ltd, the parties have made a contract and it will be implied into that contract that he should have all the powers that a managing director would normally have, unless they have expressly limited those powers. In this way one can talk of the managing director having all the authority which it is usual for a managing director to possess – in other words he has usual actual authority. Similarly when we are dealing with a case of agency by estoppel; when there is a representation to T that Mr A is managing director of P Ltd, so there is a representation that Mr A has all the usual authority of a managing director. In other words, usual apparent authority.

The representation

In *The Ocean Frost* Lord Keith stated that the most common form of ostensible authority arises when the agent is represented to be in a position which is regarded in the outside world as generally carrying authority to enter into transactions of a certain kind. This echoes what Diplock LJ said in *Freeman & Lockyer* in a passage cited above.

In *Charrington Fuel Oil v Parvant Co* (1988) The Times 28 December, the new owners of property requested suppliers of goods to continue delivering to the premises. It was held that this did not amount to a representation which could form the basis of an estoppel that the previous owners were to be considered agents of the new owners.

The following example shows the difficulties with this analysis. Assume that P Ltd appoints Mr A as its managing director, but his contract states that he may not order new office furniture for the company unless the chairman, Mr C, countersigns the order. Mr A writes to T Ltd, offering to buy a new desk at a price of £500, he types the letter himself on the company notepaper and signs it 'Mr A, Managing Director'; Mr C does not countersign. T Ltd accepts the offer and delivers the desk; but P Ltd refuses to accept delivery and pay for it. Here Mr A clearly acts outside his actual authority, so the only way in which P Ltd could be bound is if there is a representation by P Ltd to T Ltd that Mr A has authority to order the desk. But where is the representation? All that has happened is that Mr A has represented himself to have authority to order the desk, the representation he made was to describe himself as 'managing director'. If T Ltd have never dealt with the company before they will not know that Mr A is managing director, they will just be relying on his representation. Yet there is no doubt that P Ltd will be bound by the contract – why?

The answer usually adopted by the courts is that the company is said to make a representation by appointing the managing director. The representation is that he is authorised to make all contracts which a managing director may normally make. In many cases the third party would have dealt with the managing director, before, so the representation made by the company arises from its honouring of those earlier contracts made by him on its behalf. In other cases another director, for example, may have indentified the managing director to the third party, in which case there is a clear representation that the man is managing director, and unless the third party is told of limits to his authority it can be assumed that he has all the powers which a managing director usually has. In these cases it may appear at first sight that the third party only deals with the agent, but the reality is that he has dealt with the company otherwise than solely through the agent.

But, what if the third party, as in this example, has never dealt with the company before? If the third party has never dealt with the company before in any way, then the only representation that the Mr A has authority to buy office furniture has come from the agent himself. Kerr LJ has recently said that an agent may not 'pull himself up by his own bootstraps' (see *The Rafaella* [1985] 2 Lloyd's Rep 36), and Lord Donaldson MR, in *Bank of Kuwait* v *Hammoud* [1988] 3 All ER 418, used the phrase, 'He cannot pull himself up by his own shoe laces', meaning that an agent may not give himself authority which he does not in fact possess. This reflects the view of other courts on many other occasions (see, for example, *Attorney General for Ceylon* v *Silva* [1953] AC 461 (PC); *British Bank of the Middle East* v *Sun Life Assurance Co of Canada (UK) Ltd*; and *Freeman & Lockyer* v *Buckhurst Park Properties (Mangal) Ltd* where Diplock LJ said that there must be a representation by someone who has responsibility for the management of the company (other than the director whose act is in dispute)). However, in the same way that it is clear that an agent may not give himself authority, it is also clear that where a man has been appointed to a position which normally carries with it certain powers, the principal will be bound by all contracts made by the agent which fall within those usual powers. How are the two concepts reconcilable? On the one hand the managing director has an express limitation on his actual authority. On the other hand the company is bound by the purchase made in excess of that actual authority and there appears to be no representation to the third party other than the representation of the agent himself. The answer to the problem is not clear in the cases, but two explanations seem possible.

In the first place, it may be that there is a rule of law that limitations on actual authority are ineffective where the agent is appointed to an office which carries with it usual powers. This is the concept of usual authority which is examined separately in section 2.6 below. In this context usual authority extends beyond usual actual authority and usual ostensible authority and takes on a significance all its own. For reasons which are set out in the section below it is an unsatisfactory concept.

The second possible explanation of the problem is one which has not been clearly and consistently canvassed by the courts, but may, in fact, be the best explanation of several leading cases (though its apparent simplicity may be its undoing). If a man is created managing director of a company, he has implied actual authority to say: 'I am managing director'. Any third party who deals with the managing director is told, either expressly or impliedly, that he is managing director, and therefore the third party is led to believe that the managing director has all the normal authority which a managing director would have. The fact that it is the managing director himself who makes that representaton is misleading. It is necessary to examine exactly what the managing director's powers are.

He does not have actual authority to buy office furniture. But he does have actual authority to describe himself as managing director. If it were the company chairman who told the third party the name of the managing director, then there would have been a clear representation by someone with authority (the chairman) that one of the company's agents (the managing director) had certain powers. If the chairman said: 'Mr A is our managing director' and did not qualify that statement in any way, then the third party would assume that Mr A had all the powers a managing director would normally have, including the power to buy office furniture. The reason why the company would be bound is because of the chairman's actual authority to make the representation which he made. Clearly the chairman is allowed to identify the managing director to a third party, and would not be expected to inform the third party of the exact limits of the managing director's powers.

Similarly, the managing director is allowed to identify himself as managing director. When he says 'I am the managing director' he is making a statement which he is authorised to make. He would not be expected to tell all third parties of limits on his powers; after all if a company instructed its managing director not to buy office furniture, he would not be expected to describe himself in letters as 'Managing Director (who is not allowed to buy office furniture)'; that would be absurd. He would be allowed to sign himself simply as 'managing director'. That signature would be within his actual authority.

In other words when an agent is appointed to a position which usually would authorise him to do certain things and there is a limitation on his actual authority to do those things, then the position of the agent is this:

1. He has express actual authority to make all contracts a managing director could normally make, save for any restricted activities.
2. He has implied actual authority to describe himself as 'managing director'.

It is clear beyond doubt that the authorised act of the agent is seen by the law as being the act of the principal, therefore when Mr A describes himself as managing director, it is the company which says he is managing director, because he has authority to make that representation. When the company makes such a representation the third party who deals with the agent is relying on a representation made by the principal that the agent has certain authority. In all cases where the third party relies on a representation from the principal that someone is the principal's authorised agent, the principal is estopped from denying that the agent is authorised. The result of this is that Mr A has a dual capacity when he deals with T Ltd. On the one hand he is acting within his actual authority when he says that he is the managing director, in other words he is the company when he says this. On the other hand he is acting in breach of his contract of agency when he buys office furniture. This breach of his agency contract makes him liable to the company in damages for breach, but, because there is ostensible authority, the principal cannot escape liability to the third party under the sale contract.

If we look again at the leading cases mentioned, we can see this principle at work. In *The Ocean Frost* the agent describes himself as 'Chartering Manager', which was a correct description but did not represent anything about his power to make charterparty contracts because there was no standard trade practice relating to the powers of such managers. Similarly, in the *Sun Life Assurance* case, the representation that the agent was the branch manager did not represent anything about his powers. But, in *Freeman & Lockyer's* case the representation that the agent was the *de facto* managing director did make a clear representation because managing directors have a general body of management powers which the courts will recognise.

There is some judicial support for this view of representations made by agents themselves. In the *Freeman & Lockyer* case Pearson LJ said:

'The agent professes to act on behalf of the company, and he thereby impliedly represents...that he has authority from the company to do so... In this case the defendant company has known of and acquiesced in the agent's professing to act on its behalf and thereby representing that he has the company's authority to do so. The company is considered to have made the representation or caused it to be made, or at any rate to be responsible for it. Accordingly, as against the other contracting party, who has altered his position in reliance on the representation, the company is estopped from denying the truth of the representation.'

That same judge made the point even more clearly in *Hely-Hutchinson* v *Brayhead Ltd*:

'The difference and the relationship between actual authority and ostensible authority were explained by Diplock LJ in *Freeman & Lockyer* v *Buckhurst Park Properties (Mangal) Ltd*. There is, however, an awkard question arising – how the representation which creates the ostensible authority is made by the principal to the outside contractor. There is this difficulty. I agree entirely with what Diplock LJ said, that such representation has to be made by a person or persons having actual authority to manage the business. Be it suposed for convenience that such persons are the board of directors. Now there is not usually any direct communication in such cases between the board of directors and the outside contractor. The actual communication is made immediately and directly, whether it be express or implied, by the agent to the outside contractor. It is, therefore, necessary in order to make a case of ostensible authority to show in some way that such communication which is made directly by the agent is made ultimately by the responsible parties, the board of directors. That may be shown by inference from the conduct of the board of directors in the particular case, for instance, placing the agent in a position where he can hold himself out as their agent, and acquiescing in his activities, so that it can be said that they have in effect caused the representation to be made. They are responsible for it and, in the contemplation of the law, they are to be taken to have made the representation to the outside contractor.'

It must be conceded that there is a potential difficulty with this analysis. The approach adopted above says that when an agent has been appointed to an office which normally carries with it certain powers, then he has authority to represent himself as being the holder of that office, and therefore one can find a representation made by the principal that the agent has all of those normal powers. This will not work if the agent has been specifically told that he may not describe himself as the holder of the office in question. For example, if we return to the example of Mr A buying the desk; if Mr A is appointed managing director and is told that he may not buy office furniture and also that he may not describe himself as managing director, then there will not be authorised representation by P Ltd that Mr A has the authority to buy the desk. Although this may appear to be an easy way in which a principal can avoid being bound because of 'general ostensible authority', it is quite unrealistic to expect any such limitation to be put on the right of a managing director to describe himself as such. So the potential difficulty is potential only, it would not arise in practice.

In the field of ostensible specific authority few difficulties arise. When a representation is made directly to the third party that an agent is authorised to make a particular contract, there is no problem in holding the representor liable on that contract. But it will not be easy to find such a representation from conduct. For example, if Mr P lends his car to Mrs A and she sells it to Miss T, pretending to be the owner, there will be no estoppel against Mr P. He did not represent that Mrs A had authority to sell; all he did was to entrust her with possession and this is not a sufficiently clear representation to found an estoppel. After all, her possession could be explained on the ground that either she was the owner, or she had borrowed it, or she had hired it, or she was employed as a driver, or she had stolen it, or she was the owner's agent to sell it. There is no reason why it should be said that when Mr P entrusts her with possession he is representing to third parties that the last of these possibilities is the correct one (*Jerome* v *Bentley & Co* [1952] 2 All ER 114; *Eastern Distributors Ltd* v *Goldring* [1957] 2 QB 600; [1957] 2 All ER 525).

Many cases can be envisaged which would cause immense problems to the courts. For example, P Ltd receives a visit from Mr A-G, a travelling salesman. Mr A-G needs to do some paperwork in connection with the order which P Ltd makes, and is allowed to use Mr M-D's desk; Mr M-D is the managing director of P Ltd, but is out to lunch. While Mr A-G is writing at the desk, Mr T-P enters P Ltd's offices and goes straight through the door marked 'Managing Director'. He sees a man behind the desk and without checking the man's identity offers to buy certain property from P Ltd. Mr A-G accepts the offer. Is P Ltd bound?

The problem may seem unlikely to arise, but what if it did? Should we say that P Ltd is estopped from denying that Mr A-G was managing director because it allowed him to sit in the managing director's office? Such a result seems to have arisen in *Barrett* v *Deere* (1828) Moo & M 200 where a third party paid a debt owed to a merchant to a man who was in the merchant's counting house and appeared to be in charge of matters there. Lord Tenterden said, 'the debtor has a right to suppose that the tradesman has the control of his own premises, and that he would not allow persons to come there and intermeddle in his business without his authority.' This would seem a harsh result in the example given above, but *Barrett* v *Deere* is not conclusive because the extent to which the merchant acquiesced in the appearance of the man in the counting house as agent is not clear from the report of the case.

2.4 Creation by ratification

Introduction

We have already seen that the concept of ratification is that a principal can adopt an act that has been done on his behalf, even though at the time it was done the 'agent' did not have authority. Clearly if an agent makes a contract on behalf of his principal and acts within his actual or apparent authority, then the contract binds the principal; that much is elementary. Ratification is a rather different matter, though, since it involves the law in accepting that a contract made without authority can bind the principal. Necessarily this could effectively abolish the doctrine of privity of contracts if not kept within narrow limits, because if anyone could adopt a contract which has been made between two other people, then all the leading cases on privity could be discarded. For example, in *Beswick* v *Beswick* [1968] AC 58; [1967] 2 All ER 1197, no problems would have arisen if Mrs Beswick could have adopted the contract made for her benefit between her husband and their nephew.

The limits which are imposed on the ability of someone to adopt a contract made between two other people are five fold: firstly, the contract must be made by the agent as agent: any contract made by A as principal cannot be adopted by P later; secondly, P must exist at the time A acts for him; thirdly, P must have had capacity to make the contract at the time A made it; fourthly, P must have capacity to make the contract at the time he attempts to adopt it; and fifthly, the act of ratification must be unequivocal.

Agent must act as agent

The party whose contract is later adopted by another must have made the contract as an agent in the first place. The leading case is also the clearest example. In *Keighley Maxsted & Co* v *Durant* [1901] AC 240 an agent, Roberts, was appointed to buy wheat at 45s 3d. He was unable to buy at this price, so he bought at 45s 6d, but when he bought he did not disclose that he was an agent, he bought in his own name. This purchase was outside Roberts's actual authority and also outside his apparent authority, but later Keighley Maxsted & Co tried to ratify and the third party with whom Roberts had contracted attempted to enforce the contract against Keighley Maxsted & Co. The House of Lords held that this was not possible because the 'agent', Roberts, had acted in his own name. The House of Lords said quite clearly that the doctrine of ratification is an exception to the doctrine of privity and Lord MacNaughten answered the problem in the case in this way:

'By a wholesome and convenient fiction, a person ratifying the act of another, who, without authority, has made a contract openly and avowedly on his behalf, is deemed to be, though in fact he was not, a party to the contract. Does the fiction cover the case of a person who makes no avowal at all, but assumes to act for himself and for no one else?. On principle I should certainly say not.'

If someone does purport to deal as an agent, then it does not matter that he intended to defraud the principal, the doctrine of ratification can still apply. For example, in *Re Tiedemann and Ledermann Frères* [1899] 2 QB 66 the agent said that he was an agent, but his purpose in making the contract was to take the benefit of it himself and defraud his principal. The principal tried to ratify and it was held that he could, because the agent had acted as agent.

The position is different if the agent forges his principal's signature. In such a case the agent does not declare himself to be an agent, he delares himself to be the principal and that will not do for the purposes of the principal adopting the transaction or having it enforced against him (*Brook* v *Hook* (1871) LR 6 Ex 89). It must be borne in mind, however, that there may be instances where the agent defrauds his principal but, nonetheless, acts within his actual apparent authority. In such cases ratification is irrelevant, the principal will be bound.

It is not necessary that the agent names his principal, but there must be a sufficiently clear indentification of the principal for the third party to be able to discover his identity. In *Watson* v *Swann* (1862) 11 CB NS 756, Willes J said: 'It is not necessary that he should be named but there must be such a description of him as shall amount to a reasonable designation of the person intended to be bound by the contract.' Therefore, if the agent simply said, 'I am an agent' it would not be possible for a person to adopt that act. In *Lyell* v *Kennedy* (1889) 9 HLC 391 the collection of rent on behalf of 'the heir' to the property being hired was sufficient identification for the heir to be able to ratify. The point being that the identification was such that a particular person, and no other, was in a position to ratify.

The principal must exist

Contracts made on behalf of a company which has not yet been formed cannot be ratified by the company after its formation. This is a problem which only seems to arise in the field of company law. The formation of a company is only completed when certain documents have been lodged with the Registrar of Companies, and until then there is no company in existence. It has been argued that whilst it is being promoted the company should be seen to be in existence, so that after incorporation it can ratify, but the well-established rule in *Kelner* v *Baxter* (1866) LR 2 CP 174 does not allow this. In that case wine was bought on behalf of a company which had not yet been formed. Those who bought the wine did so 'on behalf of the Gravesend Royal Alexandra Hotel Co Ltd' and after it was formed that company attempted to ratify the act. The Court of Common Pleas held that the law would not allow a principal to ratify a contract if he (the principal) had not been in existence at that time the contract was made.

The promoters are personally liable on contracts made on behalf of unformed companies unless they expressly disclaim personal liability (s36(4) of the Companies Act 1985).

To get around the rule in *Kelner* v *Baxter* it is common for the promoters of a company to make contracts in their own names, but to include in the contract a provision allowing the company to adopt the contract once incorporation is completed; the result of this being that the company takes over the contract and the promoters are released from personal liability.

Principal must have capacity at the time the agent acts

The effect of ratification is that the contract made by the agent is deemed to have been made by the principal as from the beginning. Therefore, unless the principal could have made the contract himself at that time, he cannot adopt it by ratification. This is similar to the principle from *Kelner* v *Baxter*, but involves cases where the principal does exist at the time the contract is made on his behalf.

In *Boston Deep Sea Fishing and Ice Co Ltd* v *Farnham* [1957] 1 WLR 1051; [1957] 3 All ER 204, contracts made on behalf of a company which at that time was an enemy alien because of war were held not to be capable of ratification by the company after the war had ended. Harman J applied the old case of *Firth* v *Staines* [1897] 2 QB 70, where Wright J had said: 'at the time the act was done the agent must have had a competent principal'.

Similarly, if a contract made on behalf of an infant is absolutely void by virtue of the Infants' Relief Act 1874, it cannot be ratified after the infant has reached the age of majority (*Ditcham* v *Worrall* (1880) 5 CPD 410).

Also of importance here is the rule that a company cannot extend its powers in order to ratify a contract made on its behalf at a time when it did not have capacity. The principle involved is that of the doctrine of ultra vires. A company is a legal person, and it is treated as being able to make contracts even though in reality the company is just a bundle of documents in the Companies Register. The range of contracts which the company is allowed to make is limited by its Memorandum of Association. This is a document which sets out the things which the company is set up to do – its objects. Any contract made on behalf of a company which does not fall within the scope of its objects is *ultra vires*; in other words, it is outside the powers of the company and it is a contract which the company does not have capacity to make. The leading case is *Ashbury Railway Carriage Iron Co v Riche* (1875) LR 7 HL 653, where a company which was set up essentially to run railways and make locomotives made a contract to build a railway. This was outside its objects and therefore not binding on the company. A company may alter the objects set out in its Memorandum of Association, but it cannot backdate this alteration so as to ratify a contract which was ultra vires at the time it was made.

Principal must have capacity at the time of ratification

At first sight it may appear nonsensical that the principal should have to have capacity at the time he ratifies. After all, the theory about ratification is that its effect is that the principal is deemed to have made the contract right at the beginning when the agent made it, and if the principal made it at that time it should not matter what his capacity is at some future time. But the rule is well established.

It can be justified in that the fiction that the principal makes the contract as from the beginning is just a fiction; the reality is that the principal is taking over a contract which has been made at an earlier time.

The effect of this rule in practice is most likely to be felt when an insurance contract has been made and the principal tries to ratify after the property insured has been destroyed. In *Grover and Grover v Matthews* [1910] 2 KB 401 a factory was insured on behalf of its owner, but the person taking out the policy did not have authority to do so. The factory was destroyed and then the owner attempted to ratify it and take the benefit of the insurance cover. Ratification in such circumstances was held not to be effective. After the factory had been destroyed the owner could not have taken out insurance on it himself, therefore he could not ratify the insurance contract taken out before destruction. There is an exception to this in cases of marine insurance, but this is the result of statute not common law (s86 of the Marine Insurance Act 1906).

Manner and time of ratification

The effect of ratification is that the principal becomes entitled to enforce the contract which has been made on his behalf, but he is also liable on that contract to the third party. Therefore it is necessary that the principal has freely adopted the contract.

If the principal has no option but to take the benefit of what the agent has done, then there will be no ratification unless the principal makes it clear that he is adopting the contract. For example, in *Forman & Co Pty Ltd* v *The Liddesdale (Owners)* [1900] AC 190 repairs were carried out on a ship because the captain had ordered them. He had been given authority to contract for repairs which were needed because of stranding, but he went further and ordered repairs of damage due to deterioration. After all the repairs had been done the owners of the ship sold it, and necessarily part of that purchase price reflected the unauthorised repairs. The Privy Council held that the owners had not ratified because their conduct in selling the ship was not an unequivocal ratification. The position was that the owners could not fail to accept the benefit of what the captain had done – they could not have the repairs undone. Therefore, in the absence of any clear adoption of the unauthorised act, the shipowners were not bound to pay for the repairs. This, of course, gave them a profit, but there is no rule that you always have to pay for a profit which has come your way; all the law requires is that you pay for those profits for which you have contracted to pay.

A principal cannot ratify part and repudiate part of the contract made on his behalf. Ratification of part is ratification of the whole (*Cornwall* v *Wilson* (1750) 1 Ves Sen 509).

Ratification can come about by negligence, though such cases are rare. One such was *Welch* v *Bank of England* [1955] Ch 508; [1955] 1 All ER 811, in which a customer of the bank was held to have ratified certain transactions carried out by an unauthorised person in her name; the ratification was the failure of the customer to inform the bank of the wrongful nature of the agent's transaction. What is necessary in such a case is that the principal must act so carelessly that a reasonable third party would think that the act of the agent has been adopted. In the *Welch* case the customer stood by while money was drawn and other transactions undertaken in her name; she had the means to find out what was going on, but took no interest in affairs. Necessarily this sort of case does not arise very often.

Ratification must take place within a reasonable time of the agent making the contract. As in all areas of the law, what is a reasonable time depends on all the facts of the particular case being considered. In addition it used to be thought that ratification could not be effective after the time the contract was meant to take effect. So, for example, an insurance contract made without authority could not be ratified after the period which the insurance cover had begun. The old principle was set out by Fry LJ in *Metropolitan Asylums Board Manager* v *Kingham & Sons* (1890) 6 TLR 217, where he said: 'If ratification is to bind, it must be made within a reasonable time. That reasonable time can never extend after the time at which the contract is to commence.' More recently this dictum has been doubted. In *Bedford Insurance Co Ltd* v *Instituto de Resseguros do Brasil* [1985] QB 966; [1984] 3 All ER 766, Parker J doubted whether there was any principle which could sustain the view of Fry LJ and noted that there was no authority to support it. Parker J held that a contract of insurance could be ratified even after the period of cover had commenced.

The effect of ratification

It has already been mentioned that the effect of ratification is that the principal is deemed to have made the contract at the time when the agent did in fact make it. In other words ratification is retrospective. This is the rule in *Bolton Partners* v *Lambert* (1889) 41 Ch D 215 where an offer was accepted by an unauthorised agent. This acceptance was later ratified by the principal, but before the time of ratification the offeror had attempted to revoke it. The House of Lords held that on ratification the principal had become a party to the contract as from the time the agent accepted the offer, therefore purported revocation of that offer was too late because it had already been accepted by the time of revocation.

Bolton Partners v *Lambert* is a difficult case because the result of it is that the offeror could not enforce the contract against the company until ratification, but at the same time he could not revoke his offer if in fact ratification occurred later. The Privy Council doubted the rule in the *Lambert* case in *Fleming* v *Bank of New Zealand* [1900] AC 577; but there is no English case which really casts any doubt on it representing the law in this country.

It seems that as a result of a more recent Privy Council decision in *Warehousing and Forwarding Co of East Africa Ltd* v *Jafferali & Sons Ltd* [1964] AC 1; [1963] 3 All ER 571, it is possible to restrict the scope of *Bolton Partners* v *Lambert*. In *Jafferali* the agent specifically said that the contract he was making was subject to ratification. The Privy Council held that the *Bolton* v *Lambert* rule will not apply in such a case and there were indications in the Privy Council's opinion that the courts will not be slow to infer from conduct that the contract made by an agent is subject to ratification. It should not be thought, however, that this decision overrules *Bolton Partners* v *Lambert*. Indeed, it must be remembered that the rule in *Boston Deep Fishing* v *Farnham*, that one cannot allow a principal to ratify if he was incompetent at the time the agent acted, only makes sense if the effect of ratification is to make the principal a party to the contract as from the beginning. Following the decision in the *Jafferali* case we must look to see whether the third party knew that the agent was acting outside his authority; if he did then it will be presumed that the contract was made subject to ratification. If, on the other hand, the third party did not know whether the agent had the authority required to make the contract in question, then no such presumption arises and the rule in *Bolton Partners* v *Lambert* applies.

In *Kidderminster Corporation* v *Hardwicke* (1873) LR 9 Exch 13 it was held that a principal cannot sue the third party in relation to breaches which occurred before ratification, though it was not clear whether the principal would be liable for a failure to perform any of his obligations which arose before ratification.

2.5 Creation by operation of law

Introduction

There are two cases where agency is created by operation of law. We have already mentioned agency of necessity but there is also agency by cohabitation. Both of these are restricted in their application today, being nineteenth century rules which are of little relevance in the 1990s; nevertheless they occasionally arise and so must be discussed.

Agency of necessity

Agency of necessity arises when three criteria have been met: firstly, goods must have been entrusted to a bailee by a bailor; secondly, there must be a danger to the goods; and thirdly, the bailee must be unable to communicate with the bailor in order to discover what he should do. In such circumstances the bailee becomes an agent of necessity and may take reasonable steps to protect the goods from the danger. The term 'agency of necessity' is used to cover two sorts of case: firstly, come cases where the bailee has incurred expenses and wishes to be reimbursed; and secondly, some cases where the bailee has made a contract with a third party and the third party wishes to enforce that contract against the bailor. For example, if Mr P entrusts his horse to A Ltd for carriage to Glasgow and it is agreed that Mr P will collect the horse on arrival, the failure of Mr P to collect may put A Ltd in a position where they feel they must put the horse in T's stable overnight. If A Ltd pays for the stabling it will want to have this expense reimbursed; if though, A Ltd does not pay T and then A Ltd goes into liquidation, the question for the court will be whether A Ltd made the contract with T as agents of Mr P, because if they did then T can look to Mr P for the agreed cost. Lord Diplock has recently said that 'agency of necessity' should be reserved for the latter type of case (*China Pacific SA v Food Corporation of India, The Winson* [1982] AC 939; [1981] 3 All ER 688) but there are so many cases which describe the first sort of case as an example of agency of necessity, that both types will be discussed here. In the following discussion, therefore, it should be assumed that the rules laid down are applicable to both types of agency of necessity unless otherwise stated.

Agency of necessity was of great importance in the days before efficient telephonic communication systems were available to ship's captains and railway companies, and most but not all of the cases on agency of necessity have arisen out of contracts for the carriage of goods.

The first criterion gives rise to few problems. It will be clear on the facts of a case whether someone has been entrusted with possession either for carriage or as a warehouseman. But it must be remembered that there must be a consensual bailment; no agency can arise if someone takes it upon himself to look after someone else's property. For example, in *Binstead* v *Buck* (1776) 2 W Bl 1117 the finder of a dog could not claim from the owner the money he had spent looking after it because the owner had never agreed to the bailment in the first place.

The second criterion is more difficult. It is often said that agency of necessity can only arise when the goods are perishable because only then will there be a necessity to take steps to protect them, and leading cases like *Couturier* v *Hastie* (1856) 8 Exch 40, concerning a cargo of grain which was fermenting, *Sims & Co* v *Midland Railway* [1913] 1 KB 103, concerning butter which was melting in hot weather, *Springer* v *Great Western Railway* [1921] 1 KB 257, concerning tomatoes which were ripe and deteriorating and, most recently, the *China Pacific* case, concerning a cargo of wheat, are clear examples of the goods being perishable. But in fact there is no such requirement. In *Great Northern Railway* v *Swaffield* (1874) LR 9 Ex 132 a horse had been delivered by the railway to one of its stations, for collection, but had not been collected. It was held that agency of necessity arose, so that the railway company was acting as agents for the owner when it paid for the horse to be stabled and could claim reimbursement of this expense from the owner. Furthermore, there are many cases concerning agency of necessity in the context of salvage, where action taken by a ship's captain to preserve the ship and its cargo has been seen as action taken as an agent of necessity without the courts requiring that the cargo should be perishable goods (see, for example, *The Hamburg* (1863) 2 Moore PC (ns) 289). It is hard to state a general rule as to the meaning of 'danger' to the goods. Cases already cited cover deterioration of food and the risk to the health of an animal, both of which are dangers to the goods themselves and not to the financial interests of the owner, though the clearest definition of danger came in a case concerning furs where McCardie J said that there is a necessity which gives rise to agency by operation of law where the agent can prove 'an actual and definite commercial necessity for the sale' (*Prager* v *Blatspiel Stamp and Heacock Ltd* [1924] 1 KB 566). It is thought unlikely that this would usually extend to cases where there is not physical danger to the goods but, for example, the market price of such goods is falling. Clearly it could be argued that there would be a necessity in order to protect the owner's position, but it must be remembered that the times when a market falls and has no prospect of rising again are rare; though if the market is falling irreversibly, then it may be possible to hold that there was a necessity to sell.

It is worthwhile noting that, in relation to the carriage of goods by land, Lord Goddard CJ said that agency of necessity cannot arise: 'Except where the goods are perishable or where they are in a somewhat similar category, that is to say livestock which have to be tended, fed and watered.' (*Sachs* v *Miklos* [1948] 2 KB 23; [1948] 1 All ER 67). Taking this dictum in conjunction with that in *Munro* v *Willmott* [1949] 2 KB 295; [1948] 2 All ER 983, that the courts will not readily extend the scope of agency of necessity, it seems most unlikely that, in cases of carriage by land at least, a sale made because of a falling market value where there is no physical danger to the goods will come within the principle.

These days it is the third criterion which is likely to prevent agency of necessity from arising. This third requirement is that 'it must be practically impossible to get the owner's instructions in time as to what should be done' (*Sims* v *Midland Railway*). In the *China Pacific* case Lord Diplock refined this point. He showed that where goods are entrusted by a bailor to a bailee, the bailee will owe a duty of care to take reasonable steps to look after them while in his custody. The definition of what steps are reasonable does not strictly depend on whether it is possible for the bailee to contact the bailor, because if the bailee does communicate with the bailor, but the bailor gives no instructions, the duty of care will require the bailee to take steps which are reasonable in all the circumstances. In other words, as Lord Diplock put it, 'inability to communicate with the owner of the goods is not a condition precedent to the bailee's own right to reimbursement of his expenses'. But, it must be accepted that in this dictum Lord Diplock was considering the first type of agency of necessity mentioned above, and not the second type. Therefore, the position would now seem to be that in order for the bailee to make the bailor responsible for contracts made on his behalf, it is necessary that communication with the bailor is impossible; whereas the bailee may claim reimbursement of his expenses in protecting the goods whether communication was reasonably possible or not, provided that he had not received instructions not to protect the goods.

The burden of proving that communication was not reasonably possible will be on the agent, the bailee. In the *Springer* case the bailee of the tomatoes did not attempt to contact the owner and it was held that he had not proved that communicaion was not reasonably possible. It is virtually unthinkable today that the courts would look kindly on a claim by a bailee that he could not communicate with the bailor, because telephonic communication is both fast and almost universally available.

The whole question of agency by necessity needs review as a matter of some urgency, in the light of modern conditions. The case of *The Choko Star* [1990] 1 Lloyd's Rep 516 is shortly to appear before the House of Lords, who perhaps, may take the opportunity offered to examine existing law on the subject. Here the question as to whether the master of a ship had authority to sign a Lloyds Open Form for cargo (as opposed to salvage of the ship itself) arose. In the initial bearing the court held that there was implied (and hence apparent) authority to do so stemming from the authority vested in the mastership from the owners and/or shippers.

HELD: That there was no such implied authority and only the ancient rules as to agency of necessity might apply. The doctrine of agency of necessity confers, usually on shipmasters, certain authority by operation of law given certain conditions relating to emergency. Of those conditions the requirement that consultation between ship's master and owners/shippers should not be possible gives most difficulty in these days of virtually instantaneous communications. The Court of Appeal reached the decision that the doctrine of agency of necessity would apply here, given certain circumstances.

If agency of necessity is established, then the agent can take such steps as are necessary to protect the goods. This involves two elements: firstly, that unnecessary expenses undertaken need not be reimbursed; and secondly, that expenses undertaken otherwise than bona fide in the interests of the principal need not be reimbursed (see the *Prager* case). The first element is one that arises from the very nature of agency of necessity – the whole concept revolves around taking steps to protect goods, therefore any steps taken which were not in reasonable protection simply fall outside the rule. The second element arises from the relationship between principal and agent which imposes fiduciary duties on the agent. The effect of breach of these fiduciary duties is discussed in Chapter 7 below.

Presumed agency from cohabitation

There used to be a rule that a wife was the agent of her husband when making contracts for necessaries, but as a result of changing patterns of life this was abolished by s41 of the Matrimonial Proceedings and Property Act 1970.

The agency with which we are concerned is that arising from cohabitation. This agency arises from the fact of cohabitation, so there is no need for marriage (*Debenham* v *Mellon* (1880) 6 App Cas 24). The agency arises from a presumption that when a man and woman live together it is common for the woman to be responsible for the running of the household, and for her to be able to ask for credit in the man's name in order to do so. The presumption is one which originally arose as a matter of public policy at a time when it was almost universally the case that the man earned the money and the woman was responsible for the household budget. It may be that today, the courts would not easily presume that such a relationship is sufficiently general in society to be something which can be reflected by the public policy which they enforce. In any event, this form of agency is of little importance today and nothing more will be said about it.

2.6 Usual authority

We have seen above two ways in which the authority of an agent can be said to be 'usual'. Firstly, there is the case where an agent is appointed to a job which carries with it standard powers. In such a case it can be implied into his contract of agency that he will have those usual powers; this is usual actual authority and is a matter arising by presumed agreement between principal and agent. Secondly, we have seen those cases where the principal has represented to the third party that the agent holds a particular office which carries with it usual powers, so that the third party presumes that the agent has those powers; this is usual apparent authority. The matter which we are to discuss here arose in *Watteau* v *Fenwick* [1893] 1 QB 346 in which a hotel manager (the agent) was expressly told not to buy cigars on credit, yet the owners of the hotel (the principals) were held to be bound by such a purchase. There would be no problem with the case if it fitted into the estoppel principal discussed above, and it is tempting to explain the case as one of estoppel. Wills J said:

> 'Once it is established that the defendant was the real principal, the ordinary doctrine as to principal and agent applies - that the principal is liable for all the acts of the agent which are within the authority usually confided to an agent of that character, notwithstanding limitations, as between the principal and the agent, put upon that authority.'

On the face of it this dictum is consistent with the normal rules of agency by estoppel, but Wills J went on to say that he was not stating a rule of estoppel; this was clear by the two sentences following the passage just quoted:

> 'It is said that it is only so where there has been a holding out of authority, which cannot be said of a case where the person supplying the goods knew nothing of the existence of a principal. But I do not think so; otherwise in every case of undisclosed principal, or at least in every case where the fact of there being a principal was undisclosed, the secret limitation of authority would prevail, and defeat the action of the person dealing with the agent and then discovering that he was an agent and had a principal.'

Wills J's dictum would support the proposition that in cases where an agent is appointed to a job which usually carries with it certain powers, the agent will bind the principal provided he acts within this usual authority, whether or not the third party knows that he is an agent. In *Watteau* v *Fenwick* the evidence was that the third party who supplied the cigars did not know that the hotel manager was an agent, it was thought that he was the owner of the hotel. On this aspect of the case it is hard to justify the decision and, indeed, it is generally thought to have been wrongly decided.

Two earlier cases are commonly seen to have been the precursors to the rule in *Watteau* v *Fenwick*, though in fact they are not. In *Daun* v *Simmins* (1879) 41 LT 783 the manager of a public house bought spirits from someone from whom he was told he should not buy. The third party was not allowed to enforce the contract against the principal because he was held to have knowledge of the limits of the agent's authority. Though there are dicta in the case which tend to support the *Watteau* v *Fenwick* principle; these dicta should not be taken out of context. It is not the case that a rule was being laid down that an agent acting within his usual powers will bind his principal even where the third party does not know of the agency; rather that in the circumstances of a case where the third party knew that he was dealing with an agent he could not enforce a contract made outside the agent's apparent authority. In *Edmunds* v *Bushell and Jones* (1865) LR 1 QB 97 the third party dealt with an agent who acted within his apparent authority; not surprisingly it was held that the principal was bound by the agent's act. Fridman had argued that the case could have been decided on the ground that the agent was appointed to a position which carried with it usual authority, and any limitation which has been imposed on that usual authority by the principal is ineffective. There is no indication in the case that this approach to the matter is correct and, it is submitted, Fridman's view has little to commend it.

The position with regard to usual authority, then, is this:

1. The appointment of a person to a position which normally carries with it usual powers to act on behalf of the appointer will give rise to usual actual authority. This arises by virtue of the implication of authority because of the established nature of the position to which the agent is appointed.
2. A representation to a third party that a person holds a position which normally carries with it usual powers to act on behalf of the representor, will give rise to an estoppel against the representor such that any act of the agent within those usual powers will be binding on him. This is simply an example of apparent authority.
3. *Watteau* v *Fenwick* supports the view that the appointment of someone to a position which normally carries with it usual powers will bind the principal to any contract made within those usual powers whether or not the third party knows of the agency. This is unsound in principle and is unlikely to be followed by the courts today.

3

Powers of Attorney

3.1 Definition

3.2 Construction of powers of attorney

3.3 The Powers of Attorney Act 1971

3.4 Irrevocable powers of attorney

3.1 Definition

A power of attorney is a deed, the effect of which is to appoint an agent for certain purposes. Since 1971 all powers of attorney have been required to be signed and sealed (s1(1) of the Powers of Attorney Act 1971), though delivery of the deed is not required. Appointment of an agent by power of attorney is a formal appointment and strict rules of construction apply to the document by which it is made. The principal is known as the donor of the power and the agent the donee or attorney. Common uses of powers of attorney are in cases where the donor is leaving the country for a period, or is physically incapable of conducting his affairs, and he wants to appoint someone to act in the conduct of his affairs during the period of absence or inability.

There are certain statutory rules apart from those in the Powers of Attorney Act 1971, which are relevant. Probably the most important is that in s25(1) of the Trustee Act 1925 by which a trustee is allowed to appoint an agent, by power of attorney, to act as trustee in his stead for a period of up to twelve months.

By virtue of s10 of the Powers of Attorney Act 1971 a power of attorney which aims to give general authority to act in the conduct of the donor's affairs must be executed in the form laid down in Schedule I of the Act. Section 10 reads:

'(A) general power of attorney in the form set out in Schedule I to this Act, or in a form to the like effect but expressed to be made under this Act, shall operate to confer-
a) on the donee of the power; or
b) if there is more than one donee, on the donees acting jointly or acting jointly or severally, as the case may be,
authority to do on behalf of the donor anything which he can lawfully do by an attorney'.

The following is the form that a general power of attorney would take where John Smith wishes to appoint Joe Bloggs and Fred Jones to manage his affairs:

THIS GENERAL POWER OF ATTORNEY is made this 12th day of July 1990 by JOHN SMITH of 1, Albert Square, London E14.
I appoint JOE BLOGGS of 2, Coronation Street, Weatherfield, Lancashire and FRED JONES of 3, Brookside Close, Liverpool jointly and severally to be my attorneys in accordance with section 10 of the Powers of Attorney Act 1971.
IN WITNESS......................
Signed...................

A power of attorney may be for specific purposes, in which case those purposes must be set out in the body of the power.

3.2 Construction of powers of attorney

Strict rules of construction have always applied to contracts made by deed. The rules of construction are, in essence, two. Firstly, ambiguities in a power of attorney will be construed restrictively: in other words, the courts will lean in favour of limiting rather than expanding the scope of the agent's authority. Secondly, parol evidence is not admissible to alter the terms on the face of the deed.

The principal rule of construction was laid down by the House of Lords in *Re Bryant, Powis and Bryant v Banque de Peuple* [1893] AC 170:

> 'On a fair construction of the whole instrument, the authority in question is to be found within the four corners of the instrument either in its express terms or by necessary implication.'

That this is a restrictive rule was seen in *Re Dowson and Jenkins* [1904] 2 Ch 219, where a power including the right 'to sell any real and personal property now or hereafter belonging to' the donor was held not to be wide enough to authorise the donee to exercise a statutory power of sale which the donor possessed because of his position as a mortgagee in possession of land. Similarly, to authorise a donee to sell property owned by the donor 'solely or jointly with another person' did not extend to authorising sale of land held by the donor as trustee for sale (*Green v Whitehead* [1930] 1 Ch 38). In practice these difficulties are overcome by making a general appointment in the statutory form, the effect of this being to give the donee full authority to act in the donor's affairs. But even in such cases care must be taken to ensure that the power is properly executed, because it has recently been held that the Schedule 1 form, cited above, is not appropriate where a trustee wishes to authorise an agent to sell trust property (*Walia v Michael Naughton Ltd* [1985] 3 All ER 673).

Implication of authority will only be made where that is necessary in order to make sense of the deed. There can be no implication by course of dealings between donor and donee, or by trade custom (*Hawksley v Outram* [1892] 3 Ch 359).

The parol evidence rule applies strictly to deeds, so that if the document is clear on its face no evidence will be admissible to contradict its terms. This means that no prior agreement will affect the power of attorney, nor will any subsequent oral agreement.

In cases where the third party dealing with the donee knows of the limits of his authority, the donor may ratify an unauthorised act of the donee, but an attempted prior ratification will not be effective. For example, in *Midland Bank Ltd* v *Reckitt* [1933] AC 1 a solicitor was the donee of a power of attorney and was given authority to draw cheques on the donor's bank account and apply that money for the purposes of the donor. He drew cheques on the donor's account, but paid the money into his own account at the Midland Bank in order to reduce his personal overdraft. The House of Lords held that the donor was not bound by the acts of the donee because the bank knew of the limit on the authority of the donee to draw cheques on the donor's account. There was a provision in the power that the donor 'ratifies and confirms and agrees to ratify and confirm whatsoever the attorney shall do or purports to do by virtue of these presents'. This was held not to be a prior ratification of the acts of the solicitor because the third party (the bank) knew of the limit of authority.

3.3 The Powers of Attorney Act 1971

General matters

Section 1 lays down the general rule in relation to the execution of a power of attorney. It allows a power to be executed by the direction and in the presence of the donor. This is necessary for cases where the donor is not physically capable of executing the deed himself. It has already been noted above that section 1 does not require the deed to be delivered.

Section 1 reads:

> '1) An instrument creating a power of attorney shall be signed and sealed by, or by direction and in the presence of, the donor of the power.
> 2) Where such a instrument is signed and sealed by a person by direction and in the presence of the donor of power, two other persons shall be present as witnesses and shall attest the instrument.
> 3) This section is without prejudice to any requirement in, or having effect under, any other Act as to the witnessing of instruments creating powers of attorney and does not affect the rules relating to the execution of instruments of bodies corporate.'

There used to be a requirement that powers of attorney be filed at the Supreme Court or at the Land Registry, but this was abolished by section 2 of the 1971 Act.

It is not necessary to produce the original power of attorney in order to be able to prove its terms. Section 3 of the Act allows a photocopy provided it is certified as a true copy by the donor, or a solicitor, or a stockbroker.

Revocation of power

In some circumstances a power of attorney is irrevocable, these will be considered below. In cases where the power is not irrevocable, s5 provides for the protection of the donee and third party if they act on the power without notice of its revocation.

Section 5, so far as is relevant for present purposes reads:

> '1) A donee of a power of attorney who acts in pursuance of the power at a time when it has been revoked shall not, by reason of the revocation, incur any personal liability (either to the donor or to any other person) if at that time he did not know that the power had been revoked.
>
> 2) Where a power of attorney has been revoked and a person, without knowledge of the revocation, deals with the donee of the power, the transaction between them shall, in favour of that person, be as valid as if the power had then been in existence.
>
> 3) Where the interest of a purchaser depends on whether a transaction between the donee of a power of attorney and another person was valid by virtue of subsection (2) of this section, it shall be conclusively presumed in favour of the purchaser that that person did not at the material time know of the revocation of the power if:
>
> a) the transaction between that person and the donee was completed within twelve months of the date on which the power came into operation; or
>
> b) that person makes a statutory declaration, before or within three months after the completion of the purchase, that he did not at the material time know of the revocation of the power.
>
> 4) For the purposes of this section knowledge of the revocation of a power of attorney includes knowledge of the occurrence of any event (such as the death of the donor) which has the effect of revoking the power.'

Execution of instruments by the donee

The donee of a power is given authority by s7 to execute documents in his own name for the benefit of the donor. This means that the donee can act as a wholly undisclosed agent and still bind the donor by the contract made. Section 7 reads:

> '1) The donee of a power of attorney may, if he thinks fit:
>
> a) execute any instrument with his own signature and, where sealing is required, with his own seal, and
>
> b) do any other thing in his own name,
>
> by the authority of the donor of the power; and any document executed or thing done in that manner shall be as effective as if executed or done by the donee with the signature and seal, or, as the case may be, in the name, of the donor of the power.
>
> 2) For the avoidance of doubt it is hereby declared that an instrument to which subsection (3) or (4) of section 74 of the Law of Property Act 1925 applied may be executed either as provided in those subsections or as provided in this section.
>
> 3) This section is without prejudice to any statutory direction requiring an instrument to be executed in the name of an estate owner within the meaning of the said Act of 1925.'

In cases where the donee has executed an instrument in his own name, he remains liable unless he delares that he makes it solely as agent (*Tanner* v *Christian* (1855) 4 E & B 591).

3.4 Irrevocable powers of attorney

A power of attorney would be revoked at common law by the death or mental incapacity of the donor. Section 4 of the 1971 Act and the Enduring Powers of Attorney Act 1948 both create statutory exceptions to this rule.

Section 4 of the 1971 Act applies to powers of attorney which are expressed to be irrevocable and are given as security to the donee. In such cases the death or incapacity of the donor will not revoke the power. It is clear from s4(1)(i) that the only way in which the donor can revoke the power in such a case is with the agreement of the donee. Section 4 reads:

'1) Where a power of attorney is expressed to be irrevocable and is given to secure:
a) a proprietory interest of the donee of the power; or
b) the performance of an obligation owed to the donee,
then, so long as the donee has that interest or the obligation remains undischarged, the power shall not be revoked:
c) by the donor without the consent of the donee; or
d) by the death, incapacity or bankruptcy of the donor or, if the donor is a body corporate, by its winding up or dissolution.
2) A power of attorney given to secure a proprietory interest may be given to the person entitled to the interest and persons deriving title under him to that interest, and those persons shall be duly constituted donees of the power for all the purposes of the power but without prejudice to any right to appoint substitutes given by the power.'

In addition, the Enduring Powers of Attorney Act 1985 lays down the conditions in which a power of attorney can survive the mental incapacity of the donor. Much of the 1985 Act is taken up with requirements of registration and the functions of the Court of Protection, but this is not of importance for our purposes.

The 1985 Act allows a power of attorney to survive the mental incapacity of the donor if it is in the proper form and is registered. Such a power is known as an enduring power of attorney. Section 2 states the characteristics of an enduring power and section 1 the effect of a power being an enduring power. The 1985 Act refers to the 'donor' and the 'attorney', the attorney is the donee, the agent.

Section 2 reads:

'1) Subject to subsections (7) to (9) below... a power of attorney is an enduring power within the meaning of this Act if the instrument which creates the power:
a) is in the prescribed form: and
b) was executed in the prescribed manner by the donor and the attorney; and
c) incorporated at the time of execution by the donor the prescribed explanatory information.
2) The Lord Chancellor shall make regulations as to the form and execution of instruments creating enduring powers and the regulations shall contain such provisions as appear to him to be appropriate for securing:
a) that no document is used to create an enduring power which does not incorporate such information explaining the general effect of creating or accepting the power as may be prescribed; and
b) that such instruments include statements to the following effect:

i) by the donor, that he intends the power to continue in spite of any supervening mental incapacity of his;
ii) by the donor, that he read or had read to him the information explaining the effect of creating the power;
iii) by the attorney, that he understands the duty of registration imposed by this Act.
3) Regulations under subsection 2) above:
a) may include different provision for cases where more than one attorney is to be appointed by the instrument to that for cases where only one attorney is to be appointed; and
b) may, if they amend or revoke any regulations previously made under that subsection, include saving and transitional provisions.
4) Regulations under subsection 2) above shall be made by statutory instrument which shall be subject to annulment in pursuance of a resolution of either House of Parliament.
5) An instrument in the prescribed form purporting to have been executed in the prescribed manner shall be taken, in the absence of evidence to the contrary, to be a document which incorporated at the time of execution by the donor the prescribed explanatory information.
6) Where an instrument differs in an immaterial respect in form or mode of expression from the prescribed form the instrument shall be treated as sufficient in point of form and expression.
7) A power of attorney cannot be an enduring power unless, when he executes the instrument creating it, the attorney is:
a) an individual who has attained eighteen years and is not bankrupt; or
b) a trust corporation.
8) A power of attorney under section 25 of the Trustee Act 1925 (power to delegate trusts etc by power of attorney) cannot be an enduring power.
9) A power of attorney which gives the attorney a right to appoint a substitute or successor cannot be an enduring power.
10) An enduring power shall be revoked by the bankruptcy of the attorney whatever the circumstances of the bankruptcy.
11) An enduring power shall be revoked on the exercise by the court of any of its powers under Part VII of the Mental Health Act 1983 if, but only if, the court so directs.
12) No disclaimer of an enduring power, whether by deed or otherwise, shall be valid unless and until the attorney gives notice of it to the donor.
13) In this section 'prescribed' means prescribed under subsection (2) above.'

Section 1 reads:

'1) Where an individual creates a power of attorney which is an enduring power within the meaning of this Act then:
a) the power shall not be revoked by any subsequent mental incapacity of his; but
b) upon such incapacity supervening the donee of the power may not do anything under the authority of the power except as provided by subsection 2) below .... unless or, as the case may be, until the instrument ceating the power is registered by the court ...; and
c) section 5 of the Powers of Attorney Act 1971 (protection of donee and third persons) so far as applicable shall apply if and so long as paragraph b) above operates to suspend the donee's authority to act under the power as if the power had been revoked by the donor's mental incapacity.
2) Notwithstanding subsection 1)b) above, where the attorney has made an application for registration of the instrument then, until the application has been initially determined, the attorney may take action under the power:

a) to maintain the donor or prevent loss to his estate; or

b) to maintain himself or other persons in so far as section 3)(3) permits him to do so.

3) Where the attorney purports to act as provided by subsection 2) above then, in favour of a person who deals with him without knowledge that the attorney is acting otherwise then in accordance with paragraph a) or b) of that subsection, the transaction between them shall be as valid as if the attorney were acting in accordance with paragraph a) or b).'

In addition to the general rule laid down in s1, s3 is more specific about the scope of authority which can be granted under an enduring power of attorney. Section 3 reads:

'1) An enduring power may confer general authority (as defined in subsection 2) below) on the attorney to act on the donor's behalf in relation to all or a specified part of the property and affairs of the donor or may confer on him authority to do specified things on the donor's behalf and the authority may, in either case, be conferred subject to conditions and restrictions.

2) Where an instrument is expressed to confer general authority on the attorney it operates to confer, subject to the restriction imposed by subsection 5) below and to any conditions and restrictions contained in the instrument, authority to do on behalf of the donor anything which the donor can lawfully do by an attorney.

3) Subject to any conditions or restrictions contained in the instrument, an attorney under an enduring power, whether general or limited, may (without obtaining consent) execute or exercise all or any of the trusts, powers of discretions vested in the donor as trustee and may (without the concurrence of any other person) give a valid receipt for capital or other money paid.

4) Subject to any conditions or restrictions contained in the instrument, an attorney under an enduring power, whether general or limited, may (without obtaining any consent) act under the power so as to benefit himself or other persons than the donor to the following extent but no further, that is to say:

a) he may so act in relation to himself or in relation to any other person if the donor might be expect to provide for his or that person's need respectively; and

b) he may do whatever the donor might be expected to do to meet those needs.

5) Without prejudice to subsection 4) above but subject to any conditions or restrictions contained in the instrument, an attorney under an enduring power, whether general or limited, may (without obtaining any consent) dispose of the property of the donor by way of gift to the following extent but no further, that is to say:

a) he may make gifts of a seasonal nature or at a time, or on a anniversary, of a birth or marriage, to persons (including himself) who are related to or connected with the donor, and

b) he may make gifts to any charity to whom the donor made or might be expected to make gifts,

provided that the value of each such gift is not unreasonable having regard to all the circumstances and in particular the size of the donor's estate.'

The overall effect of the 1985 Act is that a clear statement is made of the authority which an attorney may have under an enduring power, in those areas of his job which could cause difficulties.

The recent case of *Re R (Enduring Power of Attorney)* [1990] 2 WLR 1219, throws some light on the powers of the court under the 1985 Act. The applicant was employed by R as a resident housekeeper and companion. R gave her nephew an enduring power of attorney with general authority to act on her behalf, which was registered under the 1985 Act. Soon afterward R became incapable of managing her own affairs and was transferred to a nursing home. The attorney terminated the applicant's employment and sought possession of R's flat. The applicant alleged that she had agreed to work for a very low rate, in the expectation that R would provide for her for the rest of her life. Her application for provision out of R's estate was dismissed at first instance. On appeal it was held that while the Court of Protection had jurisdiction under the 1985 Act to supervise the attorney's conduct, including the extensive powers needed to give consents or authorisations where required to supplement the attorney's jurisdiction, they did not have any power to enforce moral as opposed to legal obligations. Section 8(2)(b)(i) of the Act gave the Court unrestricted powers to supervise the attorney's conduct and allowed them to supplement that conduct with additional orders as needed to implement management and administration decisions on the part of the attorney (provided any such decisions by either the attorney or the Court of Protection were not inconsistent with the wishes of the donor of the power). But at no point did s8 permit the Court to give effect to moral obligations. The court had no power to dispose of R's property by way of gift or to make provision for the applicant out of R's estate. The appeal was dismissed.

Note that the Enduring Powers of Attorney (Prescribed Forms) Regulations 1990, effective as from 31 July 1990, prescribe a revised form of an enduring power of attorney. The new method of execution has been made necessary as a result of the coming into force on 31 July 1990 of s1 of the Law of Property (Miscellaneous Provisions) Act 1989 (see above).

4

Contracts Made by Agents

4.1 Introduction

4.2 Disclosed principal

4.3 Undisclosed principal

4.4 Agent acts outside his authority

4.1 Introduction

We have already seen that the acts of an agent which are within his authority are binding on the principal. This general rule is not always a full explanation of the position, however, because the agent can sometimes be personally liable. The liability of the agent may be co-existent with that of the principal, but at times the agent may be liable even when the principal is not.

An agent may contract in one of three ways with a third party: he may name his principal; or he may disclose the fact that he is an agent without naming his principal; or he may act as though he is not an agent at all. Generally there is little difference between the cases of the named principal and the disclosed but unnamed principal. The making of a contract for an undisclosed principal raises special problems and will be considered at some length below.

4.2 Disclosed principal

General rule

A disclosed principal is one whose existence is known to the third party. The only effective differences between the case of the named principal and the case of the disclosed but unnamed principal are, firstly, that if the principal is named, then only that named principal may intervene and take the benefit of the contract or be sued under it; and secondly, that it is easier to hold the agent personally liable if he acts for an unnamed principal than where the third party knows the identity of the principal. The first, though, is not really a special rule at all because even where the principal is not named it is only the true principal who may take the benefit of the contract made.

Where an agent discloses the fact of his agency the basic rule is that the agent is not liable on the contract which he makes, and, therefore, that the only privity is between principal and third party. In other words, the agent 'drops out'. But this is too simple a picture to draw because three problems may arise: firstly, the principal may not in fact exist; secondly, the agent may have undertaken personal liability on the contract; and thirdly, it may sometimes be necessary to hold the agent liable for policy reasons.

For example, see *Foalquest* v *Roberts* (1990) 21 EG 156 where a financial consultant claimed various items of remuneration for services rendered. Whether he was so entitled, depended on the true liability of the agent acting for the company with which he had dealt. The agent claimed to have acted throughout as agent for a disclosed principal and never to have assumed or accepted personal liability.

HELD: The court had looked to the objective intention of both parties, examining the form and terms of the contract and the surrounding circumstances. The Court of Appeal felt that in this case there was no reason to overturn the initial assessment of the position. There was no evidence to indicate that the agent purported to bind himself personally.

By and large, the agent's personal liability (or lack of it) would seem to depend to some extent on the expressed intention of the parties. See, for example, *Badgerhill Properties* v *Cottrell* (1991) The Independent 12 June. In making contracts for work with the defendant, T, the director of the plaintiff company, drew up contracts on headed notepaper bearing the company name. Against his own name on this paper T had written 'director' in brackets. The company sued the defendant for non-payment for work done, while the defendants counterclaimed that the work was defective.

The question arose as to whether T was personally liable, whether he had been acting on his own behalf or that of the principal company.

The Court of Appeal held that whether T was acting on his own behalf depended to some degree on the intention of the parties. The language of the contract, the fact that the company name appeared on the headed paper, the fact that the company's trading name appeared in the contract all seemed to indicate that the defendant was trading with whoever called themselves by the trade name of the company. The fact that the word agent did not appear was not enough to prevent the contract being construed as a contract of agency.

Principal does not exist

We have already seen that there can be no ratification of a contract made by a promoter on behalf of a company which has not yet been incorporated. This rule, the rule in *Kelner* v *Baxter*, carries with it a presumption that the agent should be personally liable. Indeed section 36(4) of the Companies Act 1985 makes the promoter personally liable in the absence of agreement to the contrary.

This statutory rule is only applicable where a pre-incorporation contract has been made on behalf of a company, it does not extend to other cases of non-existent principal. In other cases it is necessary to examine the manner of signature of the agent in order to discover whether he is to be personally liable. The presumption is that he will not bear personal liability on the contract unless he signs both in his own capacity and as agent. Thus, in *Kelner v Baxter* itself (which sets out the common law application to all contracts entered into on behalf of a non- existent principal) the agents of the proposed hotel company were personally liable because they had signed in their own names and had not declared that they were acting solely as agents. On the other hand, in *Newborne v Sensolid (Great Britain) Ltd* [1954] 1 QB 45; [1953] 1 All ER 708, the contract was signed by a type-written 'Leopold Newborne (London) Ltd' followed by the signature of Mr Newborne himself. The Court of Appeal held that Mr Newborne was not personally liable because giving the company name rather than signing in his own name and declaring it to be 'for and on behalf of' the company meant that the company only was undertaking liability. This also meant, as in fact was the decision in the *Newborne* case, that the 'agent' cannot enforce the contract.

The position therefore seems to depend simply on the form of signature given. If an agent's principal dies and the agent's authority is therefore terminated, this fact may not be communicated to the agent before he attempts to make a contract on behalf of his principal. If he signs in his own name declaring himself to act 'for and on behalf of' or using similar words, then he will be personally liable, but if he signs in the principal's name with his own name either not added or added merely as witness to the principal's signature, then he will not be personally liable.

In addition to the agent sometimes being personally liable because he adds his signature as an additional contracting party, the agent may also intervene and enforce the contract, or be held to it, where it is discovered that the agent is himself the principal. Clearly this will not be the case where the principal is named (see *Fairlie v Fenton* (1870) LR 5 Exch 169), but may arise where the principal is unnamed. In such cases it is clear that the agent is personally liable because it is the intention all along that the third party should deal with the principal and, therefore, if the 'agent' is in fact the principal, so is he liable because of that fact. In *Harper & Co v Vigers Bros* [1909] 2 KB 549 the plaintiff shipbrokers signed a charterparty contract for hire of a ship 'by authority of and as agents for owners', the defendants, who hired the vessel under this contract, were held to be bound to the plaintiffs because the plaintiffs were in fact the effective owners of the ship. Pickford J applied *Schmaltz v Avery* (1851)16 QB 655 which lays down the rule that an agent who is in fact the principal can enforce the contract personally by virtue of his position as the true principal.

Agent undertakes personal liability

The rule in *Kelner v Baxter* discussed in the previous paragraph is just one example of the agent undertaking personal liability on the contract which he makes. It is always possible for the agent to undertake personal liability even where the principal does exist. But it must be clear that he is undertaking such liability.

The law has consistently favoured the view that an agent who acts within his authority drops out of the picture. In *Southwell* v *Bowditch* (1876) 1 CPD 374 the agent made known that he was an agent and it was held that the principal alone was liable on the written contract. Similarly, in *The Santa Carina* [1977] 1 Lloyd's Rep 478 an oral contract made by an agent within his authority was held binding on the unnamed principal only. In neither case, however, was there any intention that the agent should be liable.

An agent will normally be personally liable under a deed which he has executed in his own name. This is the result of the rule in *Re International Contract Co* (1871) 6 Ch App 525, that a principal may not enforce a deed, and is not bound by a deed, unless he is named as a party to it; in that case the principal company was not liable for debt owed under a deed which named a director only as debtor. This rule is altered in the case of powers of attorney by section 7 of the 1971 Act, which lays down that the execution of a deed by the donee of a power is to be treated as though the donor were named in the deed. There is a further alteration of the normal rule in cases where the agent is a trustee. In such a case *Harmer* v *Armstrong* [1934] Ch 65 holds that equity will recognise that the agent was a mere trustee but only where he signs as trustee, and if he does so then the principal may enforce the deed even though not specifically named in it.

An agent will be held to have intended to be personally liable where this can objectively be seen to be the intention of both the agent and the third party. The leading case is *Universal Steam Navigation Co* v *McKelvie* [1923] AC 492 where the signature on a contract by McKelvie was said to be 'as agents'. The House of Lords held that this should be interpreted as meaning that McKelvie signed as agents alone. The House considered the possibility of the agents being jointly liable, but rejected it on the facts, saying that there was a clear declaration that they were agents only arising from the form of the signature. Therefore, something more is needed than a declaration of agency for an unnamed principal before the agent is personally liable. In *Lester* v *Balfour Williamson Merchant Shippers Ltd* [1953] 2 QB 168; [1953] 1 All ER 1146, tins of beans with sausages were sold, the labels of which did not bear the correct weight of the foods contained in the tins. The merchants who sold them declared that they did so 'for account of our principal' and the principal was named. The Divisional Court held that the declaration of agency meant that the agents had not committed an offence by selling incorrectly labelled tins. However, it was not investigated in the judgment whether the agents could have been jointly liable with the principal.

In *The Swan* [1968] 1 Lloyd's Rep 5 Brandon J held that the agent was liable jointly with the principal. The agent owned a vessel and formed a company for the purpose of operating it. The third party knew that the agent was the owner, and therefore, when he signed a contract to have the vessel repaired, objectively it was held that he signed both as agent for the company and in his own capacity as owner. He signed with his own signature and described himself as 'director' of the company, but the most important matter was the knowledge of the third party about the nature of the agent's interest in the ship.

A similar point arose in *The Santa Carina* (supra) in which the Court of Apppeal held that the burden of proof is on the third party, to prove that the agent is personally liable and that that burden will only be satisfied where there is evidence of some special facts which make it reasonable for the third party to suppose that the agent is undertaking personal liability.

There is no clear English authority on the position of the third party where both agent and principal are liable. Two lines of argument can be pursued: on the one hand, it may be that there are two separate contracts one with the principal and one with the agent, so that the third party may sue both; on the other hand, it may be that the third party must choose which to sue because he makes one contract which may be enforced against the agent or principal alternatively. We will see below that where the principal is undisclosed, so that the third party believes the agent to be acting entirely on his own account, it is well established that the third party must elect who to sue and if he elects to sue the principal he may not later take action against the agent; in other words there is one contract and the third party must elect whom he is to sue.

In *Benton* v *Campbell Parker & Co* [1925] 2 KB 410 Salter J said that two separate contracts are formed, but that election to take action against either principal or agent will prevent the third party from suing the other; however, this case did not draw a clear distinction between unnamed and undisclosed principals and Salter J in places appeared to say that they were the same. Salter J's approach was to treat the principal and agent as being alternatively liable, so that an election to sue one meant that the other could not be proceeded against. This case in not entirely clear in applying the 'one contract' rule in cases of unnamed principal.

The case most often cited on this question is *Debenham's Ltd* v *Perkins* (1925) 133 LT 252 where Scrutton LJ said:

> 'When a agent acts for a disclosed principal, it may be that the agent makes himself or herself personally liable as well as the principal. But in such a case the person with whom the contract is made may not get judgment against both. He may get judgment against the principal or he may get judgment against the agent who is liable as principal, but once he has got judgment against either the principal or the agent who has the liability of the principal, he cannot then proceed against the other party, who might be liable on the contract if proceedings had been taken against him or her first'.

In that case, a woman bought certain items from Debenhams on credit terms. Some were bought while she lived with her husband and certain others after their separation. The shop took action against the wife for the price of items bought after separation and then, in separate proceedings, wished to sue the husband for the price of certain items bought by the wife before separation. The Divisional Court held that the action taken on the post-separation contracts did not prevent the husband being sued afterwards for the price owed under the earlier contracts. The decision rested on the point that the election to sue the wife under the post-separation contracts was irrelevant to the earlier contracts because after separation she did not incur any liability as agent for her husband. It was not necessary for the decision, for the Court to decide whether the doctrine of election applies to cases of disclosed agency.

Nevertheless, it should be said that it is commonly stated in the textbooks that the doctrine of election does apply to cases of disclosed agency as well as to cases of undisclosed agency. In the absence of further clarification by the courts it should be assumed that the doctrine of election does apply, but for a powerful argument to the contrary see Reynolds, 'Election distributed' (1970) 86 LQR 318.

It is not surprising that in cases where the agent is personally liable he is also entitled personally to enforce the contract (see *Cooke* v *Wilson* (1856) 1 CB NS 153).

Agent liable for policy reasons

The rule used to exist that an agent for a foreign principal always undertook personal liability; this was based on the notion that a third party had to have someone in this country to whom he could look to ensure that the contract made was carried out. In *Elbinger Act, Fur Fabrication von Eisenbahn Material* v *Claye* (1873) LR 8 QB 313 Blackburn J said, obiter, that there was a trade custom that a person dealing in this country did not trust foreign merchants who worked through agents, and so could rely on the agent being personally liable.

These days such an approach does not reflect reality and so the old rule has been abolished. The Court of Appeal in *Teheran-Europe Co Ltd* v *ST Belton (Tractors) Ltd* [1968] 2 QB 545; [1968] 2 All ER 886 held that a foreign principal could enforce a sale contract against an English third party. It was not clear whether the principal was unnamed or undisclosed, but the Court held that it made no difference. Blackburn J's dictum from the *Claye* case was overruled and it was said that a foreign principal is to be treated in the same way as a British principal.

But, the point was also made, in the *Teheran-Europe* case that the fact that the principal is foreign may be a matter to take into consideration when construing the contract made by the agent. The point which seemed to be made was that if the principal is foreign, this may be something which leads to the agent being personally liable, though it was not stated in such clear terms. The argument here is that the agent will be personally liable if that is the proper construction of the agreement between him and the third party; and where the principal is overseas and, perhaps, unknown to the third party, it is easier to infer that the agent undertakes personal liability, to secure the position of the third party.

4.3 Undisclosed principal

Introduction

It is a rule peculiar to English law that an undisclosed principal is liable on a contract made by his agent, and can also enforce that contract in his own right against the third party. Many explanations have been attempted as to why English law allows such a rule whilst at the same time adhering vigorously to the doctrine of privity, but none sounds particularly convincing. Three leading articles between them collect and discuss all of the front-runners among these explanations. The main one of the three is the earliest, 'Undisclosed principals in contract' by Goodhart and Hamson to be found at (1931) 4 CLJ 320, but also useful are 'The undisclosed principal' (1953) 16 MLR 299 by Muller-Freienfels, which is an interesting comparative study, and 'The equity of the undislosed principal' (1965) 28 MLR 167 by Higgins, which argues for greater recognition of the rules of Equity in the treatment of cases of undisclosed agency.

It does not matter not how one attempts to explain the doctrine of the undisclosed principal, because no amount of praise will extend its scope, no amount of criticism will abolish it and no amount of scepticism over its legitimacy will alter it in any way. All that need be said is that the rule exists that an undisclosed principal may intervene in the contact made by his agent and may be sued on that contract by the third party involved.

There are three matters which fall for discussion in relation to undisclosed principals. Firstly, it must be appreciated that the whole doctrine is concerned with cases where the third party has not noticed that the agent is an agent, and this means that only contracts made within the actual authority of the agent fall within the doctrine's ambit. There can be no apparent authority without a representation that someone is an agent and necessarily, therefore, a doctrine concerned with contracts made by people who appear to be acting on their own behalf cannot involve any representation to the third party about the agent being an agent. Secondly, because the doctrine is so radical an exception to the doctrine of privity, so it must be kept within fairly narrow limits, which means that certain criteria must be fulfilled before the principal may intervene (see below: The criteria). Thirdly, we must look at the position of the agent in all this – in the eyes of the third party a contract is being made with the agent personally, so to what extent can it be enforced by or against the agent (see below: Third party election)?

The criteria

Before the doctrine of the undisclosed principal can be invoked two criteria must be fulfilled. These are: that the agent must contract personally and not as an agent; and that the identity of the agent must not be vital to the contract, nor the identity of the principal be fatal to it.

We have already seen that there is no scope for the undisclosed principal to intervene where the agent acts as agent. Clearly in many cases the principal may be able to intervene because he is the named or unnamed but disclosed principal. But if the agent says that he is acting on behalf of a named principal, no one other than that named principal may take the benefit of the agent's contract or be liable on it. It is not open to the principal to say that the agent was in fact contracting on his (the principal's) behalf where the agent has told the third party that he is in fact working for someone else. It could be argued that there would be no harm in the true principal intervening in such a case unless the identity of the named principal was of importance, but the reason why he cannot is grounded firmly in the doctrine of privity.

If A makes a contract to supply 100 tons of wheat to T, and states that P1 is his principal, then the position of the third party is that he is led to believe that the contract is being negotiated with P1. A may himself undertake liability under the contract and that would make him jointly liable with P1 in the eyes of T, but on an objective assessment of the contract made, T is buying from P1 whether or not the agent is also liable. If A is in fact working for P2 the position is no different; objectively there is no offer or acceptance passing between T and P2 and so there is no contract to which P2 is a party.

If A does not disclose that he is an agent at all the position is rather different. Here T believes that he is contracting with A alone, but where A is acting within his actual authority in making the contract he makes it in his capacity as the representative of P2, and P2 can intervene because the authorised act of A is the act of P2. Therefore, where A does not disclose that he is an agent at all, T knows that he is dealing with A and also knows that A may be dealing on his own behalf or may be dealing as the agent of an undisclosed principal. The onus is on T to ask A whether he is an agent. If A says that he is not, then the only contract which is made is between T and A personally; but if T does not bother to ask him the capacity in which he makes the sale, then T runs the risk that he may be making it in his capacity as agent.

It is sometimes a difficult question whether the agent is contracting apparently as principal or whether he is declaring that he is not an agent. The classic example is *Fred Drughorn Ltd* v *Rederiaktiebolaget Transatlantic* [1919] AC 203 where an agent hired a ship signing himself as 'charterer'. The House of Lords held that he was not asserting that he made the contract solely for his own benefit because this description was not inconsistent with him being an agent. On the other hand, in *Humble* v *Hunter* (1848) 12 QB 310 a ship was hired from someone who described himself a 'owner' and this was held to be an assertion that he was the sole owner; similarly in *Formby Bros* v *Formby* (1910) 102 LT 116 where an agent's description of himself as 'proprietor' was held to be an assertion of ownership. The distinction between the *Drughorn* case and the last two mentioned is that where an agent declares himself to be the holder of a property right (by saying he is 'owner', for example) then he is saying that he holds it personally because that is how his statement will be interpreted by a reasonable man. But, if the agent says he is the 'charterer' of a ship all he is saying is that he is the person who is signing the charterparty contract, and that signature may be made by an agent.

In *Danziger* v *Thompson* [1944] KB 654; [1944] 2 All ER 151, an agent signed as 'tenant', and the undisclosed principal wished to intervene. Lawrence J was referred to the three cases cited above and explained them on the ground given by Viscount Haldane in *Drughorn*, namely, that the capacity given by the agent will be an assertion that he is contracting solely on his own behalf where that capacity is inconsistent with him being merely an agent; a tenant can be an agent, so there was nothing inconsistent with his agency by describing himself in that way. Similarly in *Epps* v *Rothnie* [1945] KB 562; [1946] 1 All ER 146, the Court of Appeal, including Lawrence J, held that someone may be an agent even though describing himself as 'landlord' because that is no assertion that he holds any property rights in the house concerned.

The identity of the agent may be a factor which influences the third party to make the contract. Normally it can be presumed that a party to a contract does not care who he is dealing with, it will be remembered that cases concerned with mistake at common law will only allow a party to get out of an apparent contract if he can prove that the identity of the other party was so important that his mistake as to the identity undermined the very foundations of the contract (as was seen, for example, in *Boulton* v *Jones* (1857) 2 H & N 564 and *Ingram* v *Little* [1961] 1 QB 31; [1960] 3 All ER 332). A less robust approach has been taken by the courts when deciding whether the identity of the agent was so important as to prevent an undisclosed principal intervening. Similar points arise when considering whether the principal's identity is such as to prevent him from intervening and taking the benefit of the contract. The following four cases warrant discussion.

In *Said* v *Butt* [1920] 3 KB 497 there was bad feeling between the principal and the third party, so the principal used an agent to buy a ticket for entry to the first night of a play at the third party's theatre. The agent bought in his own name and when the principal turned up at the theatre he was refused admission. The Court of Kings Bench held that this was a case where the undislosed principal could not intervene to take the benefit of the contract because the third party would have refused to sell the agent the ticket if the name of the principal has been dislosed. The court took special notice that the ticket was for the first night and that the management of the theatre would be particular about those who were allowed to attend the first night performance.

The principal in *Dyster* v *Randall & Sons* [1926] Ch 932 knew that his offer to buy certain land would be rejected, so he had an agent buy it for him. The agent did not disclose that he was an agent, nor did he make any misrepresentation about his position. The principal was granted a decree of specific performance, Lawrence J holding that the absence of misrepresentation by the agent allowed any undisclosed principal to intervene and enforce the contract. The earlier case of *Archer* v *Stone* (1898) 78 LT 34 was distinguished because in that case, since the agent had declared to the third party that he was not acting as agent for his principal, with whom the third party was not prepared to deal, the misrepresentation meant that specific performance would not be granted.

A different matter arose in *Greer* v *Downs Supply Co* [1927] 2 KB 28 where a Court of Appeal refused to allow an undisclosed principal to intervene because the agent owed money to the third party for goods the third party had supplied; the contract made by the agent was to sell other goods to the third party in order to offset purchase against the debt owed. It was held that the third party was making the contract with the agent only because of the personal element.

Collins v *Associated Greyhound Racecourses Ltd* [1930] 1 Ch 1 involved the agreement by the agents to underwrite an issue of shares. This meant that when the third party offered shares to the public, if the public did not take up all of the shares offered, then the underwriters would have to take them up. The Court of Appeal held that the contract to underwrite was made between the agents and the third party only and that the principal could not intervene. The Court's decision rested on the special nature of an underwriting contract which depended on the personal integrity of the underwriters.

The result of these cases is that if the third party can prove that he was not prepared to do business with the undisclosed principal on the same terms that he offered to the agent, then the undisclosed principal will not be able to intervene. However, this explanation does not reconcile *Said* v *Butt* and *Dyster* v *Randall & Sons*. It is difficult to reconcile these two cases, because they both appear to involve a third party who would never have dealt with the principal, but in *Said* v *Butt* the principal was not allowed to intervene whereas in *Dyster* v *Randall & Sons*, he was. *Said* v *Butt* was distinguished in *Dyster* v *Randall & Sons* on the ground that the sale of tickets for a first night performance was a contract which of its nature involved the personality of the parties, in that the management of a theatre would be minded to refuse tickets to people who may do harm to the production, whereas the sale of land was an impersonal transaction. Perhaps the rule coming from all the cases involves two questions: firstly, it must be asked whether the making of the type of contract being made can objectively involve personal matters; and secondly, it should be asked whether the personality of the agent or principal is of such importance that the third party is correct in alleging that he would only deal with the agent or would never have dealt with the principal had he known his identity.

Third party election

We have seen above that when an agent acts for a disclosed but unnamed principal there are some cases where the agent is personally liable as well as the principal being liable; we have also seen that the general view is that the third party has a choice of whom to sue in such cases. If the principal is solvent he may wish to sue him; if the principal is insolvent he may wish to sue the agent. The courts have said that there are two contracts, and it is certainly the case that the third party knows that two people are liable on the contract.

Where the principal is undisclosed, however, the third party is only really led to believe that he is dealing with one party - the agent. Of course, it can be said that the third party knows that the person he deals with may be an agent, but it cannot objectively be said that he ever intends to make two contracts, one with the agent and one with the principal. The position, in fact, is that the third party makes one contract which he believes is made with the person before him, the agent, but which he knows may in fact be made on behalf of a principal whose existence has not been disclosed.

When it comes to the attention of the third party that the person he dealt with was an agent, the third party has a choice; he may enforce the contract against either the agent or the principal; but because he only ever intends to make the contract with one party, so he cannot sue both. The nature of an election is that it is an informed choice, freely made on the basis of full knowledge of relevant facts. This is normally the position in relation to the election of the third party, but not always. Two matters give rise to problems, however: firstly, how much knowledge must the third party have before he is put to his election; and secondly, when is the election made?

State of third party's knowledge

Normally, full knowledge of the identity of the principal is required before the third party can be said to have elected whom to sue. But, the position can perhaps be taken out of the hands of the third party by the action of the agent or principal. The problem which arises can be seen in a case where A contracts with T to buy certain goods, but does not pay the price immediately; T discovers that A is an agent for P and decides to take action against P but before he does this P pays A the money in order that A can pay T. There are conflicting decisions about whether the settlement between P and A prevents T from suing P. In *Armstrong v Stokes* (1872) LR 7 QB 598 Blackburn J refused to follow the earlier case of *Heald v Kenworthy* (1855) 10 Exch 739 and said that the settlement between principal and agent prevents the third party from suing the principal because such an action would have the unfair result of making the principal pay twice. But, in *Irvine & Co v Watson & Sons* (1880) 5 QBD 414 the Court of Appeal unanimously said, obiter, that Blackburn J went too far, and pointed out that it was unfair to the third party that he may be sued by the principal but can have his right to sue the principal cut down by an act between principal and agent. There is no easy answer to the problem because in *Armstrong v Stokes* it was by no means clear that the agent was an agent, so the comment of Blackburn J was obiter and the criticism of it in *Irvine & Co v Watson & Sons* was also obiter. The view of the Court of Appeal in *Irvine* is to be preferred because in the eyes of the third party he is only contracting with the agent and it is unfair for him to find that he cannot sue the person he made the contract with because of some settlement between the agent and principal which was made before the third party ever knew of the principal's existence.

What qualifies as an act of election

Once the third party has knowledge of the identity of the principal, then an unequivocal act showing his intention to pursue his remedy against either principal or agent will amount to an election, and he will not then be allowed to sue the other.

The mere institution of proceedings against the principal was held not to be an election in *Clarkson, Booker Ltd* v *Andjel* [1964] 2 QB 775; [1964] 3 All ER 260, where a writ had been issued against the principal but the third party was still allowed to sue the agent. There was the special factor in that case that the third party continued to write to the agent threatening to take action if the debt owed was not paid, but this matter was probably of little significance. The main factor in deciding that the issue of a writ is not an unequivocal election to sue the principal was that the issue of a writ is the first stage of proceedings and writs can often be served against several different parties before deciding which one to proceed against.

Principal and third party

Where the principal wishes to sue the third party he may do so without first disclosing his identity, there is nothing improper about the first contact between principal and third party being the service of a writ on the latter by the former. But, if the third party has settled with the agent, the principal may have lost his right to take action. This problem arises where the third party buys goods from the agent and pays for them but the agent does not pass the money received on to the principal; can the principal sue the third party for it?

In cases where the third party knows prior to paying the price that the agent is an agent, then the only question is whether the agent was authorised to receive payment. It may seem surprising, but an agent who is authorised to sell is not impliedly authorised to receive the purchase price. This rule dating from *Drakeford* v *Piercy* (1866) 7 B & S 515 was upheld in the context of the authority of estate agents to accept deposits in *Sorrell* v *Finch* [1977] AC 728; [1976] 2 All ER 371.

In principle, payment to an agent by the third party at a time when the third party does not know that the agent is an agent should prevent the principal from suing, but the cases are not clear. In the context of a claim by the third party to be able to set off a debt owed by the agent against a claim from the principal, *Baring* v *Corrie* (1818) 2 B & Ald 137 holds that if the agent is authorised to contract on behalf of the principal without disclosing the agency, then the third party is entitled to assume that the agent is the only party he is contracting with, and if a debt is owed by the agent to the third party this can be set-off against any claim against the third party by the principal. It is thought that a similar rule applies in the case of payments made to the agent. If the third party does not know of the existence of the principal at the time he pays the agent for the goods supplied, then this will be treated as good payment and the principal will have to look to the agent for the money.

4.4 Agent acts outside his authority

Normal rule

We have already seen that the acts of an agent outside his authority do not bind the principal and the most obvious manifestation of this is in the making of contracts by an agent - any contract made outside his authority does not bind the principal and does not entitle the principal to sue unless he ratifies.

Where the agency is undisclosed then only actual authority is relevant, but where it is disclosed, whether the principal is named or not, any contract made within apparent authority will bind the principal. The fact that the principal may have instructed the agent not to make a certain type of contract is a matter to be settled between them; it will have no effect on the right of the third party to sue the agent.

Agent's liability

The third party is not left without protection where the agent is not authorised, however. If the agency is undisclosed but the agent acts outside his actual authority then the principal cannot ratify and is neither liable nor able to sue, but the agent will be personally liable on the contract made. The third party's position is the same as though the agent had never been appointed agent for any purpose, in that the third party thinks that he is contracting with the agent and the agent is personally liable.

But, if the agent acts outside his authority in circumstances where he is not personally liable, then the third party can sue the agent for breach of warranty of authority. The liablity of the agent in such cases is contractual but it arises not from the contract which the agent purported to make as principal, but from a separate unilateral contract which he makes in his own capacity. It will be familiar that a unilateral contract is sometimes known as an 'if' contract - the offer made can be put into formula: 'if you do the act I request then I promise that a certain reward will follow', and the failure of that reward to materialise will leave the offeror liable for breach of contract. So, if in reward cases the offer is: 'if you find my lost dog, I promise that I will pay you £100', the failure to pay the £100 to the finder leaves the dog-owner liable in damages. Similarly, an agent who contracts as agent is deemed to make a unilateral offer in the form: 'if you agree to make this contract with my principal, I promise that I am authorised to make it on his behalf'. If the agent is authorised then the promise has been kept and the third party can have no complaint, but if the agent is not authorised then the agent must pay damages for breach of his promise that he was authorised. The implied promise made by the agent is known as the warranty of authority and the action against him by an aggrieved third party is an action for breach of warranty of authority.

The warranty of authority was first clearly established in *Collen* v *Wright* (1857) 8 E & B 647, in which it was recognised that the unauthorised agent can be liable for breach of warranty of authority whether he acts fradulently, knowing that he has no authority, or innocently, honestly believing that he has authority. In cases where the agent is fraudulent in asserting that he has authority which, to his knowledge, he does not possess, the third party can choose to sue in tort for damages for deceit, even if the agent believes that the principal is going to ratify, as was the case in *Polhill* v *Walter* (1832) 3 B & Ad 114.

The measure of damages for breach of warranty of authority is such as to put the third party in the position which he would have occupied if the agent had been authorised. Therefore, if the contract would have been unenforceable against the principal for some reason, or if the named principal were insolvent, then no damages would be payable because no loss would have resulted to the third party.

The agent will be liable for breach of warranty of authority even if he acted in complete good faith. For example, in *Yonge* v *Toynbee* [1910] 1 KB 215 the agent continued to act for his principal despite the termination of his authority which had happened, unknown to the agent, when his principal became insane. The agent was held liable for breach of warranty of authority despite his total innocence.

5

Torts Committed by Agents

5.1 Introduction
5.2 Fraud
5.3 Other torts

5.1 Introduction

It will be familiar to the reader that the law of tort imposes vicarious liability on an employer for those torts of his employee which are committed within the course of his employment. It will be equally familiar that the employer of an independent contractor will not be liable for the contractor's torts unless they also constitute a primary tort committed by the employer.

The difficulty for the agency lawyer is that an agent may be either an employee or an independent contractor, and it is tempting to think that once it is known whether the agent is employee or independent contractor that is the end of the matter, and that the principal's liability matches that of the employer. In fact, such an approach does not reflect the law.

There is a difference in principle between an agent and an employee or independent contractor, the difference lies in the function for which each is employed. An agent, as we have already seen, is someone who affects the legal position of his principal; which in most cases means someone who either makes or performs contracts on behalf of his principal, whereas an employee or independent contractor may work for an employer without it ever being envisaged that he will come into contact with the third parties. The rules of vicarious liability in tort have grown primarily out of situations where the employee or contractor has carelessly injured a third party whilst carrying out the job he is employed to do. However, the involvement with the third party is often not the primary function for which he is employed, and this is reflected in the tortious vicarious liability rules.

An agent, regardless of whether he is an employee or independent contractor, is by the very nature of his job likely to come across third parties, so it is easier to justify liability on the part of the principal. In the same way that an employee is under the control of the employer, so the agent is controlled by his authority. Perhaps the closest parallel which can be taken is between the employee who does the job he is employed to do but does it carelessly and the agent who acts within his actual authority in so far as making a contract is concerned, but in the course of doing so doing commits a tort; and this parallel has led the judges on occasions to liken the liability of a principal for the torts of his agent to the liability of an employer for the torts of his employee. There is, however, a significant difference in that the agent can do a job wholly different to that which he is actually authorised to do, but still act within his authority by doing something which he appears authorised to do; and if he does so he would normally bind his principal because of the concept of apparent authority, which has been discussed above. So, the law of agency must go further than that relating to employees and must ask how far the apparent authority, of an agent is relevant in the context of torts he has committed.

In the same way that a parallel can be drawn between acts within an employee's employment and acts within the scope of an agent's actual authority, so can one be drawn between the acts of an employee which are a 'frolic of his own' and the acts of an agent which are outside his actual authority. In principle it would seem right that the principal should be liable for all torts which are committed by an agent in the course of carrying out his actual authority, but should not be liable for torts commited wholly outside the agent's actual or apparent authority. But there is no easily discernable principle which should be applied to torts committed in the course of carrying out an act which is outside actual authority but within apparent authority. On the one hand it could be said that because apparent authority arises from a representation from the principal to the third party that the agent has authority to act, so the third party may be justified in looking to the principal to put right any wrong done by the agent. On the other hand it could be argued that it does not necessarily follow that, in cases where the third party has received a representation that the agent is authorised to make a contract, the third party has also received a representation that the agent is authorised to commit a tort.

The position taken by the courts is that a distinction is drawn between fraud and other torts. The principal is only liable for his agent's fraud if it was within the apparent, or perhaps actual, authority of the agent to commit fraud; this is investigated at greater length in section 5.2 below. The liability for other torts committed by his agent, however, is wider, and it is generally accepted that the principal will be liable for all torts committed within the course of the agent's employment. The difference between employees and independent contractors is ignored in both types of tort. Where non-fraud is concerned, all agents are presumed to be employees and then the normal tortious rules of vicarious liability apply; the details of this are discussed in section 5.3 below.

5.2 Fraud

Fraudulent acts of an agent can potentially affect the principal in two ways: firstly, any contract made by the agent may be voidable for fraudulent misrepresentation;

and, secondly, damages may be claimed for the tort of deceit. These two matters involve different principles. If it is argued that the principal's contract with the third party can be avoided for fraud, then it would seem that the fraud of the agent is to be seen as the direct fraud of the principal, in that the contract made is between the principal and the third party and it is only the misrepresentation of one of the contracting parties that will make the contract itself voidable. Liability in damages for the tort of deceit, however, could arise either because the fraud of the agent is looked upon as being the fraud of the principal, or because the agent is the one who commits the fraud but the principal, like an employer, is made liable as an alternative defendant.

The courts have not drawn a clear distinction between these two aspects of the agent's fraud, but it is probably just a matter of time before clear recognition is given to it. The attitude of the courts is that if the agent is acting within his actual or apparent authority in making the contract, so the manner of its making is something which must have been, or appeared to have been, authorised. In *Lloyd* v *Grace, Smith & Co* [1912] AC 716 a solicitor's clerk, acting within the course of his apparent authority, fraudulently induced a client to give him authority to sell certain property; he then sold the property and retained the proceeds. The solicitors were liable for the fraud of their agent because it was within his apparent authority to advise the client on property transactions. The House of Lords rejected the argument that because the agent was acting for his own benefit so the principal was not liable. There had been dicta to this effect in *Barwick* v *English Joint Stock Bank* (1867) LR 2 Exch 259, but these were strongly rejected. Earl Loreburn LC said that the act of the clerk 'was a tortious act committed by the clerk in conducting business which he had a right to conduct honestly'. In other words the agent induced the third party (Mrs Lloyd) to make a contract by means of a fraudulent misrepresentation; he was authorised honestly to induce her to make such a contract, therefore the fraudulent act which was within the apparent authority of the agent was as effective as if he had made a contract directly between the third party and his principal.

It must be remembered that by definition the third party will not know that a fraud is being committed; if this is known, then it is no fraud because there is no deceit. Therefore, we do not have to ask whether the agent was apparently authorised to commit fraud, all we must ask is whether he was apparently authorised to enter into the transaction into which he did enter.

The Court of Appeal reiterated this rule in *Uxbridge Permanent Benefit Building Society* v *Pickard* [1939] 2 KB 248; [1939] 2 All ER 344, where a solicitors's clerk fraudulently induced the building society to lend money to a non-existent client. The court held that it was within the actual and apparent authority of the clerk to induce the building society to lend money to a client, and therefore the building society had lost its money because the principal had represented the clerk to be authorised to make such an agreement and the building society had relied on this representation when making the loan.

The Court of Appeal has recently applied *Pickard* in *Bank of Kuwait* v *Hammoud* [1988] 3 All ER 418 which concerned a salaried partner of a firm of solicitors who was held to have the apparent authority to bind the firm regarding an undertaking to transfer money to a bank. Lord Donaldson MR stated that a practising solicitor is not to be regarded as a potential fraudster and that a bank is not obliged to regard an undertaking given by a solicitor with suspicion. Thus a practising solicitor would appear to have wide apparent authority with respect to his firm.

In both *Lloyd* v *Grace, Smith & Co* and *Uxbridge Permanent Benefit Building Society* v *Pickard* it was said that the principal would be liable where the third party had lost money because of an act of the agent which was within his actual or apparent authority. It is clear in these cases that the House of Lords and Court of Appeal respectively were holding the principal liable because his representation that the agent was authorised induced the third party to lose money. This gives rise to a problem in that the justification for holding the principal liable is that he has himself misled the third party - what happens if the agent acts within his actual authority but there is no apparent authority?

In *The Ocean Frost*, to which reference has already been made, the House of Lords did not clearly give the answer to this problem. In that case the agent of Mundogas, Mr Magelssen, signed a three-year charterparty on behalf of his principals intending to operate a fraud on both Mundogas and Armagas and to manipulate the charterparty to his own benefit. The making of this contract was outside his actual authority, and Armagas, the third party, knew this; so there was no apparent authority and accordingly Mundogas were not liable for Magelssen's fraud. Lord Keith said that the principal will be liable for his agent's fraud whenever it is fair to make him liable; it will be fair, he said, when the principal has himself represented to the third party that the agent is authorised to make the contract which causes the third party loss; but he did not say that it would be unfair where the agent is acting within his actual authority but there is no such representation.

As the authorities stand at present, therefore, it can be clearly said that a principal will be liable for the fraud of his agent where the transaction which the agent carried out fraudently was one which was within his apparent authority to carry out. Certain dicta in *Lloyd* v *Grace, Smith & Co* and *The Ocean Frost* are to the effect that a principal will also be liable for his agent's fraud where the transaction which was carried out fraudulently was within the agent's actual authority even if there is no apparent authority. A stronger case on this point is the decision of the House of Lords in *Briess* v *Woolley* [1954] AC 333; [1954] 1 All ER 909, where the managing director of a company fraudulently misrepresented that the profits of the company had been lawfully made, but there was evidence that the principals, who were shareholders in the company, actually knew of the fraud at the time it was acted on by the third party; so this case cannot be seen to lay down a general rule that all fraud within actual authority is the responsibility of the principal.

Two important export sales cases involved fraud by an agent. In *Kwei Tek Chao* v *British Traders and Shippers Ltd* [1954] 2 QB 459; [1954] 1 All ER 779 shipping agents forged the date on bills of lading so as to show that the shipment had taken place within the date stipulated in the CIF contract. Devlin J held that although the fraud had been carried out by the sellers' agents, the sellers were not responsible because the representation which the buyers alleged was fraudulent was the presentation of the documents for payment and this was done by the sellers and not the fraudulent agents; the sellers were not privy to the fraud, so there was no fraud practised by the sellers on the buyers, only by the shipping agents on the sellers. Similarly, in *United City Merchants (Investments) Ltd* v *Royal Bank of Canada* [1982] 2 WLR 1039; [1982] 2 All ER 720, the fraud of the shipping agents against the sellers was not something for which the sellers could be made responsible.

These two cases raise the interesting point of when a principal will be held to know things which are within the knowledge of his agent. The cases covered two different points: firstly, that the principal was not responsible for the fraud because he was himself a victim of it; and secondly, that the principal was treated as though he did not know of the fraud perpetrated by his agent. A principal will be held to know something within his agent's knowledge if the agent was acting on behalf of his principal and within his authority when receiving that knowledge. For example, in *Newsholme Bros* v *Road Transport and General Insurance Co Ltd* [1929] 2 KB 356 the agent of an insurance company helped a prospective customer to fill in a proposal form. The agent would put the questions on the form to the customer and would then write in the answers given. The agent in fact filled in answers different to those given and in consequence the insurance company refused to pay a claim made under the policy. This followed the rule in insurance contracts that a claim can be refused unless all relevant matters were disclosed to the insurance company by the customer. The customer argued that because the correct answers had been give to the agent, so the insurance company had been given all the relevant information and the claim should, therefore, be paid. The Court of Appeal held that when filling in the form the agent was acting on behalf of the customer, so that the customer was the principal, the agent was his agent, and the insurance company was the third party. Therefore, at no time when the agent was acting on behalf of the insurance company did he receive the knowledge to which the company was entitled.

More recently the sort of problem encountered in the *Kwei Tek Chao* case has arisen again, though in the context of the shipowner's liability for the incorrect dating of bills of lading rather than the seller's liability. In *The Saudi Crown* [1986] 1 Lloyd's Rep 261 bills of lading were signed after goods had been loaded and falsely stated that they had been loaded by 15 July 1982 when in fact the loading had not been completed until 26 July 1982. Sheen J held that the shipowners were responsible to the CIF buyers for the misrepresentation of their agents that the goods had been loaded by 15 July. It was held that the misrepresentation was made by the agents in the course of completing and issuing bills of lading, which were tasks within their actual authority. No distinction was drawn between a misrepresentation made fraudulently and one made innocently or negligently; provided it was made when doing the job which the agent was employed to do, the principal was bound.

5.3 Other torts

Where an agent commits a tort other than fraud the test of the liability of the principal is to ask whether the tort was within the course of employment of the agent. It is a matter which has received unfortunately little discussion in the cases, but the distinction between servants and independent contractors appears not to be applicable where the tortfeasor is an agent. A frequently cited dictum from Denning LJ in *Navarro v Moregrand Ltd* [1951] 2 TLR 674 is to the effect that a principal 'is responsible in tort for all wrongs done by the servant or agent in the course of his employment, whether within his actual or ostensible authority or not. The presence of actual or ostensible authority is decisive to show that his conduct is within the course of employment, but the absence of it is not decisive the other way.' In *The Ocean Frost* Lord Keith commented that this dictum is not correct in so far as fraud is concerned, but 'may have some validity in relation to torts other than those concerned with fraudulent misrepresentation'.

One important case which was not commented upon in *The Ocean Frost* is the Privy Council decision in *Kooragang Investments Pty Ltd v Richardson & Wrench Ltd* [1982] AC 462; [1981] 3 All ER 65, where the principals, a firm of estate agents, were held not to be responsible for a negligent valuation made by one of its valuers. The Privy Council said, through Lord Wilberforce, that we must ask whether the job which was done negligently was one within the scope of the agent's actual or apparent authority, and if it was, then the agent should be treated like a servant and the principal will be responsible for torts committed during the course of employment. No distinction was drawn between agents who are servants and those who are independent contractors and it seems that that distinction is of no relevance where the liability of the principal for the negligence of his agent is concerned. In that case the valuer was never authorised to undertake the valuation, so his negligence was a 'frolic of his own'.

6

Obligations of Principal to Agent

6.1 Remuneration

6.2 Indemnity

6.3 Enforcement

6.1 Remuneration

The contractual right to payment

It is often considered to be obvious that a principal must pay his agent a wage for his services, but there is no legal rule to this effect. The position between principal and agent is determined by the agreement which they make and if that does not include an express or implied promise of payment then the agent is entitled to no payment.

It must be remembered that an agent is not necessarily appointed by contract; the agreement which creates him agent may be informal. Therefore the 'right' to payment may itself be an informal matter. No one would suggest that a child who goes to the shops for his mother is legally entitled to payment, but he would nevertheless be an agent and can make a binding contract between his mother and the shop.

In some circumstances the right to remuneration will be expressly agreed, and if this is the case then normal rules of construction should be applied to the agreement. The reader will be familiar with the rule in *Re Casey's Patents* [1892] 1 Ch 104 which is that an agreement between employer and employee for the employee to do extra work on top of his contract commitment carries with it an implication that the employee will be paid for that work. This is a example of the implied right to remuneration which many agents have, it arises from the understanding between employer and employee that the work of the latter is not a gift, it is a commercial service which is given for reward. In *Way* v *Latilla* [1937] 3 All ER 759 a man was employed to obtain information about various mines in West Africa. The House of Lords held that any agreement which may have been made relating to remuneration was too vague to give rise to a contractual right to a share in the mine, but this did not prevent an award of reasonable remuneration being made on the basis of an implied term in the contract of employment. It was held that he was employed in such circumstances that he could not reasonably be expected to work for nothing, so he was entitled to a reasonable sum for his efforts. Although an agent is not necessarily an employee, because he may be an independent contractor, there is, nonetheless, a similar implication that he will be paid for what he does in many cases. But remuneration is only payable if it is agreed expressly or impliedly that it will be paid, and if it has been earned.

Express agreement for remuneration will only be enforceable where a contractual agreement has been made. We have already seen that an agent may be appointed informally, or may be someone within the family or a friend, so that there is a presumption against legally enforceable rights existing between this type of principal and agent. Where an agreement is made for remuneration to be paid at the discretion of the principal, then even if the agent does the work he has been appointed to do he will not be able to enforce the right to payment in the courts because the discretion is one for the principal, not one for the court. For example, in *Kofi Sunkersette Obu* v *Strauss & Co* [1951] AC 243 there was an agreement that the agent was to be paid a commission at a rate to be fixed by the principal; no commission was fixed and the Privy Council held that the agent was not entitled to any payment under the discretion. In other words a discretion is a discretion, even if exercised unfairly. Similarly in *Re Richmond Gate Property Co Ltd* [1965] 1 WLR 335; [1964] 3 All ER 936, where a company director was held not entitled to any payment for his services because his agreement provided that the company should pay 'such remuneration ... as the directors may determine'. In the absence of a determination there was no right to remuneration.

Sometimes the discretion to make payment will be expressed in such terms that the principal accepts the obligation of making a payment and the discretion just relates to the amount of payment. In such cases the agent can claim a reasonable reward for the services he has performed. It is not easy to know whether the terms of the agency agreement provide for a discretion whether to pay commission at all or a duty to pay commission coupled with a discretion as to the rate of payment. In *Taylor* v *Brewer* (1813) 1 M & S 290 the agreement was that the agent would receive 'such commission ... as should be deemed right'. This was held to give the principal an absolute discretion whether or not to make any payment. On the other hand in *British Bank for Foreign Trade Ltd* v *Novimex Ltd* [1949] 1 KB 623; [1949] 1 All ER 155, an agreement stating, 'we also undertake to cover you with a commission on any other business transacted', was held by the Court of Appeal to give the agent an entitlement to payment at a rate to be fixed, and in the absence of the principal fixing the commission a reasonable commission had to be paid.

Earning of commission

An agent will only be able to enforce an express or implied agreement that he should be paid if he has earned his commission. A right to salary is one which arises from the fact of employment, so long as the agent is employed he is entitled to his salary. But commission is a different matter, commission is a payment according to results so it is necessary to construe the agreement in order to discover the events which must happen before the commission is earned.

The earning of commission involves two matters: firstly, the agent must perform the act which he is asked to perform; and secondly, the event on which commission is payable must have come about because of the efforts of the agent. The first matter means that an agent is not entitled to commission merely because his principal has received some benefit from what he has done. For example, in *Toulmin* v *Millar* (1887) 12 App Cas 746 the agent was employed to find a tenant for a property; he did this and therefore had earned his commission. But, when the tenant bought the property from the principal this did not entitle the agent to a commission on the sale because he was not instructed to find a buyer, merely to find a tenant. This effectively means that an agent may not receive commission for any act outside his actual authority, even if within apparent authority. The ratification of an unauthorised act, however, may carry with it an implication that the agent will be paid.

The concept that the agent may not claim commission unless his efforts brought about the event which was required to happen prior to payment is usually expressed in the form that the agent must be the effective cause of the event. In *Millar* v *Radford* (1903) 19 TLR 575 an agent was employed to find either a tenant or a purchaser for the plaintiff's property. He found a tenant and earned commission for having done so. Some time later the tenant bought the property and the agent claimed a second commission on the ground that he had introduced a buyer and so was entitled to a commission under the original contract. It was held by the Court of Appeal that the agent was not entitled to a second commission because he had not brought about the sale.

A similar point arose in *GT Hodges & Sons* v *Hackbridge Park Residential Hotel Ltd* [1940] 1 KB 404; [1939] 4 All ER 347, where estate agents were instructed to find a buyer for a hotel. The potential purchaser found was acting on behalf of the War Office, but negotiations came to nothing. Some time later the War Office compulsorily purchased the hotel and the estate agents claimed that they had earned a commission because the purchaser whom they had introduced had bought the property. The Court of Appeal held that the commission would have been earned if there had been a voluntary sale of the hotel, but the enforced sale by way of a compulsory purchase was not the type of sale which entitled the agents to a commission.

An often difficult question when the right to remuneration is being investigated is the definition of the event which must happen before commission is payable. Particular problems have arisen with esate agents who may be employed on the basis that they will receive a commission if a sale is made, or may on the other hand be entitled to commission on introducing someone ready, willing and able to buy. Questions about the sale of land are beyond the scope of this book, but it is useful to see the way in which the courts have interpreted different estate agents' rights. The presumption is that the agent will be paid a commission if a purchaser whom he introduced to the vendor agrees to buy; it will need clear words to entitle an estate agent to commission where no sale is made.

The right to commission cannot be enforced by an agent who has breached his duties unless the principal waives the breach or the breach is unrelated to the earning of commission. The duties of an agent towards his principal are examined in detail in Chapter 7 below, but it is necessary to mention something of them now. An agent owes fiduciary duties very similar to those owed by a trustee, including a duty not to make a secret profit, which includes the taking of bribes. In *Andrew* v *Ramsay & Co* [1903] 2 KB 635 the agents, who were auctioneers, received a secret payment from the third party, and in consequence their principal refused to pay them any commission even though they had sold the principal's property as required. It was held that the breach of duty disentitled the agents from receiving a commission.

In *Harrods Ltd* v *Lemon* [1931] 2 KB 517 the principal, Mrs Lemon, instructed Harrods to sell her house. The purchaser required a survey and employed Harrod's surveying department to carry it out. This put Harrods in the position of acting for both parties; in other words they had a conflict of interest, although there was no lack of good faith on their part. When the problem was discovered Harrods contacted Mrs Lemon and explained what had happened and she said that she was quite happy for them to continue to act for her. The sale went through but she refused to pay them commission on the ground of breach of duty. The Court of Appeal held that the breach of duty had been waived, so that the right to commission was enforceable.

In *Hippisley* v *Knee Bros* [1905] 1 KB 1 auctioneers paid for the printing of advertisements and received a discount from the printers which they kept for themselves. They charged the sellers for the full cost of the advertising and also claimed a commission on the sale. The Court of Appeal held that the right to commission was not affected by the secret profit which had been received by way of the discount. The commission related to the sale of the principal's goods and the performance of the sale was in no way affected by the secret profit. Lord Alverstone CJ said:

> 'If the court is satisfied that thre has been no fraud or dishonesty upon the agent's part, I think that the receipt by him of a discount will not disentitle him to his commission unless the discount is in some way connected with the contract which the agent is employed to make or the duty which he is called upon to perform.'

A right to commission normally ceases once the agency terminates, but if appropriately worded the agency contract can extend the right to commission to things which happen after the agent's death or after other termination of the agency. In *Wilson* v *Harper Son & Co* [1908] 2 Ch 370 the commission was to be payable 'as long as we do business with those you place on our books'. It was held that this allowed the estate of the deceased agent to recover commission on orders placed after the agent's death. In contrast, there was no right to commission after the agency had been terminated in *Crocker Horlock Ltd* v *B Lang & Co Ltd* [1949] 1 All ER 526 because the commission was payable on all orders placed by those whom the agent had introduced, and 'on all repeats' and this was construed by Morris J as meaning all repeat orders received by the principal during the course of the agency.

Opportunity to earn

In most contracts an act by one party which prevents the other party from earning the benefit for which he has contracted allows that other party to claim damages for breach. If an agent is employed on terms that he should introduce customers to the principal, but will only earn commission if the principal does business with those persons who have been introduced, is it a breach by the principal if he refuses to do business with those people?

The House of Lords asserted the principal's right to choose to do business with whoever he wants in *Luxor (Eastbourne) Ltd* v *Cooper* [1941] AC 108; [1941] 1 All ER 33, where an estate agent introduced a potential purchaser but the vendor refused to accept that purchaser's offer and instead decided to withdraw the property from sale. The estate agent argued that the principal should not unreasonably prevent his agent from earning commission, but the House of Lords held that the principal does not have to sell to those who are introduced, he could refuse to do so for any reason. It was recognised in the House that an agreement could be made whereby the agent is entitled to commission on introducing a person who is ready, willing and able to buy, and if such an agreement is reached between principal and agent then the agent will earn commission whether or not the sale is made. But the agreement in that case was to pay commission on sale, and no sale was made, therefore no commission was earned.

At times the courts have held that the principal was in breach if he refused to allow the agent to earn his commission, but such cases are rare and any decided prior to *Luxor (Eastbourne) Ltd* v *Cooper* must be treated with suspicion because the decision in that case overruled several earlier cases which had held the principal to be in breach. A recent Court of Appeal decision allowed an agent damages because of his principal's obstructive behaviour. In *Alpha Trading Ltd* v *Dunnshaw-Patten Ltd* [1981] QB 290; [1981] 1 All ER 482, commission was payable to agents, who had introduced a buyer for cement, if the purchase price was paid by the buyer to the principal. The agents made an introduction and the principals agreed to sell to the third party who was introduced, but the principals then broke the sale contract and refused to supply the cement; this had the result that the agreed price was not paid and therefore the right to commission was not made out. The Court of Appeal held that in such circumstances a term was to be implied into the agency contract whereby the principal promised not to disentitle the agent from commission by breaching a contract with a third party on which the agent's right to commission depends.

Of course, the agency contract may expressly provide that the agent's right to commission survives an act of the principal which would appear at first sight to terminate that right, but this is usually a matter for express agreement and only very rarely will it be implied. The scope of the *Alpha Trading* case is limited, it only applies where the principal breaches a contract with the third party and this breach causes the agent loss. If the principal and third party agree to terminate their contract, then the agent cannot claim commission on the ground that had the contract not been terminated he would have received it. In *L French & Co Ltd* v *Leeston Shipping Co Ltd* [1921] 1 AC 451 the agent was entitled to commission on hire payments made by the third party to the principal for hire of a ship. Before the hire contract had run its full course the principal sold the ship to the third party, thereby terminating the hire contract and preventing the agent from earning commission on hire payments. The House of Lords held that the agent was not entitled to damages in such a case because the principal had not been in breach of the hire contract which had been made with the third party. In *Alpha Trading* this case was distinguished on the ground that the shipowners had not breached the hire contract by agreeing with the hirers to bring it to an end, whereas in *Alpha Trading* there was a breach of the sale contract.

6.2 Indemnity

The agent's right of indemnity arises in two contexts. Firstly, the agent may spend money in the performance of his agency contract, the normal rule is that his reasonable expenses may be recovered from the principal. Secondly, the agent may be liable in contract or tort to the third party, or may commit an offence, and the principal will be liable to indemnify the agent from the loss resulting in such cases, provided the agent acted within his actual authority.

Whether or not the agent is entitled to recover his reasonable expenses from the principal is, like so many things, a matter for their agreement. In *Adams* v *Morgan & Co* [1924] 1 KB 751 the principal was obliged to reimburse the agent the amount of super tax which the latter had had to pay when conducting business on behalf of the principal. There was no express agreement to this effect, but it was implied.

We have already discussed in Chapter 5 the circumstances in which the agent could find himself liable in contract to the third party. Liability in tort will arise whenever the agent commits a tort, whether or not the principal is vicariously liable; though, because the right of indemnity only arises if the agent acted within his actual authority, the principal will be liable as well. Of course, successful action against either principal or agent for the tort will prevent the third party from taking action against the other.

The agent will not be allowed to claim an indemnity for damages paid to third parties where he has been in breach of his duties to the principal. In *Lage* v *Siemens Bros & Co Ltd* (1932) 42 Ll LR 252 the agents did not declare all of the principal's goods which were being taken through customs. This was a breach of the duty to act with due diligence and McKinnon J held that this disentitled the agents from recovering an indemnity for fines which had to be paid. Similarly in *Barron* v *FitzGerald* (1840) 6 Bing NC 201 the agents were instructed to take out life insurance on the principal in their names, Barron and Stewart. When the policy was renewed it was taken out in the names of Barron, Stewart and Smith because the agents had taken on a new partner. The agents were in breach by taking the policy out in an incorrect name, and could not claim an indemnity from the principal.

But a liability which arises because the agent does the very thing which he is instructed to do can always be claimed from the principal. The agents in *Anglo Overseas Transport Ltd* v *Titan Industrial Corporation (United Kingdom) Ltd* [1959] 2 Lloyd's Rep 152 booked shipping space on behalf of their principals, but because of a trade custom at the port concerned, they incurred personal liability to the shipowners when the goods arrived late at port and the ship left without them. The booking made was exactly that which had been asked for, so the principals had to indemnify the agents against the loss incurred.

There is no direct authority on the point, but a dictum of Lindley J in *Thacker* v *Hardy* (1878) 4 QBD 685 is to the effect that there is no indemnity of damages paid because of the agent's negligence. In that case the agent made various contracts on the Stock Exchange for his principal, and was personally liable on them. The principal was held to be obliged to reimburse the agent because he had acted within his instructions. One question before the court was whether the contracts made were gambling contracts, because if they had been then the question would have arisen whether the agent could rightly claim to be indemnified. Lindly J held that the contracts were perfectly lawful, but added that if they had been illegal then the agent would not have been entitled to an indemnity, and added that the same is true where the agent has been negligent.

6.3 Enforcement

The agent can enforce his right to commission or indemnity in several ways. The most obvious is in an action for damages for breach of contract, but this will not be available if the agency is non-contractual. In such cases the agent can sue in restitution for an indemnity, but will not be able to sue for any remuneration because that would be to give the agency agreement contractual force.

In *Brook's Wharf & Bull Wharf Ltd* v *Goodman Bros* [1937] 1 KB 534; [1936] 3 All ER 696, warehousemen were allowed to reclaim from the owner of goods which had been stolen from the warehouse certain duties which had to be paid to the customs authorities. The basis for the Court of Appeal's decision was that it would have been unjust for the warehousemen to have to pay duty on someones else's goods, and in so far as the case lays down the restitutionary principle applicable between principal and non-contractual agent, it seems that the agent can only claim an indemnity where it is unjust for him to have to pay a third party. The court said that the warehousemen had paid the duty which was owed by the owners of the goods, and this would restrict the non-contractual agent's indemnity to cases where he had paid the principal's debt for him. If the agent was personally liable because he had chosen to incur the liability, then the indemnity would not apply. This has the effect that a non-contractual agent can claim an indemnity for expenditure which he makes, but for which the principal could have been sued directly by the third party; if the agent alone could be sued by the third party, then there is no right of indemnity.

In addition to a contractual or restitutionary claim, the agent may wish to enforce a lien over the principal's goods. The agent's lien is a possessory one, in other words it is a right to retain possession of the principal's goods until money owed has been paid.

The lien can only be exercised over goods in relation to which money is owed and only if the exercise of a lien is not inconsistent with the terms of the agency. So, in *Dixon* v *Stansfield* (1850) 10 CB 398 an agent who was regularly employed to sell his principal's goods went outside this normal function on one occasion and insured a ship for the principal. He wished to exercise a lien on the insurance policy to secure payment of money owed for previous dealings. It was held that no lien could be exercised, because the debts were not related to the agency agreement by which he came into possession of the policy.

In *Rolls Razor Ltd* v *Cox* [1967] 1 QB 552; [1967] 1 All ER 397, a salesman who was in possession of his employer's property was held not to have a lien over it because in his contract it was provided that on termination of his employment he was to hand over all property still held by him which belonged to the employer. This term was inconsistent with the salesman having a lien and so no lien could arise.

Because the purpose of the lien is to secure payment of sums due, so that payment or tender of payment of those sums will result in the lien being lost. Also, because the lien is a particular possessory lien - one which allows the agent to retain possession of the particular goods related to the debt - so an act by the agent inconsistent with these characteristics of the lien will lead to its loss: for example, if the agent sells the goods or loses possession of them, or if he waives the lien.

7

Obligations of Agent to Principal

7.1 Introduction
7.2 Obedience
7.3 Due care and skill
7.4 Conflict of interests
7.5 Secret profits
7.6 Delegation

7.1 Introduction

An agent owes duties to his principal both because of their agreement and because he is in a fiduciary position. Even a non-contractual agent is in a fiduciary position, and a fairly close comparison can be drawn between the fiduciary duties of an agent and those of a trustee. The non-contractual agent does not owe any duties arising from the agreement which he makes, because to enforce the agreement would, of course, be to make the agency contractual.

The first two duties which we will discuss below - the duty of obedience to instructions and the duty to use due care and skill - are both predominantly contractual duties, but the non-contractual agent may owe a duty of care to his principal regardless of contract, and this point should not be overlooked.

The fiduciary duties are clear and well established, but the reader should take care to acquaint himself with the agency cases in this area and not simply assume that trustee cases cover everything. By his very nature an agent is not the same as a trustee because, for example, he does not usually have legal title to any property with which he may deal on behalf of his principal.

Finally, notice that if, by conduct, the principal indicates that he no longer regards the agency as existing, the agent owes no further duty of loyalty to that principal (*Sears Investment Trust Ltd* v *Lewis's Group Ltd* [1992] TLR 459). This is the case even when the principal never formally dissolves the agency relationship.

7.2 Obedience

An agent is under a duty to obey his instructions. Disobedience will be a breach of contract, if the agency is contractual, and the normal contract remedies are available to the principal. It must be remembered that if the agent disobeys his instructions he will either be doing nothing or acting outside his actual authority; the latter leaves him able to bind his principal to third parties where the act of the agent is within apparent authority, and the liability of the principal to the third party is something which will be reflected in damages awarded to the principal.

That the duty of obedience covers cases of non-performance is clear. In *Turpin v Bilton* (1843) 5 Man & G 455 the agent failed to insure his principal's ship and was held liable for the value of the ship when it was lost and the principal was unable to claim under insurance. It is equally clear that the duty extends to mis-performance. In *The Hermione* [1922] P 162 the agents were instructed to settle a claim on behalf of a ship and its crew for at least £10,000, but they settled it for £100. They claimed in their defence that the instructions were manifestly absurd; but this was irrelevant, for the instructions were clear and if £10,000 could not be realised in the settlement then no settlement should have been made.

In *Christoforides v Terry* [1924] AC 566 Lord Sumner laid down the remedies of a principal whose agent has disobeyed instructions. The remedies are threefold: firstly, there may be a claim for damages for breach of contract; secondly, an account can be obtained so as to recover any profit which the agent may improperly have made; and thirdly, any claim by the agent for remuneration or indemnity can be resisted. We have already seen that the third of these remedies has its limitations, but there are few effective limits to the first two. The agent will be able to resist a claim for damages for non-performance where the act he was instructed to perform was illegal. 'Illegal' in this context bears its contractual meaning rather than its criminal meaning, so in *Cohen v Kittell* (1889) 22 QBD 680 the failure of an agent to place a bet was not something for which he could be sued because the betting contract if made would been void.

We have already seen how the old rule in *Ireland v Livingstone* (1872) LR 5 HL 395, that the agent acts within his actual authority where he adopts a reasonable interpretation of ambiguous instructions, was limited recently in *European Asian Bank AG v Punjab and Sind Bank (NZ) Ltd* (supra), and if the agent unreasonably takes it upon himself to interpret his instructions rather than asking the principal for clarification, then he will be in breach of his contract of agency if he adopts an incorrect interpretation and this will leave him open to an action for damages.

7.3 Due care and skill

An agent owes a duty to perform his instructions with due care and skill. In *Keppell v Wheeler* [1927] 1 KB 577 an estate agent informed his principal that an offer had been received for the principal's property, but did not inform him of an improved offer which was later received from another potential purchaser. The principal sold to the first offeror and was successful in claiming damages from the agent for his breach of duty in failing to pass on the second offer. The action in *Keppell* v *Wheeler* was for breach of contract, though in many cases an identical action could be taken in negligence.

The contractual duty of care has been supplemented recently by the Supply of Goods and Services Act 1982. Section 13 provides that where a service is supplied in the course of a business there is an implied term that the supplier will carry out the service with reasonable care and skill. This will not have any effect unless the agent who supplies a service acts in the course of his own or another's business when supplying that service. 'Business' in the Act is defined by section 18 to include profession, so the supply of professional service by an agent will be caught as well as cases where an agent is an independent contractor running a business on his own account. Where an agent is a servant of the principal the supply of the agency service will not be in the course of business. The implied term is not defined as either a condition or warranty, but simply as a term and this may mean that whether there is a right to terminate the agency contract because of a failure to take reasonable care depends on how serious is the default by the agent. In addition to this implied term, section 14 provides that the service should be provided within a reasonable time and section 15 that reasonable remuneration is to be paid for it, subject to agreement to the contrary.

A non-contractual agent will not be caught by the matters mentioned in the preceding two paragraphs, and his only duty to take care arises in negligence. A duty of care is owed by agent to principal and the standard of that duty is that reasonable care should be taken; naturally the degree of care and skill which is reasonable differs with the specialist skills which the agent possesses or professes to possess. But, there is some support for the argument that a non-contractual agent need not use as much care and skill as a contractual agent.

Most of the recent cases concerning liability for negligence on the part of an agent have concerned the principal's vicarious liability to the third party, but in *Arensen* v *Casson Beckman Rutley & Co* [1977] AC 405; [1975] 3 All ER 901, the agent himself was held liable for not exercising proper care. In that case a valuer was appointed to value shares on behalf of the seller. His valuation was unreasonably low and the seller lost money by selling at the low price recommended. The agent was liable for failing to exercise the degree of care and skill which someone who held himself out as being a professional valuer of shares should possess.

In several old cases the liability of an agent for his carelessness has been equated to the common law duties of care owed by a bailee. It has been long recognised that a person who is paid for his services as a bailee (a bailee for reward) should take greater care of goods then one who gives his services free (a gratuitous bailee), and an even lower duty of care is owed by someone who is an involuntary bailee -

someone who does not want to be in possession of another's goods at all but finds himself in possession. In outline the position is that the full negligence of the duty of care is only imposed on the bailee for reward; the gratuitous bailee must take some care but will be liable only for gross negligence, whereas the involuntary bailee is only under a duty not to do positive damage to the goods. Whether these distinctions are fully applicable to agents, by analogy, is doubtful; the closer classification of duties of care in negligence over the past fifty years or so has imposed a duty to take reasonable care whenever a duty is owed, and that once there is sufficient foreseeability of harm, the only difference between cases is in the classification of what degree of care is reasonable. Naturally all the circumstances of each case must be examined before it can be said whether an agent has acted reasonably, and whether or not he is being paid for his services is something which the reasonable man would take into account when deciding how thoroughly he should do his job.

The reader will be familiar with *Hedley Byrne & Co v Heller & Partners* [1964] AC 465; [1963] 2 All ER 575, where a distinction was drawn between professional advice given in formal circumstances, in which case a duty of care will be owed; and advice given by a professional person in an informal context, in which case no duty will be owed. The case also supports the proposition that the standard of care will vary according to the level of professional skill claimed by the adviser. It will only be in rare cases that it could be said that an agent who has instructions to bring his principal into contractual relations with a third party need not take any care, but the degree of care should differ according to the skill professed by the agent.

No recent case specifically discussed in general terms the position of the agent in the context of tortious liability for carelessness. However, the position today is likely to be that all agents owe a duty to take reasonable care in the performance of their instructions, but the standard of what is reasonable will vary depending on all the circumstances of each case. The professional agent who claims to have special skills must act in accordance with the skills which he professes. The agent who offers nothing to his principal other than his efforts will not be expected to show special skills but will be expected to reach a standard of performance commensurate with reasonable effort being applied in the job. Accordingly, an agent who offers his services for free and does not claim any special skills will not be expected to reach a very high standard of performance.

In *Chaudhry v Prabhakar* [1988] 3 All ER 718 the Court of Appeal held that a gratuitous agent owed a duty to exercise such care and skill as was reasonable in all the circumstances. The agent had offered to find a car for the principal to buy. A used car was recommended by the agent and bought by the principal but it turned out to be in poor condition having been repaired after an accident. The principal had made clear that she did not want a car which had been in an accident but the agent did not ask the seller about this. It was held that there was a breach of duty by the agent.

A useful Privy Council decision is *Gokal Chand-Jagan Nath* v *Nand Ram Das-Atma Ram* [1939] AC 106; [1938] 4 All ER 407, in which a firm of agents who had to recover money which was owed by third parties to the principal was held not to have been negligent in collecting part only of the money. The third parties were in financial difficulties and in the circumstances the Privy Council upheld the decision of the Lahore High Court that the agents had acted reasonably. It is useful to note that the Privy Council accepted that the degree of care and skill which the agents should have exercised was dependent on all the circumstances of the case; Lord Wright said that 'his duty ... is to do his best to collect all he can in the circumstances'.

7.4 Conflict of interests

The duty of an agent to avoid a conflict of interests is one which arises because of his fiduciary position, so no distinction is made between contractual and non-contractual agents. The duty is identical to that imposed on a trustee by the well known rules in *Boardman* v *Phipps* [1967] 2 AC 46; [1966] 3 All ER 721. In that case trustees had made a personal profit from investing in shares which they had learned about while acting as trustees or agents of trustees. The House of Lords held that trustees and agents alike must prevent their personal interests from conflicting with their duty to act for the benefit of others.

In *Armstrong* v *Jackson* [1917] 2 KB 822 an agent was appointed to buy some shares in a certain company for his principal. The agent owned some of these shares himself, and instead of buying for the principal in the open market he sold the principal 600 shares from his own holding. It was held that the agent had allowed his personal interest to conflict with that of the principal and so was liable to account to the principal for the profit which he made on the sale.

It is not necessary that any loss be proved to have occurred to the principal, fiduciary duties are strict and merely to put himself in a position where there was a potential conflict of interest and a potential loss to the principal will be enough to put the agent in breach of his duty. In *Industrial Development Consultants Ltd* v *Cooley* [1972] 1 WLR 443; [1972] 2 All ER 162, Cooley, the managing director of a company, IDC, resigned and took an appointment as manager of a building programme for the Eastern Gas Board. His former employers had wanted this work, but the gas board was not prepared to employ them. Cooley was held to have been in breach of the fiduciary duty he owed as a director by taking on a contract which he learned about whilst working for IDC and had to account to IDC for the profit he had made. In his defence he argued that they would not have got the contract in any event, but Roskill J held that this was irrelevant. It was held that Cooley had put himself in such a position that there was the potential for him to have put his own interests before those of his principals, IDC, and that while that potential existed he was in breach of duty and liable to account for all the profit he had made.

The agent is allowed to use his position as agent to his own advantage if he either obtains the consent of the principal before contracting personally or makes full disclosure and the principal waives the breach. But the burden of proof is on the agent and he will not escape his breach of duty if he merely puts his principal on notice that there may have been a conflict of interests, he must take positive steps to disclose the nature of the conflict (see *Dunne* v *English* (1874) LR 18 Eq 524). A similar point arises in relation to the receipt of a commission from both principal and third party because the agent is agent of both. In *Fullwood* v *Hurley* [1928] 1 KB 498 the agent was paid a commission by the seller of a hotel and claimed a second commission from the buyer under their agreement that the agent should act as his broker. The Court of Appeal held that double commission can only be obtained where there has been full disclosure, because without that dislosure the agent's interests would conflict. We have already seen that in *Harrods Ltd* v *Lemon* the full disclosure by Harrods Ltd of their unintended double-agency did not prevent them from recovering their commission.

As was seen in *Bell* v *Lever Bros Ltd* [1932] AC 161 an agent does not have to volunteer information about any breach of duty which he has committed.

Note that estate agents are not covered by the same rigid rules regarding conflict of interests. In *Kelly* v *Cooper* [1992] 3 WLR 936, the Privy Council ruled that since estate agents frequently act for numerous principals, some in competition with each other, unless the agency is in some way 'exclusive', there is no conflict of interest. An agent is not obliged to reveal each of the various principals' existence or interests to the others.

7.5 Secret profits

The duty not to make a secret profit overlaps with that just discussed. Indeed, in the recent case of *Anangel Atlas Compania Naviera SA* v *Ishikawajima-Harima Heavy Industries & Co* [1990] 1 Lloyd's Rep 167 the court held that the test as to what constitutes a bribe was to look to see if the making of a payment gave rise to a conflict of interest. In that case, since the court decided that the agent was never placed in a position to suffer any conflict of interest, the payments he received could not be described as a bribe. In *Armstrong* v *Jackson*, *Boardman* v *Phipps* and *Industrial Development Consultants Ltd* v *Cooley* the conflict of interests led to the agent making a profit which he did not disclose. The duty not to make a secret profit does not depend on the good faith of the agent. Although it was clear that there was an element of bad faith in both *Armstrong* v *Jackson* and *Industrial Development Consultants Ltd* v *Cooley*, there was none in *Boardman* v *Phipps* yet still the agents were liable for the profit they had made.

A secret profit can be made by using confidential information against the interests of the principal. For example, in *Lamb* v *Evans* [1893] 1 Ch 218 two employees of a publisher left his employment and sought to use information gained whilst working on a trade journal for the benefit of a rival publisher. Their old employer was successful in obtaining injunctions against them on the ground that the information was confidential and it would therefore be a breach of fiduciary duty to use it to the financial benefit of the agents. More recently in *Faccenda Chicken Ltd* v *Fowler* [1986] 1 All ER 617 an employer, Faccenda Chicken Ltd, failed in an action against ex-employees who had left their employment and set up in competition. The information they used was about prices which had been charged to customers of Faccenda Chicken Ltd and the names of those customers. The Court of Appeal held that the use of information gained during employment will be permitted unless the information was a trade secret or very similar to a trade secret; the names and addresses of Faccenda Chicken Ltd's customers and the prices which Faccenda Chicken Ltd had charged them was not confidential information of the same type as a trade secret, so the ex-employees were free to compete and use this information to advance their own business.

The receipt of a secret commission from the third party disentitles the agent from claiming remuneraton from the principal. We have already seen this point in *Andrew* v *Ramsay & Co* (see above: section 6.1, Earning of commission).

The receipt of a bribe carries special consequences. Not only can the agent be dismissed but the contract made with the third party is voidable at the option of the principal and the principal can claim the amount of the bribe, or damages, from either the third party of the agent. A bribe was defined by Slade J in *Industries and General Mortgage Co Ltd* v *Lewis* [1949] 2 All ER 573 as involving three elements:

1. That the person making the payment makes it to the agent of the other person with whom he is dealing.
2. That he makes it to that person knowing that that person is acting as the agent of the other person with whom he is dealing.
3. That he fails to disclose to the other person with whom he is dealing that he has made that payment to the person whom he knows to be the other person's agent.

Slade J talked of a bribe being a secret commission, but this definition does not make clear one essential matter, which is that a bribe is by its nature an inducement, so that a bribe must be paid before the agent has performed his agency, otherwise it is not a bribe, it is merely a secret profit. The receipt of a bribe is a ground for the principal dismissing the agent without notice, as in *Boston Deep Sea Fishing and Ice Co Ltd* v *Ansell* (1888) 39 Ch D 339 where a managing director was summarily dismissed for taking a bribe and the Court of Appeal upheld this as being quite proper. It is clear from the *Lewis* case that lack of corrupt motive is irrelevant to a payment being a bribe; it is the potential for corruption which needs to be avoided, so even proof of lack of corruption will not change matters.

Until 1978 it was thought that the principal could recover the amount of the bribe and damages, following a dictum to that effect in *Salford Corporation* v *Lever*

[1891] 1 QB 168, but the Privy Council in *Mahesan* v *Malaysia Government Officers' Co-Operative Housing Society Ltd* [1979] AC 374; [1978] 2 All ER 405, held that the principal cannot get double recovery and must settle for either the bribe or damages to compensate for any loss which has resulted from the acceptance of the bribe. In the *Mahesan* case the agent of a housing society which provided housing for officers of the Malaysian government accepted a bribe from one Manickam in return for agreeing that the association would buy land from Manickam. The land was not originally owned by Manickam, but he bought it for $456,000 from its owners and then sold it to the association for $944,000 having already promised Mahesan one quarter of the profit after Manickam had paid his expenses. The bribe was paid, amounting to $122,000. The housing association claimed from Mahesan both the $122,000 which he had received as a bribe and damages to cover the loss which they claimed they had incurred and which the lower court had quantified as $433,000. The Privy Council held that only one of these figures could be recovered, otherwise there would be double recovery, and because the association would clearly have chosen the larger figure, so this was the amount awarded. The result in the *Mahesan* case was cited with tacit approval in the Court of Appeal in *The Ocean Frost*, but was not discussed in the House of Lords, and can now be treated as reflecting English law. Where an agent receives a bribe, the principal is entitled to recover it from the agent whether or not the principal affirmed or rescinded the contract. When he recovers this money there is no implication that he has affirmed the contract (*Logicrose* v *Southend United Football Club* [1988] 1 WLR 1256).

In the alternative to taking action against the agent, the principal has the right to pursue his remedy against the third party for fraud. The *Mahesan* case was expressly stated to reflect the principal's rights whether he sues agent or third party.

In addition, the principal can avoid the contract which was induced by the bribe. Once the offer of a bribe has been proved, there is an irrebuttable presumption that it induced the contract; which means that even in the face of clear evidence that the agent would have made the same contract on the same terms with the third party had no bribe offered, the principal may still rescind the contract and claim either damages or the bribe.

In *Logicrose* Millet J held that a principal who discovered that his agent had obtained or arranged to obtain a bribe could treat the contract as void ab initio. The principal could also rescind the contract where, to the knowledge of the other party, the agent had placed himself in a position where there was a conflict between his interests and his duties so that he could no longer give disinterested advice; however, the other party would have to have actual knowledge or be blind wilfully to the fact that the agent intended to conceal his dealings from his principal.

The giving or taking of a bribe is a criminal offence under section 1 of the Prevention of Corruption Act 1916 where the agent works for a public body and under section 1 of the Prevention of Corruption Act 1906 it is an offence for any agent corruptly to accept a bribe. The agent or briber can avoid criminal liability by proving that there was no corrupt motive. In *R v Carr-Briant* [1943] KB 607; [1943] 2 All ER 156, the Court of Criminal Appeal held that the defendent will have to prove lack of corruption on the balance of probabilities, otherwise corruption will be presumed on evidence of payment having been made in such circumstances that it could be a bribe.

7.6 Delegation

An agent may only properly delegate his work to a sub-agent if he is authorised to do so. That authority may be authority to appoint someone else as an agent, so that the sub-agent is in a contractual relationship with the principal and is himself under all the duties of an agent; or it may be authority to appoint someone as a worker to help the agent do his job, but without creating any direct relationship between sub-agent and principal.

The first type of delegation is rare, because the creation of privity of contract between sub-agent and principal is usually only required where the sub-agent has his own work to do, not where he is merely going to do part of a job already given to the first agent. So appointments of employees by a company director creates privity between the employee and the company but it cannot be said that the employee does the director's job for him once appointed; he does his own work, and the director is merely authorised to create a new agency relationship between company and employee. In other words the new employee is not in any way a sub-agent of the director, he is a separate agent of the company.

In those cases where an agent is authorised to appoint a sub-agent to do part of his work and has authority to create privity between the sub-agent and the principal, then the principal may have a remedy against both agent and sub-agent if the latter does not perform properly. The sub-agent may be in breach of his contract or fiduciary duties, and the first agent may be negligent in the performance of his work when making the appointment; but if the appointment was a reasonable one to make and the default is entirely on the part of the sub-agent, then the principal must look to him alone for a remedy. So, in *De Bussche v Alt* (1878) 8 Ch D 286 (which sets out the general rule that an agent should not delegate unless expressly or impliedly authorised to do so), an agent was appointed to sell his principal's ship and was given express actual authority to appoint a sub-agent in Japan to make a sale there; the Court of Appeal held that the default of the sub-agent was a matter between the principal and sub-agent and did not leave the first agent liable.

It is common for an agent to be impliedly allowed to delegate in the second way explained above. The appointment of a sub-agent to do a job which does not require him to exercise a discretion and does not require any degree of confidence to be reposed in him is impliedly authorised in many circumstances. For example, in *Burial Board of the Parish of St Margaret, Rochester v Thompson* (1871) LR CP 445 a church officer was held to be entitled to employ a sub-agent to dig a grave and ring the church bell because they were jobs which anyone could do and did not require personal skills. The same principal was applied in *Allam & Co Ltd* v *Europa Poster Services Ltd* [1968] 1 WLR 638; [1968] 1 All ER 826, where notices terminating contracts were served by solicitors who were not parties to the contracts. Buckley J held that the solicitors were carrying out purely ministerial functions and so the delegation to them of the job of issuing notices was impliedly authorised. But in *John McCann & Co* v *Pow* [1975] 1 All ER 129; [1974] 1 WLR 1643, the Court of Appeal held that an estate agent was not impliedly authorised to delegate the advertising of a house to another firm of agents because the advertisement of a house is not a purely ministerial job, but requires personal skills to be employed.

An impliedly authorised delegation of the type just discussed will not create privity between principal and sub-agent, and the use of 'sub-agent' to describe those whom the agent appoints could, therefore, be misleading; perhaps they would be more accurately called delegates of the agent. The contract of appointment is between agent and delegate, not between principal and delegate, so the agent is still primarily liable to the principal to see that the job he has been given is done properly. In principle an agent does not make an absolute promise that he will execute the work which he has agreed to do, rather his contractual promise to the principal is that he will exercise reasonable care and skill in the attempted performance of the work. Therefore, in principle, the agent should only be liable for the delegate's negligence or failure to perform if the appointment of that delegate was one which it was not reasonable to make. In *Thomas Cheshire & Co* v *Vaughan Bros & Co* [1920] 3 KB 240, Atkin LJ suggested, obiter, that an agent will only be liable for his delegate's default if the choice of delegate was not a reasonable one; though Wright J in *Calico Printers' Association* v *Barclays Bank* (1931) 145 LT 51 held that the agent will be liable for the delegate's negligence. The *Calico Printers* case went to the Court of Appeal but not on this point; it is not clear from Wright J's judgement whether the appointment of the Anglo-Palestine Bank was a reasonable appointment by Barclays Bank, and therefore the conflict between Atkin LJ and Wright J is not easily solved.

The better view is that of Atkin LJ, because whenever the appointment of a delegate is authorised that appointment is part of the work being done by the agent for the principal. We have already seen that the agent does not promise that he will do his work well, merely that he will exercise reasonable care. Therefore, the exercise of reasonable care in the delegate's appointment should leave the agent free from liability for the delegate's default. If the principal wishes to protect himself, he may always provide in the agent's contract that no delegation at all is permitted.

If the appointment of a delegate is not authorised, expressly or impliedly, then the agent himself will be in breach of his contract in that he has the contractual duty to perform personally, and will also be in breach of the fiduciary duty which arises from the fact that he has been personally asked to do the job and it is inequitable for him to shirk that duty. But the principal will not be able to sue the delegate directly in contract, because there is no contract between them, nor in negligence because no duty of care is owed. In *Balsamo* v *Medici* [1984] 1 WLR 951; [1984] 2 All ER 304, Walton J held that the principal had no right to sue a delegate in negligence because the wrongful appointment gave him an action against the agent and there was no duty of care owed by delegate to principal. The affirmation of the absence of a duty of care owed by a carrier to someone who has the risk in goods but not property, in *Leigh & Sillivan Ltd* v *Aliakmon Shipping Co Ltd, The Aliakmon* [1986] AC 785; [1986] 2 WLR 902, gives weight to the decision in *Balsamo* v *Medici*. The strongest argument for the principal was that the delegate could foresee that the only person who would be injured by his negligence was the principal and this is similar to the argument of the buyer which was strongly rejected by the House of Lords in *The Aliakmon*.

8

Termination of Agency

8.1 Method and effect of termination

8.2 Irrevocable agencies

8.3 Period of notice required

8.1 Method and effect of termination

Methods of termination

Where an agency is non-contractual, there can never be a binding obligation to keep the agreement open, so either party would be able to withdraw at any time without legal liability. Contractual agencies, however, unlike many other contracts, can be revoked by either party and there is no rule that they will remain open until discharge by agreement of both parties, or repudiatory breach by one party which is accepted by the other, or frustration.

A different question which has arisen in several recent cases is whether an agency contract is automatically terminated by a breach of condition by one party. Conventional contract theory tells us that a repudiatory breach by one party will not automatically terminate the contract, and that termination will only occur once the breach has been accepted by the innocent party. But, the special feature of agency contracts is that either party can revoke his agreement to the agency and this will be effective to end the agent's actual authority. There seems no reason why the law should require a repudiatory breach by principal or agent to be accepted by the other in order for their contract to end, when at the same time it allows either to withdraw simply by giving notice that he wishes to do so.

Agreement of the parties may be built into the contract, or may take the form of an agreement to rescind the whole agreement before performance starts, or may take place after performance has started. Provided each party gives consideration for the discharge it will be binding under conventional contract rules. Termination will be built into the contract where a time is set for the expiry of the agreement, or the agency is for a particular purpose and that purpose has been achieved.

Revocation by one party will be effective to terminate the agency, but may still be a breach of contract. We have already seen that in *Luxor (Eastbourne) Ltd* v

Cooper (supra), the House of Lords refused to imply a term that the principal was obliged to allow the agent to earn his commission and this was an example of the reluctance of the courts to imply a term limiting the right to revoke the agency contract. Therefore, it is to the express terms of the contract which the parties must look if they wish for a remedy where the other has revoked before the time for the contract to run has expired. The exception in *Alpha Trading Ltd* v *Dunnshaw-Patten Ltd* [1981] QB 290; [1981] 1 All ER 482, does not impose much of a restriction on the rule in *Luxor (Eastbourne) Ltd* v *Cooper*, as we noted in Chapter 6. In *Hochster* v *De La Tour* (1853) 2 E & B 678 the revocation by the agent terminated the agency, but was also a breach of contract and the agent was liable in damages. In cases where the agent is an employee he may be entitled to damages for wrongful dismissal under the rules in *Denmark Publications Ltd* v *Boscobel Productions Ltd* [1969] 1 QB 699; [1968] 3 All ER 513.

Frustration of the agency agreement will occur when either principal or agent dies. In *Campanari* v *Woodburn* (1854) 15 CB 400 the principal died and this was a good defence to a later claim for commission which the agent claimed to have earned after the principal's death. The reason why death of the principal will frustrate the contract is because the agent cannot perform it without a principal who is capable of being bound by contracts made. An agent cannot make a contract on behalf of someone who could not make it himself. Necessarily, death of the agent frustrates the contract, as occurred in *Friend* v *Young* [1897] 2 Ch 421.

In *Yonge* v *Toynbee* (supra) the principal became mentally ill to such an extent that he no longer had capacity to appoint an agent. This terminated the existing agency contract so that the agent could not make an effective contract afterwards. It will be remembered that in that case the agent was held liable for breach of warranty of authority for making a contract after termination of his authority.

Effect of termination

That result does not always follow termination, because in some cases it will still appear to third parties that the agent is authorised even when his authority has been revoked. In *Blades* v *Free* (1829) 9 B & C 167 the third party sold goods to a woman who had been held out over a period of time as the agent of one Clarke. Clarke died but the third party did not know this and continued supplying goods on the same credit terms as before. The third party's claim against Clarke's estate failed because his death terminated actual authority and rendered ineffective the previous holding out. In contrast, the insanity of the principal in *Drew* v *Nunn* (1879) 4 QBD 661 was held not to have revoked the apparent authority of his agent. The two cases are not easy to reconcile, and there was a suggestion in *Drew* v *Nunn* that there may not have been clear apparent authority in *Blades* v *Free*.

The result in *Blades* v *Free* is in some ways more in line with the principle of the matter, in that it prevents a principal who does not have capacity to create an agency from being bound. After all, had the principal in *Drew* v *Nunn* attempted to create the agency after his insanity, this would have been ineffective and it is not right in principle that someone incapable of creating another as his agent, should nonetheless be bound by contracts made by that person. On the other hand the insanity of one party to a contract does not prevent the enforceability of the contract unless the other party knows of the insanity, and the third party will not know of the insanity where he can prove reliance on a holding-out; of course, the question in these cases is not whether the principal has created an agency but whether he is bound by a contract of sale made on his behalf.

Yonge v *Toynbee* has been challenged for its inconsistency with *Drew* v *Nunn*, but there does not seem to have been argument in *Yonge* v *Toynbee* that the agent bound his principal because of apparent authority. It could be argued that the conduct of litigation, which was what the agent did in *Yonge* v *Toynbee*, is something which an insane person has no capacity at all to do, whereas a purchase of goods, as in *Drew* v *Nunn*, can be effective; but it is by no means clear that the conduct of litigation is outside the capacity of an insane person.

A similar result to that in *Drew* v *Nunn* arose in *Summers* v *Solomon* (1857) 26 LJ QB 301 where an agent who had been held out over a period of time made a binding contract after the agency had been terminated. The decision was based on the representation which had been made earlier by the principal to the third party and which had not been rescinded. There was no question of the principal not having full capacity to make the contract which the agent made in *Summers* v *Solomon*, so the result is not open to the same doubts as *Drew* v *Nunn*.

8.2 Irrevocable agencies

In Chapter 3 we looked at the irrevocability of certain powers of attorney and the protection given to bona fide attorneys and third parties if a power is revoked. In addition to those special contracts, agency is irrevocable where the agent has an authority coupled with an interest. This means that where the agent is given authority in order to secure some property right, the principal cannot deprive the agent of his security.

In *Re Hannan's Express Gold Mining and Development Co Ltd, ex p Carmichael* [1896] 2 Ch 643 Carmichael agreed to buy any shares in Phillips' new mining company which the public did not buy and gave Phillips authority to buy shares in his (Carmichael's) name in order to ensure that all the shares were paid for. Carmichael attempted to revoke Phillips's authority but it was held by the Court of Appeal tht the agency was irrevocable because it was designed to protect an interest of the agent. This case was distinguished in *Frith* v *Frith* [1906] AC 254 where a general manager had his authority revoked. He argued that because he was entitled to a benefit under the contract, namely, employment and a salary, so the contract could not be revoked; but the Privy Council disagreed. They held that the essence of authority coupled with an interest is that the purpose of the agency is to confer a benefit on the agent, so that once that benefit has been conferred the agency ceases.

This will arise, for example, in cases where the principal owes the agent a debt and employs him as agent in order to raise the money to pay the debt, as happened in *Spooner* v *Sandilands* (1842) 1 Y & C 390 where the agent was put in charge of the principal's land in order to manage it so that money could be raised to pay the principal's debt to the agent. This authority to manage was irrevocable. Similarly in *Clerk* v *Laurie* (1857) 2 H & N 199 where the authority given to a bank to claim dividends on the principal's investments was irrevocable because the bank's authority was to take as much in dividends as was required to secure loans made to the principal's husband.

On the other hand the authority to sell goods given to the agent in *Smart* v *Sandars* (1848) 5 CB 895 could be revoked despite the fact that the agent made a loan to the principal and the proceeds of sale were to be used to pay off the loan, because the loan was only advanced after the agency had been created and the rule is that an agency will be irrevocable only if the purpose of its creation was to secure the agent's position.

8.3 Period of notice required

We have already seen that authority may usually be revoked by the principal with or without the consent of the agent, and vice versa. Normally the rule in *Levy* v *Goldhill Co* [1917] 2 Ch 297 applies and the agency may be revoked without any period of notice. In that case a claim for damages for wrongful dismissal was rejected by Peterson J because the agent had no right to notice of revocation.

But where the relationship between principal and agent is that of master and servant the agent is entitled to reasonable notice. In *Martin-Baker Aircraft Co Ltd* v *Murison* [1955] 2 QB 556; [1955] 2 All ER 722, McNair J held that the contract of service required notice which he determined to be 12 months.

Index

Acceleration clauses. *See* Consumer credit
Advertisements, consumer credit, for, *298–299*
Agency
    authority, creation of, *397–423*. *See also* Agent, creation of authority
    cohabitation, from, *421*
    consent model, *390, 394–395*
    creation, *393–394*
    definition, *389–393*
    general principle, *395–396*
    sale, and, *17*
    termination, *471–474*. *See also* Termination of agency
    usual authority, *421–423*
Agency of necessity, *418–421*
Agent, creation of authority, *397–423*
    actual authority, *400*
    agreement, by, *398–403*
    estoppel, *403–412*
        authority created, *403–404*
        leading cases, *404–407*
        representation, *407–412*
    implied, *399–400*
    implied actual authority, *400–401*
    operation of law, by, *418–421*
    ratification, by, *412–417*
        agent must act as agent, *413*
        effect, *417*
        manner and time, *415–417*
        principal must exist, *414*
        principal must have capacity at time agent acts, *414–415*

Agent, ratification by (*contd.*)
        principal must have capacity at time of ratification, *415*
    usual authority, *401–403*
Agents
    acting outside authority, *444–445*
    commission, *453–456*
    contracts made by, *432–445*
    delegation, *468–470*
    disclosed principal, *432–437*
        agent liable for policy reasons, *437*
        agent undertakes personal liability, *434–437*
        principal does not exist, *433–434*
    enforcement of right to commission or indemnify, *458–459*
    fraud, *447–451*
    indemnity, *457–458*
    obligations to principal, *460–470*
        conflicts of interests, *464–465*
        due care and skill, *461–464*
        obedience, *460*
    opportunity to earn, *456–457*
    principal's obligations to, *452–459*
    remuneration, *452–457*
        contractual right to, *452–453*
    sale by, *182*
    secret profits, *465–468*
    torts committed by, *446–451*
    undisclosed principal, *438–443*
        criteria, *438–441*
        principal and third party, *443*
        third party election, *441–443*

Agreements to sell, *5–6*
Antecedent impossibility, *160–164*
   'perished', meaning, *161–162*
Ascertained goods, *12*
Auction sales, *21–22*

Bailment
   risk, and, *158*
   sale, and, *17–18*
Bankruptcy
   buyer, of, *6*
   seller, of, *5–6, 164*
Barter, contract of
   sale distinguished, *13–14*
Buyer in possession, sale by, *196–204*

Canvassing, consumer credit, and, *315*
Carrier, duty to, *58*
Charge cards, *18*
City of London, sales in, *178–179*
Cohabitation, presumed agency from, *421*
Condition, damages for breach, *244–246*
'Conditional sale' agreements, *16*
   motor vehicle subject to, *204–206*
Conditions, *39–41*
Consideration, sale of goods, and, *19*
Consumer credit
   acceleration clauses, *342–345*
   additional charges, *292–293*
   advertisements, *298–299*
   amendment of agreements, *374–375*
   breach of contract, *330–356*
   cancellation of agreements, *307–315*
      time for, *309–310*
   canvassing, *315*
   charges not included, *293*
   classification of agreements, *285–288*

Consumer credit (*contd.*)
   conditional orders, *373–374*
   copies of documents, *303–305*
   'credit', *282–283*
   creditor's obligations, *316–329*
   damages for late or non-payment, *332–334*
   debtor-creditor credit, *286–287*
   debtor-creditor-supplier credit, *286–287*
   deposits, *300*
   debtor's remedies, *319–327*
      creditor's liability, *321–323*
      damages, *325–326*
      dealer, position at common law, *319–320*
      debtor rescinding, *323*
      exclusion clauses, *326–327*
      negotiator, position of, *320–321*
      rejection of goods, *324–325*
   debtor's protection, *372–375*
   default by debtor, *330–356*
   default notices, *335–337*
   definitions, *281–289*
   duty to pay, *330–331*
   duty to take care of goods, *334–335*
   early settlement, *357–359*
   enforcement orders, *365–372*
      making application, *367–368*
      powers of court, *368–369*
      supplementary, *370–372*
   exemptions, *283–285*
   fixed sum credit, *285*
   form of agreement, *302–303*
   formalities, *302–306*
   formation of contract, *298–315*
   implied terms, *316–318*
      description and sample, *318*
      quality, *318*
      title, *316–318*
   'individuals', *281–282*

Consumer credit (*contd.*)
   information, *328–329*
   judicial control, *365–381*
   licensing, *294–297*
   linked transactions, *290–292*
   making contract, *299–302*
   minimum payment clauses, *345–351*
      compensation for depreciation, *349–350*
      payments on breach, *348–349*
      penalty rule, *345–346*
      termination by debtor, *346–347*
   multiple agreements, *289–290*
   negotiations, *289*
   notice of cancellation rights, *305*
   offer and acceptance, *299–300*
   pre-existing and future arrangements, *288*
   regulated agreements, *281–285, 301*
   repossession, *337–342*
      effect of protection, *338–340*
      third parties, from, *340–341*
   repossession for late or non-payment, *331–332*
   restricted or unrestricted use credit, *286*
   running account credit, *285*
   security, *351–356*
      Act of 1974, under, *353–355*
   suspended orders, *373–374*
   termination, *357–364*
      breach, and, *364*
      creditor, by, *359–360*
      debtor, by, *360–364*
      settlement, and, *364*
   time orders, *372–373*
   total charge for, *292–293*
   transfer of ownership, *327–328*
   variation of agreements, *293–294, 305–306*

Consumer credit (*contd.*)
   withdrawal from contract, *306–307*
Consumer Credit Act 1974, *279–280*
Consumer protection, *248–260*
Consumer Protection Act 1987, *249–255*
   damage, *255*
   defect, *254*
   defences, *254–255*
   key provision, *252*
   Part II, *257–258*
   persons liable, *252–254*
   time limits, *255*
Contracts uberrimal fidei
   misrepresentation, and, *27*
Credit, consumer. *See* Consumer credit
   meaning, *282–283*
Credit cards, *18, 382–386*
   agreement, *382–385*
   credit limit, *384*
   formalities, *383–384*
   goods, *385*
   loss, *386*
   misuse, *386*
   repayment, *384–385*
'Credit-sale' agreements, *16*

Damages
   breach of condition or warranty, for, *244–246*
   fraudulent misrepresentation, and, *32–33*
   misrepresentation, for, *246*
   negligent misrepresentation, and, *34–35*
   non-acceptance of goods, for, *225–228*
   non-delivery, for, *242–244*
   tort, in, *246*
Delivery, *49–60*
   carrier, to, *58*
   contract goods mixed with goods of different description, *61–62*

Delivery (*contd.*)
  duty of buyer to take, *101*
  excessive, *61*
  expenses of, *53*
  goods in transit, *58–60*
  instalment, *53–58*
    contract severable or non-severable, *54–58*
    single or separate contracts, *54*
  insufficient, *60–61*
  methods, *50–51*
  place, *51*
  time, *52*
Description, *64–69*
  breach of section 13, *68–69*
  exclusion of section 13, *69*
  implied terms about, *64–69*
  relationship between sections 13 and 14, *69*
  sale by, *64–66*
  terms included in, *66–67*
Document of title, meaning, *192*

Estoppel, *166–175*
  creation of agency by. *See* Agent, creation of authority
  negligence, by, *171–175*
  nemo dat quod non habet, and, *166–175*
  representation, by, *167–171*
Exchange, contract of sale distinguished, *13–14*
Exclusion of liability, *102–132*
  contra preferentem rule, *109–110*
  fundamental breach, *110*
  incorporation, *104–109*
    course of dealing, by, *108–109*
    document contractual, whether, *105–106*
    no document signed, where, *105–109*
    notice, *106–108*
    signature, by, *104–105*
  interpretation, *109–111*

Exclusion of liability (*contd.*)
  prejudicial control: incorporation, *104–109*
  judicial control: interpretation, *109–111*
  negligence, *110–111*
  strict construction, *109–110*
  third parties, *111*
  Unfair Contract Terms Act 1977, *111–116*. *See also* Unfair Contract Terms Act 1977
Existing goods, *10*
Extortionate credit bargains, *375–381*
  Consumer Credit Act 1974, *377–378*
  fair dealing, principles of, *379–380*
  grossly exorbitant payments, *378–379*
  Moneylenders Acts 1900 and 1927, *375–377*
  undue influence, *380–381*

Fair trading legislation, *259–260*
Fiduciary relationship, misrepresentation, and, *27–28*
Fitness for purpose, *85–94*
  communication of purpose, *89*
  'expressly or by implication makes known to the seller any particular purpose for which the goods are being bought', *87–89*
  'in the course of a business', *85*
  liability of seller, *92–93*
  'reasonably fit for that purpose', *89–90*
  reliance by buyer on seller's skill and judgment, *90–92*
  'the goods supplied under the contract', *85–86*
  time at which goods must be reasonably fit, *93–94*

Fixtures, goods, and, *10*
Food and drugs legislation, *258*
Fraud, agent, by, *447–451*
Fraudulent misrepresentation, *30*
    damages, *32–33*
    remedies for, *32–34*
    rescission, *33–34*
Fructus industriales, *9*
Fructus naturales, *9*
Frustration, *160–164*
    specific goods, *162–163*
    unascertained goods, *163–164*
Future goods, *11*

Gift, sale, and, *16–17*
Goods, *8–13*
    ascertained, *12*
    categories, *8–13*
    existing, *10*
    fixtures, *10*
    future, *11*
    growing crops, *9–10*
    interests in land, distinguished, *8–9*
    specific, *11–12*
    unascertained, *12*
Goods in transit, damage or deterioration, *58–60*
Growing crops, *9–10*

Hire, contracts of, *266–270*
    correspondence with description, merchantable quality and fitness for purpose, *270*
    exclusion of liability, *269–270*
    fitness for purpose, *268–269*
    hire by sample, *269*
    merchantable quality, *268*
    right to transfer possession, *267–268*
Hire purchase, *278–279*
Hire purchase agreements, *16*
    motor vehicle subject to, *204–206*

Implied terms
    consumer credit. *See* Consumer credit
    description, about. *See* Description
    fitness for purpose, *85–94*. *See also* Fitness for purpose
    sale by sample. *See* Sale by Sample
    trade usage, *99*
Impossibility, antecedent, *160–164*
In the course of a business, meaning, *70–71*
Innocent misrepresentation, *32*
    remedies, *35–37*
    rescission for, *241*
Innominate terms, *41–42*
Interests in land, goods distinguished, *8–9*
Intermediate stipulations, *41–42*

Lien, unpaid seller's. *See* Unpaid seller

Manufacturer's guarantees, *255–256*
Market overt, sale in, *177–179*
    City of London, *178–179*
    sunrise and sunset, between, *179*
Mercantile agent, *182–192*
    disposition in ordinary course of business, *190–191*
    'document of title', meaning, *192*
    meaning, *183–186*
    ostensible authority, *186*
    possession as, *187*
    possession with consent of owner, *187–190*
        consent, meaning, *187–190*
        owner, meaning, *190*
    purchaser must prove good faith and lack of notice of lack of agent's authority, *192*
    sale by, *182–192*
Merchantable quality, *74–85*
    'contract description', *78*
    cosmetic defects, *81–82*

Merchantable quality (*contd.*)
    durability,   83
    exceptions,   74–75
    exclusions,   84
    implied terms,   74–85
    meaning,   75–80
    minor defects,   81–82
    part of goods unmerchantable,   80
    product having to undergo further process,   84
    reform,   84–85
    second-hand goods,   83–84
Mere puffs,   24
Misrepresentation
    categories,   29–32
    contracts between parties in fiduciary relationship,   27–28
    contracts of insurance,   27
    contracts uberrimae fidei,   27
    damages for,   246
    fact, of,   24–26
    family arrangements,   27
    fraudulent. *See* Fraudulent misrepresentation
    future, as to,   25
    innocent,   32
    made false by later events,   27
    material,   28
    'mere puffs',   24
    Misrepresentation Act 1967, section 3,   37
    must have induced contract,   28–29
    negligent. *See* Negligent misrepresentation
    not affecting judgment of representee,   28–29
    opportunity to test,   29
    plaintiff aware of,   28
    plaintiff unaware of,   28
    silence amounting to,   26–27
        distorting positive representation,   26–27

Misrepresentation (*contd.*)
    statements of law,   26
    statements of opinion,   24–25
Mistake, sale of goods, and,   20–21
Motor vehicles, hire purchase or conditional sale agreement, subject to,   204–206

Negligence, estoppel by,   171–175
Negligent misrepresentation,   30–32
    damages,   34–35
    rescission,   35
Nemo dat quod non habet,   165–207
    agent, sale by,   182
    bailee, powers of,   176
    buyer in possession, sale by,   196–204
        consent,   198
        documents of title, relevance of,   199–201
        meaning,   196–197
        possession of goods, requirement of,   198–199
        requirements of good faith and absence of notice,   201
        section 9, effect of,   201–204
    Customs and Excise Act 1952, sale under,   176–177
    estoppel,   166–175. *See also* Estoppel
    innkeeper's power to sell goods,   176
    market overt, sale in,   177–179
    meaning,   165–166
    mercantile agent, sale by,   182–192. *See also* Mercantile agent.
    miscellaneous exceptions,   207
    motor vehicles subject to hire purchase or conditional sale agreement,   204–206
    pawning,   176
    sale by order of court,   177

Nemo dat quod non habet (contd.)
   sale by unpaid seller exercising statutory rights, *206*
   sale under common law powers, *175*
   sale under statutory powers, *175–177*
   sale under voidable title, *179–182*
   seller, in possession, sale by, *192–196*
   sheriff's power to seize and sell goods, *175–176*
Non acceptance of goods
   damages for, *225–228*
Non-delivery, damages for, *242–244*

Passing of property, *133–156*
   acceptance, *155–156*
   assent for appropriation, *142–143*
   reservation of rights of disposal, *151–155*. See also Reservation of rights of disposal
   specific goods, *143–150*
     'act adopting the transaction', *149–150*
     'deliverable state', *145–146*
     intention of parties, *143*
     Rule 1, *144–146*
     Rule 2, *146*
     Rule 3, *147–148*
     Rule 4, *148*
     'unconditional contract', *144*
   unascertained goods, *134–143*
   'unconditional appropriation', *136–142*
     internal organisation, *137*
     shipbuilding contracts, *141*
     shipment, *139*
     unconditional, *138*
Perished, meaning, *161–162*
Powers of attorney, *424–431*
   Act of 1971, *426–427*
   construction, *425–426*

Powers of attorney (*contd.*)
   definition, *424–425*
   irrevocable, *428–431*
Price, *6–7*
   action by seller for, *223–225*
   duty of buyer to pay, *100–101*
   recovery by buyer, *247*
   vagueness as to, *6–7*
   valuation by third party, *7*
Principal. See Agency; Agent
Product liability, *249–255*
Property in goods, *4–5*

Quality, *63–99*
   implied terms
     goods to which section 14 applies, *72–74*
     in the course of a business, *70–71*
     seller liable, *72*
     strict liability, *71–72*
     terms are conditions, *72*
   implied terms about descriptions, *64–69*. See also Description
   merchantable, *74–85*. See also Merchantable quality
Quantity, *60–62*
   delivery of contract goods mixed with goods of different description, *61–62*
   excessive delivery, *61*
   insufficient delivery, *60–61*
Quiet possession, *47–49*

Rejection of goods by buyer, *229–240*
   acceptance of goods, and, *232–234*
   acceptance of part of goods, and, *239–240*
   'an act inconsistent with the ownership of the seller', *235–238*

Rejection of goods by buyer (*contd.*)
  effect, *230–231*
  instalment contracts, *231–232*
  intimation of acceptance, *235*
  loss of right, *232–239*
  method of, *229–230*
  reasonable opportunity to examine goods, *234–235*
  retention of goods by buyer after lapse of reasonable time, *238–239*
  time of, *229–230*
Representations, *23–39*. See also Misrepresentation
Rescission
  affirmation of contract by representee, and, *38*
  fraudulent misrepresentation, and, *33–34*
  innocent misrepresentation, for, *241*
  lapse of time, and, *38*
  limits on right, *37–39*
  negligent misstatement, and, *35*
  restitutio in integrum no longer possible, *38*
  third party rights, *38–39*
Reservation of rights of disposal, *151–155*
  export/shipping contracts, *154–155*
  fulfilment of conditions, and, *151*
  goods sent by sea, *153–154*
  Romalpa clauses, *151–152*
Risk, *157–160*
  bailment, and, *158*
  CIF contract, *159*
  FOB contract, *159*
  party at fault, *158*
  passing before property, *158–159*
  remaining with seller, *159*
  'unless otherwise agreed', *157–158*

Romalpa clauses, *151–152*
Sale, *5–6*
  agency, and, *17*
  buyer's bankruptcy, and, *6*
  bailment, and, *17–18*
  contracts of barter or exchange distinguished, *13–14*
  contracts for work and materials distinguished, *14–16*
  gift, and, *16–17*
  other transactions distinguished, *13–18*
  seller's bankruptcy, and, *5–6*
Sale by description. See Description
Sale by sample, *94–99*
  exclusions, *99*
  goods sold by description as well as sample, *99*
  meaning, *95–96*
  section 15(2)(a), *96–97*
  section 15(2)(b), *97*
  section 15(2)(c), *97–98*
Sale of goods
  antecedent impossibility, *160–164*
  auction sales, *21–22*
  buyer, duties of, *100–101*
    duty to pay, *100–101*
    duty to take delivery, *101*
  consideration, *19*
  delivery, *49–60*. See also Delivery
  exclusion of liability, *102–132*. See also Exclusion of liability
  fitness for purpose, *85–94*. See also Fitness for purpose
  formal requirements for contracts, *22*
  formation of contract, *19–22*
  frustration, *160–164*
  mistake, *20–21*
  passing of property, *133–156*. See also Passing of property

Sale of goods (*contd.*)
   personal remedies of seller, 223–228. *See also* Seller, personal remedies of
   quality, 63–99. *See also* Quality
   quantity, 60–62. *See also* Quantity
   remedies, 208 *et seq.*
   right of buyer to reject goods, 229–240. *See also* Rejection of goods by buyer
   risk, 157–160. *See also* Risk
   sale by sample, 94–99. *See also* Sale by sample
   seller, duties of, 43 *et seq.*
   title, 43–49. *See also* Title
   trade usage, 99
   transfer of title by non-owner. *See Nemo dat quod non habet*
   types of obligations created, 23–42
Sale of Goods Act 1893, 3
Sale of Goods Act 1979
   agreements to sell, 5–6
   categories of goods, 8–13
   interpretation, 3–4
   price, 6–7
   property in goods, 4–5
   sales, 5–6
   scope, 3–18
Sample, sale by. *See* Sale by sample
Second-hand goods, merchantable quality, 83–84
Seller in possession, sale by, 192–196
Seller, personal remedies of, 223–228
   action for damages for non-acceptance of goods, 225–228
   action for price of goods sold, 223–225
Services, contracts to supply, 271–273

Services, contracts to supply (*contd.*)
   contracts concerned, 271
   exclusion of implied terms, 273
   implied term about care and skill, 271–272
   implied term about consideration, 273
   implied term about time for performance, 272–273
Silence, misrepresentation, and. *See* Misrepresentation
Specific goods, 11–12
   frustration, 162–163
Specific performance, 246–247
Stoppage in transit, unpaid seller's right, 214–220
Supply of Goods and Services Act 1982, 261–273
   agreements within, 263
   contracts to supply services, 271–273. *See also* Services, contracts to supply
   contracts which are not sale of goods, 262–266
   correspondence with description, 264
   fitness for purpose, 265–266
   hire, contracts of, 266–270. *See also* Hire, contracts of
   implied conditions and warranties, 263
   merchantable quality, 265
   title, 263–264
   transfer by sample, 266

Termination of agency, 471–474
   effect, 472–473
   irrevocable agencies, 473–474
   methods, 471–472
   period of notice required, 474
Terms, implied. *See* Implied terms
Title, 43–49
   breach of condition, and, 44–45

Title (*contd.*)
   freedom from encumbrances, 47–49
   nemo dat exceptions, 44–45
   quiet possession, 47–49
   seller's right to sell, 43–47
      exclusion of section 12(1), 47
      time at which condition must be satisfied, 47
   total failure of consideration, and, 46
   transfer by non-owner. *See Nemo dat quod non habet*

Torts
   agents, committed by. *See* Agents
   damages in, 246

Trade Descriptions Act 1968, 258

Trade usage, 99

Unascertained goods, 12
   frustration, 163–164
   passing of property, 134–143

Unconditional appropriation, meaning, 136–142

Unfair Contract Terms Act 1977, 111–116
   anti-avoidance provisions, 128–129
      evasion by use of choice of law clauses, 129
      evasion by use of secondary contracts, 128–129
   background, 111
   businessmen, and, 131–132
   consumer goods, guarantees relating to, 116
   consumers, and, 130–131
   dealing as a consumer, 114–116
   exclusions, 112–114
   hire purchase contracts, 116–117
   international supply contracts, 129

Unfair Contract Terms Act 1977 (*contd.*)
   personal injury or death, liability for, 116
   reasonableness test, 118–127
      choice, relevance of, 125
      dual test, 118–119
      'guidelines', 121–123
      hire purchase contracts, 119
      misrepresentation, 120, 126–127
      nature of, 120–121
      sale of goods, 119
      section 4, 120
      section 7, 119–120
      section 9, 120
   sale of goods contracts, 116–117
   scope, 112
   sea carriage of passengers, 129 130
   supply of goods, 117
   terms rendered void by, 116–117

Unpaid seller, 209–222
   exercise of statutory rights of sale, 206
   lien, right of, 210–214
      conditions for exercise, 210–212
      loss of, 212–214
      waiver by seller, 214
   meaning, 209
   right of resale, 220–222
   right of stoppage in transit, 214–220
      conditions necessary for exercise, 215–219
      method of exercising, 219–220

Voidable title
   sale under, 179–182

Warranty, *39–41*
 damages for breach, *244–246*
Work and materials, contracts for
 sale distinguished, *14–16*